Identifying German Character Dolls

First edition/First printing

Copyright © 2008 Mary Gorham Krombholz. All rights reserved.
No part of the contents of the book may be reproduced without the written permission of the publisher.

To purchase additional copies of this book, please contact:
Reverie Publishing Company, 130 South Wineow Street, Cumberland, Maryland 21502
888-721-4999
www.reveriepublishing.com

Library of Congress Control Number 2008925200
ISBN 978-1-932485-55-4

Project Editor: Krystyna Poray Goddu

Design: Jaye Medalia

Front cover:
Two rare bisque socket-head dolls by Kämmer & Reinhardt: 22-inch girl, GM 1909, marked K*R//105;
21-inch boy, marked K*R//106. For a full description of these dolls, see page 63.
(Photo Courtesy of the Rosalie Whyel Museum of Doll Art)

Back cover:
Clockwise from top left: Bisque socket head, so-called "Winker," by Gebrüder Heubach (see page 293); bisque socket head by Hertel, Schwab & Co. (see page 148); Bisque socket-head googly by Kestner (see page 175); bisque socket head by Armand Marseille (see page 254). Beth Karp Collection. (Photos: Lee Krombholz)

Printed and bound in Korea

Identifying German Character Dolls

Mary Gorham Krombholz

Reverie
PUBLISHING COMPANY

Acknowledgments

I couldn't have written this book without the help of many, many friends. First and foremost, I'd like to thank the two people who made all of my special days in Germany possible. Susan Bickert and Roland Schlegel arranged every one of my tours through the old porcelain factories, planned and helped me dig in the dumping grounds of the factories and introduced me to many dollmakers who once made dolls in Thuringia.

Next, I'd like to thank my fellow German doll researcher and friend Christiane Gräfnitz for the countless hours of time she spent photographing antique dolls for this book. Christiane knows most of the curators of the Thuringian doll museums, and she traveled to many museums to photograph dolls on permanent display, as well as some of the dolls in the storage areas. Christiane also spent a great deal of time on my behalf locating German books and magazines that contained information on the character-doll movement.

My deepest thanks to Astrid Ledbetter for the many, many hours she spent translating German documents, articles and books for me. This original source material was very important to the overall accuracy of this book.

I sincerely appreciate the generosity of the following collectors of antique German dolls for allowing me to include their dolls in this book: Georgia Alarcon, Julie Blewis, Ann Cummings, Christiane Gräfnitz, Hannelore Henze-Döllner, Christa Dorner, Kenneth Drew, Katharina Engels, Kathy and Mike Embry, Ursula Gauder, Andrea Jones, Beth Karp, Anita Ladensack, Antje Lode, Dr. and Mrs. Lossnitzer, Roswitha Lucke, Evi Maiwald, Susan Moore, Ferna Nolte, Donilee Popham, Georgia Rank, Beth Riley, Norah Stoner, Karen Schmelcher, Christel Wonneberg and Carol Wood.

This identification book would be worthless without the talent and dedication of the following photographers who are responsible for photographing the dolls pictured on these pages: Frank McAloon, Gene Abbott, Susan Bickert, John Cummings, Pierre Dutertre of Red Kite Studios, Christiane Gräfnitz, Jill Gorman, Fanilya Gueno, Ann M. Hanat of Black Cat Images, Estelle Johnston, Andrea Jones, Lee Krombholz, Anita Ladensack, Antje Lode, Carol Nagel, Scott Popham, Michael Rank, Gregg Smith, Norah Stoner and Charles W. Walker.

I would like to extend my sincere appreciation to the following Thuringian doll museums and curators for their willingness to share important dolls from the collections with the readers of this book: Deutches Spielzeugmuseum, Sonneberg, curator, Sonja Gürtler; Dorfmuseum, Nauendorf; Hessisches Puppenmuseum, Hanau-Wilhelmsbad, curator, Mareen Raetzer; Historisches Coburger Puppenmuseum/Lossnitzer Collection; Museum der Stadt Nürnberg, Spielzeugmuseum Lydia Bayer, Dr. Marion Faber, Director; Heimatmuseum Schloss Ehrenberg, Ohrdruf, curator Peter Cramer; Museum Schloss Tenneberg, Waltershausen, curator Thomas Reinecke and the Rothenburg Puppenmuseum/Katharina Engels Collection. Thanks too, to the Rosalie Whyel Museum of Doll Art in Bellevue, Washington, for allowing me to include some of the museum's rare character dolls in this book.

The curators of several German museums helped me in major ways. I'd like to thank Sonja Gürtler, curator of the Sonneberg Doll Museum, for giving me permission to include Christiane's photographs of the Munich Art Dolls and the Dressel carousel dolls. Frau Gürtler also let Christiane photograph many other dolls in the museum for this book and copy the inventory sheets of each of the dolls for me. Thomas Reinecke, curator of the Waltershausen Doll Museum has also been a major help with all my books. The museum has a very fine collection of Waltershausen-area character dolls, many of which are included in this book. Peter Cramer, curator of the Ohrdruf town museum, is a serious researcher of the porcelain and doll factories that were once located in the area, and he shared some of his important research with me. He also gave me permission to include the archival photos of the Hertel, Schwab & Co. porcelain factory in this book.

Special thanks are due to Goetz Seidel for allowing me to include some of the dolls in one of the Ladenburger Spielzeugauktions in this book. I'd also like to thank Richard Ritchie of Robin Imaging Services for all his help with the book. I am very grateful for the many hours of time my friend Jane Serrianne spent hand coloring the illustrations from the Kämmer & Reinhardt twenty-fifth-and fiftieth-anniversary booklets, as well as the Hertel, Schwab and Co. porcelain factory illustrations. I'd also like to acknowledge the very special help John Cummings gave to me.

And last, but definitely not least, I'd like to thank my son Lee for the many hours he spent photographing dolls for me as well as solving all of my computer problems; and, a huge thank you to my husband Herb for fifty years of helping me every day in so many ways.

Dedication

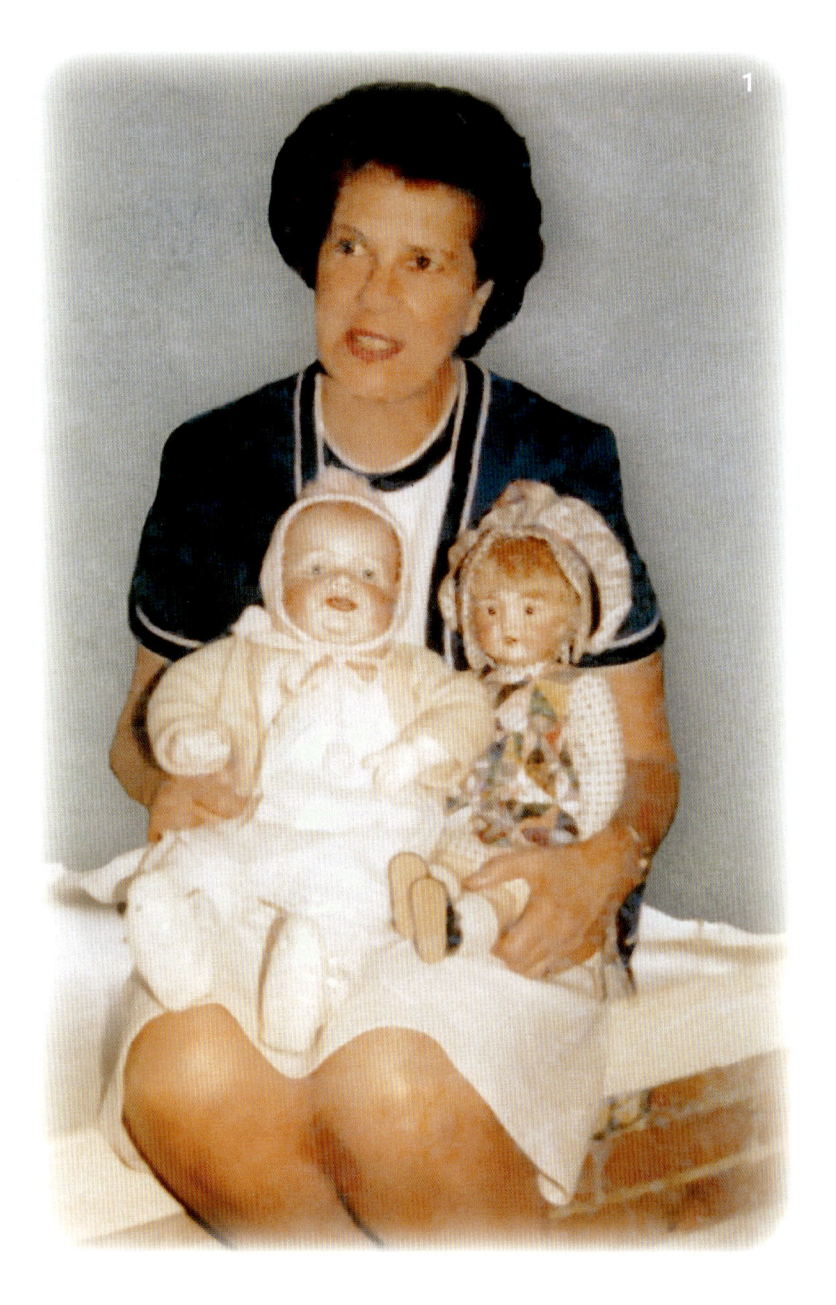

1. Jane Walker holds two of her favorite character dolls. (Photo: C.W. Walker)

2. The bookshelves in Jane Walker's 1804 house in Waynesville, Ohio, held a tantalizing group of collectible character dolls. (Photo: C.W. Walker)

This book is dedicated to my doll friend and mentor, Jane Walker. I first met Jane many years ago at a doll auction. We became friends, and before long I was making visits to Jane and George Walker's 1804 house in Waynesville, Ohio. The time I spent with Jane was always a delight, especially when we had "show and tell" with recent doll purchases. German character dolls were Jane's favorites by far, and I learned to appreciate their unique characteristics by studying the examples in her collection.

Jane began collecting antique dolls in the 1950s, and her excellent library of antique doll books was my first source of information on the history of German dolls. In 1989, when I began to write a monthly doll article for the weekly newspaper *Antique Week*, Jane suggested topics and gave me photographs of many of the dolls in her collection to use to illustrate my articles. Jane's son photographed all of the dolls in her collection, and his photographs were my favorite study guides.

Jane Walker now lives with her son and daughter-in-law in New England. I will always treasure the time I spent with Jane and her dolls. No student ever had a better teacher.

Tribute to Rosalie Whyel Museum of Doll Art

Rosalie Whyel, her daughter Shelley and grandchildren Alec and Evelyn Helzer hold their favorite character dolls: Rosalie has chosen a bisque character lady, circa 1920, marked: "**B&D Ltd.//213/3;**" Shelley has a bisque Kewpie designed by Rose O'Neill, circa 1920; Alex is holding a Kestner bisque-head boy, circa 1915, marked "**143,**" and Evelyn's selection is a Shirley Temple composition doll, circa 1930s.

The Rosalie Whyel Museum of Doll Art is a magical place for collectors of antique as well as modern dolls. From the time the doors opened in the fall of 1992 until today, doll lovers continue to be enchanted by the permanent collections as well as the special exhibits showcasing specific types of dolls.

The Rosalie Whyel doll collection contains examples from the earliest dolls made to contemporary dolls by today's artists. The special exhibits of early papier-mâché and wooden dolls were visited by collectors from all over the world. Each special exhibit is a cause for celebration, because we know we will see dolls we have never seen before. We never tire of studying the permanent collections, especially the collection of German character dolls, which is without equal in any museum in the world.

There are many antique dolls in private collections today. But they are inaccessible to the majority of doll collectors. It is only by visiting doll museums that collectors can see and study doll collections that most of us can only dream of owning. Rosalie's museum is just such a place. During my visits to the museum I continue to leave nose-prints on every glass case, as I try to look at each detail of every single doll.

It is no wonder that the Rosalie Whyel Museum of Doll Art was awarded the Jumeau Award for Best Private Museum Worldwide in 1994 and the United Federation of Doll Clubs (UFDC) Outstanding Preservation Award in 1993.

Table of Contents

Acknowledgments 4
Dedication 5
Tribute to Rosalie Whyel Museum of Doll Art 6
Foreword 9
Introduction 10

Part One: WALTERSHAUSEN AS A DOLLMAKING CENTER

Introduction 16
CHAPTER 1: Munich Art Dolls 20
CHAPTER 2: Kämmer & Reinhardt Doll Factory and Heinrich Handwerck Doll Factory 48
CHAPTER 3: Simon & Halbig Porcelain Factory and Franz Schmidt & Co. Doll Factory 86
CHAPTER 4: Alt, Beck & Gottschalck Porcelain Factory 106
CHAPTER 5: Baehr & Proeschild Porcelain Factory and Bruno Schmidt Doll Factory 124
CHAPTER 6: Hertel, Schwab & Co. Porcelain Factory and Kley & Hahn Doll Factory 142
CHAPTER 7: Kestner Doll & Porcelain Factory and Catterfelder Doll Factory 160

Part Two: SONNEBERG AS A DOLLMAKING CENTER

Introduction 188
CHAPTER 1: Cuno & Otto Dressel Doll Factory 194
CHAPTER 2: Arthur Schoenau Doll Factory and Schoenau & Hoffmeister Porcelain Factory 214
CHAPTER 3: Armand Marseille Porcelain Factory and Arthur Krauss Doll Factory 230
CHAPTER 4: Ernst Heubach Porcelain Factory 264
CHAPTER 5: Gebrüder Heubach Porcelain Factory 276
CHAPTER 6: Hertwig & Co. Porcelain Factory 302
CHAPTER 7: Other Sonneberg-Area Porcelain Factories 318
 Wm. Und F. & W. Goebel Porcelain Factory
 Gebrüder Knoch Porcelain Factory
 Recknagel Porcelain Factory
 Swaine & Co. Porcelain Factory

Bibliography 338
Index of Mold Markings 340
General Index 342

This 19-inch Munich Art Doll was made in 1908. For a full descrition, see page 42. Courtesy Deutsches Sielzeugmuseum, Sonneberg. (Photo: Christiane Gräfnitz)

Foreword

In the doll world one is either dreaming about writing a good informative book about dolls or dreaming about reading one. Usually, the process of writing doesn't get much past a little research when reality sets in and the enormity of the task seems overwhelming.

Not so for Mary Krombholz. Her research involves front-end loaders, annual sojourns to Germany, doll tours of Europe, untold friends with untold collections and a fervent devotion to her subject. All this is held together with one constant—enthusiasm, but intermingled are the dedication and energy few possess.

Addressing the subject of Character Dolls as a whole is daunting. One company's production alone could easily fill a book. That we are privileged to see the wealth and breadth of the dolls that tilted the doll-manufacturing business at the beginning of the twentieth century is exhilarating. The story of Character Dolls is as compelling as their collective faces. Mary's desire to document facts and bring the truth to doll collectors will make this, as her books that precede it, an invaluable resource as well as a beautiful account of some of the world's most beloved dolls.

As you enter these pages, the familiarity of the human family will probably entice you like no other dolls do. Savor this adventure of new-found friends or long-lost playmates. The creators of the Character Dolls imbued them with a charisma that still lures us today. Few could facilitate this "Family Reunion" as well as the ebullient Mary Krombholz.

Thank you, Mary for writing the book of which we have all dreamed—in one way or another.

Rosalie Whyel, Director
Rosalie Whyel Museum of Doll Art

Introduction

1. This 1900 original postcard pictures a young girl who closely resembles a dolly-faced doll. Her sweet, placid expression personifies the idealized child. Author's Archival Paper Collection.

In 1908 an exciting event took place in Munich, Germany, that changed dollmaking forever. Max Schreiber, manager of the doll and toy department at the Hermann Tietz department store in Munich, decided to hold a doll-design contest to increase doll sales. He believed that declining doll sales were due to the similarity of dolls currently on the market so, following a friend's suggestion, Schreiber asked a group of artists not connected to dollmaking to design dolls. The only condition of the contest was that the dolls resemble realistic "street" children.

The May 18, 1908, *Münchner Zeitung* (Munich newspaper) described the event in an article titled "A Walk Through the Exhibit," writing: "The doll and toy display is a continuation of Munich's rich toy history. It responds to the individual child's ability to learn, and presents dolls and toys in good taste. A big group of children are assembled in the room that looks like a child's room, adoring all of the beautiful things they have never seen before."

Throughout the history of dollmaking, character-like portrait dolls have been made from a variety of different materials, including wood, papier-mâché, wax and porcelain. A few were designed for trade exhibitions like the London International Exhibition of 1851. English dollmaker Augusta Montanari entered realistic wax-head portrait dolls in a competition in London's Great Exhibition of 1851, with hopes of winning a gold medal—and was unanimously awarded the Prize Medal. But these special-exhibition dolls were never produced in any quantity, and only served to showcase dolls made by a particular doll and/or porcelain factory

The Munich Art Dolls made under the direction of Marion Kaulitz and displayed as part of the 1908 Hermann Tietz exhibition (see Part One: Chapter 1) were the first group of character dolls offered for sale to the general public. These realistic childlike dolls did not immediately reward their creators with an outpouring of orders and resulting financial success. But the Hermann Tietz doll exhibit of 1908 can be compared to dropping a pebble in a pond: the ripples radiate outward long after the pebble has disappeared from view.

These new dolls arrived on the scene at just the right time and place. Many material goods were within the reach of men and women of moderate means. Children were pampered as never before, and given dolls and toys their parents never had. Dolls were soon being made in record numbers. German dollmaking flourished until the outbreak of World War I.

"all gone"

Could I have another glass of that
Hires' Rootbeer?

2. The smiling boy pictured on an 1895 original advertising postcard helped increase sales for Hires Root Beer. His expressive facial expression resembles the Munich children of the street who served as models for the 1908 Munich Art Dolls. Author's Archival Paper Collection.

(Bisque-head character dolls were made after the war, but in much smaller numbers.)

Taking note of the outpouring of praise for the Munich Art Dolls, the Kämmer & Reinhardt doll factory began to make character dolls. Their bisque-head examples were introduced at a private showing for a small number of guests at the Hermann Tietz department store in Berlin in 1909. (See Part One: Chapter 2) In the following years, bisque character heads were made by the majority of porcelain factories in Thuringia that had been making doll-related porcelain products. Soon large and small doll factories throughout the Sonneberg and Waltershausen areas added these lifelike doll heads to their standard dolly-faced doll lines.

The introduction of German bisque character dolls marked a major change in the type of porcelain-head dolls made in Thuringia from the 1840s on. From the 1840s until the early 1900s, facial modeling on dolls resembled the idealized image of a child. The dolls were created from the artist's or modeler's perception of an imagined child with a sweet placid expression rather than from a true-to-life child. From 1908 on, modelers made slight modifications of their original sketches and created new dolls with completely different expressions.

The *Random House Dictionary of the English Language, Second Edition Unabridged* defines the word "character" as follows: "the aggregate of features and traits that form the individual nature of a person…character, individuality and personality refer to the sum of characteristics possessed by a person." I will use the words "character" and "dolly-faced" rather than the word "child" to distinguish between these vastly different bisque-head dolls because both types can be described as child dolls. The primary facial feature that separates these two types can be summed up with one word: "expression." Dolly-faced dolls portray ideal beauty in a soft, passive way. Character dolls portray children exhibiting realistic emotions, like laughing and crying.

Three different types of factories in two areas of Thuringia were responsible for the production of bisque-head character dolls. The top tier was made up of the porcelain factories that made all of the bisque heads. The second tier was comprised of the hundreds of large and small doll factories that made doll parts and assembled dolls. The third tier consisted of home workers who made parts for doll bodies, clothing, wigs and accessories.

For many years, books and magazine articles have credited the Waltershausen area for making dolls that were superior in quality to those made in the Sonneberg area. But this comparison is impossible to establish because the exchange of porcelain doll heads and composition bodies was seldom documented. Doll factories in the Sonneberg area ordered many bisque doll heads from porcelain factories in the Waltershausen area and doll factories in the Waltershausen area ordered many bisque doll heads from porcelain factories in the Sonneberg area.

The Waltershausen dollmaking area is very different from the Sonneberg dollmaking area. In 1896 the German government conducted an important survey of workers employed by the factories making dolls and toys in Germany. The results are surprising. In 1896, 40,829 German residents had jobs relating to doll and toy making. Of this number, 34,622 workers lived in the Sonneberg area. In 1896, there were 1,536 porcelain factories in Germany; 878 of these were in Thuringia. Of this number, sixty-one porcelain factories made doll-related porcelain in the Sonneberg area and seventeen porcelain factories made doll-related porcelain in the Waltershausen area. Turning to the number of doll factories in Thuringia, we find that there were more than five hundred doll factories located within a twenty-five-mile radius of Sonneberg, and 278 of these were located in the Sonneberg area. The number of Waltershausen area doll factories listed in the commercial registers from 1800 to 1939 was only eighty-seven.

Why did Thuringia produce more dolls and toys than any

Introduction

other area of the world? The primary reason was the availability of natural resources in this German region. The dense forests provided ample wood for making wooden dolls and toys. Wood was also used to stoke the beehive kilns during the earliest years that porcelain-head dolls were made. The many mountain streams provided a regular supply of water for the porcelain factories, which was necessary for many reasons, especially as a component of porcelain slip. But the most important reason Thuringia led the world in porcelain doll-head production was the availability of kaolin, quartz and feldspar. Large deposits of kaolin were located in the Thuringian towns of Steinheid and Neuhaus, while quartz and feldspar were found in many of the Thuringian mountainous regions. And finally, Thuringia boasted a workforce that was easily trained and motivated to work. Because many of its mountainous areas were not suited to farming, residents were grateful to have year-round employment in the doll and porcelain factories.

It is impossible today to determine the amount or the complete line of doll-related products sold by any doll factory in the Sonneberg or Waltershausen areas. Therefore, it is fortunate that original catalogs and anniversary booklets are still in existence to document a small part of dollmaking in Thuringia. Although they do not provide accurate figures on the total number of dolls sold, or on every type of doll sold, during any given year, they are important because they illustrate a sample of the dolls sold by individual doll and porcelain factories. My original 1918 catalog published by the J.D. Kestner, Jr. doll and porcelain factory includes a large variety of character dolls, clothing and accessories that illustrate the factory's production during the years after World War I.

The twenty-fifth and fiftieth-anniversary booklets published by the Kämmer & Reinhardt doll factory document the production of character dolls in a unique way. Because they were written by factory employees, we learn important facts about the doll factory from a completely original source. These two booklets provide the most accurate information possible on the history of the Kämmer & Reinhardt doll factory and the doll-related products made before 1911 and from 1911 to 1936. Photographs in the booklets show how dolls were made in this doll factory, but the assembly process in all of the factories was the same, regardless of their location or size. I have included some of these original photographs, which have been hand-colored, of workers in the Kämmer & Reinhardt doll factory in this book so that readers may visually enter each workroom and observe the dollmaking process from start to finish.

It is certain that the introduction of character dolls had a major impact on overall doll production. One of the earliest references to the boost in doll sales credited to character dolls can be found in a book written by Max von Boehn in 1929, published by F. Bruckmann in Munich, Germany, titled *Puppen und Puppenspiele*. (It was translated and republished by Dover Publications in New York in 1972 as *Dolls*.) Max von Boehn provides the following statistics: "The total value of dolls and toys produced in Germany was 36 million Marks in 1894, and it was 140 million Marks in 1913. In 1910, Germany's dolls dominated the world's market; of the total European products, more than two-thirds were supplied by Germany."

The Sonneberg and Waltershausen areas were the two main centers of dollmaking in the world from the 1840s until the onset of World War II. Thanks to the dedicated workers in both of those areas, who made bisque heads and parts in the porcelain factories, and bodies and other doll-related components in doll factories and home factories, many thousands of dolls were made each year. Many of the dollmakers' families were related to each other, and the exchange of bisque heads between the porcelain factories is well-documented in original business letters and documents. While it is not possible to document that any one character doll was made in its entirety in the Sonneberg or Waltershausen areas, my research on the former grounds of many of the factories in both regions has made it possible to properly identify the makers of many previously unidentified dolls' heads.

More than eight hundred dolls are shown and identified, in individual and group photographs, in the pages of this book, which I have organized in two parts. Part One describes the factories and production of the Waltershausen region, and Part Two describes the factories and production of the Sonneberg region. There are few traces of dollmaking visible in Thuringia now, but the dolls that remain in museum and private collections are tangible reminders of the millions that were once made in this picturesque area of Germany.

3

Introduction

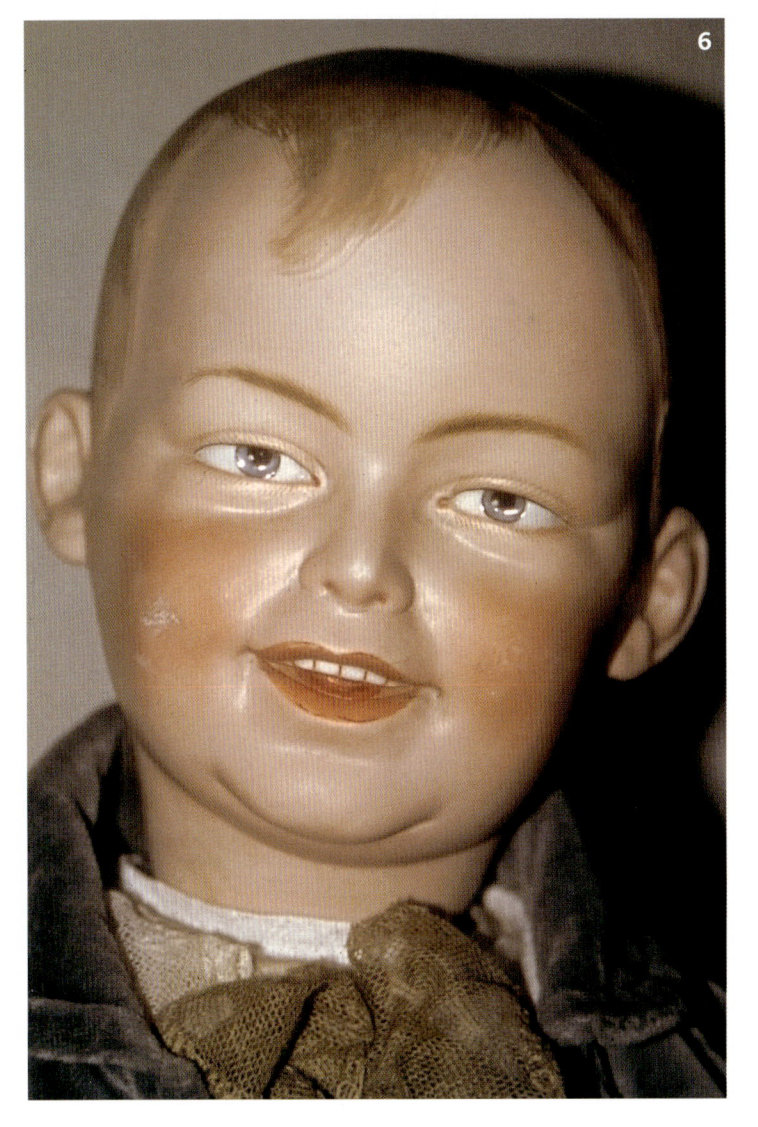

3. The 1908 German character-doll movement revolutionized doll-making because, for the first time, dolls were designed to look like real children. Lauren Emily Jacobs, born August 3, 2005, has the same smile and captivating personality that was captured by sculptors employed by Thuringian porcelain factories during the character-doll era. Lauren's look-alike character head is the Kämmer & Reinhardt mold number 126; see illustrations 85, 87 and 88 in Part One: Chapter 2. (Photo: Courtesy of Lauren's parents)

4. Three Munich Art Dolls on permanent display in the Sonneberg Doll Museum illustrate the appeal of the dolls that initiated the German character-doll movement. All three dolls are pictured and described in Part One: Chapter 1. Courtesy Deutsches Spielzeugmuseum, Sonneberg. (Photo: Christiane Gräfnitz)

5. Käthe Kruse's cloth character dolls were introduced at the 1910 Christmas display held at the Hermann Tietz department store in Berlin. The title of the exhibit was Handmade Toys. This 16.77-inch Käthe Kruse doll No. 1, dressed in original clothing, is marked with the Kruse signature and control number on the sole of the left foot. The model for the first Käthe Kruse cloth doll was a sculpture of a child's head by Francois Duquesnoy (1597-1643), a prominent Brussels-born Baroque sculptor in Rome, referred to as Il Fiammingo in Italy. Author's Collection. (Photo: Gregg Smith)

6. This bisque-headed character doll, marked PR, was made by the Paul Rauschert porcelain factory in Pressig. It showcases the talent of the sculptors who worked in the Sonneberg-area porcelain factories during the character-doll era, which lasted from 1908 until the 1940s. Historisches Coburger Puppenmuseum/Lossnitzer Collection. (Photo: Christiane Gräfnitz)

Introduction

7. One of only two existing bronze busts that served as the model for the Kämmer & Reinhardt character doll mold number 100 stands next to a bisque-character head mold number 100 made from a plaster mold of the model. Franz Reinhardt, inspired by the exhibition of Munich Art Dolls at the Hermann Tietz Department Store in Munich, had a bronze bust of a six-week-old baby sculpted by the artist and sculptor Arthur Lewin-Funcke. Courtesy Rothenburg Puppenmuseum/Katharina Engels Collection. (Photo: Christiane Gräfnitz)

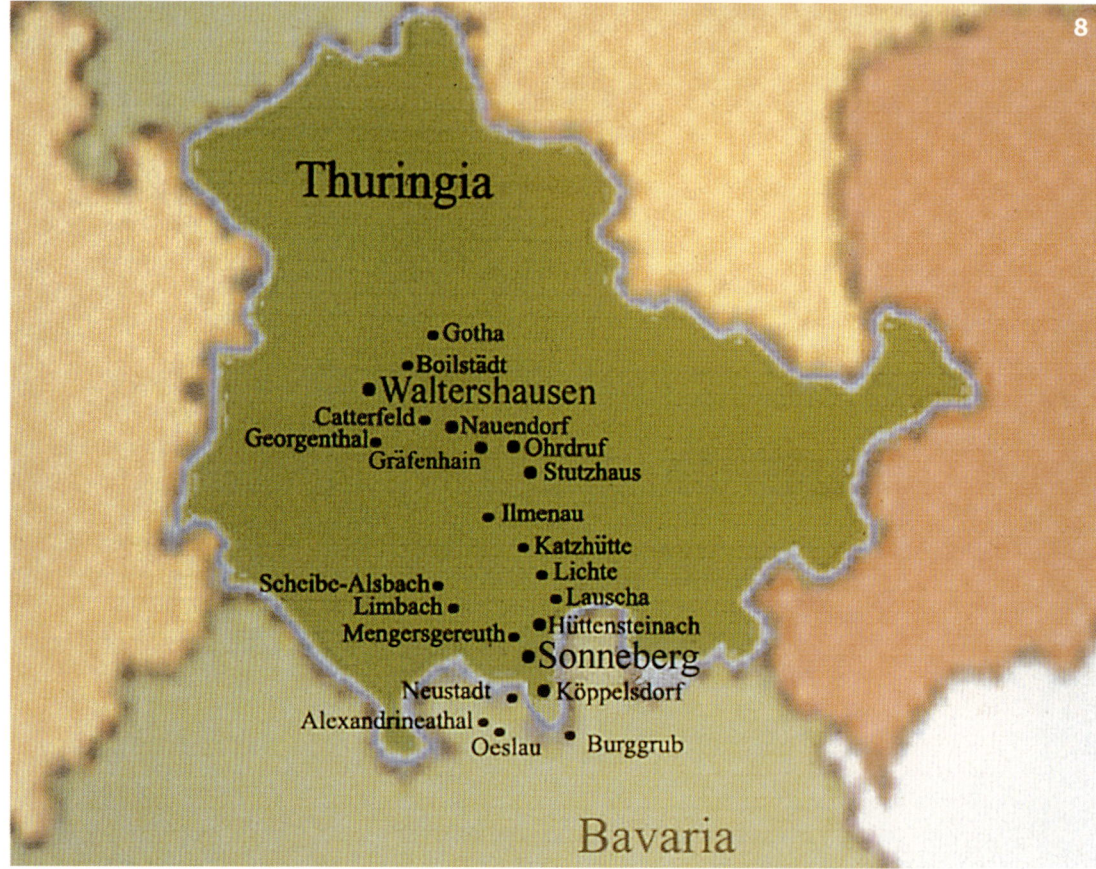

Introduction

8. The majority of Thuringian towns where doll and/or porcelain factories were once located are on this map. According to German commercial records from 1800 to 1939, about five hundred doll factories and sixty-one porcelain factories were located within a twenty-five-mile circle of Sonneberg. Of the five hundred Sonneberg-area doll factories, 278 were located in Sonneberg. About eighty-seven doll factories and seventeen porcelain factories were located within a twenty-five-mile circle of Waltershausen. The doll and porcelain factories located within these two twenty-five-mile circles form the Sonneberg and Waltershausen dollmaking areas I discuss in this book.

The locations of the towns and villages vary slightly on this map as compared to other maps, so that the names of the dollmaking sites could be shown larger. (Computer-generated map by Paul Serrianne and Stephanie Maddrill.)

9. This map of Germany shows the German states, including Thuringia, known as the "Green Heart of Germany" because of its wooded hillsides and green valleys. From the 1500s on, more dolls and toys were made in Thuringia than in any other area of the world. (Computer-generated map by Paul Serrianne and Stephanie Maddrill.)

Part One

INTRODUCTION

Waltershausen as a Dollmaking Center

Waltershausen was an important dollmaking center from 1816 until the 1940s. According to the town archives, the town was an early Frankish settlement. Sometime between the seventh and ninth centuries, it was named "Walthershaus" because a settler named "Walther" built a house near a creek at the foot of the Burgberg (Castle Mountain). Soon more families settled in the woods near his home. The town was first mentioned in historic records in 1209, when it had a population of approximately two thousand.

It was originally a farming town; later, furriers, potters and fabric makers settled there. The book *Von der Waltershausen Pferdebahn Zur Waldsaumbahn, 1848-1998 (From the Waltershausen Horse-Drawn Train to the Train Along the Forest's Edge)* by Michael Weisser and Mario Möller describes the town as having been "a farming and beer-brewing town located at the Schweinaer Strasse, a pass through the Thueringer Woods, and at the Waldrandstrasse from Eisenach to Ilmenau."

A new tourist booklet titled *Waltershausen, the Gateway to the Thuringian Forest* provides the following description: "Once belonging to the duchy of Sachen-Coburg-Gotha, Waltershausen is an industrial town today. It has about 13,000 inhabitants and is the second largest town in the district of Gotha. Waltershausen is located in a highly attractive landscape at the foot of the Burgberg and the Ziegenberg Mountains, at the northwest border of the Thuringian forest. The historic walking trail leads visitors from the Waltershausen train station through the center of the town, past City Hall, the market place, and the oldest church up to castle hill where Castle Tenneberg is located."

The town developed slowly over the course of 775 years and suffered greatly due to a number of devastating fires. The layout of the old town, however, has been preserved without any significant changes. A few historical buildings provide a link to the past. The church tower, which is actually a city tower, contains a stone plaque documenting its construction to 1458.

According to the tourist information office, Waltershausen became a "booming industrial city" by the nineteenth century. The booklet also lists the town's products in the following way: "In the last century, Waltershausen gained importance because of its sausage factories, the processing of alabaster, the production of pipes and figures of clay. Waltershausen is also well-known as a doll town. The production of dolls began in 1816. The good reputation of dolls from Waltershausen is still alive in Germany and abroad."

Credit for the town's success as a dollmaking center from the early 1800s on must be given to Johann Daniel Kestner, Jr. Kestner was born in Waltershausen on September 4, 1787. In 1824 he built a doll factory in the center of town. By 1830 his annual sales totaled more than $15,000. As his production of wooden and papier-mâché dolls and toys increased, he hired more and more workers who lived in Waltershausen and the surrounding villages. The sale of blackboards, wooden animals, jack-in-the-boxes and dolls brought increasing income to the early residents of this mountain region.

By the onset of the character movement in 1908, the town of Waltershausen was in a good position to make and ship large numbers of dolls without difficulty. In 1900 Waltershausen had about seven thousand residents; the surrounding villages provided an excellent dollmaking work force. The network of railroad lines allowed for efficient shipment of dolls from Waltershausen to the large German ports of Hamburg and Bremen.

In 1911 the Kämmer & Reinhardt doll factory in Waltershausen celebrated its twenty-fifth anniversary. The description of Waltershausen in my original Kämmer & Reinhardt twenty-fifth-anniversary booklet is as follows: "The busy town of Waltershausen is located in the most beautiful area of the Thuringian Forest. Beeches are everywhere; Castle Tenneberg is located on top of the hill. Although it is located very close to the most beautiful area of the mountains, the town does not get any tourism. The inhabitants do not live off of tourists, but rather are a very productive people that rely on themselves for work and food."

In 1938, for the twenty-fifth anniversary of his doll factory, Adolf Huelss wrote a slightly biased description of Waltershausen dollmaking: "Waltershausen, the 12,000 inhabitant strong town at the foothills of the beech-lined Castle Mountain with its storybook castle Tenneberg, is the home of the doll industry. Some of the companies here have achieved world recognition through their long existence. In these factories top quality and average quality is professionally produced in contrast to the competition in Sonneberg which is known as the center of the doll industry, and whose cheaper products are manufactured by home businesses and home workers."

The Castle (Schloss) Tenneberg dates back to 1176. It was named after the spruces (Tannen) that originally covered the Burgberg, and was first occupied by Thuringian counts. Count Balthesar built a large addition to the existing castle in 1391. The castle has been a local heritage museum since 1929, supported by the Waltershausen Town Council and private donations. The first collections were donated by Bruno Kestner. The changing exhibits are very well-attended by townspeople and visitors from all over the world. Since 1992 more than three hundred antique dolls have been added to the permanent collection, some of them on loan from private collectors. The doll museum is an excellent place to study examples of the dolls made by the Waltershausen-area doll and porcelain factories.

The chapters in Part One will discuss the doll and porcelain factories that produced the majority of bisque-head character dolls in the Waltershausen area.

1. This 1911 photograph of Waltershausen, which has been hand colored, is pictured in my Kämmer & Reinhardt twenty-fifth-anniversary booklet. Approximately ten thousand people lived in Waltershausen during the many years bisque-head character dolls were made; today there are more than seventeen thousand residents. Ohrdruf is about fifteen miles from Waltershausen, and Sonneberg is about seventy miles away. Author's Archival Paper Collection.

2. One of the oldest streets in Waltershausen provides a view of the old Klauster gate in the distance. (Photo: Mary Krombholz)

Introduction

5. The Kestner & Co. porcelain factory made the 200 mold number series of bisque character heads, marked with the CP initials, for the Catterfelder doll factory in Catterfeld, Thuringia. This head features: wig; multi-stroke eyebrows; black-outlined upper eyelids; painted eyes with white highlights; closed mouth; 19-inch doll; circa 1910; marked: **CP 210//50**. Julie Blewis Collection. (Photo: Fanilya Gueno)

Waltershausen Dollmaking Center

3. This 1390 medieval Klauster gate was part of the original series of gates and towers that once enclosed the Waltershausen market area. The Waltershausen trademark, three rooted evergreen trees and a fish, is still visible on one side of the building. (Photo: Mary Krombholz)

4. A 2006 photograph of a typical street scene in Waltershausen shows that many of the streets are unchanged since dollmaking was the principal occupation of the townspeople. (Photo: Mary Krombholz)

6. The beautiful old Tenneberg castle has been the town's Heritage Museum since 1929. It houses a large collection of memorabilia and artifacts relating to the town's history. The outstanding antique-doll collection features hundreds of dolls originally made in the Waltershausen area. (Photo: Mary Krombholz)

7. The C.M. Bergmann doll factory is one of the nineteen doll factories that still exist in Waltershausen. The Bergmann factory workers assembled dolls with bisque heads made by the Simon & Halbig, Alt, Beck & Gottschalck and Armand Marseille porcelain factories in this factory building from 1888 to 1931. Thomas Reinecke, longtime curator of the Waltershausen Doll Museum, provided important information on the locations of the doll factories that were once part of the dollmaking scene for the January 25, 1996, issue of the Ciesliks' *Puppenmagazin*. (Photo: Mary Krombholz)

8. The worn black letters spelling "Otto Gans" are barely visible on the front of this large red brick building in Waltershausen. The Gans doll factory was founded in 1901 and was well known for patents relating to "flirting" eyes. A number of porcelain factories made bisque heads for the Gans factory, including the Armand Marseille factory. The circa-1922 bisque-head doll marked with the 975 mold number pictured in illustration 76 in Part Two: Chapter 3 is an excellent example of an Otto Gans character doll. (Photo: Mary Krombholz)

9. The Simon & Halbig porcelain factory made this beautiful bisque character head with the following features: wig; multi-stroke eyebrows; painted lower eyelashes and upper eyelashes of hair; glass sleep eyes, open/closed mouth with upper teeth and molded tongue; 16-inch doll; circa 1912; marked: **S&H 5**. Courtesy Rosalie Whyel Museum of Doll Art. (Photo: Christiane Gräfnitz)

Part One

Chapter 1

Munich Art Dolls

MARION KAULITZ   PUPPENZIMMER (I, 56
PUPPEN MODELLIERT VON MARIE MARC-SCHNÜR, JOSEPH WACKERLE UND PAUL VOGELSANGER; GEKLEIDET VON MARION KAULITZ
ALICE HEGEMANN UND LILIAN FROBENIUS ♠ AUSSTELLER WARENHAUS HERMANN TIETZ

Visitors admiring a display of dolls in a 1908 exhibit at the Munich branch of the Hermann Tietz department store had no idea that the dolls they were viewing would serve as the primary catalyst for the entire German character doll movement. The person responsible for this first Munich Art Doll display was Max Schreiber, manager of the doll and toy departments for the main Hermann Tietz department store in Berlin, as well as the branches in Munich and Hamburg. In an effort to increase doll sales, Schreiber acted upon a friend's advice to hold a doll design contest. Although he had worked in the doll field before his association with the Tietz stores, Schreiber believed that the most creative designs would come from artists and sculptors who had never designed dolls, so he invited only those not involved with dollmaking to enter the contest. His sole request to the participants was that the dolls must look like the children who played in the streets of Munich. The contest was a great success, and the dolls received much acclaim from visitors—especially those credited to Countess Marion Magdalena Kaulitz. Fortunately, Max Schreiber's description of the event is recorded in the Ciesliks' *German Doll Encyclopedia*.

1. The Munich Art Dolls on display in Room 58 of Exhibit Hall I are pictured in this important archival photograph from the original 1908 Fairgrounds catalog. Professor Richard Riemerschmid, director of Munich's 750th anniversary celebration, asked Marion Kaulitz to decorate the doll room in the Fairgrounds exhibit with the theme "the artistic doll reform." Marie Marc-Schnür, Joseph Wackerle and Paul Vogelsanger are listed as modelers in the caption; Marion Kaulitz is credited for dressing the dolls, and the department store (*Warenhaus*) Hermann Tietz is listed as *Aussteller* (exhibitor). (Photo: Courtesy City of Munich Museum Archives)

2. This photograph pictures Exhibit Hall I on the Munich Fairgrounds, the site of the May 17, 1908, exhibit of Munich Art Dolls. The dolls were exhibited as part of a commemoration of Munich's 750th anniversary. The German words on the bottom of the photograph translate as: "Munich Exhibit 1908//Middle Building of Exhibit Hall I//Built by Wilhelm Bertsch". The May 18, 1908, issue of the Munich newspaper *Münchner Zeitung* described the event in an article titled "A Walk Through the Exhibit:" "Room 58 displays a collection of dolls. A large group of dolls are assembled in the room; so simple and yet so original a doll has never been seen before." (Photo: Courtesy City of Munich Museum Archives)

The exhibited dolls and designs caused a sensation since they represented a completely new doll type, and because of their simple way of fabrication, were to a child no longer stereotype factory goods, but small personalities and friends. Especially of interest to the public were the dolls of Marion Kaulitz of Gmund on Tegernsee, which included the cheeky girl, gentle Rose, enchanting Helene in a blue and white striped dress and white apron. Others were the baby designed by Josef Wackerle, the Dutch boy with clogs, green vest and black and white checkered cap and Donatelli head, and the schoolboy with his Tyrolean hat, decorated with feathers.

(The mention of the Donatelli head refers to the choice of Renaissance paintings and sculptures of children as a source for doll-head models. Marion Kaulitz was said to have been influenced by the work of the Renaissance artist Donatelli.)

Following the acclaim given the Munich Art Dolls in the Tietz design contest, Marion Kaulitz joined Hermann Tietz in another exhibit. She showed her dolls in exhibit hall number 1, room number 58, at the Munich Fairgrounds, as part of a

Chapter 1

display in celebration of Munich's 750th anniversary. The Kaulitz dolls were described in an article titled "A Walk Through the Exhibit" in the May 18, 1908, *Münchner Zeitung* (Munich Newspaper). "Room 58 also features a collection of toys. It is a continuation of the rich history of Munich's toy industry. A big group of children admired all the beautiful things with gleaming eyes. A wooden crocodile opens its red throat and lifts its tail, so simple and original and yet so unprecedented. And next door are dolls, and what dolls they are! The artists have worked successfully on their perfection."

In 1992 author Ulrike Zeit wrote a well-researched book titled *Künstler Machen Puppen für Kinder* (Artists Create Dolls for Children). Zeit's research sheds much-needed light on the Munich Art Dolls. She describes Marion Kaulitz and the Munich Art Dolls on display at the Munich Fairgrounds as follows:

> Marion Kaulitz was born in Braunschweg in 1865. In 1908, she gained her first publicity with her background as a portrait painter and children's book author. The reason for her dolls was that Munich was celebrating its 750th anniversary, and was presenting an exhibit on the modern Munich, the Munich of 1908. The director of the anniversary celebration was Professor Richard Riemerschmid, who was an architect, designer, Art Nouveau admirer and co-founder of the *Vereingte Werstaetten* (United Workshops). Riemerschmid asked Marion Kaulitz, a member of the *Deutscher Werkbund* (German Work Federation), to decorate the doll room of the exhibit with the theme 'the artistic doll reform.' Also in 1908, the Munich department store Tietz had its own exhibit. The director of the doll and toy department Max Screiber had commissioned Munich artists to make 'artist dolls' and design them as close to a real child as possible.

The official catalog for the 1908 Munich Fairgrounds exhibition contains a great deal of information about the Munich Art Dolls. The doll room decorated by Marion Kaulitz is pictured in the catalog and is also pictured in illustration 1 on page 20. The participants in the creation of the room and its contents are listed as follows: "*Entwurf und Künstlerische Leitung* (Design and Head Artist): Marion Kaulitz. *Aussteller* (Exhibitor): Hermann Tietz. *Innebeinrichtung* (Interior Design): Hermann Tietz. *Raumausschmueching* (Interior Decoration) *Frieze, Entworfen und Ausgefuehrt* (Designed and Executed by) Marion Kaulitz." The Frieze was the hand-painted border of stylized trees, pull toys and farm animals that encircled the doll room. The first line in the picture caption printed under the doll display photograph in the Fairgrounds exhibit catalog reads: "Marion Kaulitz." Under her name are the following credits: "*Puppen Modelliert von* (dolls modeled by) Marie Marc-Schnür, Joseph Wackerle *Und* Paul Vogelsanger; *Gekleidet von* (dressed by) Marion Kaulitz, Alice Hegemann und Lillian Frobenius. *Aussteller* (exhibitor): *Warenhaus* (department store) Hermann Tietz."

The Munich Fairgrounds was a perfect venue for the display of Munich Art Dolls. The landscaped grounds featured more than fifty buildings, which included a marionette theater; a post office; a fire house; many restaurants, including a tea and beer house; a dance hall and seven large exhibit halls. The grounds themselves included a "foliage" walk; a park of figures and benches; tennis courts; large bleachers and a bazaar. The architect's original black-and-white drawings of the 1908 Munich Fairgrounds are in the archives of the Munich Town Museum. They are very similar in size and staging to the drawings of a number of World Expositions, including the one held in Brussels in 1910.

Following the two initial displays in 1908 of the Munich Art Dolls at the Munich branch of the Hermann Tietz department store and at the Munich Fairgrounds, acclaim for the group of artists and sculptors responsible for making the dolls began to appear in books and magazine articles. Author Max von Boehn provides a very accurate description of the part the Munich Art Dolls played in the German doll reform movement in his 1929 book *Puppen und Puppenspiele* (*Dolls*). Boehn writes:

> The first real success was achieved by Munich artists, who in 1908 instituted an exhibition of toy dolls in the warehouse of Hermann Tietz; here they aimed at and reached simplicity, naturalness and genuine childishness. The dolls exhibited were equally far removed from triviality and from coarseness; the golden mean between the rude naturalistic style and the sweetly unreal style in the formation of dolls was gained at last.
>
> For the first time the name of Marion Kaulitz was heard as a doll artist. Her dolls are full of individuality and character and yet remain children, so true-hearted and bright, so charmingly pert and rakish. The heads of papier-mâché were modelled by Paul Vogelsanger and painted by the artist, who also made the dresses. The same heads, when given different wigs and dresses, provided a series of entirely different impressions.
>
> With her, Lillian Frobenius, Alice Hegemann and Marie Mare-Schnür won distinction with their dolls, made lovingly and with insight. While it could be believed, when looking at Kaulitz's dolls, that one was gazing at real boys and girls, the dolls of Joseph Wackerle move in a clever, piquant realm which, it is true, gives them charm for grown-ups, but debars them from the sphere of toys…Wackerle's dolls glided into the field of some ingenious delicacy which makes them attractive to adults, but they are not toys at all.

The reference to "heads of papier-mâché" in Boehn's sec-

Munich Art Dolls

3. A 1908 photograph, which has been hand colored, pictures Marion Kaulitz at the age of forty-three. She is surrounded by twelve Munich Art Dolls, dressed in original clothing. The hand-embroidered hat band and buttoned coat on the clothing of the boy standing next to her show the attention to detail typical of the original clothing worn by Munich Art Dolls. (Photo: Courtesy City of Munich Museum, including the Museum of Photography)

Chapter 1

ond paragraph brings up the question as to the difference between papier-mâché and composition. The Munich Art Dolls' heads are usually described as being made of "hard composition." The words "papier-mâché" and "composition" describe the same type of material, *Masse*. But, there are many component parts of both papier-mâché and composition, and the recipes vary in hardness. Paper pulp (soaked and cooked paper) is the most important part of papier-mâché heads. The basic recipe also includes three additives: liquid glue, plaster of Paris and ground chalk (whiting). Many other ingredients were added to the mixture by different dollmakers, and the recipes were not shared. According to doll historians, the recipe for Sonneberg papier-mâché was paper pulp, glue, kaolin (clay soil) and chalk. The mixture was very durable.

Composition heads also contain a variety of ingredients, very similar to the ingredients in papier-mâché mixtures. But often the paper pulp is left out, and finely ground wood, plaster of Paris, ground chalk, kaolin and glue are used. Composition is generally much harder and more durable than papier-mâché.

The third showing of Munich Art Dolls took place in the Hermann Tietz department store in Berlin, at the 1908 Christmas show titled "*Die Puppe einst und jetzt*" (The Doll in Times Past and Now). Alfred Goldschiner, manager of the toy purchasing department of the Tietz stores, directed this display of dolls and toys. A description of this Christmas display is in the Sonneberg Doll Museum archives. Curt Neumann was the custodian of the dolls and toys owned by the Sonneberg School of Industry, founded in 1883. The doll and toy collection was made up of the students' early works, as well as examples from foreign competitors, which were used in the training of the students who wished to become dollmakers. In August 1909 Curt Neumann gave a report on the 1908 Berlin Christmas show to the general assembly of the Sonneberg Association of the Museum of Trade. Neumann stated:

> In September 1908 we were asked by Mr. Goldschiner, a representative of the Tietz department stores in Berlin, Hamburg and Munich, to make available to him and his company, on the company's charge and responsibility, some artifacts from the Sonneberg Museum to demonstrate the historical development of Sonneberg dolls. The Tietz president expressly requested a short report about the development of Sonneberg dolls, and for that a gentleman came to Berlin and exhibited the dolls in historical sequence. I moved into the Tietz department store with more than 100 dolls and some older dolls' house furniture. My stay there was particularly interesting because of the busy times we spent to prepare this exhibition before Christmas.

The original bill of lading in the Sonneberg Doll Museum archives lists the number of Sonneberg dolls and toys in the 1908 Berlin Christmas display as 182. The dolls were shipped by train in five wooden crates.

This exhibition proved to be fortuitous for the Sonneberg Doll Museum because after the 1908 doll show, with the help of the Hermann Tietz department stores, the museum was able to include some Munich Art Dolls in their own 1910 display that celebrated the opening of the Sonneberg Industry and Trade Museum building. The important letters relating to the Sonneberg display and the resultant museum ownership of many Munich Art Dolls are well documented in letters preserved in the Sonneberg Doll Museum archives. A letter dated April 13, 1910, from the Munich Tietz department store is addressed to the Sonneberg Industry and Trade Museum in care of Curt Neumann and reads as follows:

> We are taking the liberty to send you today per rush shipment 13 original Munich artist dolls as an addition to your exhibit. Of those you don't already have as part of your collection, we would donate those dolls hoping to make a valuable contribution. Those dolls can't be omitted from your exhibit because they are originals from the Munich 1908 exhibit and are the basis of the artistic art reform. The dolls you don't wish to keep, we ask you politely to return to us. (Signed) With best regards, Hermann Tietz.

In the one hundred years since Marion Kaulitz introduced the Munich Art Dolls, doll researchers have provided many descriptions of the dolls, but little information on Kaulitz and her life as an artist and dollmaker. Kaulitz's birthplace, Braunschweg, is located in the northern part of Germany between Hannover and Berlin. She later moved near Munich to the town of Gmund on Lake Tegernsee, Bavaria, where she lived until 1924. From 1924 on Kaulitz lived in the small town of Bayrisch Gmain with her friend Aline Stickl, who is listed as a "painter of art" in the town archives. The archives also provide the following information: "Marion Kaulitz, born in Braunsweig on March 9, 1865, died in Bayrisch Gmain on June 6, 1948, at the age of 83."

One of the most interesting descriptions of Marion Kaulitz was written by Hartl Mitius for the July 1909 issue of *Leipziger Illustrierten Zeitung* (Leipzig Illustrated Newspaper). Mitius writes:

> Schwabing, which is the El Dorado for artists, is home to a modern doll mother. She is the inventor of 'doll individuality.' Her address is Ungerstrasse 16, up four flights of stairs. Once you climb those steps you reach a friendly studio with a big window with flowers blooming on the sill. They mirror the warm demeanor of their owner Marion Kaulitz. The studio is the rave of all children and a joy to the artistic. The beauty of this reformed doll is the fact that she does not have the

Munich Art Dolls

4. The Munich Art Dolls were displayed in many showrooms following their introduction in 1908. A group of them can be seen on the draped showroom table in the left foreground of this original photograph. The dolls on display all have Paul Vogelsanger-sculpted heads. The German words on the back of the photograph read: "*Berliner Illustrations-Gesellschetl, m.b.H., Berlin Koeniggraetzerstr. 67, 27. Nov. 1913.*" The translated German words are: "Photography Berliner Illustrations Company," followed by the street address and date. (Author's Archival Paper Collection)

usual face with the rosy cheeks and the batting eyes. Normal children want little friends not ladies that go to the ball.

Joining Marion Kaulitz in the design and sculpting of the hard-composition heads and the sewing of the costumes for the 1908 Munich displays were the following artists and sculptors: Alice Hegemann, Marie Marc-Schnür, Lillian Frobenius, Joseph Wackerle and Paul Vogelsanger. Sculptor Joseph Wackerle is credited with designing the more expressive heads. He was born on May 15, 1880, in Partenkirchen, Bavaria. He became an academic professor in Munich in 1923, and later created models for china figurines and other glazed porcelain products for the Nymphenburg porcelain factory. He also created majolica (earthenware) figurines and figurine groups. The 1908 Munich Fairgrounds catalog includes a photograph of two terracotta figures sculpted by Joseph Wackerle. The life-size figures of a girl holding a basket and a boy holding a cage are very realistic, and the heads closely resemble the expressive Wackerle dolls in the Sonneberg Doll Museum. Joseph Wackerle also designed felt marionettes, a few of which can still be seen in the City of Munich Museum.

Sculptor Paul Vogelsanger was born in Munich on November 24, 1882. His doll-head sculpting and his association with Kaulitz are described in the July 1909 *Leipzig Illustrated Newspaper* as follows: "Calmer, harmonic, friendly children's faces, and mainly the heads with modeled hair." Even in 1909-1910, after the other Munich artists are no longer mentioned as being instrumental in the making of Marion Kaulitz's dolls, Vogelsanger is still noted as working with her.

The majority of Munich Art Dolls had painted eyes and closed or open/closed mouths. They were often dressed in German provincial costumes or in colorful children's play clothing. The clothes were beautifully detailed, using a variety of fabrics including silk, cotton, velvet and knitted wool. Although many of the Vogelsanger heads are alike, they never seem the same because of the differences in painting, hairstyles and clothing.

The Munich Art Dolls' clothing is described in a July 1910 Paris issue of *Art & Decoration* as follows:

Chapter 1

Marion Kaulitz charmingly varies the clothes, dressing some grandly in silk while others wear cotton or knitted wool. Some are dressed for school, some are urchins wearing sabots [wooden shoes]. These realistic dolls represent children of all classes and colors. Many of the dolls wear accurate provincial costumes. For Brittany there is a whole series of dolls with headdresses of Nantes, Pluvinier, Auray, the isle of Moines, Rosporden, Vannes or Quimperle, and with aprons and fichus [triangular shawls] of brilliant colors that are separate from the somber dresses. And there are the 'bigoudaines' of Pont-l Abbé with their strange coiffures and dresses embroidered in bright colors. Also dolls dressed as all the swell young lads with their short, round jackets, beautifully embroidered vests and round hats with velvet ribbons. There are similar provincially dressed dolls for Normandy, the Basque country, Provence, Savoy and Vendee. These costumes are simple but accurate and greatly surpass the dolls usually seen in France.

Responding to the universal praise for Marion Kaulitz's Munich Art Dolls, in 1909 Franz Reinhardt, sole director of the Kämmer & Reinhardt doll factory, introduced his company's first character dolls at a small exhibition for invited guests only at the Berlin Tietz department store. According to a description in my Kämmer & Reinhardt twenty-fifth-anniversary booklet, published by the company in 1911: "The Company showed all of their products, including those in the series of 'art dolls' as character dolls were called at the time." The Ciesliks describe the reaction to the first Kämmer & Reinhardt character dolls shown in 1909 in their *German Doll Encyclopedia* as follows: "Specialists were moved to enthusiasm. Here somebody had combined both realism and graciousness. The new dolls were partly of porcelain, partly of an unbreakable material, artfully oil painted. These new 'character dolls,' a name created by Kämmer & Reinhardt, had no sleeping eyes, but painted eyes only."

Following the initial slow sales of 1909, the Kämmer & Reinhardt character series became a huge success. The first public display of Kämmer & Reinhardt character dolls, as well as the introduction of Käthe Kruse's cloth dolls took place in 1910 at the Berlin branch of the Hermann Tietz Department Store. The display was titled *"Spielzeug aus eigener Hand"* (Handmade Toys), and a whole floor was cleared for the December *Weihnachts Ausstellung* (Christmas Exhibition) of dolls and toys.

In a 1910 article in the Sonneberg newspaper, the Sonneberg Chamber of Trade and Commerce describes the increase in the sales of character dolls: "The Teddy Bear as the most attractive doll and toy article has been replaced by the character doll which, by pushing away all other doll types, had an unexpected success, particularly in England and Germany, and all orders have not been filled." Also in 1910, the building that now houses the Sonneberg Doll Museum was completed. The Ciesliks describe the founding of the doll and toy museum in their *German Doll Encyclopedia* as follows:

After the School of Industry had been established in 1883 by the efforts of the members of the chamber of commerce and trade, nobody had thought about establishing a museum of toys, in which could be collected the students' early works of sculpturing, modeling and also foreign products. The reason for founding the museum was the lack of a new generation trained in the arts. The industry of Sonneberg, however, concentrated on exporting, requiring well-trained special workers, mainly sculptors and artists, able to do models and drawing of new toys. Studying the products of foreign competitors was also part of the training. As a result, many interesting models were collected since the school's founding in 1883, which were kept and served as illustrative material for school lessons. Toys from all over the world were stored.

Verlegers and factory workers, after returning from a business trip abroad, brought samples of foreign toy products to Sonneberg and made them available to the School of Industry. From this collection, enlarged by samples donated by Sonneberg factory owners, arose the Museum of Industry and Trade for the town of toys. In addition to dolls and toys, they also systematically collected and cataloged goods of porcelain and glass. The toy museum was first moved into in 1910, and it became exclusively available as a museum and for exhibitions in 1938.

In March 1910 the following article written by the Sonneberg Industry and Trade Museum appeared in the Sonneberg newpaper.

Our trade museum exhibits a large group of older dolls as well as a valuable collection of modern dolls which demonstrate the doll reform of the recent years. This collection proves the following: "The goal to make character heads for dolls, which means heads that have individual facial expression, is not a new one. The attempt was made with a so-called lady's head from 1840; a carved boy's head from the 1850s; the so-called Fingers Taufling, with a papier-mache head and wax-covered facial features similar to a modern baby was also made in the 1850s.

The latest idea to make character heads came from the Tietz department store in Munich in 1908. The sculptors Joseph Wackerle, Paul Vogelsanger and artist Marie Marc-Schnür from Munich modeled a

Munich Art Dolls

5. According to the original Sonneberg Doll Museum inventory sheet, this 19¼-inch Munich Art Doll with a Paul Vogelsanger-sculpted head is the Marion Kaulitz Emblem Doll. It is listed as doll # 4 on the Marion Kaulitz invoice pictured in illustration 6. The doll's shoe is marked with the name of the dressmaker, Aline Stickl. The hand-knit gloves that hang around the doll's neck complete the "children-of-the-street" image. Kaulitz lived with Stickl in Bayrisch Gmain from 1924 until her own death in 1948. Courtesy Deutches Spielzeugmuseum, Sonneberg. (Photo: Christiane Gräfnitz)

Chapter 1

whole line of character dolls for the Tietz Company. From this reform movement we own many dolls.

In response to the success of the first group of Kämmer & Reinhardt character dolls, Marion Kaulitz claimed, in a 1911 newspaper advertisement, to be the inventor of character dolls. She also accused Kämmer & Reinhardt of copying her doll faces, clothing and hairstyles. She asserted, too, that she was the first doll designer to use the twisted-plaits-over-each-ear hairstyle. Kämmer & Reinhardt issued a challenge to Kaulitz to accuse them if she felt she had been wronged. Max Schreiber entered the controversy by siding with Kämmer & Reinhardt, saying he remembered earlier dolls made for the Tietz store with the same twisted-plait hairstyle. Following this assertion, Kaulitz asked her attorney to intervene.

The outcome of the controversy over the name "character doll" as well as the facial modeling and hairstyles disputes can be found in Kämmer & Reinhardt's twenty-fifth-anniversary booklet, published in 1911, in the following text: "Unfortunately we had law suits in regard to the copying of our products, and of course we won them. Under the Jena High Court order our heads are now legally protected. Copies can be confiscated. So far we have not make use of that right, but we will if we have to."

The 1911 newspaper advertisement controversy between Marion Kaultiz and the Kämmer & Reinhardt doll factory over the first use of the phrase "character dolls" did not prevent either party from introducing new doll models in 1911 and 1912. Kämmer & Reinhardt continued to introduce new character doll models during these years. And according to the Ciesliks' *German Doll Encyclopedia*, in 1911 Kaulitz introduced fourteen models for dolls, GM numbers 21 thorough 34. Also in 1911, she was awarded the prize for the most original artist doll at the Frankfurt International Doll Exhibit.

Marion Kaulitz continued to make dolls in 1912, according to her advertisement in the catalog for the 1912 Bavarian Trade Show in Munich (see below). She also received a well-deserved honor in Paris that year; she was named a member of the International Union of Arts and Science. This prestigious society was founded in 1912 by the well-known French sculptor Auguste Rodin.

A December 14, 1911, handwritten letter, signed by Marion Kaulitz, is preserved in the archives of the Sonneberg Doll Museum. The letterhead on this important letter contains a line drawing of the Kaulitz Emblem Doll. It is pictured in illustrations 7, 8 and 9 on pages 29 and 30. Even in the uncolored letterhead, there is no mistaking the unique checkerboard design of the original shoes. To the right of the letterhead drawing one can read the following words: "*Gmund am Tegernsee 167 – TEL – 45//Marion Kaulitz – Mitglied des Deutschen//Werkbundes – Brüssel 1910 Gold – Medaille//Münchner Künstler Kaulitz Puppen.*" The German words translate as: "Gmund on (Lake) Tegern #167 – Telephone #45 – Marion Kaulitz – member of the German Work Federation – Brussels (World Exposition) 1910 Gold Medal – Munich Artist Kaulitz Dolls." (The village of Gmund is located south of Munich in the foothills of the Bavarian Alps.)

Marion Kaulitz addressed this 1911 letter to the: "Industry and Trade Museum of the Meininger Upper Country, Sonneberg." It reads: "In response to your honorable letter, I will be happy to put together a group of artist dolls. I will only charge my cost, postage and packaging. As soon as I put together the group, I will give you the necessary information. Since I know the good reputation the museum has, I will do my best. I remain with best regards. (Signed) Marion Kaulitz."

An invoice dated January 15, 1912, handwritten and signed by Marion Kaulitz, accompanied the four dolls she sold to the Sonneberg Doll Museum. This invoice is pictured in illustration 6 on page 29 and has the same letterhead as the 1911 letter described above. Kaulitz wrote the following below the letterhead: "2% discount if paid within four weeks, goal: 30 days. She also noted that: "empty crates will be taken back at 2/3s of the value." Under *Factura* (the old German word for invoice) Kaulitz lists the four dolls she sold to the museum. She addressed the invoice to the Industry and Trade Museum of the Meininger Upper County, Sonneberg, with the following notation: "In response to your inquiry I am sending you today at your expense and liability: "V9, Kaulitz doll, 7.20 Mark; M9, Kaulitz doll, 7.00 Mark; K9I, 9.50 Mark; I9II, Kaulitz doll, 7.40 for a total of 31.10 Mark." In the left column, below the four listed dolls, are the numbers 2965, 2966, 2967 and 2968. On the right side of the numbers she wrote: "I kindly would like to add that this only covers my costs and at the same time I would like to ask you if you find an interested party to direct him to me. Always at your service, respectfully yours, Marion Kaulitz."

Marion Kaulitz advertised her dolls in the *Bayrische Gewerbeschau, Amtlicher Katalog, Munich, 1912 (Anzeigenteil)* (Bavarian Trade Show, Official Catalog, Munich 1912 (Advertisements) with the following words: "Kaulitz Artist Dolls//Gold Medal 1910 Brussels; International Doll Exhibit in Breslau, 1st Prize 1911; Frankfurt on Main, Prize for most original Artist doll; Handpainted, wipeable, almost unbreakable. To order original Kaulitz dolls, contact the originator of the doll reform, Marion Kaulitz."

In 1912 Kaulitz registered the numbers 21 through 34, thus indicating fourteen new doll head models. To my knowledge, doll researchers have not uncovered any information concerning the total number of Munich Art Dolls made. Marion Kaulitz did not consider the dolls to be works of art, but rather toys for children. She made them to last and priced them in the lower range of doll prices. It is certain that she was a fine portrait artist who became interested in designing a new type of doll that children would love. In my opinion, she asked some of her Munich artist and sculptor friends to join her in this endeavor. They worked together to

Munich Art Dolls

create the head designs, paint the heads and dress the dolls.

I thought it would be difficult to determine, one hundred years after the initial showing of the Munich Art Dolls, which of the dolls in the Sonneberg Doll Museum's permanent collection were made by Paul Vogelsanger and which by Joseph Wackerle, the primary Munich Art Doll sculptors. But I was wrong. The detailed inventory sheets preserved in the museum offer conclusive proof as to the artist responsible for creating each of the doll heads. Although a few of the dolls are not identified on the inventory sheets, their facial sculpting and painting are so similar to dolls identified on the inventory sheets that the maker of every head can be identified. I am very grateful to Sonja Gürtler for allowing my friend Christiane Gräfnitz to photograph the Munich Art Dolls in storage and for allowing me to have photocopies of the original inventory sheets and the Munich Art Doll acquisition letters.

Although one hundred years have passed since the Munich Art Dolls were made, the dolls in the Sonneberg Doll Museum look exactly as they did when they were originally created. The clothing and accessories are in perfect condition. The dolls are as appealing today as they were when first seen in the summer of 1908, on the display tables of the Hermann Tietz department store in Munich. Their charming waif-like innocence is appreciated by doll collectors worldwide, but their real importance lies in the fact that they heralded a new style of dollmaking, one that portrayed a true-to-life child rather than an idealized child. The 1908 Munich exhibit would not be so important to today's doll collectors if the Kämmer & Reinhardt doll factory had not responded to the idea of this new type of realistic doll. The far-reaching influence of the dolls shown at the Tietz stores is evident in the work of today's doll artists and designers.

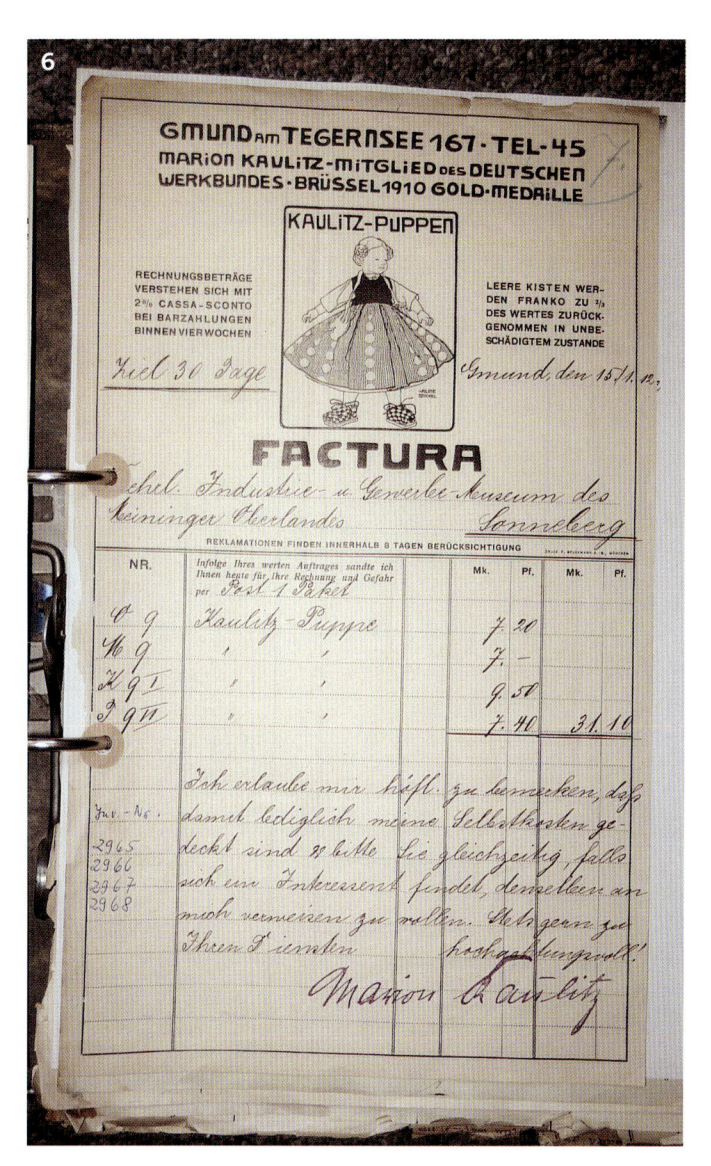

6. This original January 15, 1912, invoice, hand-written by Marion Kaulitz, accompanied the four dolls Kaulitz sold to the Sonneberg Doll Museum. The letterhead includes a drawing of her Emblem Doll, pictured in illustration 4. The translated words above the doll read: "Gmund on (Lake) Tegern #167; Telephone #45; Marion Kaulitz, Member of the German Work Federation; Brussels (World Exposition) 1910 Gold Medal; Munich Artist Kaulitz Dolls." The German Work Federation was an artistic movement dedicated to improving sales for traditional crafts as well as mass-produced products, which put Germany on a competitive footing with England and the United States. The association, founded in 1907, was made up of architects, designers and industrialists. Courtesy Deutches Spielzeugmuseum, Sonneberg. (Photo: Christiane Gräfnitz)

7. The doll's handmade shoes, marked with the name Aline Stickl, are an important part of her charming "children-of-the-street" image. The unique checkerboard shoes can be seen on the drawing of the Emblem Doll on the Kaulitz company letterhead, seen on the invoice pictured at left. Courtesy Deutsches Spielzeugmuseum, Sonneberg. (Photo: Christiane Gräfnitz)

Chapter 1

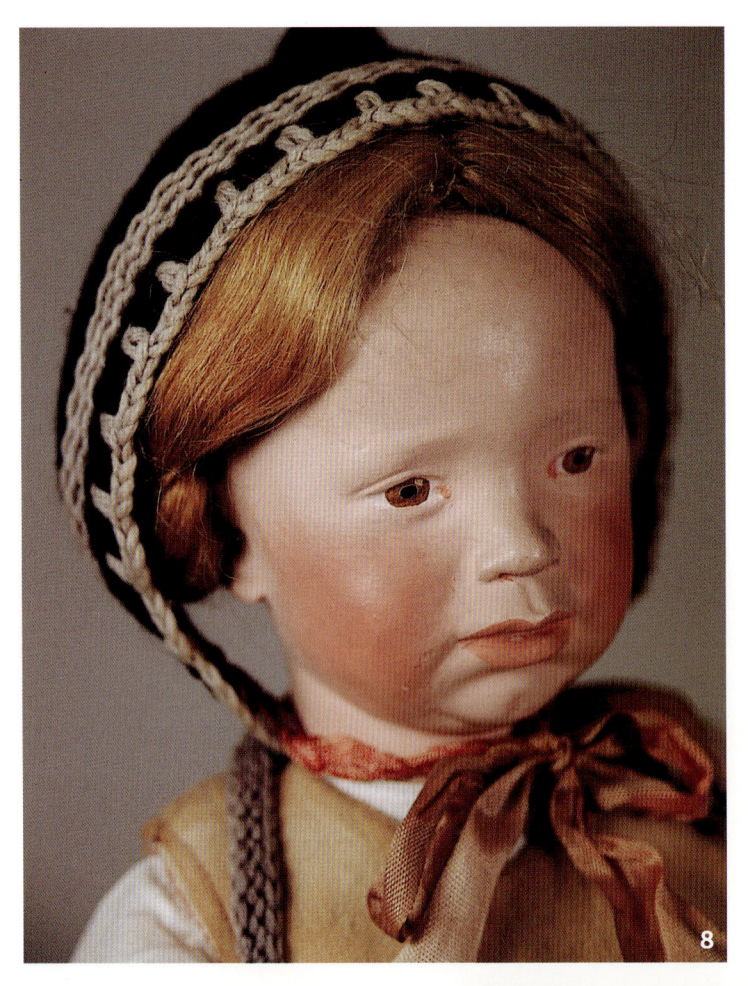

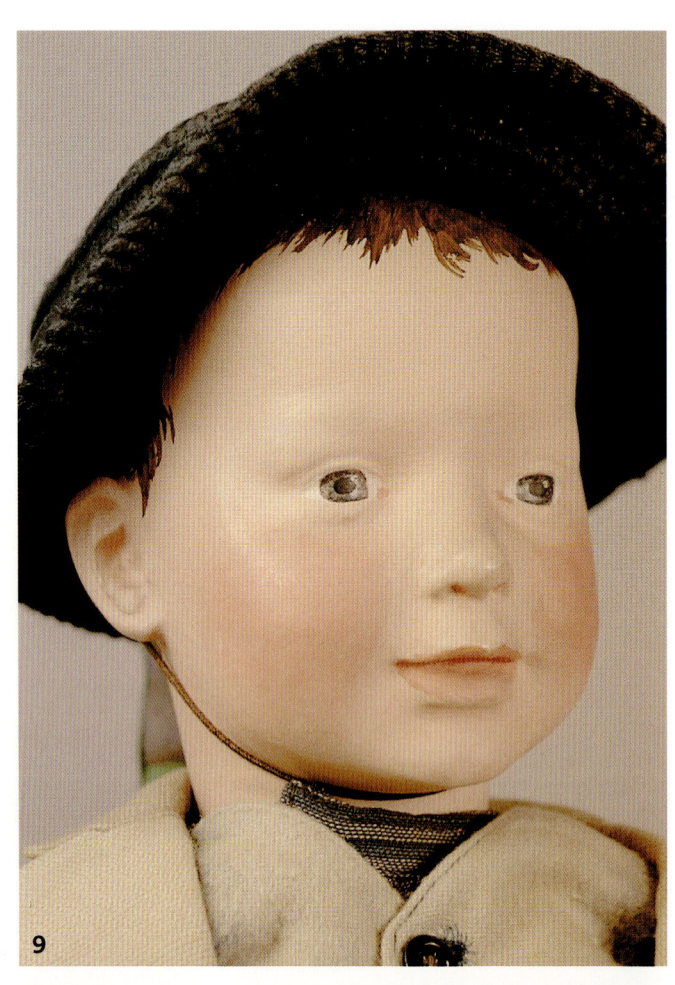

8. A closer view of the head of the Emblem Doll shows the full cheeks, pouty expression and typical German hairstyle with braids wound around each ear. This hairstyle was referred to as the "snail-shell hairstyle" on the inventory sheet that describes the doll's hairstyle and clothing. Courtesy Deutsches Spielzeugmuseum, Sonneberg. (Photo: Christiane Gräfnitz)

9. This is doll #1 on the January 15, 1912, invoice listing the four dolls (including the Emblem Doll) sold by Marion Kaulitz to the Sonneberg Industry and Trade museum, which later became the Sonneberg Doll and Toy Museum. Paul Vogelsanger sculpted the head of this 19¾-inch boy with painted hair. Courtesy Deutsches Spielzeugmuseum, Sonneberg. (Photo: Christiane Gräfnitz)

10. This 18¼-inch undressed Munich Art Doll, with a head sculpted by Paul Vogelsanger, resembles the Emblem Doll pictured in illustration 5. The pouty mouth, deep chin dimple and pigtails complete the childish look. Courtesy Deutsches Spielzeugmuseum, Sonneberg. (Photo: Christiane Gräfnitz)

11. The well-modeled ears and chubby cheeks on this Munich Art Doll, also pictured in illustration 10, are sculpting details often found on Vogelsanger heads. Courtesy Deutsches Spielzeugmuseum, Sonneberg. (Photo: Christiane Gräfnitz)

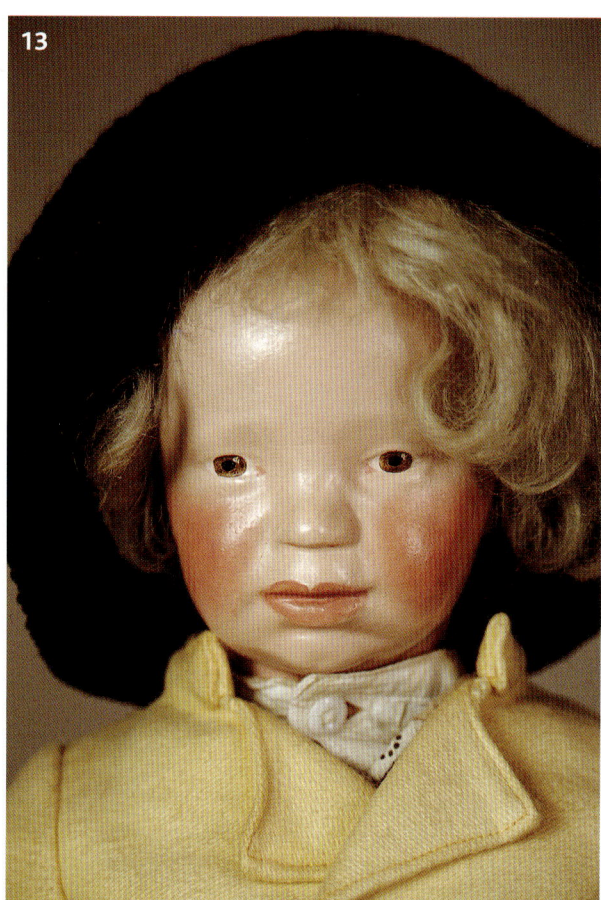

Munich Art Dolls

12. The hard-composition head of this 18½-inch Munich Art doll was also sculpted by Paul Vogelsanger, according to the original inventory sheet in the Sonneberg Doll Museum. This doll is #2 on the January 15, 1912, invoice of four dolls sold to the museum by Marion Kaulitz. It is apparent that Vogelsanger sculpted the entire group of dolls that accompanied the invoice pictured in illustration 6. Courtesy Deutsches Spielzeugmuseum, Sonneberg. (Photo: Christiane Gräfnitz)

13. A closer view of the Vogelsanger head seen in illustration 14 shows the sculpted similarity of this doll to the Emblem Doll in illustration 5. The facial features include pale eyebrows, highlighted brown painted eyes, a full open/closed mouth and deeply blushed cheeks. Courtesy Deutsches Spielzeugmuseum, Sonneberg. (Photo: Christiane Gräfnitz)

14. This 20-inch Munich Art Doll is doll #3 on the January 15, 1912, invoice of the four dolls sold to the museum by Marion Kaulitz. The boy's original clothing is described in the July 1910 Paris issue of *Art & Decoration* as follows: "Dolls dressed as swell young lads with their short round jackets." Courtesy Deutsches Spielzeugmuseum, Sonneberg. (Photo: Christiane Gräfnitz)

Chapter 1

15. A closer view of the Vogelsanger head seen in illustration 12 shows the typical "calmer, harmonic, friendly children's faces" credited to him in the July 1909 *Leipzig Illustrated Newspaper*. The newspaper article also notes that: "Vogelsanger of Munich delivered by far the most heads." The head on this doll is identical to the heads on my two Munich Art Dolls pictured in illustration 18. Courtesy Deutsches Spielzeugmuseum, Sonneberg. (Photo: Christiane Gräfnitz)

16. This 20-inch Munich Art Doll with a Vogelsanger head is very similar to the heads pictured in illustrations 13 and 15. It shows the similarity of modeling details evident on Vogelsanger-sculpted heads. This doll is in the permanent collection of a doll museum located in an old Hanau-Wilhelmsbad castle. Courtesy Hessisches Puppenmuseum, Hanau-Wilhelmsbad. (Photo: Christiane Gräfnitz)

18. This pair of 13-inch Munich Art Dolls with identical molded heads illustrates the differences in appearance due to facial painting. The doll in original clothing has molded eyelids, large gray/blue painted eyes and full light-red painted lips. The undressed doll lacks eyelid definition, and has much smaller painted eyes and very pale pink lips. The well-made composition jointed bodies are marked with the Dressel winged-helmet trademark. The Cuno & Otto Dressel doll factory made the majority of composition bodies found on Munich Art Dolls, including the majority of the examples pictured in this chapter, and also marketed as Munich Art Dolls. Author's Collection. (Photo: Gregg Smith)

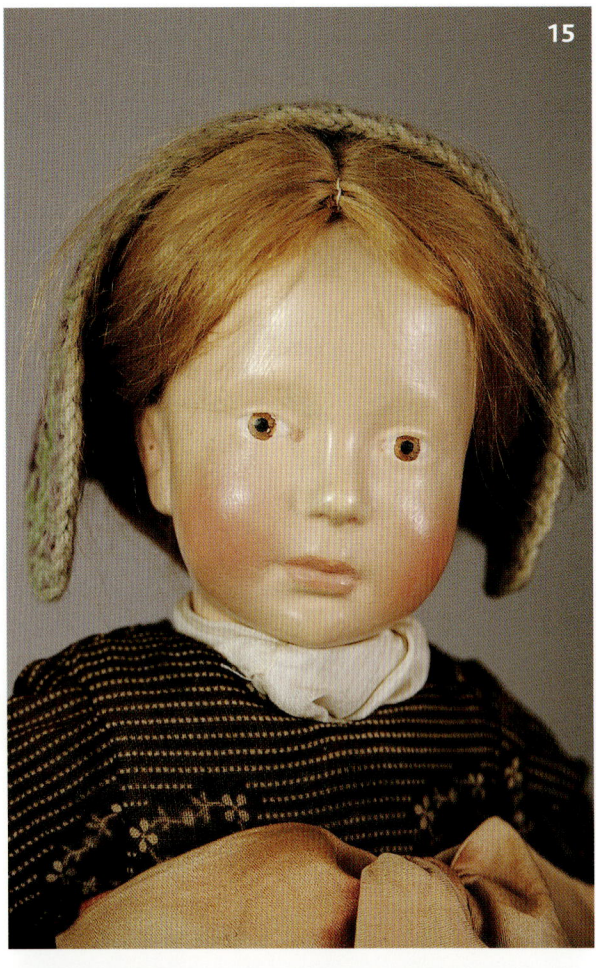

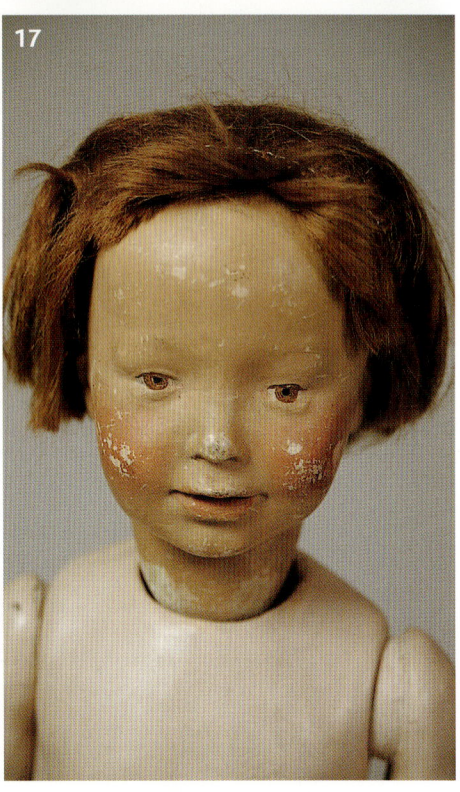

17. The hard-composition head on this 18½-inch Munich Art Doll is similar in styling to the Vogelsanger-sculpted heads shown in the preceding Munich Art Doll photographs in this chapter. The slightly smiling open/closed mouth and high forehead are sculpting details that change the appearance of this doll. Courtesy Deutsches Spielzeugmuseum, Sonneberg. (Photo: Christiane Gräfnitz)

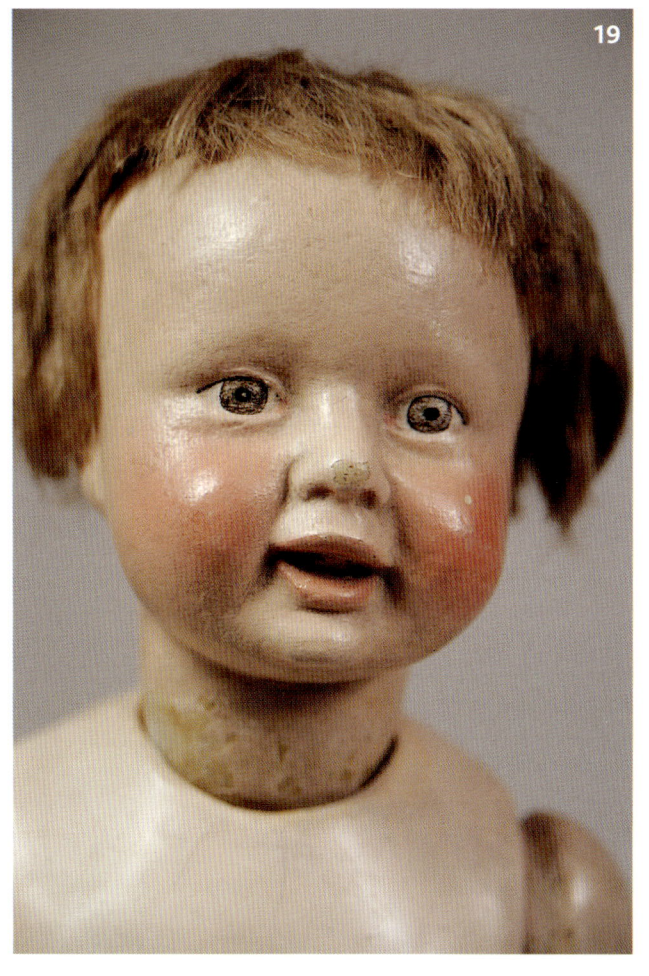

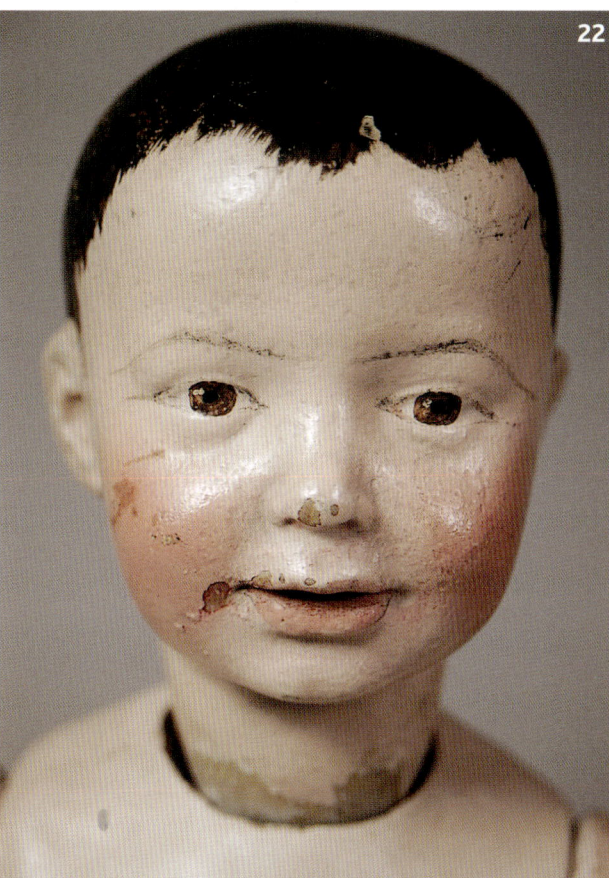

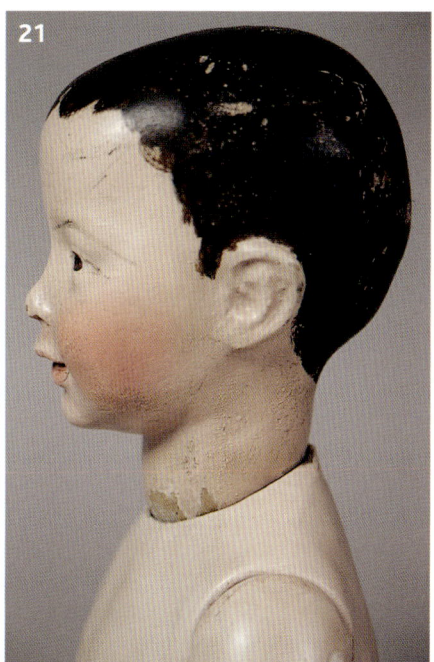

Munich Art Dolls

19. This 18¼-inch Munich Art Doll with a Vogelsanger sculpted head has a very different expression from the other Munich Art Dolls, due to its well-modeled open/closed laughing mouth. Courtesy Deutsches Spielzeugmuseum, Sonneberg. (Photo: Christiane Gräfnitz)

20. This 18¼-inch Munich Art Doll has a smooth head and painted hair. The facial modeling is similar to several other heads credited to Vogelsanger on the Sonneberg Doll Museum inventory sheets. The composition-jointed body differs slightly from the body pictured in illustration 18; the arms and legs are longer and thinner. Courtesy Deutsches Spielzeugmuseum, Sonneberg. (Photo: Christiane Gräfnitz)

22. A closer view of the boy doll seen in illustration 20 shows the painted hair with uneven forehead brushstrokes that resemble the hairstyle of a child playing outside on a windy day. This doll has expressive painted eyebrows. Some Vogelsanger-sculpted Munich Art Doll heads, including the pair pictured in illustration 18, lack painted eyebrows. The dolls pictured in illustrations 16 through 20 are described on the Sonneberg Doll Museum inventory sheets as follows: "*Puppe; Deutschland; Marion Kaulitz; Tegernsee, um 1910.*" The translated German words are: "Doll; Germany; Marion Kaulitz in 1910." The word "Tegernsee" refers to the Kaulitz home and doll factory in the small town of Gmund on Lake Tegernsee, Bavaria where she lived until 1924. Courtesy Deutsches Spielzeugmuseum, Sonneberg. (Photo: Christiane Gräfnitz)

21. The side profile of the doll seen in illustrations 20 and 22 shows the similarity of Vogelsanger-sculpted ears, which differ greatly from the shape of Wackerle-sculpted ears (see illustration 38). Courtesy Deutsches Spielzeugmuseum, Sonneberg. (Photo: Christiane Gräfnitz)

33

Chapter 1

23. The Sonneberg Doll Museum original inventory sheet credits the head on this Munich Art Doll to Joseph Wackerle in 1908. The 18-inch doll, a 1909 donation to the museum from the Hermann Tietz Department Store in Munich, bears the name "The Munich Child." Wackerle was employed as a sculptor at the Königliche Porzellan Manufaktur Nymphenburg (King's porcelain factory in Nymphenburg, Bavaria) before sculpting the Munich Art dolls. Courtesy Deutsches Spielzeugmuseum, Sonneberg. (Photo: Christiane Gräfnitz)

24. A closer view of the 18-inch doll seen in illustration 23 shows the wide-spaced eyes, curved eyebrows and full lips. Courtesy Deutsches Spielzeugmuseum, Sonneberg. (Photo: Christiane Gräfnitz)

26. This 25½-inch Munich Art Doll with a Joseph Wackerle head has a very different expression from the Wackerle head pictured in illustration 23. The original inventory sheet lists the doll as a 1909 donation by the Hermann Tietz, Department Store in Munich. Courtesy Deutsches Spielzeugmuseum, Sonneberg. (Photo: Christiane Gräfnitz)

25. The side view of the doll shown in illustraitions 26 and 27 shows the typical Wackerle full lips that feature a protruding upper lip. Many Wackerle heads have the same type of sculpted lips. Courtesy Deutsches Spielzeugmuseum, Sonneberg. (Photo: Christiane Gräfnitz)

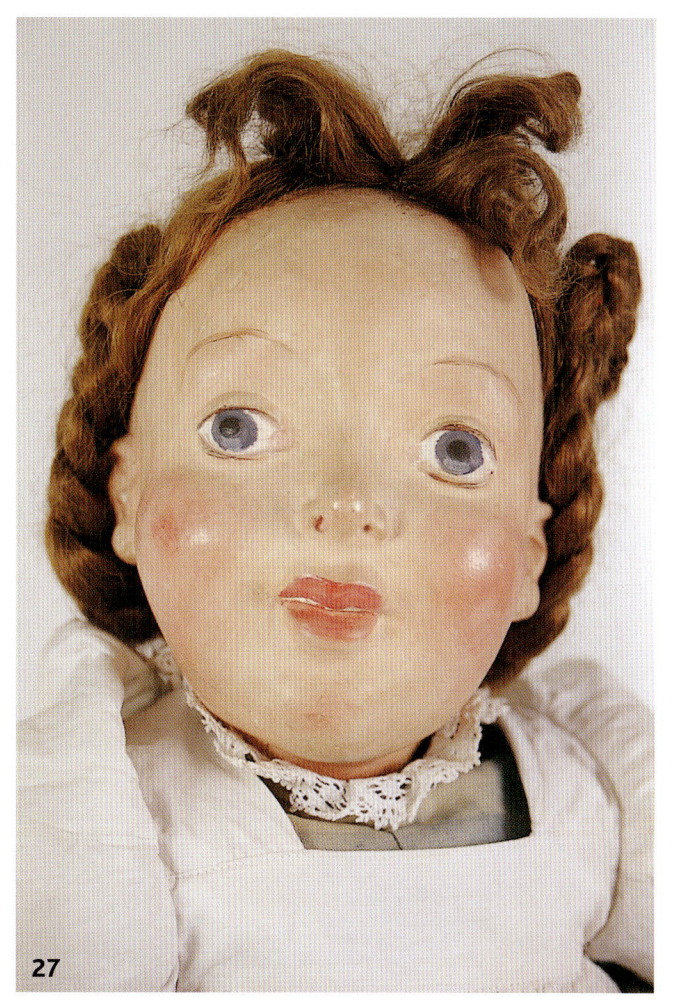

Munich Art Dolls

27. A closer view of the Wackerle head seen in illustration 26 shows the full lips, rounded cheeks and high-arched eyebrows that create an expressive, wide-eyed facial expression. Courtesy Deutsches Spielzeugmuseum, Sonneberg. (Photo: Christiane Gräfnitz)

28. This 25½-inch Munich Art Doll, with a Joseph Wackerle-sculpted shoulder head, has a leather body and jointed arms. It was donated to the Sonneberg Doll Museum in 1909 by Ernst Friedrich Dressel. According to hand-written notes on the original inventory sheet, Ernst Friedrich Dressel was a patron of the Sonneberg Doll Museum and mediated/arranged for the donation of thirteen heads to the museum by the Hermann Tietz Department Store chain. A letter in the museum archives dated February 10, 1909, explains the donation. The letter is described in the text of this chapter. Courtesy Deutsches Spielzeugmuseum, Sonneberg. (Photo: Christiane Gräfnitz)

29. The molded blond hair on the Munich Art Doll seen in illustration 28 features a row of large, vertical molded curls. A comparison of this head with the head of the baby pictured in illustration 64 shows the similarity of the Wackerle-sculpted mouth and nose. Courtesy Deutsches Spielzeugmuseum, Sonneberg. (Photo: Christiane Gräfnitz)

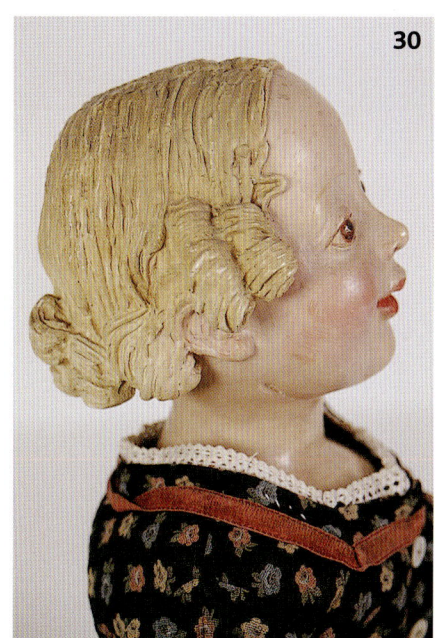

30. The side profile of the Wackerle head seen in illustrations 28 and 29 shows the difference in modeling as compared to the Vogelsanger heads, expecially in the modeling of the noses and ears (see illustration 21). Courtesy Deutsches Spielzeugmuseum, Sonneberg. (Photo: Christiane Gräfnitz)

Chapter 1

31. A closer view of the head seen in illustration 34 shows the unusual open/closed mouth with painted teeth and molded tongue. The painted eyes are similar to the eyes on many Vogelsanger-sculpted heads, including the painted eyes on my pair of Munich Art Dolls pictured in illustration 18. Courtesy Deutsches Spielzeugmuseum, Sonneberg. (Photo: Christiane Gräfnitz)

32. The open/closed mouth with painted teeth of the Vogelsanger doll seen in illustration 33 is very different in sculpting from the Wackerle mouths pictured in illustrations 23, 25 and 28. Courtesy Deutsches Spielzeugmuseum, Sonneberg. (Photo: Christiane Gräfnitz)

34. This 18-inch Munich Art Doll has a Paul Vogelsanger-sculpted head. This doll was also a 1910 donation to the Sonneberg Doll Museum from the Hermann Tietz Department Store in Munich. Courtesy Deutsches Spielzeugmuseum, Sonneberg. (Photo: Christiane Gräfnitz)

36

Munich Art Dolls

33. This 20½-inch Munich Art Doll has a Vogelsanger composition shoulder head, and a leather body with jointed arms. The doll was donated to the Sonneberg Doll Museum in 1909 by the Hermann Tietz Department Store in Munich. Sales records in the Sonneberg Doll Museum indicate that the Cuno & Otto Dressel doll factory made composition-jointed bodies for Munich Art Dolls with socket heads, and kid bodies for Munich Art Dolls with shoulder heads. Courtesy Deutsches Spielzeugmuseum, Sonneberg. (Photo: Christiane Gräfnitz)

35. A closer view of the head seen in illustration 36 shows the beautiful eye sculpting that lends such a pensive expression to the face. Courtesy Deutsches Spielzeugmuseum, Sonneberg. (Photo: Christiane Gräfnitz)

36. This beautiful 18½-inch Munich Art Doll was a 1910 donation to the Sonneberg Doll Museum from the Hermann Tietz Department Store in Munich. The museum inventory records indicate the original clothing worn by this doll is typical of the clothing worn by women in the Bavarian town of Straubing. The doll was dressed by Wanda V. Cranach, who owned the *Atelier f. Künstlerishche* (Artistic Studio for Lady Dressing) in Straubing. Marion Kaulitz also lived in Straubing, a suburb of Munich, when the Munich Art Dolls were introduced. Courtesy Deutsches Spielzeugmuseum, Sonneberg. (Photo: Christiane Gräfnitz)

Chapter 1

37. A full-length photograph of the Munich Art Doll seen in illustration 39 shows the long pheasant feather trimming its cone-shaped hat. Its clothing is similar to the clothing worn by a doll in the center of the photograph pictured in illustration 1 of the dolls on exhibit in the 1908 display at the Munich Fairgrounds. (Photo: Courtesy of Dr. Marion Faber, director of the Spielzeugmuseum der Stadt Nuernberg, Lydia Bayer Puppenmuseum)

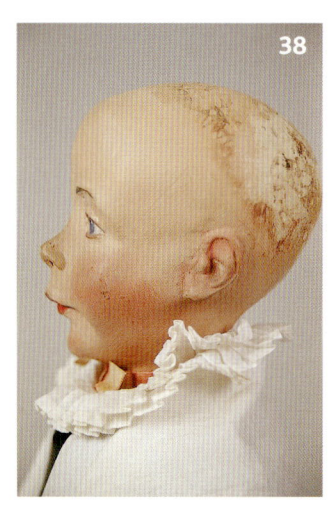

38. The side profile of the doll seen in illustrations 40 and 41 shows the Wackerle typical lip sculpting, which includes a protruding upper lip. Courtesy Deutsches Spielzeugmuseum, Sonneberg. (Photo: Christiane Gräfnitz)

39. This 18-inch Munich Art doll with a Joseph Wackerle-sculpted head is in the permanent collection of the Lydia Bayer Museum in Nuremberg. Courtesy Spielzeugmuseum der Stadt Nürnberg, Lydia Bayer Puppenmuseum. (Photo: Christiane Gräfnitz)

Munich Art Dolls

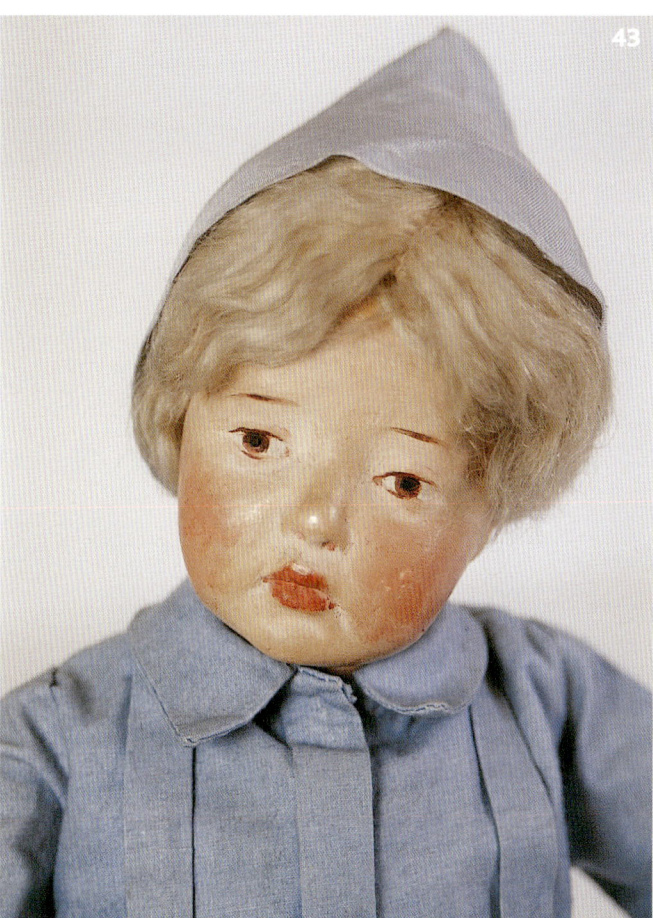

40. The slim-faced Wackerle-designed head of the doll in illustration 41 has a serious expression, arched eyebrows, molded upper eyelids, a thin nose and a closed mouth with long painted lines between the lips. Courtesy Deutsches Spielzeugmuseum, Sonneberg. (Photo: Christiane Gräfnitz)

41. This 18½-inch Munich Art Doll has a shoulder head sculpted by Josef Wackerle, and an original leather body with curved one-piece wooden arms. The doll was dressed by Wanda V. Cranach to represent a girl from the Spree (river that runs through Berlin) Forest area. It was also a 1910 donation from the Herman Tietz Department Store in Munich to the Sonneberg Doll Museum. Courtesy Deutsches Spielzeugmuseum, Sonneberg. (Photo: Christiane Gräfnitz)

42. This 16-inch doll with a 1908 Paul-Vogelsanger head is dressed like a coach driver. It was donated to the Sonneberg Doll Museum by the Cuno & Otto Dressel doll factory in 1909, according to this doll's original inventory sheet. Courtesy Deutsches Spielzeugmuseum, Sonneberg. (Photo: Christiane Gräfnitz)

43. A closer view of the doll in illustration 42 shows the painted eyes, distinctive mouth and smooth complexion often found on dolls sculpted by Paul Vogelsanger. Courtesy Deutsches Spielzeugmuseum, Sonneberg. (Photo: Christiane Gräfnitz)

Chapter 1

43. A closer view of the doll in illustration 44 shows the similarity of sculpting to the Vogelsanger head pictured in illustration 35. Courtesy Deutsches Spielzeugmuseum, Sonneberg. (Photo: Christiane Gräfnitz)

44. This 20½-inch doll with a 1909 Vogelsanger-sculpted head was donated to the Sonneberg Doll Museum in 1909 by the Hermann Tietz Department Store in Berlin. The clothing was created by well-known Munich Art Doll seamstress Klara Siewert. Her specialty was designing clothing that resembled that worn by children from the "Eastern provinces." The doll is identified on the inventory card as *Rumänin I*, because it is dressed in ethnic clothing typically worn by a girl from Rumania. Courtesy Deutsches Spielzeugmuseum, Sonneberg. (Photo: Christiane Gräfnitz)

45. A closer view of the doll in illustration 46 shows the smooth facial sculpting that is typical of Vogelsanger-sculpted heads. Courtesy Deutsches Spielzeugmuseum, Sonneberg. (Photo: Christiane Gräfnitz)

46. This 20½-inch doll, with a 1909 Vogelsanger-sculpted head, has slightly different facial sculpting to the doll pictured in illustration 44. Identified as *Rumänin II*, it was donated to the museum in 1909 by the Hermann Tietz Department Store in Berlin, and the clothing was designed by Munich Art Doll seamstress Klara Siewert. Courtesy Deutsches Spielzeugmuseum, Sonneberg. (Photo: Christiane Gräfnitz)

Munich Art Dolls

47. The facial sculpting on a third 20½-inch doll dressed to represent a Rumanian girl, varies slightly from the dolls pictured in illustrations 43 through 46. This doll was also a gift to the Sonneberg Doll Museum in 1909 from the Hermann Tietz Department Store in Berlin. The doll, with a 1909 Vogelsanger head, is identified as *Rumänin III* on the original inventory sheet, and it was also dressed by Klara Siewert. Courtesy Deutsches Spielzeugmuseum, Sonneberg. (Photo: Christiane Gräfnitz)

48. A closer view of the doll in illustration 47 shows the similarities of the dolls identified as *Rumänin I, II and III*. Courtesy Deutsches Spielzeugmuseum, Sonneberg. (Photo: Christiane Gräfnitz)

49. This 14½-inch Munich Art Doll is dressed like a child from Weissenburg in Alsace-Lorraine. The facial sculpting is very similar to the sculpting of the Vogelsanger heads on the *Rumänin I, II and III* dolls. The doll was donated to the Sonneberg Doll Museum by the Hermann Tietz Department Store in Munich on April 13, 1910. Courtesy Deutsches Spielzeugmuseum, Sonneberg. (Photo: Christiane Gräfnitz)

50. A closer view of the doll in illustration 49 shows the calm sweet expression typical of Vogelsanger's sculpting. Courtesy Deutsches Spielzeugmuseum, Sonneberg. (Photo: Christiane Gräfnitz)

Chapter 1

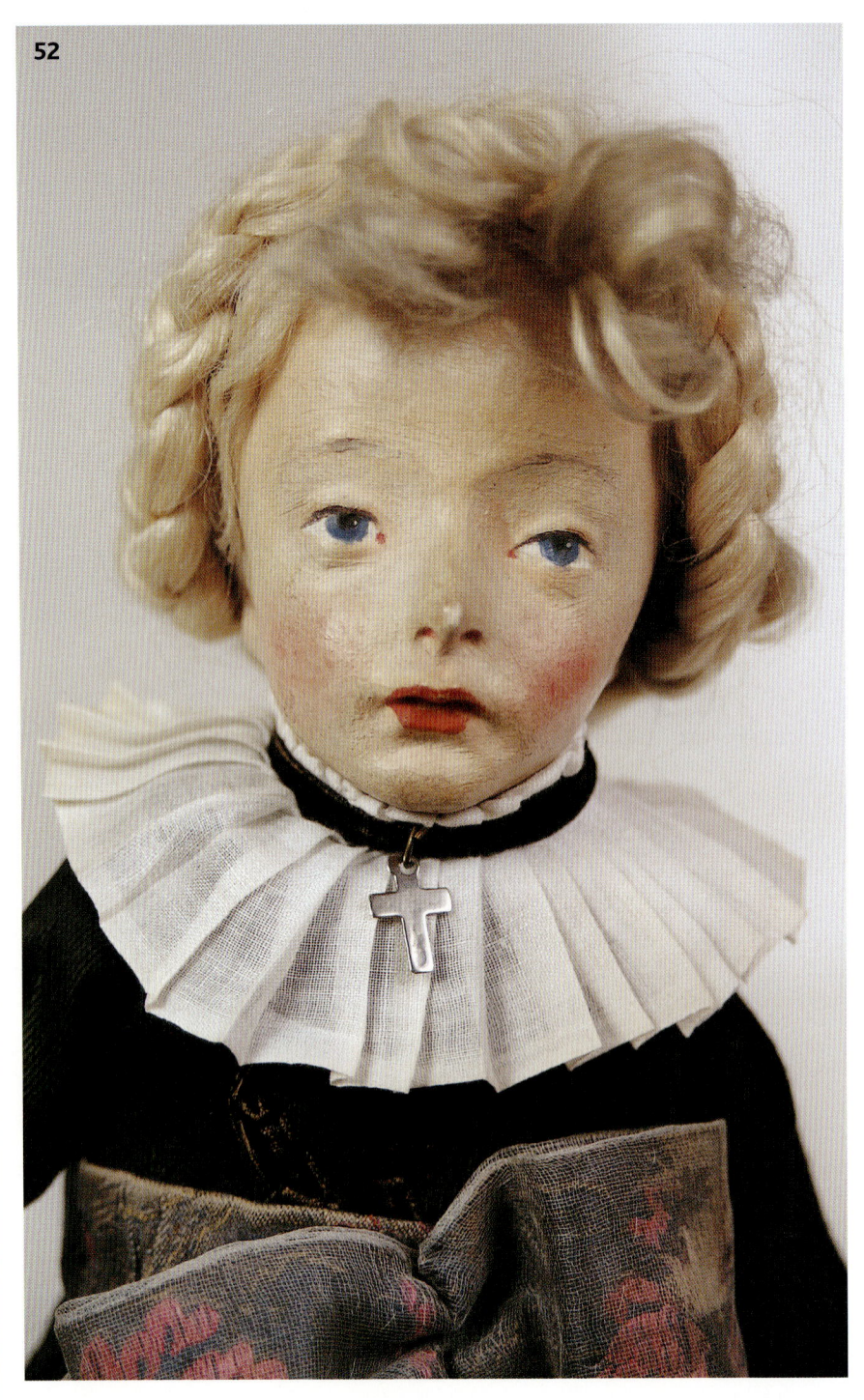

51. An April 13, 1910, letter addressed to the Sonneberg Doll Museum lists this 19-inch Munich Art Doll, made in 1908, as one of thirteen dolls donated to the museum by the Hermann Tietz Department Store in Munich. The facial modeling is very similar to the heads sculpted by Wackerle. The doll is identified as a *Schlierseer* girl on the museum's inventory sheet, indicating it was dressed to resemble a girl living near Lake Schlier in the Bavarian Alps. Courtesy Deutsches Spielzeugmuseum, Sonneberg. (Photo: Christiane Gräfnitz)

52. A closer view of the head in illustration 51 shows the typical Wackerle wide-spaced eyes, thin nose and mouth. Courtesy Deutsches Spielzeugmuseum, Sonneberg. Photo: Christiane Gräfnitz)

53. The side profile of the doll in illustrations 51 and 52 shows another view of the typical Wackerle-sculpted nose and protruding upper lip that resembles a person with an overbite. Courtesy Deutsches Spielzeugmuseum, Sonneberg. (Photo: Christiane Gräfnitz)

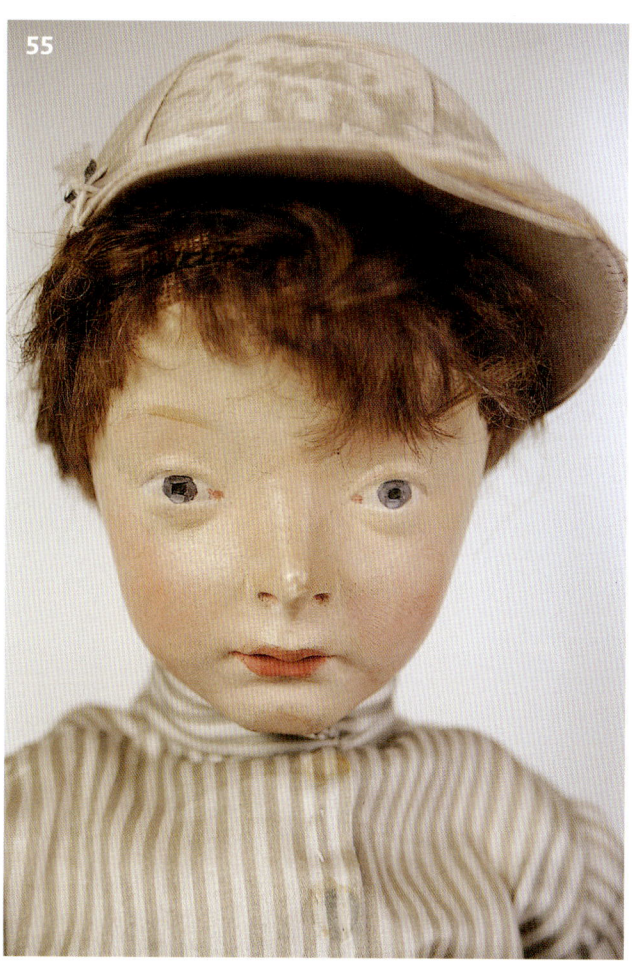

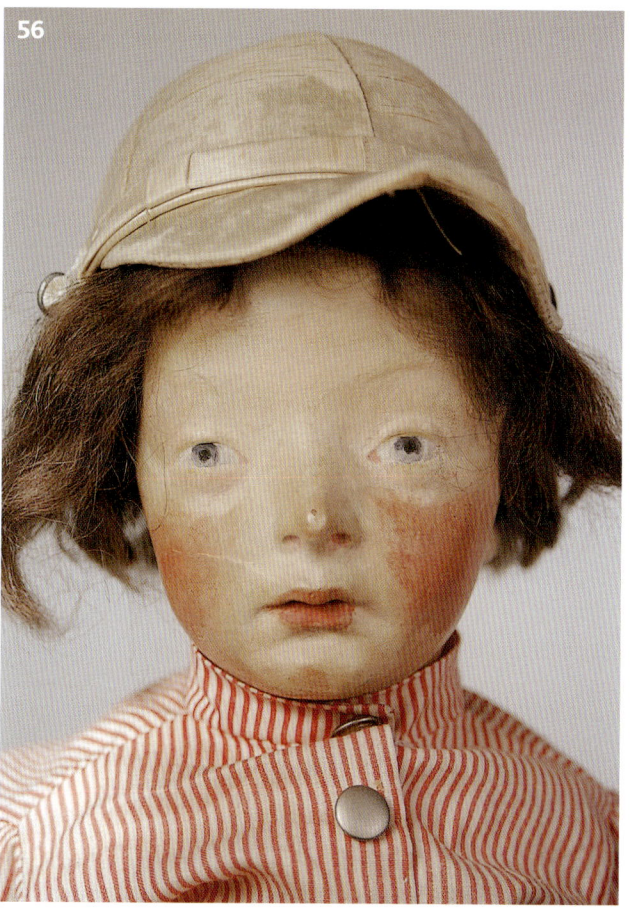

Munich Art Dolls

54. A side view of the doll in illustration 55 shows the typical Wackerle thin nose and protruding upper lip. Courtesy Deutsches Spielzeugmuseum, Sonneberg. (Photo: Christiane Gräfnitz)

55. This 20½-inch Munich Art doll was also donated to the Sonnberg Museum in 1909 by the Hermann Tietz Department Store in Berlin. The doll was redressed in 1963 because the original jockey jacket was destroyed, according to the original inventory sheet. The original jockey-styled clothing was created for a 1909 doll competition at the Kaufhaus des Wessens (Department Store of the West) in Berlin in 1909 by Mrs. Thomaelen, a member of the Artisans School in Magdeburg. Courtesy Deutsches Spielzeugmuseum, Sonneberg. (Photo: Christiane Gräfnitz)

56. A closer view of the doll in illustration 57 shows the molded eye sockets, full, down-turned mouth and chin dimple. Courtesy Deutsches Spielzeugmuseum, Sonneberg. (Photo: Christiane Gräfnitz)

57. A similar 20½-inch jockey was originally dressed for the doll competition in Berlin by seamstress Mrs. Thomaelen, and redressed in identical clothing is 1963. This jockey's face is fuller than the face of the jockey pictured in illustration 55, but the Wackerle nose is similar. Courtesy Deutsches Spielzeugmuseum, Sonneberg. (Photo: Christiane Gräfnitz)

Chapter 1

58. This 16½-inch Tyrolean schoolboy with a Wackerle-sculpted head, was donated to the Sonneberg Doll Museum in 1910 by the Munich branch of the Hermann Tietz Department Store. He is dressed to represent a typical Tyrolean schoolboy with lederhosen, a felt jacket and a straw hat trimmed with a long pheasant feather (the hat was removed for the photograph). Courtesy Deutsches Spielzeugmuseum, Sonneberg. (Photo: Christiane Gräfnitz)

59. The head sculpting of the doll in illustration 58 closely resembles Wackerle's expressive sculpting as opposed to the calm facial expressions typical of Vogelsanger. The nose and mouth sculpting is very similar to the Wackerle head pictured in illustration 40. Courtesy Deutsches Spielzeugmuseum, Sonneberg. (Photo: Christiane Gräfnitz)

60. A closer view of the facial sculpting of the doll in illustration 61 shows the similarity to the Vogelsanger heads identified as *Rumaenin I, II and II*, pictured in illustrations 44-48. Courtesy Deutsches Spielzeugmuseum, Sonneberg. (Photo: Christiane Gräfnitz)

61. This 13½-inch doll is part of the Munich Art Doll group currently on display in a glass showcase on the second floor of the Sonneberg Doll Museum. The head was sculpted by Joseph Vogelsanger and donated to the museum in 1909 by the Hermann Tietz Department Store in Munich. The hairstyle is identified as *Schnecken* (pinned-up braids, resembling the inside of snail shells). Courtesy Deutsches Spielzeugmuseum, Sonneberg. (Photo: Christiane Gräfnitz)

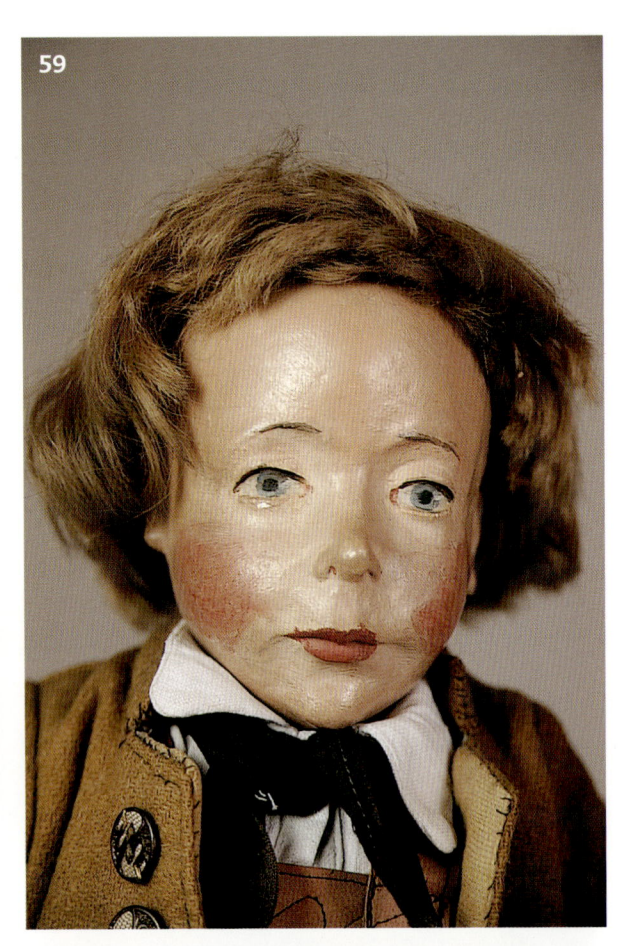

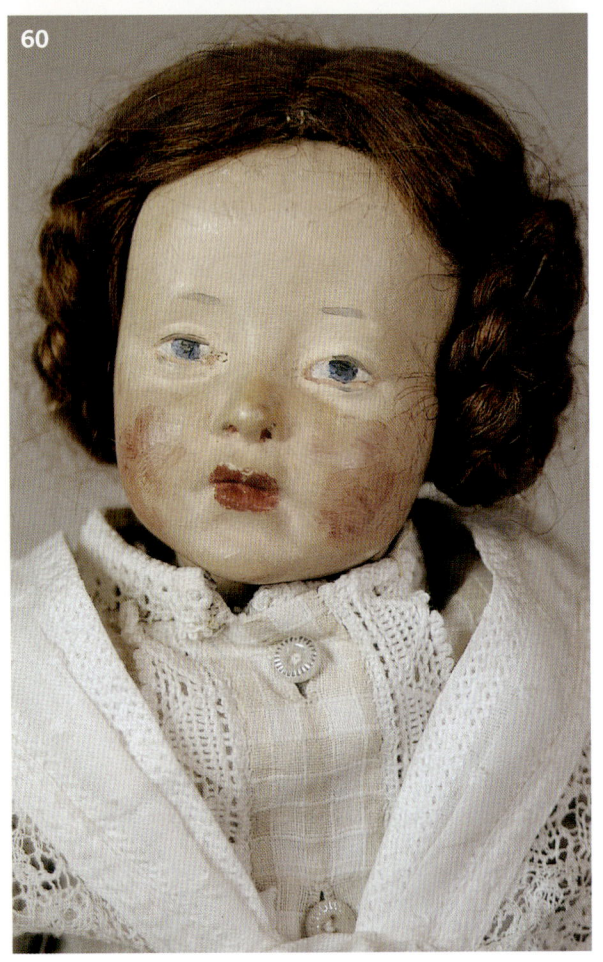

Munich Art Dolls

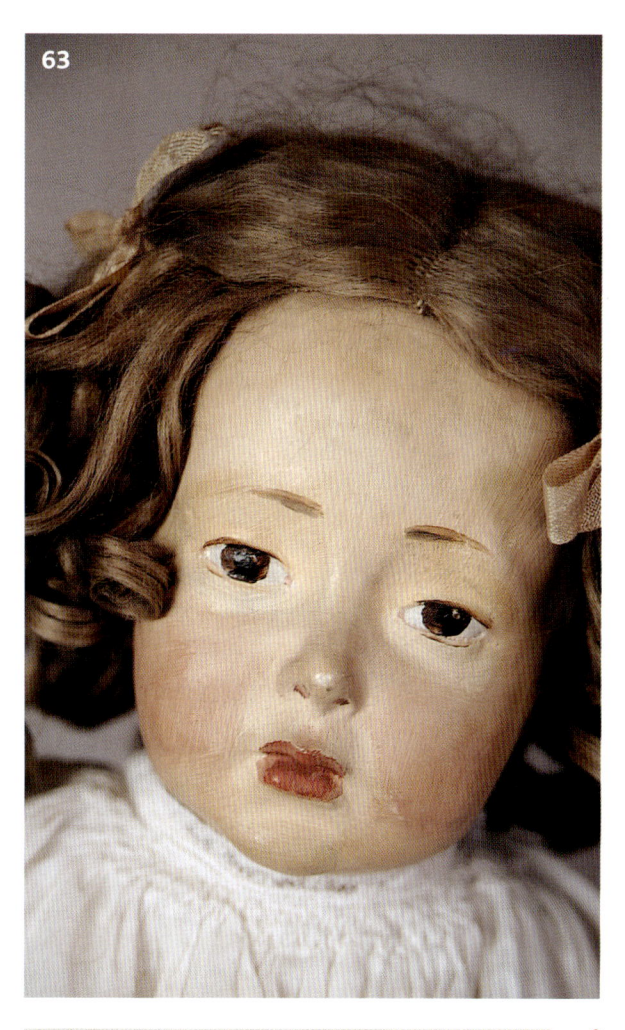

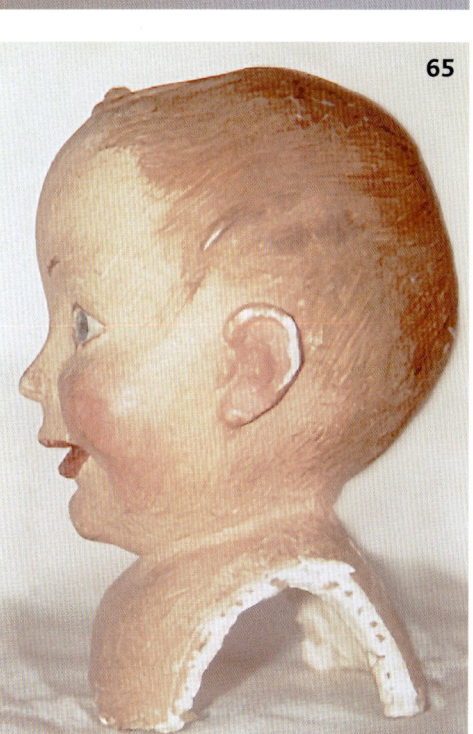

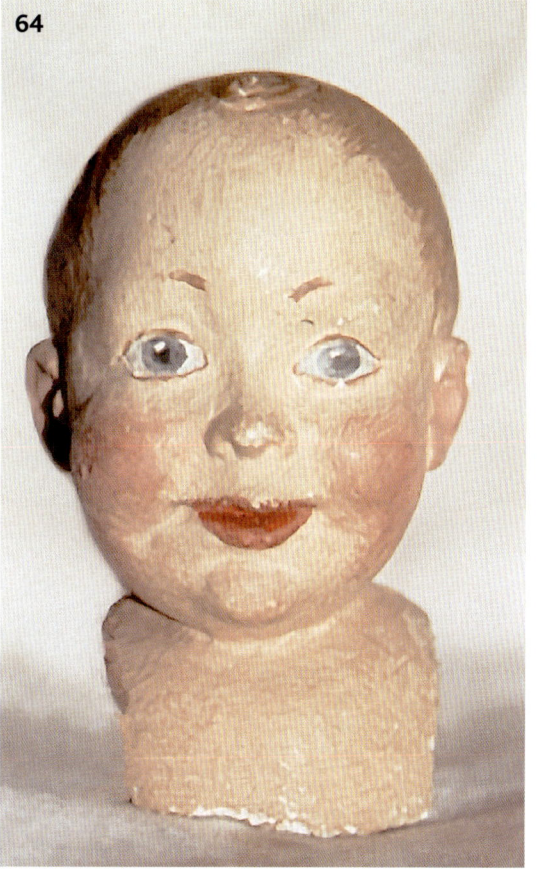

62. This 16½-inch Munich Art Doll was donated to the Sonneberg Doll Museum in 1909 by the Hermann Tietz Department Store in Berlin. The shoulder head is mounted on a cloth body with bisque arms. The doll, identified as *Mädchen Gärtnerin* (Girl Gardener) on the original inventory sheet, was dressed in 1909 by an original Munich Art seamstress identified as Frau Koch for the 1909 Department Store of the West doll competition in Berlin. Courtesy Deutsches Spielzeugmuseum, Sonneberg. (Photo: Christiane Gräfnitz)

63. This 20¾-inch Volgelsanger-sculpted head has the same mouth sculpting as the head pictured in illustrations 60 and 61. The large painted eyes and full mouth give this Munich Art Doll a particularly sweet expression. The doll was donated to the Sonneberg Doll Museum by the Hermann Tietz Department Store in Munich. Courtesy Deutsches Spielzeugmuseum, Sonneberg. (Photo: Christiane Gräfnitz)

64. This unusual 3¼-inch Munich Art Doll shoulder head baby was sculpted by Joseph Wackerle. Marie Marc-Schnür also sculpted a Munich Art Doll baby head, which is pictured in a November 1908 article in *Welt der Frau* (*Woman's World*), written by Ernst Veil. This very rare baby shoulder head shows the variety of dolls sculpted by Wackerle. Although the mouth is fuller on this baby, the nose is very similar to the Wackerle-sculpted head with molded vertical curls pictured in illustration 29. Ferna Nolte Collection. (Photo: Christiane Gräfnitz)

65. A side view of the head in illustration 64 shows the unusual sculpting and slightly rougher Joseph Wackerle complexion as compared with the smooth composition heads made by Paul Vogelsanger. Ferna Nolte Collection. (Photo: Christiane Gräfnitz)

Chapter 1

66. This 13½-inch doll is identified as *Kleine Schwäben* (Little Swabian), according to the original Sonneberg Doll Museum inventory sheet. The original clothing represents a girl living in Swabia, a region near Stuttgart. This Munich Art Doll was donated to the museum on April 13, 1910, by the Hermann Tietz Department Store in Munich. Courtesy Deutsches Spielzeugmuseum, Sonneberg. (Photo: Christiane Gräfnitz)

67. The unusual facial sculpting of the doll in illustration 66 includes a wide nose, upper and lower molded eyelids and far-spaced painted eyes, similar to other sculpted heads credited to Wackerle. Courtesy Deutsches Spielzeugmuseum, Sonneberg. (Photo: Christiane Gräfnitz)

68. The Wackerle wide-spaced painted eyes and mouth of the doll in illustration 69 are similar to those of the doll pictured in illustrations 66 and 67. The nose is smaller, but shaped much like the nose on the baby pictured in illustration 64. Courtesy Deutsches Spielzeugmuseum, Sonneberg. (Photo: Christiane Gräfnitz)

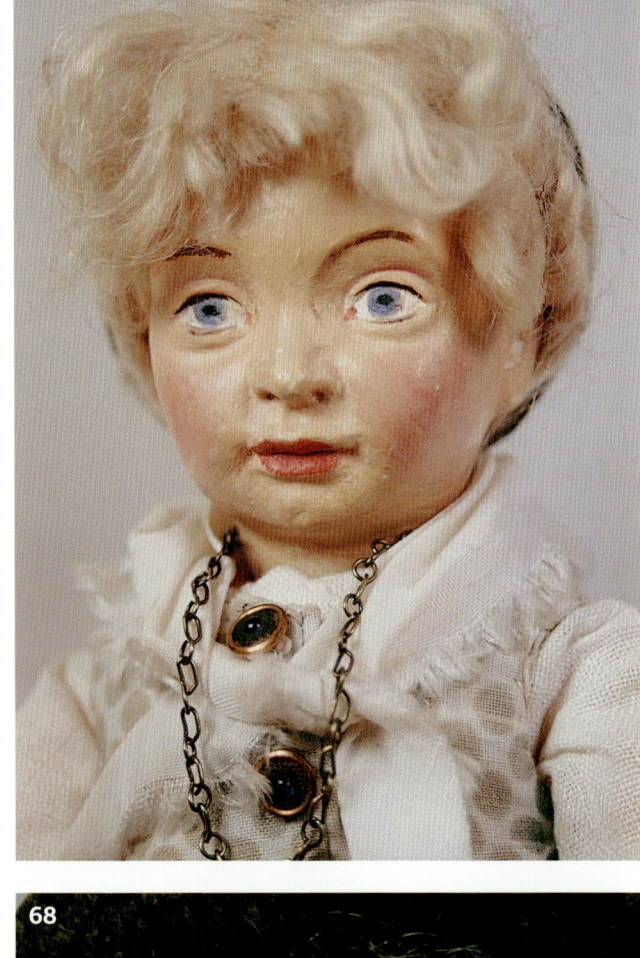

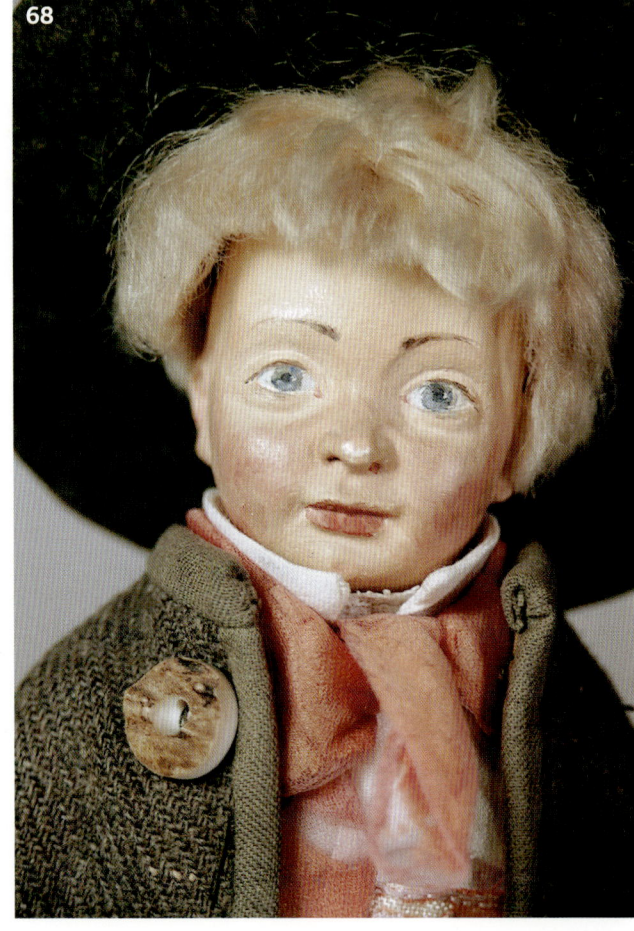

69. This 17-inch Munich Art Doll is wearing the traditional lederhosen, jacket and large hat of the Schliersee area. Lake Schlier is located in upper Bavaria, south of Munich. This doll was donated to the Sonneberg Doll Museum in 1910 by the Hermann Tietz Department Store in Munich. The Wackerle-sculpted head has a similar, but smaller, sculpted nose as the baby pictured in illustration 64. Courtesy Deutsches Spielzeugmuseum, Sonneberg. (Photo: Christiane Gräfnitz)

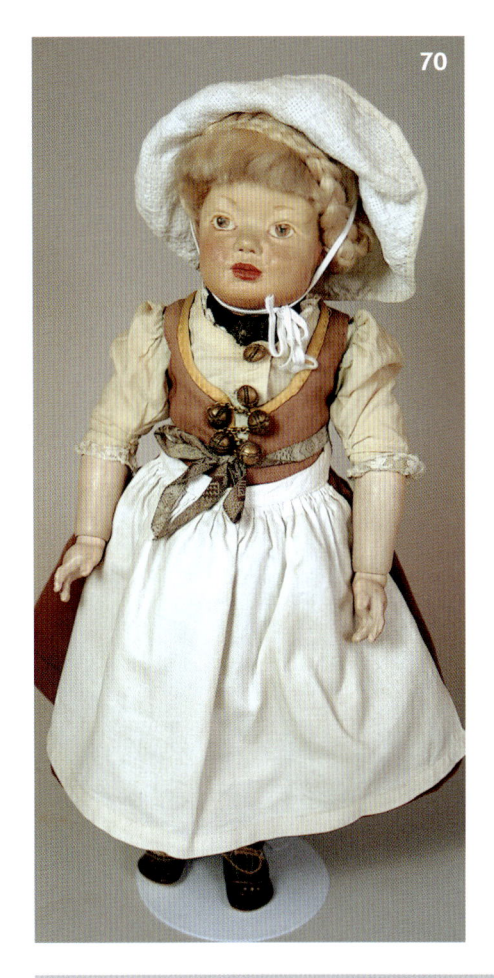

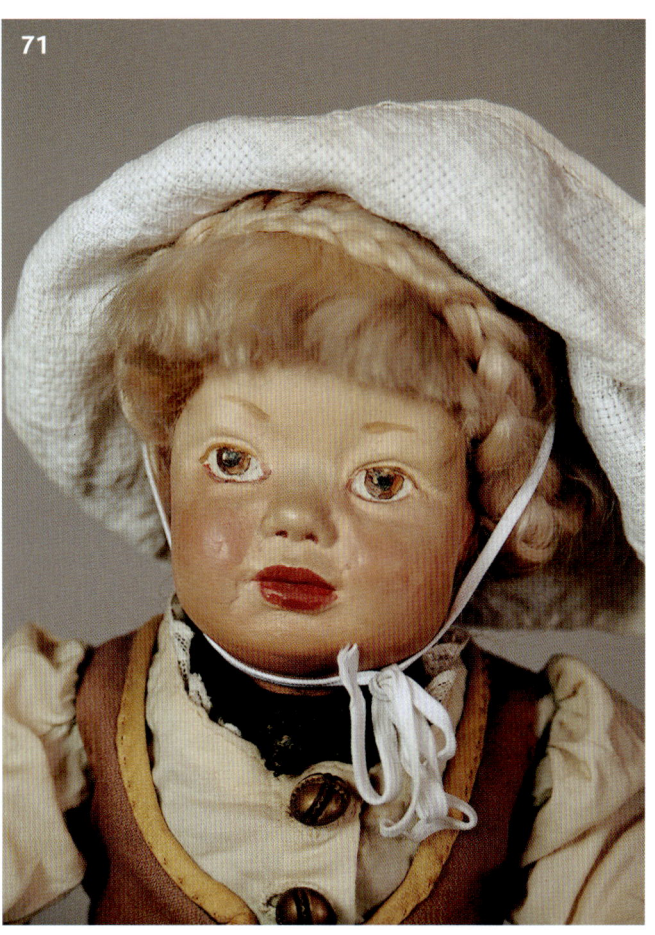

Munich Art Dolls

70. This 16½-inch Munich Art Doll, donated to the Sonneberg Doll Museum by the Hermann Tietz Department Store in Munich on April 13, 1910, is identified on the original inventory sheet as a gardener. Many of the Munich Art Dolls were originally dressed in what is described as work-related clothing. The wide-spaced painted eyes, the painted eyebrows and the facial shape resemble the Wackerle-sculpted head pictured in illustration 67. Courtesy Deutsches Spielzeugmuseum, Sonneberg. (Photo: Christiane Gräfnitz)

71. A closer view of the head of the doll in illustration 70 shows the difference in nose and mouth sculpting, although the painted eyes are still widely spaced, like many of the eyes on Wackerle-sculpted heads. Courtesy Deutsche Spielzeugmuseum, Sonneberg. (Photo: Christiane Gräfnitz)

72. This 18½-inch Munich Art Doll also has a Marie Marc-Schnür-sculpted wax head. She was dressed by Wanda V. Cranach to represent a woman from Bregenz, a city on Lake Constance's eastern corner on the Austrian side. The wax-head doll was also donated to the Sonneberg Doll Museum on April 13, 1910, by the Hermann Tietz Department Store in Munich. Courtesy Deutsches Spielzeugmuseum, Sonneberg. (Photo: Christiane Gräfnitz)

73. This unusual 19¼-inch Munich Art Doll has a wax head sculpted by Marie Marc-Schnür, according to the original Sonneberg Doll Museum inventory sheet. The doll, wearing original clothing made by Wanda V. Cranach, is dressed to represent women in the Ziller Valley, located in the Austrian Alps east of Innsbruck. The doll was donated to the Sonneberg Doll Museum on April 13, 1910, by the Hermann Tietz Department Store in Munich. Courtesy Deutsches Spielzeugmuseum, Sonneberg. (Photo: Christiane Gräfnitz)

Part One
CHAPTER 2
Kämmer & Reinhardt Doll Factory

1. This photograph of modeler Ernst Kämmer, co-founder of the Kämmer & Reinhardt doll factory was taken in 1901. Author's Archival Paper Collection.

2. Franz Reinhardt, seen in this 1911 photograph, co-founded the Kämmer & Reinhardt doll factory, and led the factory from the death of his partner in 1901 until his own death on March 28, 1933. Author's Archival Paper Collection.

The Kämmer & Reinhardt doll factory in Waltershausen sold some of the finest dolls in the world that imitated the features of a real child, in varying moods. Sculptor Ernst Kämmer directed the creative side of the business while merchant Franz Reinhardt handled the practical side of the company. My original copy of the Kämmer & Reinhardt 1911 twenty-fifth-anniversary booklet provides accurate history of the doll factory as well as important information about the first character dolls introduced by the company. The following introductory information describes the founding of the company.

At the end of 1885, two busy people got together, the modeler Ernst Kämmer, who had worked for another doll factory and young business man Franz Reinhardt. It was their goal to manufacture jointed dolls with little money and a lot of work. On January 5, 1886 they registered at the court of trades as 'Kämmer & Reinhardt.' This is the birthday of the company,

3. The twenty-fifth-anniversary booklet published by the Kämmer & Reinhardt doll factory in 1911 includes this 1885 photograph of the first doll factory building. According to information in the booklet, increasing doll orders forced the company to build a larger doll factory. Author's Archival Paper Collection.

Chapter 2

although preparations to start the company began many weeks before. Ernst Kämmer was known to be an excellent modeler and craftsman, so the company achieved great success in just a short time, supported of course by the business knowledge of well-educated Franz Reinhardt. They started the business in a very frugal way.

The words written in December 1910 are unchanged by time, and represent the thoughts of a person who was closely connected to the doll factory. His last three words are: "Waltershausen December 1910." The date indicates that all of the words in the booklet were written in 1910 rather than 1911, the actual twenty-fifth anniversary of the doll factory. In this chapter I have included a few of the paragraphs that pertain to the history of the factory, and the words that describe the production of character dolls. From the Kämmer & Reinhardt booklet we learn the following history.

Our business kept growing without any major interruptions. This is especially important because all that growth carried over in the private sector, to the home workers, which increased their workload. That was not always without difficulties because there would be shortages among the skilled home workers, people had to be found and trained. With that other problems arose, people had to be hired but could not get used to working neatly and had to be let go again. The base for the whole business was to produce high quality products.

Through the years, we added other novelties, the following are the most important ones: 'Porcelain heads with teeth (before that the heads were made with their mouths closed); oval-shaped wooden joints that don't turn too far; stiff joints that don't spread too far apart while in the sitting position; wooden heads with a face mask, bathing children with movable arms and eye lashes made from real hair.

All these inventions, as well as some technical improvements, like pouring the paint instead of brushing it on, are now common in the industry. Hardly anybody remembers to thank the genius Ernst Kämmer for these inventions. Unfortunately, we lost him way too early. In 1901 he died on a vacation to another country. He was not only very talented but also a man with integrity, a very industrious co-worker, a true friend and he gave advice to his partner as well as the lowest worker, who loved and honored him.

When examining the sales graph for our company one can note that the quickest and most successful development regarding sales numbers happened right after the years of the death of the expert Herr Kämmer. The reason for this was, although Kämmer was a very industrious man, he was an older man and he was very careful regarding the increase of production. The old house had become too small for the factory and after Herr Kämmer died, we built a new and bigger factory, which now has been added on again. This of course allowed a much bigger production. Production was especially increased early in the year to fill the storage rooms. We would have to add on even more if we would not have all our home workers and we would not get all our wooden parts and stamped doll parts from our sister company Heinrich Handwerck.

Another important reason the sales numbers increased surprisingly was the invention of the 'non-fading and matte' celluloid heads. Our Franz Reinhardt was the only one in the business who envisioned correctly that the celluloid heads would be more successful if they were prettier and did not fade. After many attempts, Karl Krausser, the factory's technical director, achieved success in making celluloid heads that met those criteria. The factory Rheinische Gummi und Celluloidwarenfabrik agreed to make heads after our beautiful models, deliver them unfinished and we would finish them here with our new methods and thus excite the world.

We had made our bisque heads (legally protected by the D.R.P.) with eyes moving to the side. We called them 'The Flirt,' and they were especially successful in America. Another reason why the jointed dolls were so successful might have been that we gave them names like 'Mein Liebling' which was 'My Darling' in English. One of the most successful lines of that doll type was 'My One and Only Darling.' With names like that and adding little tags, again we were the front runners for the whole doll industry. All these successes, however, are put to shame by our latest success: the 'Character dolls.'

In the summer of 1908 at the Munich Fair, we saw a group of artist dolls, which created a stir because they actually offered something new. The Munich artists criticized the uniformity of the doll heads – they all looked the same, they were made to look idealistic, therefore unrealistic without any expressions. We could not argue with their opinion, as we could not argue the fact that there was a stagnation in the doll industry. Twenty three years we had dominated the market with one doll model. The group of dolls that was exhibited was to promise some success, after all it was a new idea, but we found that most of that attractiveness was due to the artistic arrangement and the colors of the costumes. Most of the heads, when we looked closely, we found to be ugly. We hope the artists will forgive our judgments because we were unsure about our own criticism – it could have been that we were just

Kämmer & Reinhardt Doll Factory

4. A photograph of the second, and last, Kämmer & Reinhardt doll factory is also included in the factory's twenty-fifth-anniversary booklet. The large historic building is now listed in the Register of Historic Properties, and is therefore protected from demolition. Author's Archival Paper Collection.

5. A recent photograph of the first Kämmer & Reinhardt doll factory building in Waltersausen shows how little it has changed. (Photo: Mary Krombholz)

6. A 1911 photograph from the twenty-fifth-anniversary booklet pictures Franz Reinhardt's villa, automobile and personal chauffeur. The villa is still standing near the second factory. It has been converted into a four-family apartment building. Author's Archival Paper Collection.

7. A recent photograph of the large Kämmer & Reinhardt doll factory in Waltershausen shows the difference in size between the first and second factory buildings. Two factory mottos can still be seen under the arched 1907-dated entrance. The translated German words read: "Only the best is good enough for our children" and "Always ahead, never backwards." Kämmer & Reinhardt occupied the building from 1907 until the 1930s. (Photo: Mary Krombholz)

Chapter 2

prejudiced. We did realize the fact and we chose to follow the idea that the Munich artists voiced.

We turned to a Berlin artist who had sculpted a bronze bust of an about 6 week old child. He recommended it for our doll production. This is our famous baby head! It took us a while to come to terms with using this model for production. It was absolutely beautiful but it seemed too realistic. It was so surprising to find out how successful we were with it, and this success was unsurpassed in the doll manufacturing chronicles. In addition to the baby head, the Berlin artist made some other models after having great interest in the new movement. We have to thank Mr. Secret Commerce Counselor Halbig because he gave us his full support throughout our venture.

In 1909, we brought the new dolls on the market and called them, unlike the Munich artists, 'Character Dolls.' They are now famous all over the world. Our samples caused us to have a strange experience. Our customers had a hard time deciding on our new product. Even in 1909, at the Berlin Fair, we were only able to sell a few samples. There was one friend who was gutsy enough to order a few dozen. We went ahead and sent him the few he had ordered.

Then the unthinkable happened. Everybody that had bought a sample wrote soon after they had received the dolls and said they had already sold. They ordered more, which soon were also sold. That went on until soon we were inundated with orders and we were unable to meet all the orders in 1909. This was mainly the case for the baby doll, but also the dolls 'Peter' and 'Marie,' which were modeled by our Berlin artist, quickly became favorites.

Besides the pretty heads, we also put a lot of effort into making the character doll unique. The dolls were coated with a matte lacquer. This is the only natural component. Years ago, we had tried to make matte lacquered dolls popular on the European market. In America they had caught on right away. Now it seemed this was the only way. Instead of frilly clothes we dressed the dolls in practical and natural shirts. We gave them natural yet nice looking hairdos. Now we put our own modelers in charge to make a head. Franz Reinhardt's grandson was the model for the 'Hans' and 'Gretchen' doll, which were the big successes of 1910!

The character dolls would have become more popular sooner, if the sleeping eyes had not changed the facial expression. This question remains unanswered, but it is probably the main reason why the old fancy dolls are still selling well and always will.

Having great success with the character dolls was very honoring, yet very embarrassing, too. Just after the March fair we had to recall our traveling sales person due to the fact that we already had too many orders which would take all year to fill. We had to withdraw business from our sales people, storage businesses and clothing stores. We even had to block orders from our best, oldest and dearest customers. We were very sorry, but hoped people would understand.

Nevertheless, we take credit for helping the whole doll industry to a new high thanks to the character dolls. Every worker in the doll industry profits from this. We don't expect any thanks, but we would appreciate tactfulness on behalf of the other doll manufacturers not to copy our products. This is not always maintained. We also expect from our noble customers not to purchase those copies. This is the end of the chronicles! We have reached the present! We are sailing into the new quarter century with a thousand masts! Kämmer & Reinhardt. Waltershausen, December 1910.

The identity of the "Berlin artist who sculpted a bronze bust of a six-week-old child" was a mystery for many years. It was finally solved in 1987 by researchers Jürgen and Marianne Cieslik, who found an article in the newspaper *Thüringer Allegemeine Zeitung* dated April 24, 1928. The article contained the information that the well-known Berlin sculptor Professor Lewin-Funcke created the original model for the first Kämmer & Reinhardt character head, the 100 mold number. The Ciesliks write in a 1987 issue of their *Puppenmagazin*: "Professor Lewin-Funcke was afraid he would tarnish his reputation as a famous sculptor and art teacher in Berlin if it became known that he modeled doll heads." Professor Lewin-Funcke also created the original models for the 101, 102 and 107 Kämmer & Reinhardt bisque character heads.

Shortly after Käthe Kruse introduced her first cloth character doll, Number 1, at the 1910 Christmas display at the Berlin Hermann Tietz department store, she was approached by a representative of the Kämmer & Reinhardt doll factory to consider letting them make her dolls according to her own specifications. She agreed, and the Kämmer & Reinhardt doll factory sent men to the Käthe Kruse doll factory to learn the techniques she had worked out for her own doll production. The dolls were sold as *Baby Bauz* but, unfortunately, they did not come up to her standards, and the contract was cancelled. The dolls were only made for a few months in 1911 and are rarely found today. The Kämmer & Reinhardt head is similar, but not identical, to the early Kruse cloth dolls. The dolls are easily identified because, unlike the Kruse dolls' bodies, the Kämmer & Reinhardt bodies have jointed knees. The Käthe Kruse museum in Donnauworth, Germany, has an example on permanent display.

The Kämmer & Reinhardt doll factory made a number of character dolls with celluloid heads. Identical plaster molds

Kämmer & Reinhardt Doll Factory

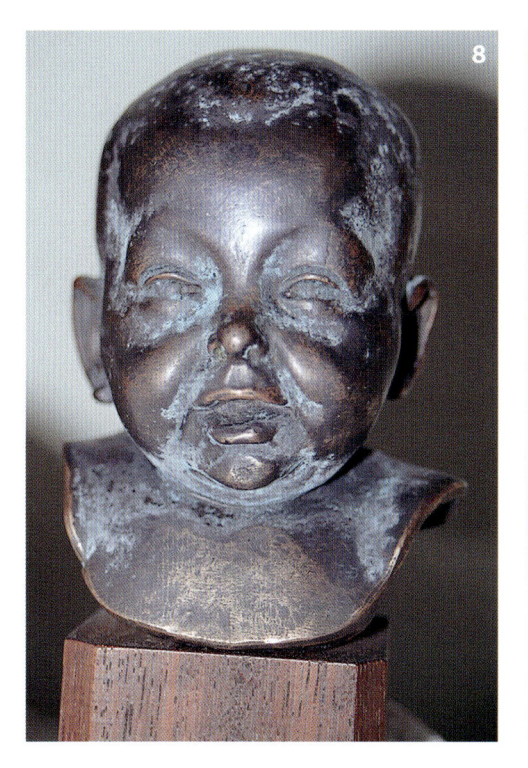

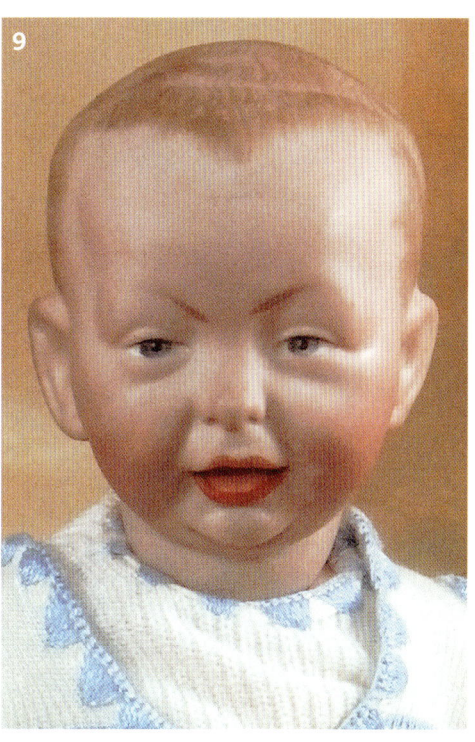

8. This original 4-inch bronze bust of Kämmer & Reinhardt's mold number 100 baby is on permanent display in the Rothenburg doll museum. It is one of only two existing bronze sculptures of the factory's first character doll, from which the original plaster bust was made. Courtesy Rothenburg Puppenmuseum/ Katharina Engels Collection. (Photo: Christiane Gräfnitz)

9. Bisque socket head by Simon & Halbig; baby body parts by Heinrich Handwerck; assembly by Kämmer & Reinhardt; molded hair; large, realistic ears; well-defined eye sockets; single-stroke, slanted eyebrows; molded, black-outlined upper eyelids; painted eyes with white highlights, open/closed mouth with molded tongue; chin dimple; 11-inch doll; GM 1909; marked: K*R//100//28. In the 1911 twenty-fifth-anniversary booklet, Franz Reinhardt described the first display of his character dolls in the Berlin Hermann Tietz department store in 1909: "Only invited guests were permitted to view the small exhibit that presented the whole product line, including the new doll type." Beth Karp Collection. (Photo: Lee Krombholz)

10. This photograph of the mold number 100 baby is on page 15 of the Kämmer & Reinhardt twenty-fifth-anniversary booklet. The caption lists the trademark name of the doll: "Baby." Note the unusual position of the left arm on the composition five-piece, jointed-baby body. Author's Archival Paper Collection.

11. In 1908 Arthur Lewin-Funcke (1866-1937) created the original plaster bust for Kämmer & Reinhardt's first character baby, mold number 100. It was named *Lachendes Baby* (Laughing Baby). A six-month-old baby served as the model for this plaster bust, total height 13 cm (5 inches). This casting, made from the original plaster bust, was ordered by Karen Lewin-Funcke, granddaughter of Arthur Lewin-Funcke. Antje Lode Collection. (Photo: Antje Lode)

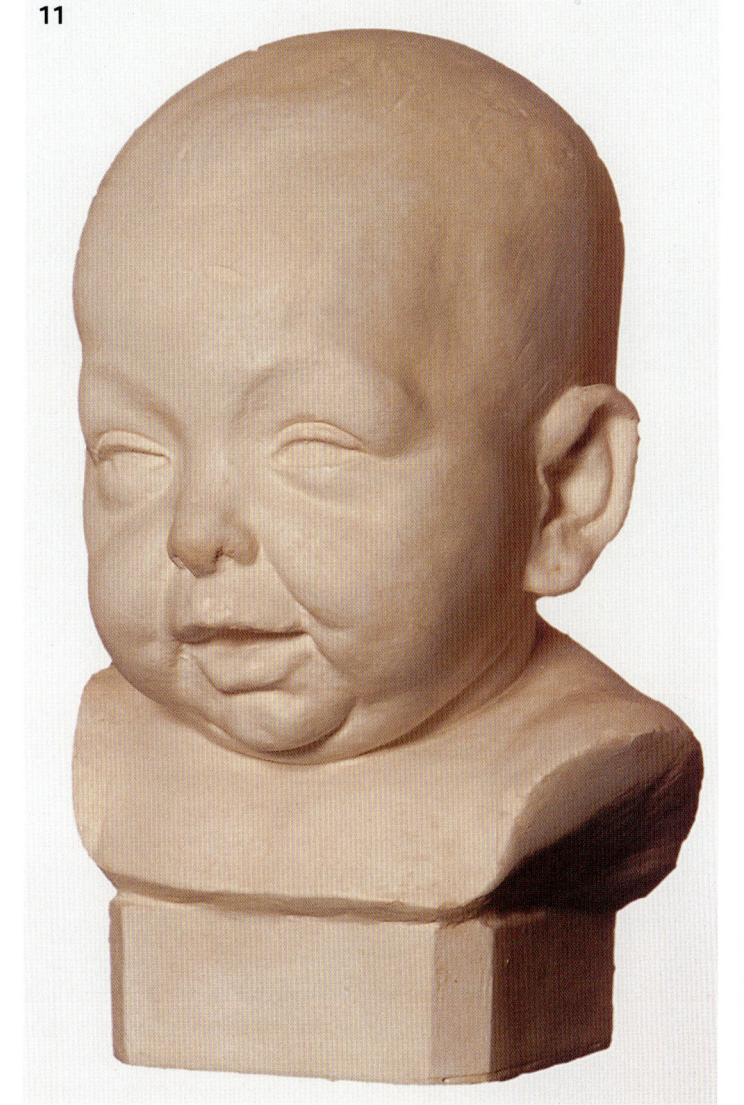

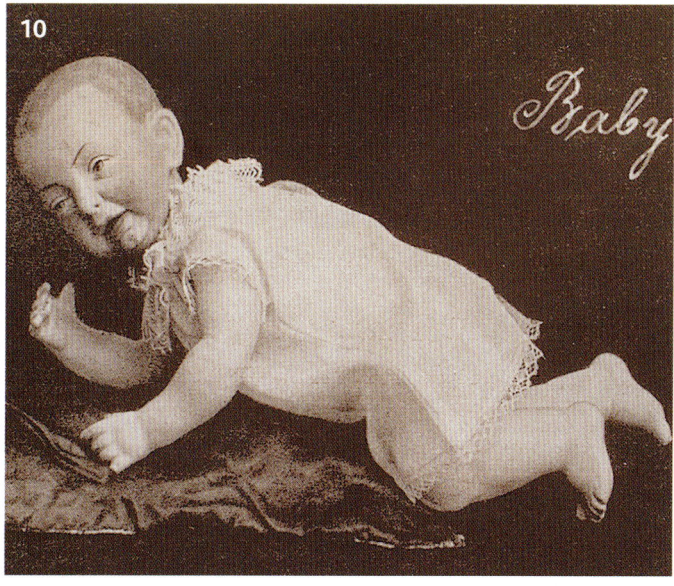

Chapter 2

were used to make the factory's celluloid heads; only the number identifying the doll head was changed. Karl Krausser designed the Kämmer & Reinhardt celluloid character heads, and perfected the process for coloring and giving a durable finish to the heads. The actual heads were made by the factory that used the famous turtle mark trademark, Rheinische Gummi und Celluloidwarenfabrik. The celluloid heads arrived, unpainted, at the Waltershausen Kämmer & Reinhardt doll factory where they were painted and coated with a dulling product by workers. The celluloid example of the Kämmer & Reinhardt mold number 101 is mold number 701.

The Kämmer & Reinhardt doll factory was not the only Thuringian doll factory to make celluloid-head character dolls. A few others include Baehr & Proeschild, J.D. Kestner Jr., Koenig & Wernicke, Bruno Schmidt, Franz Schmidt & Co. and Karl Standfuss.

Various methods were used to limit the shine on the celluloid heads. Some doll factories wax-coated the doll heads, while others tried to create a matt finish by rubbing the completed head with a fine pumice stone or powder. Kestner claimed that all of their celluloid heads were of a soft matt-finished type and would not fade in the sun. My 1918 Kestner & Co. sample book pictures many pages of celluloid-head character dolls. Celluloid heads are mounted on jointed celluloid children's bodies, toddler and bent-limb baby bodies. The heads are also found on composition, leather and cloth bodies. Eyes are painted, made of glass or of celluloid. Some Thuringian dolls were originally made of thin celluloid, which was easily crushed, while others were made as finely as their bisque counterparts.

The Kämmer & Reinhardt doll factory also made cloth dolls in the 1920s. They represent various personalities and the clothing is extremely well made.

My Kämmer & Reinhardt fiftieth-anniversary booklet contains much of the same information that is printed in the twenty-fifth-anniversary booklet, while also providing the continuing history of the porcelain factory and describing the types of dolls sold from 1911 to 1936. A few additional paragraphs in the fiftieth-anniversary booklet explain the reason the Munich Art dolls did not sell well.

> During the summer of 1908, which was during the naturalist movement, a number of artist dolls were on exhibit in Munich. These artist dolls stood in direct contrast to the existing dolls, which schematically did not have any expression and were the so-called 'sweet-realistic' dolls. The artist dolls were unsuccessful, though, and their initial impact at the exhibit was due to the artistic arrangements of the dolls and their dresses. Their heads had been too realistic.
>
> The dolls were supposed to be played with by children and their imagination was different than that of the artists. Not only the adults but also the children would call these artist dolls ugly. Kämmer & Reinhardt did recognize the basic idea, though, and transformed it to the children's world and taste.
>
> From this time on the company's business kept growing steadily. Even the war did only do little harm. In 1916, Commerce Counselor Reinhardt sold his shares to the Bing Works. Being part of the Bing Company led to even greater exports. Commerce Counselor Reinhardt kept a position on the Board of Directors and it was very important that he pass on his wealth of knowledge in the doll industry. It was in 1930 that a severe blow hit the export as well as the inland business of Kämmer & Reinhardt manufacture which also impacted the Bing Works. The company had to deal with a severe world economic crisis. In 1932, Otto Eichhorn became director and in 1933, 95% of all shares were transferred to Otto Eichhorn and Max Kritschgau. Both have been the shareholders since then.

The first volume of *The Collector's Encyclopedia of Dolls* by Dorothy S., Elizabeth A. and Evelyn J. Coleman provides important information on the early history of the Gebrüder Bing Company, which became the Bing Werke. The encyclopedia entry reads: "Gebrüder Bing, A.G. (Joint Stock Co.) 1882-1919. Nuremberg, plus branches all over the world, 1920-25 plus, successor of Gebrüder Bing was Bing Werke. Bing, one of the largest German toy manufacturers made and distributed all kinds of dolls. Before World War I, they had as many as 4,000 employees." There is no question that Bing Werke had the proper facilities and marketing skills to promote and sell Kämmer & Reinhardt dolls following Franz Reinhardt's sale of his Kämmer & Reinhardt shares of stock to Bing Werke in 1916.

The fiftieth-anniversary booklet updates the history since 1933 as follows:

> Since then, the company is starting to regain strength in more ways than one. The products themselves are being changed, the inland business is changing and so is especially the export. Over the last few years, the inventory has changed, and since this spring we have brought out some novelties that will please the best of all tastes. The development of Waltershauser dolls is more than the doll head and limb design. It is concentrating on maintaining a taste for the finest clothing.
>
> Special recognition needs to be paid to the new one-of-a-kind 'infant babies.' They have already gained fame under the names 'Putz' and 'Pumpelchen' and 'Putz Learns to Walk.' The 'standing sitting babies' have also been changed into a highly refined series which will please each customer.
>
> Our dolls in dresses are wearing the latest fashions each year. One doll series is the 'My Sweet Darling.' It

Kämmer & Reinhardt Doll Factory

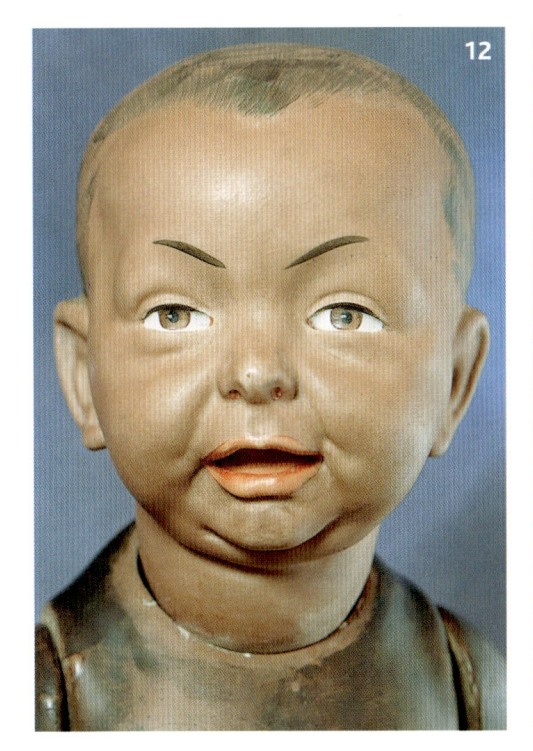

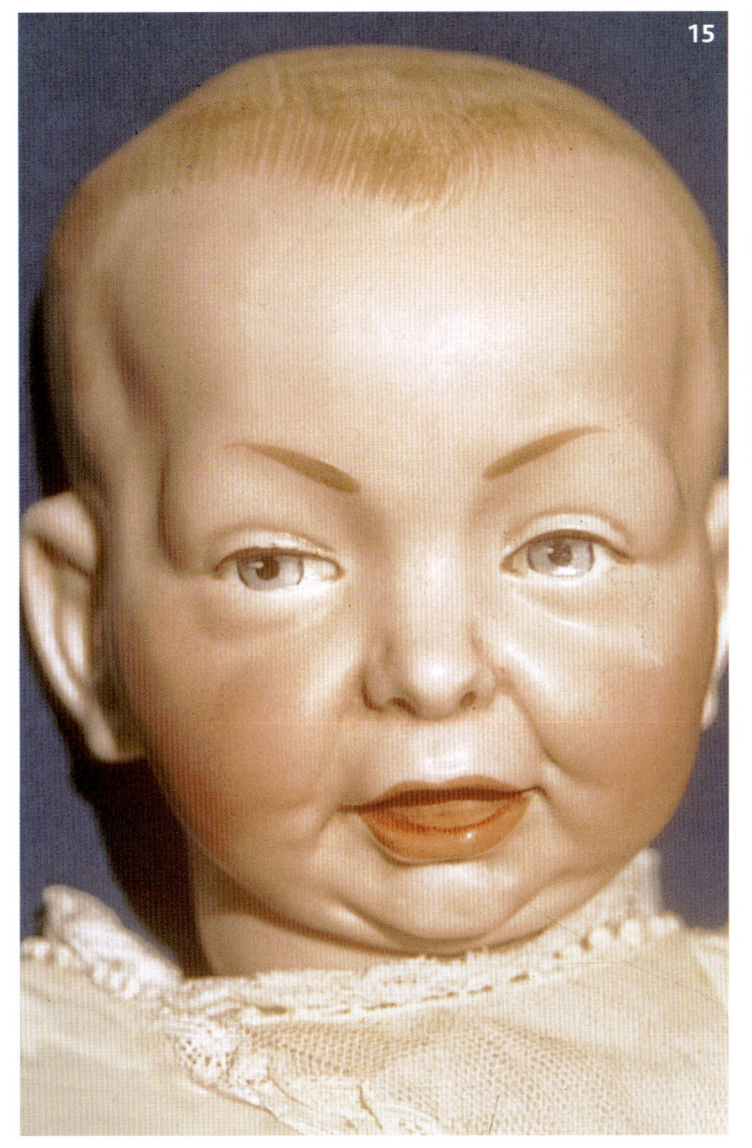

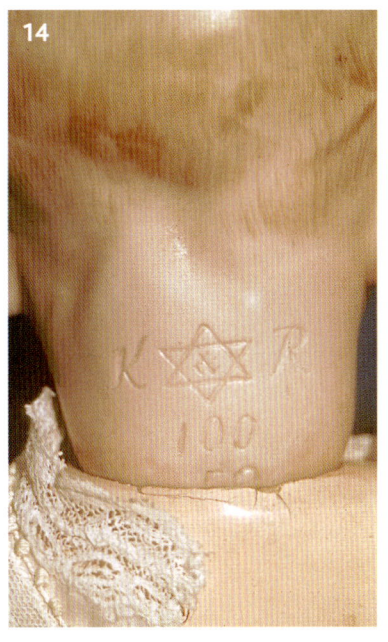

12. Brown bisque socket head by Simon & Halbig; baby body parts by Heinrich Handwerck; assembly by Kämmer & Reinhardt; molded hair; large, realistic ears; well-defined eye sockets; single-stroke, slanted eyebrows; molded, black-outlined upper eyelids; painted eyes with white highlights; open/closed mouth with molded tongue; chin dimple; 18½-inch doll; GM 1909; marked: K*R//100//58. Author's Collection. (Photo: Gregg Smith)

13. On this 1912 postcard, a young girl holds a Kämmer & Reinhardt mold number 100 bisque-head character baby. The doll is wearing a long christening dress. Author's Archival Paper Collection.

14. The back of the head seen in illustration 15 shows the incised mold marks, including the trademark star which contains the "&" mark between the "K" and "R." Ferna Nolte Collection. (Photo: Christiane Gräfnitz)

15. Bisque socket head by Simon & Halbig; baby body parts by Heinrich Handwerck; assembly by Kämmer & Reinhardt; molded hair; large, realistic ears; well-defined eye sockets; single-stroke, slanted eyebrows; molded, black-outlined upper eyelids; painted eyes with white highlights; open/closed mouth with molded tongue; chin dimple; 19½-inch doll; GM 1909; marked: K*R//100//50. Ferna Nolte Collection. (Photo: Christiane Gräfnitz)

Chapter 2

has a slender body, just like the latest fashion. It also wears the latest hairdos and gained special recognition at this year's Leipzig Fair. This series shows the way for the doll in the near future. Even the doll of highest quality and taste does not have the right impact if it is not displayed in the correct way. It can look boring and only half as pretty. Dolls have to be displayed in a lively arrangement that makes them look alive and attractive. Unfortunately, many store owners do not recognize this basic idea.

Author Christa Langer provides the following information on the Kämmer & Reinhardt doll factory following the 1933 death of Franz Reinhardt, in her book titled *Charakterpuppen*.

> He didn't live to see his company awarded a Certificate of Honour at the World Exhibition in Paris in 1937. The production was almost brought to a standstill during the Second World War, and finally the Reich's Office of Surveying Technology moved into the buildings of Kämmer & Reinhardt.
>
> At the end of the Second World War, the doll industry of Waltershausen, which had previously employed thousands of workers, had a work force of about two hundred. After the War, tentative steps to start production were made again in the doll factories (they were still in private hands at this time). Otto Gan's doll factory was sequestered in 1946 and it became the VEB Puppenfabrik Waltershausen, a state-owned property on the 13th of February 1948.
>
> At the same time the industrial organization of the Sozialistiche Einheitpartei Deutschlands was established. Employees of Kämmer & Reinhardt decided to convert the firm to a state-owned company at the end of 1957. The state-owned company Biggi was established on the 1st of January 1958 and was integrated with the VEB Puppenfabrik. This meant that it became the largest company of its kind in Waltershausen. Otto Eichhorn, the son of the last owner of Kämmer & Reinhardt, passed on his rights for the re-founding of the company to Juliane and Werner Hoefner in 1983. They continued using the old brand marks.

Heinrich Handwerck Doll Factory

Heinrich Handwerck founded his doll factory in Waltershausen in 1855. The Simon & Halbig porcelain factory in Gräfenhain made most of the doll heads Handwerck mounted on his factory's composition bodies. The untimely death of Handwerck, at the age of forty-three, shortly after the 1902 Leipzig Fair, was the result of an incurable kidney disease. Soon after his death, Kämmer & Reinhardt bought the Heinrich Handwerck doll factory. By purchasing the Handwerck doll factory, Kämmer & Reinhardt was able to arrange for Simon & Halbig to make all of their bisque doll heads from 1902 on.

The twenty-fifth-anniversary booklet of the Kämmer & Reinhardt doll factory presents some background on the purchase of their "sister company."

> In 1902, soon after Mr. Kämmer died, Mr. Heinrich Handwerck also died. He was the founder of the doll factory here in Waltershausen 26 years ago, which now has our name. Mr. Handwerck had also started very small and achieved great success. Not only was he a very industrious business man but also was a man of great character.
>
> His main principle was always to go his own way. He had invented an excellent way to mechanically make doll parts. He had it patented and it is still used successfully at the Heinrich Handwerck doll company today. This way of manufacture was the main reason for Franz Reinhardt to buy the Handwerck factory. Mr. Nuessle became an invaluable experienced expert and industrious partner who took over the leadership of that factory independently while Franz Reinhardt stayed head of our company. Both companies worked hand in hand, yet independently – which turned out to be a worthwhile way. Another reason to buy the Heinrich Handwerck company was to get in touch with the well known porcelain factory Simon & Halbig in Gräfenhain. Once the lovely heads were made by Simon & Halbig, the heads reached their absolute perfection.

As this passage explains, when Kämmer & Reinhardt bought the Heinrich Handwerch doll factory in 1902, the purpose was to have Heinrich Handwerck make all of the parts for the composition bodies used by Kammer & Reinhardt on the bisque-head dolls assembled at their own factory. Simon & Halbig made all of the bisque character heads in the 100-mold-number series and Kämmer & Reinhardt assembled the majority of the bisque-head dolls in their own doll factory in Waltershausen. The above passage from the booklet also explains that following the purchase by Kämmer & Reinhardt, the Handwerck doll factory continued to operate as a separate company, under the leadership of Gottlieb Nuessle. Although the Handwerck doll factory was owned by Kämmer & Reinhardt, the factory continued to make their own dolls with

16. Marie bisque socket head by Simon & Halbig; body parts by Heinrich Handwerck; assembly by Heinrich Handwerck; wig; single-stroke eyebrows; molded, black-outlined upper eyelids; painted eyes with white highlights; closed mouth; 19-inch doll; GM 1909; marked: **K*R//101//49**. The original model for the 101 mold number heads was also made by sculptor Arthur Lewin-Funcke. Beth Karp Collection. (Photo: Lee Krombholz)

Kämmer & Reinhardt Doll Factory

Chapter 2

Simon & Halbig bisque heads in their Waltershausen doll factory. The section on Heinrich Handwerck in the *German Doll Encyclopedia* by Jürgen and Marianne Cieslik notes that in 1910 it was advertised as being: "Factory for fine ball-jointed dolls, heads, spare parts, wigs, 'Bebe Cosmopolite,' speciality: character dolls."

The Ciesliks wrote an excellent article on the Heinrich Handwerck doll factory in the August 1989 issue of *Puppenmagazin*. One illustration in the article is of a character doll that has recently been credited to the Heinrich Handwerck doll factory. The caption under the photograph of the dolls reads: "A series of charming Simon & Halbig character dolls, with the marks '111' in the back of the head. All of the dolls examined until now have a marked Handwerck body."

Several examples of these rare dolls are part of the Rosalie Whyel collection, on display in the Rosalie Whyel Museum of Doll Art in Bellevue, Washington. The dolls are marked with mold numbers 111, 120 and 128. They are pictured on pages 192 and 193 of the book *The Rose Unfolds, Rarities of the Rosalie Whyel Museum of Doll Art*. The text that accompanies the three dolls on page 192 of that book notes: "Very little is known about the character dolls from Heinrich Handwerck after the company was purchased by Kämmer & Reinhardt in 1902. We propose several dolls, which do not 'fit' into any other series by Simon & Halbig or Kämmer & Reinhardt, for attribution to the Handwerck series. The dolls numbers – 111, 120 and 128 could easily fit into the Handwerck series of 'near character' dolly-faced dolls such as numbers 99, 109 and 119. In fact, the attributed dolls often have marked Handwerck bodies and original shoes marked 'HH' for Heinrich Handwerck."

Side views of the three dolls are pictured on page 193 of Rosalie Whyel's book. The text under the picture reads: "The dolls were photographed to show their family resemblance and then we removed their wigs and caught their profiles. Voila! The proof! Look at the high crown cuts, the sloping noses and the similar chins and ear shapes."

The doll pictured on the left on page 192 in *The Rose Unfolds* is identical to the doll pictured with the Ciesliks' article on Heinrich Handwerck in the August 1989 *Puppenmagazin*. Examples of these beautiful Heinrich Handwerck character-like dolls are pictured in this book in illustrations 108, 110, 111, 112, 113 and 114 on pages 84 and 85. The modeling is exquisite, and it is evident that the partnership between Simon & Halbig and Heinrich Handwerck resulted in some of the most beautiful dolls ever made in Thuringia. In my opinion, the number of dolls found with Simon & Halbig heads on marked Heinrich Handwerck composition bodies offer proof that the mold numbers 111, 120, 128 and 129, which, until the Ciesliks' 1989 article had not been attributed to any specific doll factory, are indeed Heinrich Handwerck dolls. These mold numbers do not belong to the Kämmer & Reinhardt series.

In all of the captions for the Kämmer & Reinhardt character dolls pictured in this book, I credit the Simon & Halbig porcelain factory for making the bisque heads, the Heinrich Handwerck doll factory for making the composition body parts and the Kämmer & Reinhardt doll factory for assembling the dolls. But the Heinrich Handwerck doll factory cannot be credited for making all of the body parts on the Kämmer & Reinhardt character dolls pictured in this chapter of the book. It is impossible for us today, a century later, to know whether bodies made by other Thuringian porcelain factories are an integral part of the Kämmer & Reinhardt dolls pictured. The Kämmer & Reinhardt doll factory sold many bisque character heads to a variety of Thuringian doll factories in both the Waltershausen and Sonneberg areas. One such factory was the Gustav Schmey doll factory in Sonneberg. Illustration #1536 in the Ciesliks' *German Doll Encyclopedia* pictures a large group of Schmey bisque-head dolls on a 1911 advertising postcard. The promotional postcard was sent out as an invitation to visit the Schmey booth at the 1911 Leipzig Spring Fair. The back of the postcard reads: "A novelty, character dolls dressed in delightful fashion and of the largest selection, furthermore dolls in sport and traditional costume."

The most recognizable bisque character-head dolls pictured on the Schmey post card include a mold number 100 Kämmer & Reinhardt baby, two examples of a Kämmer & Reinhardt mold number 101 (Peter) and one example of a Kämmer & Reinhardt mold number 107 (Carl). Examples of Gebrüder Heubach character dolls are also pictured on the postcard.

The Gustav Schmey doll factory was founded in 1853 and was still advertising dolls for sale in the 1930s. Like so many other Thuringian doll factories, the Schmey doll factory bought bisque heads from a number of porcelain factories and assembled and dressed the dolls with the help of home workers and their own doll-factory workers.

The Heinrich Handwerck doll factory closed in 1918 when the Kämmer & Reinhardt doll factory was purchased by Bing Works. But the closing was not permanent. In 1921 Heinrich Handwerck, Jr. reopened his father's doll factory in a different location. His mother, Minna Handwerck, helped her son operate the business. Their registered trademarks included: "dolls, doll heads, doll bodies, dresses and wigs." Heinrich Handwerck, Jr. did not succeed in reviving his father's old doll factory. He declared bankruptcy in 1926 and tried to reopen the factory in 1927 and again in 1929, before closing the factory permanently in 1930.

Kämmer & Reinhardt Doll Factory

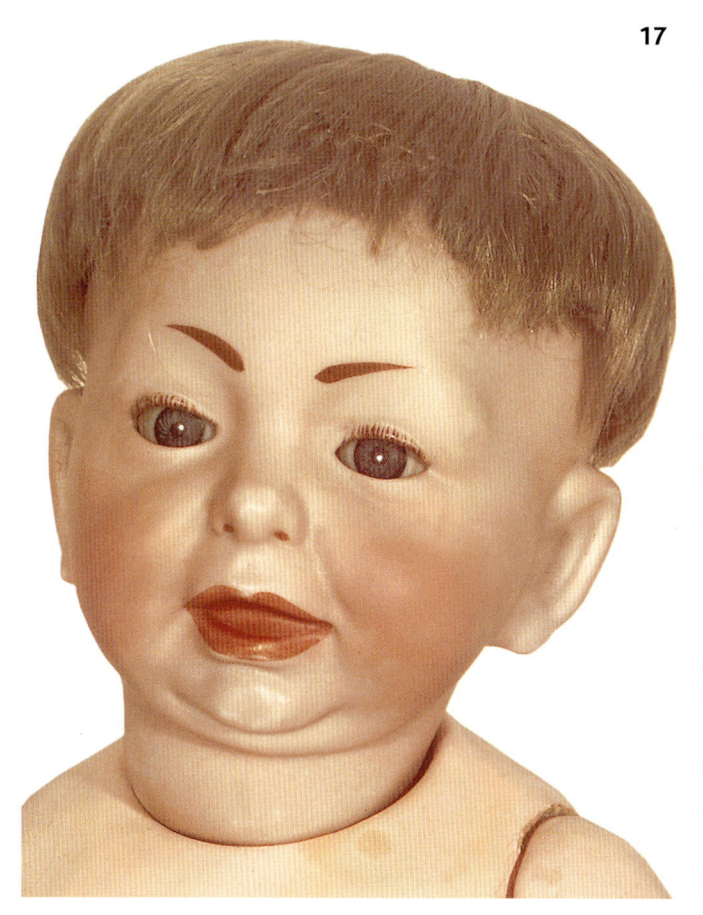

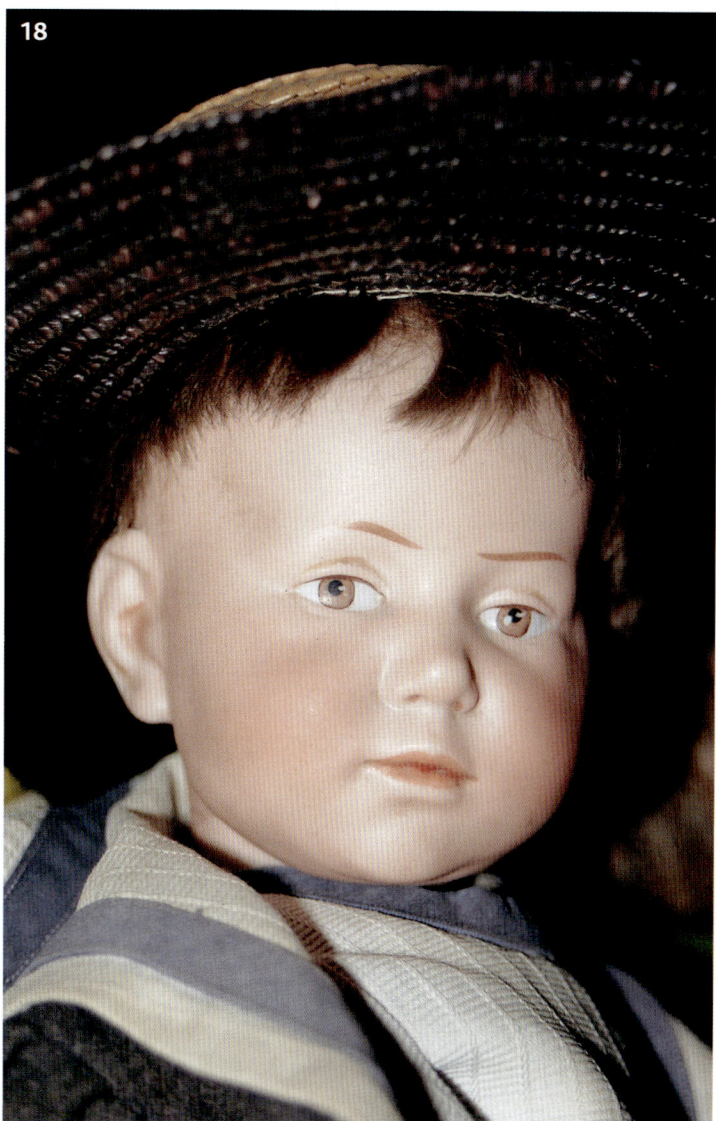

17. Bisque socket head by Simon & Halbig; baby body parts by Heinrich Handwerck; assembly by Kämmer & Reinhardt; wig; large, realistic ears; well-defined eye sockets; single-stroke, slanting eyebrows; short, closely spaced upper eyelashes; glass sleep eyes; open/closed mouth with molded tongue; 14-inch doll; GM 1909; marked: **36** (height in centimeters). Glass-eyed, wigged versions of mold number 100, like this one, are uncommon. Antje Lode Collection. (Photo: Antje Lode)

18. Peter bisque socket head by Simon & Halbig; body and assembly by the Cuno & Otto Dressel doll factory in Sonneberg; original wig and clothing; single-stroke eyebrows; molded, black-outlined upper eyelids; painted eyes with white highlights; closed mouth; 18¾-inch doll; GM 1909; marked: **K*R//101**. This doll sits on the carousel in the basement of the Sonneberg Doll Museum. The entire exhibit, entered in competition at the Brussels World Exposition of 1910, was moved to the basement of the museum, where it can still be seen. Courtesy Deutsches Spielzeugmuseum, Sonneberg. (Photo: Christiane Gräfnitz)

19. Marie bisque socket head by Simon & Halbig; body parts by Heinrich Handwerck; assembly by Kämmer & Reinhardt; wig; single-stroke eyebrows; molded, black-outlined upper eyelids; painted eyes with white highlights; closed mouth; 16½-inch doll; GM 1909; marked: **K*R//101//43**. Beth Karp Collection. (Photo: Lee Krombholz)

Chapter 2

20. Peter bisque shoulder head by Simon & Halbig; body parts by Heinrich Handwerck; assembly by Kämmer & Reinhardt; wig; single-stroke eyebrows; molded, black-outlined upper eyelids: painted eyes; closed mouth; 17-inch doll; GM 1909; marked: **K*R//201**. The mold number 201 is the shoulder-head version of mold number 101. Ursula Gauder Collection. (Photo: Christiane Gräfnitz)

21. Marie bisque socket head by Simon & Halbig; body parts by Heinrich Handwerck; assembly by Kämmer & Reinhardt; original wig; single-stroke eyebrows; slightly molded, black-outlined upper eyelids; painted eyes; closed mouth; 8¼-inch doll; GM 1909; marked: **K*R//101//21**. Susan Moore Collection. (Photo: John Cummings.)

23. Marie bisque socket head by Simon & Halbig; body parts by Heinrich Handwerck; assembly by Kämmer & Reinhardt; original wig and clothing; single-stroke eyebrows; molded, black-outlined upper eyelids; painted eyes; closed mouth; 15-inch doll; GM 1909; marked: **K*R//101//39**. Larger Kämmer & Reinhardt doll heads in the 100 mold number series usually have white highlights on the left side of each pupil, but the highlights are absent on many smaller doll heads. Ann Cummings Collection. (Photo: John Cummings)

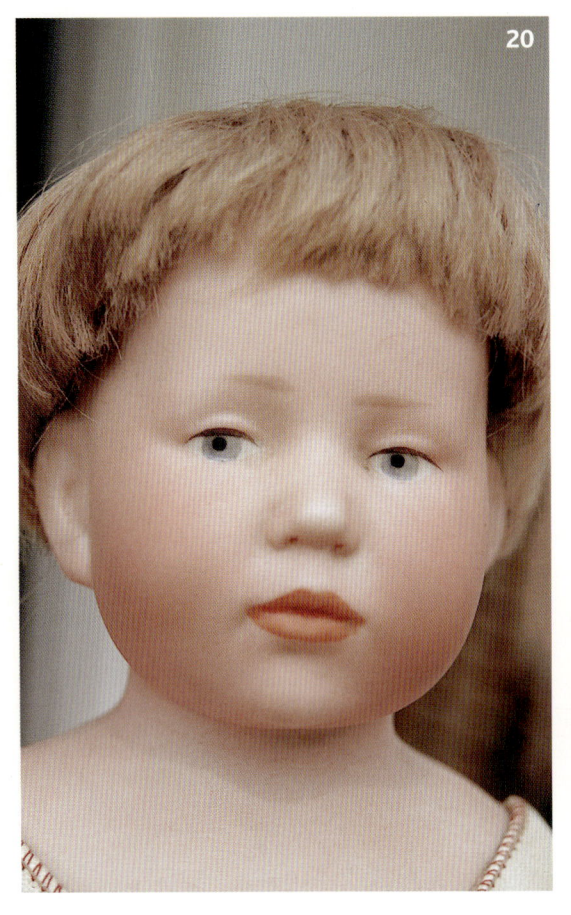

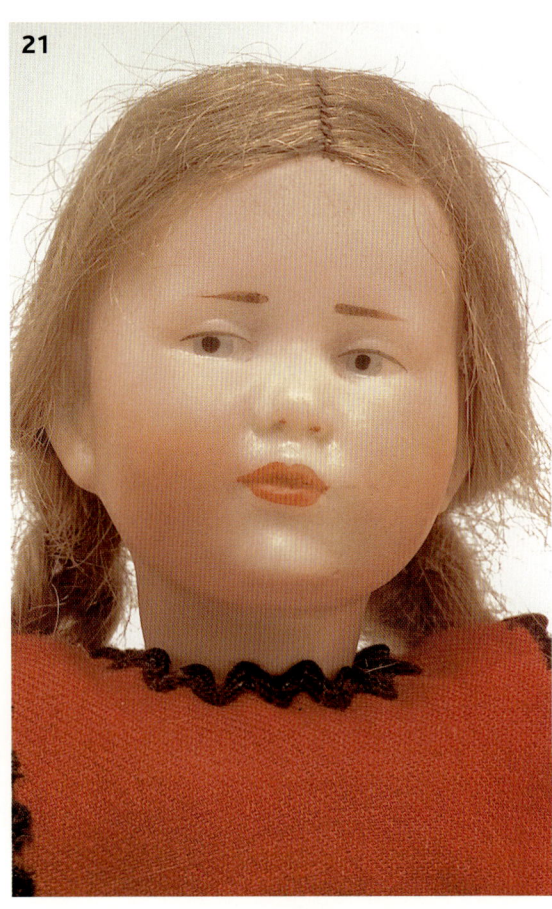

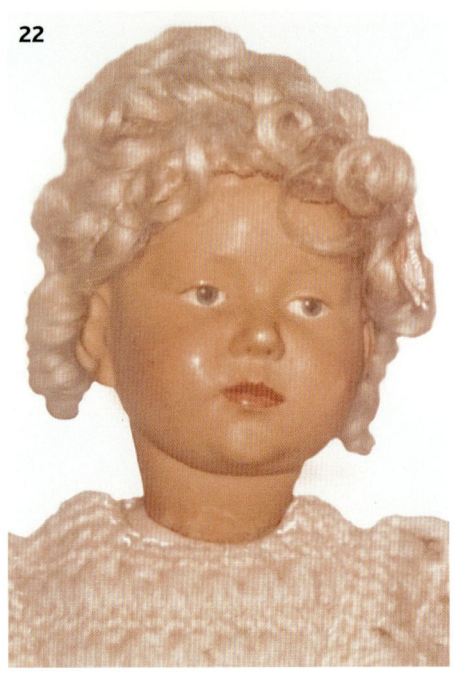

22. Marie celluloid head by Rheinische Gummi und Celluloid-Fabrik; unfinished head painted by Kämmer & Reinhardt factory artists; wig; single-stroke eyebrows; painted eyes; closed mouth; 12-inch doll; circa 1910; marked: **K*R//701**. The Kämmer & Reinhardt 700 series is the celluloid-head version of the 100 mold number series. Courtesy Museum Schloss Tenneberg, Waltershausen. (Photo: Christiane Gräfnitz)

Kämmer & Reinhardt Doll Factory

24. Peter bisque solid domed head by Simon & Halbig; body parts by Heinrich Handwerck; assembly by Kämmer & Reinhardt; thin, reddish-brown, flocked wig, glued on; single-stroke eyebrows; slightly molded, black-outlined upper eyelids; painted eyes with white highlights; closed mouth; 18-inch doll; GM 1909; marked: **K*R//101x//46**. According to this doll's owner, a well-known German researcher of Kämmer & Reinhardt dolls: "The 'x' after the mold number does not always mean 'flocked hair' but also stands for an intermediate size, as in the case of the 117x doll which was available in 34 cm only." Antje Lode Collection. (Photo: Antje Lode)

25. In 1898 sculptor Arthur Lewin-Funcke created the original shoulder head plaster bust *Knabenbüste* (boy bust), which was the model for Kämmer & Reinhardt mold numbers 102 and 107. These mold numbers are two versions of the same model. The dolls in 102 mold number series have molded hair, while the dolls marked with the 107 mold number are wigged. This casting was ordered by Karin Lewin-Funcke, granddaughter of Arthur Lewin-Funcke. According to the Ciesliks's research published in their book, *German Doll Studies*: "Only a boy portrait bust, owned by the family, gives a clue to the further Lewin-Funcke models. It is a portrait of a boy, Walter, which has been sold as model 102 by K&R. This head is completely identical with model 107, Karl, except that it has a wig." Antje Lode Collection. (Photo: Antje Lode)

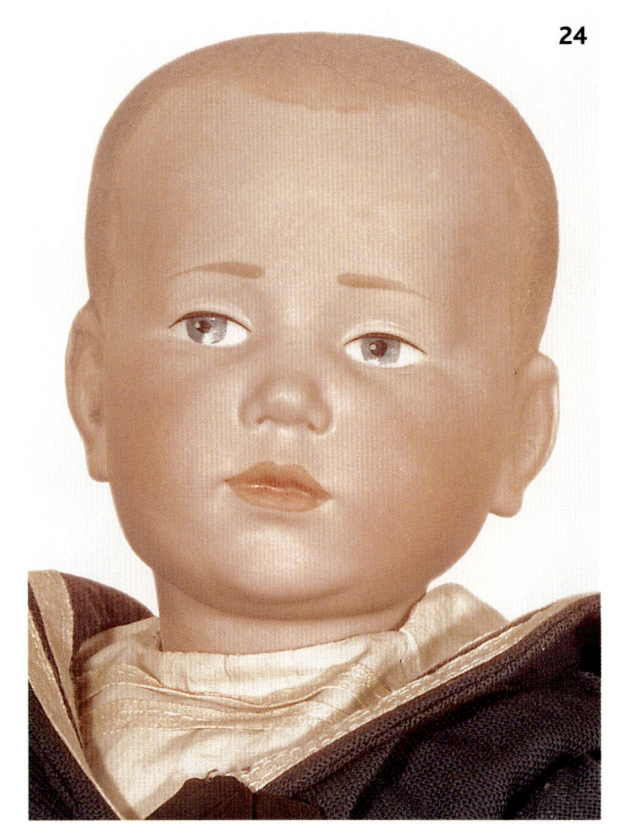

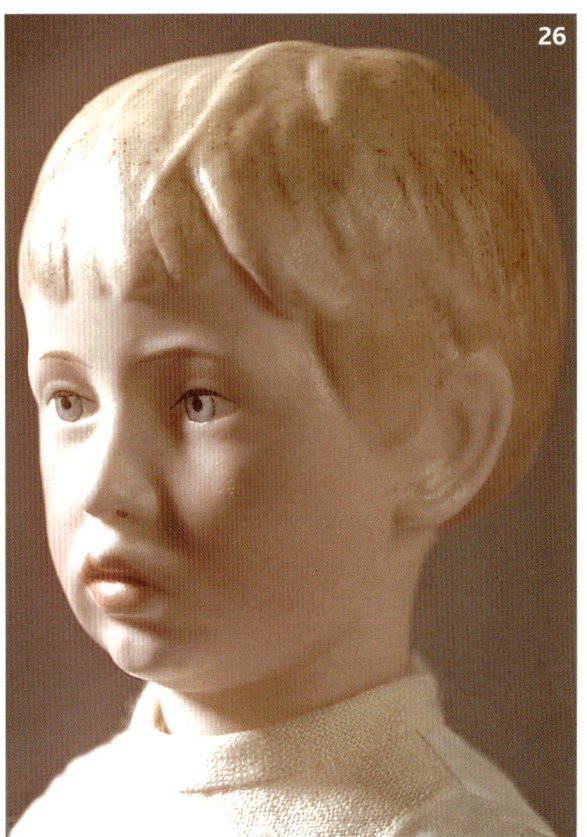

26. Walter bisque socket head by Simon & Halbig; molded hair; single-stroke eyebrows; molded, black-outlined upper eyelids; painted eyes; closed pouty mouth; 12-inch doll; GM 1909; marked: **102//K*R//30**. The side view shows the deeply molded hair, large well-modeled ear and chin dimple. Antje Lode Collection. (Photo: Antje Lode)

Chapter 2

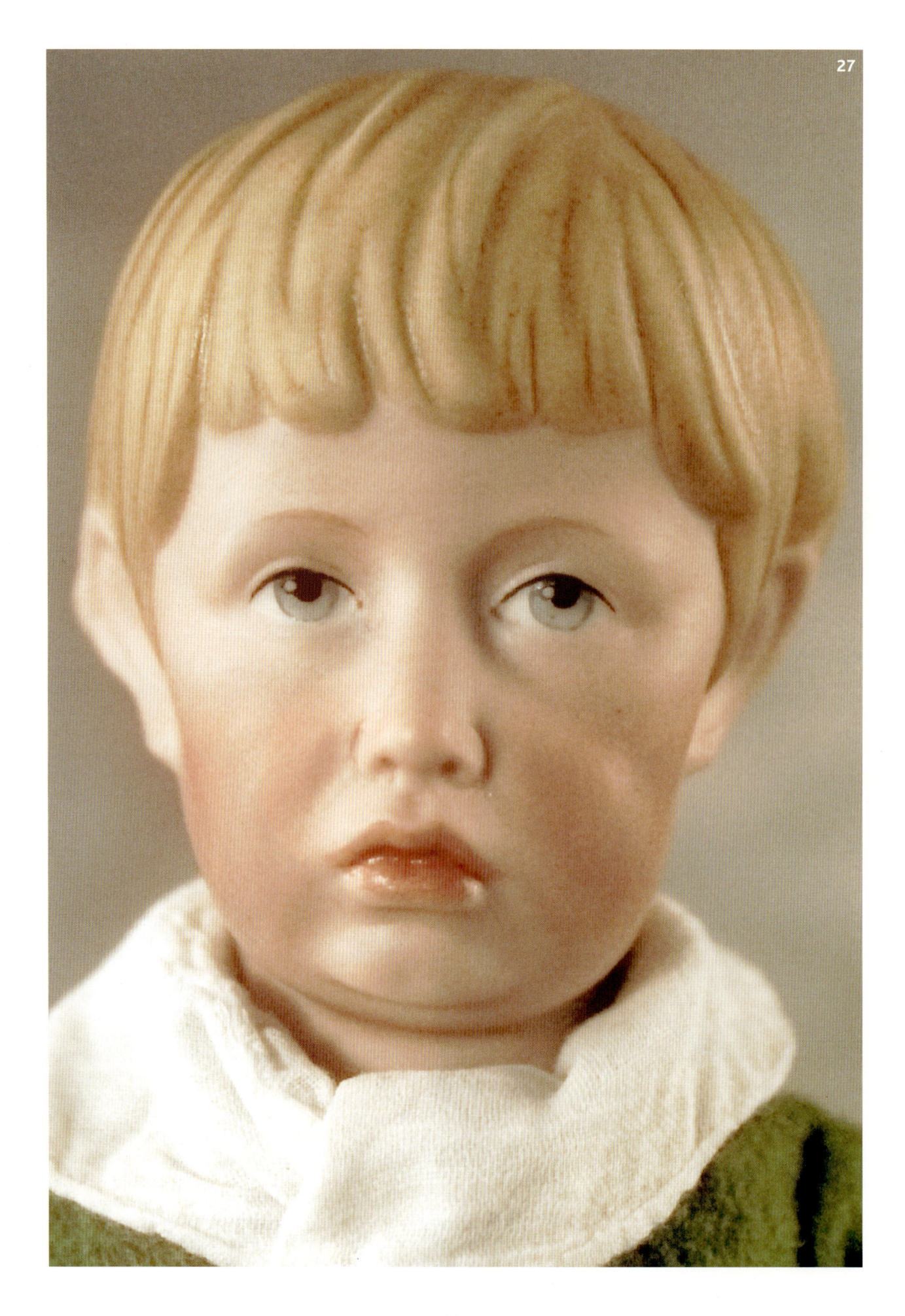

Kämmer & Reinhardt Doll Factory

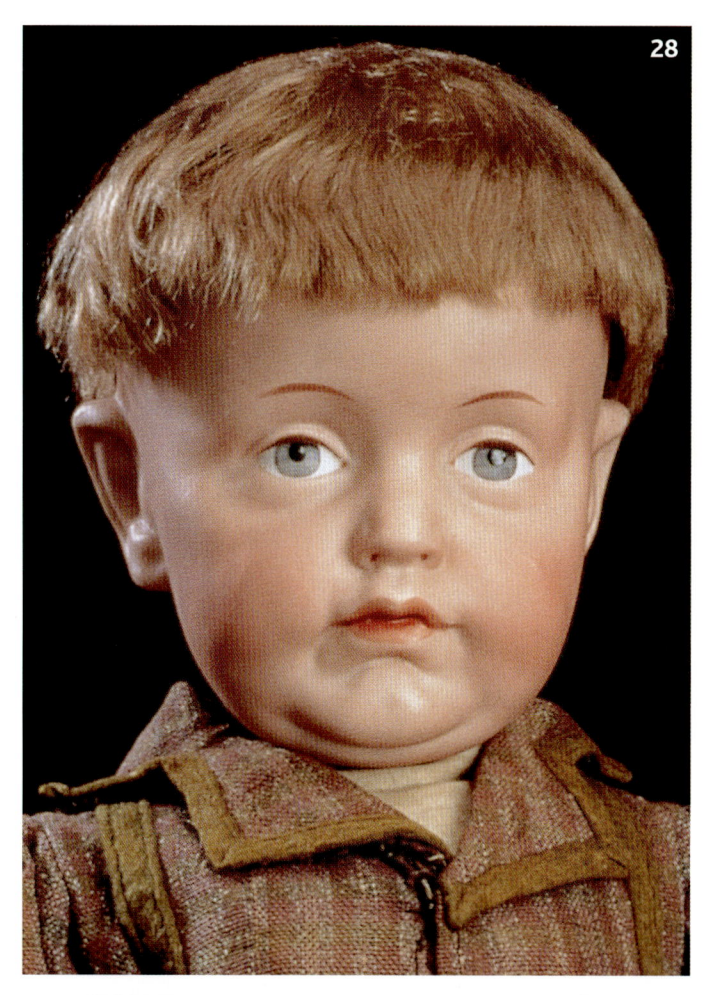

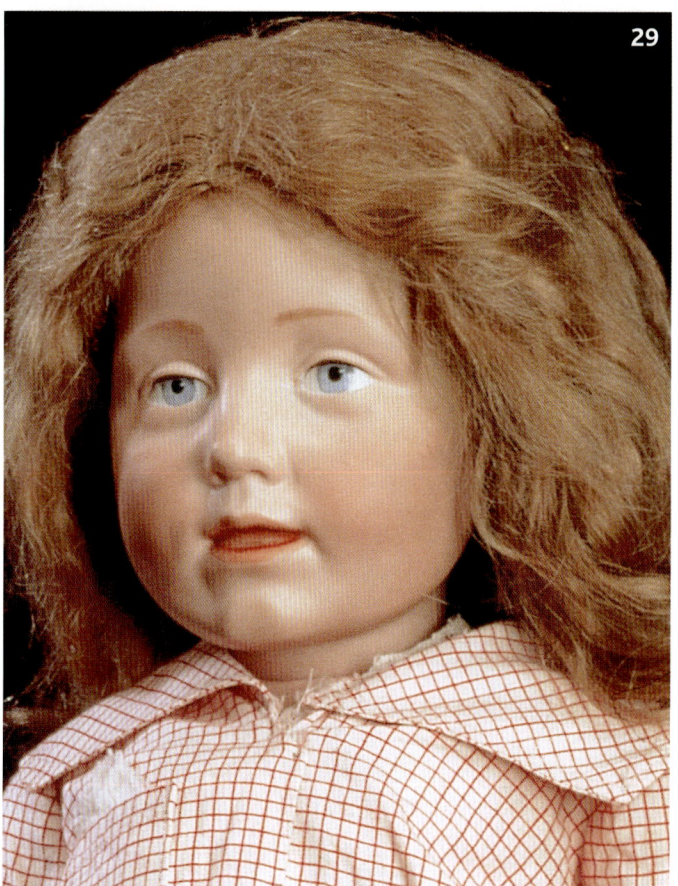

27. Walter bisque socket head by Simon & Halbig; body parts by Heinrich Handwerck; assembly by Kämmer & Reinhardt; deeply molded hair and realistic facial modeling; single-stroke eyebrows; molded, black-outlined upper eyelids; painted eyes with white highlights; closed pouty mouth; chin dimple; 12-inch doll; GM 1909; marked: K*R//102. Beth Karp Collection. (Photo: Lee Krombholz)

28 and 29. Two rare bisque socket heads by Kämmer & Reinhardt; mold number 105 girl, left, features: wig; single-stroke eyebrows; molded and black-outlined upper eyelids; painted eyes; open/closed mouth with molded tongue; 22-inch doll; GM 1909; marked K*R//105. Mold number 106 boy features: wig; single-stroke eyebrows; molded and black-outlined upper eyelids; large painted eyes with a tiny white highlight on the edge of each pupil; closed mouth; 21-inch-doll; marked: K*R//106. Courtesy Rosalie Whyel Museum of Doll Art. (Photo Courtesy of the Rosalie Whyel Museum of Doll Art)

30. This 1908 6-inch plaster bust of Heinz Burkowitz, nephew of modeler Arthur Lewin-Funke was the original model for the Kämmer & Reinhardt mold number 106 bisque head. This casting was ordered by Karin Lewin-Funcke, granddaughter of Arthur Lewin-Funcke. Antje Lode Collection. (Photo: Antje Lode)

Chapter 2

31. Rare composition socket head of mold number 102, probably one of the first Kämmer & Reinhardt prototypes; molded red hair; single-stroke eyebrows; painted eyes with white highlights; closed pouty mouth; 18-inch doll; GM 1909; unmarked. Courtesy Rosalie Whyel Museum of Doll Art. (Photo: Christiane Gräfnitz)

32. Carl bisque socket head by Simon & Halbig; body parts by Heinrich Handwerck; assembly by Kämmer & Reinhardt; wig; single-stroke eyebrows; molded and black-outlined upper eyelids; painted eyes with white highlights; closed pouty mouth; 19-inch doll; GM 1909; marked: K*R//107. Courtesy Rosalie Whyel Museum of Doll Art. (Photo: Christiane Gräfnitz)

33. Elise bisque socket head by Simon & Halbig; body parts by Heinrich Handwerck; assembly by Kämmer & Reinhardt; wig; single-stroke eyebrows; molded and black-outlined upper eyelids; painted eyes with white highlights; closed smiling mouth with darker shading between lips; 17-inch doll; GM 1909; marked: K*R//109//46. Beth Karp Collection. (Photo: Lee Krombholz)

34. Carl bisque socket head by Simon & Halbig; body parts by Heinrich Handwerck; assembly by Kämmer & Reinhardt; wig; single-stroke eyebrows; molded, black-outlined upper eyelids; painted eyes; closed pouty mouth; 21½-inch doll; GM 1909; marked: K*R//107. According to Jan Foulke's *Simon & Halbig Dolls: The Artful Aspect*, a Kämmer & Reinhardt character doll with the mold number 107 was pictured and identified as Carl in the February 1910 *Playthings* magazine advertisement for the American importers Strobel & Wilken Co. Carl is often listed as "Karl" in German doll books. Private Collection. (Photo: Christiane Gräfnitz)

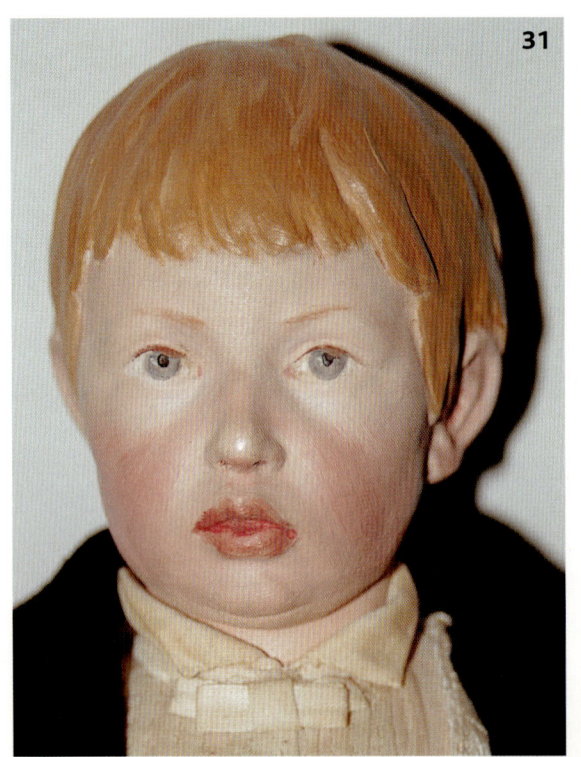

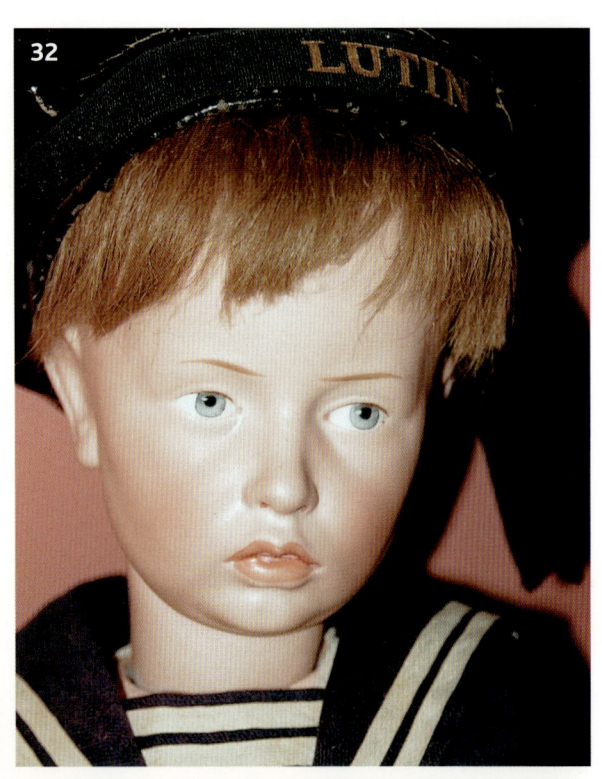

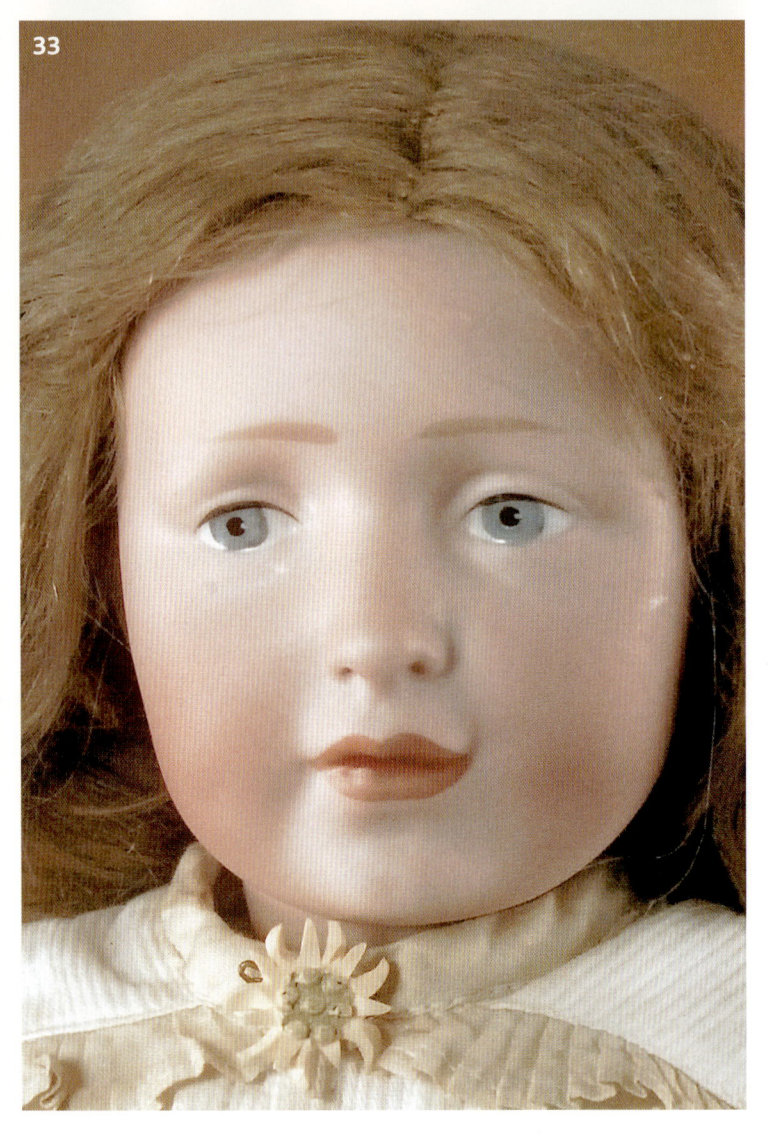

Kämmer & Reinhardt Doll Factory

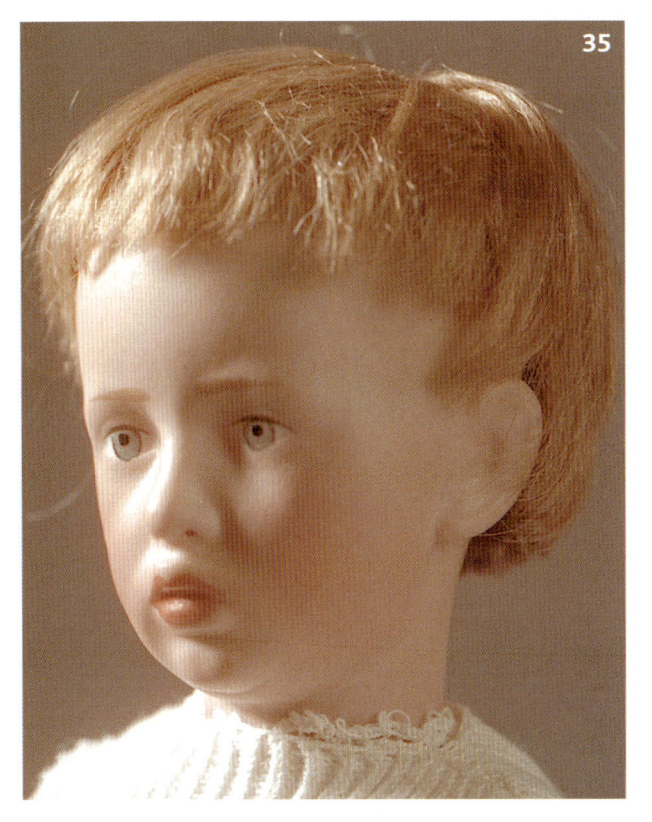

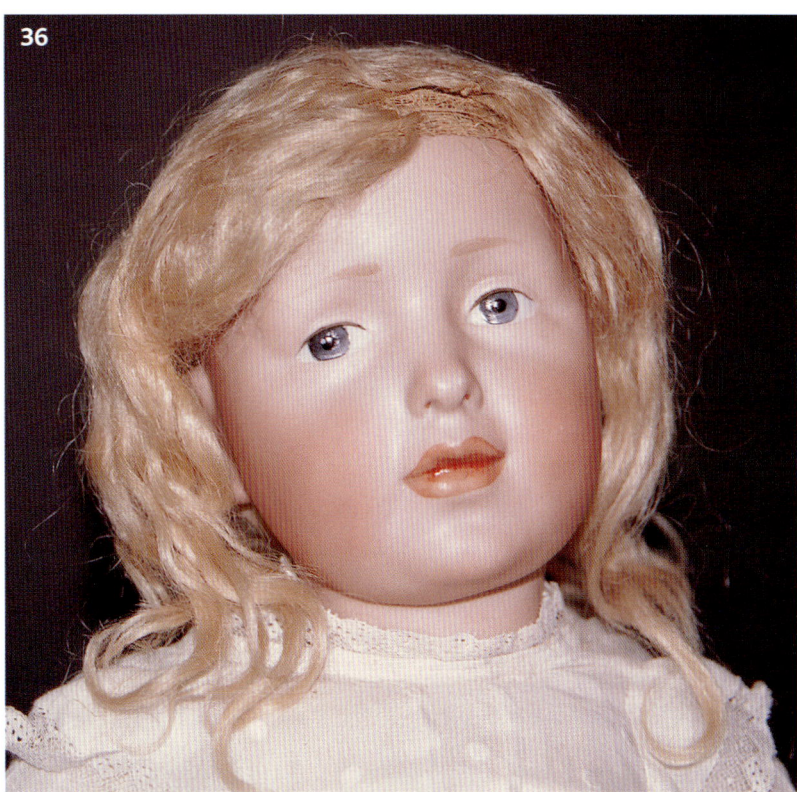

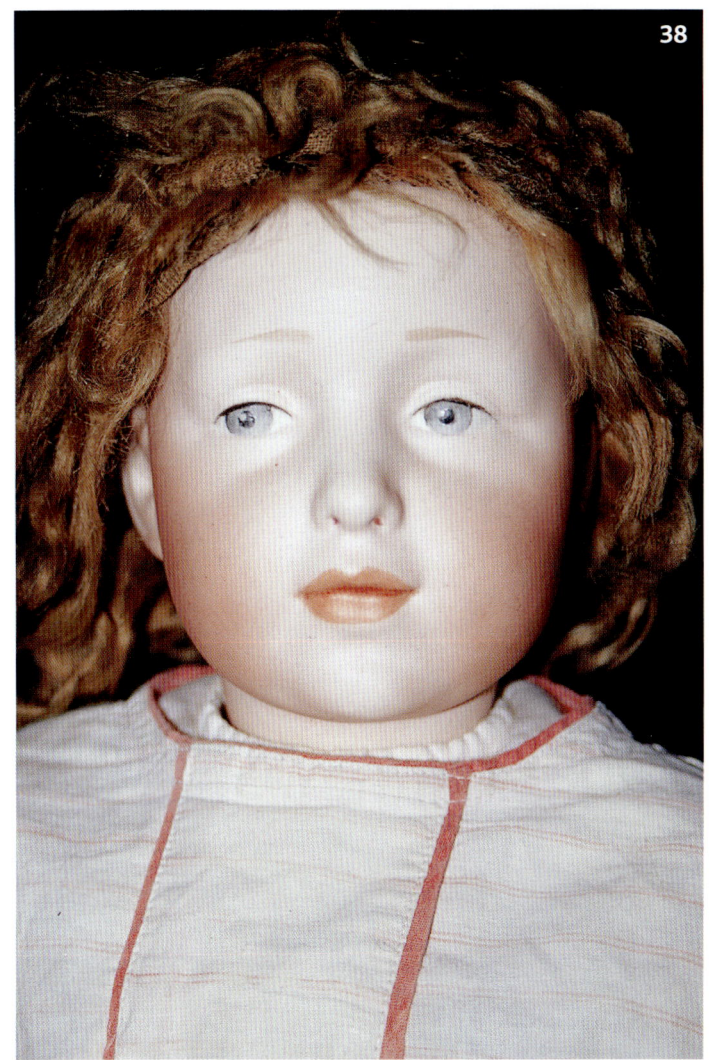

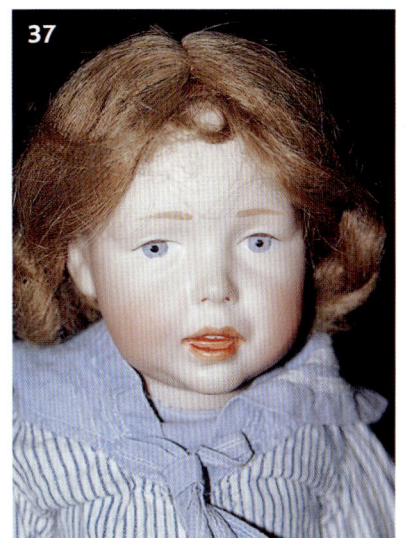

35. Carl bisque socket head by Simon & Halbig; body parts by Heinrich Handwerck; assembly by Kämmer & Reinhardt; wig; single-stroke eyebrows; molded, black-outlined upper eyelids; painted eyes; closed pouty mouth; 12-inch doll; GM 1909; marked: **K&R//107//30**. Antje Lode Collection. (Photo: Antje Lode)

36. Elise bisque socket head by Simon & Halbig; body parts by Heinrich Handwerck; assembly by Kämmer & Reinhardt; wig; pale-blond single-stroke eyebrows; molded and black-outlined upper eyelids; painted eyes with white highlights; closed smiling mouth; 19-inch doll; GM 1909; marked: **K*R//109//49**. Kathy and Mike Embry Collection. (Photo: Kathy Embry)

37. Bisque socket head by Simon & Halbig; body parts by Heinrich Handwerck; assembly by Kämmer & Reinhardt; wig; single-stroke eyebrows; molded, black-outlined upper eyelids; painted eyes; open/closed mouth with upper teeth and molded tongue; 18-inch doll; GM 1909; marked: **K*R//112**. Courtesy Ladenburger Spielzeugauktion/Goetz Seidel. (Photo: Christiane Gräfnitz)

38. Elise bisque socket head by Simon & Halbig; body parts by Heinrich Handwerck; assembly by Kämmer & Reinhardt; wig; single-stroke eyebrows; molded, black-outlined upper eyelids; painted eyes with white highlights; closed smiling mouth; 21¼-inch doll; GM 1909; marked: **K*R//109**. Courtesy Ladenburger Spielzeugauktion/Goetz Seidel. (Photo: Christiane Gräfnitz)

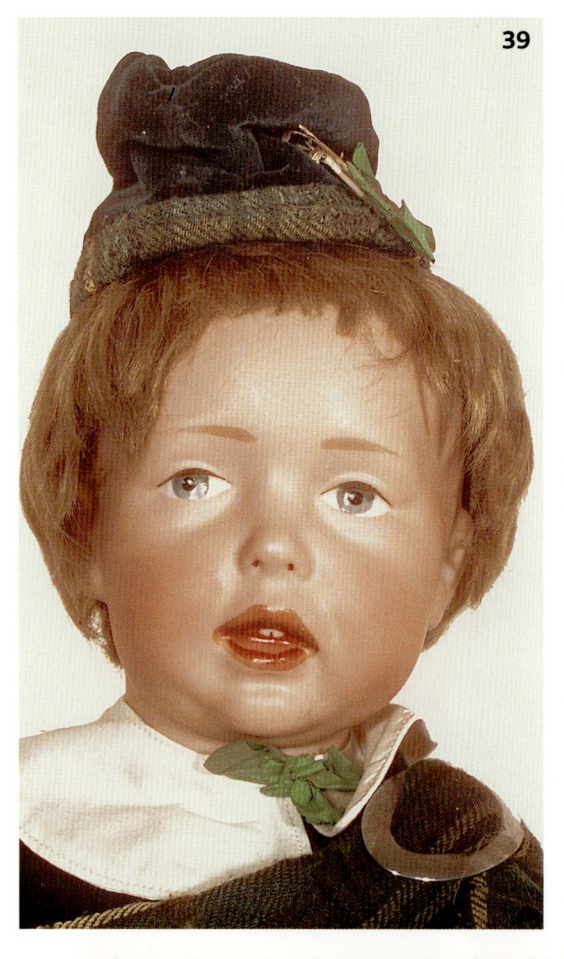

Chapter 2

39. Bisque socket head by Simon & Halbig; body parts by Heinrich Handwerck; wig; single-stroke eyebrows; molded, black-outlined upper eyelids; painted eyes with white highlights; open/closed mouth with upper molded teeth and tongue; 18-inch doll; GM 1909; marked: K*R//112//46. Antje Lode collection. (Photo: Antje Lode)

40. Bisque socket head by Simon & Halbig; body parts by Heinrich Handwerck; assembly by Kämmer & Reinhardt; flocked hair; single-stroke eyebrows; slightly molded, black-outlined upper eyelids; painted eyes; open/closed mouth with upper painted teeth and molded tongue; 9-inch doll; GM 1909; marked: K*R//112x. Norah Stoner Collection. (Photo: Norah Stoner)

41. A photograph in my Kämmer & Reinhardt twenty-fifth-anniversary booklet pictures Gretchen, dressed in an original slip made by the factory's home workers. The mold number 114 dolls were first on display at the 1910 Easter Fair in Leipzig. Author's Archival Paper Collection.

42. This photograph, shown on page 27 of the Kämmer & Reinhardt twenty-fifth-anniversary booklet, is of the original model for the factory's mold number 114 bisque heads, with the trade name Hans for the dolls dressed like boys, and Gretchen for those dressed like girls. Franz Reinhardt's grandson was the model for the 114 mold number. According to the twenty-fifth-anniversary booklet, Kämmer & Reinhardt's best-selling dolls in 1910 were the mold number 114 series. Author's Archival Paper Collection.

Kämmer & Reinhardt Doll Factory

43. Bisque socket head by Simon & Halbig; body parts by Heinrich Handwerck; assembly by Kämmer & Reinhardt; wig; single-stroke eyebrows; short, closely spaced upper painted eyelashes; glass sleep eyes; open/closed mouth with upper teeth and molded tongue; 15-inch doll; GM 1909; marked: K*R//112//43. Glass-eyed versions of the 112 mold number, such as this example, are uncommon. Beth Karp collection. (Photo: Lee Krombholz)

Chapter 2

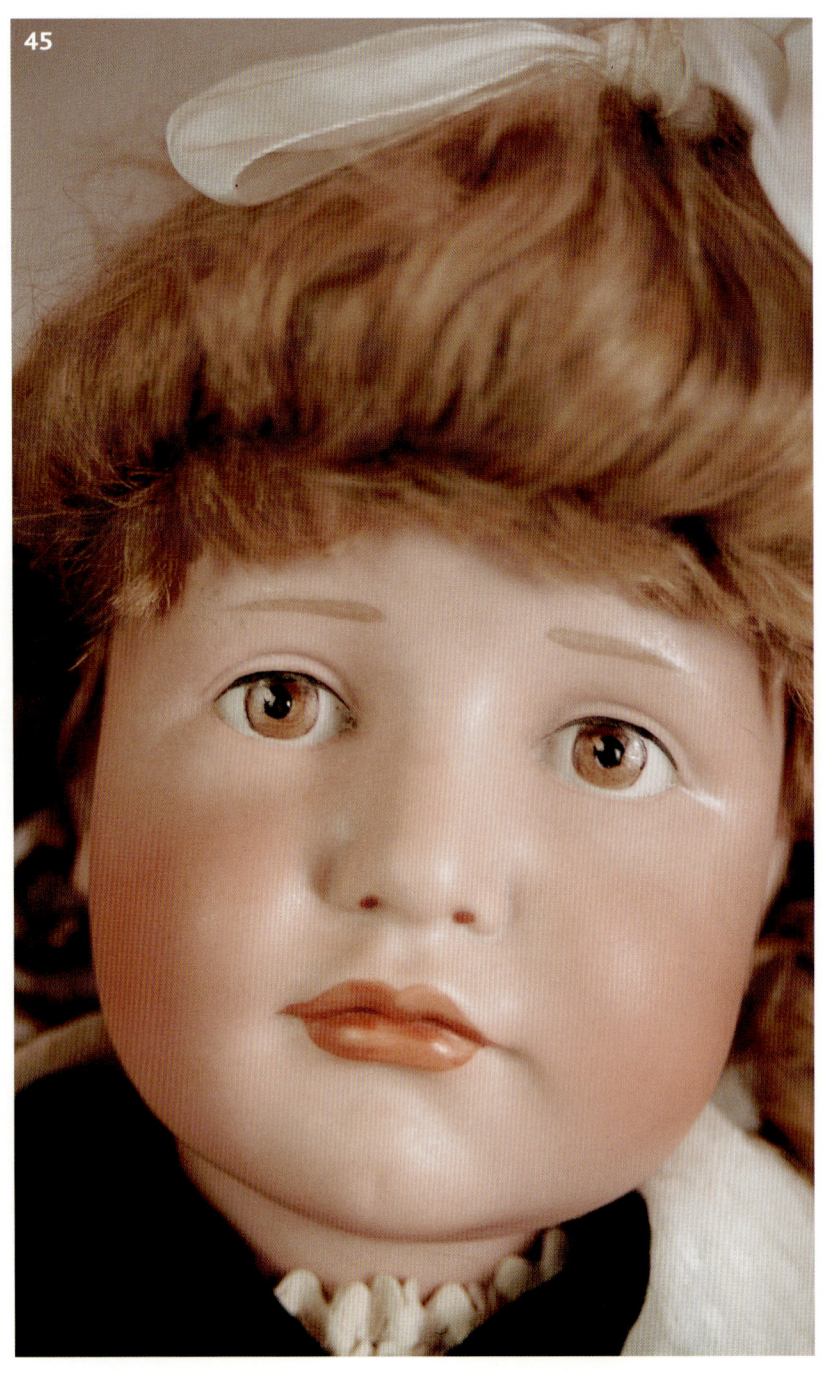

44. Gretchen bisque socket head by Simon & Halbig; original wig and clothing; single-stroke eyebrows; slightly molded, black-outlined upper eyelids; painted eyes; closed pouty mouth; chin dimple; 10-inch doll; GM 1909; marked: **K*R//114//26**. Author's Collection. (Photo: Gregg Smith)

45. Gretchen bisque socket head by Simon & Halbig; body parts by Heinrich Handwerck; assembly by Kämmer & Reinhardt; wig; single-stroke eyebrows; molded, black-outlined upper eyelids; painted eyes with white highlights; closed pouty mouth; chin dimple; 23¾-inch doll; GM 1909: marked: **K*R//114**. Courtesy Deutsches Spielzeugmuseum, Sonneberg. (Photo: Christiane Gräfnitz)

46. Gretchen bisque socket head by Simon & Halbig; body parts by Heinrich Handwerck; assembly by Kämmer & Reinhardt; wig; single-stroke eyebrows; molded, black-outlined upper eyelids; painted eyes with tiny, white highlights; closed pouty mouth; chin dimple; 18-inch doll; GM 1909; marked: **K*R//114//46**. Norah Stoner Collection. (Photo: Norah Stoner)

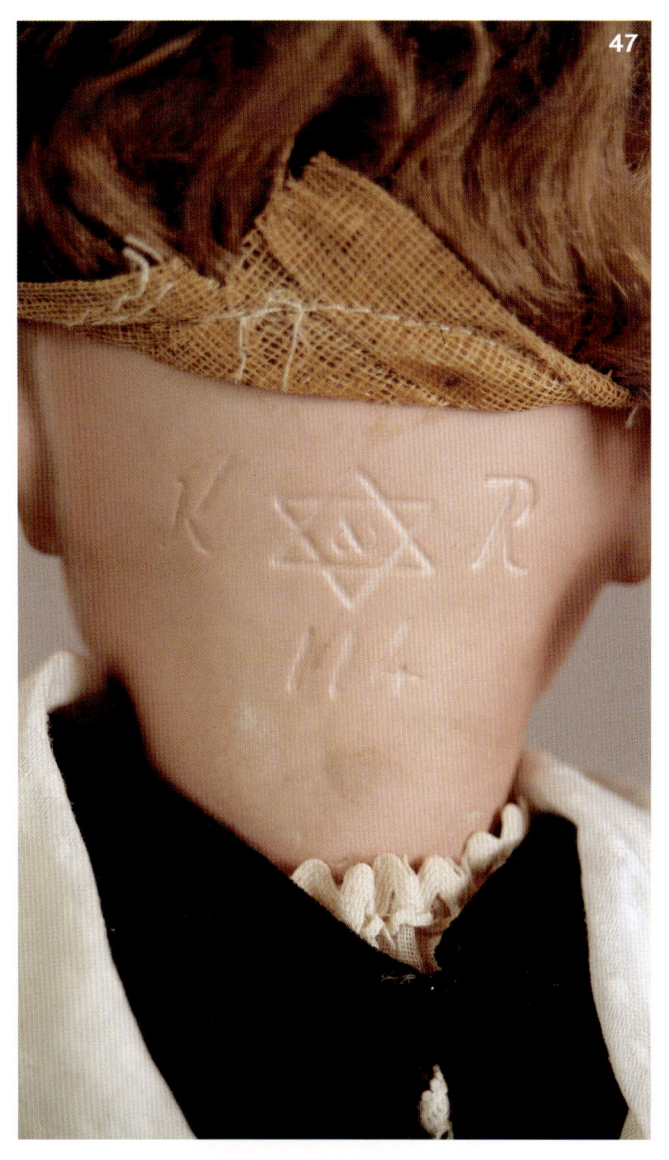

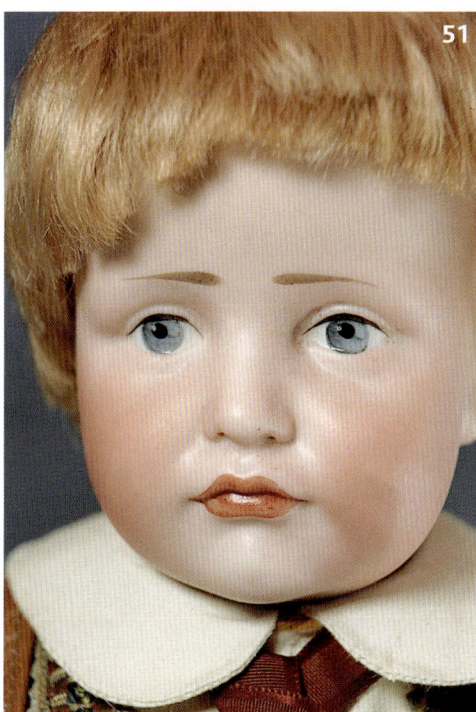

Kämmer & Reinhardt Doll Factory

47. The back of the head of the doll in illustration 45 shows the incised Kämmer & Reinhardt trademark star and mold number 114. Courtesy Deutsches Spielzeugmuseum, Sonneberg. (Photo: Christiane Gräfnitz)

48. Gretchen bisque socket head by Simon & Halbig; body parts by Heinrich Handwerck; assembly by Kämmer & Reinhardt; wig; single-stroke eyebrows; molded, black-outlined upper eyelids; painted eyes with white highlights; closed pouty mouth; chin dimple; 17-inch doll; GM 1909: marked: K*R//114. Ursula Gauder Collection. (Photo: Christiane Gräfnitz)

49. Hans bisque socket head by Simon & Halbig; body parts by Heinrich Handwerck; assembly by Kämmer & Reinhardt; wig; single-stroke eyebrows; molded, black-outlined upper eyelids; painted eyes; closed pouty mouth; chin dimple; 12-inch doll; GM 1909; marked: K&R//114. Ursula Gauder Collection. (Photo: Christiane Gräfnitz)

50. Hans bisque socket head by Simon & Halbig; body parts by Heinrich Handwerck; assembly by Kämmer & Reinhardt; flocked hair; single-stroke eyebrows; slightly molded, black-outlined upper eyelids; painted eyes with white highlights; closed pouty mouth; chin dimple; 14-inch doll; GM 1909; marked: K*R//314//36. Antje Lode Collection. (Photo: Antje Lode)

51. Hans bisque socket head by Simon & Halbig; body parts by Heinrich Handwerck; assembly by Heinrich Handwerck; wig; single-stroke eyebrows; molded, black-outlined upper eyelids; painted eyes with white highlights; closed pouty mouth; chin dimple; 17-inch doll; GM 1909; marked: K*R//114//43. Beth Karp Collection. (Photo: Lee Krombholz)

Chapter 2

53. Bisque socket head by Simon & Halbig; body parts by Heinrich Handwerck; assembly by Kämmer & Reinhardt; molded hair combed to one side in front; single-stroke eyebrows; painted upper and lower eyelashes; glass sleep eyes; open/closed pouty mouth; chin dimple; 15-inch doll; GM 1911; marked: **K*R//S&H//115//38**. The models for the Kämmer & Reinhardt mold numbers 115 and 115A were based on a child's head sculpture by the Brussels-born Italian Baroque sculptor Francois Duquesnoy, known in Italy as Il Fiammingo. Antje Lode Collection. (Photo: Antje Lode)

54. Bisque socket head by Simon & Halbig; body parts by Heinrich Handwerck; assembly by Kämmer & Reinhardt; wig; single-stroke eyebrows; painted upper and lower eyelashes; glass sleep eyes; closed pouty mouth; chin dimple; 18-inch doll; GM 1911; marked: **S&H//K*R//115A**. Christa Dorner Collection. (Photo: Christiane Gräfnitz)

56. Bisque socket head by Simon & Halbig; body parts by Heinrich Handwerck; assembly by Kämmer & Reinhardt; wig; multi-stroke eyebrows; painted upper and lower eyelashes; glass sleep eyes; closed pouty mouth; chin dimple; 16 inches; GM 1911; marked: **K*R//S&H//115A//42**. Mold number 115A, produced from 1911 to 1927, is the wigged version of the molded-hair mold 115. Beth Karp Collection. (Photo: Lee Krombholz)

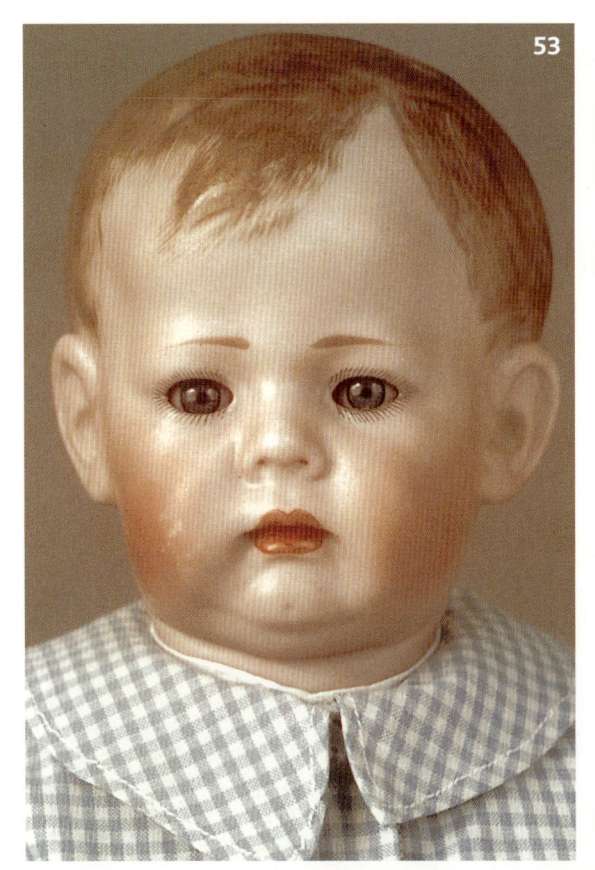

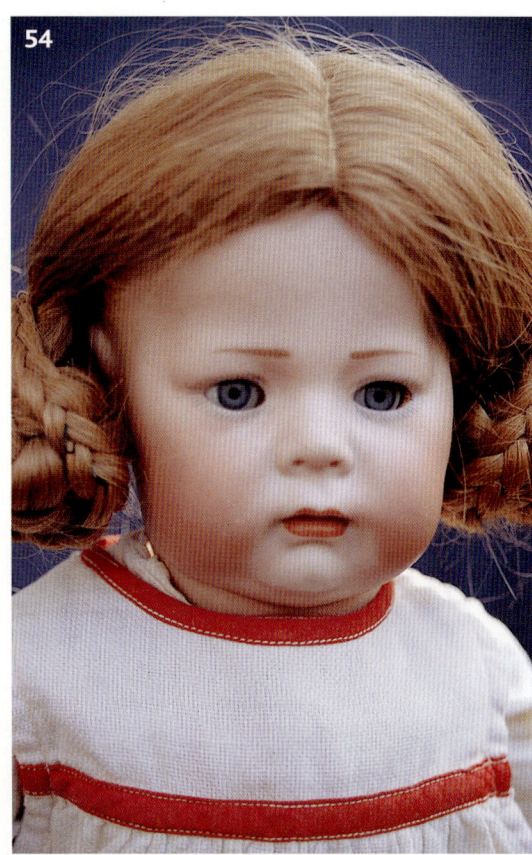

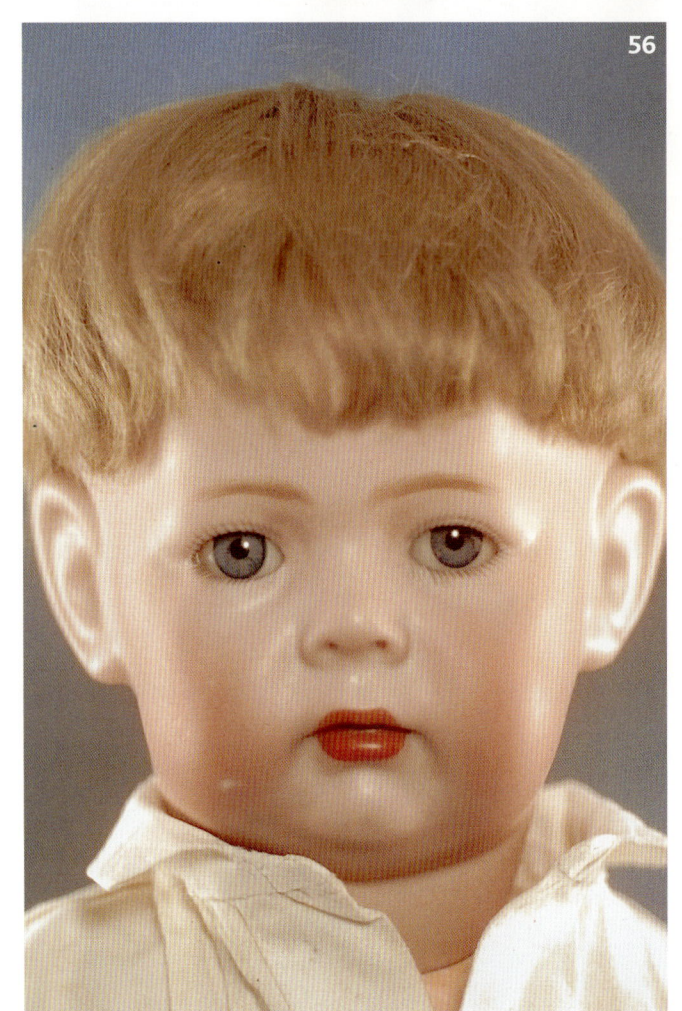

55. Bisque socket head by Simon & Halbig; baby body parts by Heinrich Handwerck; assembly by Kämmer & Reinhardt; wig; multi-stroke eyebrows; painted upper and lower eyelashes; glass sleep eyes; closed pouty mouth; chin dimple; 13½-inch doll; GM 1911; marked: **11 K*R//SIMON & HALBIG//115A//34**. Antje Lode Collection. (Photo: Antje Lode)

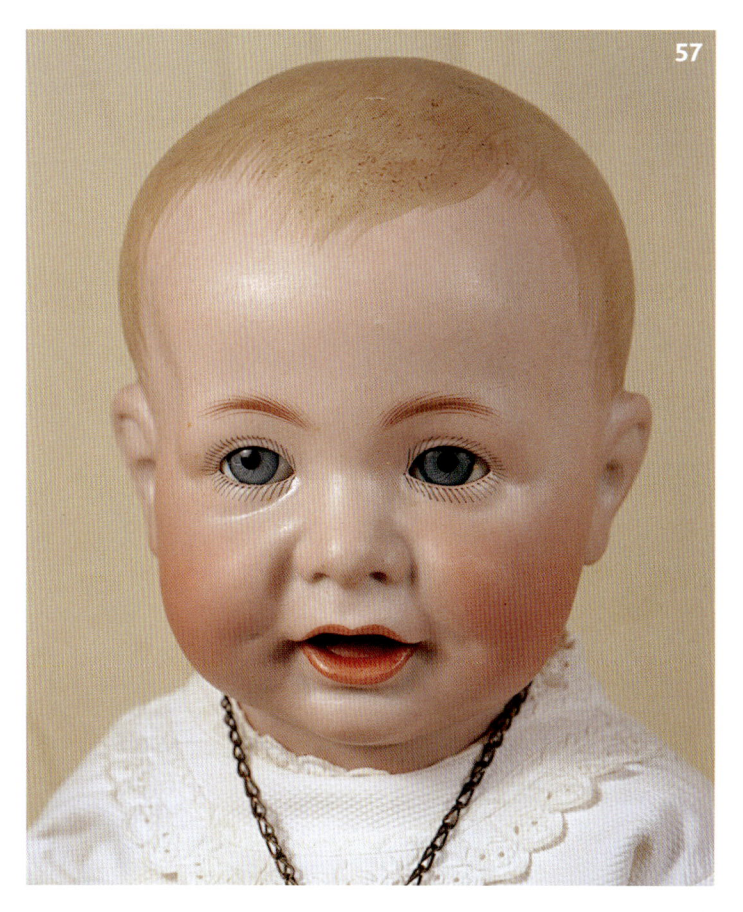

Kämmer & Reinhardt Doll Factory

57. Bisque socket head by Simon & Halbig; body parts by Heinrich Handwerck; assembly by Kämmer & Reinhardt; molded hair combed to one side in front; multi-stroke eyebrows; painted upper and lower eyelashes; glass sleep eyes; open mouth with molded upper teeth and tongue; cheek dimples; 20-inch doll; GM 1911; marked: **K*R//S&H//116//50**. Georgia Alarcon Collection. (Photo: Estelle Johnston)

58. Bisque socket head by Simon & Halbig; body parts by Heinrich Handwerck; assembly by Kämmer & Reinhardt; wig; multi-stroke eyebrows; painted upper and lower eyelashes; glass sleep eyes; open/closed mouth with molded tongue; cheek dimples; 19¾-inch doll; GM 1911; marked: **K*R//116A**. Courtesy Historisches Coburger Puppenmuseum/Lossnitzer Collection. (Photo: Christiane Gräfnitz)

- **59.** Bisque socket head by Simon & Halbig; body parts by Heinrich Handwerck; assembly by Kämmer & Reinhardt; wig; multi-stroke eyebrows; painted upper and lower eyelashes; glass sleep eyes; open/closed mouth with molded tongue; cheek dimples; 21¼-inch doll; GM 1911; marked: **K*R//116A**. Mold number 116A is the wigged version of the molded-hair mold 116. Courtesy Ladenburger Spilzeugzuktion/Goetz Seidel. (Photo: Christiane Gräfnitz)

- **60.** Bisque socket head by Simon & Halbig; baby body parts by Heinrich Handwerck; assembly by Kämmer & Reinhardt; wig; multi-stroke eyebrows; painted upper and lower eyelashes; glass sleep eyes; open mouth with upper teeth and molded tongue; 11-inch doll; GM 1911; marked: **K*R//S&H//116A//28**. Antje Lode Collection. (Photo: Antje Lode)

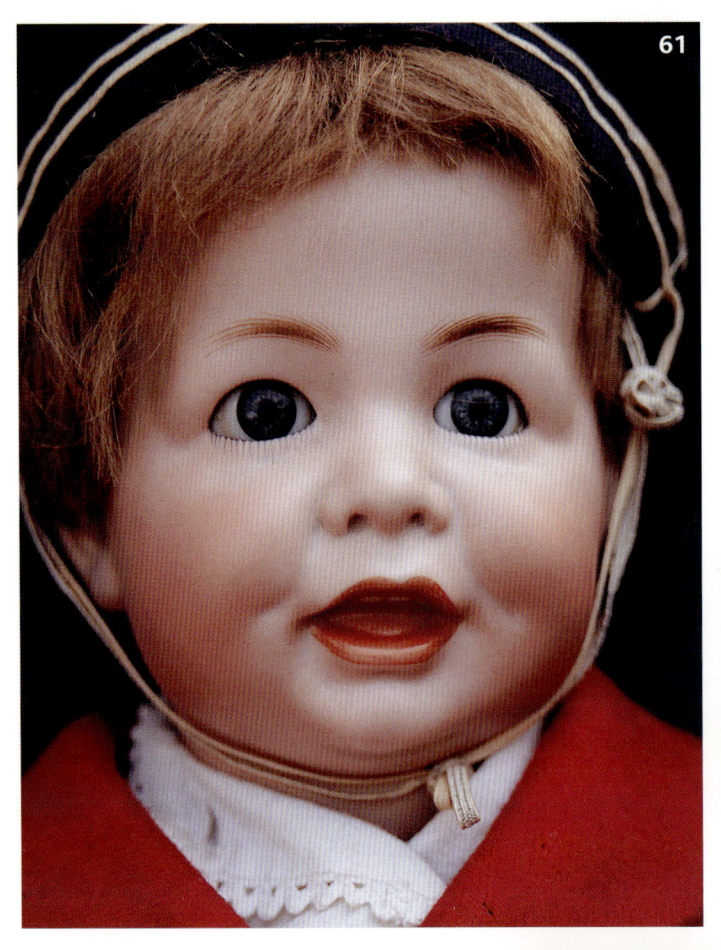

Chapter 2

61. Bisque socket head by Simon & Halbig; body parts by Heinrich Handwerck; assembly by Kämmer & Reinhardt; wig; multi-stroke eyebrows; painted upper and lower eyelashes; glass sleep eyes; open/closed mouth with upper teeth and molded tongue; cheek dimples; 19-inch doll; GM 1911; marked: **S&H//K*R//116A**. Christa Dorner Collection. (Photo: Christiane Gräfnitz)

62. *Mein Lieblingsbaby* (My Darling Baby) bisque socket head by Simon & Halbig; body parts by Heinrich Handwerck; assembly by Kämmer & Reinhardt; wig; multi-stroke eyebrows; painted upper and lower eyelashes; glass sleep eyes; closed mouth; 27-inch doll; GM 1911; marked: **K*R//SIMON & HALBIG//117//68**. The mold numbers 117 and 117A are generally referred to as *Mein Leibling* by antique-doll collectors, although the Kämmer & Reinhardt doll factory named many bisque heads in 100 mold number series *Mein Leibling*, with the insertion of other descriptive names like *Mein Neuer Liebling* (My New Darling, #117n) and *Mein Lieblingsbaby* (My Darling Baby, #126). Beth Karp Collection. (Photo: Lee Krombholz)

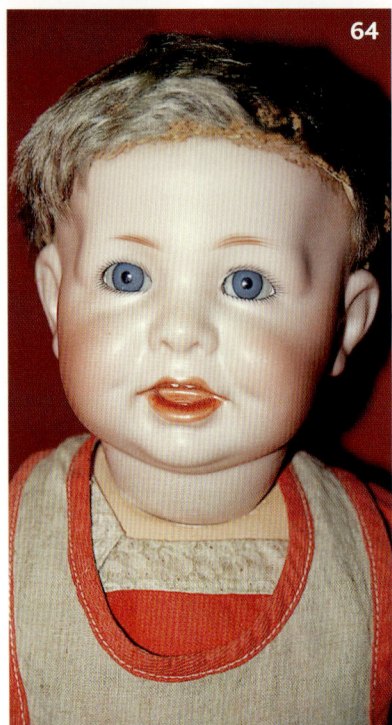

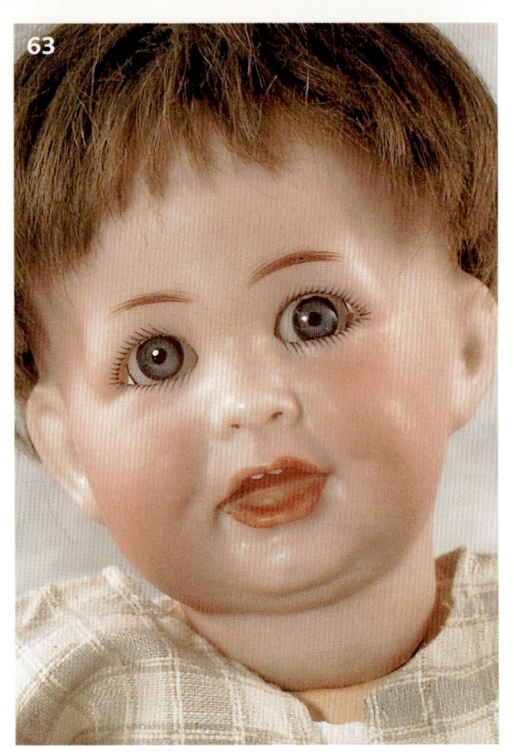

64. Bisque socket head by Simon & Halbig; body parts by Heinrich Handwerck; assembly by Kämmer & Reinhardt; wig; multi-stroke eyebrows; painted upper and lower eyelashes; glass sleep eyes; open/closed mouth with upper teeth and molded tongue; cheek dimples; 16½-inch doll; GM 1911; marked: **K*R//116//A**. Courtesy Hessisches Puppenmuseum, Hanau-Wilhelmsbad. (Photo: Christiane Gräfnitz)

63. Bisque socket head by Simon & Halbig; body parts by Heinrich Handwerck; assembly by Kämmer & Reinhardt; wig; multi-stroke eyebrows; painted upper and lower eyelashes; glass sleep eyes; open/closed mouth with upper teeth and molded tongue; 9-inch doll; GM 1911; marked: **K*R//SIMON & HALBIG//116A//26**. Beth Karp Collection. (Photo: Lee Krombholz)

72

Kämmer & Reinhardt Doll Factory

65. *Mein Liebling* bisque socket head by Simon & Halbig; body parts by Heinrich Handwerck; assembly by Kämmer & Reinhardt; wig; multi-stroke eyebrows; painted upper and lower eyelashes; glass sleep eyes; closed mouth; 29½-inch doll; GM 1911; marked: K*R//117A. The primary differences between the mold numbers 117 and 117A are the rounder eye cuts and smaller mouth on the 117 mold. Courtesy Hessisches Puppenmuseum, Hanau-Wilhelmsbad. (Photo: Christiane Gräfnitz)

66. *Mein Neuer Liebling* (My New Darling) bisque socket head by Simon & Halbig; body parts by Heinrich Handwerck; assembly by Kämmer & Reinhardt; wig; multi-stroke eyebrows; painted upper and lower eyelashes; flirty, glass sleep eyes; open mouth with upper teeth; 23½-inch doll; GM 1916; marked: K*R//117n. Courtesy Historisches Coburger Puppenmuseum/Lossnitzer Collection. (Photo: Christiane Gräfnitz)

67. *Mein Liebling* bisque socket head by Simon & Halbig; body parts by Heinrich Handwerck; assembly by Kämmer & Reinhardt; wig; multi-stroke eyebrows; painted upper and lower eyelashes; glass sleep eyes; closed mouth; 31½-inch doll; GM 1911; marked: K*R//S&H//117//80. Examples of mold number 117, ranging in height from 7 to 31 inches, were introduced at the Leipzig autumn fair in 1912. Courtesy Deutsches Spielzeugmuseum, Sonneberg. (Photo: Christiane Gräfnitz)

68. *Mein Liebling* bisque socket head by Simon & Halbig; body parts by Heinrich Handwerck; assembly by Kämmer & Reinhardt; wig; multi-stroke eyebrows; painted upper and lower eyelashes; glass sleep eyes; closed mouth; 15½-inch doll; GM 1911; marked: K*R//SIMON & HALBIG//117//39. Antje Lode Collection. (Photo: Antje Lode)

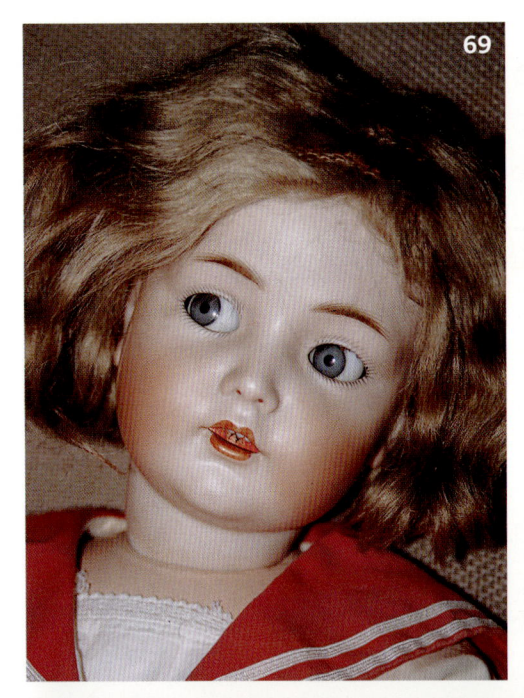

Chapter 2

69. *Mein Neuer Liebling* (My New Darling) bisque socket head by Simon & Halbig; body parts by Heinrich Handwerck; assembly by Kämmer & Reinhardt; wig; multi-stroke eyebrows; painted upper and lower eyelashes; flirty, glass sleep eyes; open mouth with upper teeth and separate tongue; 23-inch doll; GM 1916; marked: **K*R//SIMON & HALBIG//117n**. Courtesy Museum Schloss Tenneberg, Waltershausen. (Photo: Christiane Gräfnitz)

70. These two dolls, made from identical master molds, were sold by the Kämmer & Reinhardt doll factory. The doll on the left has a celluloid head marked **717**, circa 1920; the doll on the right has a bisque head marked **117n**. The bisque-head doll in this photograph is described in illustration 69, while the celluloid-head doll is described in illustration 72. The 700 mold series is the celluloid version of the 100 mold number series. Courtesy Museum Schloss Tenneberg, Waltershausen. (Photo: Christiane Gräfnitz)

71. *Mein Liebling* (My Darling) bisque socket head by Simon & Halbig; body parts by Heinrich Handwerck; assembly by Kämmer & Reinhardt; wig; multi-stroke eyebrows; painted upper and lower eyelashes; glass sleep eyes; closed mouth; 23-inch doll; GM 1911; marked: **K*R//SIMON & HALBIG//117A**. Ann Cummings Collection. (Photo: John Cummings)

72. Kämmer & Reinhardt celluloid head with wig; multi-stroke eyebrows; upper eyelashes made of hair; flirty, glass sleep eyes; open mouth with upper teeth; 24½-inch doll; circa 1920; marked: **K*R//717//62**. Kämmer & Reinhardt bought unpainted celluloid heads from Rheinische Gummi und Celluloid-Fabrik (the Rhenania factory of rubber and celluloid) in Mannheim-Neckarau. The celluloid heads were painted at the K&R factory. Courtesy Museum Schloss Tenneberg, Waltershausen. (Photo: Christiane Gräfnitz)

Kämmer & Reinhardt Doll Factory

73. *Mein Neuer Leibling* (My New Darling) bisque socket head by Simon & Halbig; body parts by Heinrich Handwerck; assembly by Kämmer & Reinhardt; wig; multi-stroke eyebrows; painted upper and lower eyelashes; flirty, glass sleep eyes; open mouth with open mouth and separate tongue; 18-inch doll; GM 1916; marked: K*R//SIMON & HALBIG//117n. Note the difference between the mouth sculpting and eyebrow painting on the 117A in illustration 71 and this 117n. Ann Cummings Collection. (Photo: John Cummings)

74. Bisque socket head by Simon & Halbig; baby body parts by Heinrich Handwerck; assembly by Kämmer & Reinhardt; wig; multi-stroke eyebrows; painted upper and lower eyelashes; glass sleep eyes; open mouth with upper teeth; cheek and chin dimples; 20-inch doll; circa 1911; marked: K*R//SIMON & HALBIG//118//50. Antje Lode Collection. (Photo: Antje Lode)

75. Bisque socket head by Simon & Halbig; body parts by Heinrich Handwerck; assembly by Kämmer & Reinhardt; wig; multi-stroke eyebrows; painted upper and lower eyelashes; flirty, glass sleep eyes; open mouth with upper teeth; 13½-inch doll; GM 1911; marked: K*R//SIMON & HALBIG//117x//Germany//34. Antje Lode Collection. (Photo: Antje Lode)

76. *Mein Neuer Leibling* (My New Darling) bisque socket head by Simon & Halbig; body parts by Heinrich Handwerck; assembly by Kämmer & Reinhardt; wig; multi-stroke eyebrows; painted upper and lower eyelashes; flirty, glass sleep eyes; open mouth with upper teeth and separate tongue; 19-inch doll; GM 1916; marked: K*R//117n. Beth Karp Collection. (Photo: Lee Krombholz)

Chapter 2

77. Bisque socket head by Simon & Halbig; baby body parts by Heinrich Handwerck; assembly by Kämmer & Reinhardt; 25-inch doll; circa 1913; marked: **K*R//SIMON & HALBIG//119 Baby//62**. This five-piece composition baby body is a good example of the well-modeled durable bodies made by the Heinrich Handwerck doll factory, which was owned by the Kämmer & Reinhardt doll factory from 1901 until 1920. Beth Karp Collection. (Photo: Gregg Smith)

78. A closer view of the doll shown in illustration 77 head shows the features of the head: wig; multi-stroke eyebrows; painted upper and lower eyelashes; glass sleep eyes; open/closed mouth with upper teeth; chin dimple. Beth Karp Collection. (Photo: Gregg Smith)

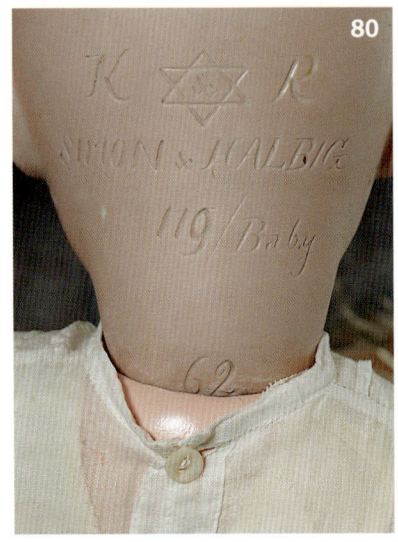

79. *Mein Klein Liebling* (My Little Darling) bisque socket head by Simon & Halbig; baby body parts by Heinrich Handwerck; assembly by Kämmer & Reinhardt; wig; multi-stroke eyebrows; painted upper and lower eyelashes; glass sleep eyes, open mouth with upper teeth and separate tongue; cheek dimples; 16-inch doll; GM 1912; marked: **K*R//SIMON & HALBIG//121//36**. Beth Karp Collection. (Photo: Lee Krombholz)

80. The back of the doll head pictured in illustrations 77 and 78 has the incised markings, including the factory's trademark star and the word "Baby." Beth Karp Collection. (Photo: Gregg Smith)

Kämmer & Reinhardt Doll Factory

81. Moritz bisque socket-head googly by Simon & Halbig; body parts by Heinrich Handwerck; assembly by Kämmer & Reinhardt; wig; single-stroke eyebrows; full, short upper eyelashes; side-glancing glass eyes; closed laughing mouth; cheek dimples; 15¾-inch doll; GM 1913; unmarked. Moritz, usually marked with the K&R mold number 124, is wearing a wig and clothing that depicts *Struwwelpeter* (Shock-headed Peter, a character in a German children's book by the same name). Note the difference in eyebrow painting and mouth size between Max seen in illustration 82 and this doll. Courtesy Rosalie Whyel Museum of Doll Art. (Photo: Christiane Gräfnitz)

82. Max bisque socket-head googly by Simon & Halbig; body parts by Heinrich Handwerck; assembly by Kämmer & Reinhardt; wig; thick, black single-stroke eyebrows; short, closely-spaced upper painted eyelashes; glass stationary eyes; closed laughing mouth; cheek dimples; 15¾-inch doll; GM 1913; marked: **K*R//123**. Kämmer & Reinhardt's Max and Moritz character dolls resemble the illustrations of the mischievous boys in the 1865 book titled *Max and Moritz* by German author and artist Wilhelm Busch. Courtesy Historisches Coburger Puppenmuseum/Lossnitzer Collection. (Photo: Christiane Gräfnitz)

83. Bisque socket head by Simon & Halbig; baby body parts by Heinrich Handwerck; assembly by Kämmer & Reinhardt; wig; multi-stroke eyebrows; painted upper and lower eyelashes; glass sleep eyes; open mouth with upper teeth and separate tongue; cheek dimples; 17-inch doll; GM 1912; marked: **K*R//SIMON & HALBIG//122//42**. Ann Cummings Collection. (Photo: John Cummings)

84. *Mein Klein Liebling* (My Little Darling) bisque socket head by Simon & Halbig; baby body parts by Heinrich Handwerck; assembly by Kämmer & Reinhardt; wig; multi-stroke eyebrows; painted upper and lower eyelashes; glass sleep eyes; open mouth with upper teeth and separate tongue; chin dimples; 21-inch doll; GM 1912; marked: **K*R//SIMON & HALBIG//121**. Christa Dorner Collection. (Photo: Christiane Gräfnitz)

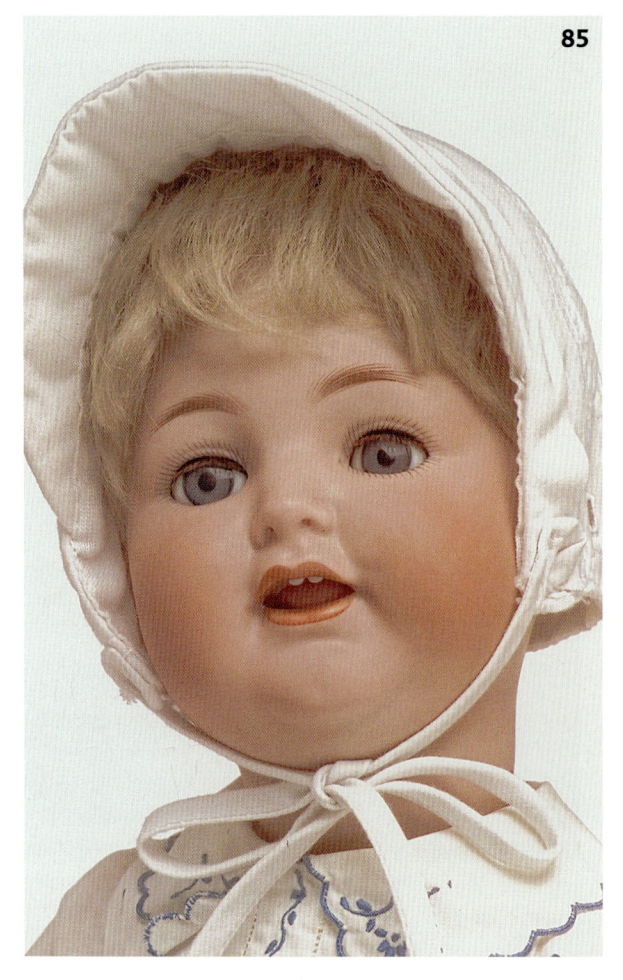

Chapter 2

85. *Mein Lieblingsbaby* (My Darling Baby) bisque socket head by Simon & Halbig; body parts by Heinrich Handwerck; assembled by Kämmer & Reinhardt; wig; multi-stroke eyebrows; painted upper and lower eyelashes; glass sleep eyes; open mouth with upper teeth and separate tongue; chin dimple; 16½-inch doll; circa 1914; marked: **K*R//SIMON & HALBIG//126//42**. Ann Cummings Collection. (Photo: John Cummings)

86. Bisque socket heads by Simon & Halbig; body parts by Heinrich Handwerck; assembly by Kämmer & Reinhardt; jointed composition bodies with rounded stomachs. Head features include wigs; multi-stroke eyebrows; upper and lower painted eyelashes (smallest one has single-stroke eyebrows); glass sleep eyes; open mouths with upper teeth and separate tongues; two 10-inch dolls, one 8½-inch doll; circa 1914; two marked: **K*R//SIMON & HALBIG//126//23**; smallest marked: **K*R//SIMON & HALBIG//126//19**. The 126 mold number group was trademarked *Mein Lieblingsbaby* (My Darling Baby) as part of the *Mein Liebling* series. The three dolls pictured here, all mold number 126, were marketed in 1927 as *Mein Fett Klein Liebling* (My Fat Little Darling). Beth Karp Collection. (Photo: Lee Krombholz)

87. *Mein Lieblingsbaby* (My Darling Baby) bisque socket head by Simon & Halbig; body parts by Heinrich Handwerck; assembled by Kämmer & Reinhardt; original skin wig; multi-stroke eyebrows; painted upper and lower eyelashes; glass sleep eyes; open mouth with upper teeth and separate tongue; chin dimple; 22-inch doll; circa 1914; marked; **K*R//SIMON & HALBIG//126//50**. Beth Karp Collection. (Photo: Lee Krombholz)

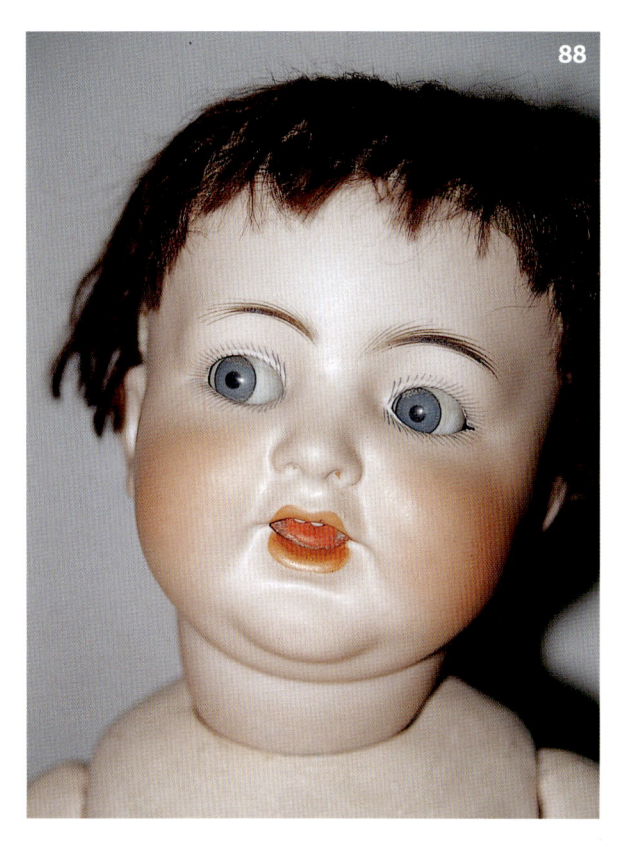

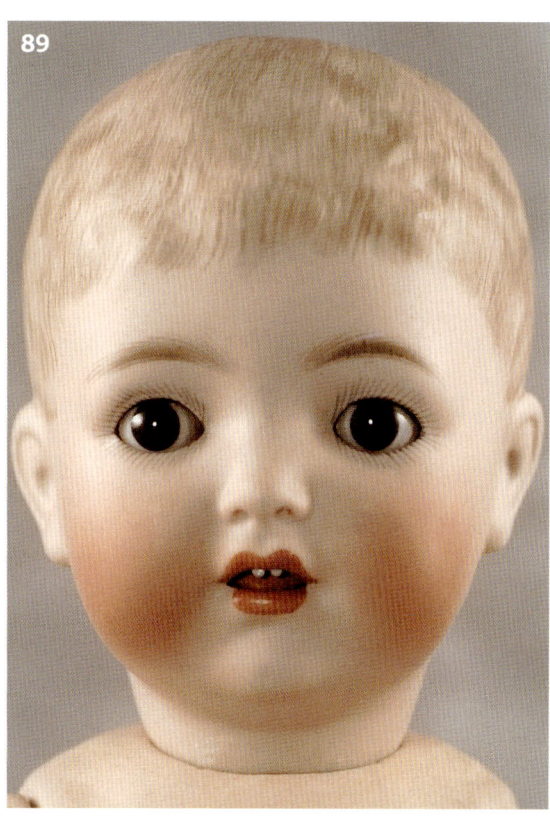

Kämmer & Reinhardt Doll Factory

88. *Mein Lieblingsbaby* (My Darling Baby) bisque socket head by Simon & Halbig; jointed baby body with voice box by Heinrich Handwerck; assembled by Kämmer & Reinhardt; wig; multi-stroke eyebrows; painted upper and lower eyelashes; glass flirty eyes; open mouth with upper teeth and separate tongue; chin dimple; 15-inch doll; circa 1914; marked: K*R//126//38. Courtesy Hessisches Puppenmuseum, Hanau-Wilhelmsbad. (Photo: Christiane Gräfnitz)

89. Bisque socket head by Simon & Halbig; body parts by Heinrich Handwerck; assembly by Kämmer & Reinhardt; molded hair; multi-stroke eyebrows; painted upper and lower eyelashes; glass sleep eyes; open mouth with upper teeth and separate tongue; 14½-inch doll; GM 1914; marked: Germany//SIMON & HALBIG//K*R//36//127n. Beth Karp Collection. (Photo: Lee Krombholz)

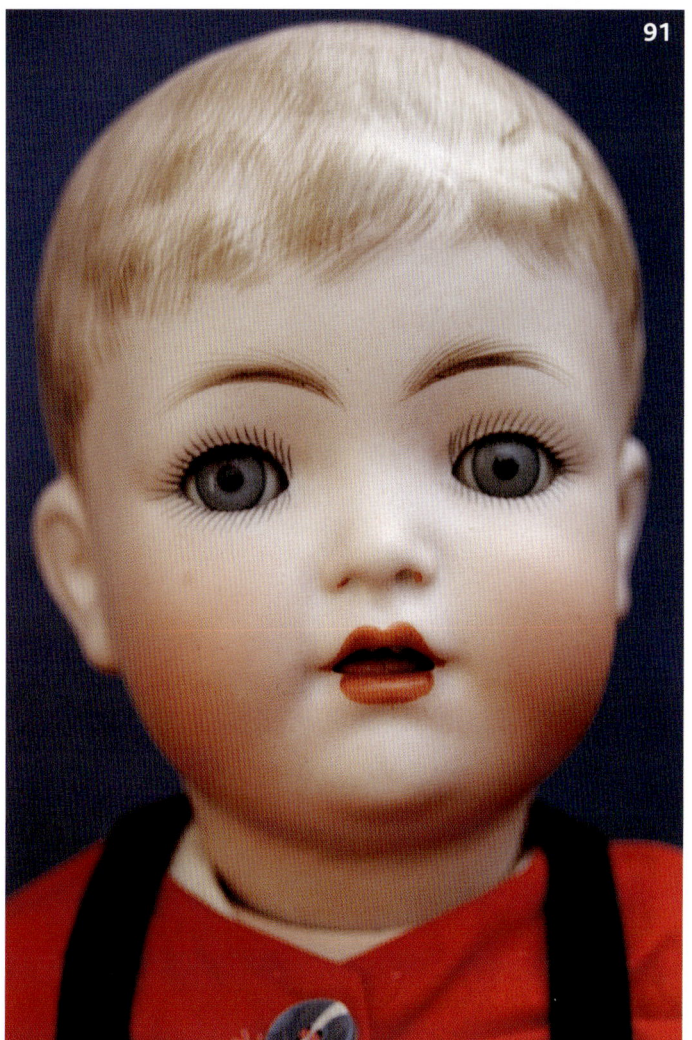

90. Bisque socket head by Simon & Halbig; body parts by Heinrich Handwerck; assembly by Kämmer & Reinhardt; molded hair; multi-stroke eyebrows; molded upper eyelids; painted upper and lower eyelashes; glass sleep eyes; open mouth with upper teeth and separate tongue; chin dimple; 18-inch doll; GM 1914; marked: K*R//127//42. Courtesy Ladenburger Spielzeugauktion/Gotz Seidel Auctions. (Photo: Christiane Gräfnitz)

91. Bisque socket head by Simon & Halbig; body parts by Heinrich Handwerck; assembly by Kämmer & Reinhardt; molded hair; multi-stroke eyebrows; painted upper and lower eyelashes; glass sleep eyes; open mouth with upper teeth and separate tongue; 15¾-inch doll; GM 1914; marked: K*R//SIMON & HALBIG //127n//36. Christa Dorner Collection. (Photo: Christiane Gräfnitz)

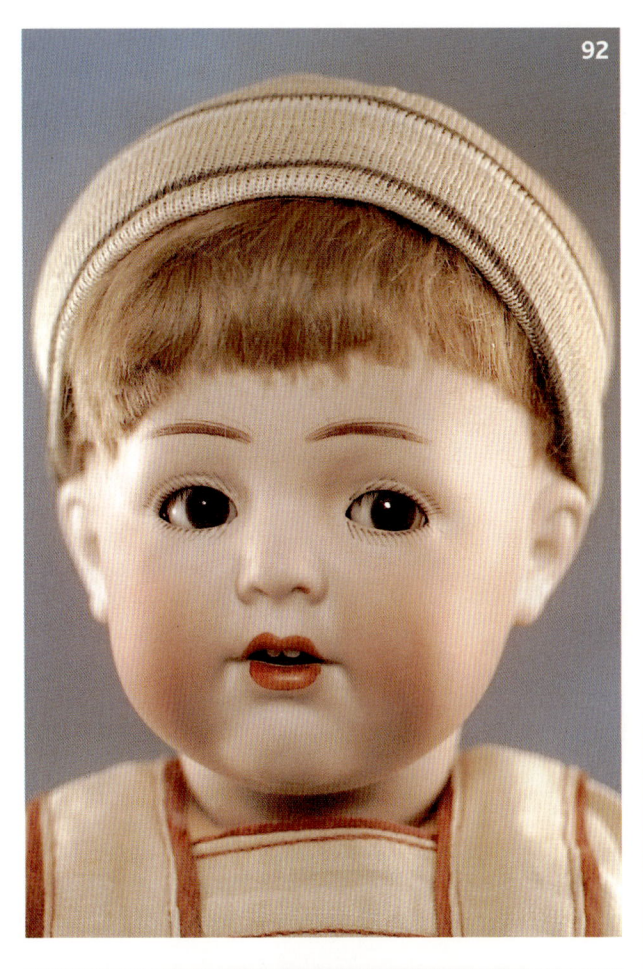

CHAPTER 2

92. Bisque socket head by Simon & Halbig; body parts by Heinrich Handwerck; assembly by Kämmer & Reinhardt; wig; multi-stroke eyebrows; painted upper and lower eyelashes; upper eyelashes made of hair; glass, side-glancing flirty eyes (Otto Gans patented mechanism); open mouth with upper teeth and separate tongue; 15-inch doll; GM 1914; marked: **K*R//SIMON & HALBIG//128//32**. Beth Karp Collection. (Photo: Lee Krombholz)

93. Bisque socket-head googly by Simon & Halbig; body parts by Heinrich Handwerck; assembly by Kämmer & Reinhardt; multi-stroke eyebrows; upper half of eye socket outlined in black; large, side-glancing sleep eyes; closed smiling mouth; 15½-inch doll; circa 1914; marked: **K*R//SIMON & HALBIG//131**. Anita Ladensack Collection. (Photo: Anita Ladensack)

94. Bisque socket-head googly by Simon & Halbig; body parts by Heinrich Handwerck; assembly by Kämmer & Reinhardt; original wig and clothing; multi-stroke eyebrows; upper half of eye socket outlined in black; large, side-glancing, glass sleep eyes; closed, smiling mouth; 13-inch doll; circa 1914; marked: **K*R//SIMON & HALBIG//131//Germany//2**. According to Jan Foulke's research published in her book *Simon & Halbig Dolls: The Artful Aspect*, the 131 was still listed in the 1927 catalog, and may have been one of the last molds designed by Kämmer & Reinhardt modelers. Kathy and Mike Embry Collection. (Photo: Ann Hanat)

Kämmer & Reinhardt Doll Factory

95. Bisque head by Simon & Halbig; body parts by Heinrich Handwerck; assembly by Kämmer & Reinhardt; flange neck; slightly molded hair; single-stroke eyebrows; painted upper and lower eyelashes; glass sleep eyes; closed mouth; 15-inch doll; GM 1925; marked: K*R//S&H//172. The Kämmer & Reinhardt succeeding mold number 173 is also listed as a character newborn with flange neck in the Ciesliks' book *German Doll Marks and Identification Book*. Courtesy Rosalie Whyel Museum of Doll Art. (Photo: Christiane Gräfnitz)

96. Original Kämmer & Reinhardt cloth doll; wire legs and arms; wooden feet; stockinet head; shaped nose, yarn eyebrows, mustache and beard; felt clothing sewed with great attention to detail; 13½-inch doll; circa 1920s; unmarked. The Kämmer & Reinhardt doll factory made a large variety of realistic cloth dolls that were dressed to represent German townspeople, including this man smoking a typical German pipe with a porcelain bowl for holding tobacco. Beth Karp Collection. (Photo: Lee Krombholz)

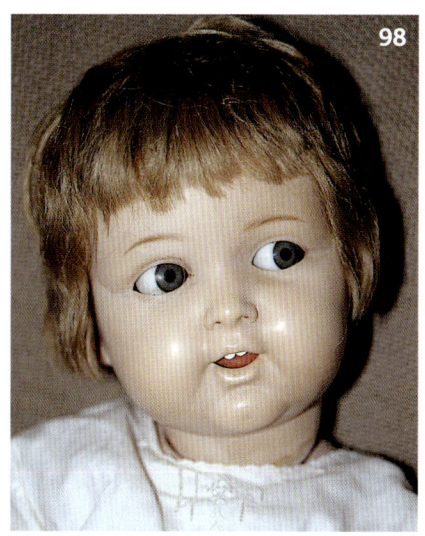

97. Bisque socket head by Simon & Halbig; body parts by Heinrich Handwerck; assembly by Kämmer & Reinhardt; molded hair; multi-stroke eyebrows; molded upper eyelids; painted upper and lower eyelashes; glass sleep eyes; open mouth with upper teeth and separate tongue; 13-inch doll; GM 1914; marked: SIMON & HALBIG//K*R//127//32. Beth Karp Collection. (Photo: Lee Krombholz)

98. Celluloid socket head by Rheinische Gummi und Celluloid-Fabrik for Kämmer & Reinhardt purchased unpainted, then painted by Kämmer & Reinhardt artists at the factory; wig; single-stroke eyebrows; side-glancing glass eyes; open mouth with upper teeth and separate tongue; 20-inch doll; GM 1915; marked: K*R//728. Courtesy Museum Schloss Tenneberg, Waltershausen. (Photo: Christiane Gräfnitz)

Chapter 2

99 and 100. Two photographs of the Kämmer & Reinhardt doll factory sample room in 1936 combine to create one large image. The photographs, which have been hand colored, are pictured in the factory's fiftieth-anniversary booklet. A variety of dolly-face and character dolls are on display. Author's Archival Paper Collection.

101. This 1900 photograph of Heinrich Handwerck is pictured in the Kämmer & Reinhardt's twenty-fifth-anniversary booklet. Following Handwerck's death in 1902, Franz Reinhardt bought the Heinrich Handwerck doll factory. It was led by Gottlieb Nussle as a separate "sister" factory until 1918, when the factory closed. The factory was re-founded in 1921 by Heinrich Handwerck Jr. and closed permanently in 1930. Author's Archival Paper Collection.

102. This 1911 photograph, which has been hand colored; is pictured on page 12 of the factory's twenty-fifth-anniversary booklet. It shows the Kämmer & Reinhardt sample room filled with standing dressed dolls. The room, decorated with a brass light fixture and a patterned border at ceiling level, contains a large table, chairs and several rows of shelves. Bisque shoulder heads are arranged on a separate, slanted shelf, which has a wooden border to keep the heads in place. Author's Archival Paper Collection.

103. This photograph of the large Heinrich Handwerck doll factory in Waltershausen is pictured on page 26 of the Kämmer & Reinhardt twenty-fifth anniversary booklet. It has been hand-colored to show the trees and other buildings that originally surrounded the factory. The signage on the top of the building reads: *Puppen Fabrik* (doll factory). Following the purchase of the factory by Reinhardt, the Handwerck doll factory made all of the composition body parts for Kämmer & Reinhardt bisque-head dolls. As a separate company, the Heinrich Handwerck doll factory continued to assemble and sell dolls with Simon & Halbig bisque heads to other Thuringian doll factories. Author's Archival Paper Collection.

Kämmer & Reinhardt Doll Factory

103

HEINRICH HANDWERCK.   ANSICHT DER FABRIK.

104

HEINRICH HANDWERCK.   MECHANISCHE DREHEREI DER HOLZTEILE.

106

HEINRICH HANDWERCK.   SCHNEIDEN DER STÄMME.

105

HEINRICH HANDWERCK.   MECHANISCHES STANZEN UND ZUSAMMENFÜGEN GROSSER PUPPENTEILE.

104. This photograph and the three that follow, which have all have been hand colored, are also pictured in the 1911 Kämmer & Reinhardt twenty-fifth-anniversary booklet. They show how the Heinrich Handwerck doll factory made composition bodies for Kämmer & Reinhardt and other Thuringian doll factories. The German text on this photograph reads: "Mechanical Turning of Wooden Parts." The four factory workers inside the Handwerck doll factory are operating lathes connected by a line shaft. The large tubes in the upper-left section of the photograph are part of a venting system that collects sawdust, much like a giant vacuum cleaner. Author's Archival Paper Collection.

105. The German words on this photograph read: "Mechanical Stamping and Assembly of Big Doll (body) Parts." Large composition body parts in various stages of production are pictured. In their *German Doll Encyclopedia*, the Ciesliks provide the following information on the production of bodies in the Heinrich Handwerck doll factory at Tiergartenstrasse: "In 1888, the factory expanded and moved into a new factory building in order to make faster machine-made doll parts. All wooden parts for arms and legs, balls for joints, were also manufactured in one factory." Author's Archival Paper Collection.

106. This photograph shows a factory worker in the Handwerck doll factory cutting up a large tree trunk with an axe, in order to make wooden body parts such as balls for ball joints and upper and lower limbs. Author's Archival Paper Collection.

Chapter 2

107. This photograph, which is labeled in German to read: "Making of the Crates," shows workers making wooden crates in the Heinrich Handwerck doll factory. The majority of large Thuringian doll and porcelain factories made their own cardboard boxes and shipping crates in the factory, especially those that concentrated on exports to the United States. Author's Paper Collection.

108. Bisque socket head by Simon & Halbig, body parts by Heinrich Handwerck; assembled and sold by Heinrich Handwerck; wig; multi-stroke eyebrows; painted upper and lower eyelashes; glass sleep eyes; open/closed mouth; 17-inch doll; circa 1912; marked: **120/3**. Courtesy Rosalie Whyel Museum of Doll Art. (Photo: Christiane Gräfnitz)

109. Heinrich Handwerck dolly-faced dolls, marked with the circa 1900 factory mold numbers that jump in increments of 10 and end with the number "9" (79, 89, 99, and 109) are well known to antique-doll collectors, but the factory also assembled and sold dolls with Simon & Halbig bisque character heads. This is an example of an unmarked 18-inch Heinrich Handwerck character doll with a Simon & Halbig bisque head and a marked Heinrich Handwerck body. The head features include multi-stroke eyebrows, painted eyes with white highlights and a closed mouth. Courtesy Rothenburg Puppenmuseum/Katharina Engels Collection. (Photo: Christiane Gräfnitz

110. The Heinrich Handwerck doll factory is also credited with the assembly and sale of an exquisite group of character dolls with Simon & Halbig heads, marked with the mold numbers 111, 120, 128 and 129. The features on this bisque character head include original wig; multi-stroke eyebrows; painted upper and lower eyelashes; glass sleep eyes; closed mouth; 16-inch doll; circa 1912; marked: **111//3**. The Handwerck bisque head dolls marked 111, 120, 128 and 129 fit into the known Handwerck mold number series; and, the dolls are usually found on marked Heinrich Handwerck bodies, wearing marked Heinrich Handwerck shoes. Courtesy Rosalie Whyel Museum of Doll Art. (Photo: Christiane Gräfnitz)

Kämmer & Reinhardt Doll Factory

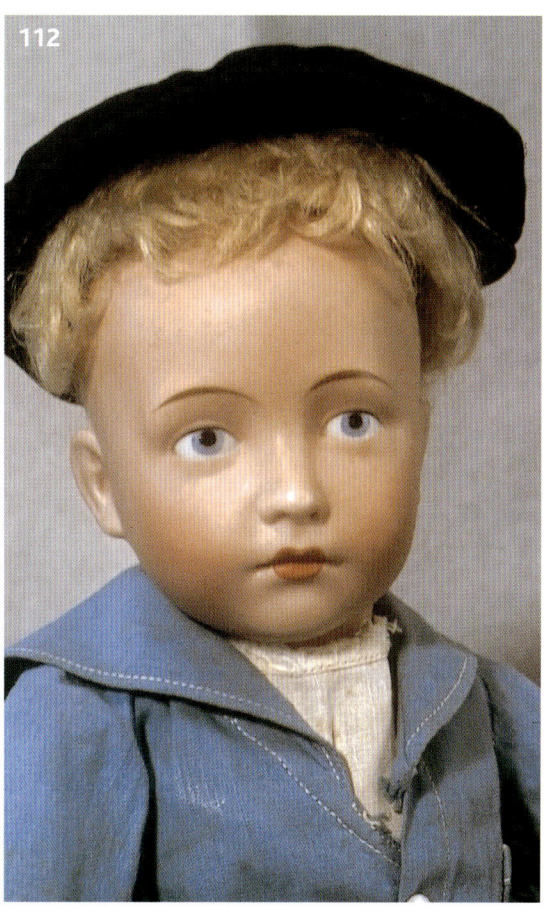

111. Bisque socket head by Simon & Halbig; body parts by Heinrich Handwerck; assembled and sold by Heinrich Handwerck; wig; multi-stroke eyebrows; painted upper and lower eyelashes; glass sleep eyes; closed mouth; 16½-inch-doll; circa 1912; marked: **111/4**. Julie Blewis Collection. (Photo: Fanilya Gueno)

112. Bisque socket head by Simon & Halbig, body parts by Heinrich Handwerck; assembled and sold by Heinrich Handwerck; wig; single-stroke eyebrows; painted eyes; closed mouth; 15-inch doll; circa 1912; marked: **111/5**. Julie Blewis Collection. (Photo: Fanilya Gueno)

113. Bisque socket head by Simon & Halbig, body parts by Heinrich Handwerck; assembled and sold by Heinrich Handwerck; wig; single-stroke eyebrows; painted eyes; open/closed mouth with molded tongue; chin dimple; 19-inch doll; circa 1912; marked: **120**. Julie Blewis Collection. (Photo: Fanilya Gueno)

114. Bisque socket head by Simon & Halbig, body parts by Heinrich Handwerck; assembled and sold by Heinrich Handwerck; wig; single-stroke eyebrows; intaglio-painted eyes with white highlights centered close to the upper eyelid; closed mouth; 15½-inch doll; circa 1912; marked: **129**. Another doll in the Handwerck series, marked **128/5**, is pictured on page 192 of the book *The Rose Unfolds, Rarities of the Rosalie Whyel Museum of Doll Art*. Julie Blewis Collection. (Photo: Fanilya Gueno)

Part One
Chapter 3

Simon & Halbig Porcelain Factory

1. This photograph of Carl Halbig hangs in the Dorf Museum in the neighboring village of Nauendorf, home of the Alt, Beck & Gottschalck porcelain factory. The photograph was taken in 1919, as part of the celebration marking the fiftieth anniversary of the porcelain factory and Carl Halbig's eightieth birthday. (Photo: Carol Nagel)

Carl Halbig and Wilhelm Simon founded the Simon & Halbig porcelain factory in Gräfenhain in 1869. In 1859 Carl Halbig, then eighteen years old, had begun to work as an accountant for the Alt, Beck & Gottschalck porcelain factory in Nauendorf. Following the death of Johann Theodor Gottschalck on November 7, 1865, he became a director of the porcelain factory. After her husband's death, Gottschalck's widow began to direct the factory with co-founder Beck. In the following months, she and Carl Halbig began dating and eventually married.

In the 1860s, Wilhelm Simon was a very successful merchant and a well-respected citizen in his hometown. His Simon ancestors had settled in Hilburghausen in 1711. He founded the Wilhelm Simon doll factory in Hildburghausen in 1846, and directed it for forty-eight years, until his death in 1894. (After his death, his son became the sole owner of the Simon doll and toy factory.) Wilhelm Simon was a client of the Alt, Beck & Gottschalk porcelain factory, and he and Carl Halbig became business acquaintances. After Halbig became a director of the factory, the two men decided to found a porcelain factory in Gräfenhain. Halbig's wife and Simon provided most of the money required to configure an old parish church into a porcelain factory. According to Jürgen and Marianne Cieslik in the March 2001 issue of *Puppenmagazin*, "Carl Halbig took with him the best Nauendorf workers and the best recipes for biscuit porcelain, and was off to a good start."

The history of Gräfenhain is closely tied to that of Nauendorf, home of the Alt, Beck & Gottschalck porcelain factory. The villages are such close neighbors it is hard to tell where one village starts and the other ends. Both are located in the foothills of the Thuringian mountains, at the rim of the "Zechstein" formation. This formation of sediment rock from the Upper Permian defines the hilly landscape. In 1130, due to its geological conditions, Gräfenhain became an excellent area in which to mine cobalt and slate. Ore mining was the principal reason both Gräfenhain and Nauendorf developed and thrived over the

2. This 1911 photograph, which has been hand colored, is pictured in my Kämmer & Reinhardt twenty-fifth-anniversary booklet. It shows the Kämmer & Reinhardt sculptor Karl Krausser creating an original model for the Simon & Halbig porcelain factory. Simon & Halbig made all of Kämmer & Reinhardt's bisque doll heads from 1902 on. Author's Archival Paper Collection.

87

Chapter 3

next few centuries. (Ore mining had ceased in the region by 1780.)

In 1168 the village of Gräfenhain became the property of Duke Erwin von Gleichen. The first year the village is mentioned in history books is 1230. The first settlers of Gräfenhain were from the areas that later became the German states of Thuringia, Franken and Eastphalia. In 1292 the first Gräfenhain church was built and in 1593 the first school was built. In 1690 residents began to drive their covered wagons to neighboring towns in order to find buyers for their wares. Both Gräfenhain and Nauendorf continued to grow over the next few centuries, and by the late nineteenth century the majority of residents worked at porcelain production, papier-mâché mask making or in cigar factories. The population of Gräfenhain is about fifteen hundred today, while Nauendorf residents number about five hundred.

Very little information has surfaced concerning Carl Halbig's personal life during his first marriage to the widow Gottschalck. They had a son and two daughters before her death in 1887. Halbig's second wife was Minna Seyferth. They had a daughter named Elisabeth, nicknamed Lisa. For many years, the growing Halbig family lived in the small house that adjoined the porcelain factory.

In 1900 Carl Halbig built a new home, a villa directly across the street from his porcelain factory. The villa, featuring English Tudor styling, still dominates the Gräfenhain landscape on the main highway between Gräfenhain and Nauendorf. An article by Adrian Weber in the *Kreis Gotha* newspaper dated April 17, 1999, provides an excellent description of the Halbig villa, and includes many important references to the porcelain factory during the years character dolls were made.

> The four-floor building has a wonderful view of Ohrdruf and Gotha. Together with a barn and a smaller building it is located on the northeast corner of a big park. The cellar foundation is 27 inches thick and the outer walls are 15 inches thick. The western tower and big window in the former parlor dominate the street view of the house. Wrought iron railings and two little leaded glass windows still remind one of the 'good old days.' The interior of the house was furnished in the style of the early 1900s. Wall rugs, paintings and valuable furniture were part of the appropriate furnishings of a successful manufacturer back then. Today, only the restored staircase and doors remain from the former luxury.
>
> The Halbig family lived happily in these surroundings until 1914. Earlier, Carl Halbig's daughter Elisabeth married the German officer Ernst Rosenstock, and the company continued to flourish. But with the beginning of the First World War, the lucrative exporting business collapsed. By the end of 1918, Halbig was forced to sell the biggest part of his porcelain factory to the Bing Werke (Works) of Nuremberg. At about the same time, his son-in-law returned highly decorated from the war.

The Bing Werke, founded in 1917, was a large conglomerate of doll and porcelain factories. The full name of the company was "Continental Supplies Center Concentra AG." It was the largest doll and toy company in the world from 1917 until 1932, when it declared bankruptcy. The company did an excellent job of selling the products of its many "sister" doll and porcelain factories, due to permanent sample stores in many cities worldwide and a permanent trade building in Leipzig.

The Kämmer & Reinhardt doll factory became a joint stock company in 1916, following owner Franz Reinhardt's sale of the majority of his shares of stock to the Bing Werke in Nuremberg. From 1916 on, Bing handled all of the doll-related sales, including those that involved Simon & Halbig products. In 1920 the Kämmer & Reinhardt factory bought the Simon & Halbig porcelain factory.

Author Adrian Weber's 1999 article continues the history of the Simon & Halbig porcelain factory.

> Despite all efforts during the following years of inflation, the doll production would never reach the pre-war position again. A further big blow for the entrepreneur was the sudden death of his son Arno in 1923, which he never got over. Three years later, on June 23, 1926, Carl Halbig died from complications of a stroke. He was 86 years old. At the funeral, almost all of his employees and residents of Gräfenhain gave him his last farewell. His funeral urn was buried, as he wished, in the park by his house next to the grave of his son Arno.
>
> With the peak of the World Economy Crisis came the end for the last parts of the doll factory. Under the National Socialists, Ernst Rosenstock advanced to the rank of Captain and was transferred to Berlin. During the Second World War, he supposedly had a leading function. In April of 1945, the first American troops reached Ohrdruf. Since there was still resistance in Gräfenhain, they began firing on the town. Along with the church, the 'villa' was hit by shapnel; the repairs can still be seen today. Three months later, the Soviet Secret Service deported Ernst Rosenstock. Nobody has heard from him since.
>
> Halbig's daughter Elisabeth lived in the house by herself for about a year after the end of the war, until the Russian occupation of 1945 forced her to share her house with less-fortunate Gräfenhain residents. Beginning in the 1950s, she had to tolerate the division

Simon & Halbig Porcelain Factory

3. This contemporary photo shows a typical street in Gräfenhain, population about fifteen hundred. The current population is much the same as it was during the years the Simon & Halbig factory made doll-related porcelain products in this small Thuringian town. (Photo: Mary Krombholz)

4. This photograph of the Carl Halbig villa and large barn mentioned in the description of the home-site by author Adrian Weber in the 1999 *Kreis Gotha* newspaper was taken in May 2007. (Photo: Ann Cummings)

5. Carl Halbig bought the old pastor's house on Main Street in Gräfenhain in March 1868, and remodeled it into this porcelain factory. From 1869 until 1900, the Halbig family lived in the small house on the right in this photograph. The factory and house were torn down in 1994. (Photo: Carol Nagel)

6. Wilhelm Simon's home/doll factory in Hildburghausen still stands close to the main Town Square. (Photo: Mary Krombholz)

7. This old photograph of the Carl Halbig villa in Gräfenhain has been hand colored. The villa is still standing on Karl Halbig Street. Gräfenhain church records indicate that Halbig spelled his name "Carl" rather than "Karl," the more common German spelling of the name. Courtesy Dorf Museum in Nauendorf.

Chapter 3

of the house into separate apartments. Elisabeth lived in the villa until her death in 1980.

Jürgen and Marianne Cieslik's *German Doll Encyclopedia* includes entries for the years 1919 to 1930 that help explain the ownership of the porcelain factory during the years following World War I. In 1919 Carl Halbig celebrated his eightieth birthday. The same year, the porcelain factory celebrated its fiftieth anniversary, and Carl Halbig, his son Arno and Nuremberg resident Leo Benarie were listed as owners. In 1923, following the death of Carl Halbig's son Arno, Elisabeth's husband Ernst Rosenstock became a director of the Simon & Halbig porcelain factory. In 1927 and in 1930 (following Carl Halbig's death in 1926), the sole owner of the factory is listed as Kämmer & Reinhardt and the director is listed as Ernst Rosenstock. In 1913 there were two hundred and twenty porcelain factory workers; by 1930 the number had dropped to one hundred. In 1927 the Simon & Halbig porcelain factory advertised the following products: "Bisque heads, all-bisque dolls, and unfired doll heads made of composition." Production in 1930 is described as: "Bisque doll heads, export to all countries." During this period of time, the Simon & Halbig porcelain factory was also making bisque animal figurines and bathing children.

The Simon & Halbig porcelain factory and the Wilhelm Simon doll factory were always completely separate factories. It seems unlikely that the Simon doll factory ever assembled or dressed dolls for the doll-related products sold by Simon & Halbig. Beginning in 1869, however, the Simon doll factory bought bisque heads from the Simon & Halbig porcelain factory. In 1900 the Simon factory advertised "fine toys, music toys, dolls and porcelain services for children."

Wilhelm Simon is buried in the Simon family cemetery, located just outside the town of Hildburghausen. His former home/factory is still standing today in Hildburghausen, a block away from the main Town Square. In the *Chronicles of Hildburghausen*, the following sentences describe the Simon doll and toy factory: "The well-known toy factory of Wilhelm Simon exports to all European countries, to North and South America, Java and East India." The Simon doll factory moved from Hildburghausen to Nuremberg in 1910. That year its products were listed as character dolls, miniature dolls and doll clothing.

The Simon & Halbig porcelain factory made bisque heads for more German doll factories than any other Thuringian porcelain factory. In the *German Doll Encyclopedia*, the Ciesliks list the following doll factories for which Simon & Halbig manufactured bisque doll heads: "C.M. Bergmann, Waltershausen ('Eleanor' and 'Columbia'); Carl Bergner, Sonneberg (double and multi-face dolls); Cuno & Otto Dressel, Sonneberg ('Jutta'); Edison phonograph doll (Nos. 719 and 917); R. Eekhoff, Groningen, Holland; Fleishmann & Bloedel, Fürth (heads marked 'DEP' for the French market); Hamburger & Co., Berlin ('Imperial' and 'Santa'); Heinrich Handwerck, Waltershausen; Adolf Huelss, Waltershausen; Emile Jumeau, Paris (number series 200); Kämmer & Reinhardt, Waltershausen (from 1902 on all heads); Louis Lindner & Sohne, Sonneberg; Roullet & Decamp, Paris ('Ondine'); Franz Schmidt, Georgenthal; S.F.B.J., Paris (from 1900 to 1914); Carl Trautmann, Finstergergen; Welsch & Co., Sonneberg; Hugo Wiegand, Waltershausen; Wiesenthal, Schindel & Kallenberg, Waltershausen and Adolf Wislizenus, Waltershausen (Old Glory)."

The Simon & Halbig porcelain factory made a number of dolls with two or more faces. The first German two-faced doll was patented in 1880 by Fritz Bartenstein. Bartenstein was an inventor as well as a doll factory owner in Sonneberg. His laughing/crying doll was improved in 1881 by the addition of "Mama" and "Papa" voices. Bartenstein heads were available in either bisque or wax. In 1903 Carl Bergner of Sonneberg made his first multi-faced doll. It had a sleeping, laughing and crying face. The faces were well-modeled, and the crying face included a molded tear on each cheek. Bergner also advertised a three-faced doll that represented Red Riding Hood, the Grandmother and the Wolf. The Simon & Halbig porcelain factory made all of the multi-faced bisque heads for Carl Bergner.

Outstanding portrait-like character dolls were made by Simon & Halbig in 1898. Equal in every way to the Spanish-American War heroes with Simon & Halbig bisque heads introduced the same year, Uncle Sam bisque socket heads are also excellent examples of the fine modeling and painting created by the factory's artists and modelers. Character heads made from similar master molds include Uncle Sam, Old Rip, Hexe, Buffalo Bill and Farmer Brown. Although the bisque heads were very similar, the facial painting and clothing differed. As Uncle Sam, the doll was originally dressed in red-and-white-striped pants, a blue-cloth vest covered with white stars and a top hat with stars on the hatband. The bisque heads marked "Hexe" were made from a master mold similar to the Uncle Sam mold, but warts were added to the face to change the appearance. The Simon & Halbig doll factory used the New York importing company Butler Brothers for the sales and distribution of some of their dolls. Uncle Sam dolls were still listed in the Butler Brothers' 1899 Wholesale Catalog for Christmas.

Simon & Halbig also created a portrait doll of George Washington with a cloth-and-wood body designed to ride a horse. My example of the Simon & Halbig George Washington portrait doll is dressed in felt, complete with white knickers and a gray/blue coat trimmed in gold. A lace-ruffled blouse and a tri-corner hat complete the costume. The body is wooden with wooden limbs attached

Simon & Halbig Porcelain Factory

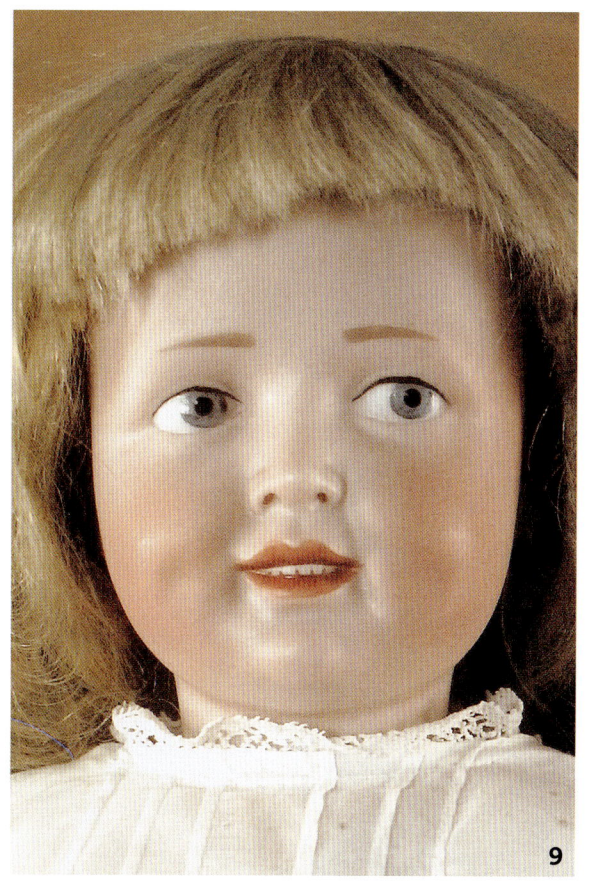

8. Bisque socket head by Simon & Halbig for the Kämmer & Reinhardt doll factory in Waltershausen; original wig, pierced ears; multi-stroke eyebrows, painted upper and lower eyelashes; glass sleep eyes; open mouth with upper teeth; 16-inch doll; circa 1910; marked: K*R//HALBIG//290. This is the only Kämmer & Reinhardt bisque-head doll pictured in this chapter. I have included it to serve as a reminder of the many thousands of bisque dolly-faced and character heads the Simon & Halbig porcelain factory made for the Kämmer & Reinhardt doll factory. Private Collection, formerly Jane Walker Collection. (Photo: Gene Abbott)

9. Bisque socket head by Simon & Halbig; wig; single-stroke eyebrows; black accent line on upper eyelids; painted eyes; open/closed smiling mouth with upper-painted teeth; cheek dimples; 16-inch doll; circa 1912; marked: 151//S&H//0½. The side-glancing painted eyes are uncommon on 151 heads. Note the similarities in facial painting between this head and the Kämmer & Reinhardt 100 mold number series, especially the single-stroke painted eyebrows and black-outlined upper eyelids. (See Part One: Chapter 2) Beth Karp Collection. (Photo: Lee Krombholz)

10. Bisque socket head by Simon & Halbig; wig; pierced ears; multi-stroke eyebrows; painted upper and lower eyelashes; large, stationary glass eyes; open mouth with upper teeth; 23-inch doll; circa 1888; marked: 919//S14H. Karin Schmelcher Collection. (Photo: Christiane Gräfnitz)

11. Dark-brown bisque socket head by Simon & Halbig; wig; multi-stroke eyebrows; molded upper eyelids; painted upper and lower eyelashes; glass sleep eyes; closed mouth with upper teeth; chin dimple; 13½-inch doll; GM 1888; marked; S6H//759//DEP. Beth Karp Collection. (Photo: Gregg Smith)

12. Bisque socket head by Simon & Halbig; original wig and clothing; multi-stroke eyebrows; painted upper and lower eyelashes; glass sleep eyes; open mouth with upper teeth; chin dimple; 16-inch doll; circa 1912; marked: SIMON & HALBIG//600//6½. Ann Cummings Collection. (Photo: John Cummings)

Chapter 3

by wires. The black wooden-heeled boots are well carved, as are the wooden hands with separate thumbs. The painted facial features, chin and generous nose create a close resemblance to George Washington.

The number of doll factories, toy stores and American department stores that sold dolls with Simon & Halbig bisque heads indicates the importance of this porcelain factory from a worldwide standpoint. In volume two of *The Collector's Encyclopedia of Dolls*, Dorothy S., Elizabeth A. and Evelyn J. Coleman state that the following companies sold dolls with Simon & Halbig bisque heads: Bawo & Dotter; C.M. Bergmann; Bing Works; Geo. Borgfeldt & Co.; Cuno & Otto Dressel; Eekhoff; Fleischmann & Bloedel; Gimbel Brothers, Hamburger; Heinrich Handwerck; Adolf Huelss; Kämmer & Reinhardt; Kley & Hahn; Louis Lindner & Sons; Franz Schmidt & Co.; F.A.O. Schwarz; S.F.B.J.; Strobel & Wilken; Wagner & Zetsche; Wiesenthal, Schindel & Kallenberg and Adolf Wislizenus. Each of these companies had their own groups of customers located all over the world.

Included among the numerous Thuringian doll factories for which Simon & Halbig made all of the bisque heads was the Franz Schmidt & Co. doll factory in Georgenthal, a tiny village located a few miles from Waltershausen. Franz Schmidt worked for the Kestner doll and porcelain factory before founding his own doll factory with sculptor Traugott Schmidt in 1890. He was the first dollmaker to insert glass eyes, as well as sleeping eyes, in character dolls, and used his own designs for the bisque doll heads made for him by the Simon & Halbig porcelain factory. Schmidt died in 1942, and his son directed the doll factory until it closed in 1945.

The Dorfmuseum in Nauendorf had a temporary display of Simon & Halbig and Alt, Beck & Gottschalck doll-related porcelain products in June 1999. I was fortunate to be able to visit the museum and study the doll heads and doll-head shards on display, which included several Simon & Halbig 1940s composition heads. According to the museum signage, Keramisches Werk GmbH made the Simon & Halbig composition character heads. The 'Keramisches Werk GmbH' entry in the Cieslik's *German Doll Encyclopedia* contains the following information about the company: "The Simon & Halbig workshops started in the early 1930s with sculptor Kühnert from Nauendorf; and, Hofmann, Reinhardt and Nüchter from the earlier Simon & Halbig porcelain factory in Gräfenhain. Since 1943 they produced doll heads of composition and papier-mâché."

The Halbig family owned the Simon & Halbig porcelain factory from the death of Wilhelm Simon in 1894 until the Kämmer & Reinhardt doll factory purchased it in 1920. That year, the Kämmer & Reinhardt doll factory was a joint stock company because of a merger with Bing Werke (see Part One: Chapter 2). From 1920 until 1932, when Bing Werke declared bankruptcy, all of Simon & Halbig's doll-related porcelain products were marketed and sold by this large conglomerate. In the Thuringian commercial registers, Carl Halbig continued to be listed as a director of the Simon & Halbig porcelain factory from 1920 until his death in 1926. Elisabeth Halbig's husband, Ernst Rosenstock, was listed as a director until the Bing Werke bankruptcy in 1932, and the resulting permanent closure of the Simon & Halbig porcelain factory.

13. Bisque socket head by Simon & Halbig with lady composition body; pierced ears; original wig; multi-stroke eyebrows; upper eyelashes of hair and painted lower eyelashes; glass sleep eyes; open mouth with upper teeth; 18-inch doll; GM 1894; marked: **SIMON & HALBIG//1159**. Ann Cummings Collection. (Photo: John Cummings)

14. Light-brown bisque socket head by Simon & Halbig; original wig and clothing; pierced ears; multi-stroke eyebrows; painted upper and lower eyelashes; glass sleep eyes; open mouth with upper teeth; 17-inch doll; circa 1910; marked: **Germany//Halbig//S&H**. Kenneth Drew Collection. (Photo: Ann Hanat)

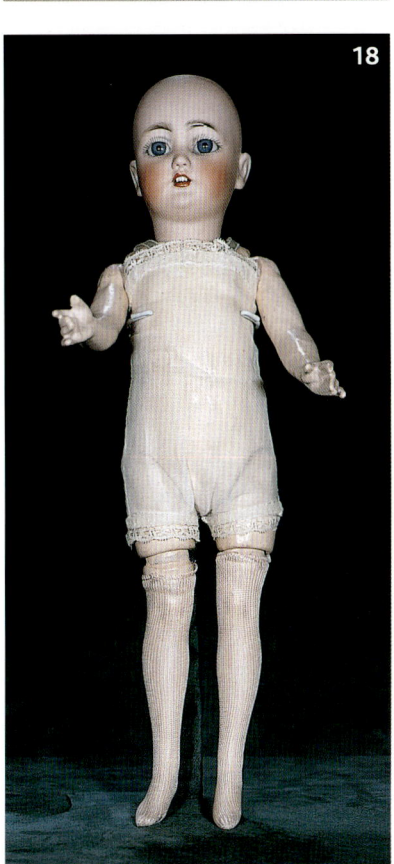

Simon & Halbig Porcelain Factory

15. Light-brown bisque socket head by Simon & Halbig with Asian-style facial painting; pierced ears; original wig; Asian clothing; molded upper eyelids; multi-stroke eyebrows follow the eye slant; narrow, slanted, glass sleep eyes; open mouth with upper teeth; 12-inch doll; circa 1898; marked: SH/1199/DEP//3//Germany. Beth Karp Collection. (Photo: Lee Krombholz)

16. Bisque socket head by Simon & Halbig; original wig; pierced ears; molded, multi-stroke eyebrows; painted upper and lower eyelashes; glass sleep eyes; open mouth with upper teeth; cheek and chin dimples; 23-inch doll; GM 1899; marked: S&H//1279//DEP//Germany//12. Ann Cummings Collection. (Photo: John Cummings)

17. Bisque socket head by Simon & Halbig for the Franz Schmidt & Co. doll factory; wig; multi-stroke eyebrows; painted upper and lower eyelashes; glass sleep eyes; open mouth with upper teeth; 10-inch doll; circa 1912; marked: 1299//Simon & Halbig//3½. Beth Karp Collection. (Photo: Lee Krombholz)

18. Bisque socket head with multi-stroke eyebrows; painted long upper and lower eyelashes; glass sleep eyes; open mouth with upper teeth; 13-inch doll; marked 1159//Simon & Halbig//S.H.5. This bisque dolly-faced socket head by Simon & Halbig is mounted on a "flapper" body with a long torso, thin un-jointed arms, legs jointed above the knees, and feet molded to wear high-heeled shoes. The design patent for the mold number 1159 was registered in 1894, but the bisque-head dolls with original flapper bodies were sold in the 1920s. The use of the 1159 mold number in the 1920s proves a production span of at least thirty years and indicates that dolly-faced dolls continued to sell well during the character-doll era. Author's Collection. (Photo: Gene Abbott)

19

Simon & Halbig Porcelain Factory

19. Slightly tinted, bisque socket head by Simon & Halbig; wig and original seventeenth-century court clothing; molded, multi-stroke eyebrows; original upper eyelashes and straight lower eyelashes; prominent nose; large closed lips; chin dimple; 19-inch doll; circa 1902; marked: **1301//S&H**. Julie Blewis Collection. (Photo: Fanilya Gueno)

20. White-bisque socket head by Simon & Halbig; clown-like appearance; original wig and clothing; black, multi-stroke eyebrows; lower eyelashes painted with straight brushstrokes; glass sleep eyes; closed, smiling mouth; 12-inch doll; circa 1902; marked: **4//1304//SH**. Beth Karp Collection. (Photo: Lee Krombholz)

21. Bisque socket head by Simon & Halbig; lady composition body; wig and original clothing; well-modeled cheekbones; pierced ears; multi-stroke eyebrows; traces of upper hair eyelashes; lower eyelashes painted with short, straight brushstrokes; glass sleep eyes, closed mouth with reddish-brown thin, shaded lips; 22-inch doll; circa 1902; marked: **1303//S&H//8.5**. Julie Blewis Collection. (Photo: Fanilya Gueno)

22

Simon & Halbig Porcelain Factory

22. Reddish-brown, tinted bisque socket head by Simon & Halbig; original wig and clothing; pierced ears; single-stroke eyebrows; molded upper eyelids; molded, realistic painted eyes; closed mouth; 23½-inch doll; circa 1902; marked: **1303//S&H//70**. Julie Blewis Collection. (Photo: Fanilya Gueno)

23. Bisque socket head by Simon & Halbig; original wig and clothing representing a lady from India with red-painted mark in center of forehead; pierced ears; multi-stroke eyebrows; straight lower eyelashes; glass sleep eyes; closed mouth; 23½-inch doll; circa 1902; marked: **1303//S&H//70**. Julie Blewis Collection. (Photo: Fanilya Gueno)

Chapter 3

24. Bisque socket head by Simon & Halbig; lady composition body; pierced ears; original wig and clothing; multi-stroke eyebrows; painted upper and lower eyelashes; glass sleep eyes; closed mouth; chin dimple; 25-inch doll; circa 1902; marked: **1307//S&H**. Julie Blewis Collection. (Photo: Fanilya Gueno)

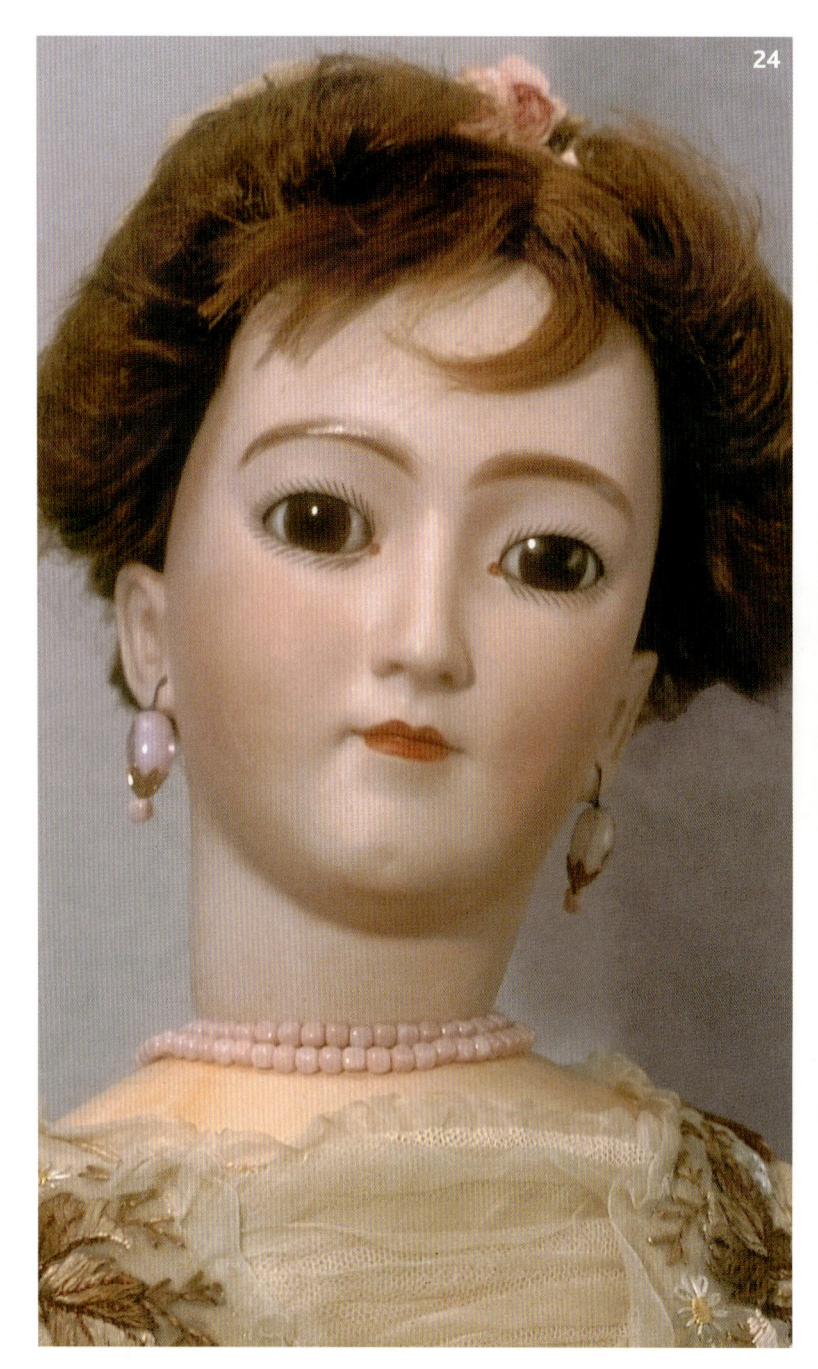

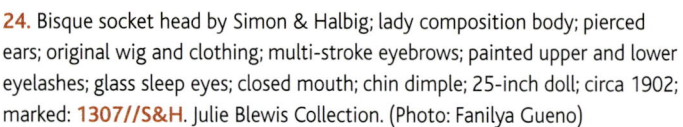

25. Light-yellow/tan bisque socket head by Simon & Halbig; original wig and clothing; multi-stroke eyebrows; painted upper and lower eyelashes; glass sleep eyes; open mouth with upper teeth; 15-inch doll; circa 1910; marked: **1329//Germany//SIMON & HALBIG//S&H**. Beth Karp Collection. (Photo: Lee Krombholz)

26. Light-brown bisque socket head by Simon & Halbig; pierced ears; wig; molded, glossy, black multi-stroke eyebrows; painted upper and lower eyelashes; glass sleep eyes; full, glazed lips with open mouth and upper teeth; 13½-inch doll; circa 1910; marked: **1358//Germany//SIMON & HALBIG//S&H//3**. Beth Karp Collection. (Photo: Gregg Smith)

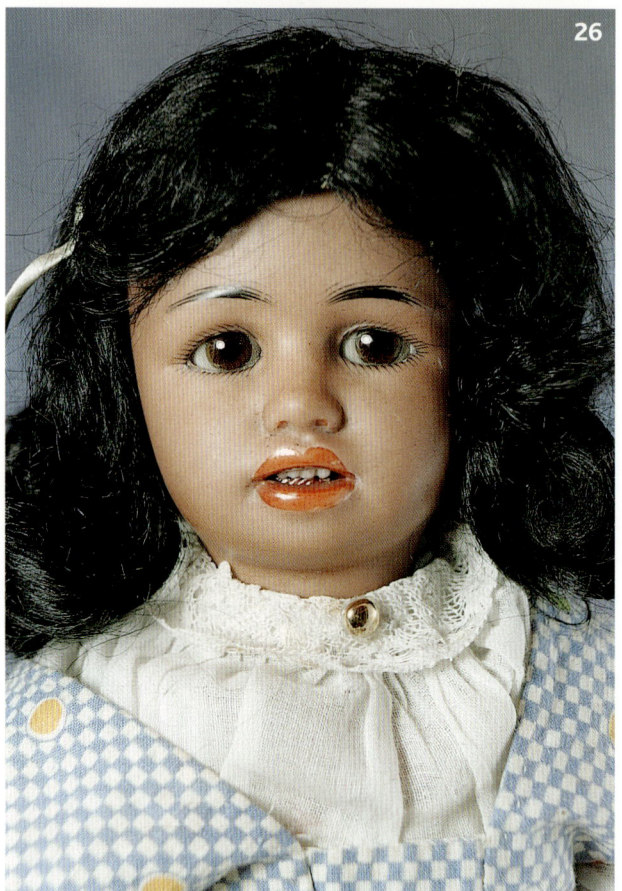

Simon & Halbig Porcelain Factory

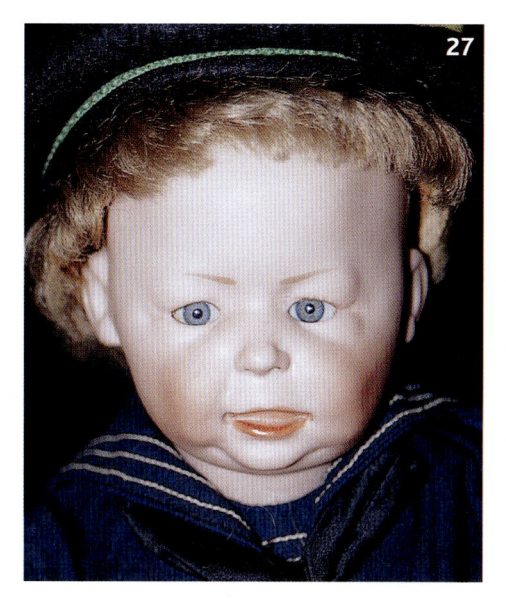

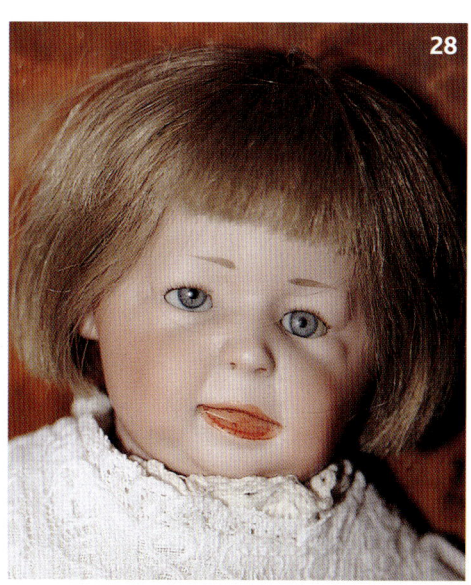

27. Bisque socket head by Simon & Halbig; wig; single-stroke, slanted eyebrows; painted short, closely spaced, upper eyelashes; small, glass sleep eyes; open/closed mouth with molded tongue; double chin; 15-inch doll; circa 1914; marked: **S&H//1428**. Courtesy Ladenburger Spielzeugauktion/Goetz Seidel. (Photo: Christiane Gräfnitz)

28. Bisque socket head by Simon & Halbig; wig; single-stroke eyebrows; painted short, closely-spaced, upper eyelashes; small, glass sleep eyes; open/closed mouth with molded tongue; double chin; 11½-inch doll; circa 1914; marked: **S&H//1428**. Roswitha Lucke Collection. (Photo: Christiane Gräfnitz)

29. Bisque socket head by Simon & Halbig; wig; single-stroke eyebrows; painted upper and lower eyelashes; glass sleep eyes; closed mouth; 9½-inch doll; circa 1914; marked: **S&H//1448**. Note the eyebrows are painted like some of the 100 series Kämmer & Reinhardt character dolls. (See Part One: Chapter 2) Norah Stoner Collection. (Photo: Norah Stoner)

30. Bisque socket head by Simon & Halbig; wig; single-stroke, slanted eyebrows; painted short, closely spaced, upper eyelashes; small, glass sleep eyes; open/closed mouth with molded tongue; double chin; 23½-inch doll; circa 1914; marked: **1428//15**. Beth Karp Collection. (Photo: Lee Krombholz)

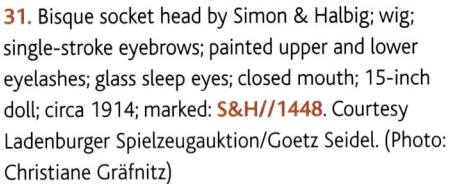

Chapter 3

31. Bisque socket head by Simon & Halbig; wig; single-stroke eyebrows; painted upper and lower eyelashes; glass sleep eyes; closed mouth; 15-inch doll; circa 1914; marked: **S&H//1448**. Courtesy Ladenburger Spielzeugauktion/Goetz Seidel. (Photo: Christiane Gräfnitz)

32. Bisque socket head by Simon & Halbig for the Cuno & Otto Dressel doll factory; wig; pierced ears; multi-stroke eyebrows; painted upper and lower eyelashes; glass sleep eyes; closed mouth; flapper body with molded bust, jointed at the elbows and knees; slender arms and legs, feet molded to wear high-heeled shoes; 15-inch doll; circa 1920; marked: **1468//S&H**. Ursula Gauder Collection. (Photo: Christiane Gräfnitz)

33. Bisque socket head by Simon & Halbig for the Cuno & Otto Dressel doll factory; wig; pierced ears; multi-stroke eyebrows; painted upper and lower eyelashes; glass sleep eyes; closed mouth; flapper body with feet molded to wear high-heeled shoes; 15 inches; circa 1920; marked: **SIMON & HALBIG// S&H//1469//2**. Susan Moore Collection. (Photo: John Cummings)

34. Bisque socket head by Simon & Halbig; wig; multi-stroke eyebrows; molded upper eyelids; painted upper and lower eyelashes; glass sleep eyes; open/closed pouty mouth; 19½-inch doll; circa 1920; marked: **S&H//1488**. Courtesy Ladenburger Spielzeugauktion// Goetz Seidel. (Photo: Christiane Gräfnitz)

Simon & Halbig Porcelain Factory

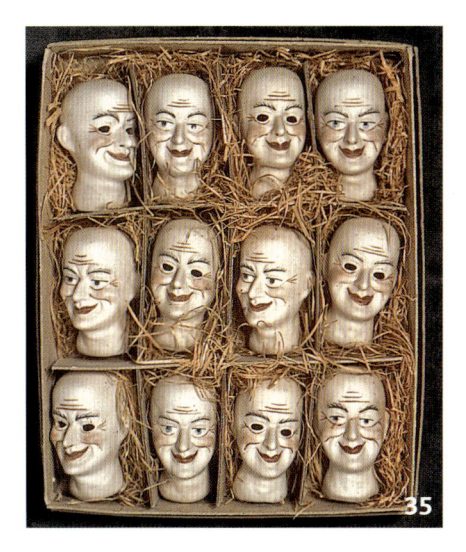

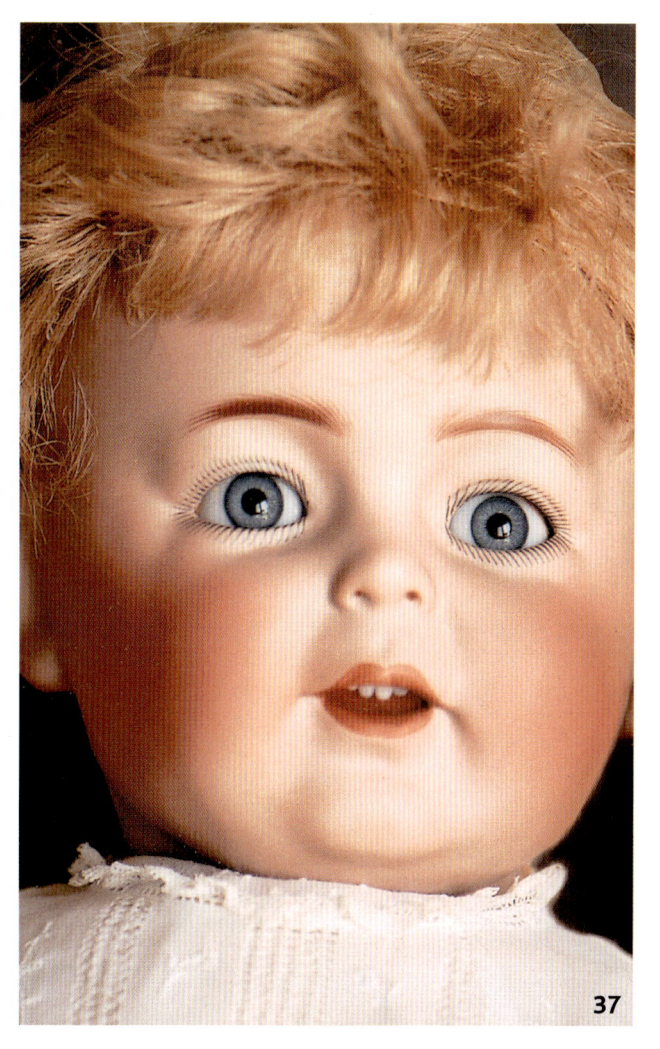

35. Twelve Simon & Halbig bisque heads with flange necks, in original cardboard box, made for the Cuno & Otto Dressel Portrait Series; bald heads; red-painted wrinkles on faces; multi-stroke eyebrows; six of the heads have eye cuts for glass eyes; the other six heads have painted eyes; closed smiling mouths; 2-inch heads; GM 1895; each marked: **D**. Author's Collection. (Photo: Gregg Smith)

36. A close view of Uncle Sam seen in illustration 38 shows the fine modeling and facial painting. Author's Collection. (Photo: Gene Abbott)

37. Bisque socket head by Simon & Halbig for the Neustadt doll factory of Carl Hartmann; wig; multi-stroke eyebrows; painted upper and lower eyelashes; glass sleep eyes; open mouth with upper teeth and separate tongue; 22-inch doll; circa 1925; marked: **Erika//1489//SIMON & HALBIG**. Georgia Rank Collection. (Photo: Michael Rank)

38. Uncle Sam bisque socket head by Simon & Halbig for the Cuno & Otto Dressel Portrait Series; original gray wig and clothing, with metal medal hanging at waist; painted red-age wrinkles; multi-stroke gray eyebrows; painted upper and lower eyelashes; prominent nose; stationary glass eyes; closed smiling mouth; 12½-inch doll; GM 1895; marked: **S1**. Author's Collection. (Photo: Gene Abbott)

Chapter 3

39. Three bisque socket heads by Simon & Halbig for the Cuno & Otto Dressel Portrait Series; original wigs and clothing; molded warts and red painted wrinkles; single-stroke eyebrows; stationary glass eyes; open/closed mouths with witch-like painted teeth; 6-inch doll and 8½-inch dolls; GM 1895; marked; **Hexe//**with different size numbers. Author's Collection. (Photo: Gregg Smith)

40. George Washington bisque socket head by Simon & Halbig for the Adolf Wislizenus doll factory in Waltershausen; original wig and clothing; single-stroke eyebrows; sculpted eye sockets, with upper and lower molded eyelids; painted eyes; closed mouth; 9-inch doll; GM 1895; marked: **13//AW**. The gray wig is styled to look like the military hairstyles worn by American officers in the 1700s. Author's Collection. (Photo: Gregg Smith)

41. Light reddish-brown bisque socket head by Simon & Halbig for the Cuno & Otto Dressel doll factory's Portrait Series; original wig and clothing; red painted wrinkles; multi-stroke eyebrows; painted upper and lower eyelashes; stationary glass eyes; open/closed smiling mouth with painted teeth; red painted smile lines near mouth; 10-inch doll; GM 1895; marked: **H1**. Beth Karp Collection. (Photo: Lee Krombholz)

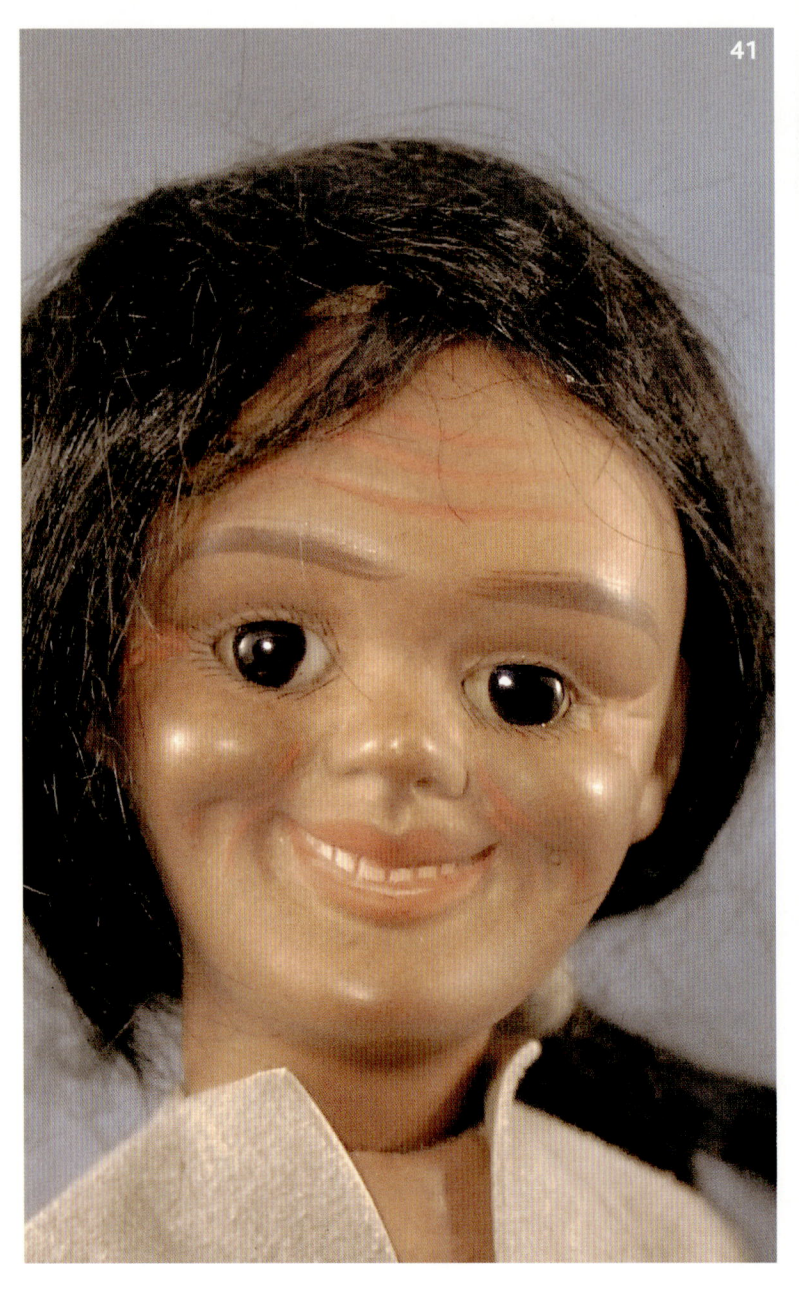

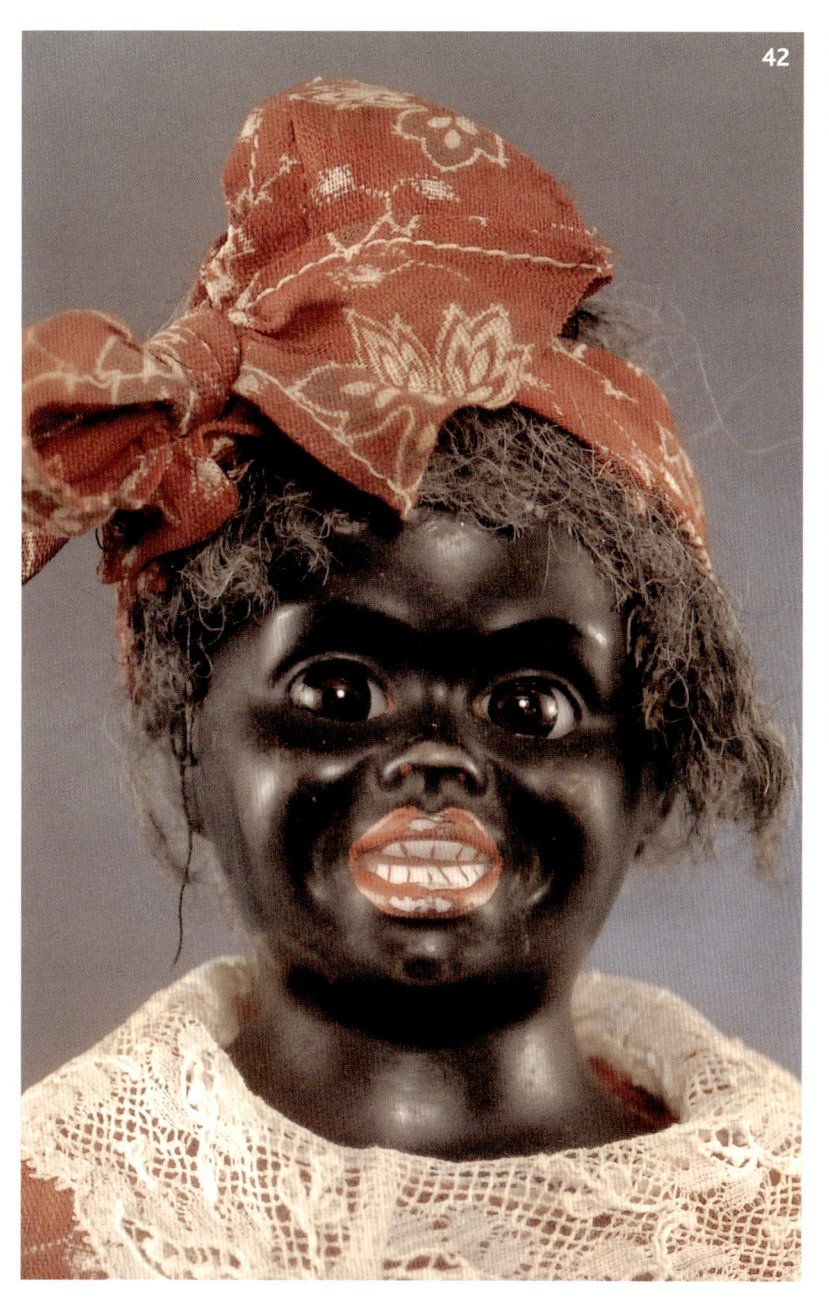

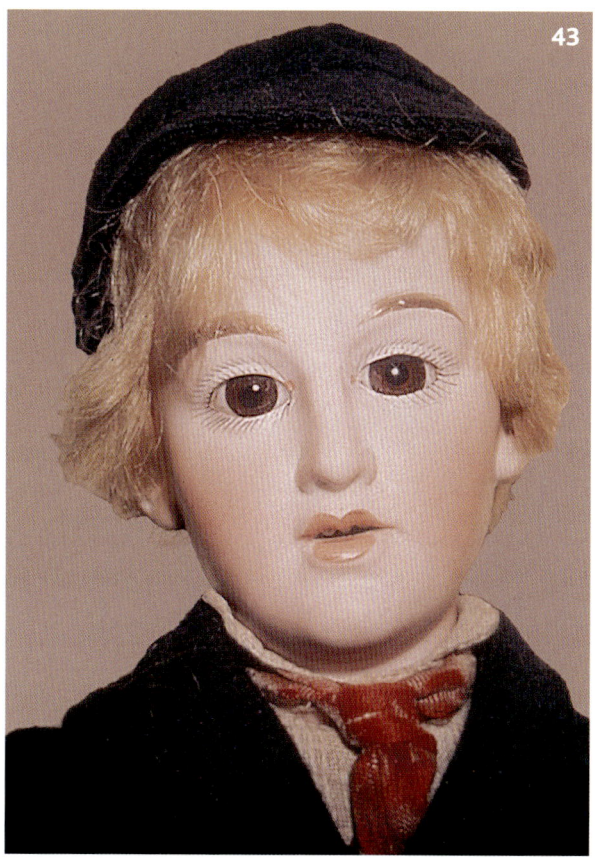

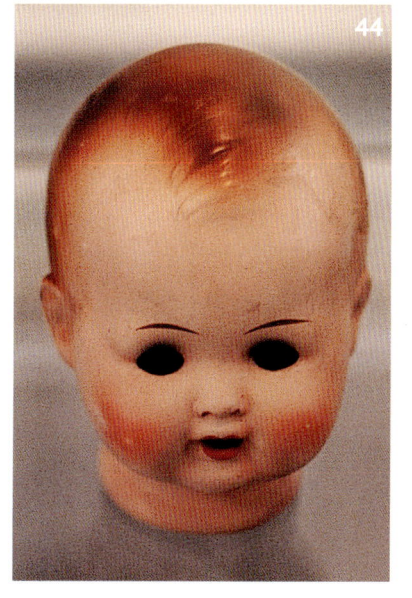

Simon & Halbig Porcelain Factory

42. Black-bisque shoulder head by Simon & Halbig for the Cuno & Otto Dressel Portrait Series; original wig and clothing; multi-stroke eyebrows; molded upper eyelids; stationary glass eyes; large open/closed mouth with upper and lower painted teeth; 13-inch doll; GM 1895; marked: **N1**. Beth Karp Collection. (Photo: Lee Krombholz)

43. Bisque socket head by Simon & Halbig for the Cuno & Otto Dressel Portrait Series; original wig and wool clothing appropriate for a bicyclist; multi-stroke eyebrows; painted upper and lower eyelashes; stationary glass eyes; prominent nose; open mouth with upper teeth; 14-inch doll; GM 1895: marked: **M1**. This doll was purchased in 1897 from Hanke's Department Store in Cincinnati, Ohio. Private Collection, formerly Jane Walker Collection. (Photo: C.W. Walker)

44. Composition baby head with flange neck by Simon & Halbig; single-stroke eyebrows; eye cuts for glass eyes; open mouth with upper teeth; 4-inch head; unmarked. See Illustration 45 for more information on this head. Courtesy Dorf Museum in Nauendorf. (Photo: Mary Krombholz)

45. Composition head with flange neck credited to Simon & Halbig by Dorf Museum curators; molded hair; single-stroke eyebrows; eye cuts for glass eyes; open mouth with upper teeth; 4-inch head; unmarked. The Keramisches Werk GmbH Company produced this composition doll head circa 1943. Former Simon & Halbig sculptors Kühnert and associates Reinhardt and Nüchert opened a ceramic workshop in the early 1930s and used Simon & Halbig molds to make composition heads. Courtesy Dorf Museum in Nauendorf. (Photo: Mary Krombholz)

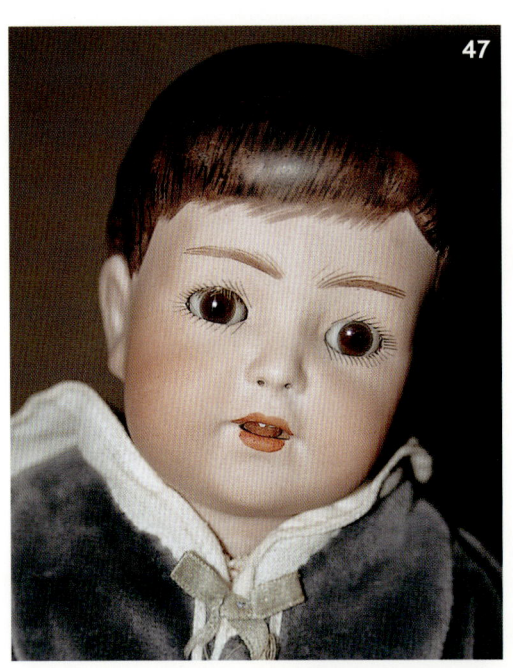

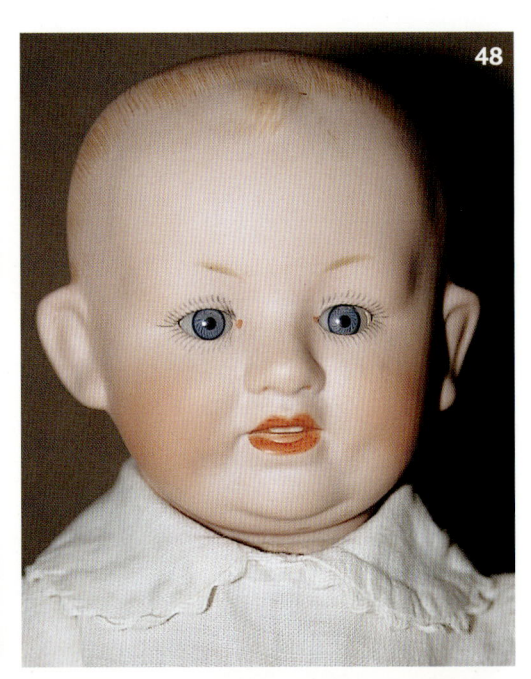

Chapter 3

46. Four-faced bisque socket head by Simon & Halbig for the Carl Bergner doll factory in Sonneberg; all faces have multi-stroke eyebrows; painted upper and lower eyelashes; stationary glass eyes; black face and one white face have closed mouths, other two faces have open/closed mouths; 3½-inch heads; unmarked. Courtesy Museum Schloss Tenneberg, Waltershausen. (Photo: Christiane Gräfnitz)

47. Bisque socket head by Simon & Halbig for the Franz Schmidt & Co. doll factory in Georgenthal; molded hair; multi-stroke eyebrows; painted upper and lower eyelashes; glass sleep eyes; open mouth with upper teeth and separate tongue; 12-inch doll; circa 1912; marked: **F.S.&Co.//1257//25**. The Simon & Halbig porcelain factory made all of Franz Schmidt's bisque doll heads from 1890 on. Courtesy Museum Schloss Tenneberg, Waltershausen. (Photo: Christiane Gräfnitz)

48. Bisque socket head by Simon & Halbig for the Franz Schmidt & Co. doll factory; molded hair; single-stroke, slanted eyebrows; painted upper and lower eyelashes; glass sleep eyes; open/closed mouth with molded upper teeth and tongue; cheek dimples; double chin; 15¾-inch doll; GM 1910; marked: **F.S.&Co.//1271//21Dep**. Courtesy Museum Schloss Tenneberg, Waltershausen. (Photo: Christiane Gräfnitz)

49. Bisque socket head by Simon & Halbig for the Franz Schmidt & Co. doll factory; wig; molded upper eyelids with black outlines; single-stroke eyebrows; painted eyes; closed mouth; well-modeled and blushed cheeks; chin dimple; 23-inch doll; circa 1912, marked: **F.S.&Co.//1262/56**. Julie Blewis Collection. (Photo: Fanilya Gueno)

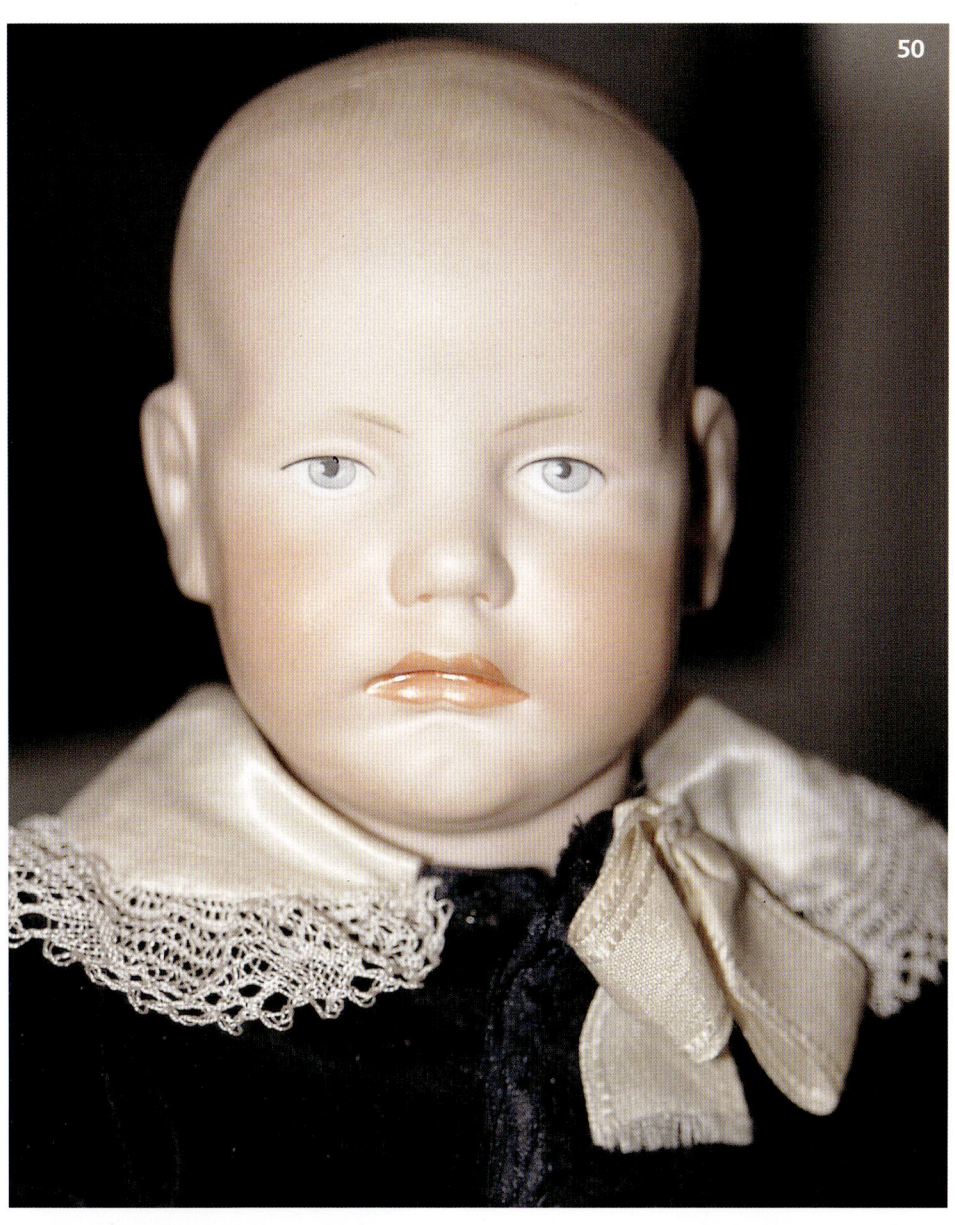

Simon & Halbig Porcelain Factory

50. Bisque socket head by Simon & Halbig for the Franz Schmidt & Co. doll factory; molded hair; single-stroke, slanted eyebrows; black outline of upper eyelids; painted eyes with white highlights; slightly open/closed mouth; 12½-inch doll; circa 1912; marked: F.S.&Co.//1267//32. Rothenburg Puppenmuseum/Katharina Engels Collection. (Photo: Christiane Gräfnitz)

51. Bisque socket head by Simon & Halbig for the Franz Schmidt & Co. doll factory; wig; molded, multi-stroke eyebrows; painted upper and lower eyelashes; glass sleep eyes; open mouth with upper teeth; chin dimple; 20-inch doll; circa 1912; marked: S&H//1299//8. Kenneth Drew Collection. (Photo: Ann Hanat)

52. Bisque socket head by Simon & Halbig for the Franz Schmidt & Co. doll factory; wig; multi-stroke eyebrows; painted upper and lower eyelashes; glass sleep eyes; pierced nostrils; open mouth with upper teeth; 11¾-inch doll; circa 1912; marked: F.S.&Co.//26. Roswitha Lucke Collection. (Photo: Christiane Gräfnitz)

53. Bisque socket head by Simon & Halbig for the Franz Schmidt & Co. doll factory; wig; multi-stroke eyebrows; painted upper and lower eyelashes; glass sleep eyes; pierced nostrils; open mouth with upper teeth and separate tongue; chin dimple; 15-inch doll; circa 1912; marked: 1295//F.S.&Co.//34. Author's Collection. (Photo: Gregg Smith)

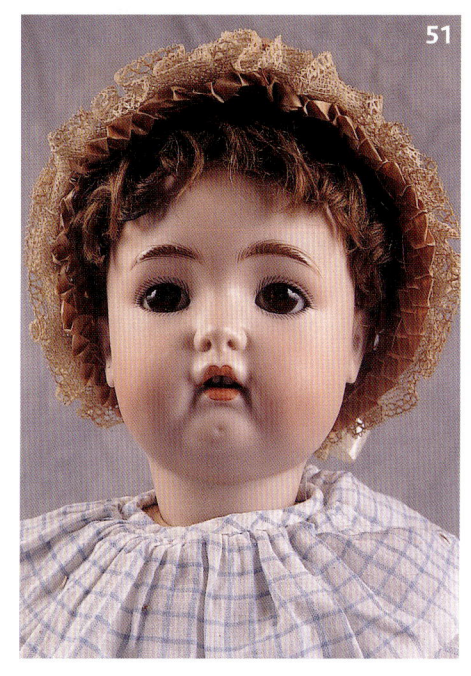

Part One

Chapter 4

Alt, Beck & Gottschalck Porcelain Factory

The Alt, Beck & Gottschalck porcelain factory in Nauendorf is closely tied to the Simon & Halbig porcelain factory in Gräfenhain because so many of the factory workers lived in the two adjoining villages. Nauendorf's population of about five hundred residents and Gräfenhain's population of about fifteen hundred have changed little since dollmaking was the principal occupation. Nauendorf is slightly older than Gräfenhain. The first monastery was built in Nauendorf in 1152 and the village had its own mayors since 1525.

The Alt, Beck & Gottschalck porcelain factory was founded by four workers who were unhappy with their jobs at the C. F. Kling & Co. porcelain factory in the nearby town of Ohrdruf. Gottlieb Beck from Ohrdruf, a modeler, and three porcelain turners, Carl Ehrenberger from Nauendorf, Theodor Gottschalck from Ohrdruf and Heinrich Völker from Gotha, decided to form their own porcelain factory. In 1854 they received permission from the Count's "Justice Ministry" in Georgenthal to do so. Carl Ehrenberger allowed his three friends to build the porcelain factory on a piece of property he owned in Nauendorf. The first Alt, Beck & Gottschalck factory contained a forming room and a small round kiln where the first Thuringian bisque doll heads were fired in 1854. The first porcelain factory building is still standing directly behind the second Alt, Beck & Gottschalck porcelain factory in Nauendorf today.

During the initial six months of factory production, the co-owners had problems making group decisions. The first group of factory workers was fired and co-founder Carl Ehrenberger resigned. Co-owners Beck and Gottschalck bought all of Ehrenberger's shares in the porcelain factory. In the following months, co-founder Heinrich Völker, who had sent the factory into heavy debt, was forced to resign by the remaining co-founders, Beck and Gottschalck.

Because of a lack of capital due to Völker's debt, Beck and Gottschalck had to paint dishes for another porcelain factory in order to continue to make their own porcelain products. They were not financially able to buy a masse mill in the early years of production, and so they had to grind all of the kaolin, quartz and feldspar (components of a porcelain mixture) by hand. The finely ground porcelain ingredients created a very fine quality bisque, resulting in ever-increasing orders for the small factory.

Much of the historical information concerning the founding of the Alt, Beck & Gottschalck porcelain factory is found in an article titled "White Gold from Nauendorf" in the March 2001 issue of Jürgen and Marianne Cieslik's *Puppenmagazin*. The Giesliks state in the article that the Alt, Beck & Gottschalck porcelain factory was probably the first Thuringian porcelain factory to make bisque-head dolls. The quote they used to establish this claim is from the 1888 book *The Thuringian Industry in 1888*: "With the introduction of this progressive innovation, the little company turned out to be successful." The progressive innovation referred to was the use of a porcelain board and a grinding stone to grind the kaolin, quartz and feldspar. The Giesliks comment: "These historic sources do not prove, but they suggest that, according to the known quotes in this book, Beck and Gottschalck were the inventors of bisque porcelain."

By 1856, the porcelain factory had twenty-eight employees and orders continued to increase. By 1864 the factory was so

1. The oldest Alt, Beck & Gottschalck porcelain factory is still standing today in Nauendorf. The first Thuringian bisque doll heads were fired in a kiln on the ground floor of this building, according to the book *The Thuringian Industry in 1888*. (Photo: Mary Krombholz)

successful that Alt, Beck & Gottschalck bought and remodeled the Stutzhaus porcelain factory in Stutzhaus, a suburb of Ohrdruf. The Nauendorf-based Alt, Beck & Gottschalck factory made glazed and unglazed porcelain shoulder heads, all-bisque, all-china and all-bisque dolls in the oldest building on the Stutzhaus factory site.

Many shards were recently found in the old Alt, Beck & Gottschalck porcelain factory building by Wolfgang Ortlepp, the current owner of the property. These important shards document the production of 1860s and 1870s chinas and parians by the Alt, Beck & Gottschalck porcelain factory. Until Ortlepp found the doll-head shards between the ceiling and floorboards of the oldest factory building, the bisque shoulder heads made in Nauendorf in the 1880s were considered the earliest Alt, Beck & Gottschalk doll-related porcelain products.

Following the death of co-owner Johann Theodor Gottschalck's death in 1865 and the loss of employee Carl Halbig in 1869 (see Part One: Chapter 3), the factory was forced to reorganize. Christian E. Reinhold Weingart, who had been working as director of the commercial department of the factory since 1868, became the new manager. In 1881 he became co-owner with Friedrich Alt. Formerly a co-owner of the Stutzhaus porcelain factory, he had been experienced in porcelain factory management and ownership when he was hired by the Alt, Beck & Gottschalck porcelain factory.

The two Alts died within a short time of each other: Friedrich Alt died in 1884 and Johann Georg Wilhelm Alt in 1885. This caused a reorganization that allowed Weingart to take over the management of the porcelain factory. Because the majority of stock shares were still owned by the Alt family, the children of Friedrich and Johann Alt were part owners of the factory, but they left most of the management responsibilities to Weingart.

The Alt, Beck & Gottschalck porcelain factory employed two hundred and twenty workers in 1886. By 1890 the factory had three hundred workers and one hundred home workers. Weingart died that year and his sons Wilhelm and Ernst became managers of the porcelain factory. In 1909 the Alt, Beck & Gottschalck porcelain factory became a limited liability company and in 1920 it became a holding company.

The Alt, Beck & Gottschalck porcelain factory continued to be listed as a large porcelain manufacturer in 1930, when their products included: "Biscuit dolls, nanking dolls, bathing children, figurines, animals, vases, religious figures and holy basins." In 1953 the porcelain factory was expropriated by the communist German Democratic Republic (GDR or, in German, DDR—*Deutsche Demokratische Republik*) and became so-called 'people-owned,' according to the Ciesliks's research,

Chapter 4

as published in their March 2001 article: "The factory was operated during this time by the VEB (People Owned Business) Keramik (Ceramics) in Georgenthal, Werk II (Factory #2) under the leadership of Bernd Ilgen." The Alt, Beck & Gottschalck porcelain factory closed permanently in 1962.

Today the Alt, Beck & Gottschalck porcelain factory in Nauendorf looks much as it did when it was converted into apartments in the late 1990s. During the remodeling, the factory grounds yielded many porcelain shards that offer irrefutable proof of the doll-related porcelain products made by the factory. A 1999 display of Alt, Beck & Gottschalck doll-related products at the Dorf Museum, which is located across the street from the factory, included many of these shards. I have included photographs of a few of the shards in this chapter. The most recognizable all-bisque doll shards were the Orsini character dolls and an all-bisque Bye-Lo Baby.

The Alt, Beck & Gottschalck porcelain factory made many character dolls for the American importers Geo.Borgfeldt & Co. Dorothy S. and Evelyn J. Coleman wrote an excellent article on this company for the April 1990 issue of *Doll Reader* magazine. From their research we learn that George Borgfeldt was born near Hamburg in 1833 and first came to America in 1853 when he has twenty years old. After working in New York for four years, he moved to Nashville, Tennessee, where he worked for the next five years before moving to Indianapolis, Indiana, in 1862. After the Civil War was over, in late 1865, Borgfeldt returned to New York and started a hosiery business with a partner. The name of the company was Good & Borgfeldt.

During the years 1873 to 1880, Borgfeldt was a managing partner of the New York City toy company Strasburger, Pfeiffer & Company, which distributed dolls made of wood, composition, wax, glazed porcelain and cloth. The company also distributed other doll-related products such as doll parts, dollhouses, London rag dolls, paper dolls and dressed dolls, including French dolls sold with trunks of clothing and accessories.

In 1880 Borgfeldt left Strasburger, Pfeiffer & Company to start his own company. In 1881 he founded the Geo. Borgfeldt & Co. importing firm, specializing in dolls, toys and related items. Geo. Borgfeldt & Co. was located on Leonard Street in New York City. The co-partnership was made up of Borgfeldt and Marcelle and Joseph Kahle. The partners came up with a unique idea to stimulate business. They began to gather samples from the top European manufacturers to show in their New York City sample rooms. This allowed American doll and toy stores to buy European goods without the expense and language problems of buying in foreign countries. It seems impossible, but descriptions of his sample rooms indicate that Borgfeldt may have had as many as one hundred thousand samples on display.

In just six years Geo. Borgfeldt & Co. had branches in Berlin, Fürth, Bodenbach (Bohemia) and London. The company also opened a branch in Sonneberg in 1887. In 1886 fifteen-year-old Fred Kolb had become an employee of the company and in 1892 he became its manager. He directed the doll department in 1905. When he died in 1960, he was chairman of the Geo. Borgfeldt & Co. board of directors. George Borgfeldt, after serving as president of the Geo. Borgfeldt & Co. for nearly twenty years, made his home in the town of Doebling, near Vienna, Austria. He died on November 20, 1903.

It is well known that the Borgfeldt company arranged for the manufacture of Rose O'Neill's Kewpies and Grace Storey Putnam's Bye-Lo Babies. Borgfeldt also had the exclusive rights to distribute the Bye-Los with bisque heads made by Alt, Beck & Gottschalck; Hertel, Schwab & Co.; Kestner & Co.; and C.F. Kling & Co.

Bisque-head Bye-Lo Babies have the following incised marks on the back of their flange necks: "Copr. by Grace Storey Putnam." The popularity of this doll is based on its appeal to the mother in each of us, according to Stella Burke May who, in the 1920s, wrote an article titled "Women and Dolls" for *Everybody's Magazine*. It was reprinted in the November 1984 issue of *Doll Reader*. The author begins her description of the Bye-Lo Baby with the following words.

> Grace Storey Putnam's three-day-old baby doll is moving so fast that at this writing it may not be too optimistic to say that she may realize fifty thousand dollars in royalties from this year's sale of dolls. The doll trade has been completely reeducated since the fall of 1924 when Mrs. Putnam first offered her infant doll, only to be frowned upon by manufacturers and salesmen alike, who threw up their hands and exclaimed with fierce unanimity: 'That doll won't sell. It looks too much like a live baby.' But it went well and is still going. All of which proves that this is an age of realism and that women who bring children into the world are pretty good judges of what all children like to play with.

Grace Storey Putnam sculpted the dolls in her studio on Staten Island. In Stella Burke May's article, she described the reason she began to make dolls.

> When my husband's illness made breadwinning a necessity for me, I entered the art department of Mills College. I can't tell you where the idea came to me to model a newborn baby. The doll idea kept growing within me. I must make a doll with universal appeal. And what appeal is as general as that of a new-born infant.
>
> So, everywhere I went I studied babies. In maternity wards, in hospitals, in the homes of friends who had new babies I made a study of babies from life. And yes, I studied the little ones whose feeble spark

Alt, Beck & Gottschalck Porcelain Factory

2. The second Alt, Beck & Gottschalck porcelain factory building was built in front of the first factory, pictured in illustration 1. I visited Nauendorf again in May 2007, and was happy to see that the first and second porcelain factory buildings are still standing on the original factory site. (Photo: Mary Krombholz)

had fluttered out. It was all part of my work. You must know the tragedy of things before you can appreciate the joy of them; because you can give them verity. It is like getting sand in your work. Like the coarse fiber in tapestry. Otherwise life and its expressions would be too sugary sweet. This is why I did not want a pretty baby, why I did not want a perfect baby.

I wanted to reproduce the baby that all mothers would recognize as their new-born infant. And I found it – three days old in an Oakland, California hospital. I knew the minute I saw the babe that he was the one I was looking for. He was simply adorable. For two hours I worked feverishly modeling the infant's face. I returned to work all day for the following two days on the head – working directly from life as the tiny thing, awake or asleep, lay before me on the hospital pillow. My Bye-Lo is as he was when three days old. From that model I perfected one in wax and with the wax model and many letters to toy manufacturers, I came out East.

The sculptress faced rejection at first because the dollmakers she approached thought the doll was too realistic to sell well. Eventually Geo. Borgfeldt & Co. patented the doll under the Bye-Lo Baby trade name in 1923. The first Christmas the doll was advertised, buyers in large numbers lined up to buy it, and it became known as the "Million Dollar Baby."

The original head was modeled to fit a body socket, but it was commercially made with a flange neck on a cloth body. The majority of bisque-head Bye-Lo Babies were sold with the Putnam-designed cloth body. It is unique, with its cloth legs curved inward and heels touching. The hands are usually made of celluloid, rather than composition. The bisque head came in seven sizes, from nine to twenty inches in length. Occasionally an original Bye-Lo Baby has been found with straight cloth legs.

Putnam explains the success in the following way: "His wide, flat nose, his funny little high forehead with its scanty hair, his drowsy eyes, his wrinkled neck and button mouth appealed to the mother urge in childhood."

Because of the great success of the By-Lo Babies, Geo. Borgfeldt & Co. persuaded Grace Putnam to create another doll. She envisioned a fairy-like doll with huge exotic wings. The original design was modified by the Borgfeldt creative department, which decided on a more realistic type of baby doll, with smaller wings. The doll was marketed as the "Fly-Lo Baby." The permanently-seated body was not popular, and few were made.

One of the most desirable Alt, Beck & Gottschalck bisque-head dolls, Pretty Peggy, was designed by Grace Corry Rockwell in 1926 and distributed by Geo. Borgfeldt & Co. Rockwell designed and made dolls for various companies. The molded-hair example pictured on page 114 is marked: "Copr. By//Grace C. Rockwell//Germany//1391/30."

Another character baby with an Alt, Beck & Gottschalck bisque head, distributed by Geo. Borgfeldt & Co., was Baby Bo Kaye. The circa-1925 bisque-head doll, designed by Joseph Kallus, had molded blond hair, sleep eyes and an open mouth with two lower teeth. The K&K Toy Company, a subsidiary of Geo. Borgfeldt & Co., made the body and assembled the dolls. The Baby Bo Kaye head was also made in composition and celluloid. The celluloid heads were made by Rheinesche

Chapter 4

Gummi und Celluloid-Fabrik, and marked with their trademark turtle.

Another American designer, Jeanne I. Orsini, created designs for a group of appealing all-bisque dolls, marked with various dates, including 1919 and 1920. Orsini copyrighted her first doll in 1916. For many years the dolls, named Didi, Mimi and Vivi, were credited to the Kestner porcelain factory. But the Dorf Museum in Nauendorf documented the production of the all-bisque dolls during their 1999 exhibit. During the remodeling of the Alt, Beck & Gottschalck factory in the late 1990s, a number of Orsini all-bisque shards were found, and they were on display when I visited the museum in June 1999. Genevieve Angione describes the unusual Didi, Mimi and Vivi bisque hands in her book titled *All-Bisque and Half-Bisque Dolls*: "The right hand has a raised forefinger out of a closed fist, both of which made the porcelain handling and finishing more difficult. The left hand is cupped and the thumb is bent inward, which made it necessary to open up a hole between the thumb and fingers."

The first bent-limb character babies were introduced in 1909. In 1912, the standing baby doll was introduced on a toddler body. Many different dolls were made using these two distinct body types. The majority of bodies made in the first few decades of the 1900s represented a baby in a sitting or a crawling position. The bent-limb baby body was a dollmaker's dream because the modeling was simple and the assembly was fast; there were just five body parts to string together. Some of the bodies were quite realistic with much modeling detail, such as rolls of fat on the arms and legs. The difference in modeling between the left and right arms also helped create a very realistic baby doll.

One Alt, Beck & Gottschalck character baby with a very expressive face, Bonnie Babe, was designed by Georgene Hendren Averill. Averill was born on May 21, 1876, in Denver, Colorado. She married James P. Averill in 1914. She took out her first doll copyright in 1926. Originally named Baby Smiles, it was later trademarked by Geo. Borgfeldt & Co. as Bonnie Babe. The original design for the doll's face was for dimples in each cheek, but no teeth. Before the doll was produced, two lower teeth were added to the facial modeling. Georgene Averill died in Santa Monica, California, in 1961.

Borgfeldt bought the rights to Bonnie Babe from Georgene Averill and an advertisement in a 1927 Geo. Borgfeldt & Co. sales catalog for Bonnie Babe reads: "The One Year Old Baby Doll. We are responsible for many innovations in dolls that have definitely affected and advanced the entire industry. The latest achievement is Madame Georgene's Bonnie Babe, the friendly One Year Old Baby Doll little girls are receiving with such enthusiasm. Bonnie Babe is so delightful, so appealing and so different from other dolls, that it is sure to be another outstanding success in the doll world. Bisc Head, glass moving eyes, moving tongue and two pearly lower teeth."

Many character babies with Alt, Beck & Gottschalck bisque heads were assembled by K&K Toy Company and then distributed by Geo. Borgfeldt & Co. Pretty Peggy, Bonnie Babe, Baby Bo-Kaye and the Bye-Lo Baby were very popular with buyers during the years they were originally marketed, and they are just as popular with antique doll collectors today.

3. In the 1990s the second factory building was remodeled into apartments. Some of the shards dug up at the site were on temporary display at the Dorf Museum in Nauendorf in 1999, when I visited the museum and photographed the Alt, Beck & Gottschalck doll-related shards pictured in this book. (Photo: Courtesy Dorf Museum, Nauendorf)

Alt, Beck & Gottschalck Porcelain Factory

4. Bisque socket head by Alt, Beck & Gottschalck; wig; multi-stroke eyebrows; painted upper and lower eyelashes; glass sleep eyes; open mouth with upper teeth; 12½-inch doll; circa 1910; marked: **1321//32**. Private Collection. (Photo: Christiane Gräfnitz)

5. Bisque socket head by Alt, Beck & Gottschalck; wig; multi-stroke eyebrows; painted upper and lower eyelashes; glass sleep eyes; open mouth with upper teeth and separate tongue; 10-inch doll; circa 1912; marked: **ABG//1353//26**. Kenneth Drew Collection. (Photo: Ann Hanat)

6. A closer view of the head seen in illustration 7 shows the dimpled cheeks and expressive smile. Georgia Alarcon Collection. (Photo: Estelle Johnston)

7. Bisque socket head by Alt, Beck & Gottschalck; molded hair; multi-stroke eyebrows; upper eyelids outlined in black; painted eyes with white highlights; open mouth with upper teeth; dimples; 13-inch doll; circa 1912; marked: **23//13ABG57**. Georgia Alarcon Collection. (Photo: Estelle Johnston)

Chapter 4

8. Uncommon bisque socket head by Alt, Beck & Gottschalck; wig; multi-stroke eyebrows; painted upper and lower eyelashes; glass sleep eyes; open/closed laughing mouth with long row of upper teeth; cheek dimples; 14-inch doll; circa 1914; marked: **1450**. Julie Blewis Collection. (Photo: Fanilya Gueno)

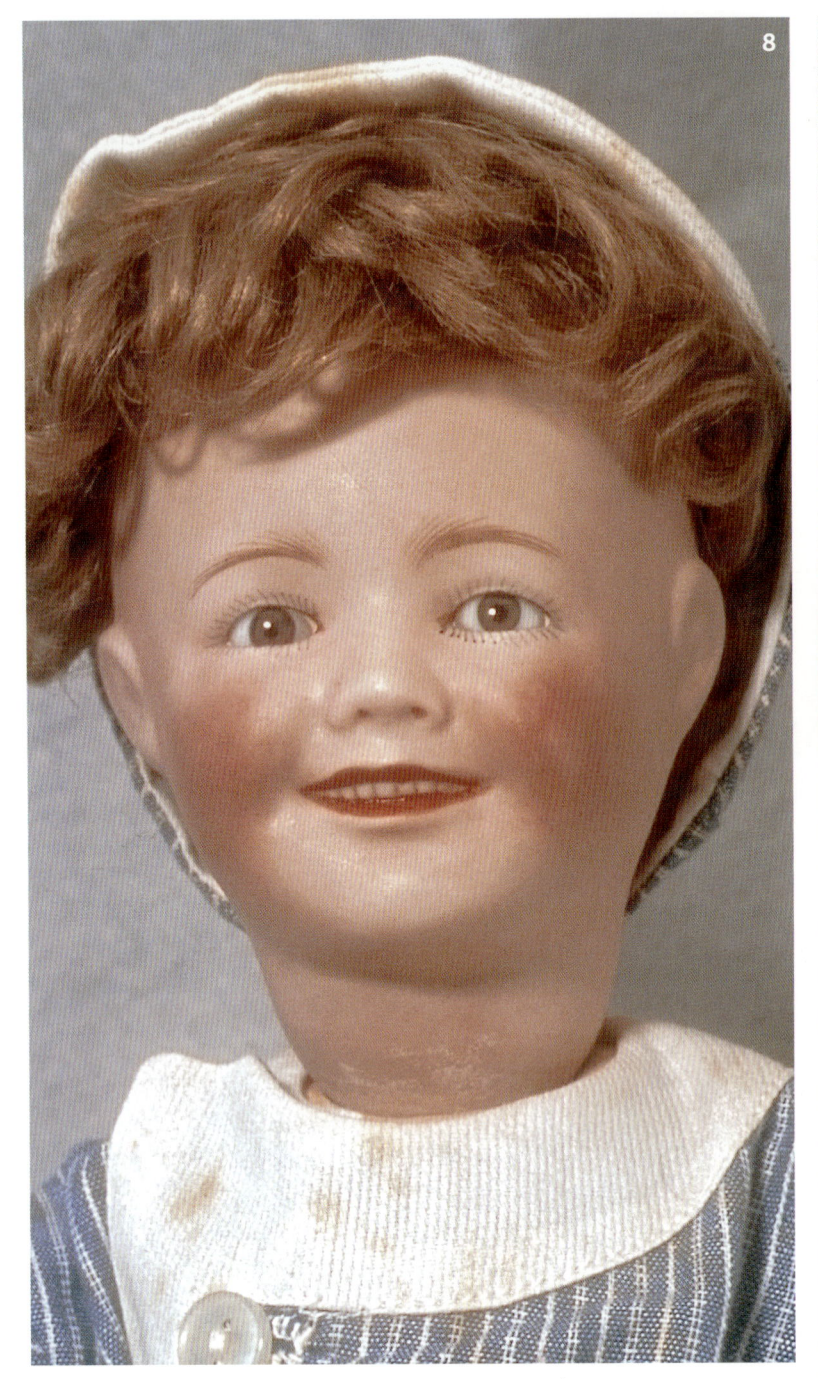

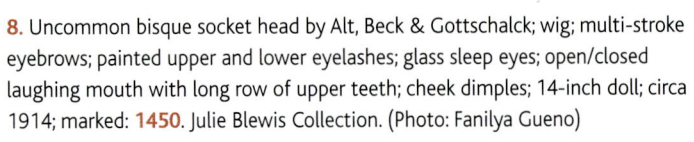

9. Bisque socket head by Alt, Beck & Gottschalck; multi-stroke eyebrows; painted lower eyelashes; glass sleep eyes; open mouth with upper teeth and separate tongue; 17¾-inch doll; circa 1912; marked: **ABG//1361//35**. This bisque head was made from a master mold identical to the 1361 head pictured in illustration 10. Roswitha Lucke Collection. (Photo: Christiane Gräfnitz)

10. Bisque socket head by Alt, Beck & Gottschalck; open crown; multi-stroke eyebrows; painted upper and lower eyelashes; open mouth; 5-inch head; circa 1912; marked: **ABG//1361//38**. The factory trademark has the entwined, fancy-script letters "A" and "G" with the letter "B" incised sideways over the other letters. Author's Collection. (Photo: Gregg Smith)

Alt, Beck & Gottschalck Porcelain Factory

11. Bisque socket head by Alt, Beck & Gottschalck; original wig; multi-stroke eyebrows; painted upper and lower eyelashes; glass sleep eyes; open/closed laughing mouth with upper teeth; cheek dimples; 18-inch doll; circa 1914; marked **1448/I//Made in Germany**. This uncommon bisque-head doll is very similar to the Alt, Beck & Gottschalck mold number 1450 doll pictured on page 33 of Jan Foulke's *16th Blue Book, Dolls and Values* under the Alt, Beck & Gottschalck heading. Courtesy Rosalie Whyel Museum of Doll Art. (Photo: Christiane Gräfnitz)

CHAPTER 4

12. The Alt, Beck & Gottschalck porcelain factory made this seldom-seen 18-inch bisque-head doll with a flange neck designed by American designer Grace Corry Rockwell. The molded-hair examples of Rockwell-designed bisque heads, circa 1926-1928, are often marked with the Alt, Beck & Gottschalck mold number 1391. The beautifully sculpted head features include: molded hair; single-stroke eyebrows; painted upper and lower eyelashes; glass sleep eyes and a closed mouth. The doll was copyrighted by Rockwell as Pretty Peggy, produced and sold by Geo. Borgfeldt & Co. and marked: **Copr.by//Grace C. Rockwell//Germany1391/30**. Courtesy Rosalie Whyel Museum of Doll Art. (Photo: Christiane Gräfnitz)

13. This area of the porcelain factory site yielded the most doll-head shards during the 1990s remodeling of the old Alt, Beck & Gottschalck factory building into apartments, according to the curators of the Dorf Museum. Many doll-head shards were also found in a storage building that adjoins the oldest factory building, in the space between the attic floor and the floor below. Photo courtesy Dorf Museum, Nauendorf.

14. These two DiDi all-bisque Orsini shards, found on the Alt, Beck & Gottschalck factory site, measure 3 and 3½ inches. The larger shard, marked **41//17** on the head and **JIO©1920** on the back, has multi-stroke eyebrows; upper and lower painted eyelashes and an open/closed smiling mouth with painted teeth. The smaller shard, marked **JIO©1920//41** on the back of the body, has single-stroke eyebrows; upper and lower painted eyelashes and an open/closed smiling mouth with painted teeth. Author's Collection. (Photo: Gregg Smith)

114

Alt, Beck & Gottschalck Porcelain Factory

15. All-bisque MiMi by Alt, Beck & Gottschalck; designed by Jeanne I. Orsini; wig; multi-stroke eyebrows; painted upper and lower eyelashes; stationary glass eyes; open/closed mouth with painted teeth; 7-inch doll; circa 1916 on; marked: **J.I.O.(c)1919**. Courtesy Rothenburg Puppenmuseum/Katharina Engels Collection. (Photo: Christiane Gräfnitz)

16. This group of Alt, Beck & Gottschalck bisque doll shards was found on the factory site during the remodeling of the factory building. They were shown in a temporary display at the Dorf Museum in 1999. Note the Orsini all-bisque dolls, each with a different sculpted mouth. An all-bisque Bye-Lo Baby body is attached to the top right corner of the board. (Photo: Mary Krombholz)

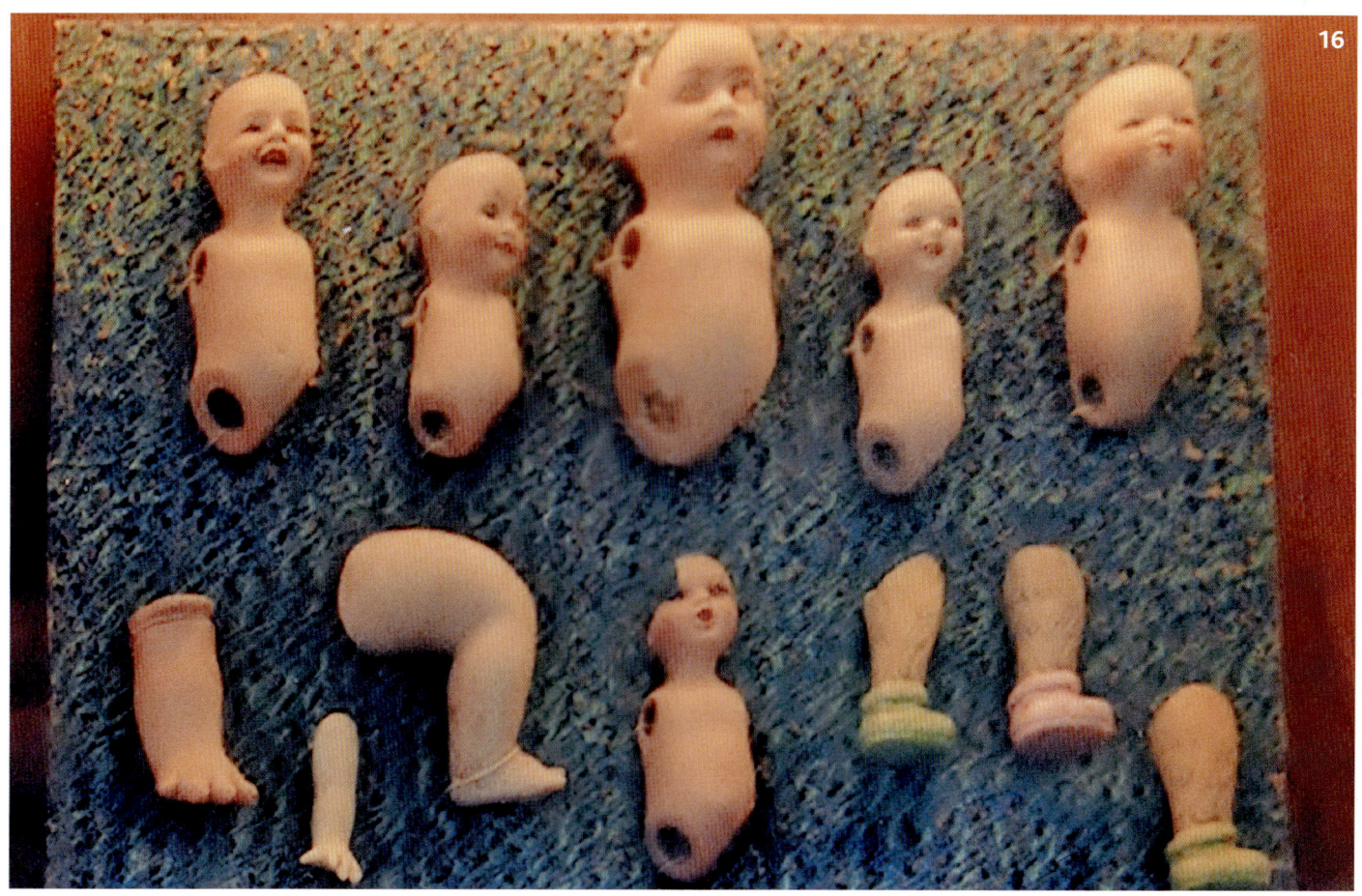

Chapter 4

17. All-bisque MiMi by Alt, Beck & Gottschalck; designed by Jeanne I. Orsini; jointed arms and legs; white painted stockings that end over the knees; one-strap flat black shoes; 7 inches; marked: **J.I.O.©1920**. Roswitha Lucke Collection. (Photo: Christiane Gräfnitz)

18. A closer view of MiMi shows the wig, multi-stroke eyebrows; painted upper and lower eyelashes; stationary glass eyes and open/closed mouth with painted teeth. Roswitha Lucke Collection. (Photo: Christiane Gräfnitz)

19. These two Alt, Beck & Gottschalck all-bisque dolls were designed by Jeanne I. Orsini. DiDi, left in photo, has the typical Orsini straight index finger on the hand that is touching her lips. MiMi, right in photo, has a round open/closed mouth. Both dolls have multi-stroke eyebrows; painted upper and lower eyelashes; stationary glass eyes; open/closed mouths; and are 7 inches high. Hennelore Henze-Doellner Collection. (Photo: Christiane Gräfnitz)

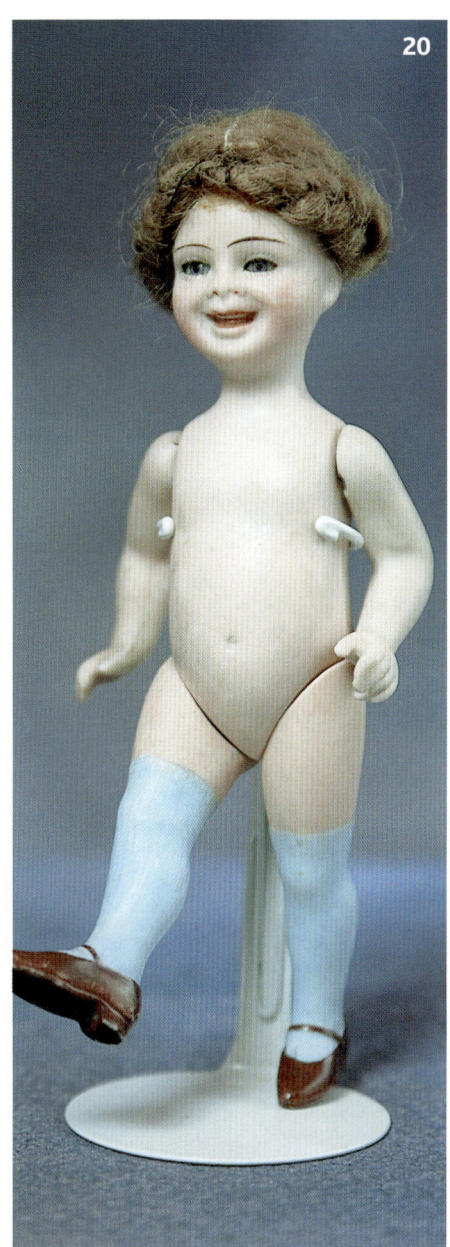

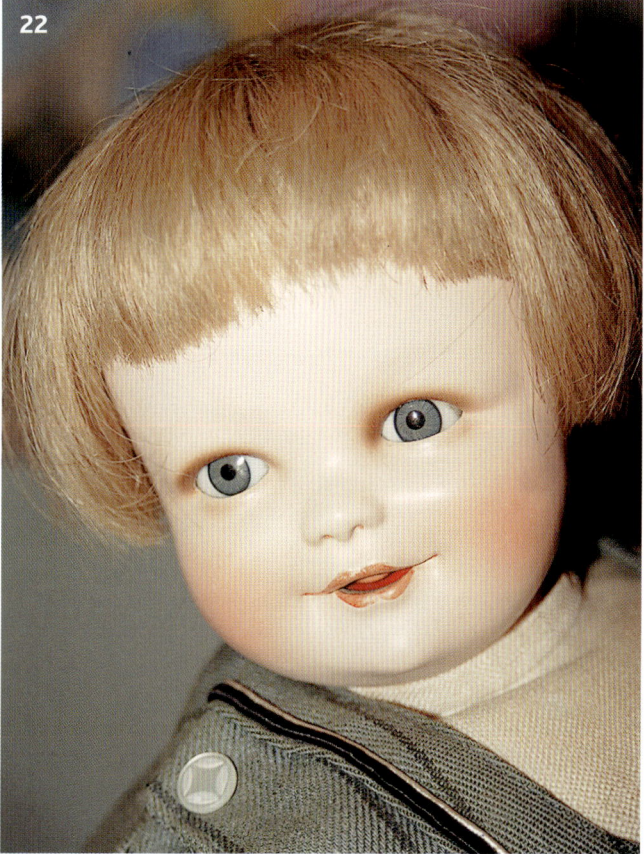

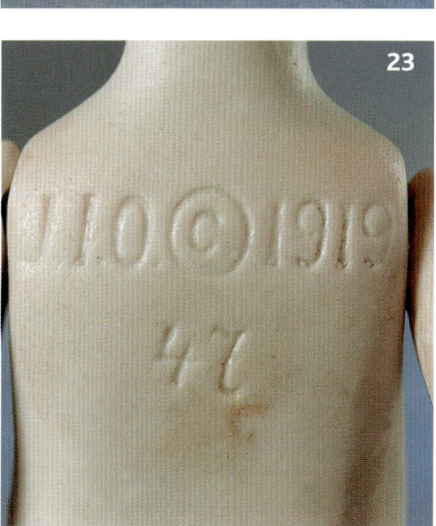

Alt, Beck & Gottschalck Porcelain Factory

20. This all-bisque 5-inch Alt, Beck & Gottschalck ViVi Orsini doll has uncommon long blue stockings that end above the knees. Beth Karp Collection. (Photo: Gregg Smith)

21. A close view of the head of the doll in illustration 20 shows the original wig, with braids across the top of the head; single-stroke eyebrows; painted upper and lower eyelashes; stationary glass eyes; open/closed mouth with upper teeth and molded tongue; 5-inch doll; circa 1916 on; marked: **JIO©1919//47**. Beth Karp Collection. (Photo: Gregg Smith)

22. Earthenware swivel head designed by Jeanne I. Orsini; wig; single-stroke eyebrows; glass eyes with flirty mechanism and shading around eye sockets; open smiling mouth with teeth and movable tongue; 21-inch doll; circa 1925; marked: **Copr.by J.I. Orsini//Germany**. An identical earthenware-head Orsini doll is pictured in the Summer 1982 issue of *Doll News*. It is marked **Copr.by//J.I. Orsini//Germany//1430/2/**. The 1430 mold number is in the Alt, Beck & Gottschalck series; the ABG Albego composition-head character doll is marked 1432. Courtesy Rosalie Whyel Museum of Doll Art. (Photo: Christiane Gräfnitz)

23. The back of the upper body shows the incised marks of the doll pictured in illustrations 20 and 21. Beth Karp Collection. (Photo: Gregg Smith)

CHAPTER 4

24. These two Alt, Beck & Gottschalck all-bisque dolls were designed by Jeanne I. Orsini. The doll on the left in photo is marked: **J.I.O.(c)1920**; the doll on the right in photo is marked: **J.I.O.(c)1919**. Note the varying expressions of the four dolls shown in this illustration and illustration 19, which have been accomplished by skilled mouth sculpting. These two dolls have single-stroke eyebrows; painted upper and lower eyelashes; side-glancing painted and glass stationary eyes; open/closed mouths with upper teeth; and are 5 inches high. The comparison of the smiling Orsinis shows ViVi on the left with painted eyes, a narrow upper lip and a wide open smiling mouth while DiDi on the right has glass eyes and a less open mouth with higher upper-lip peaks. The original circular paper label on chest reads: "ViVi//Reg. U.S. Patent Office//Copr. 1920//J.I.O. Orsini//Patent Applied For//Germany." Hennelore Henze-Doellner Collection. (Photo: Christiane Gräfnitz)

26. George Borgfeldt & Co., New York importers and distributors, used a number of advertising devices to promote their products. My Borgfeldt celluloid advertising calendar is important because it provides information on the company's products in 1933. The back of the celluloid card contains a calendar for the year 1933. Below the calendar is another small advertisement, which reads: "American//Nifty Toys//And//Doll Specialties//Mickey and Minnie Mouse//Felix Cat//Skippy Novelties//Bye-Lo Baby and Daisy Dolls//Margaret Steiff Stuffed//Animals//J.W. Spear's Games." The card is signed: Geo. Borgfeldt & Co. Author's Collection. (Photo: Robin Imaging Services)

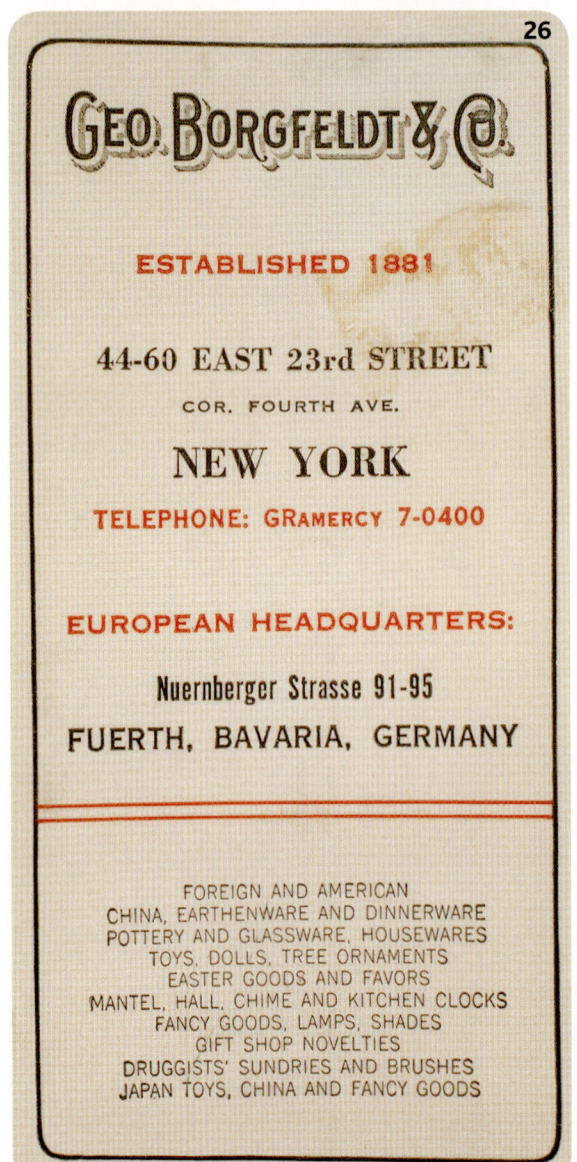

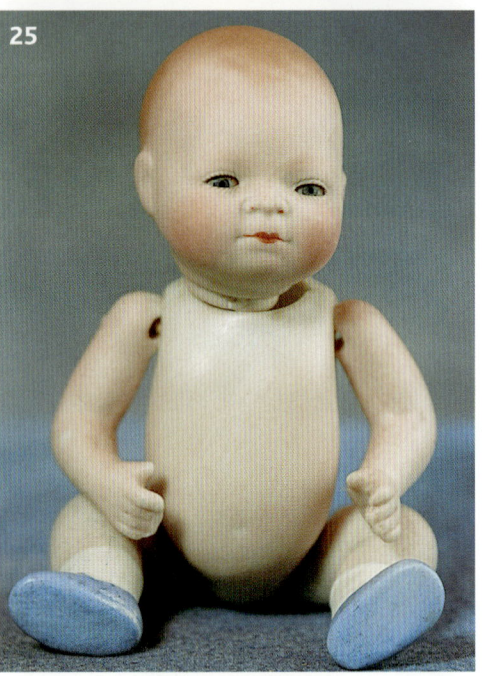

25. All-bisque Bye-Lo Baby by Alt, Beck & Gottschalck for Geo. Borgfeldt & Co. An identical all-bisque head and attached body, pictured in illustration 16, was found during the remodeling of the Alt, Beck & Gottschalck porcelain factory into apartments. The Kestner & Co. porcelain factory also made all-bisque Bye-Lo Babies for Borgfeldt. The body, jointed at the shoulders and hips, has well-modeled hands, white painted socks and blue molded shoes. Head features include flange swivel neck; single-stroke eyebrows; painted upper and lower eyelashes; tiny, glass sleep eyes; closed mouth; 5-inch doll; circa 1925; marked: **6-22//Copr.by// Grace S. Putnam//Germany**; **20//12** incised inside the upper arms. Original paper label read: "Bye-lo-Baby © Germany//G.S. Putnam." Author's Collection. (Photo: Gregg Smith)

Alt, Beck & Gottschalck Porcelain Factory

27. Four Thuringian porcelain factories made Bye-Lo Babies for Geo. Borgfeldt & Co., including, Alt, Beck & Gottschalck, Hertel, Schwab & Co., Kestner & Co. and C.F. Kling & Co. Marked Bye-Lo Baby heads contain the Alt, Beck & Gottschalck mold numbers 1369 (socket head, circa 1925), 1373 and a rare 1415 with painted eyes and a smiling mouth. To my knowledge, no Bye-Lo Baby heads marked with the names or mold numbers of other porcelain factories have surfaced. The majority of original Bye-Lo Baby dolls are found on cloth bodies with celluloid hands and frog-like shaped legs with touching heels. This Bye-Lo Baby is 14 inches tall and marked: **Copr.by//Grace S. Putnam//MADE IN GERMANY**. Author's Collection. (Photo: Gregg Smith)

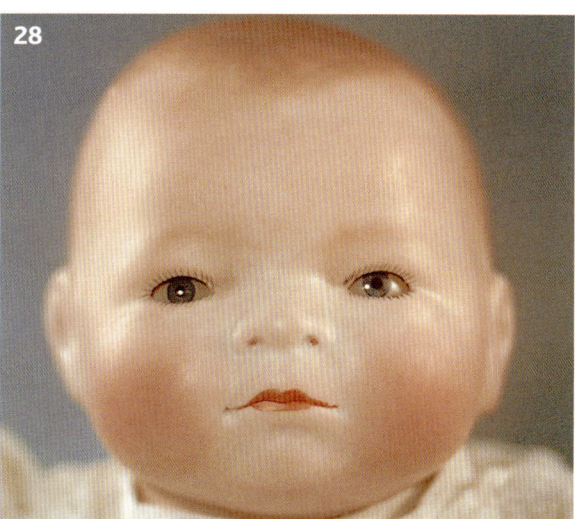

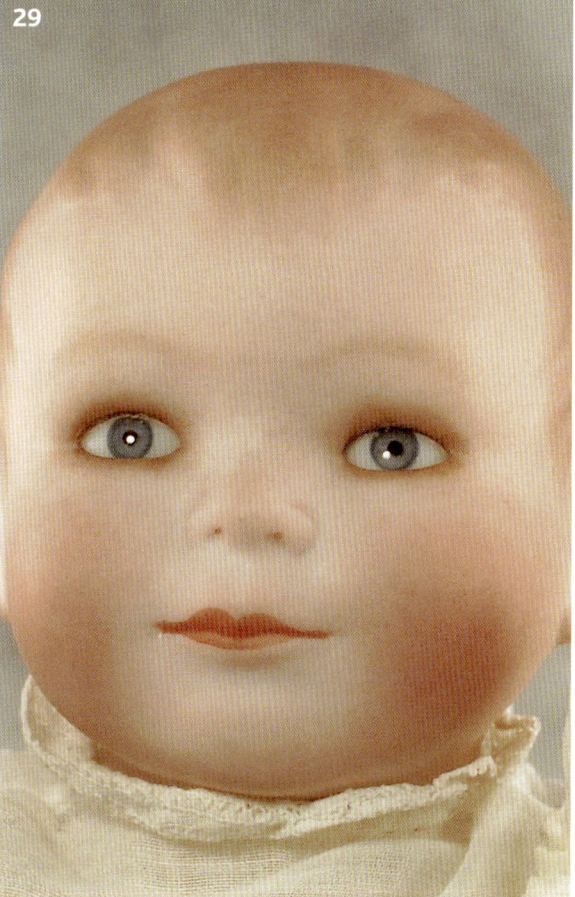

28. Bye-Lo Baby bisque head by Alt, Beck & Gottschalck for Geo. Borgfeldt & Co.; flange neck, molded hair; single-stroke eyebrows; painted upper and lower eyelashes; tiny, glass sleep eyes; closed mouth; 10½-inch doll; circa 1922 on; marked: **Copr.by//Grace S. Putnam//MADE IN GERMANY**. The original round paper label attached to the clothing reads: BYE-LO BABY//Reg. U.S. Pat. Off.//PATENT APPLIED FOR//K and K//Copyright 1922//By GRACE STOREY//PUTNAM. Beth Karp Collection. (Photo: Lee Krombholz)

29. Fly-Lo Baby bisque head by Alt, Beck & Gottschalck for Geo. Borgfeldt & Co.; designed by Grace Storey Putnam; flange neck; molded hair; single-stroke eyebrows; brown shading above and below eyes; glass sleep eyes; closed mouth with straight, narrow lips; 3¼-inch head; circa 1926; marked: **Copr. by//Grace S. Putnam//Germany//1418/25**. Originally, the dolls had wings with wired edges that were attached to the wrists. Beth Karp Collection. (Photo: Lee Krombholz)

30. Bye-Lo Baby bisque head by Alt, Beck & Gottschalck for Geo.Borgfeldt & Co.; flange neck; molded hair; single-stroke eyebrows; upper and lower painted eyebrows; glass sleep eyes; closed mouth; 8-inch doll; circa 1922 on; marked: **Copr.by//Grace S. Putnam// MADE IN GERMANY**. A Geo. Borgfeldt & Co. 1925 advertisement listed the doll for sale in seven sizes from 9 to 20 inches in height. Ann Cummings Collection. (Photo: John Cummings)

Chapter 4

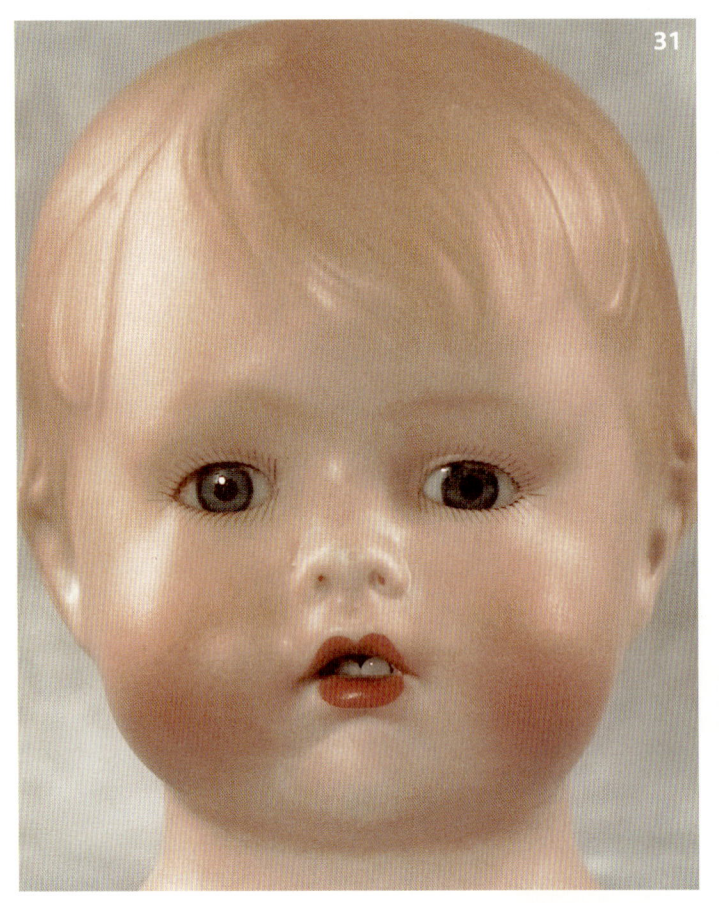

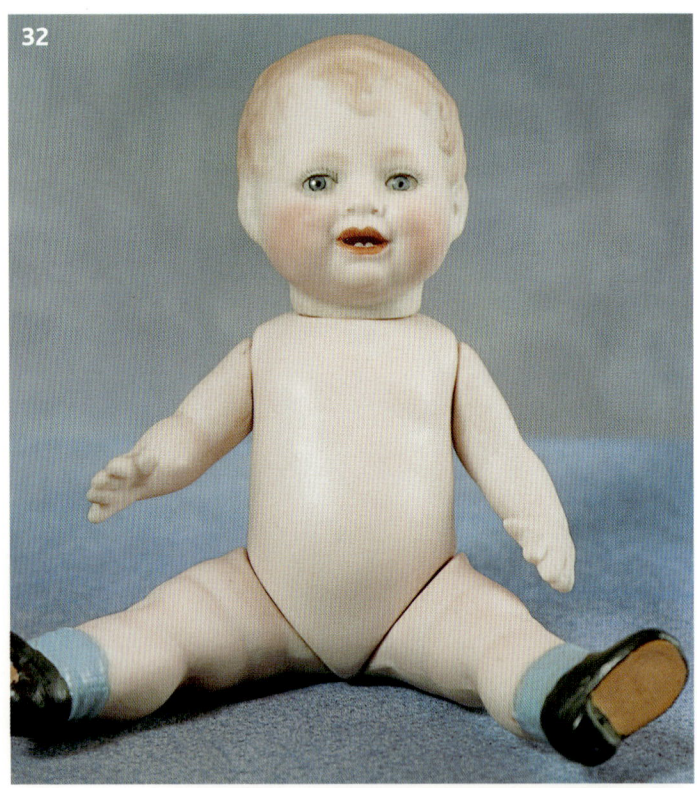

31. Baby Bo Kaye bisque head by Alt, Beck & Gottschalck for Geo. Borgfeldt & Co.; designed by American designer Joseph L. Kallus; bodies by K&K Toy Co.; flange neck; molded hair; single-stroke eyebrows; painted upper and lower eyelashes; glass sleep eyes; open mouth with lower teeth; 4-inch head; circa 1925; marked: **Copr. by J.L. Kallus//Germany//1394/30**. Beth Karp Collection. (Photo: Lee Krombholz)

32. All-bisque Bonnie Babe by Alt, Beck & Gottschalck for Geo. Borgfeldt & Co.; swivel flange neck marked **15**; jointed at hips and shoulders; dimpled knees; molded blue socks and one-strap black-heeled shoes; 6¼-inch doll; circa 1926; marked **179-2/0** (inside upper legs); **H98//15** (inside upper arms). Alt, Beck & Gottschalck made thousands of bisque character heads for Borgfeldt, as well as all-bisque Kewpies and Bye-Lo Babies. The modeling and facial painting on my 2-inch Bonnie Babe head (with a flange neck and all-bisque body), and my 6-inch Bonnie Babe head (with a flange neck and cloth body) indicate that both dolls were made by Alt, Beck & Gottschalck. Author's Collection. (Photo: Gregg Smith)

34. Bonnie Babe bisque head by Alt, Beck & Gottschalck for Geo. Borgfeldt Co.; designed by American designer Georgene Averill; bodies by K&K Toy Co.; flange neck; molded hair; single-stroke eyebrows; painted upper and lower eyelashes; glass sleep eyes; open mouth with lower teeth and separate tongue; cheek and chin dimples; 22-inch doll; GM 1929; marked: **Copr.by //Georgene Averill//1005/3652//Germany**. Averill transferred the United States trademark for Bonnie Babe to Borgfeldt, giving him full distribution rights. The heads were made in six sizes, and most of the cloth bodies were made by the Borgfeldt subsidiary K & K Toy Co. Author's Collection. (Photo: Gene Abbott)

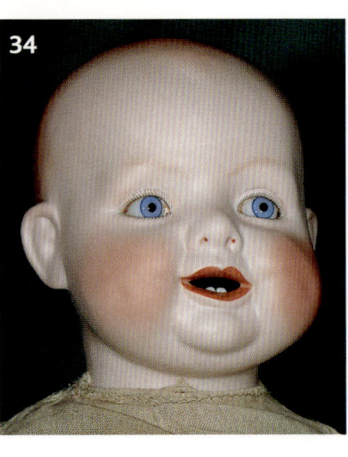

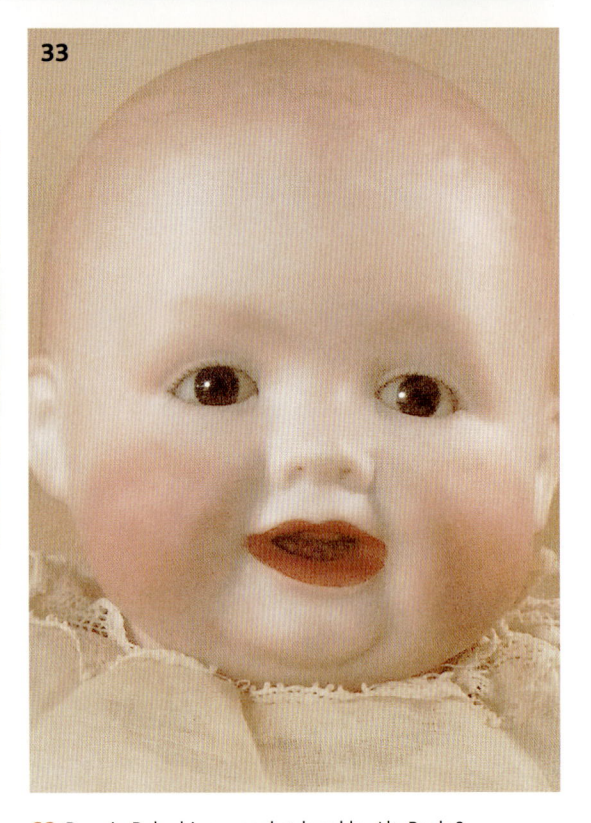

33. Bonnie Babe bisque socket head by Alt, Beck & Gottschalck for Geo. Borgfeldt; original clothing; molded hair; single-stroke eyebrows; painted upper and lower eyelashes; glass sleep eyes; open mouth with lower teeth and separate tongue; cheek and chin dimples; 9½-inch doll; GM 1929; marked: **Copr.by//Georgene Averill//1005 1420//14/0**. Original cloth tag on clothing reads: "BONNIE BABE//COPYRIGHTED BY//GEORGENE AVERILL//MADE BY K AND K TOY CO." Beth Karp Collection. (Photo: Lee Krombholz)

120

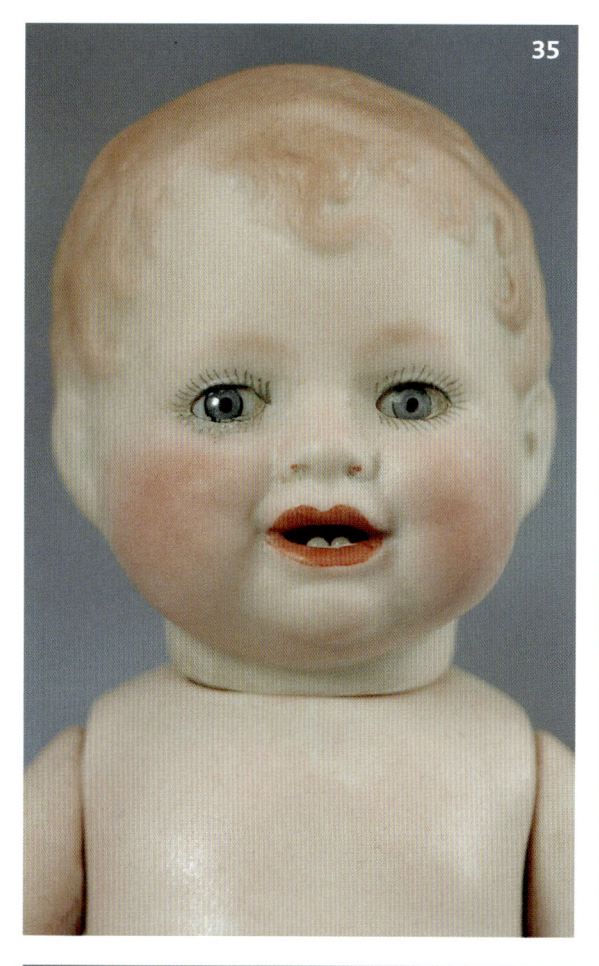

Alt, Beck & Gottschalck Porcelain Factory

35. A closer view of the head of the doll in illustration 32 shows the molded curly hair; single-stroke eyebrows; painted upper and lower eyelashes; glass sleep eyes and open laughing mouth with lower teeth. Author's Collection. (Photo: Gregg Smith)

36. A closer view of the all-bisque googly in illustration 37 shows the original wig; single-stroke eyebrows; side-glancing glass eyes and open/closed mouth with painted teeth. The modeling and facial painting is very similar to the Orsini all-bisque dolls pictured earlier in this chapter. Roswitha Lucke Collection. (Photo: Christiane Gräfnitz)

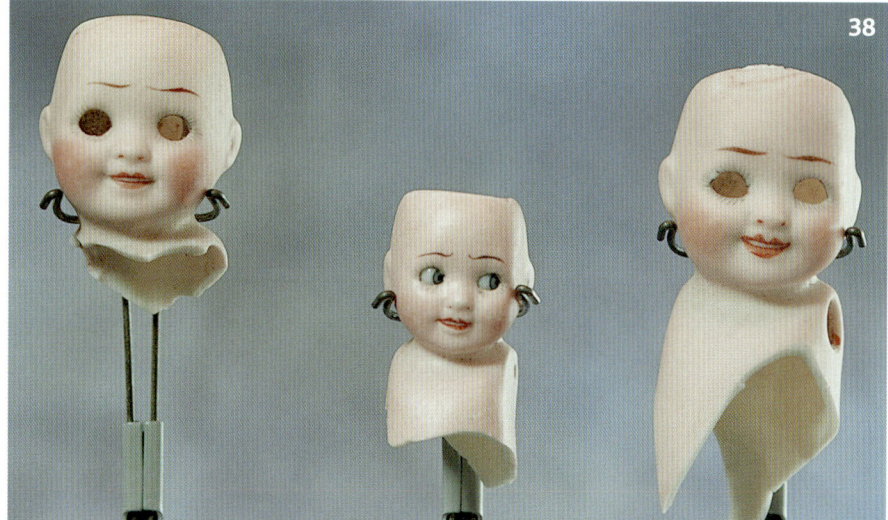

38. Alt, Beck & Gottschalck all-bisque Orsini-type doll shards with ViVi molded mouths were found in the factory dumping grounds. They measure from 1½ to 3½ inches in height. The shard in the middle has side-glancing glass stationary eyes. All three shards have single-stroke wavy eyebrows, upper and lower painted eyelashes and open/closed mouths with painted teeth. The Orsini all-bisque dolls marked DiDi, MiMi and ViVi were made by Alt, Beck & Gottschalck for Geo. Borgfeldt & Co. Author's Collection. (Photo: Gregg Smith)

37. All-bisque barefoot googly by Alt, Beck & Gottschalck; jointed at the hips and shoulders; 4½-inch doll; circa 1920s, unmarked. The all-bisque dolls pictured in illustrations 36, 37, 39, 40, 41, 42 and 43 were made by the Alt, Beck & Gottschalck porcelain factory in the 1920s, during the years Ernst Weingart directed the factory. Roswitha Lucke Collection. (Photo: Christiane Gräfnitz)

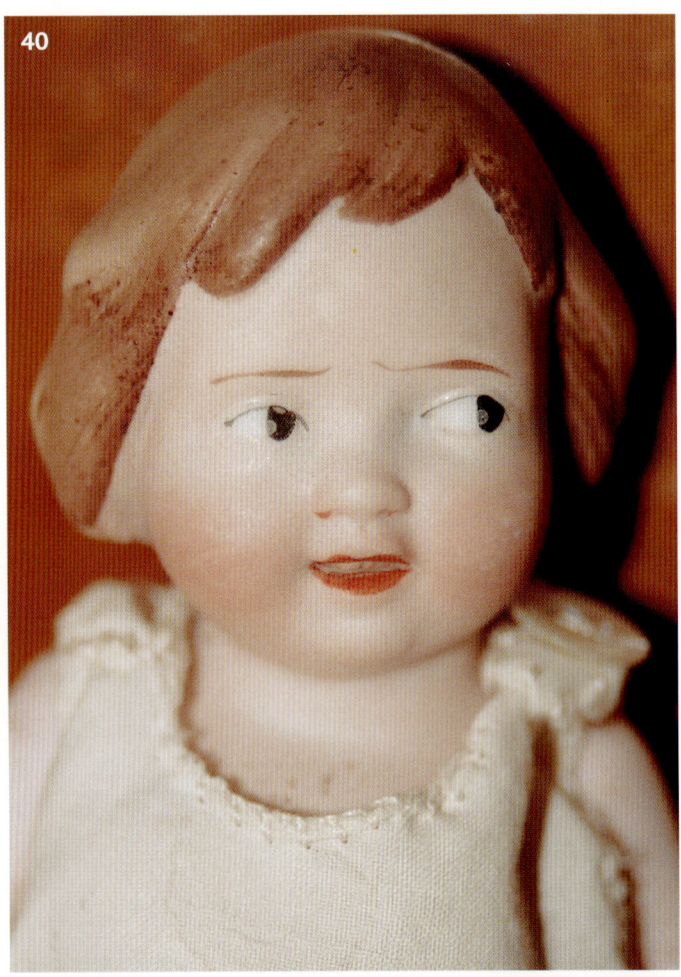

Chapter 4

39. A closer view of the all-bisque googly in illustration 42 shows the wig; single-stroke eyebrows; large side-glancing painted eyes and open/closed mouth with painted teeth. Roswitha Lucke Collection. (Photo: Christiane Gräfnitz)

40. A closer view of the all-bisque doll pictured in illustration 41 shows the molded hair; single-stroke eyebrows; side-glancing painted eyes and open/closed mouth with painted teeth. Roswitha Lucke Collection. (Photo: Christiane Gräfnitz)

41. All-bisque googly by Alt, Beck & Gottschalck; jointed at shoulders only; bare feet; 4½-inch doll; circa 1920s; unmarked. Roswitha Lucke Collection. (Photo: Christiane Gräfnitz)

42. All-bisque googly doll by Alt, Beck & Gottschalck, jointed at the shoulders only; blue painted socks and one-strap black flat shoes; 4-inch doll; circa 1920s; unmarked. Roswitha Lucke Collection. (Photo: Christiane Gräfnitz)

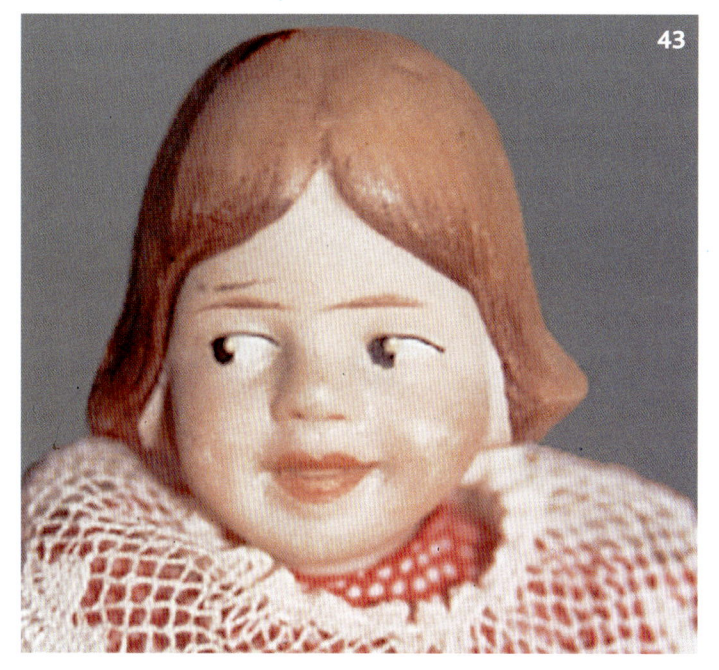

Alt, Beck & Gottschalck Porcelain Factory

43. All-bisque googly by Alt, Beck & Gottschalck; jointed at the shoulders only; molded hair; single-stroke eyebrows; side-glancing painted eyes with white highlights; open/closed mouth with painted teeth; 4-inch doll; circa 1920s; marked **37-10**. Roswitha Lucke Collection. (Photo: Christiane Gräfnitz)

44. Kewpie by Alt, Beck & Gottschalck and other Thuringian porcelain factories for Geo. Borgfeldt & Co.; original box; marked O'Neill on bottom of feet; jointed at the shoulders only; molded hair with topknot and molded wisps of hair over each ear; tiny, single-stroke eyebrows; short, straight, upper-painted eyelashes; large, side-glancing eyes with white highlight on top edge of each large black pupil; impish smiling mouth; 5-inch doll; circa 1913. Original circular red-heart label on chest reads: "KEWPIE//Germany." Ann Cummings Collection. (Photo: John Cummings)

45. This original Kewpie box was found on the grounds of the Alt, Beck & Gottschalck/Hertel, Schwab & Co. factory site in Stutzhaus. Alt, Beck & Gottschalck, Hertel, Schwab & Co., Kestner & Co. and many other Thuringian porcelain factories made Kewpies for Geo. Borgfeldt & Co. from 1913 on. Author's Archival Paper Collection. (Photo: Robin Imaging Services)

46. Two all-bisque doll head shards, measuring 2½ and 3½ inches, were found on the Alt, Beck & Gottschalck factory site. The doll shard on the left in the photo is marked **28//14** and the other, larger, head is marked **150**. Both heads have multi-stroke eyebrows, upper and lower painted eyelashes and open/closed mouths with upper teeth. Author's Collection. (Photo: Gregg Smith)

Part One

CHAPTER 5

Baehr & Proeschild Porcelain Factory

Stone pillars still mark the entrance of the old Baehr & Proeschild porcelain factory in Ohrdruf, which has a population of about sixty-five hundred people. The factory buildings where bisque doll heads were once made are now used by another Ohrdruf company. But traces still remain of the years that dolls were made on this site, including several storage buildings built of discarded plaster molds and support timbers. The loading dock is a visible reminder of the years when horse-drawn wagons and, later, trucks, were loaded with boxes of dolls ready to be delivered to customers all over the world. Water is still flowing through the concrete trough that originally brought water into the factory from a nearby mountain stream. The large valve that once controlled the water flow is still in place.

When I visited the factory in June 1999, a large dumping area was visible behind one of the buildings. Hundreds of bisque doll-head shards had been brought up to the surface of the ground by the spring rains. When I visited the site again in 2002, the ground that once contained so many reminders of the past had been leveled and grass covered the shards.

1. The old water valve that once channeled the flow of water from a nearby mountain stream into the factory buildings is still on the grounds of the former Baehr & Proeschild porcelain factory. (Photo: Mary Krombholz)

Of all the large factories in Thuringia that once made doll-related products, the Baehr & Proeschild porcelain factory is the only one with multiple buildings that remains standing today. Most of the other old factories have been replaced by new buildings that are less expensive to maintain.

Georg Baehr and August Proeschild founded the Baehr & Proeschild porcelain factory in Ohrdruf in 1871. From an original sales order in the Sonneberg Doll Museum archives, we learn that the Baehr & Proeschild porcelain factory made bisque shoulder heads for the Sonneberg dollmaker Heinrich Stier in 1875. The "unmovable heads with human eyes, mohair wigs and earrings" were mounted on leather bodies. August Proeschild died in 1888 and by 1893 the porcelain factory was directed by partners Georg Baehr, Hans Baehr and Carl Engelke. In 1894 Georg Baehr died and his son Hans became the only liable partner. In 1905 the following porcelain products were advertised: "Bisque doll heads with wigs, with and without sleeping eyes, natural eyelashes of hair, movable dolls, babies, Nanking dolls, bathing dolls, bisque angels, porcelain figures, arms and legs, bisque figures and

2. The small town of Ohrdruf has a population of about sixty-five hundred today, similar to the population during the time porcelain doll heads were made here. Three Thuringian porcelain factories made doll-related porcelain products in Ohrdruf. The Kestner & Co. and C.F. Kling & Co. porcelain factories made glazed and unglazed porcelain-head dolls from the late 1840s on; the Baehr & Proeschild porcelain factory made bisque-head dolls from the 1870s on. Georg Baehr and August Proeschild founded the Baehr & Proeschild porcelain factory in 1871, and it is the only doll-related Thuringian porcelain factory with multiple buildings that are still standing now. (Photo: Mary Krombholz)

beautiful knick-knacks." (The information in this paragraph is from the Ciesliks' research as published in the *German Doll Encyclopedia*.)

The Baehr & Proeschild porcelain factory had a close business relationship with the Bruno Schmidt doll factory. From the 1900 founding of the Schmidt doll factory until 1918, when Schmidt purchased the Baehr & Proeschild porcelain factory, all of Schmidt's bisque doll heads and parts were made by Baehr & Proeschild.

The Bruno Schmidt home and doll factory, located directly behind the home, are still standing in Waltershausen. Before founding the doll factory, Schmidt was a co-owner of a toy factory with Hugo Giesler.

In 1904 Schmidt registered a heart-shaped trademark, which contained the initials "BSW" (Bruno Schmidt, Waltershausen). The factory used the following advertising phrase to promote their heart-shaped trademark: "This is what the doll stork said 'Listen little doll mother, this enchanting doll is yours and its name shall be Heart of Gold.'"

In 1910 the Bruno Schmidt doll factory advertised character dolls, including babies; standard dolly-faced dolls with bisque and celluloid heads; doll bodies; spare parts for dolls; doll wigs; doll shoes and stockings; and doll clothing in many styles.

The Baehr & Proeschild porcelain factory made a large number of dolly-faced heads, including bisque heads in the 200 and 300 number series. The mold series begins with the number 201, which was introduced circa 1888, and ends with number 394, circa 1897. One group of Baehr & Proeschild character dolls was made for the Kley & Hahn doll factory in Ohrdruf. These are marked with the 500 series mold numbers. Bisque character heads bearing the mold numbers 520, 525, 553, 568, 585 and 592 are especially expressive.

The factory also made many Native American, Black, Asian and googly dolls. The Baehr & Proeschild mold number 244 is a Native American Belton bisque head with three stringing holes on a flattened crown, scowling black-painted eyebrows and pierced ears. In addition to making heads for Bruno Schmidt, Baehr & Proeschild made bisque heads for the Waltershausen doll factories of Wiesenthal, Schindel

Chapter 5

3. Several buildings on the factory site were constructed of discarded plaster molds and wooden timbers. Many doll heads are still visible in the plaster molds that were used to construct the walls of the building on the right in this photograph. (Photo: Mary Krombholz)

& Kallenberg and Adolf Wislizenus. The Joseph Bergmann doll factory in Sonneberg sold character dolls with Baehr & Proeschild bisque heads, including those marked with the 224 mold number.

The earliest bisque heads made by Baehr & Proeschild are marked with incised mold numbers only. In 1888 the factory added "dep" to the incised mold numbers. The trademark initials "B&P" were added in about 1895. The dolly-faced dolls made before 1910 contain incised marks in the 200 or 300 mold numbers only. The "crossed swords" trademark was used with the B&P initials from 1900 to 1919. In 1919, due to the purchase of Baehr & Proeschild by the Bruno Schmidt doll factory, a heart accompanied the B&P letters. It is also important to point out that the Bruno Schmidt doll factory used a heart trademark before the purchase of Baehr & Proeschild, and that the heart contained the initials "BSW" for Bruno Schmidt, Waltershausen.

An excellent example of a doll assembled with a Baehr & Proeschild bisque head and an Adolf Wislizenus jointed composition body is on permanent display in the Waltershausen Doll Museum. It always causes comments, especially from doll collectors who marvel at the unusual body with rib delineation. The Adolf Wislizenus doll factory specialized in unusual bodies. They are easily recognized because they contain modeling details that are unique to this doll factory.

No other Thuringian doll factory included body modeling like molded ribs and well-defined fat wrinkles on both the upper and lower limbs.

The Adolf Wislizenus doll factory was the second oldest doll factory in Waltershausen. From 1816 until 1851, the J.D. Kestner, Jr. doll factory was the only doll factory in Waltershausen. The Wislizenus doll factory was founded in Waltershausen by Gottlob Schafft in 1851. Adolf Wislizenus was Schafft's partner for sixteen years, until he became the sole owner in 1877. From 1894 until about 1909, William Heinecke was the owner of the doll factory. Hans Heinecke bought the factory in 1909. Both Heineckes retained the Wislizenus name.

The doll factory assembled and sold a wide variety of dolls, including swimming dolls powered by clock mechanisms, dolls with wax heads and multi-faced dolls. In 1910 the doll factory advertised a character baby. In 1911 the Wislizenus factory advertised that they held a record for their assortment of character dolls made from their own designs. The factory closed permanently in 1931, due to poor sales, and a short time later it was bought by the Koenig & Wernicke doll factory in Waltershausen.

The Wislizenus doll factory bought many bisque heads from the Simon & Halbig porcelain factory. The only marks on the back of the head of my Simon & Halbig bisque-head George Washington are the Adolf Wislizenus trademark

Baehr & Proeschild Porcelain Factory

initials: "AW." (See Part One: Chapter 3 for a photo of this doll.) The Wislizenus doll factory also assembled and sold dolls with Gebrüder Heubach heads and Ernst Heubach heads. Both of these porcelain factories are located in the Sonneberg area.

As doll collectors, we are most interested in the porcelain products that relate to our hobby. But it is important to remember that the Thuringian factories that made doll-related porcelain products also made a variety of other porcelain products such as figurines, tableware, religious items and powder boxes. It is often difficult to create a mold number sequence because the mold numbers of many products not related to dolls are interspersed with the doll-head mold numbers.

Although the Thuringian porcelain factories differed in appearance, the rooms inside served the same purpose. In each porcelain factory, porcelain products were made in a very similar way. Because the Baehr & Proeschild porcelain factory is the only one with multiple buildings still standing today, it is easiest for us to imagine the dollmaking process of long-ago taking place there. By taking an imaginary walk through the Baehr & Proeschild porcelain factory, it is possible to picture how bisque-head character dolls were made in porcelain factories throughout this dollmaking area.

Author Clara L. Mateaux provides an excellent description of the steps required in making an original clay model in a porcelain factory like the Baehr & Proeschild porcelain factory in her 1898 book *Wonderland of Work*.

> The first person we notice as we enter the large, well-lighted workroom is a brown-haired blue-bloused young man with a pipe in his mouth. He is sitting at a tall work-bench with a top that can be screwed up and down or around in any way he requires.
>
> He is the artist, or modeler, the one who first invents the features of a new doll; and so we must consider him an important person in the establishment and watch him closely as he pats and dabs away at a lump of softish wet clay, not much with his fingers but with one of his little bone tools, a large supply of which are stuck in another handy slab of wet clay, which serves him as a kind of tool cushion.
>
> After some time the shapeless gray mass gradually assumes a form and presently we see that of a pretty, though expressionless face. When he has turned it about and improved it to his heart's content, the modeler proceeds to mark it with a piece of red chalk, a few careful lines, and then he hands the little bust over to worker number two, whose business it is to get an exact mold or copy of it.
>
> As soon as the clay model is dry, the modeler lays it face upwards in a dish of wet clay, carefully pressing this clay into every corner and up to those red guiding lines which the modeler draws for the purpose of a sort of boundary. Next, he builds a regular clay wall around the mass, but somewhat higher than the uncovered face of the model, so that it now looks like a box half-full of clay with a pale-gray face staring out of it.
>
> Then another worker comes to assist in the work by holding those clay walls together while the first one fetches a big vessel full of plaster of Paris; the contents of the pot he pours all over the face, and so hides it from our view, apparently spoiling it forever. But as soon as the plaster of Paris is dry, the box is turned over and the clay is removed, leaving a plaster mold of the front of the doll's head. Then they build up the clay walls again, and pour plaster of Paris in again to make a mold of the back of the head.

The amount of room needed for porcelain production cannot be emphasized enough. The top floor or attic of a porcelain factory was often used as mold storage space. Usually the molds were stacked on numbered shelves and the shelf numbers were listed in a large inventory book. Every morning, workers located and carried the plaster molds that were going to be in use that day down to the slip-pouring room. Ideally, this room would be filled with light from large windows. During the years character dolls were made, the porcelain slip was often transported in porcelain tubes suspended almost at ceiling height to the long wooden worktables. Hoses attached to the porcelain tubes fed the porcelain slip to the workers at each of the worktables.

The thick porcelain slip was poured into the plaster working molds and allowed to stand for about ten minutes. During this initial settling and absorption by the porous plaster molds, more slip was often added. When the liquid slip had slightly hardened, the superfluous slip was then poured out of the hole on one end of the two-part mold. The excess slip was poured into a trough in the center of the worktable, and the troughs were connected to a container in which the slip could be recycled by adding more water. After the worker waited for another ten minutes or so, the doll head was hard enough to withstand removal from the mold. When the doll head was in the leather stage, the doll-head seams that resulted from the slight space between the two separate parts of the doll-head mold were removed with a tool, and the eye and mouth openings were cut out. The doll head had to dry completely before it was fired in the kiln because air pockets created by the stirring of the porcelain mixture could easily destroy the head. The head was then placed inside a fireproof ceramic container (*Chamotte*) to be fired at the temperature required to make hard-paste porcelain. The beehive kilns used throughout the character dollmaking years could hold hundreds of doll heads in one firing. After the first firing, the dull white porcelain doll head was sanded and painted. A flesh color was applied first, and when it was dry, the cheeks,

Chapter 5

eyebrows, eyelashes and lips were painted. The facial painting became permanent when the doll heads were fired again at a lower kiln temperature.

The rooms necessary to sculpt, make and paint porcelain were not the only rooms on the factory site. In addition to the rooms for sculpting the original models, the slip-making and pouring rooms, the assembling and painting rooms, porcelain factories had to have rooms for many other jobs related to the day-to-day operation of the factory. These included offices used by the president of the factory and his staff. Many porcelain factories also had company doctors who treated workers for a variety of medical problems.

Robert R. Roentgen provides the following information on the closing of the Baehr & Proeschild porcelain factory, including a short list of products made there: "Baehr & Proeschild, 1871 – defunct before 1945, figurines, dolls and doll heads, decorative porcelain."

Thuringian porcelain factories like Baehr & Proeschild were standing all over Germany in 1989 when the Berlin Wall fell. Almost all of the factories have been torn down in the past nineteen years. But the porcelain factory sites have been the source of important product information. Doll heads that were rejected by factory inspectors were disposed of in many ways. They were usually dumped outside, on the factory site, but a distance away from the porcelain factory buildings. Dumping grounds are very important because they contain shards that identify the variety of products made by every porcelain factory. In winter, when snow covered the ground, many products that did not pass inspection were used as filler beneath the factory floorboards. These shards have proven to be the most valuable source of product identification because they remained in place for such a long period of time, perhaps even one hundred years.

Because of the large numbers of doll heads that were made year after year, there were also large numbers of plaster molds that had to be discarded after a certain number of uses. Rather than filling up the dumping grounds with them, porcelain factories offered the molds to their employees to use as inexpensive building material. They were mortared into interior and exterior walls of houses, barns and storage sheds. They remain in plain view as reminders of the years that dolls were made. The plaster molds still in place on the Baehr & Proeschild porcelain factory site have not been damaged by the passing years. It is a joy to walk past a wall of plaster molds and see doll faces staring back at you. But it is even better to hold an antique doll with a bisque head marked with a Baehr & Proeschild mold number, and to marvel at the permanent legacy left by factory workers so long ago.

4. The area behind these factory buildings once contained a large dumping ground filled with bisque doll-head shards. (Photo: Mary Krombholz)

Baehr & Proeschild Porcelain Factory

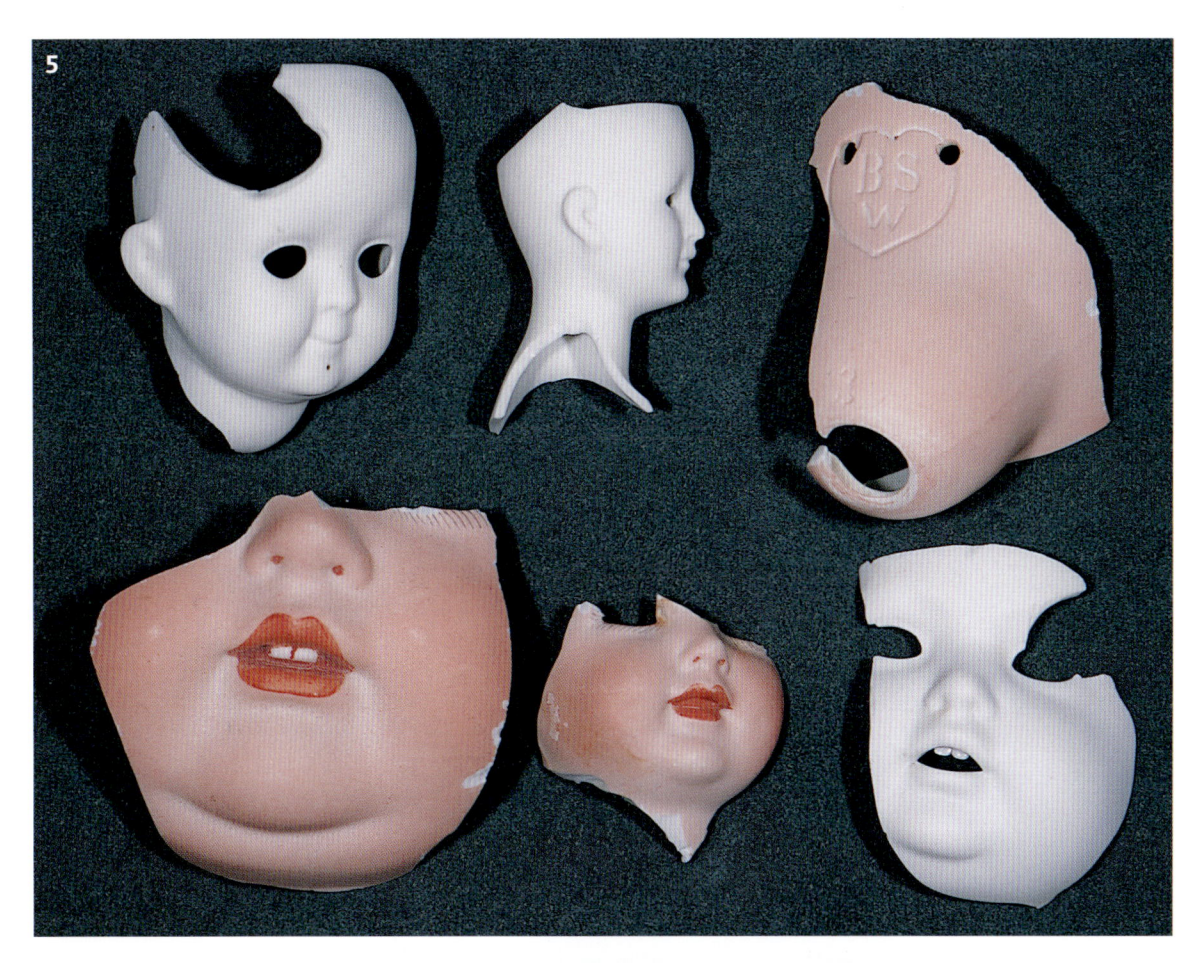

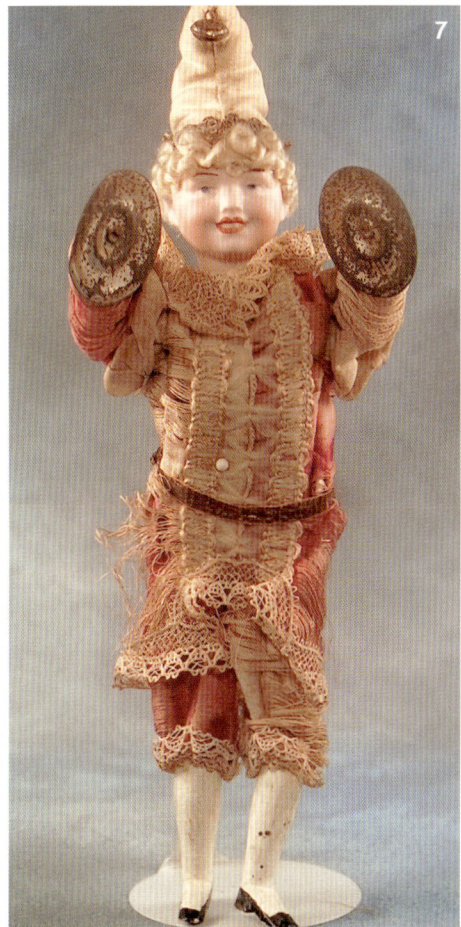

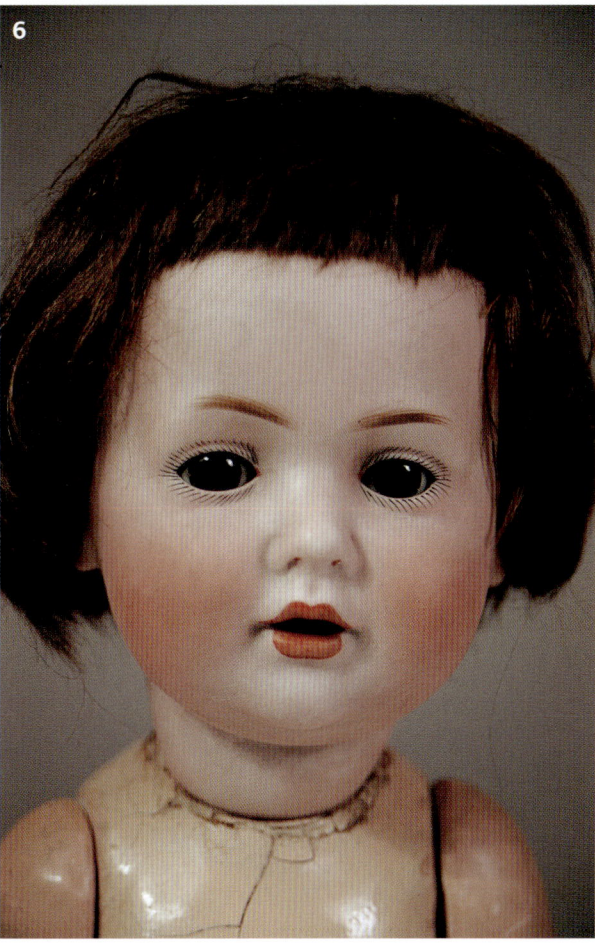

5. These six doll-head shards are a sample of the bisque shards I found on the factory grounds in 1999. The googly shard on the top row is made of thin, finely textured bisque. The large neck shard on the top row is marked with the Bruno Schmidt heart trademark. The "W" under the letters "BS" is for Waltershausen, home of the Bruno Schmidt doll factory. The three head shards on the bottom row illustrate the variety of molded mouths found on Baehr & Proeschild character dolls. Author's Collection. (Photo: Gene Abbott)

6. Bisque socket head by Baehr & Proeschild; wig; multi-stroke eyebrows; painted upper and lower eyelashes; glass sleep eyes; open mouth with upper teeth; 14½-inch doll; marked: **B&P** (with **crossed swords**). Courtesy Deutsches Spielzeugmuseum, Sonneberg. (Photo: Christiane Gräfnitz)

7. Bisque socket head by Baehr & Proeschild for a wood-and-wire Cymbalier body with clapping arms; original wig and clothing; single-stroke eyebrows; painted eyes; open/closed smiling mouth with upper teeth; 10-inch doll; GM 1888; marked **73//225**. The brass cymbals clang when the bellows mechanism in the center of the body is pressed. Beth Karp Collection. (Photo: Lee Krombholz)

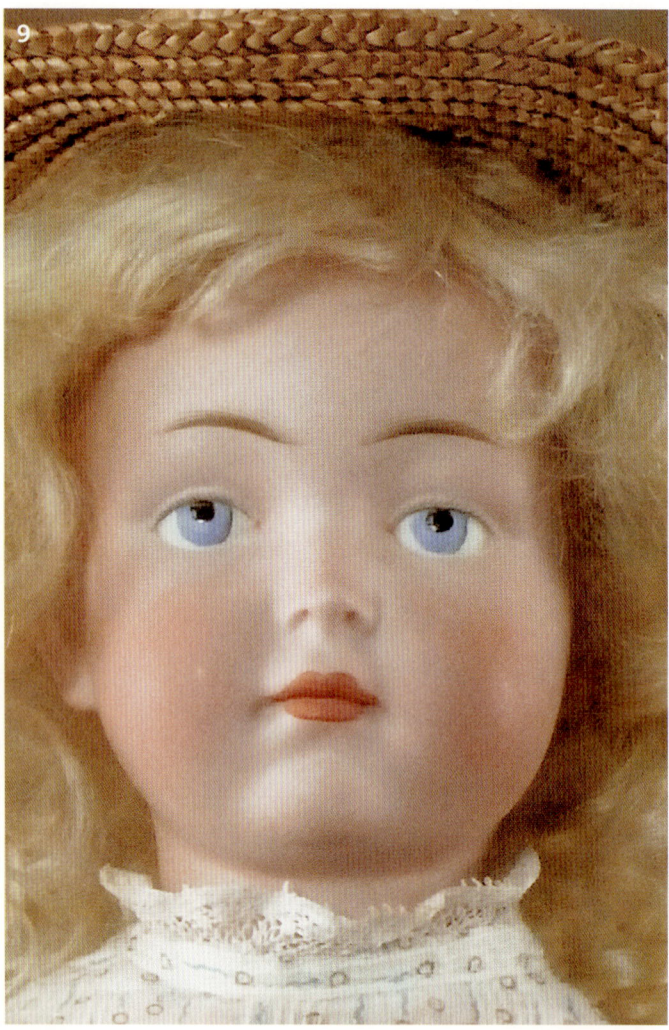

Chapter 5

8. Bisque socket head by Baehr & Proeschild for the Kley & Hahn doll factory; wig; multi-stroke eyebrows; short, closely spaced, painted upper eyelashes; outlined upper eyelid; painted eyes with white highlights; closed smiling mouth, partially outlined upper and lower lips; cheek dimples; 17-inch doll; circa 1910; marked: **K&H//520//4½//Germany**. Beth Karp Collection. (Photo: Lee Krombholz)

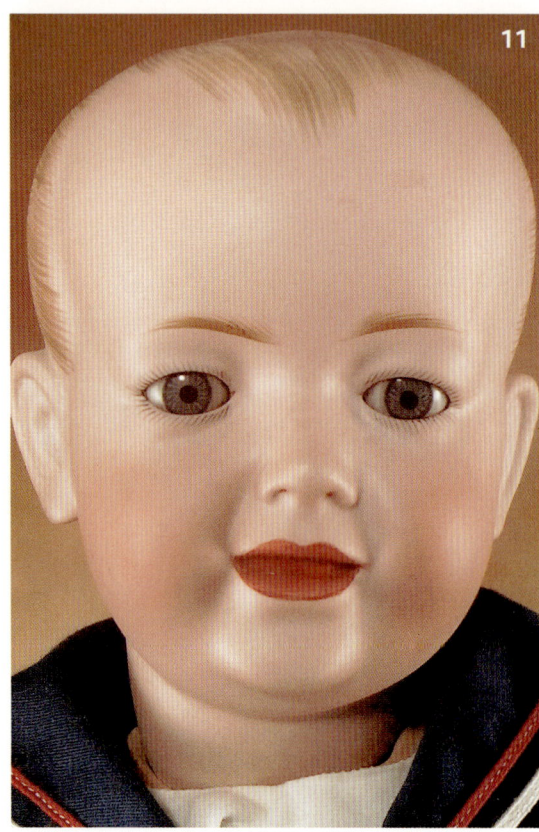

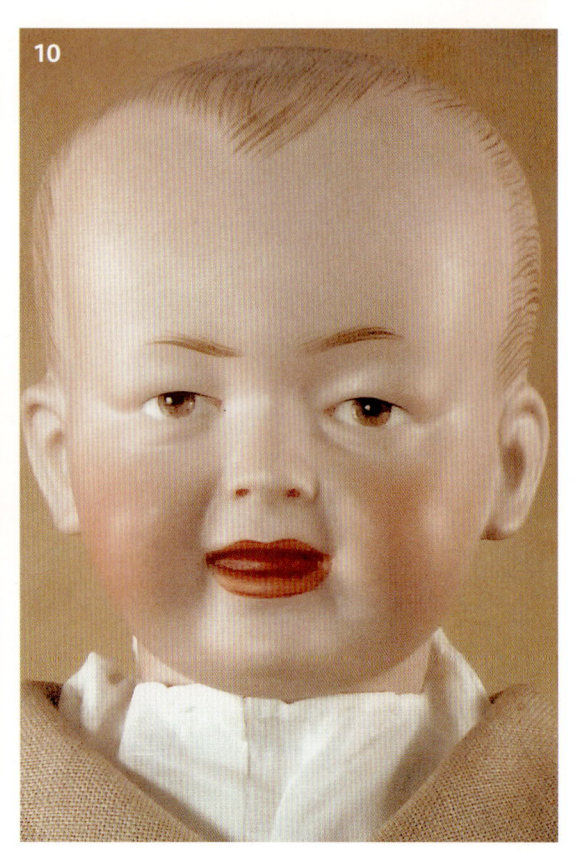

Baehr & Proeschild Porcelain Factory

9. Bisque socket head by Baehr & Proeschild for the Kley & Hahn doll factory; wig; multi-stroke eyebrows; upper eyelids outlined in black; short, closely-spaced upper eyelashes; painted eyes with white highlights; closed mouth; 15-inch doll; circa 1912; marked: **K&H** (inside **banner**)**//526//3½**. Beth Karp Collection. (Photo: Lee Krombholz)

10. Bisque socket head by Baehr & Proeschild for the Kley & Hahn doll factory; molded hair; well-defined eye sockets; multi-stroke eyebrows; painted eyes with white highlights on pupils; open/closed mouth with molded tongue; 14-inch doll; circa 1912; marked: **525**. Beth Karp Collection. (Photo: Lee Krombholz)

11. Bisque socket head by Baehr & Proeschild for the Kley & Hahn doll factory; molded hair; multi-stroke eyebrows; painted upper and lower eyelashes; glass sleep eyes; open/closed mouth with molded tongue; 17-inch doll; circa 1912; marked: **Germany//K&H** (inside **banner**)**//9//525**. Beth Karp Collection. (Photo: Lee Krombholz)

12. Brown bisque Native-American-type socket head by the Baehr & Proeschild porcelain factory in Ohrdurf; wig; original clothing; pierced ears with large hoop earrings; scowling multi-stroke eyebrows; painted upper and lower eyelashes; stationary glass eyes; closed mouth; 12-inch doll; circa 1888; marked: **244//0**. Beth Karp Collection. (Photo: Lee Krombholz)

131

Chapter 5

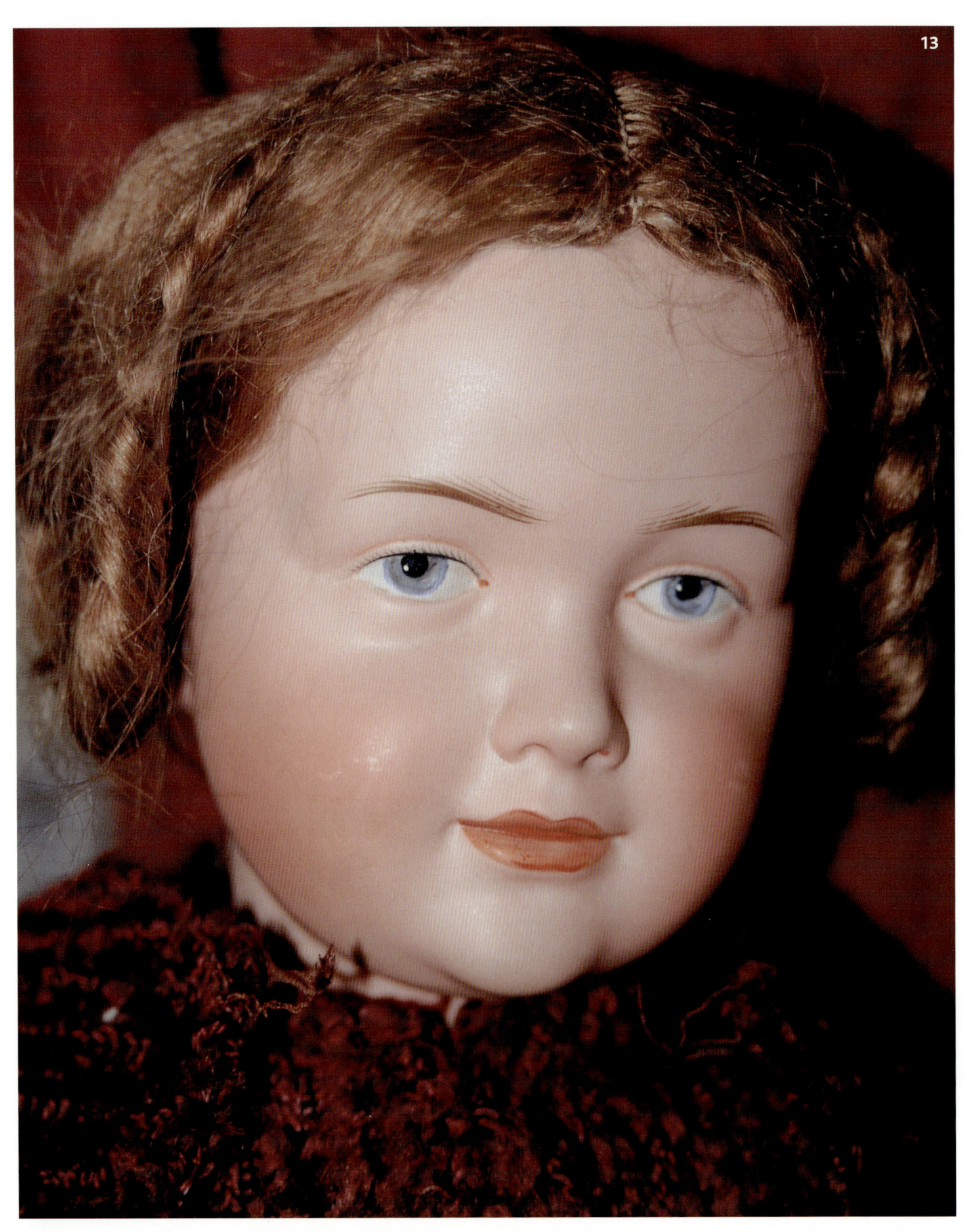

13. Bisque socket head by Baehr & Proeschild for the Kley & Hahn doll factory in Ohrdruf; wig; well-defined eye sockets; multi-stroke eyebrows; short, closely spaced upper eyelashes; painted eyes with white highlights on pupils; closed smiling mouth; 20½-doll; circa 1910; marked: **BSW** (inside **heart**)**//520**. Rothenburg Puppenmusuem/Katharina Engels Collection. (Photo: Christiane Gräfnitz)

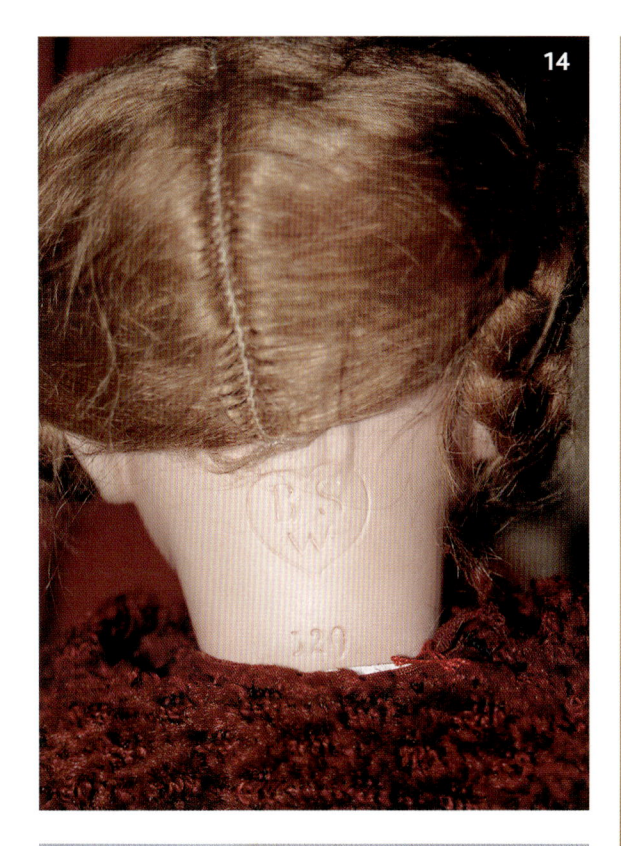

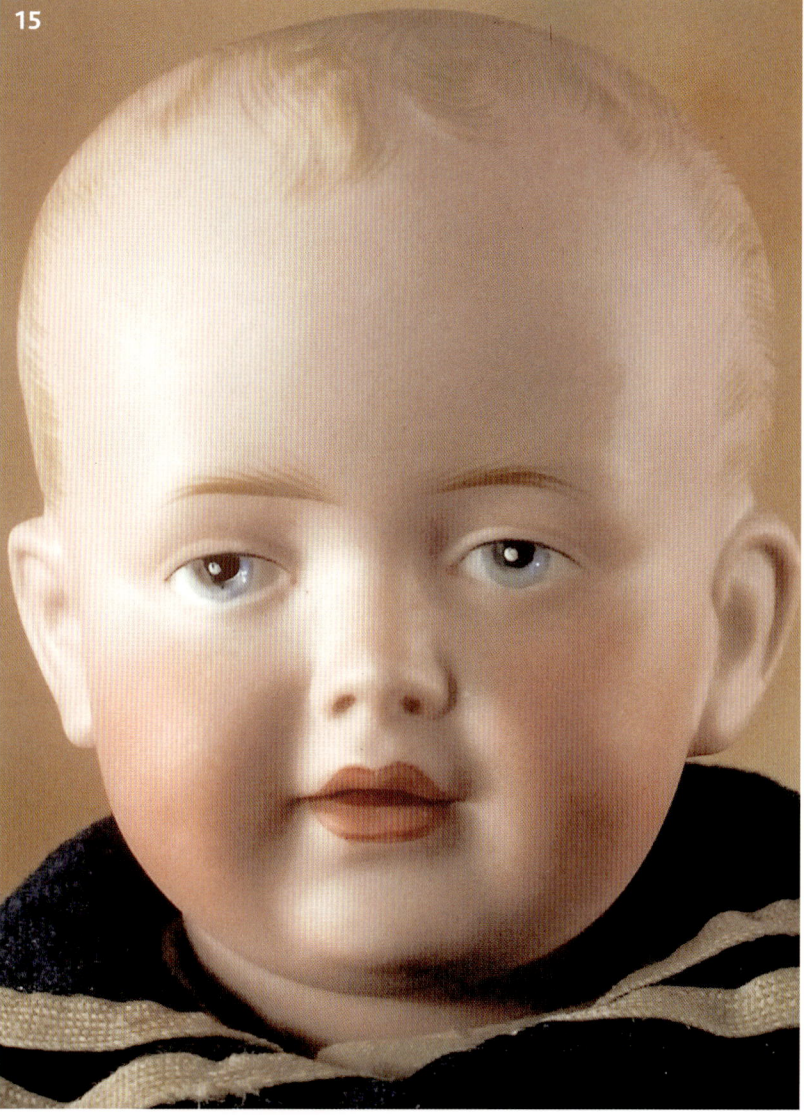

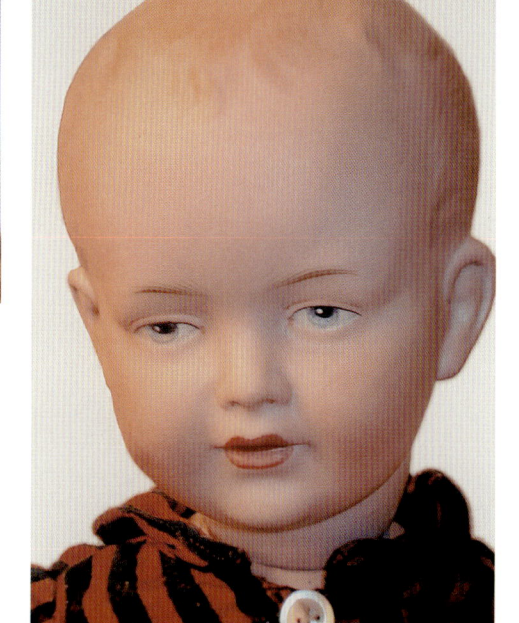

Baehr & Proeschild Porcelain Factory

14. The back of the head shown in illustration 13 bears the Bruno Schmidt trademark heart enclosing the initials "BS" above the initial "W." Rothenburg Puppenmuseum/Katharina Engels Collection. (Photo: Christiane Gräfnitz)

17. Bisque socket head by Baehr & Proeschild; wig; multi-stroke eyebrows; painted upper and lower eyelashes; glass sleep eyes; open/closed mouth; cheek dimples; 9-inch doll; circa 1912; marked **536**. Christiane Gräfnitz Collection. (Photo: Christiane Gräfnitz)

15. Bisque socket head by Baehr & Proeschild for the Kley & Hahn doll factory; molded hair; multi-stroke eyebrows; intaglio-painted eyes with white highlights on pupils; open/closed mouth; 13-inch doll; circa 1912; marked **531//6**. Beth Karp Collection. (Photo: Lee Krombholz)

16. Bisque socket head by Baehr & Proeschild for the Kley & Hahn doll factory; molded hair; well-defined eye sockets; multi-stroke eyebrows; painted eyes with white highlights on pupils; open/closed mouth; 15-inch doll; circa 1912; marked: **531**. Norah Stoner Collection. (Photo: Norah Stoner)

133

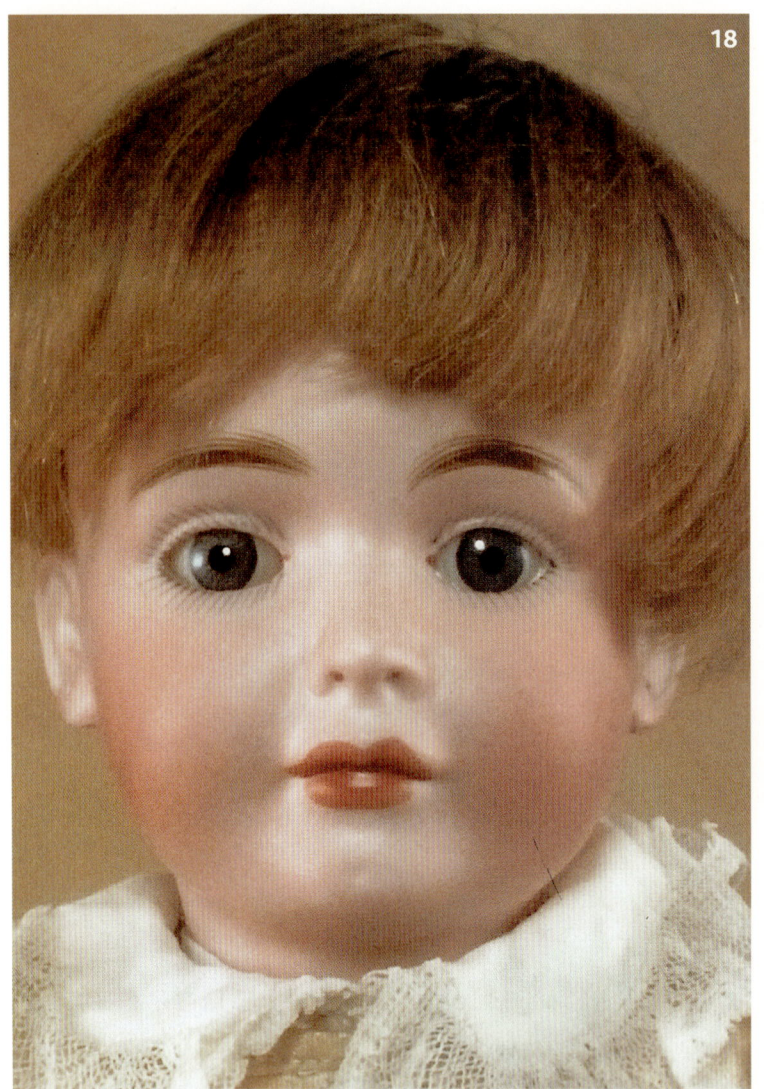

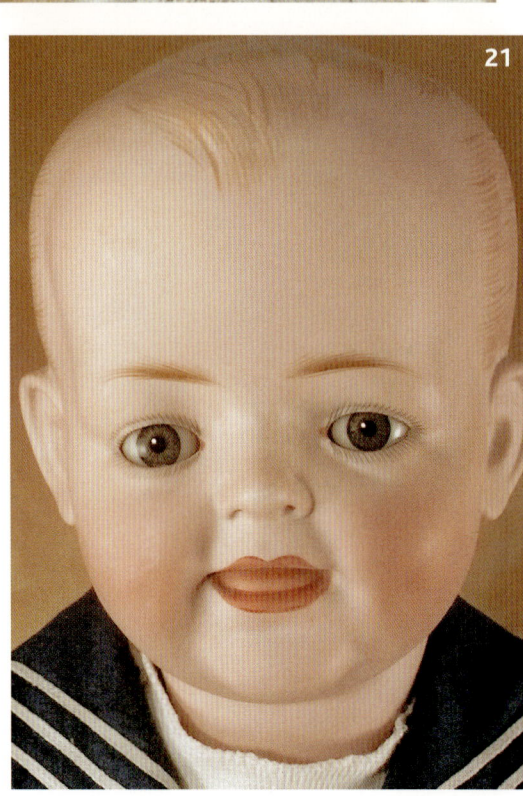

CHAPTER 5

18. Wendy bisque socket head by Baehr & Proeschild for the Bruno Schmidt doll factory; wig; multi-stroke eyebrows; painted upper and lower eyelashes; glass sleep eyes; closed mouth; 13½-inch doll; circa 1912; marked: **2033//BSW** (inside **heart**)**//537**. Beth Karp Collection. (Photo: Lee Krombholz)

134

Baehr & Proeschild Porcelain Factory

19. Wendy bisque socket head by Baehr & Proeschild for the Bruno Schmidt doll factory; wig; multi-stroke eyebrows; painted upper and lower eyelashes; glass sleep eyes; closed mouth; 14½-inch doll; circa 1912; marked: **BSW** (inside **heart**)**//537**. Christa Dorner Collection. (Photo: Christiane Gräfnitz)

20. Bisque socket head by Baehr & Proeschild for the Kley & Hahn doll factory; wig; multi-stroke eyebrows; painted upper and lower eyelashes; glass sleep eyes; closed mouth; 17-inch doll; circa 1912; marked: **K&H** (inside **banner**)**//546//5// Germany**. Beth Karp Collection. (Photo: Lee Krombholz)

21. Bisque socket head by Baehr & Proeschild for the Kley & Hahn doll factory; molded hair; multi-stroke eyebrows; painted upper and lower eyelashes; glass sleep eyes; smiling open/closed mouth with large molded tongue; 22-inch doll; circa 1912; marked: **Germany//K&H** (inside **banner**)**//548**. Beth Karp Collection. (Photo: Lee Krombholz)

22. Bisque socket head by Baehr & Proeschild for the Kley & Hahn doll factory; molded hair; multi-stroke eyebrows; painted upper and lower eyelashes; glass sleep eyes; closed mouth; 15½-inch doll; circa 1912; marked: **K&H** (inside **banner**)**//546//4**. Norah Stoner Collection. (Photo: Norah Stoner)

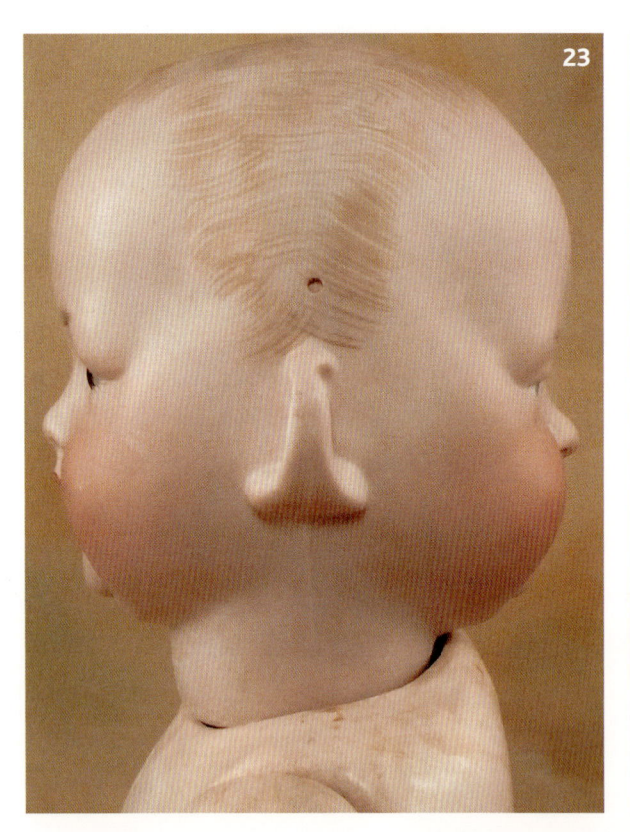

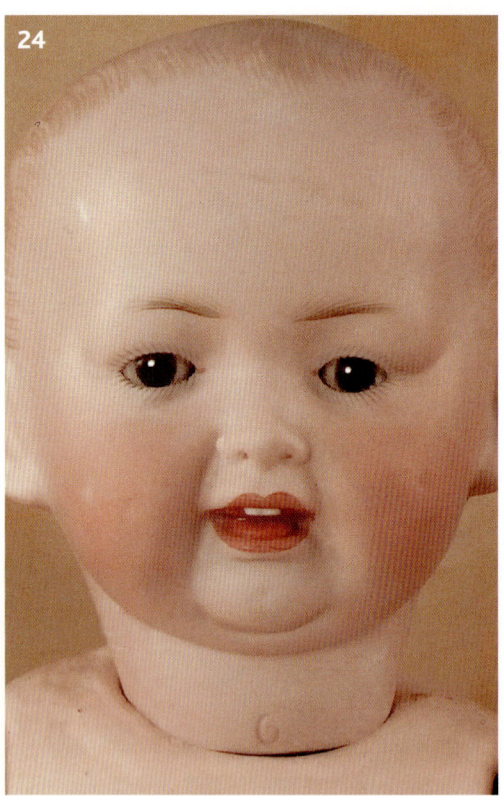

Chapter 5

23. A side view of the laughing/crying two-faced Baehr & Proeschild bisque socket head shows the single ear that is molded to look natural with either face. Beth Karp Collection. (Photo: Lee Krombholz)

24. Laughing face of two-faced Baehr & Proeschild bisque socket head for the Kley & Hahn doll factory; molded hair; multi-stroke eyebrows; painted upper and lower eyelashes; glass sleep eyes; open mouth with upper teeth and molded tongue; 13-inch doll; marked: **6** on front neck of laughing-face side. Beth Karp Collection. (Photo: Lee Krombholz)

26. Bisque socket head by Baehr & Proeschild; molded hair; multi-stroke eyebrows; painted upper and lower eyelashes; glass sleep eyes; open/closed mouth with upper teeth; 10½-inch doll; circa 1914; marked: **582**. Courtesy Historisches Coburger Puppenmuseum/Lossnitzer Collection. (Photo: Christiane Gräfnitz).

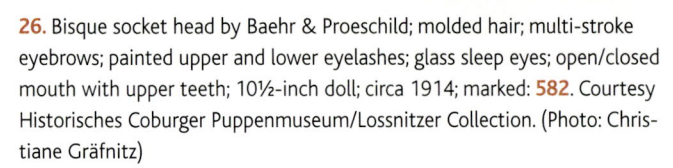

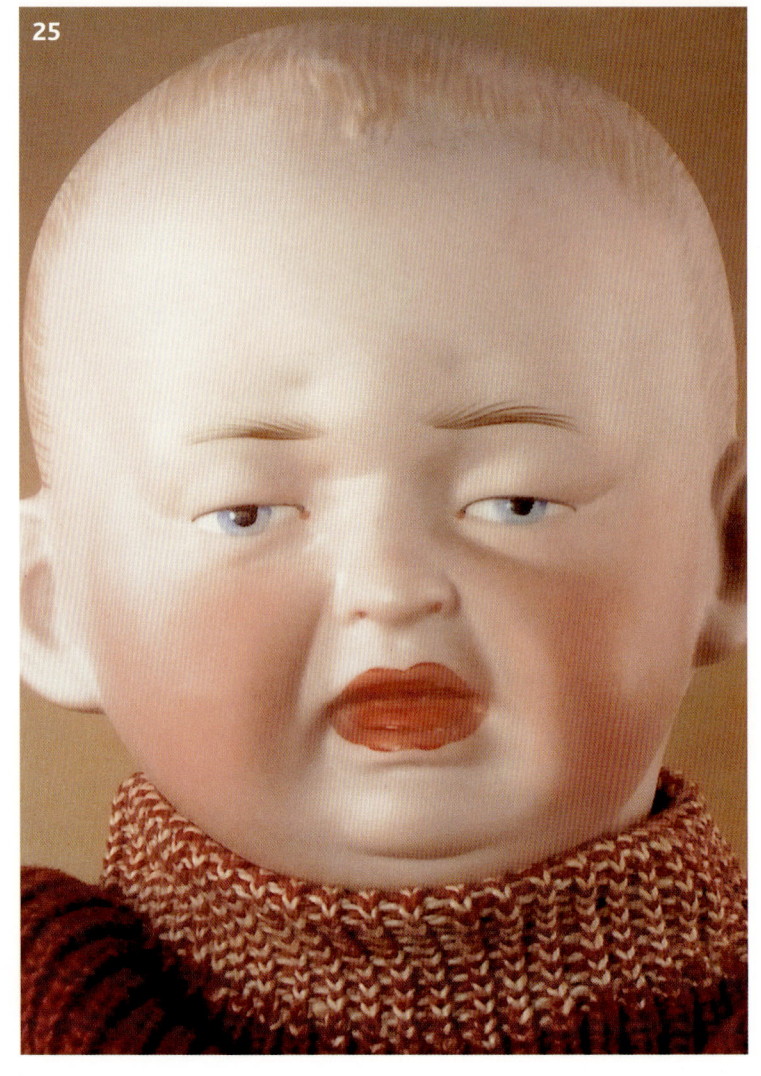

25. Crying face of two-faced bisque socket head by Baehr & Proeschild for the Kley & Hahn doll factory; molded hair; well-defined eye sockets; multi-stroke eyebrows; painted eyes with white highlights on edge of pupils; open/closed mouth with large molded tongue; 13-inch doll; GM 1911; marked: **567** on front neck of crying-face side. Beth Karp Collection. (Photo: Lee Krombholz)

Baehr & Proeschild Porcelain Factory

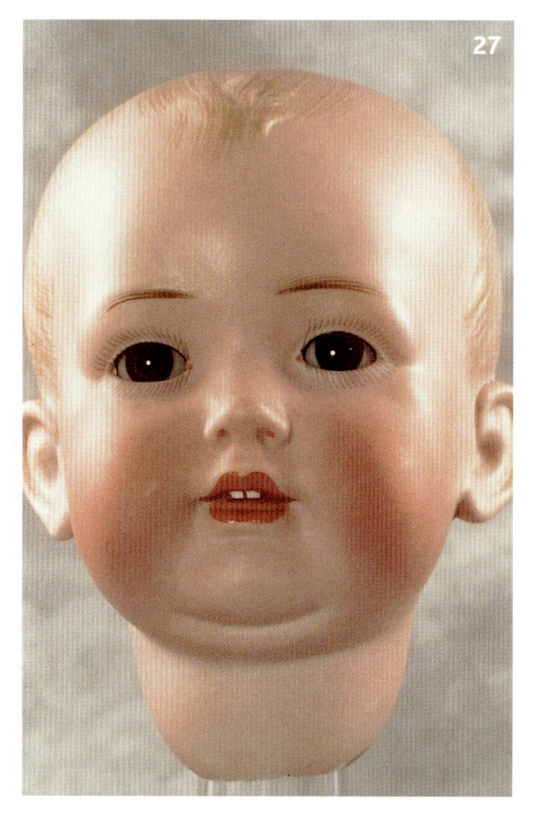

27. Bisque socket head by Baehr & Proeschild; molded hair; multi-stroke eyebrows; painted upper and lower eyelashes; glass sleep eyes; open/closed mouth with upper teeth and tongue; 14-inch doll; circa 1914; marked: **584.8**. Beth Karp Collection. (Photo: Lee Krombholz)

28. Bisque socket head by Baehr & Proeschild; wig; multi-stroke eyebrows; painted upper and lower eyelashes; glass sleep eyes; open/closed mouth with upper teeth; 10-inch doll; circa 1912; marked: **B&P** (with **crossed swords**)**//585//2/0//Germany**. Ann Cummings Collection. (Photo: John Cummings)

29. Bisque socket head by Baehr & Proeschild; wig; multi-stroke eyebrows; painted upper and lower eyelashes; glass sleep eyes; open/closed mouth with upper teeth; 17-inch doll; circa 1920; marked: **604//G**. Kenneth Drew Collection. (Photo: Ann Hanat)

30. Bisque socket head by Baehr & Proeschild; wig; multi-stroke eyebrows; painted upper and lower eyelashes; glass sleep eyes; open/closed mouth with upper teeth; 12-inch doll; circa 1912; marked: **585**. Beth Karp Collection. (Photo: Lee Krombholz)

Chapter 5

31. Bisque socket-head googly by Baehr & Proeschild; wig; single-stroke eyebrows; painted upper and lower eyelashes; large side-glancing eyes; closed smiling mouth; cheek and chin dimples; 8½-inch doll; circa 1914; marked: **BP** (inside **heart**)**//686**. Rothenburg Puppenmuseum/ Katharina Engels Collection. (Photo: Christiane Gräfnitz)

32. The large Bruno Schmidt doll factory is located directly behind the Schmidt home. The Baehr & Proeschild porcelain factory made bisque heads for the Bruno Schmidt doll factory from 1898 on. (Photo: Mary Krombholz)

33. The 1910 Bruno Schmidt home is still standing in Waltershausen. My May 2007 trip to Waltershausen confirmed the restored condition of both the home and factory. The home looks much like it did originally. (Photo: Mary Krombholz)

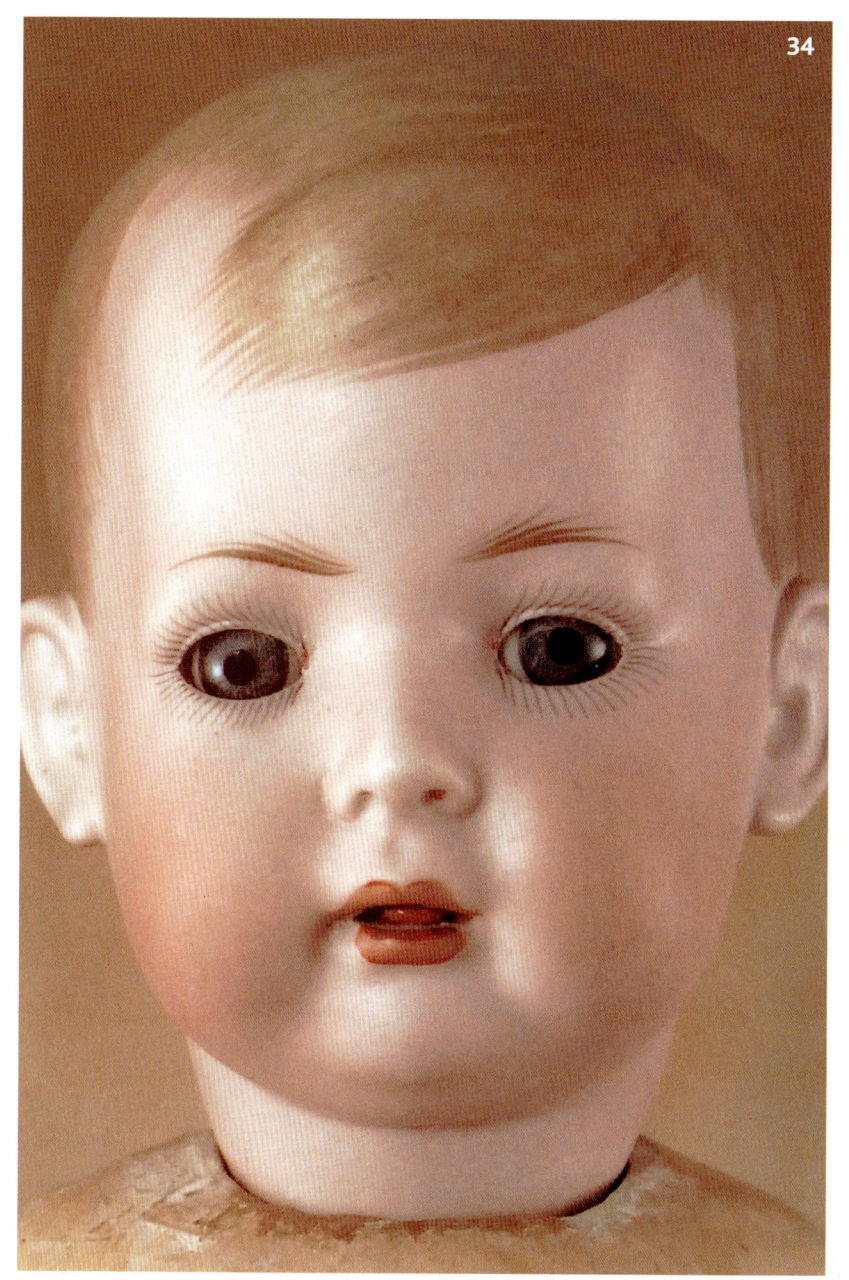

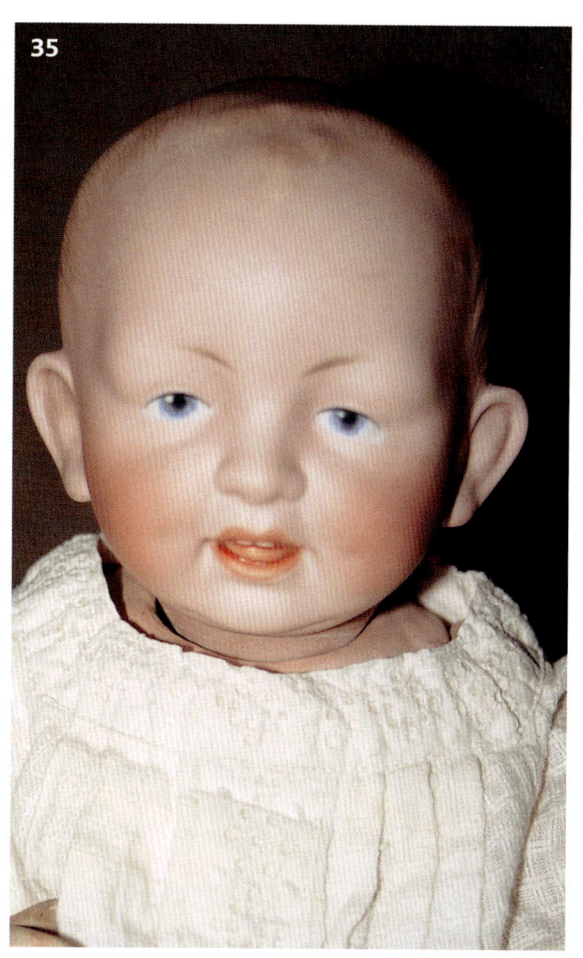

Baehr & Proeschild Porcelain Factory

34. Bisque socket head by Baehr & Proeschild for the Bruno Schmidt doll factory; molded hair; multi-stroke eyebrows; painted upper and lower eyelashes; glass sleep eyes; open mouth with upper teeth and separate tongue; 18-inch doll; circa 1912; marked 2048//4. The original model for the 2048 mold number was a sculpture by the Brussels-born Italian sculptor Francois Duquesnoy, known as Il Fiammingo in Italy. The Ciesliks picture the bronze model for the 2048 mold number on page 266 of their *German Doll Encyclopedia* and describe it as follows: "Bronze model for Herzbaby, trademarked *Mein Goldherz* (My Goldheart), surprisingly similarity to the model head of Käthe Kruse." Below the model is a separate photograph of the mold number 2048 bisque character head with glass eyes, identical to the doll in this photo. If we compare the photographs of the model and doll head, there is no question that the Fiammingo bronze model was the model for Baehr & Proeschild's trademark Heart Baby. Beth Karp Collection. (Photo: Lee Krombholz)

35. Bisque socket head by Baehr & Proeschild for the Bruno Schmidt doll factory; molded hair; multi-stroke eyebrows; painted eyes with white highlights on edge of pupils; open/closed mouth with upper teeth and molded tongue; 11-inch doll; circa 1912; marked: BSW (inside heart)//2046. Courtesy Museum Schloss Tenneberg, Waltershausen. (Photo: Christiane Gräfnitz)

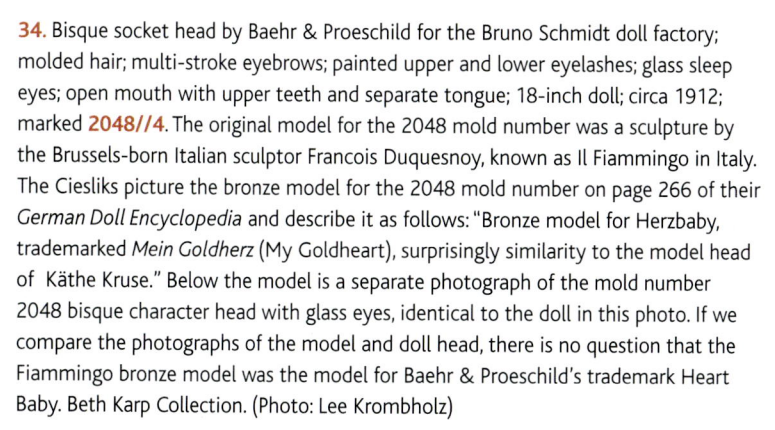

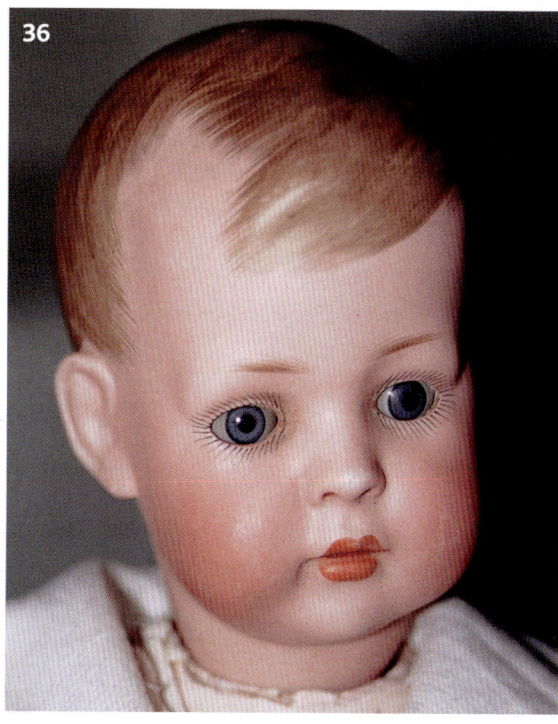

36. Bisque socket head by Baehr & Proeschild for the Bruno Schmidt doll factory; molded hair; multi-stroke eyebrows; painted upper and lower eyelashes; glass sleep eyes; open/closed mouth; 12-inch doll; circa 1912; marked BSW (inside heart)//2048. Rothenberg Puppenmuseum/Katharina Engels Collection. (Photo: Christiane Gräfnitz)

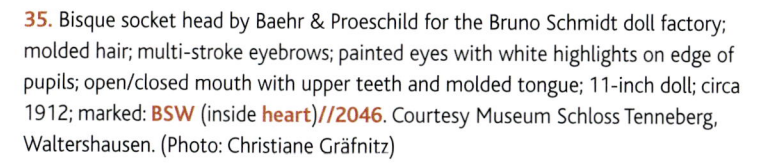

Chapter 5

37. Bisque socket head by Baehr & Proeschild for the Bruno Schmidt doll factory; wig; multi-stroke eyebrows; painted upper and lower eyelashes; glass sleep eyes; closed mouth; 18-inch doll; GM 1927; marked: **BSW** (inside **heart**)//2072. Courtesy Rothenberg Puppenmuseum/Katharina Engels Collection. (Photo: Christiane Gräfnitz)

38. Bisque socket head by Baehr & Proeschild for the Bruno Schmidt doll factory; molded hair; multi-stroke eyebrows; painted upper and lower eyelashes; glass sleep eyes; open mouth with upper teeth and tongue; 24-inch doll; circa 1920; marked: **BSW** (inside **heart**)//2094. Courtesy Rothenberg Puppenmuseum/Katharina Engels Collection. (Photo: Christiane Gräfnitz)

39. The old Adolf Wislizenus home/factory is still standing in Waltershausen today. The large doll factory is located behind the home, through the arched opening. (Photo: Mary Krombholz)

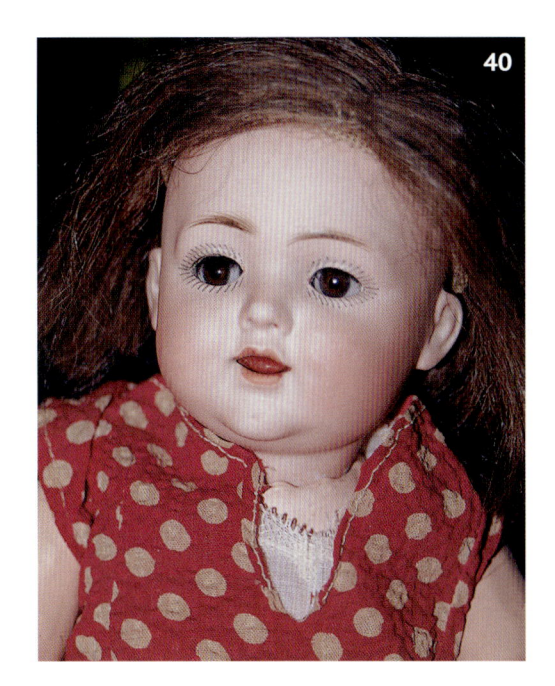

Baehr & Proeschild Porcelain Factory

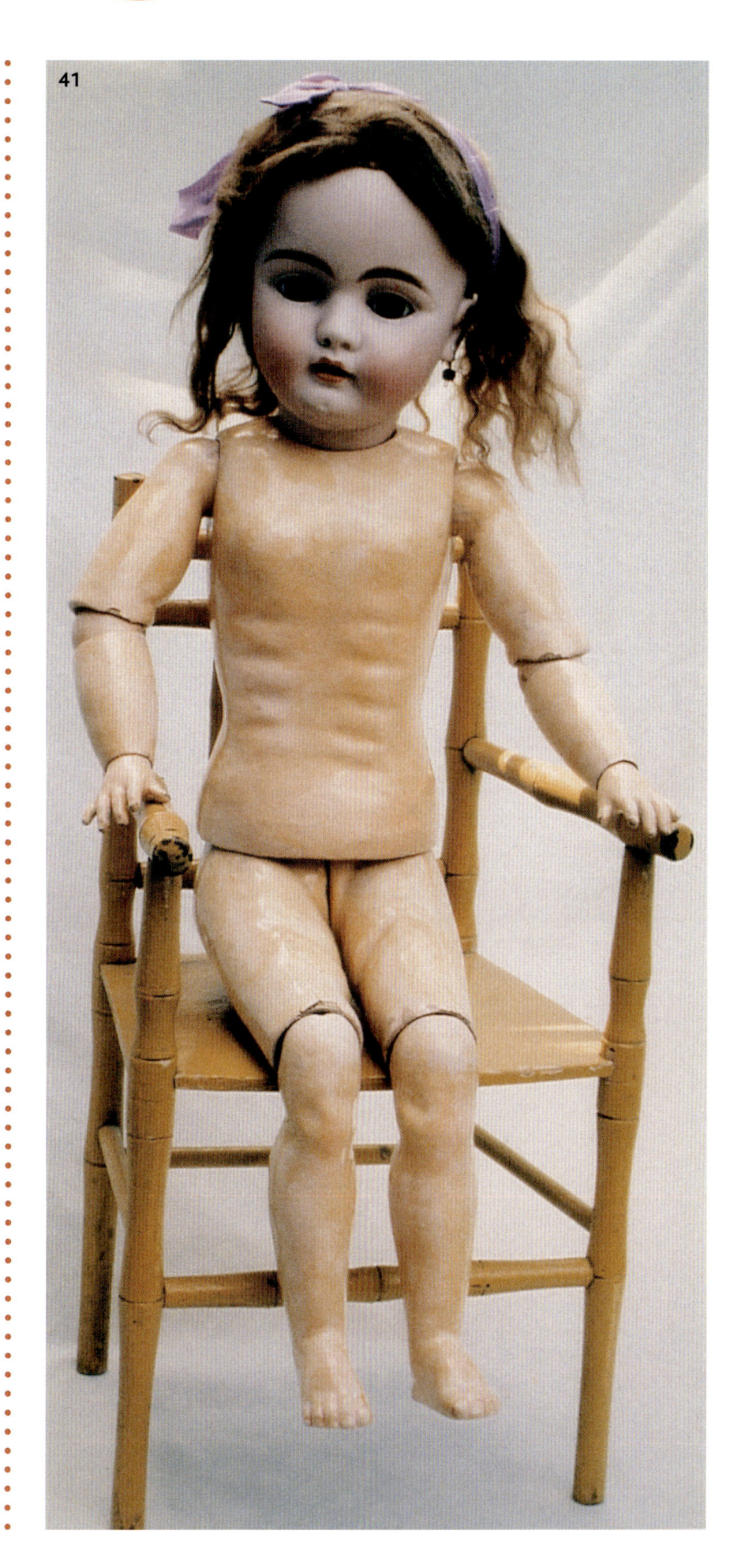

40. Bisque socket head by Baehr & Proeschild for the Bruno Schmidt doll factory; wig; multi-stroke eyebrows; painted upper and lower eyelashes; glass sleep eyes; open mouth with separate tongue; 11½-inch doll; circa 1914; marked: **BP** (inside heart)**//692**. Courtesy Ladenburger Spielzeugauktion/Goetz Seidel. Photo: (Christiane Gräfnitz)

41. This bisque socket head by Baehr & Proeschild is mounted on an unusual, and very realistic, composition-jointed body by the Adolf Wislizenus doll factory. The body has a delineated rib cage and jointed shoulders, elbows, hips and knees. Courtesy Museum Schloss Tenneberg, Waltershausen. (Photo: Christiane Gräfnitz)

42. Bisque dolly-faced socket head by Baehr & Proeschild; wig; multi-stroke eyebrows; painted upper and lower eyelashes; glass sleep eyes; open mouth with upper teeth; 22½-inch doll; circa 1897; marked **394//11**. Courtesy Museum Schloss Tenneberg, Waltershausen. (Photo: Christiane Gräfnitz)

Part One

CHAPTER 6

Hertel, Schwab & Co. Porcelain Factory

The Hertel Schwab & Co. porcelain factory was founded in 1910 by three sculptors, August Hertel, Friedrich Müller and Heinrich Schwab, and a porcelain painter, Hugo Rosenbusch. Only fifteen workers were employed during the founding year, but by 1920 the number had risen to one hundred. The Hertel, Schwab porcelain factory was located in Stutzhaus, a suburb of Ohrdruf. The oldest building on the factory site was used by two other porcelain factories. The Stutzhaus porcelain factory made porcelain products in the oldest Hertel, Schwab building before the Alt, Beck & Gottschalck porcelain factory purchased the factory buildings in 1864. The first letter in the Orhdruf Town Museum archives that bears a Hertel, Schwab & Co. letterhead with the Stutzhaus address is dated 1911. Hertel, Schwab & Co. added a large addition to the factory in 1913-1914, including a very large kiln, which is still inside the building.

The Nauendorf-based Alt, Beck & Gottschalck porcelain factory (See Part One: Chapter 4) made glazed and unglazed porcelain shoulder heads, all-bisque and all-china dolls in the oldest Stutzhaus factory building from 1864 until the factory was sold to the Hertel, Schwab porcelain factory in the late 1890s. An 1895 letter bearing an Alt, Beck & Gottschalk letterhead and the Stutzhaus address was found in the Ohrdruf Town Museum archives by Peter Cramer, curator of the Ohrdruf Town Museum, proving that Alt, Beck & Gottschalck was making porcelain products at the Stutzhaus factory in 1895. Many shards were recently found in this building to prove the production of 1860s and 1870s chinas and parians by Alt, Beck & Gottschalck.

Some bisque character heads, the circa-1912 mold numbers 150, 151 and 152, made by the Hertel, Schwab porcelain factory were formerly attributed to the Kestner porcelain factory.

In the 1980s, when they published the *German Doll Encyclopedia*, Jürgen and Marianne Cieslik corrected the research that had been commonly accepted by doll collectors worldwide, stating that after careful research and study of old catalogs, they had come to the conclusion "these mold numbers were exclusively produced by Hertel, Schwab & Co." Bisque character babies were the first products of the Hertel, Schwab porcelain factory. The difference in appearance between Kestner character babies and those made by Hertel, Schwab centers on two features, the eyebrow painting and the color of the glass eyes. Hertel, Schwab character babies have very unusual painted eyebrows that are unlike the eyebrows of bisque character dolls made by any other Thuringian porcelain factory. The "wavy" eyebrows are painted to indicate a surprised expression. Hertel, Schwab glass eyes are often a very unusual shade of blue.

The Kley & Hahn doll factory in Ohrdruf was one of the main customers of the Hertel Schwab & Co. porcelain factory, which also made bisque character heads for the Koenig & Wernicke doll factory in Waltershausen, the Rudolph Walch doll factory near Frankfurt, the Albert Schachne doll factory in Nuremberg and the Wiesenthal, Schindel & Kallenberg doll factory in Waltershausen. In addition, the factory made a large number of doll heads for American department and toy stores. Included in the list of dolls exported to the United States are the Bye-Lo Baby for Geo. Borgfeldt & Co.; Our Baby (mold #152) and Our Fairy (mold #222) for Louis Wolf and the Jubilee Doll mold number series 163, 165, 172 and 173 with googly eyes for the Strobel & Wilken importing company with offices in Cincinnati and New York. All of these importers listed branch offices in Sonneberg and bought directly from the porcelain factories. Pricing was highly competitive.

Archival photographs in the Ohrdruf Town Museum show

1. The Hertel, Schwab & Co. porcelain factory in Stutzhaus, near Ohrdruf, is pictured in this 1914 photograph, which has been hand colored. The large letters on the side of the building spell out the name: "Porzellanfabrik Hertel, Schwab & Co." (Photo: Courtesy Heimatmuseum Schloss Ehrenburg, Ohrdruf)

artists in the Hertel, Schwab & Co. porcelain factory in a painting room. It is possible to form a mental picture of the work done by artists in this porcelain factory by studying the old photographs in the Ohrdruf Town Museum archives. The text in Clara L. Mateaux's 1898 book *Wonderland of Work* describes the process of painting doll heads.

> Let us go to the dolls' painting room and watch their cheeks grow rosy, and their lips and eyebrows appear. This is a nice cool, comfortable room with a long table running along its side, and busy people waiting to receive their batch of new doll heads, which will pass round from hand to hand, each worker doing his or her own particular share of perfecting them, according to the rule observed in all this German Toyland, as in their other industries.
>
> The first doll's head being handed to worker number one, he will, with a stroke and a flourish, leave two little bowed cherry-colored lips, and then he pops it down on the other side ready for his neighbor to catch up and decorate the eyebrows and eye outlines. Thus the heads proceed on their way, growing prettier at every step, until at last they are set down with blushing cheeks and pink-lined nostrils.

In 2004 my friend, fellow antique-doll researcher Christiane Gräfnitz, traveled to Stutzhaus to take photographs of the Hertel, Schwab & Co. porcelain factory for me. The owner of property gave her some doll-head shards and molds, which she shared with me. One of the most interesting plaster molds found on the property is of a character doll that resembles the dolls American collectors refer to as the Campbell Kids. They were designed by Grace G. Drayton, an American artist responsible for the original Campbell Kid sketches.

The artist was born Viola Grace Gebbie in the small town of Darby, Pennsylvania, near Philadelphia, on October 14, 1877. Her father owned the successful art-book publishing house Gebbie and Company. As a child, Drayton drew many versions of her own image, which she named "funny babies." She continued to draw her round "roly-polys" into adulthood, and later said: "When I thought of a career, I found I had one in just keeping alive these youngsters I had created in and from my own childhood."

Drayton was married twice, first for eleven years to Theodore E. Widerseim, a salesman for Ketterlinus Lithographers and then to W. Heyward Drayton III, a wealthy and socially prominent man who encouraged her artistic talents. She died on January 31, 1936, at the age of fifty-eight.

Diane M. Goff and Margaret Dowling wrote about Drayton's life for the 1988 Spring issue of *Doll News*, in an article titled "The Life and Art of Grace G. Drayton." They explained: "As Mrs. Drayton (1911 to 1923), Grace continued

Chapter 6

2. This 2005 photograph of the factory buildings once occupied by the Hertel, Schwab porcelain factory shows that part of the building pictured in illustration 1 has been recently restored. (Photo: Courtesy Heitmatmuseum Schloss Ehrenburg, Ohrdruf)

to draw for postcards, books, prints, magazine covers and illustrations, comics and embroidery pieces. She also designed Dolly Dingle paper dolls, composition dolls and cloth dolls." Drayton began her twenty-year relationship with the Campbell Soup Company in 1904. In 1914, George Borgfeldt & Co. introduced the Drayton-designed all-bisque doll named September Morn.

The American importer Strobel & Wilken distributed many examples of the Campbell Kids in doll form. One group was made by the Hertel, Schwab & Co. porcelain factory especially for the fiftieth anniversary of the Strobel & Wilken company in 1914. The company had been founded in 1864 in Cincinnati, Ohio, and opened a branch office in New York City in 1886. The anniversary celebration prompted the production of a special series of Jubilee googly dolls. A two-faced bisque character head pictured in illustrations 45, 46 and 47 is marked with the mold number 168 and the size number 4. A socket-head Campbell Kid that looks like one side of the two-faced doll (which, as a single head, is usually marked with the mold number 163) is pictured in illustration 43. The matching Campbell Kid googly mold found on the grounds of the Hertel, Schwab factory site is pictured in illustration 41.

A Hertel, Schwab & Co. bisque-head character doll is a good representation of Drayton's talents. Thuringian porcelain factory modelers often used American magazine and advertising illustrations for ideas for creating new lines of dolls. Many doll researchers believe that Grace Drayton's images provided the inspiration for googly dolls made by a number of Thuringian porcelain factories. The appealing image of a child with round googly-type eyes, expressive eyebrows, a pug nose and chubby cheeks is a lasting legacy from this American artist.

The Ohrdruf porcelain factories Baehr & Proeschild and Kestner & Co. also made bisque character heads for Kley & Hahn. The bisque heads made for Kley & Hahn by these factories differ in styling details and are easily identified. The Baehr & Proeschild porcelain factory made the 500 mold number series; the Hertel, Schwab & Co. porcelain factory made the 100 mold number series; and the Kestner & Co. porcelain factory made the 200 mold number series. (The Kestner Kley & Hahns are shown in Part One: Chapter 7 and the Baehr & Proeschild Kley & Hahns are shown in Part One: Chapter 5). The Kley & Hahn doll factory assembled and sold dolls primarily for the United States market. The factory sold character dolls in all price ranges from 1911 on and continued to sell dolly-faced dolls until closing down in the late 1930s.

The earliest Kley & Hahn character dolls were made by Hertel, Schwab. The 158 mold number was introduced in 1911 and the 160 mold number was introduced in 1912. The Hertel, Schwab number 100 series often featured large molded ears. A very unusual two-faced Kley & Hahn character baby, with a bisque head by the Hertel, Schwab porcelain factory, bears the 159 mold number. The doll has expressive crying and laughing faces. The laughing face is reflected in a showcase mirror in the Waltershausen Doll Museum. The unusual sculpting of the double ears allows each face to have the same ear shape.

The Kley & Hahn doll factory was founded in 1902 by Albert Kley and Paul Hahn. In 1922 founder Albert Kley died and Paul Hahn became the sole owner. In 1924 Kley & Hahn had a booth at the Leipzig Fair. A January 1927 advertisement in *Playthings* magazine provides important information about the factory's products during this time period. The advertisement reads: "Manufacturers of Jointed Dolls and Character Babies dressed and undressed in all qualities from the cheapest to the first quality, also all parts for repairing dolls." The trademarks listed include: *Walküre*, *Schneewittchen* (Snow White) and *Meine Einzige* (My Only One). The address for their Leipzig Fair booth is: "Messhaus Union Fourth Floor, Room 591." In 1930 the Kley & Hahn doll factory advertised porcelain dolls, bisque heads, body parts and Nanking dolls.

The large Kley & Hahn doll factory is still standing on the outskirts of Ohrdruf today. The large letters that spell out the word *Puppenfabrik* are barely visible behind the trees on the side of the factory that faces the railroad track. The large factory building has been converted into apartments. When I visited the site in May 2007, a woman was looking out of her upstairs window. She was probably wondering why anyone would be

Hertel, Schwab & Co. Porcelain Factory

taking photographs of the building. The records of the factory that are preserved in the Ohrdruf Town Museum provide important glimpses into the past. A hand-colored illustration of the first factory workers is pictured in this chapter.

The Hertel, Schwab porcelain factory concentrated on exports, especially to the United States. Factory representatives succeeded in establishing business relationships with large New York importers like Geo. Borgfeldt & Co., who ordered Bye-Lo Babies; Strobel & Wilken, who ordered the Jubilee googly series and Louis Wolf who ordered the popular number 152 bisque character heads. Hertel, Schwab resumed bisque character-head production after World War I, with the help of Geo. Borgfeldt & Co., which became a shareholder in the porcelain factory in 1918 and continued to be a shareholder until 1928. The factory advertised the following products in 1930: "Bisque doll heads, including babies; shoulder heads to be used on Nanking cloth bodies; pin cushion dolls and all-bisque dolls."

The year of the closing of the Hertel, Schwab porcelain factory is difficult to determine. Even the current owner of the property, Wolfgang Ortlepp, has not been able to find a specific answer in his records, and can only confirm that the porcelain factory had been closed sometime prior to his grandfather's purchase of the buildings in 1937.

3. The storage building in front of the porcelain factory is constructed of old plaster molds and wooden timbers. Alt, Beck & Gottschalck made doll-related porcelain products on this site from 1864 until the late 1890s, when the factory was sold to Hertel Schwab & Co. (Photo: Christiane Gräfnitz)

4. This 1914 photograph, which has been hand colored, shows one hundred and three men and women workers in front of the Hertel, Schwab addition to the Alt, Beck & Gottschalck porcelain factory. In June 1999 I met the great-granddaughters of founder Hugo Rosenbusch in Ohrdruf, who let me photograph their framed photograph of the factory. They identified their great-grandfather as the gentleman dressed in a dark suit sitting on the left side of the front row of this original factory photograph. (Photo: Mary Krombholz)

Chapter 6

5. This is the 1914 Hertel, Schwab addition to the old Alt, Beck & Gottschalck factory building. (Photo: Christiane Gräfnitz)

6. Three male factory workers are painting bisque heads inside the Hertel, Schwab porcelain factory in this 1915 original photograph, which has been hand colored. The long worktable is next to a group of windows that provide natural light for the detailed artwork. (Photo: Courtesy Heitmatmuseum Schloss Ehrenburg, Ohrdruf)

7. Factory owner August Hertel is standing behind a large desk in the left foreground of this hand-colored 1915 photograph, which pictures the business office in the Hertel, Schwab porcelain factory. (Photo: Courtesy Heitmatmuseum Schloss Ehrenburg, Ohrdruf)

8. In this 1915 hand-colored photograph, four female factory workers on the left are painting doll-body parts in a workroom inside the Hertel, Schwab factory. Composition body parts fill the shallow wooden trays at each worktable. The male worker on the right is painting bisque heads. Unpainted bisque doll heads are lined up on wooden trays, and also fill the large wooden box on the floor. (Photo: Courtesy Heitmatmuseum Schloss Ehrenburg, Ohrdruf)

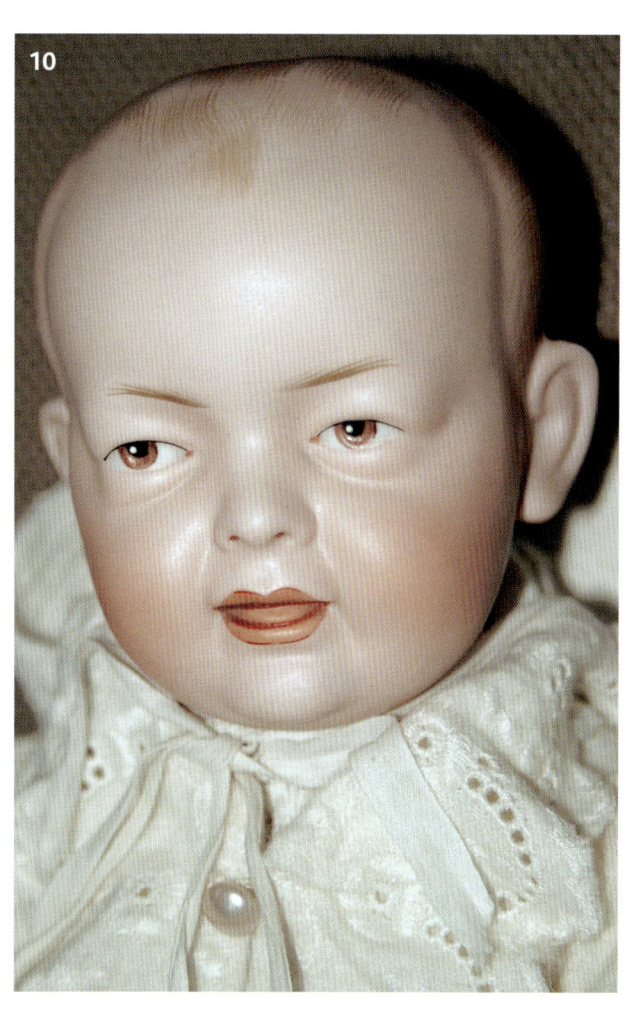

Hertel, Schwab & Co. Porcelain Factory

9. Bisque socket head by Hertel, Schwab for the Kley & Hahn doll factory in Ohrdruf; molded hair; wavy multi-stroke eyebrows; painted eyes; open/closed mouth with realistic molded tongue; 12-inch doll; circa 1912; marked: **Germany//K&H//138**. Courtesy Museum Schloss Tenneberg, Waltershausen. (Photo: Christiane Gräfnitz)

10. A closer view of the doll head seen in illustration 9 shows one well-sculpted ear, defined eye sockets and expressive painted eyes with white highlights on pupils. Courtesy Museum Schloss Tenneberg, Waltershausen. (Photo: Christiane Gräfnitz)

12. Bisque socket head by Hertel, Schwab; wig; wavy multi-stroke eyebrows; black outline of upper eyelids; painted eyes with white highlights on the pupils; slightly-parted mouth; 14-inch doll; circa 1912; marked: **140**. Courtesy Rosalie Whyel Museum of Doll Art. (Photo: Jill Gorman)

11. Bisque socket head by Hertel, Schwab; wig; wavy multi-stroke eyebrows; painted eyes with white highlights on pupils; slightly parted mouth; 16-inch doll; circa 1912; marked: **140//3**. Beth Karp Collection. (Photo: Gregg Smith)

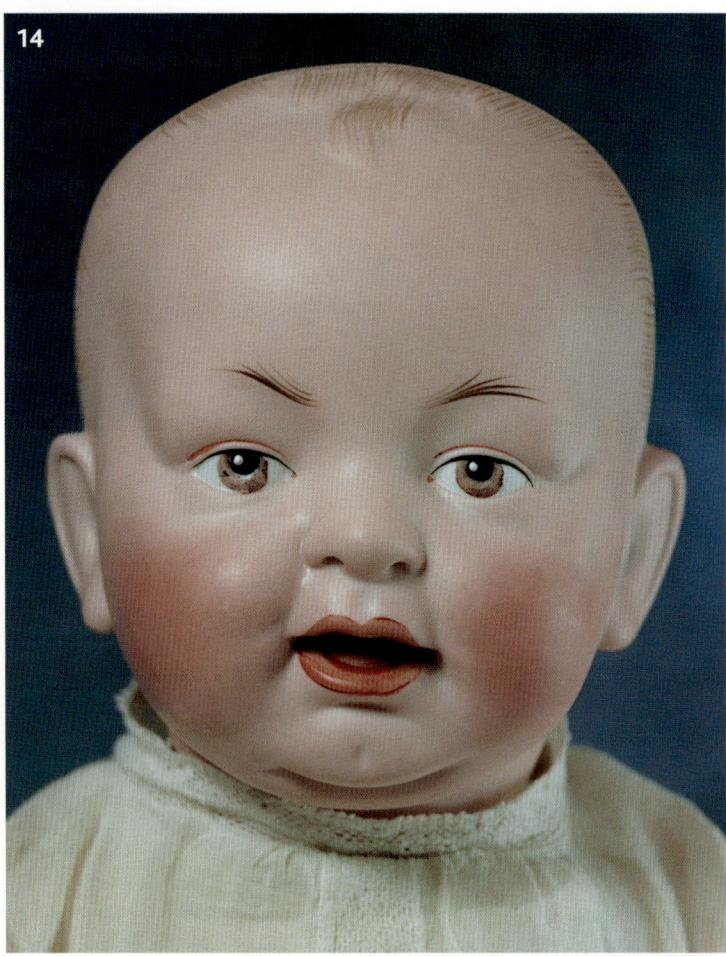

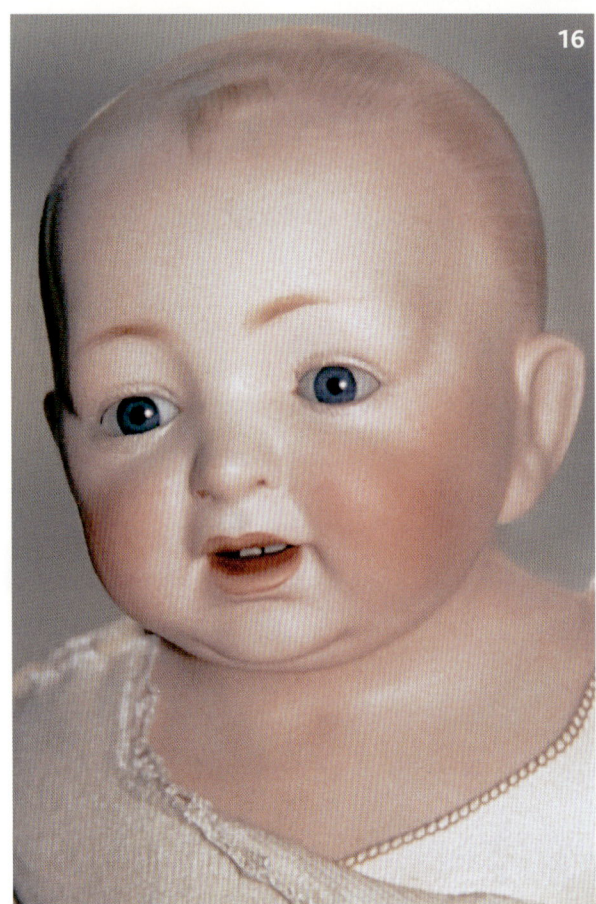

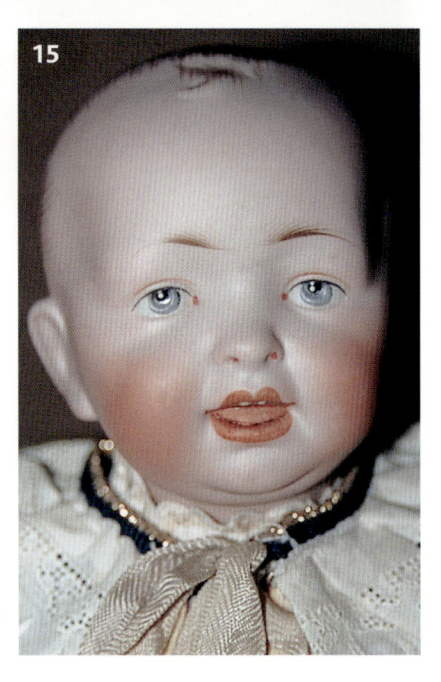

Chapter 6

13. Bisque socket head by Hertel, Schwab; wig; wavy multi-stroke eyebrows; painted upper and lower eyelashes; glass sleep eyes; open/closed mouth with molded tongue; 13-inch doll; circa 1912; marked: **141//0**. Beth Karp Collection. (Photo: Lee Krombholz)

14. Bisque socket head by Hertel, Schwab; molded hair; wavy multi-stroke eyebrows; painted eyes with white highlights on pupils; open/closed mouth with molded tongue; chin dimple; 14-inch doll; circa 1912; marked: **142//7**. Beth Karp Collection. (Photo: Gregg Smith)

16. Bisque shoulder head by Hertel, Schwab; molded hair; multi-stroke eyebrows; painted upper and lower eyelashes; glass sleep eyes; open mouth with upper teeth and molded tongue; 14-inch doll; circa 1912; marked: **142**. Courtesy Rothenburg Puppenmuseum// Katharina Engels. (Photo: Christiane Gräfnitz)

15. Bisque socket head by Hertel, Schwab; molded hair; wavy multi-stroke eyebrows; painted eyes with white highlights on pupils; open/closed mouth with upper teeth and large molded tongue; 12½-inch doll; circa 1912; marked: **142**. Courtesy Museum Schloss Tenneberg, Waltershausen. (Photo: Christiane Gräfnitz)

Hertel, Schwab & Co. Porcelain Factory

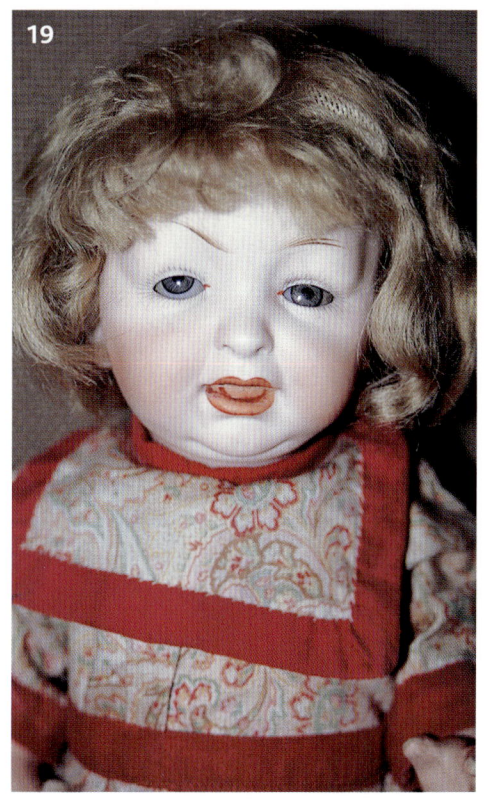

17. Bisque socket head by Hertel, Schwab; wig; wavy, multi-stroke eyebrows; painted upper and lower eyelashes; glass sleep eyes; open/closed mouth with molded tongue; 14½-inch doll; circa 1912; marked: **150//5**. Kenneth Drew Collection. (Photo: Ann Hanat)

18. Bisque socket head by Hertel, Schwab for the Wiesenthal, Schindel & Kallenberg doll factory; wig; multi-stroke eyebrows; painted upper and lower eyelashes; glass sleep eyes; open/closed mouth with upper teeth and molded tongue; 16-inch doll; circa 1912; marked: **150//4**. Courtesy Museum Schloss Tenneberg, Waltershausen. (Photo: Christiane Gräfnitz)

19. Bisque socket head by Hertel, Schwab for the Wiesenthal, Schindel & Kallenberg doll factory in Waltershausen; wig; wavy multi-stroke eyebrows; painted upper and lower eyelashes; glass sleep eyes; open/closed mouth with molded tongue; 17-inch doll; circa 1912; marked: **150**. Courtesy Museum Schloss Tenneberg, Waltershausen. (Photo: Christiane Gräfnitz)

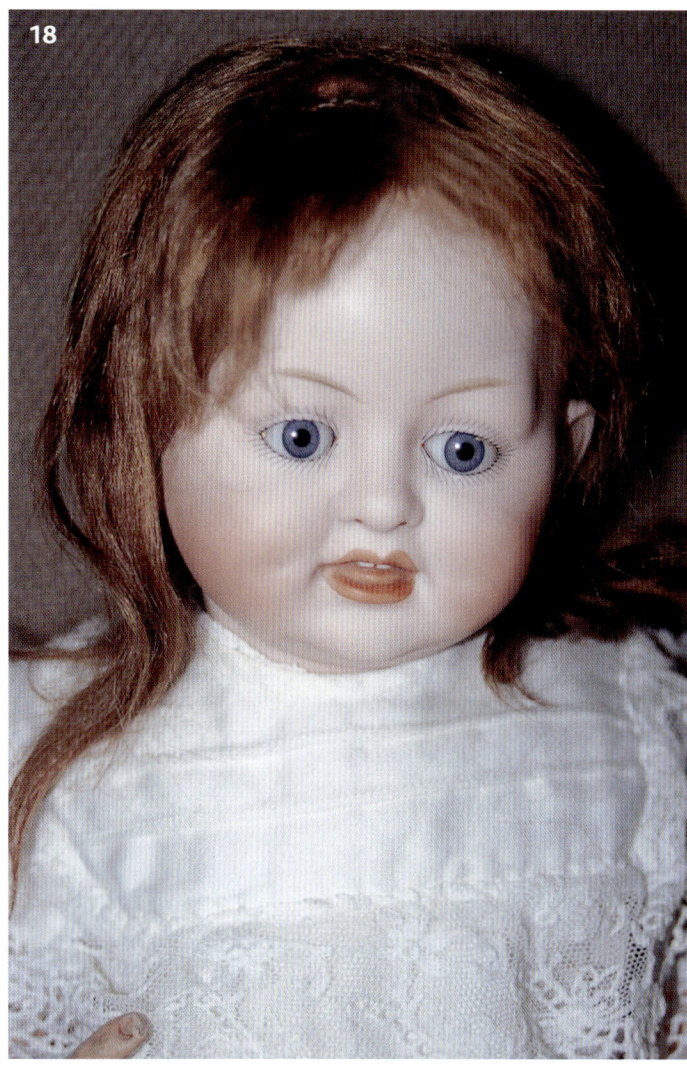

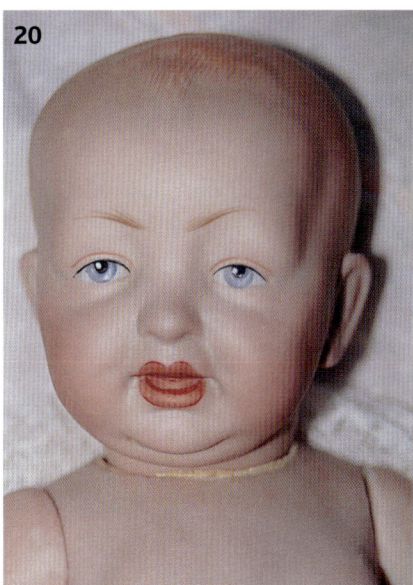

20. All-bisque baby by Hertel, Schwab; molded hair; wavy multi-stroke eyebrows; black outline of upper eyelids; painted eyes with white highlights on pupils; open/closed mouth with molded tongue; 11½-inch doll; unmarked. Roswitha Lucke. (Photo: Christiane Gräfnitz)

Chapter 6

21. Bisque socket head by Hertel, Schwab; molded hair; multi-stroke eyebrows; painted upper and lower eyelashes; glass sleep eyes; open/closed mouth with upper teeth and molded tongue; 26-inch doll; circa 1912; marked: **151/4**. Kenneth Drew Collection. (Photo: Ann Hanat)

23. Bisque socket head by Hertel, Schwab; wig; multi-stroke eyebrows; painted upper and lower eyelashes; glass sleep eyes; open mouth with upper teeth and separate tongue; 15-inch doll; circa 1912; marked: **152//6**. Ann Cummings Collection. (Photo: John Cummings)

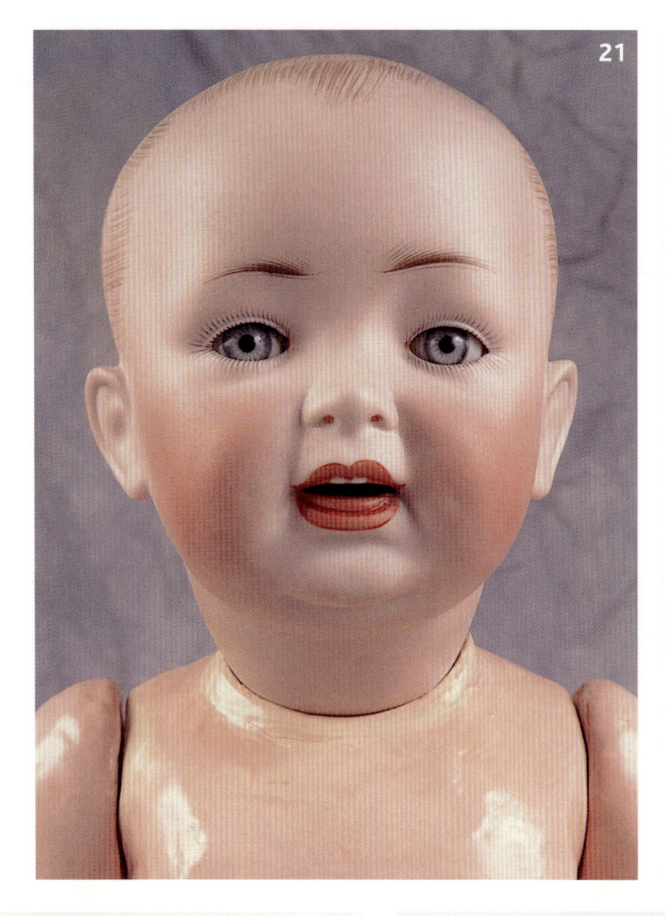

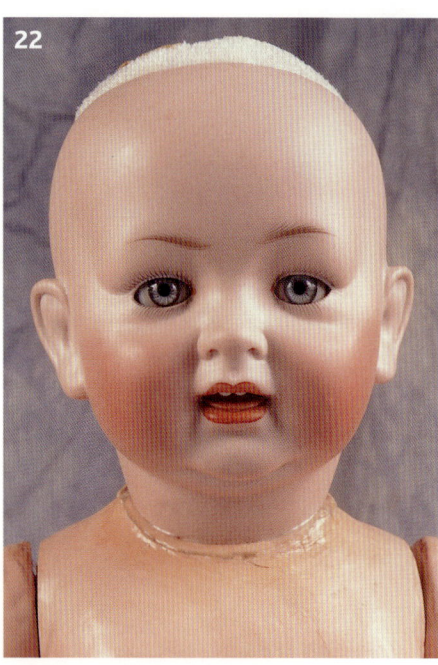

22. Bisque socket head by Hertel, Schwab; multi-stroke eyebrows; painted upper and lower eyelashes; glass sleep eyes; open/closed mouth with molded tongue; cheek dimples; 25-inch doll; circa 1912; marked: **151//13//Made in Germany**. Kenneth Drew Collection. (Photo: Ann Hanat)

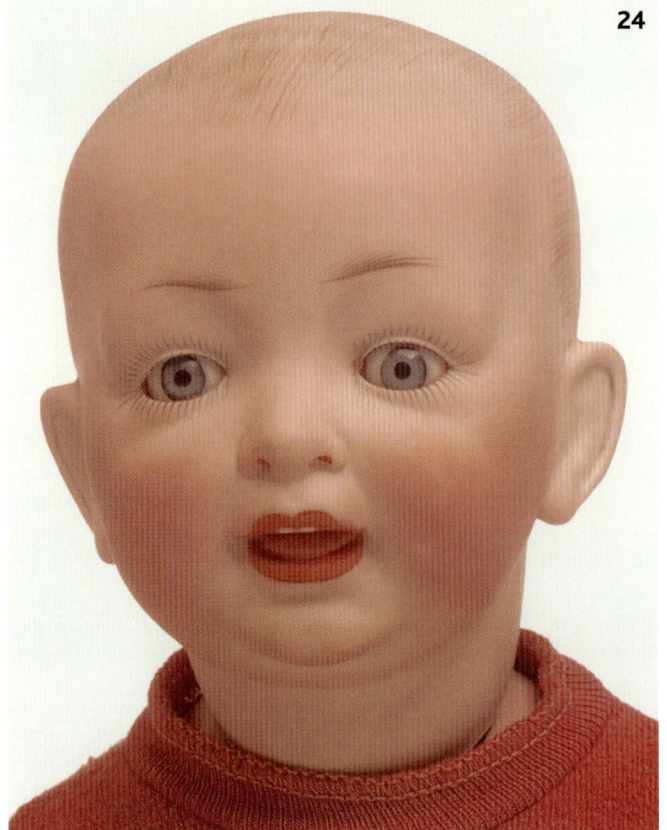

24. Bisque socket head by Hertel, Schwab; molded hair; multi-stroke eyebrows; painted upper and lower eyelashes; glass sleep eyes; open/closed mouth with upper teeth and molded tongue; 13½-inch doll; circa 1912; marked: **6/152**. Ann Cummings Collection. (Photo: John Cummings)

Hertel, Schwab & Co. Porcelain Factory

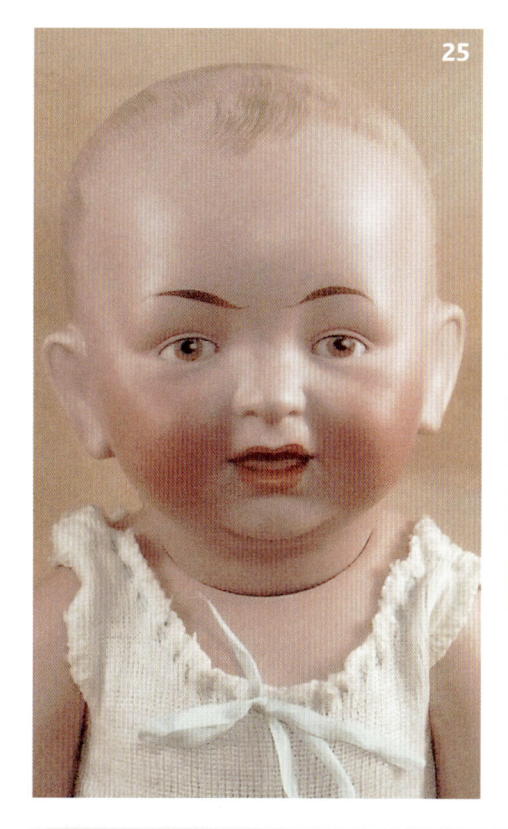

26. Nine female workers at the Hertel, Schwab & Co. porcelain factory are sanding wooden body parts in this 1915 photograph, which has been hand colored. Workers in the majority of Thuringian porcelain factories that made doll-related porcelain products sanded, painted and assembled composition doll bodies inside the factories. Most of the composition and wooden body parts were made by home workers. (Photo: Courtesy Heimatmuseum Schloss Ehrenberg, Ohrdruf)

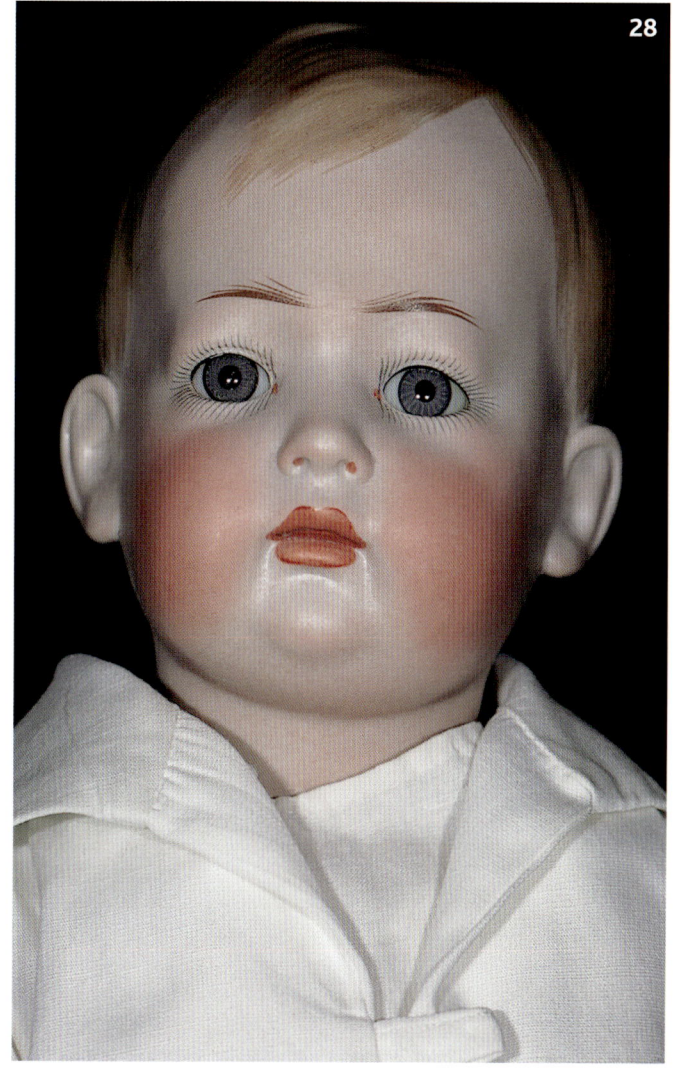

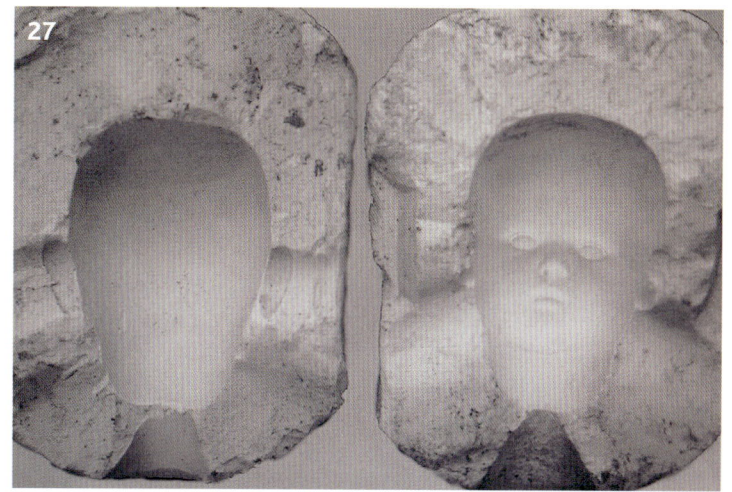

25. Bisque socket head by Hertel, Schwab; molded hair; wavy single-stroke eyebrows; painted upper and lower eyelashes; painted eyes with white highlights on right side of pupils, rather than the typical left side; open/closed mouth with molded tongue; 11-inch doll; circa 1912; marked with size number 7. Beth Karp Collection. (Photo: Lee Krombholz)

27. These two parts of a Hertel, Schwab plaster working mold, measuring 6 x 6 x 2½ inches, were found on the grounds of the factory by the current owner, Wolfgang Ortlepp. The factory made a large number of character babies from 1912 on. (Photo: Christiane Gräfnitz)

28. Bisque socket head by Hertel, Schwab for the Kley & Hahn doll factory; molded hair; wavy multi-stroke eyebrows; painted upper and lower eyelashes; glass sleep eyes; slightly parted, open/closed mouth; 18-inch doll; circa 1912; marked: **IV 154//6**. The original model for the 154 mold number head was a child's head sculpture created by the Brussels-born Italian sculptor Francois Duquesnoy, known in Italy as Il Fiammingo. Mold number 157 is the wigged version of 154. Private Collection. (Photo: Gene Abbott)

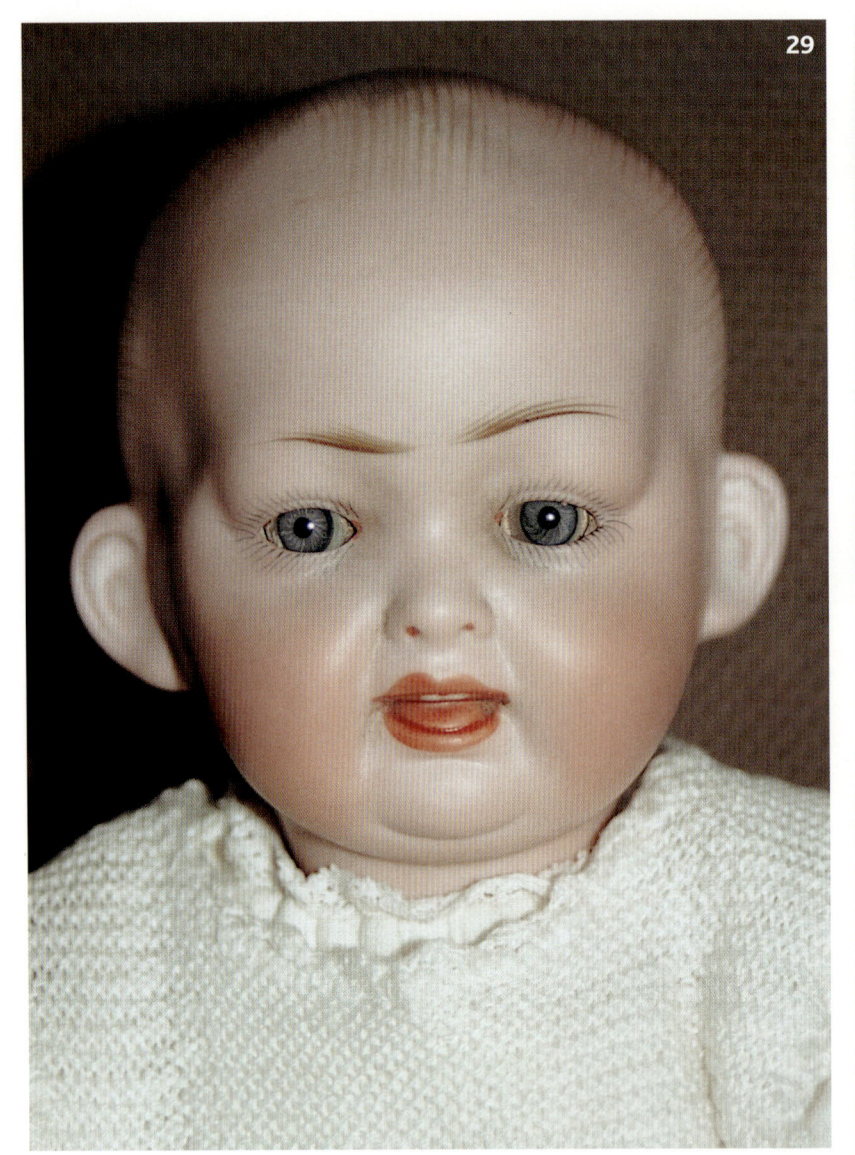

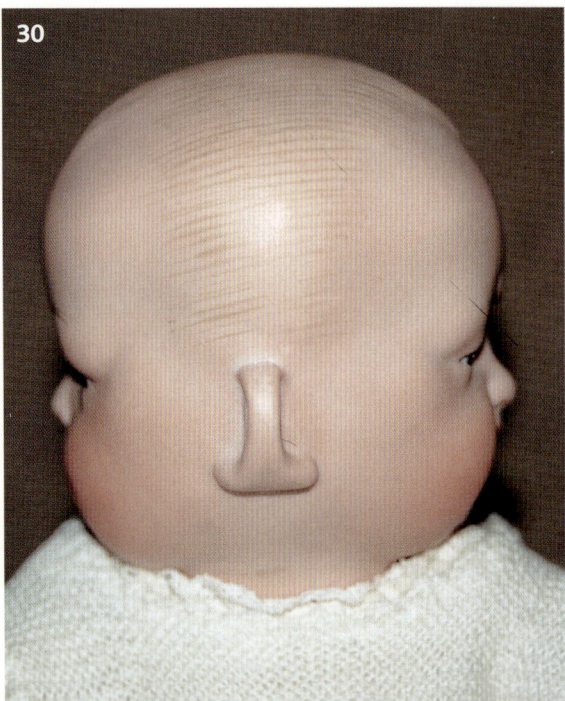

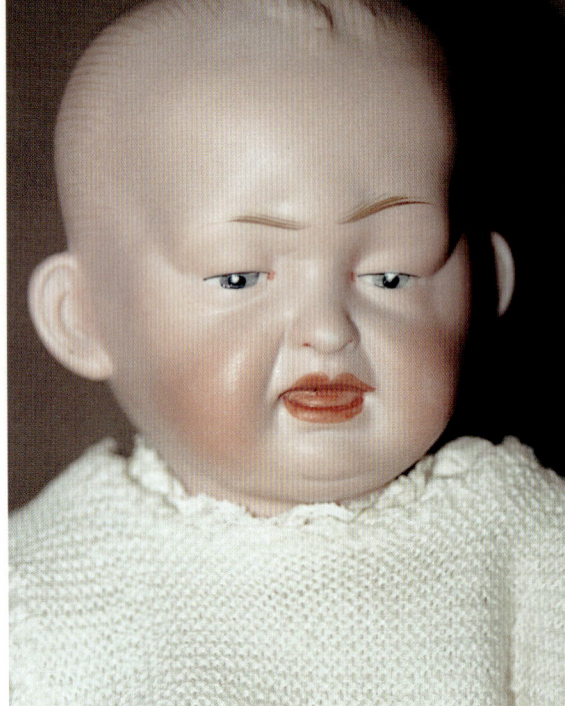

Chapter 6

29. Laughing face of a two-faced bisque socket head by Hertel, Schwab for the Kley & Hahn doll factory; molded hair; large molded ears; wavy multi-stroke eyebrows; painted upper and lower eyelashes; open/closed mouth with upper teeth and molded tongue; 11 inches; GM 1911; marked: **159**. Courtesy Museum Schloss Tenneberg, Waltershausen. (Photo: Christiane Gräfnitz)

32. This Hertel, Schwab character-head plaster working mold was found on the factory grounds by the current owner of the property, Wolfgang Ortlepp. The mold measures 6 x 6 x 2½ inches. (Photo: Christiane Gräfnitz)

30. The side view of the Hertel, Schwab two-faced bisque head shows the single sculpted ear that looks natural with either face. Courtesy Museum Schloss Tenneberg, Waltershausen. (Photo: Christiane Gräfnitz)

31. Crying face of the two-faced bisque socket head by Hertel, Schwab for the Kley & Hahn doll factory; molded hair; large molded ears; wavy multi-stroke eyebrows; painted eyes with white highlights on pupils; open/closed mouth with molded tongue; 11-inch doll; GM 1911; marked: **159**. Courtesy Museum Schloss Tenneberg, Waltershausen. (Photo: Christiane Gräfnitz)

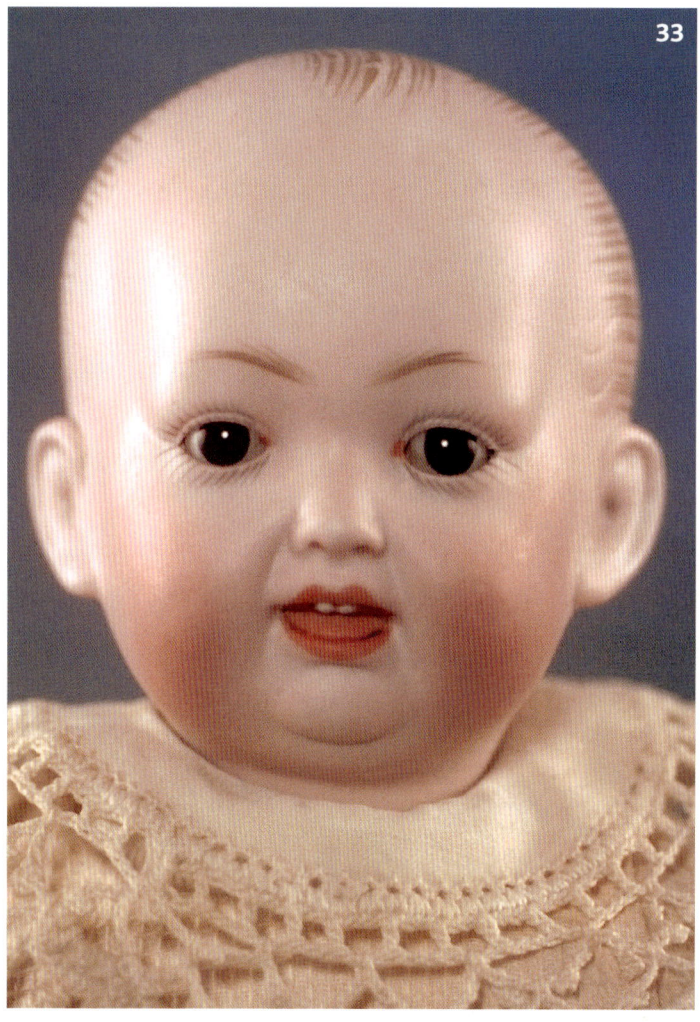

Hertel, Schwab & Co. Porcelain Factory

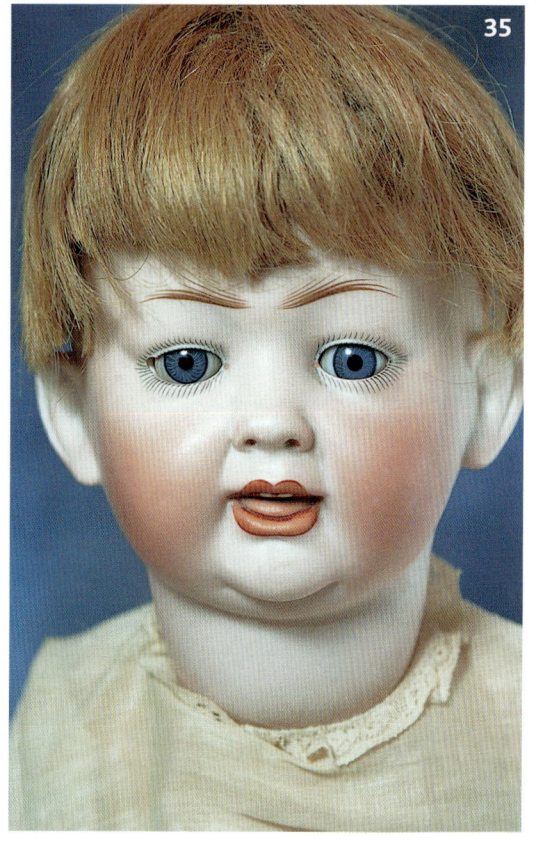

33. Bisque socket head by Hertel, Schwab for the Kley & Hahn doll factory; molded hair; wavy multi-stroke eyebrows; painted upper and lower eyelashes; glass sleep eyes; open/closed mouth with upper teeth and molded tongue; 11-inch doll; circa 1911; marked: **Germany//K&H** (inside **banner**)//158-210. Beth Karp Collection. (Photo: Lee Krombholz)

34. Bisque socket-head googly by Hertel, Schwab; wig; single-stroke eyebrows; painted upper and lower eyelashes; side-glancing glass eyes; open/closed smiling mouth; 10½-inch doll; circa 1914; marked: **165.1**. Beth Karp Collection. (Photo: Lee Krombholz)

35. Bisque socket head by Hertel, Schwab for the Kley & Hahn doll factory; wig; wavy multi-stroke eyebrows; painted upper and lower eyelashes; glass sleep eyes; open/closed mouth with upper teeth and molded tongue; chin dimple; 16-inch doll; circa 1912; marked: **K&H** (inside **banner**)//**Germany**//**160/9**. Author's Collection. (Photo: Gregg Smith)

36. This googly mold was also found on the grounds of the old Hertel, Schwab porcelain factory site by the current owner, Wolfgang Ortlepp. The plaster working mold measures 7 x 5½ x 2½ inches. (Photo: Christiane Gräfnitz)

Chapter 6

37. A closer view of the head of the doll pictured in illustration 38 shows the fine facial painting and modeling. Christa Dorner Collection. (Photo: Christiane Gräfnitz)

39. Bisque socket head by Hertel, Schwab for the Kley & Hahn doll factory; molded hair; wavy multi-stroke eyebrows; painted upper and lower eyelashes; glass sleep eyes; open/closed mouth; 14-inch doll; circa 1912; marked: **K&H** (inside **banner**)**//166-6**. The Fiammingo sculpture of a young boy (also used as the model for Käthe Kruse's No. 1 doll and other bisque-head dolls) was the model for the 166 mold number series. Beth Karp Collection. (Photo: Lee Krombholz)

38. Bisque socket-head googly by Hertel, Schwab; wig; single-stroke eyebrows; painted upper and lower eyelashes; side-glancing glass eyes; open/closed smiling mouth; 14½-inch doll; circa 1914; marked: **165.5**. Christa Dorner Collection. (Photo: Christiane Gräfnitz)

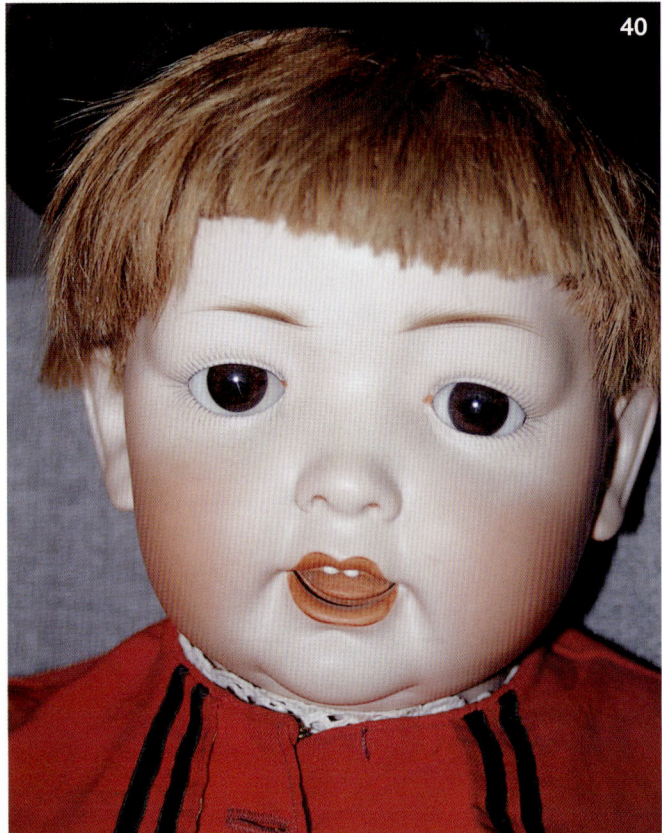

40. Bisque socket head by Hertel, Schwab for the Kley & Hahn doll factory; wig; multi-stroke eyebrows; painted upper and lower eyelashes; glass sleep eyes; open/closed mouth with upper teeth and molded tongue; 25½-inch doll; circa 1912; marked: **167//14**. Courtesy Ladenburger Spielzeugauktion/Goetz Seidel. (Photo: Christiane Gräfnitz)

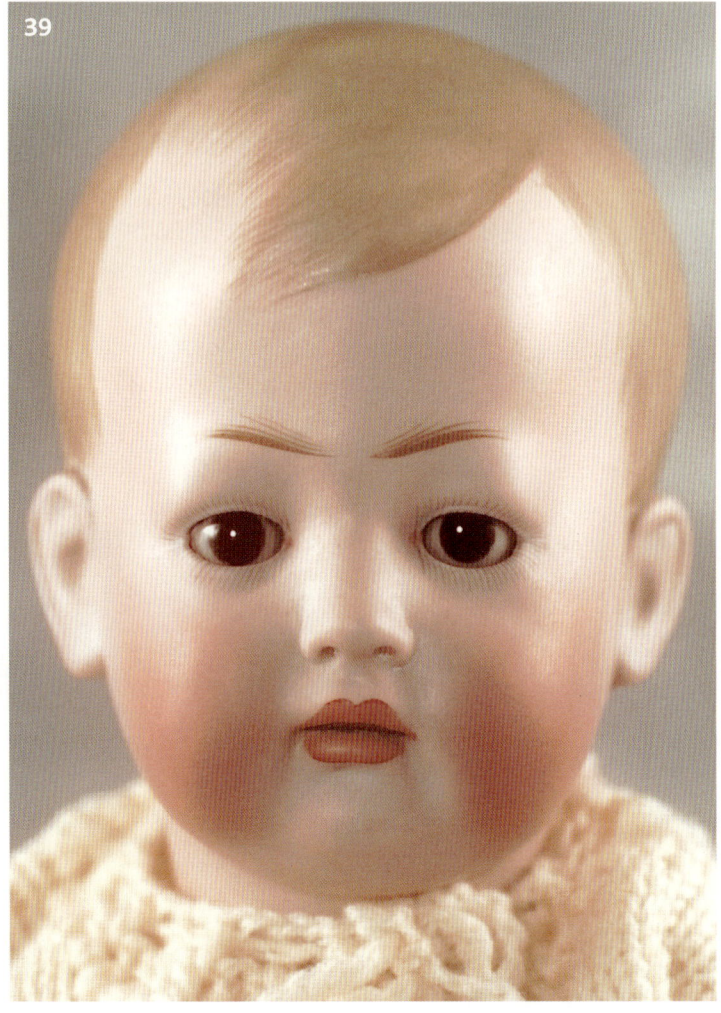

Hertel, Schwab & Co. Porcelain Factory

41. This googly plaster working mold was found on the grounds of the Hertel, Schwab porcelain factory by the current owner, Wolfgang Ortlepp. The distinctive molded hair is similar to the molded hair on the dolls pictured in illustrations 43 and 46. (Photo: Christiane Gräfnitz)

42. Bisque socket head by Hertel, Schwab for the Kley & Hahn doll factory; wig; wavy multi-stroke eyebrows; painted upper and lower eyelashes; upper hair eyelashes; glass sleep eyes; open/closed mouth with molded tongue; 16-inch doll; circa 1912; marked: K&H (inside banner)//169-6. Beth Karp Collection. (Photo: Lee Krombholz)

43. Bisque socket-head googly by Hertel, Schwab; molded hair; single-stroke eyebrows; painted upper and lower eyelashes; side-glancing glass eyes; open/closed smiling mouth; 3-inch head; circa 1912; unmarked. Courtesy Deutsches Spielzeugmuseum, Sonneberg. (Photo: Christiane Gräfnitz)

44. Bisque socket-head Jubilee googly by Hertel, Schwab for the New York importers Strobel & Wilken; molded hair; multi-stroke eyebrows; painted upper and lower eyelashes; side-glancing glass eyes; closed smiling mouth; 15-inch doll; circa 1914; marked: 172.3. The Jubilee dolls were made by German porcelain factories to commemorate special anniversaries of doll-distributing companies. This series of Jubilee dolls marked the fiftieth anniversary of the Strobel & Wilken importing company. Historisches Coburger Puppenmuseum/ Lossnitzer Collection. (Photo: Christiane Gräfnitz)

CHAPTER 6

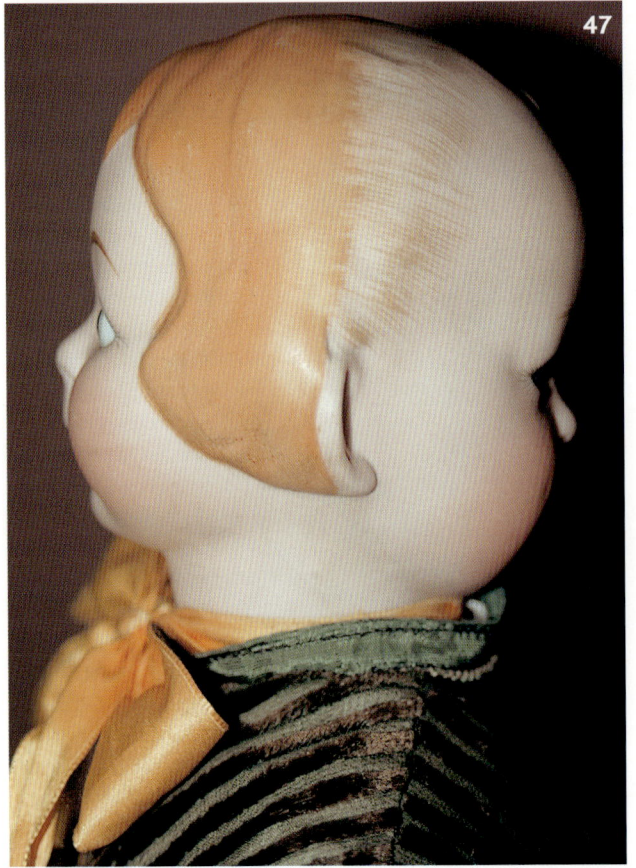

45. Character-boy side of a two-faced bisque socket head by Hertel, Schwab; molded hair; large molded ears; wavy multi-stroke eyebrows; painted upper and lower eyelashes; glass stationary eyes; open/closed mouth with molded teeth and tongue; 14½-inch doll; circa 1912; marked: **168/4**. Courtesy Museum Schloss Tenneberg, Waltershausen. (Photo: Christiane Gräfnitz)

46. Googly-girl side of a two-faced bisque socket head by Hertel, Schwab; molded red hair; single-stroke eyebrows; painted upper and lower eyelashes; side-glancing glass eyes; open/closed smiling mouth with protruding upper lip; 14½-inch doll; circa 1912; marked: **168/4**. The head sculpting resembles Grace Drayton's Campbell Kid illustrations. Courtesy Museum Schloss Tenneberg, Waltershausen. (Photo: Christiane Gräfnitz)

47. A side view of the two-faced bisque socket head shows the single sculpted ear that is visible only on the character-boy side of the head. Courtesy Museum Schloss Tenneberg, Waltershausen. (Photo: Christiane Gräfnitz)

Hertel, Schwab & Co. Porcelain Factory

48. This is a closer view of the Jubilee googly head pictured in illustration 44. Historisches Coburger Puppenmuseum/Lossnitzer Collection. (Photo: Christiane Gräfnitz)

Chapter 6

49. This all-bisque 6-inch googly, made by the Hertel, Schwab porcelain factory for the New York importing company Louis Wolf & Co., has an original label that reads: "Our Fairy" inside an oval wreath. The word "Germany" is written below the wreath. The doll's features include jointed arms; original wig; single-stroke eyebrows; painted upper and lower eyelashes; side-glancing glass eyes and a open/closed mouth with upper teeth and a molded tongue. The doll was first announced in the January 1914 issue of *Playthings* magazine, and listed in four sizes from 7 to 11½ inches. Marked: **222//16**. Author's Collection. (Photo: Gregg Smith)

50. The large Kley & Hahn doll factory is still standing on the outskirts of Ohrdruf. I visited the site in May 2007 and found it had been subdivided into apartments since my last visit. (Photo: Mary Krombholz)

51. Two unpainted googly-head shards were also found on the Hertel, Schwab factory site by the current owner, Wolfgang Ortlepp. The back of the mold on the left is marked with the mold and size numbers: **222//12**. (Photo: Christiane Gräfnitz)

Hertel, Schwab & Co. Porcelain Factory

52. This 1911 photograph, which has been hand colored, pictures the sixteen women and eleven men who made up the first group of employees hired by the factory. Co-owners Albert Kley and Paul Hahn are seated in the middle of the front row. After the factory was enlarged, the name of the factory and *"Puppenfabrik"* were written in large letters on the side of the building that faces the railroad track. Only a few letters are visible today. (Photo: Courtesy Heimatmuseum Schloss Ehrenberg, Ohrdruf)

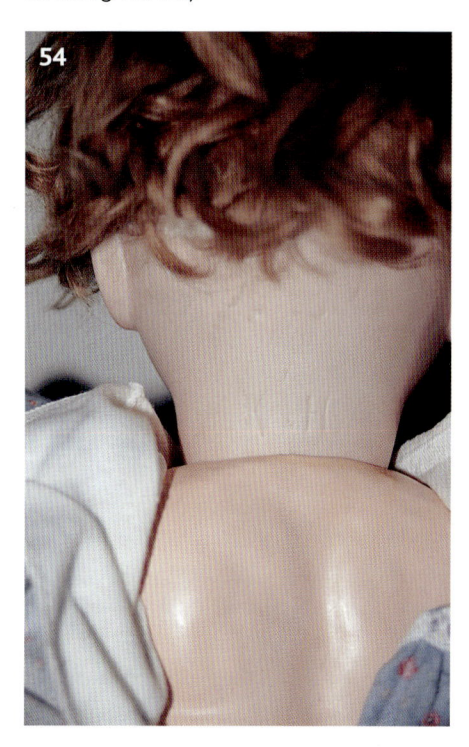

54. This view of the back of the head pictured in illustration 53 shows the solitary marking: **K&H**. Courtesy Heimatmuseum Schloss Ehrenberg, Ohrdruf (Photo: Christiane Gräfnitz)

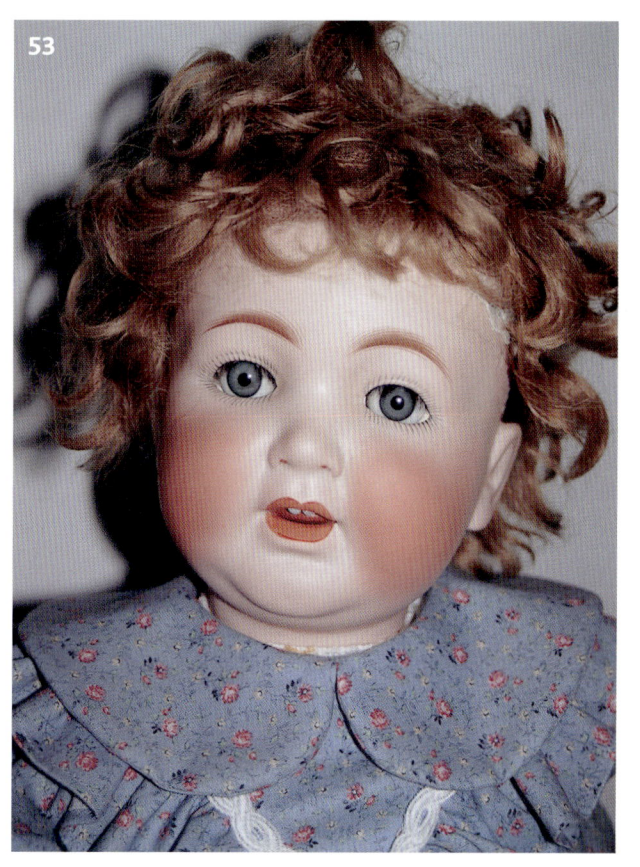

53. The Hertel, Schwab porcelain factory made the 100 series mold numbers for the Kley & Hahn doll factory; Baehr & Proeschild made the 200 series for the factory and Kestner made the 600 series. Bisque heads made by these three Ohrdruf-area factories are easy to attribute to the proper porcelain factory if they are marked with a mold number. But it is difficult to attribute heads that are only marked with the letters "K&H," like this bisque socket head. The features on this 20-inch doll include a wig; multi-stroke eyebrows; painted upper and lower eyelashes; glass sleep eyes and an open mouth with upper teeth and separate tongue. Courtesy Heimatmuseum Schloss Ehrenberg, Ohrdruf (Photo: Christiane Gräfnitz)

Part One
Chapter 7
Kestner Doll & Porcelain Factory

1. The metal sign in the shape of the Kestner "crown of superiority" is still visible between the windows on the 1824 home/factory. The Kestner trademark was once covered with gold paint, but it is no longer visible. (Photo: Mary Krombholz)

Johann Daniel Kestner, Jr. left a permanent legacy unequaled by any other dollmaker in Waltershausen. Doll books and magazines are full of accounts of his interesting life. Kestner was the only dollmaker in Waltershausen from 1816 until 1851, when Gottlob Schafft founded a doll factory there.

Kestner was born on September 4, 1787, the second son of a Waltershausen master butcher and innkeeper named Bernhard Heinrich Kestner. When Johann was just ten years old, his parents sent him to Erfurt to work in a small shop. He must have developed good merchandising and communication skills as a shopkeeper's assistant, because in 1803, at the age of sixteen, he started his own business. During the Napoleonic wars, he began to buy lard, cow hides and horns from soldiers in Napoleon's army, who camped nearby. Kestner then sold the cow-related by-products in order to purchase a variety of useful items which he sold to the troops. When the troops left the area, he began to make papier-mâché blackboards and wooden shirt buttons. Because a lathe was required to make the thin, wooden-button rings, Kestner decided it would be economical to use the lathe to make other wooden items, as well. As a result, the young entrepreneur added jointed wooden dolls to his inventory. On October 30, 1815, at the age of twenty-eight, Kestner married Sabrina Friederike Buschmann. During the following years, he and Sabrina had five children: three daughters and two sons.

On February 4, 1823, the Gotha newspaper *Privaten Gothaer Zeitung* published the following advertisement: "Johann Daniel Kestner, Waltershausen, also supplies in addition to doll heads and figures from papier mâché, figures from white leather (leather bodies) to go with the doll heads, sheets of parchment, black boards with or without wooden frames, embroidered and wrapped little buttons to match white shirts, ladies shirts and ladies clothing." The buttons referred to in this advertisement are *Zwirn* buttons. To make these intricate buttons, home workers in the Waltershausen area wound cotton thread around small wooden rings. They were paid very low wages.

Kestner's sales rapidly increased, and in 1824 he was able to build a doll factory in Waltershausen. In 1830 his sales totaled more than $15,000. By the 1850s, his annual sales had risen to $150,000. From 1824 until the factory closed in 1938, dolls were assembled, dressed and packed for sale or export there. One reason for his increasing profit from doll sales was Kestner's focus on improving the quality of his dolls while steadily increasing prices. From the beginning, he concen-

2. The original Kestner home/doll factory, built by Johann Daniel Kestner, Jr. in 1824, is still standing near the town square in Waltershausen. Following its initial construction, additional factory buildings were built that encircled the oldest factory building. The dark, three-story building on the right in this photograph was the second factory building. (Photo: Mary Krombholz)

trated on finding buyers for dolls of top quality rather than making and selling large quantities of inexpensive dolls.

One of the most interesting facts about J.D. Kestner, Jr. is in the book *Reise ins Spielzeugland* (A Journey to Toyland). Author Marion Christiana Mueller writes that in 1846 Kestner employed 1,264 workers, including 423 children younger than fourteen. Children were always an important part of the Thuringian home work force in both the Waltershausen and Sonneberg areas because they were considered "free" labor. The more children a family had, the larger a work force they had to make doll-related products. Children began to work at the age of three or four. Young children often sat under their mother's sewing machine, cutting thread hour after hour. As a child grew older, he or she would be asked to do jobs like sanding, painting, hand sewing, knitting, matching and setting stationary glass eyes and packing the finished products into cardboard or wooden boxes. Children usually delivered the doll parts or finished products because their parents had to work twelve or more hours a day to support their families. On January 1, 1904, the German government enacted the "Children's Work Act." From this date on, children eight and older were allowed to do the following doll-related work: "Painting and brushing of doll joints; sorting and inserting of doll eyes; operating the bellows to help blow doll eyes; sewing, crocheting and knitting of doll dresses; sewing of doll bodies, making curls for doll wigs with cleaned hair of wool or mohair and packing dolls in boxes."

Home workers did not have much disposable income for food or clothing. Clothing and shoes were often passed down from older to younger members of the family. Potatoes were an important part of the daily diet. They were even eaten raw. Meat was a very special treat for the majority of home workers. Most Thuringian home workers rented their houses, as well as small pieces of ground on which they grew food necessary for survival, like potatoes and cabbage. The community cottage gardens used to grow potatoes and other fruits and vegetables are still used by residents of many Thuringian towns and villages today.

Kestner was instrumental in establishing the first railroad line into Waltershausen. On May 15, 1849, the line that connected Frottstetten and Waltershausen provided the link to the Eisenach and Gotha lines. Improved railway connections allowed Kestner to increase production and charge less for his goods. Shortly after the first railroad line was connected, American buyers began to travel to Waltershausen to visit Kestner's sample rooms.

Chapter 7

In 1842 Kestner divorced his first wife and married Maria Debes. It must have been an amicable divorce because his first and second wives lived together in the Kestner home. His son, Johann Christian Adolf Kestner, died in 1847. Following his son's death, J.D. Kestner, Jr. adopted his grandson Adolf. After Kestner's death on December 11, 1858, at the age of seventy-one, his two wives continued to live together and manage the doll and porcelain factory. They were assisted by the company secretary H. Osten and Eduard Reitz. In 1872 twenty-four-year-old Adolf assumed the leadership of the Kestner doll and porcelain factory, which he held until his death in 1918.

In 1860 the Kestner doll factory bought the Steudinger, Müller & Co. porcelain factory in Ohrdruf. Ohrdruf and Waltershausen are less than seven miles apart, and the proximity of the doll and porcelain factories was important for filling doll orders on time. It is probable that glazed porcelain shoulder heads were made for the Kestner doll factory in the Müller porcelain factory during the late 1840s and 1850s. Seven glazed porcelain shoulder heads on permanent display in the Waltershausen Doll Museum have been attributed to the Kestner porcelain factory by museum curators. The earliest chinas on display have hairstyles with molded buns, which date the shoulder heads to the late 1840s or early 1850s.

Descriptions of day-to-day work in the Thuringian porcelain factories are almost nonexistent. It is fortunate for doll collectors that the American magazine *Playthings* included articles about German doll production during the early 1900s. One article, published in April 1906, provides the following history of the Kestner & Co. porcelain factory in Ohrdruf.

> Since about 1816, the Kestner factory has made fame for itself the world over with its popular Kestner dolls. As early as 1850, the dolls were exported to the United States, and are now recognized as one of the leading lines in this country.
>
> Early in its history the Kestner factory started with the home industry system, having workmen with homes in neighboring villages furnish various doll parts to be assembled at the main factory. In 1860, a porcelain factory was acquired at Ohrdruf, making the plant complete in every respect for the manufacture of all kinds of dolls.
>
> The factory is now operated by the grandson of the founder, and employs nearly a thousand workers, inclusive of home operators to manufacture the enormous output. The main products consist of kid dolls, extra fine jointed dolls, bisque and celluloid doll heads, bisque babies, toy tea and dinner sets, figures, busts, etc.

Playthings also provides the following information on the process of making Kestner composition bodies: "The jointed dolls require hollow molds, the pieces being made in two parts of paper pulp, which are fastened together and provided with the necessary sockets for ball joints. After this a flesh color is poured over them and they are put on sticks to dry before being varnished. The finished bodies, arms and legs are turned over to the joiners who fasten the heads, arms and legs together by means of rubber cords and hooks."

The Kestner doll and porcelain factory sold doll-related porcelain from the 1840s until it closed permanently in 1938. The dolls included china, parian-like and bisque shoulder heads (with and without molded hair), bathing dolls in china and bisque, all-bisque dolls, bisque socket heads to be used on composition bodies, bisque character dolls and celluloid dolls. Original sample books provide the most accurate information on the porcelain products made by the factory. I was fortunate to have the opportunity to buy an original Kestner sample book distributed from 1918 on. The front cover includes a raised gold crown with the following words: "*Kronen Puppen*" (King Dolls) and "*Kestner.*" Below the crown are the following words: "*J.D. Kestner, jun. Puppenfabrik*" (doll factory) and "*Kestner & Comp. Porzellanfabrik*" (porcelain factory).

Dating a sample book like mine is not easy because Thuringian porcelain factories did not issue new sample books every year they produced porcelain products. Sample books were expensive to print and distribute. In the majority of porcelain factories, products that sold well were included in succeeding sample books long after the products were originally introduced. This is very evident from the study of sample books in my archival paper collection.

It is fortunate that the current directors of the Kestner doll

3. The doll-factory buildings that surrounded the original building were torn down a few years ago, and new apartment buildings now stand on the site. This photograph shows the factory buildings that filled the entire block behind the oldest factory building. (Photo: Mary Krombholz)

Kestner Doll & Porcelain Factory

4. The 1824 doll factory is no longer encircled by the massive Kestner doll factory buildings. The building has been designated a historic landmark, and will thankfully be saved from future demolition. Johann Daniel Kestner, Jr. lived in this house for many years, and is believed to have died here in 1858, at the age of seventy-one. (Photo: Mary Krombholz)

and porcelain factory, Ernst Bufe, Eduard Prechtl and Ernst Florschuetz, are listed in my sample book. These three men directed the factory following the death of Adolf Kestner in 1918. From the sample book we now know that bisque dolly-face dolls, character dolls and dollhouse families were still in the sales line following World War I. The sample book is also important because it pictures many types of dolls in original clothing, including character dolls with socket heads, babies, dollhouse dolls and all-bisque dolls.

The first page of the sample book shows a picture of all of the buildings that once made up the original Ohrdruf porcelain factory site. Only one porcelain factory building is still standing today. The sample book contains thirty-two pages of color and black-and-white photographs of the factory's products. Following the pictures of bisque-head dolls on composition bodies, the book shows wigged and molded-hair half-dolls, all-bisque dolls, dollhouse dolls, bisque socket heads without bodies and a page of bodies with stringing devices.

Following the pictures of composition bodies, the sample book features a page of assorted wigs, a page of baby-doll clothing and a page of doll shoes. Each pair of shoes is in an individual box. After these pages are seven pages of tea and coffee sets for children. Each tea and coffee set is individually boxed, and each set contains a different configuration of china cups, saucers, plates and pouring pieces. The bisque-head doll photographs include googlies and many other character dolls.

The sample page of wigs is especially important because it illustrates a variety of original Kestner wigs. Kestner wigs were made in the Waltershausen doll factory as well as by the factory's home workers. An article in Clara L. Mateaux's 1898 book *Wonderland of Work* provides insight as to the type of hair used to make wigs during the years the Kestner doll factory sold dolly-faced dolls and character dolls.

> At length the hair strands reach the hands of the 'Frau Hair Dressers,' blue-eyed, busy girls, whose own neat, fair hair generally hangs down in long plaited braids, and whose nimble fingers will soon effect a complete transformation of these staring little faces, which they will soften and make gentle and pleasant looking by means of a wig of some sort. So this hair dressing is really a turning point in Miss Dolly's career, and one worth knowing about.
>
> The manufacturers informed us that doll hair is nearly the costliest part of her composition, and that the material which forms these varied tresses is very different in texture and value. Black hair, not by any means the favorite color with young customers, is really human hair; but the shining, glossy curls, or the flowing barley-sugar-like locks, which little misses love to comb and plait, is a soft, silky kind of mohair, prepared especially for this purpose.
>
> However, let's return to our work room, and see the bald heads, all collected now before the damsels who have undertaken to cover them with wigs. The wigs are mostly made of hair, glued to a net foundation, or perhaps raw wool, braided and then boiled to keep in the waves, or curled around hot tubes, and stuck to the head curl by curl. Some of these doll beauties are made more German looking to our eyes, by numbers of little fair plaits which are twisted and braided, and then pinned and tied under a cap in the local fashion.

Antique dolls originally belonged to a child's world of fantasy, which is part of their charm. But quite often, they teach us facts that are even more exciting than the fantasy. Dolls give us an insight into the childhood lives of our ancestors. They show us changes in taste and what people considered beautiful at various periods of time. And they are our very best source of information on clothing styles through the years. This is especially true of the dolls pictured in my original Kestner sample book. The clothing is identical to the clothing that would have been worn by children during this particular time period.

There is no other toy more influenced by fashion than a doll. The dating and identification of an originally dressed doll is possible because of fashion details. While a popular doll-head mold would be produced year after year, doll factory owners tried to dress their dolls in the newest fashions every year. A well-stocked doll factory, like the Kestner factory, kept their products in sample rooms. It was common

Chapter 7

5. This lithograph of J.D. Kestner, Jr. is on permanent display in the Waltershausen doll museum. The Kestner family donated many of Kestner's original sample books and business records to the museum. The sample books identify the Kestner & Co. late 1840s glazed-porcelain shoulder heads on display in the museum. Courtesy Museum Schloss Tenneberg, Waltershausen. (Photo: Christiane Gräfnitz)

for large Thuringian doll factories to have thousands of different doll-related samples in their sample rooms. The Dressel doll factory in Sonneberg often had between twenty thousand and thirty thousand samples on display in their large sample rooms, year after year.

One of the most spectacular success stories of any bisque doll is that of the American artist Rose O'Neill's Kewpie, which was first produced by Kestner. In 1909 an enterprising editor of *Ladies Home Journal* envisioned a children's section of the magazine featuring the drawings of Rose O'Neill. The editor encouraged O'Neill to adapt the baby faces that she had initially drawn as magazine illustrations. In reply to the suggestion, O'Neill wrote: "For such a Palmer-Coxy page as you have in mind these persons should perform a series of exploits, shouldn't they? I have for a long time called these persons 'Kewpies,' diminutive for Cupids, and it seems to me the name spelled so might be amusing to children."

Rose O'Neill had an appealing personality, according to her peers. From early childhood on, her artistic talent was apparent. Her main ambition was to become a professional artist. Her success came early when she won a competition for a drawing she submitted as a Nebraska schoolgirl. At the age of fourteen, she submitted poems and drawings to local newspapers. Her serious art training took place at the Convent of St. Regis in New York. Following these art lessons, she soon paid her own way for three years of art-based study by selling drawings to magazines such as *Truth, Collins Weekly* and *Harper's Bazar.*

The secret to Rose O'Neill's success was no doubt her great love of children, coupled with sound business sense. In May of 1938, speaking to her niece about the Kewpies in an interview published in the *Kansas City Star*, O'Neill said:

> I dreamed them...they were bouncing about all over the coverlet chirping their little newborn name. One perched on my hand like a bird. Its little sit-down wasn't warm like a human baby's, it was oddly cool. So I knew they were elves, but of a new kind. I had the strange impression that their intentions were of the best. In fact, I knew at once they were bursting with kindness, and that their hearts were as well rounded as their tummies. I meditated on them for days afterwards, and bit by bit, I saw they had philosophy.

Her personal life, apart from the success of her artwork and the fame she later won as a result of her Kewpie dolls, was not always a happy one. Her two marriages ended in divorce, and her greatest consolation in later life seems to have been her beautiful family home, Bonniebrook, located in the Ozark Mountains of Missouri.

The first copyright for a Kewpie doll was filed by Rose O'Neill on December 17, 1912, and the doll was patented on March 4, 1913. The first dolls were manufactured by the Kestner & Co. porcelain factory in Ohrdruf. Recalling the exciting first production, the artist wrote:

> The drawings and verses began in 1909. By 1913, the dolls were all over the world. First many children began to write to me, asking if I couldn't make them a Kewpie they could hold in their hands. Just for fun, I molded a little statue of a Kewpie. Then the doll factories got the idea. I selected a factory and the whole thing was done. The first bisque Kewpies were manufactured in Germany. I went over there, molded nine statues of different sizes, saw that they came out right, and before World War I began there were many factories turning them out as fast as they could pull them out of the ovens.

The Kestner porcelain factory made the initial group of Kewpies under O'Neill's supervision. When it was evident that the Kestner porcelain factory could not keep up with the demand, a number of other Thuringian porcelain factories began to make Kewpies for Geo. Borgfeldt & Co., including Hertwig & Co., A.W. Fr. Kister, Gebrüder Voigt, Hermann Voigt, and Alt, Beck & Gottschalck.

In the early twentieth century, the Kestner factory also made the majority of the bisque character-doll heads found on dolls sold by the Catterfelder doll factory. The small town of Cat-

Kestner Doll & Porcelain Factory

terfeld is located just below Ohrdruf. The doll factory was founded in 1906 by Hugo and Richard Gross. The factory was formerly the Carl Trautmann doll factory of Finsterbergen. The Catterfelder doll factory registered the trademark initials "CP" in 1910. The trademark is very easy to identify because the letters are in fancy script that looks very much like Old English calligraphy. The following words were used by the Catterfelder doll factory in 1910 to advertise their character dolls. "Particular attention has to be drawn to the character babies, who left the path of tradition and express completely new ideas."

The character doll mold numbers made by Kestner for Catterfelder include: 200, 201, 207, 208, 209, 218, 219, 220, 262 and 270. My original 1918 Kestner sample book contains the photograph of a bisque character-head doll that is in my collection. It is marked with the Catterfelder fancy script letters "CP" and the mold number "262."

Unlike most Thurigian factories, Kestner & Co. made complete character dolls with their own bisque heads and body parts. The variety and quality of dolls made by the Kestner porcelain factory is unsurpassed. From the jointed wooden dolls made beginning in 1816 to the last bisque-head dolls made before the factory closed in 1938, this prolific factory created a lasting legacy of dolls that are treasured by collectors today.

6. Three bisque socket heads by Kestner; wigs; multi-stroke eyebrows; painted upper and lower eyelashes; glass sleep eyes; open mouths with upper teeth; 9½, 12½, and 16 inches in height; GM 1897; dolls marked with a size number and an alphabet letter from the well-known Kestner series, and the words: **Made in Germany//143**. (See illustrations 9 and 10 for examples of full markings.) Beth Karp Collection. (Photo: Lee Krombholz)

Chapter 7

7. A.T.-type bisque socket head by Kestner; wig; multi-stroke eyebrows; painted upper and lower eyelashes; large glass stationary eyes; slightly open/closed mouth with upper and lower lip outlines; 12-inch doll; circa 1880s; marked: **7**. Kathy and Mike Embry Collection. (Photo: Ann Hanat)

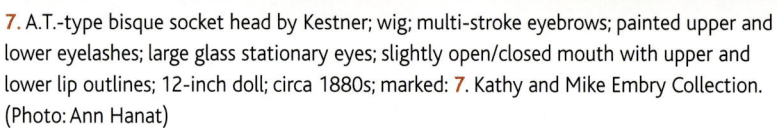

8. Bru-type bisque socket head by Kestner; wig; multi-stroke eyebrows; painted upper and lower eyelashes; glass sleep eyes; open/closed mouth with upper teeth; 13¾-inch doll; marked **8**. Ursula Gauder Collection. (Photo: Christiane Gräfnitz)

10. Bisque socket head by Kestner; wig; multi-stroke eyebrows; painted upper and lower eyelashes; glass sleep eyes; open mouth with upper teeth; 18-inch doll; GM 1897; marked: **F. made in Germany 10.//143**. Ann Cummings Collection. (Photo: John Cummings)

9. Bisque socket head by Kestner; original wig; multi-stroke eyebrows; painted upper and lower eyelashes; glass sleep eyes; open mouth with upper teeth; 13-inch doll; GM 1897; marked: **A. made in Germany 8.//143**. Ann Cummings Collection. (Photo: John Cummings)

166

Kestner Doll & Porcelain Factory

11. Gibson Girl 16-inch bisque socket-head doll, left in photo, is mounted on its original seldom-seen composition-lady body. The unmarked-head features include: original wig; single-stroke eyebrows; painted upper and lower eyelashes; glass sleep eyes and a closed mouth. Gibson Girl 19½-inch shoulder-head doll, right in photo, has its original leather jointed body with bisque lower arms; original wig; single-stroke eyebrows; painted upper and lower eyelashes; glass sleep eyes; closed mouth and is marked: **172**. Both dolls are circa 1900; note the long necks, which are typical of the illustrations from the Gibson-Girl era. Doll on left in photo: Mike and Kathy Embry Collection; Doll on right in photo: Courtesy Evansville, Indiana Museum of Arts, History and Science. (Photo: Ann Hanat)

12. Gibson Girl bisque socket head by Kestner; original wig; multi-stroke eyebrows; painted lower eyelashes; glass sleep eyes; closed mouth; 22-inch doll; circa 1900; marked: **172//7**. The hairstyle and haughty upturned chin resembles the drawings of well-known artist Charles Dana Gibson, who captured women's features and clothing styles during the early 1900s. Beth Karp Collection. (Photo: Lee Krombholz)

13. Gibson Girl bisque socket head by Kestner; original wig; single-stroke eyebrows; upper and lower eyelashes; glass sleep eyes; closed mouth; 20-inch doll; circa 1900; marked: **172//5 made in Germany**. Ann Cummings Collection. (Photo: John Cummings)

167

Chapter 7

14. *Das Wunderkind* (The Wonder Child) original box with bisque socket heads by Kestner; redressed doll; original wig; multi-stroke eyebrows; painted upper and lower eyelashes; glass sleep eyes; open mouth with upper teeth; 11 inches; circa 1900; marked: **made in//A Germany 3//174**. The box also contains two of the original three additional bisque socket heads that fit the same body; they are pictured in illustrations 15 and 16. Original directions stated the heads could be changed with a buttonhook. In translation, a few lines of the poem on the box lid read: "Out of far-away fairyland, I come as a doll child. Give me a different head, a boy I will be. Again change my head, and as if by magic, a little girl with a smile will come to you. Isn't this like a fairy tale?" Ursula Gauder Collection. (Photo: Christiane Gräfnitz)

15. *Das Wunderkind* boxed bisque socket head by Kestner; original wig with plaits; multi-stroke eyebrows; short closely-spaced upper eyelashes painted on the molded upper eyelid; painted eyes; open/closed mouth with upper teeth; cheek dimples; circa 1910; marked: **185**. Ursula Gauder Collection. (Photo: Christiane Gräfnitz)

16. *Das Wunderkind* boxed bisque socket head by Kestner; original boyish wig; multi-stroke eyebrows; short closely-spaced eyelashes painted onto the molded upper eyelid; painted eyes; closed mouth; circa 1910: marked: **184**. Ursula Gauder Collection. (Photo: Christiane Gräfnitz)

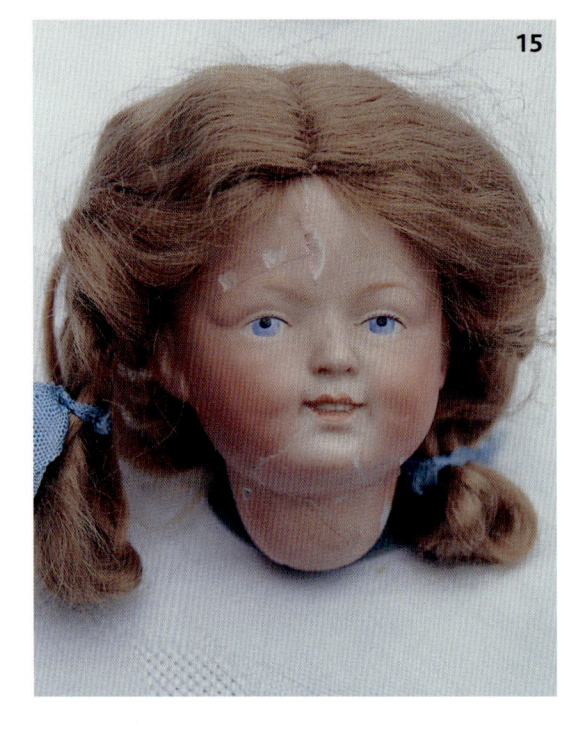

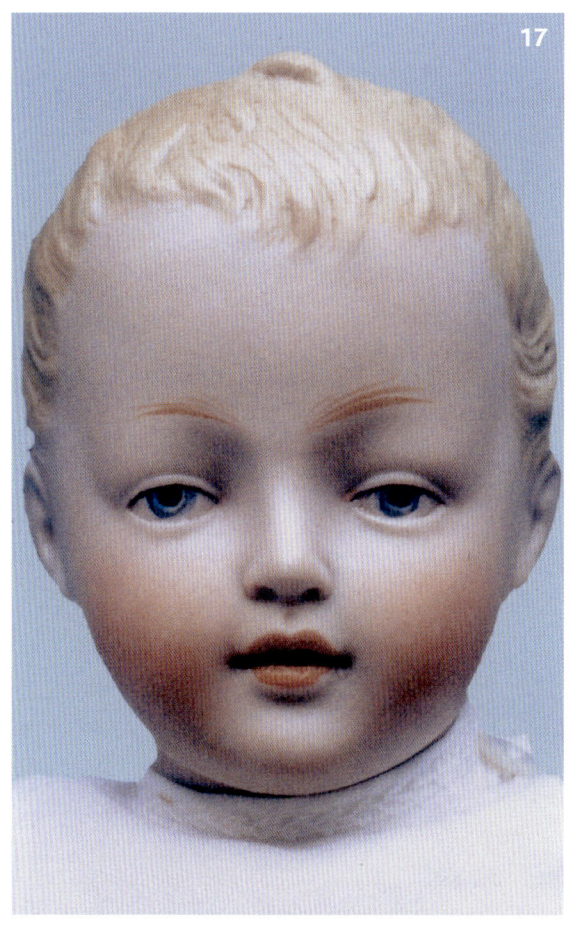

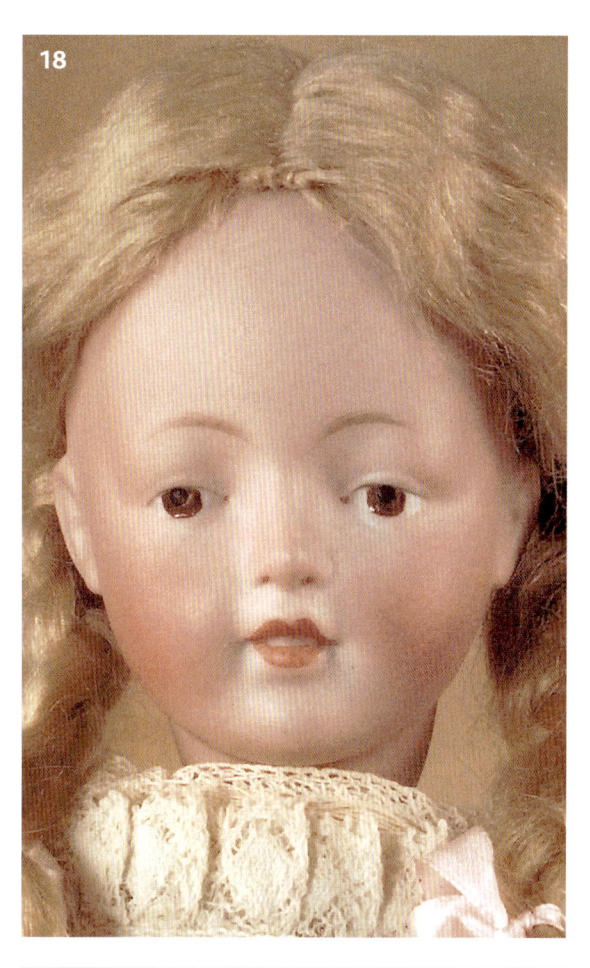

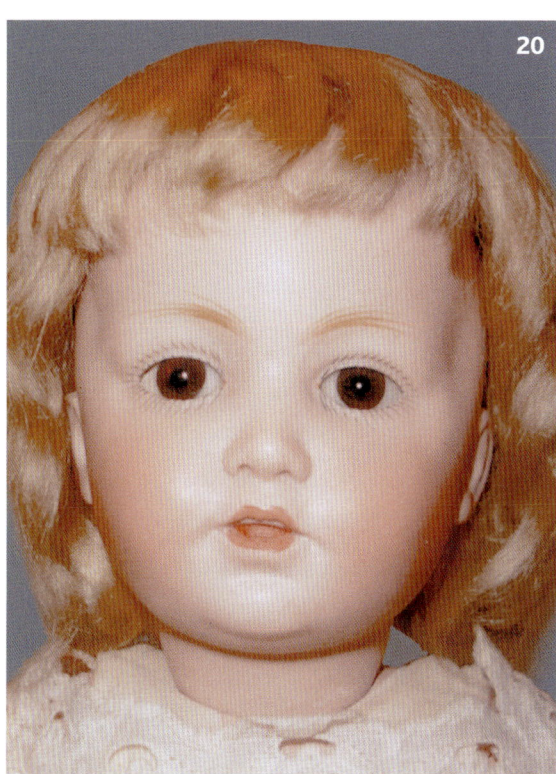

Kestner Doll & Porcelain Factory

17. This Kestner bisque socket-head character boy may be the first in the factory's character doll series, according to Jan Foulke, in whose book entitled Kestner, *King of Dollmakers* it is pictured (page 120). To my knowledge, it is the only recorded example of a #177 mold number. Bisque socket head; molded hair; well-defined eye sockets; multi-stroke eyebrows; intaglio-painted eyes; open/closed mouth; 11-inch doll; circa 1909; marked: **177**. Private Collection, formerly Jane Walker Collection. (Photo: C.W. Walker)

18. Bisque socket head by Kestner; original wig; multi-stroke eyebrows; painted eyes with glazed brown irises; open/closed mouth with white space between lips; 11 inches; circa 1909; marked: **178**. Beth Karp Collection. (Photo: Lee Krombholz)

19. Bisque socket head by Kestner; wig; multi-stroke eyebrows; painted eyes; open/closed mouth with white space between lips; 11-inch doll; circa 1909; marked: **178**. Kathy and Mike Embry Collection. (Photo: Ann Hanat)

20. Bisque socket head by Kestner; original wig; multi-stroke eyebrows; painted upper and lower eyelashes; large, stationary glass eyes; open/closed mouth with white space between lips and molded tongue; 15-inch doll; circa 1909; marked: **179**. Beth Riley Collection. (Photo: Andrea Jones)

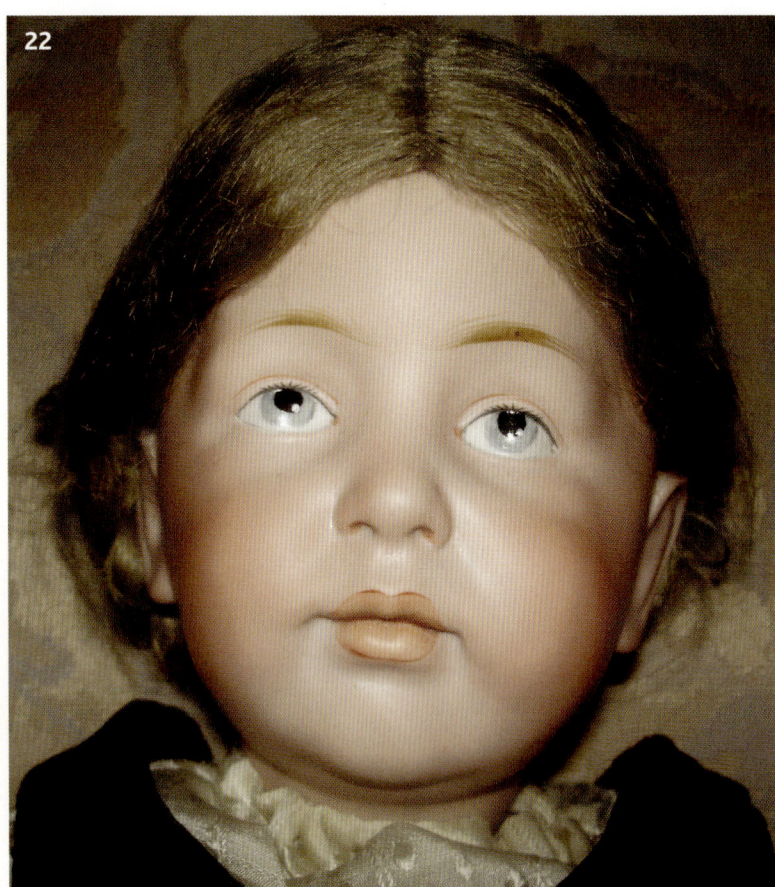

Chapter 7

21. Bisque socket head by Kestner; wig; multi-stroke eyebrows; short, closely spaced upper painted eyelashes; painted eyes with typical factory white iris highlight; open/closed mouth with upper teeth; 15-inch doll; circa 1910; unmarked. The bisque character head closely resembles the Kestner mold number 181. Kathy and Mike Embry Collection. (Photo: Ann Hanat)

22. Bisque head by Kestner; wig; multi-stroke eyebrows; short closely spaced upper painted eyelashes; painted eyes with white highlights; closed mouth; 19-inch doll; circa 1910; marked: **208**. Courtesy Rosalie Whyel Museum of Doll Art. (Photo: Jill Gorman)

23. Bisque socket head by Kestner; original wig and clothing; multi-stroke eyebrows; short, closely spaced, painted upper eyelashes; painted eyes with white highlights; open/closed mouth with white space between lips; 21-inch doll; circa 1910; marked: **186**. Courtesy Rosalie Whyel Museum of Doll Art. (Photo: Jill Gorman)

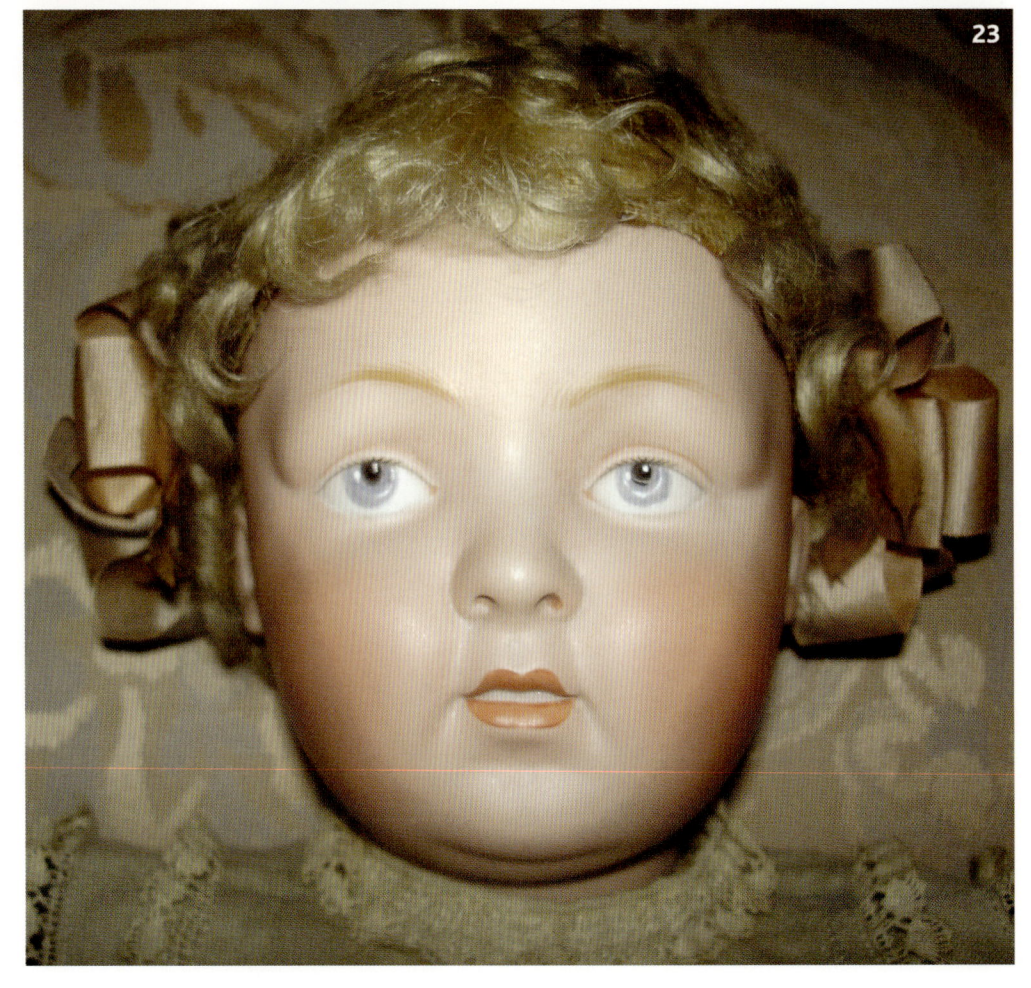

Kestner Doll & Porcelain Factory

24. Bisque socket head by Kestner; wig; multi-stroke eyebrows; short, closely spaced painted upper eyelashes; painted eyes with white highlights; closed mouth; 15 inches; circa 1910; marked: **182**. The white highlights are painted on the left side of each pupil in the identical position as the highlights on Kestner chinas and parians with painted eyes. Beth Karp Collection. (Photo: Lee Krombholz)

Chapter 7

25. Bisque socket head by Kestner; wig; multi-stroke eyebrows; painted upper and lower eyelashes; glass sleep eyes; open/closed mouth with molded upper teeth and accented lips; 18-inch doll; circa 1910; marked: **made in//F. Germany 10.//185**. Beth Karp Collection. (Photo: Lee Krombholz)

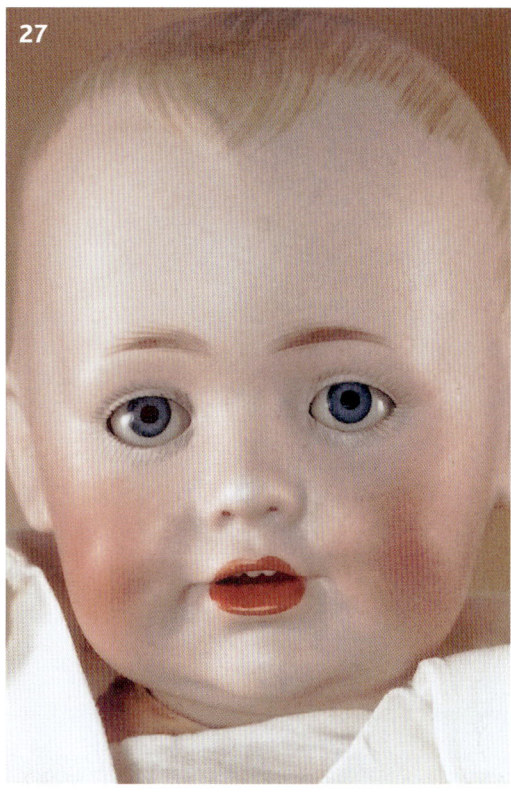

Kestner Doll & Porcelain Factory

26. Bisque socket head by Kestner for the Catterfelder doll factory in Catterfeld, Thuringia; wig; single-stroke eyebrows; painted eyes with white highlights; open/closed mouth with upper teeth; 13½-inch doll; circa 1912; marked: **CP//219**. The Kestner & Co. porcelain factory made the entire group of bisque character heads marked with the CP initials and 200 series mold numbers, for the Catterfelder doll factory. Courtesy Historisches Coburger Puppenmuseum/Lossnitzer Collection. (Photo: Christiane Gräfnitz)

27. Bisque socket head by Kestner; molded hair; multi-stroke eyebrows; painted upper and lower eyelashes; glass sleep eyes; open mouth with upper teeth; 15½-inch doll; marked: **JDK//made in Germany**. Beth Karp Collection. (Photo: Lee Krombholz)

28. Four bisque socket heads by Kestner; two with molded hair, two with wigs; multi-stroke eyebrows; painted upper and lower eyelashes; glass sleep eyes; open mouths with upper teeth; from 9 to 26 inches in height; circa 1912; marked **JDK 211**. Beth Karp Collection. (Photo: Gregg Smith)

Chapter 7

29. Bisque socket-head googly by Kestner; wig; raised, slanted and shaded multi-stroke eyebrows; black outline of eye socket; short, closely spaced, painted upper eyelashes; large, side-glancing glass stationary eyes; closed smiling mouth; 14-inch doll; circa 1913; marked: **made in Germany//J.D.K.//221//ges. gesch.** "*Ges.*" is the abbreviation of the German word *Gesetzlich* and "*gesch.*" is the abbreviation of *geschuetzt*. The two words mean patented. Courtesy Ladenburger Spielzeugauktion/ Gotz Seidel. (Photo: Christiane Gräfnitz)

30. Hilda bisque socket head by Kestner; wig; multi-stroke eyebrows; painted upper and lower eyelashes; glass sleep eyes; open mouth with upper teeth and separate tongue; 16-inch doll; GM 1914; marked: **No.12 made in 12.//Germany//237//J.D.K.//1914//©//Hilda//ges. gesch. 1070**. This version has a cry box. The face is the same as mold number 245, but the expression seems slightly sweeter and the tongue is not as prominent. Georgia Alarcon Collection. (Photo: Estelle Johnston)

31. Two Hilda bisque socket heads by Kestner; one with molded hair, one with wig; multi-stroke eyebrows; painted upper and lower eyelashes; glass sleep eyes; open mouths with upper teeth and separate tongues; 10½-and-12-inch dolls; GM 1914; wigged doll marked: **made in//B. Germany. 6.//J.D.K.//237**; baby doll marked: **Hilda//©//J.D.K.Jr.1914//ges.gesch.//7//made in Germany**. GM 1914. According to Jan Foulke's research in her book "*Kestner, King of Dollmakers,*" the mark on the back of the head does not have to say "Hilda" for her to be genuine, but the wigged version must be mold number 245 or 237; the bald-head version has the German registration number 1070. Beth Karp Collection. (Photo: Lee Krombholz)

174

Kestner Doll & Porcelain Factory

32. Bisque socket-head googly by Kestner; original plaster pate, wig and clothing; raised, slanted and shaded multi-stroke eyebrows; black outline of eye socket; closely spaced painted upper eyelashes; large, side-glancing glass stationary eyes; closed smiling mouth; 11½-inch doll; circa 1913; marked: **made in //A.Germany.5.// J.D.K.//221//ges. gesch**. Beth Karp Collection. (Photo: Lee Krombholz)

Chapter 7

33. Light yellow-brown bisque socket head by Kestner; wig; multi-stroke eyebrows; painted upper eyelashes; Asian-type eye cuts; glass sleep eyes; open mouth with upper teeth and separate tongue; 13-inch doll; circa 1914; marked: **made in//J. Germany 10//243//JDK// made in Germany**. Beth Karp Collection. (Photo: Gregg Smith)

34. Hilda bisque socket head by Kestner; wig; multi-stroke eyebrows; painted upper and lower eyelashes; glass sleep eyes; open mouth with upper teeth and separate tongue; 11-inch doll; GM 1914; marked: **C. made in Germany 7.//245//J.D.K. Jr.//1914//© Hilda**. Ann Cummings Collection. (Photo: John Cummings)

36. Hilda bisque socket head by Kestner; wig; multi-stroke eyebrows; painted upper and lower eyelashes; glass sleep eyes; open mouth with upper teeth and separate tongue; 20½-inch doll; GM 1914; marked: **No.16. made in 16.//Germany// 245//J.D.K. Jr.//1914//©// Hilda//ges. gesch. N. 1070**. This mold number was the first in the Hilda series. Some of the separate tongues in the Hilda series are on springs. Georgia Alarcon Collection. (Photo: Estelle Johnston)

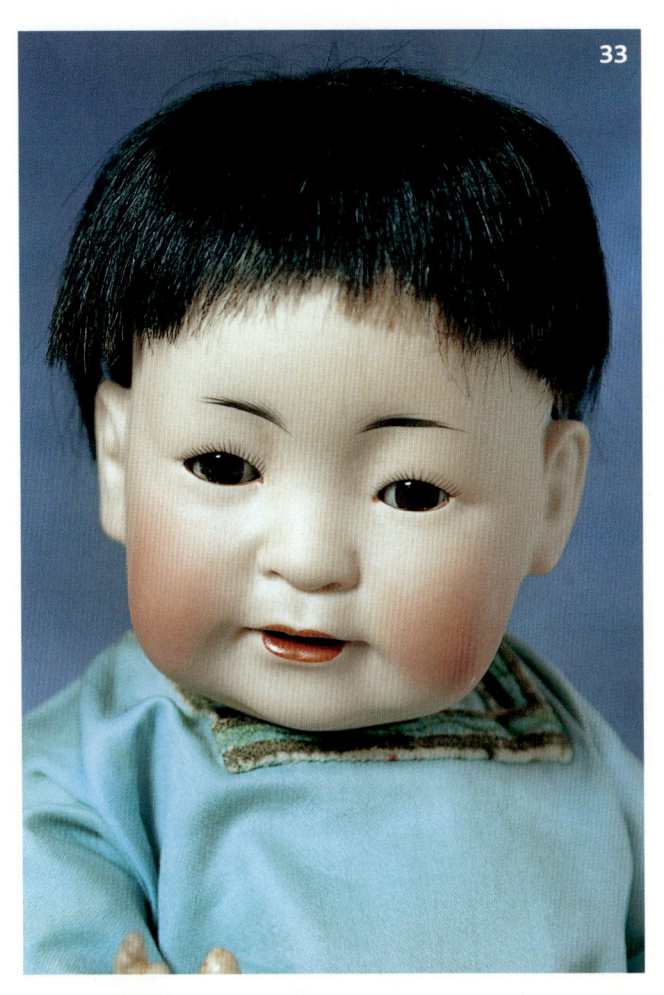

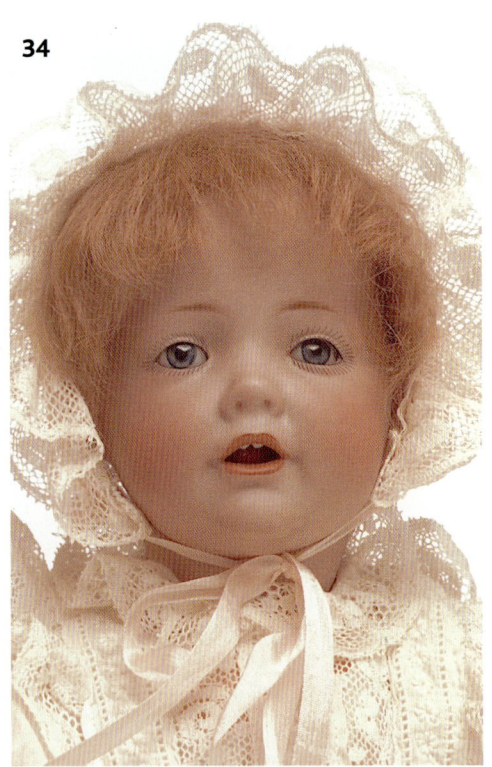

35. Hilda-type bisque socket head by Kestner; skin wig; multi-stroke eyebrows; painted upper and lower eyelashes; glass sleep eyes; open mouth with upper teeth and separate tongue; cheek dimples; 16-inch-doll; GM 1915; marked: **No.12. made in 12.//Germany//247//J.D.K.//12**. The mold number 247 was made right after the mold number 245. Georgia Alarcon. (Photo: Estelle Johnston)

Kestner Doll & Porcelain Factory

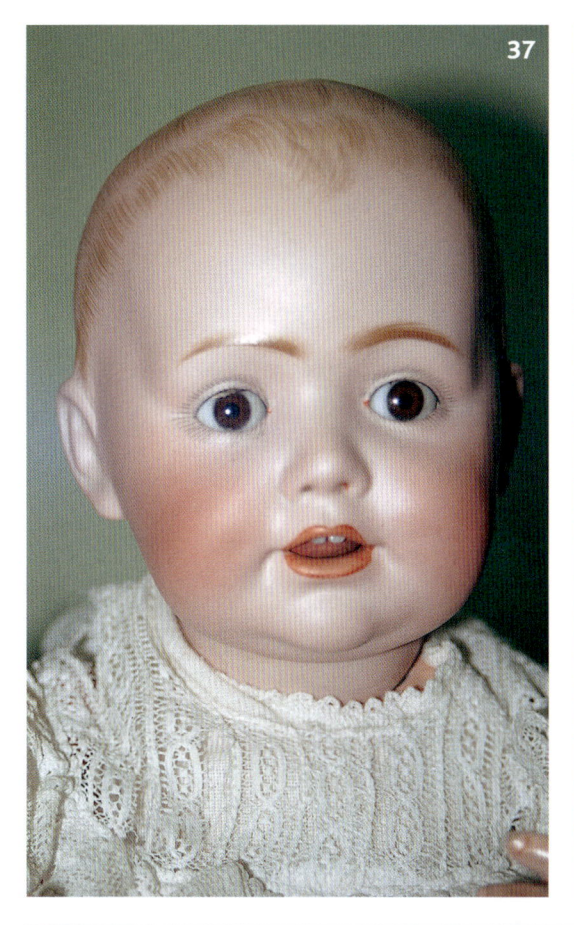

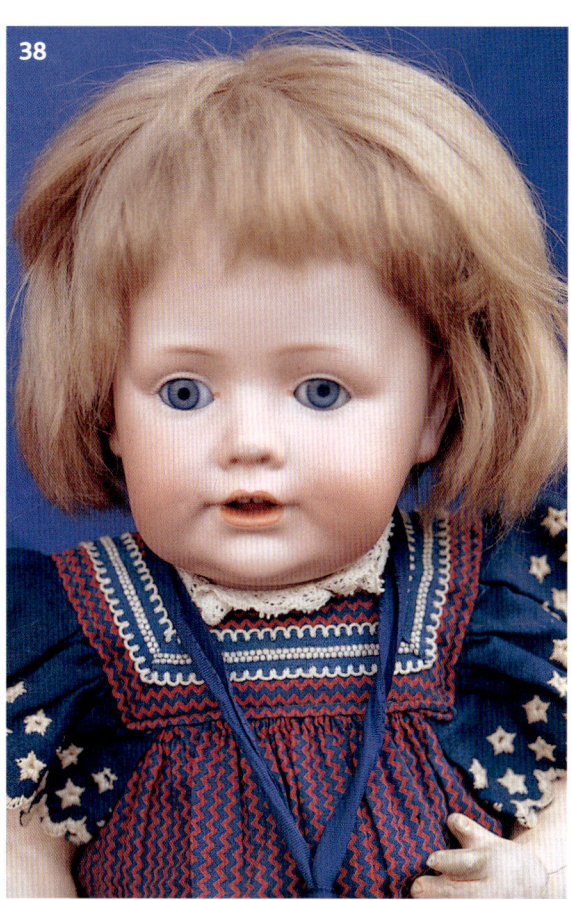

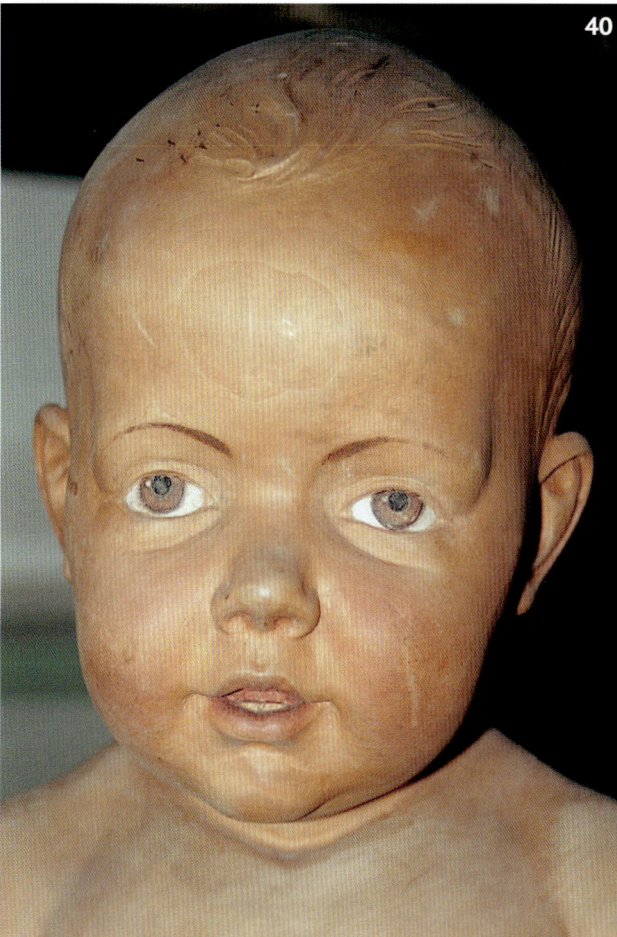

37. Hilda-type bisque socket head by Kestner; molded hair; multi-stroke eyebrows; painted upper and lower eyelashes; glass sleep eyes; open mouth with upper teeth and separate tongue; 15½-inch doll; unmarked. Courtesy Museum Schloss Tenneberg, Waltershausen. (Photo: Christiane Gräfnitz)

38. Hilda-type bisque socket head by Kestner; wig; multi-stroke eyebrows; painted upper and lower eyelashes; glass sleep eyes; open mouth with upper teeth and separate tongue; 13¾-inch doll; GM 1915; marked: **JDK//247**. Christa Dorner Collection. (Photo: Christiane Gräfnitz)

39. Bisque socket head by Kestner; bald-headed version of Hilda; molded hair; multi-stroke eyebrows; painted upper and lower eyelashes; glass sleep eyes; open mouth with upper teeth and separate tongue; 15-inch doll; GM 1915; marked: **ges. gesch// JDK//N. 1070//11// made in Germany**. Georgia Alarcon Collection. (Photo: Estelle Johnston)

40. Original Hilda wooden head and shoulders model. Note the molded wooden tongue and lower teeth. Courtesy Museum Schloss Tenneberg, Waltershausen. (Photo: Christiane Gräfnitz)

177

Chapter 7

41. Hilda-type bisque socket head by Kestner; multi-stroke eyebrows; painted upper and lower eyelashes; glass sleep eyes; open/closed mouth with upper teeth and separate tongue; cheek dimples; 11-inch doll; GM 1915; marked: **JDK//7//made in Germany**. Georgia Alarcon Collection. (Photo: Estelle Johnston)

42. Bisque socket head by Kestner; wig; multi-stroke eyebrows; painted upper and lower eyelashes; glass sleep eyes; open mouth with upper teeth and separate tongue; 13½-inch doll; circa 1916; marked: **made in//Germany//J.D.K.//257**. Ferna Nolte Collection. (Photo: Christiane Gräfnitz)

44. Bisque socket head by Kestner; wig; multi-stroke eyebrows; painted upper and lower eyelashes; side-glancing, flirty glass eyes; open mouth with upper teeth and separate tongue; 15¾-inch doll; circa 1916; marked: **made in//Germany//J.D.K.//257**. Christa Dorner Collection. (Photo: Christiane Gräfnitz)

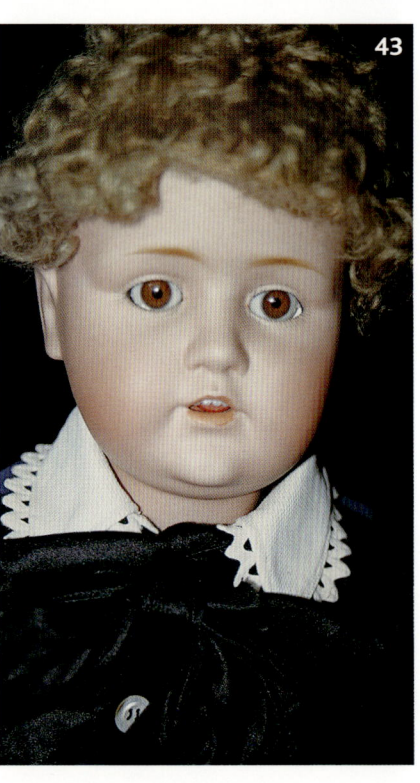

43. Bisque socket head by Kestner; wig; multi-stroke eyebrows; painted upper and lower eyelashes; glass sleep eyes; open mouth with upper teeth and separate tongue; 20-inch doll; circa 1915; marked: **a½.made in Germany.4½.//Germany//249//J.D.K.** Courtesy Museum Schloss Tenneberg, Waltershausen. (Photo: Christiane Gräfnitz)

178

Kestner Doll & Porcelain Factory

45. Two bisque socket heads by Kestner; wigs; multi-stroke eyebrows; painted upper and lower eyelashes; glass sleep eyes; open mouths with upper teeth and molded tongues; 21½-and-14-inch dolls; circa 1916; both marked: **made in Germany// JDK//260//Germany**, and a size number in centimeters. Beth Karp Collection. (Photo: Lee Krombholz)

46. Bisque socket head by Kestner for the Kley & Hahn doll factory in Ohrdruf; wig; multi-stroke eyebrows; painted upper and lower eyelashes; glass sleep eyes; open mouth with upper teeth and molded tongue; 23¾-inch doll; circa 1920; marked: **266 K&H//680**. Private Collection. (Photo: Christiane Gräfnitz)

47. Bisque socket head by Kestner: wig; multi-stroke eyebrows; painted upper and lower eyelashes; glass sleep eyes; open mouth with upper teeth and molded tongue; 16½-inch doll; circa 1916; marked: **JDK//260**. Courtesy Schloss Tenneberg, Waltershausen. (Photo: Christiane Gräfnitz)

48. Bisque socket head by Kestner; wig; multi-stroke eyebrows; painted upper and lower eyelashes; side-glancing, flirty glass eyes; open mouth with upper teeth and molded tongue; 20-inch doll; circa 1916; marked: **made in Germany//JDK//260**. Ann Cummings Collection. (Photo: John Cummings)

Chapter 7

50. Bisque socket head by Kestner for the Century Doll Company; flange neck; molded hair; single-stroke eyebrows; painted upper and lower eyelashes; glass sleep eyes; closed mouth; 13-inch doll; marked: **Germany// Century Doll & Co.** In 1925, the Century Doll Company of New York advertised a group of bisque baby heads made by the Kestner porcelain factory. Ann Cummings Collection. (Photo: John Cummings)

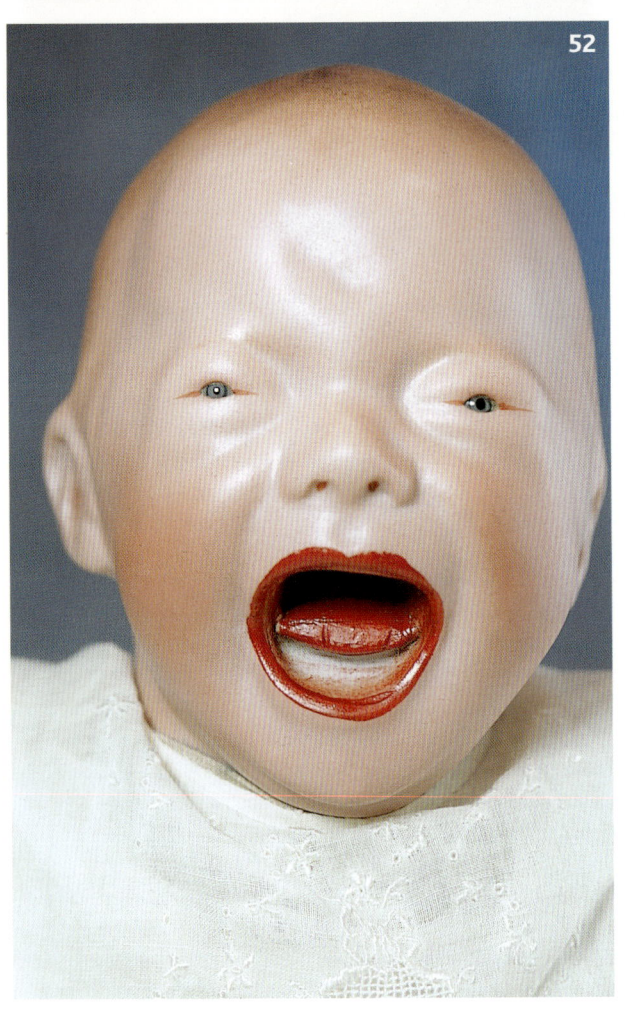

- **49.** Sweetums bisque socket head by Kestner for the Century Doll Company; flange neck; smooth painted head; single-stroke eyebrows; painted upper and lower eyelashes; glass sleep eyes; closed mouth; 13-inch doll; circa 1925; marked: **Century Doll Co.//Kestner//Germany**. Original circular paper hangtag reads: "A CENTURY BABY DOLL//*Sweetums*//Century Dolls." Christa Dorner Collection. (Photo: Christiane Gräfnitz)

- **51.** All-bisque googly by Kestner; jointed at the knees, hips, elbows and shoulders; 6 inch doll; unmarked. Kathy and Mike Embry Collection. (Photo: Kathy Embry)

- **52.** Bisque socket head with reddish complexion by Kestner; flange neck; smooth painted head; single-stroke eyebrows; tiny, stationary glass eyes; open/closed crying mouth with molded tongue and painted circle of lower teeth; 13-inch doll; circa 1916; marked: **255//2//O.I.C.//made in Germany**. Author's Collection. (Photo: Gregg Smith)

Kestner Doll & Porcelain Factory

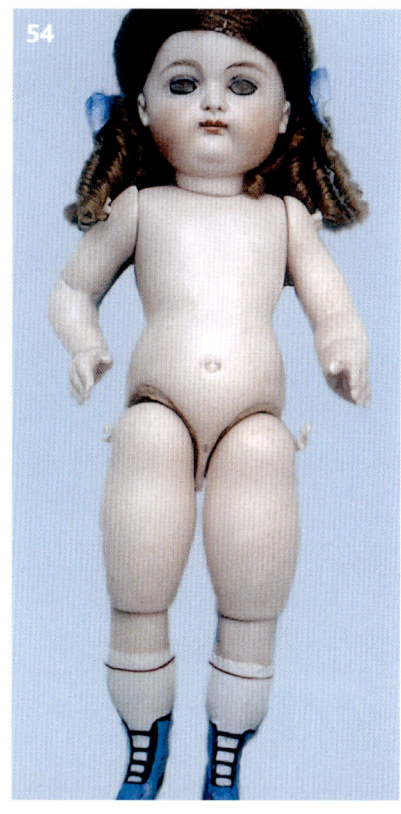

53. A closer view of the unmarked Kestner googly pictured in illustration 51 shows the bisque socket head; wig; single-stroke eyebrows; painted upper and lower eyelashes; side-glancing glass eyes; closed smiling mouth. Kathy and Mike Embry Collection. (Photo: Kathy Embry)

54. All-bisque doll by Kestner; jointed at the knees, hips and shoulders; wig; multi-stroke eyebrows; painted upper and lower eyelashes; glass sleep eyes; closed mouth; 9-inch-doll; unmarked. The bulbous lower legs, with white stockings and these laced high-heeled boots are identification features of some Kestner all-bisque dolls. Private Collection, formerly Jane Walker Collection. (Photo: C.W. Walker)

55. This 1910 original postcard features the German comic characters Max and Moritz. Illustrations of the mischievous boys, drawn by German humorist Wilhelm Busch, first appeared in his 1865 book titled *Max und Moritz*. The book was translated into English in 1962 and titled *Max and Moritz, the Story of Two Rascals in Seven Pranks*. Author's Archival Paper Collection.

56. All-bisque Max and Moritz googlies by Kestner; molded hair; single-stoke eyebrows; smiling mouths; 5 and 5½ inches in height; circa 1918; unmarked. The two dolls are pictured on page 8 of my 1918 Kestner original sample book. Kathy and Mike Embry Collection. (Photo: Ann Hanat)

Chapter 7

57. Max bisque socket-head googly by Kestner; black molded hair with bangs; single-stroke eyebrows; intaglio side-glancing eyes; closed smiling mouth. Kathy and Mike Embry Collection. (Photo: Ann Hanat)

58. Moritz bisque socket-head googly by Kestner; red molded hair with topknot; single-stroke eyebrows; intaglio side-glancing eyes; open/closed smiling mouth. Kathy and Mike Embry Collection. (Photo: Ann Hanat)

60. All-bisque googly by Kestner; molded hair; single-stroke eyebrows; side-glancing painted eyes; closed smiling mouth; white painted socks and one-strap black molded shoes; 5½-inch doll; unmarked. Doll resembles Horseman's Peterkin, designed by Helen Trowbridge. Susan Moore Collection. (Photo: Digital Images)

59. All-bisque Kewpie action figure by Kestner and other Thuringian porcelain factories; 5-inch doll; marked: Rose O'Neill circle and name on bottom of feet. The Kewpie is holding a molded satchel and umbrella. Beth Karp Collection. (Photo: Lee Krombholz)

Kestner Doll & Porcelain Factory

61. Bisque socket head by Kestner for the Catterfelder doll factory in Catterfeld, Thuringia; wig; multi-stroke eyebrows; painted upper and lower eyelashes; open mouth with upper teeth and separate tongue; 11-inch doll; circa 1910; marked: **CP//208**. Courtesy Rothenburg Puppenmuseum/Katharina Engels Collection. (Photo: Christiane Gräfnitz)

62. Bisque socket head by Kestner for the Kley & Hahn doll factory in Ohrdruf; wig; multi-stroke eyebrows; painted upper and lower eyelashes; glass sleep eyes; open mouth with upper teeth and separate tongue; chin dimple; 13-inch doll; circa 1920; marked: **680//36//K&H//made in// Germany**. Author's Collection. (Photo: Gregg Smith)

63. Bisque socket head by Kestner for the Catterfelder doll factory; wig; multi-stroke eyebrows; painted upper and lower eyelashes; glass sleep eyes; open mouth with upper teeth and separate tongue; 20-inch doll; circa 1916; marked: **CP//262//50//Made in Germany//made in Germany//50**. The words "made in Germany" are incised in two different places on the back of the head, with an upper and a lower case letter "M" on the word "made." The Catterfelder trademark on the back of the head is difficult to decipher because the initials are incised with double lines, and a large spiral circle is incised below the initials. This head is pictured on page 15 of my Kestner sample book, with a group of bisque character heads sold separately by the factory. Author's Collection. (Photo: Gregg Smith)

Chapter 7

64. This photograph of the Kestner & Co. porcelain factory in Ohrdruf is pictured in my 1918 original sample book, printed shortly after World War I ended. The single remaining factory building on the site is pictured with the other factory buildings. The book can be dated because the names of the 1918 company directors are listed on the left side of the crown under the words "J.D. Kestner jun." The three former employees led the Kestner factory from the death of Adolf Kestner in 1918 until the factory closed in 1938. Author's Archival Paper Collection.

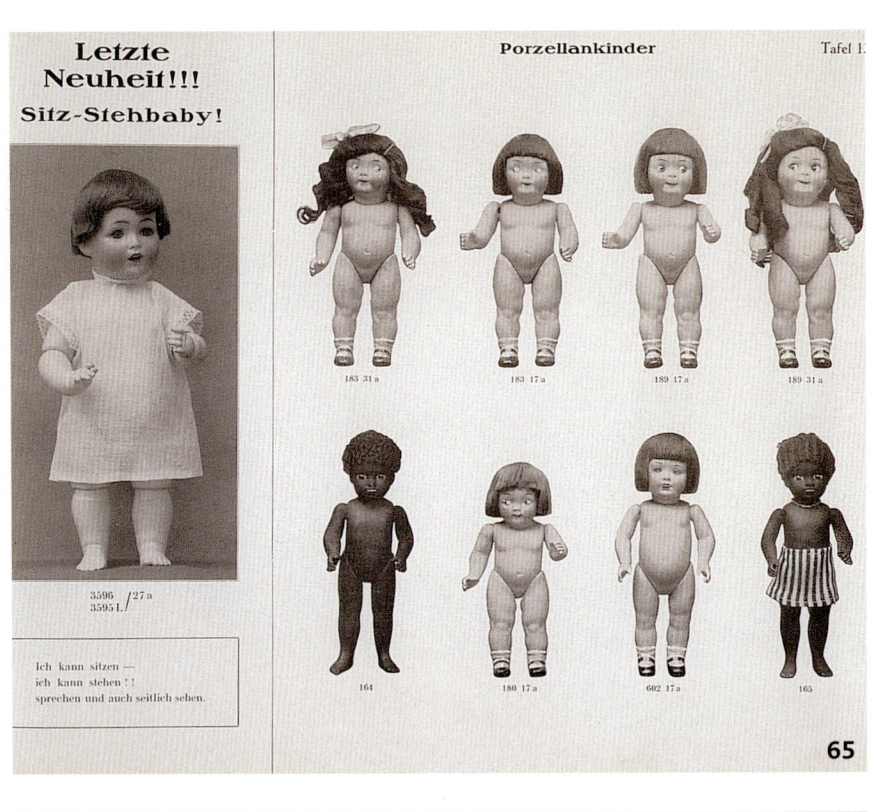

65. Page 12 of the 1918 sample book pictures nine Kestner character dolls with jointed bodies. The heading over the eight all-bisque dolls is *Porzellankinder* (porcelain children). Five all-bisque googlies, with painted and glass eyes, have white-molded socks and one-strap black shoes. The two dark-brown all-bisque dolls have glass stationary eyes and molded teeth. The standing doll with a jointed composition body and original chemise on the left side of the page is described as a "sitting and standing baby." Author's Archival Paper Collection.

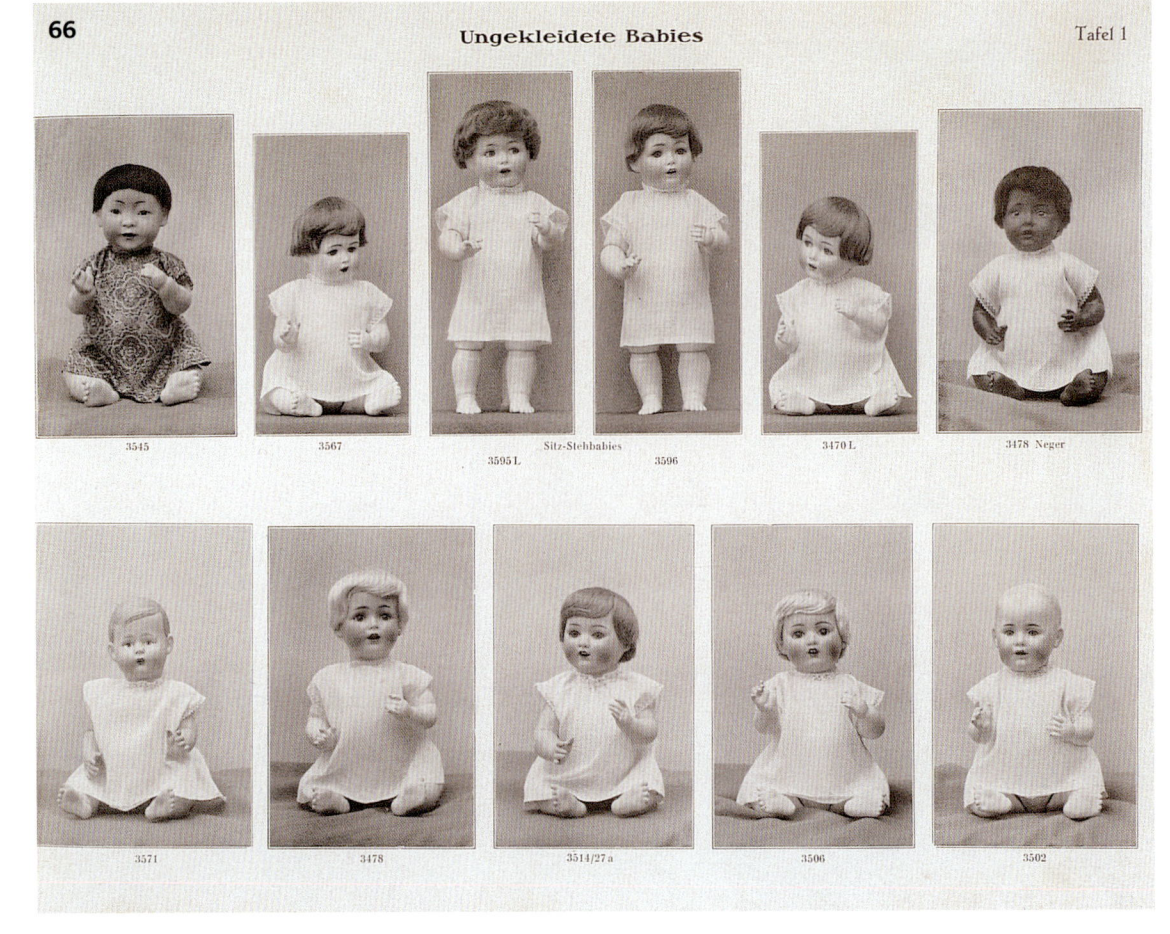

66. Eleven dolls with five-piece jointed composition baby bodies and bisque character heads are pictured on page one of my Kestner sample book. Many of the babies are marked with the mold number 257 and wear original chemises. An Asian baby in a flowered chemise, marked 243, is identical to a bisque-headed doll dressed in an Asian jacket pictured in illustration 33 of this chapter. A dark-brown bisque-head Hilda is pictured on the far right of the top row, and a bald-headed Hilda is pictured on the far right of the bottom row. Author's Archival Paper Collection.

184

Kestner Doll & Porcelain Factory

67. Page 5 of the sample book pictures seven dolls dressed in white slips. The doll in the center of the top row is wearing a Kestner crown paper label and the undressed boy on the right top row has a celluloid character head and body. The two small dolls in the middle of the bottom row have 1920s flapper-type bodies. Although this sample book was not distributed before 1918, it was probably reprinted for many years following the initial printing. Each page has three punched holes so that sample books in succeeding years could easily be made by changing and adding pages to the original book. Author's Archival Paper Collection.

68. Twenty bisque socket heads, fourteen with wigs and six without wigs, are pictured on page 15 of the sample book. The wigs include boyish side-parted hairstyles (top row) as well as girls' hairstyles with straight short hair and bangs and some featuring longer side-parted hair. Bisque heads with molded hair and open crowns are also pictured on this page of the sample book. The Kestner porcelain factory sold large amounts of bisque character heads without bodies to a variety of doll factories in the Sonneberg and Waltershausen areas, including the bisque head in this chapter's illustration 63, which is also pictured on this page of the Kestner sample book. Author's Archival Paper Collection.

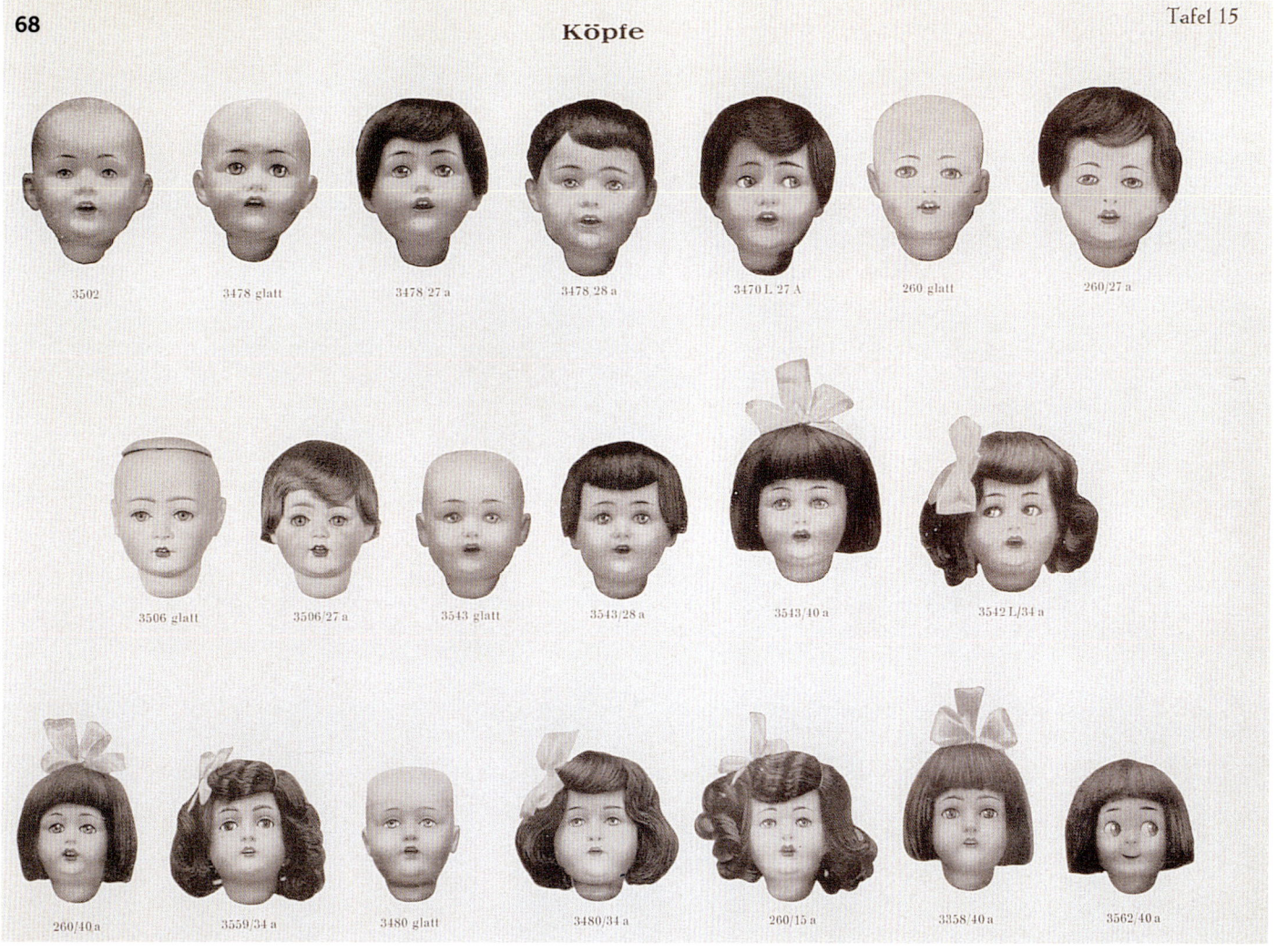

Chapter 7

69. A variety of composition body parts are pictured on page 17 of the sample book, including a standard child's body, a narrow more-adult-type body and a chubby baby body. The molded composition arms and legs strung on the bodies vary in size and design. Weighted glass sleep eyes are pictured, along with rubber cord and wire. Author's Archival Paper Collection.

70. Page 18 of the sample book is titled "*Perücken*," the German word for wigs. This important page shows the variety of hairstyles worn by original Kestner dolls. The wigs on the top row from left to right include: a center-parted wig with short loose curls; a wig with smooth crown and long braids; a wig with very long straight hair; a wig with short curly hair featuring a barrette and a large silk hair ribbon; and a wig with a center-parted hairstyle and long corkscrew curls. The remainder of wigs pictured include: short boyish wigs, short straight-haired wigs with bangs; a center-parted wig with coiled braids on each side of a center part; a wig with a long circular roll of hair; and, a wig made up of dozens of small tight curls. Author's Archival Paper Collection.

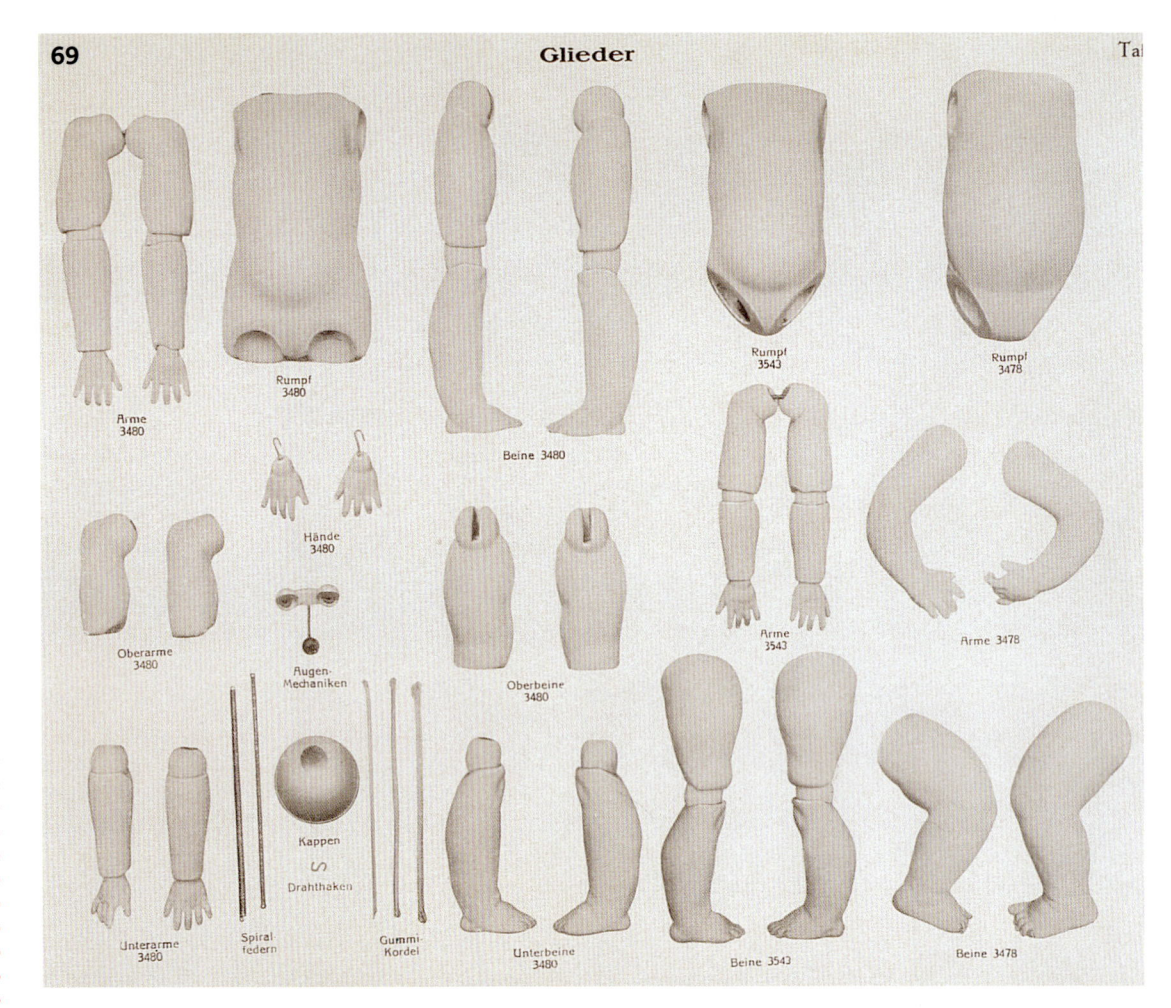

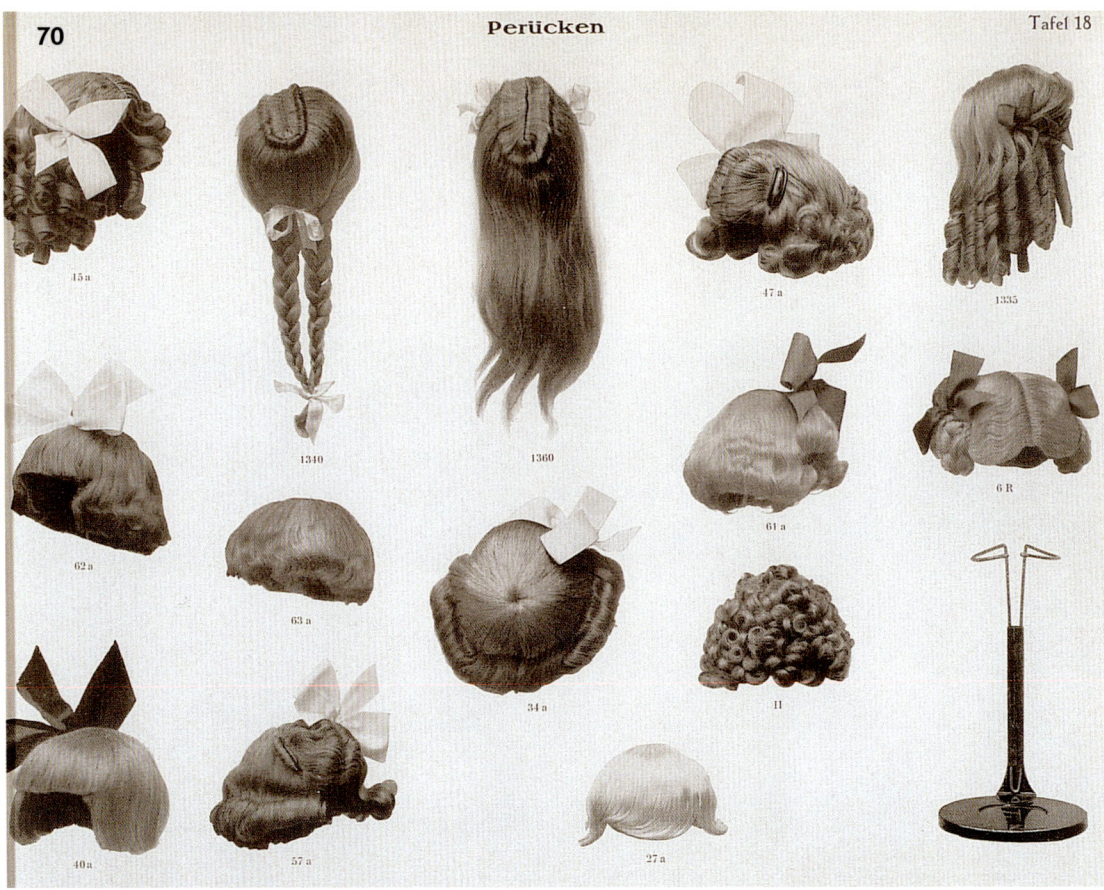

186

Kestner Doll & Porcelain Factory

Puppenschuhe

71. Seventy-two pairs of boxed doll shoes are pictured on page 20 of the sample book, varying in color and style, including fifty-three pairs with rounded toes and shoelaces. Most of the shoes have shoelaces, except for the one-strap shoes with metal-snap fasteners. The high-heeled shoes with pointed toes stand out because they resemble French-type shoes. Author's Archival Paper Collection.

Part Two

INTRODUCTION

Sonneberg as a Dollmaking Center

Sonneberg was a large dollmaking center long before Waltershausen became a successful center for assembling dolls. It is difficult to understand how such a small town could become the world's largest producer of dolls and toys. By studying the history of Sonneberg from the 1200s on, we can understand the events that influenced dollmaking in this area. One of the first recorded buildings in Sonneberg was a castle built on top of a hill in 1207 by a family named Von Sonneberg. In 1350 the town became a stop on the trading routes between Nuremberg and Erfurt. Although trading continued, the population of Sonneberg numbered less than one thousand residents for the next three hundred years.

Farming was difficult because of the poor, rocky soil, so residents were forced to turn to other occupations to support themselves. The mountains surrounding Sonneberg contained large slate deposits, offering a valuable source of income. Slate was used to cover the sides and roofs of buildings, and also to make slate blackboards and slate pencils. Slate was harvested only when the Thuringian mountains were free of snow. In order to generate income during the winter months, the industrious German families began carving wooden spoons, saucers and other household items to sell to the Nuremberg merchants who stopped to spend the night before going through the nearby mountain pass on their way to the Leipzig fairs.

Sonneberg wooden items were sold as Nuremberg Wares until the Thirty-Years War, which was fought from 1616 to 1648. The small town of Sonneberg lost three-fourths of its residents during the war, and Nuremberg also suffered greatly. But Sonneberg was able to recover before Nuremberg and for the first time, Sonneberg wood carvers were forced to sell their own products. They traveled throughout the surrounding countryside in search of buyers and soon found a strong market for their well-made wares.

In the late 1600s, a wood carver added small wooden dolls and toys to his sales line and other carvers followed suit. But the major impetus to the new doll and toy production was the introduction of a bread-dough mixture in about 1740. Low-grade flour and gum water were combined with bread to make faces of bread dough which were pressed onto small wooden bodies. Bread-dough products were an excellent source of income because the bread dough was inexpensive and very easy to mold. The 1805 introduction of papier-mâché by Johann Friedrich Mueller also increased the variety of Sonneberg dolls and toys offered for sale.

The Sonneberg *Beausirers* (bread-dough makers) and *Puppenhersteller* (dollmakers) decided to found a Trade Guild in the late 1700s. But arguments between members of the Guild limited production. In an effort to stop the bickering and stimulate the doll and toy industry, Duke Georg the First signed The Great Sonneberg Privilege of Trade on February 24, 1789. The Privilege gave twenty-six Sonneberg merchants and four merchants from neighboring villages the exclusive right of trade. All doll and toy production came under the complete control of these thirty men. They were called *Verlegers*, and met weekly with the Lord Mayor and the brewery owners to develop a feeling of unity. In 1817 a private association made up of this group of influential citizens was founded in Sonneberg under the name *Casino-Gesellschaft* (Casino Society).

In the decades following 1789 there were many marriages between sons and daughters of the merchants who belonged

1. This 1910 original postcard of Sonneberg shows all of the red-tile roofed buildings that were located in this picturesque dollmaking town when bisque-head character dolls were introduced. Author's Archival Paper Collection.

to the Casino Society. These strong family and Lutheran Church ties formed a very solid base for the rapidly growing doll industry. By 1826 some of the Sonneberg doll and toy makers had yearly sales totaling nearly two million dollars and inventories of more than one thousand doll- and toy-related items.

Unfortunately, the preferential treatment of a few merchants created large differences in income between the residents of Sonneberg. Three very distinct working groups emerged, with completely different and very defined responsibilities. For the seventy-three years that the The Great Sonneberg Privilege of Trade was in effect, the *Verlegers* became quite wealthy. Although *Verlegers* were not allowed to own a doll or toy factory until the Privilege was rescinded in 1862, they were completely responsible for the growth of their own doll companies. Therefore, *Verlegers* concentrated on generating business and securing orders by introducing new doll designs. They traveled all over the world to find potential customers. *Verlegers* also placed orders, financed and arranged for delivery of their own products. Basically, they financed the dollmaking process from beginning to end.

Directly under the *Verlegers* were the factory owners. In Sonneberg, doll production was carried out by a large number of specialized home and factory workshops. Doll-factory owners received doll orders from the *Verlegers* and then assigned their own factory and home-trade workers to produce the dolls. The home-trade workers picked up supplies from the factories, like composition body and limb molds, which they used to mold body parts at their own homes. They then delivered the body parts to doll factories, where the parts were assembled into a complete doll. While the assembly took place in workshops referred to as doll factories, quite often these were comprised of only one or two rooms in a worker's home. There were often as many as thirty-eight workers responsible for making a single doll from start to finish.

The home-trade workers in Sonneberg made up the largest part of the Sonneberg work force. For hundreds of years, Thuringian towns and villages were filled with a largely unseen work force. These home workers, known as *Hausindustrielle*, made doll body parts, wigs, shoes and everything else necessary for the assembly of complete dolls, from morning to night, year after year, in the privacy of their own homes. At the turn of the nineteenth century, there were more than fifty thousand home-trade and factory workers living in Sonneberg and the surrounding villages. The valley in which the town of Sonneberg lies measures only six square miles. During the years bisque-head character dolls were made, about twenty-five thousand men, women and children lived in Sonneberg. The numerous villages surrounding Sonneberg provided the remaining work force.

One two-story home in Sonneberg held as many as seventy workers during the six weeks before Christmas, forcing the workers to eat and sleep in shifts. During the early 1900s, the majority of orders were needed for Christmas. And there was scarcely a house in Sonneberg that was not connected to doll and toy making during the years character dolls were made.

It is fortunate for antique-doll collectors that a group of children and grandchildren of the original Sonneberg home

INTRODUCTION

2. Home workers' houses filled the hillsides surrounding Sonneberg during the dollmaking years, and they still stand, reminding townspeople and visitors of the important work carried out by hundreds of dollmaking families. (Photo: Mary Krombholz)

workers agreed to give oral histories of their memories relating to dollmaking in the Sonneberg area. These were published in 1995 in a book titled: *Sonneberger Geschichten Von Puppen, Griffeln und Kuckuckspfiefen (Sonneberg Stories of Dolls, Slate Pencils and Cuckoo Whistles)*. This important book, in which the children and grandchildren of original home workers share the stories of their lives during the years their parents and grandparents made dolls, toys, slate pencils and cuckoo whistles in home workshops, documents the lives of many home workers in the Sonneberg area.

Author Angelika Tessmer explains the stories on the first page of the book.

> To collect and convey pictures of the workaday world of our parents and grandparents, as long as the knowledge of the handcraft tradition, native works and old techniques are still able to be found, is the concern of this book.
>
> Much that is today scarcely yet known – never assembled and described, took shape again through long conversations. Much, at first glance, may seem long-winded and confusing, but the old work techniques should be preserved as exactly as possible. Who amongst us has yet played with a ratchet, knows the artistic qualifications for braiding, or can describe the layout or atmosphere of an old workroom? We don't want to create a monument to our parents and grandparents, for they have already done so, long ago, through their work. We want to preserve a portion, which the people of our region have written with us, which leaves us proud, to conquer life through tradition, capability and personal fortitude. To all who helped with the portrayal, and brought the past near, we would like to thank. We will guard your inheritance.

To protect the privacy of the home workers and their families, I have not listed any of the names of the men and women who gave the oral histories included in this book.

The first oral history in the book is titled: "Sonneberg the Toyland." The town of Sonneberg is described in the following way.

In Sonneberg and the surrounding region various handcrafts already developed around the year 1600; the first toymakers settled in here because of the abundance of wood. They founded the beginning of the toy industry. Already in 1735 there were about 30 different kinds of wooden toy wares. In addition to the whetstones, they built a visible Sonneberg trade region for the Nürnberg tradesmen who traveled the old trade route from Nürnberg to Leipzig. Wooden dolls, dancing and pull-toys (dolls made of wood), forest horns, flutes, small pipes, riders and horse teams were the first toys Sonneberg sent into the world.

Can you envision that in Sonneberg there was scarcely a house in which toy products were not either produced, or bought up and packed for export? Also in the outlying sections of the city and villages there were a great many families whose livelihoods were toy production. Here the home workshops or small family factories worked on production of parts which were then assembled in the factories of Sonneberg.

Another oral history describes the work of a dollmaker: "The dollmaker completed the masterful preliminary work of the molder, the body maker, the head maker, the painter, the eye maker, the wig maker, the shoe maker, the voice maker, the cardboard processor and the box maker, who delivered their products to him twice a week."

The chapters in Part Two of this book provide specific information on the types of character dolls made by Sonneberg-area dollmakers from 1910 until the 1940s. The town's entry in the 1910 Brussels' World's Fair calls it the "World's Largest Doll & Toy Center;" by studying the Sonneberg-area dolls pictured in this book, we can revisit the dollmaking years in the town that was exactly that for more than four hundred years.

Sonnenberg as a Doll Making Center

3. A home worker known as a "hair dresser" created hair strands in a room that looked much like this one. Hair strands and bisque heads are grouped on the typical type of worktable once found in the small kitchen of a Sonneberg home worker. Several home workers' rooms have been reproduced for the dollmaking exhibits located in the basement of the Sonneberg doll museum. (Photo: Courtesy Deutsches Spielzeugmuseum, Sonneberg)

4. Several families shared each of these two-story workers' houses in Sonneberg during the years dollmaking was the principal occupation. (Photo: Mary Krombholz)

5. A closer view of the worktable shows the wooden pegs and knotted hair strands. Children often did this type of work because their tiny fingers could quickly knot the hair. (Photo: Christiane Gräfnitz)

6. In this hand-colored photograph a Sonneberg home worker is delivering a large stack of boxes that are tied on top of her *Schanzen* (delivery basket). It was a common sight during the dollmaking years to see women of all ages delivering doll parts with large delivery baskets strapped to their backs. (Photo: Courtesy Deutsches Spielzeugmuseum, Sonneberg)

INTRODUCTION

7. The German text below this 1911 photograph, which has been hand colored, translates to read "Home Industry" and "Cleaning and Scraping Stamped Doll Parts." A grandmother and one of her grandsons are sanding the rough edges on the small wooden doll parts piled in their work aprons, while the grandson on the right is scouring the rough edges with a knife.

8. This 1910 original postcard pictures Untere Marketstrasse in Sonneberg, which was the center of activity for more than one hundred years. Outdoor booths filled the area on Saturdays, when home workers from the surrounding villages delivered their doll parts to the Sonneberg doll factories. After receiving money for their work, men and women often bought food and other necessities from vendors. Author's Archival Paper Collection.

9. This 1910 original Sonneberg postcard shows two child-sized wagons "parked" on one side of the muddy street. Children often used their wagons to deliver dolls and doll parts made and/or assembled by their families in the small home factories located on every street in Sonneberg. Author's Archival Paper Collection.

10. The 1910 Sonneberg Doll Museum building once housed the Sonneberg School of Industry, where students learned all of the skills relating to dollmaking, including drawing, modeling, painting, wood carving and mechanics. In 1838 the Sonneberg Association of Trade was founded; in 1883 the School of Industry was founded. The building became the site of the doll museum in 1929. The museum's doll collection, which covers hundreds of years of dollmaking, is the finest collection of Sonneberg-area dolls in the world. (Photo: Mary Krombholz)

11. This bisque-head character doll was sold by the Sonneberg dollmaker Theodor Hornlein, who assembled dolls in Sonneberg from 1879 until the 1930s with bisque heads made by unidentified Thuringian porcelain factories. An identical doll was purchased at the F.A.O. Schwarz toy store in New York in 1915. Head features include a wig; multi-stroke eyebrows; intaglio-painted eyes; dimples and a smiling open/closed mouth with teeth and tongue. The 12-inch, circa-1912 doll is marked **T.H.7**. Julie Blewis Collection. (Photo: Fanilya Gueno)

HAUSINDUSTRIE.   ABPUTZEN GESTANZTER PUPPENHÄNDE.

Sonnenberg as a Doll Making Center

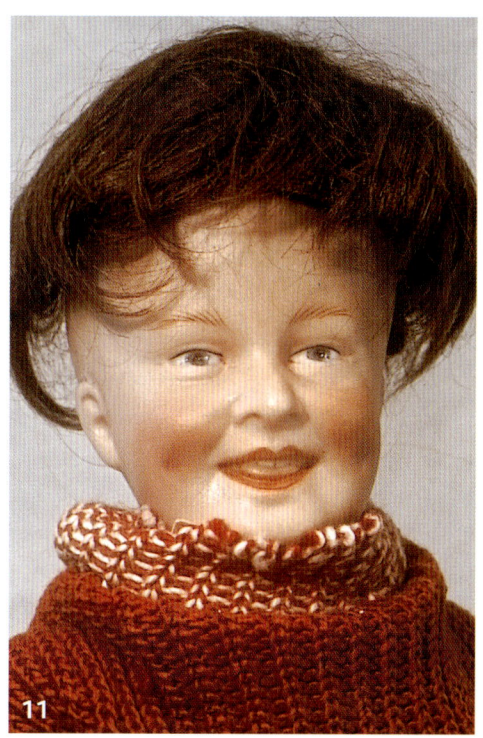

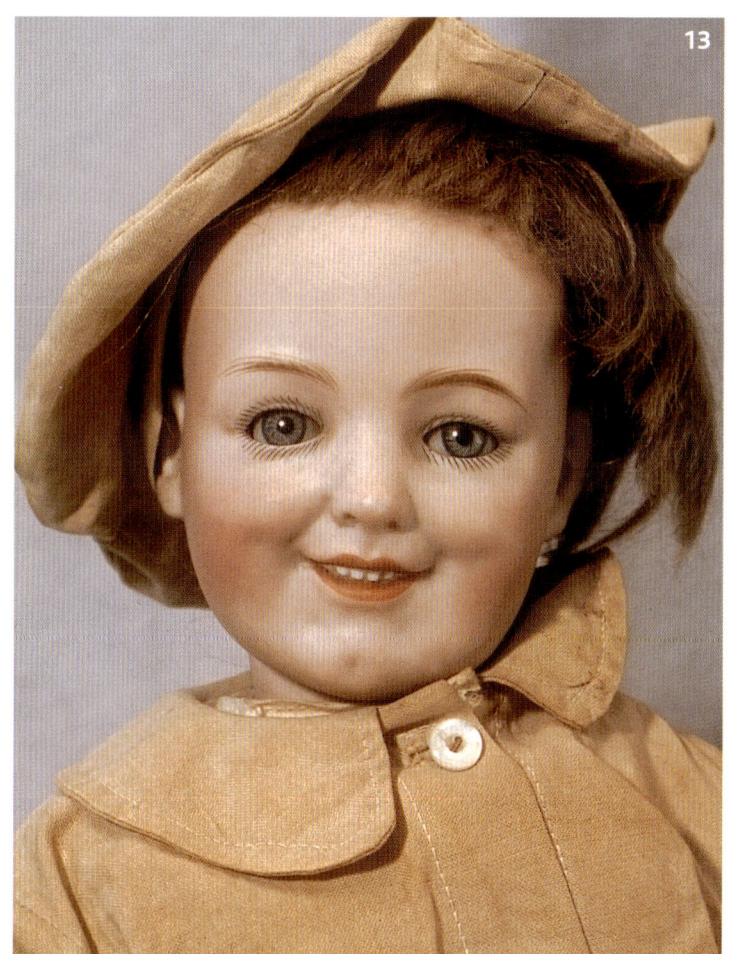

13. This uncommon 12-inch bisque character-head doll was made by Armand Marseille, circa 1912. Head features include a wig; multi-stroke eyebrows; upper and lower painted eyelashes; glass sleep eyes; cheek and chin dimples and an open/closed mouth with upper teeth. The doll is marked A0M//570. Julie Blewis Collection. (Photo: Fanilya Gueno)

12. Most of the 278 original doll factories in Sonneberg are still standing. This bisque character-head doll was sold by the Sonneberg dollmaker Fritz Bierschenk, who assembled dolls with bisque heads made by unknown Thuringian porcelain factories from 1906 until the 1930s. Head features include the original wig; single-stroke eyebrows; intaglio eyes with white highlights and open mouth with upper teeth and tongue. The 18-inch doll, GM 1910, is marked FB//616/2. Courtesy Rosalie Whyel Museum of Doll Art. (Photo: Christiane Gräfnitz)

193

Part Two

Chapter 1

Cuno & Otto Dressel Doll Factory

The Cuno & Otto Dressel doll factory was founded circa 1700 by Johann Georg Dressel. This important Sonneberg doll factory made dolls and toys for a longer period of time than any other doll factory in Thuringia. In the early years of production, the Dressel doll factory made wooden and papier-maché dolls and toys. The factory continued to make wooden and papier-maché dolls in the ensuing years, but also produced large numbers of dolls made of wax, glazed porcelain, bisque, composition and celluloid. The company name "Cuno & Otto Dressel" was first used in 1873. In 1875 the doll factory registered a stylized helmet with wings as a trademark. The oval below the wings contained the words *Holz Masse*, which means wood mass.

It is difficult to attribute even a small portion of the dolls assembled and sold by the factory to Dressel with any certainty because the bodies were seldom marked, and also because the factory bought heads and doll parts from so many doll and porcelain factories in both the Sonneberg and the Waltershausen areas. The New York importers Butler Brothers acted as distributor for the majority of products made by the Cuno & Otto Dressel doll factory. Butler Brothers had branches in Sonneberg, St. Louis, Chicago, Minneapolis, Dallas, San Francisco and Boston. The Dressel factory assembled a large number of doll- and toy-related products in their own doll factory, but they also bought and sold products made by many Sonneberg-area doll factories and home workers.

1. This photograph pictures Ernst Friedrich Dressel (1797-1870), youngest son of Johann Friedrich Dressel, founder of the Dressel doll factory. Ernst Dressel was one of the original Sonneberg *Verlegers*. His wife, Henriette Bishop, was a descendant of Gotthelf Greiner, who is credited with producing the first Thuringian hard-paste porcelain at the Limbach porcelain factory on November 10, 1772. (Photo: Courtesy Deutsches Spielzeugmuseum, Sonneberg)

A large number of Dressel bisque-head character dolls featured heads made by the Simon & Halbig porcelain factory. They were often marked with the "Jutta" trademark, which was patented in 1907. The following porcelain factories also made bisque shoulder and/or socket heads for the Dressel doll factory: Armand Marseille, Ernst Heubach and Hering & Sohn in Köppeldorf, Schoenau & Hoffmeister in Burggrub and Gebrüder Heubach in Lichte.

From the 1884 book *Wonderland of Work* by Clara L. Mateaux, we learn important facts about the home workers who

2. Ernst Friedrich Dressel Jr.'s villa is still standing in Sonneberg, across the street from the Lutheran church attended by the Dressel family. (Photo: Mary Krombholz)

were employed by a large doll factory like Cuno & Otto Dressel. Mateaux writes:

> Two million dolls are annually exported from Thuringia. The largest number of dolls come from Sonneberg, a thriving town near the northern corner of Bavaria, a neighborhood which is the very center of a real Wonderland of Playthings; for here men and women spend their lives in inventing, improving and making all sorts of pretty and ingenious things of the kind, though the specialty is most decidedly dolls – dolls of every sort and quality, for Dolldom here is a power which keeps many fingers and heads busy.
>
> There is a large school of design, where novelties are continually being studied and treated as a serious business of life; at which we cannot wonder how in Thuringia thirty thousand pairs of hands are employed in doll and toy making, and that Sonneberg alone keeps thousands of men, women and children busy. After this we must look with interest and almost respect at these German 'trifles.' The real makers of the toys live in busy Sonneberg, or in the villages near it, more especially in Friedenbach, Neustadt or Schalkau, where each family has its own particular line of business, and each member of the family does some special portion of it, never attempting to accomplish anything else.
>
> You will see how completely this system of division of labor is carried out in Toydom, the result being that each part is thoroughly done without any waste of time, imperfections or awkwardness; so thus it is that the simplest of these German toys go through a great many hands before they reach those of your little brothers and sisters, for them to play with and break.
>
> For even when they are made and ready, they have to meet with the approval of the merchant who first buys them from the manufacturer, and who, most likely, sells them again wholesale to another dealer, who sells them to the retail shops, from which the little customers will in turn buy them for themselves.

In 1789 Johann Philipp Dressel was awarded the Great Sonneberg Privilege of Trade (see Part Two: Introduction). In 1843 his son Ernst Friedrich Dressel founded the Sonneberg Federation of Trade, an organization made up of ten Sonneberg merchants interested in promoting overseas contacts with the aim of supplying doll-related products to a larger group of customers. Sonneberg-area doll factories used many promotional methods to enlarge their customer base. One of

Chapter 1

3. This is an early-1900s photograph of Otto Dressel (7/30/1831-7/24/1907), co-partner of the Cuno & Otto Dressel doll factory in Sonneberg. In 1873 the Dressel doll factory changed its name from the Ernst & Carl Dressel doll factory to the Cuno & Otto Dressel doll factory. Two years later, the doll factory registered its well-known trademark: a stylized helmet with an oval containing the word *Holzmasse* (wood pulp). (Photo: Courtesy Deutsches Spielzeugmuseum, Sonneberg)

the most effective promotions was a German advertising postcard announcing a new line of doll samples and mailed to customers of American wholesale companies.

An original postcard in my archival paper collection illustrates this type of advertising. The front of the postcard pictures a group of dolls and toys on shelves decorated for Christmas. The valley town of Sonneberg is shown in the distance. Under the Sonneberg doll and toy picture is the following message: "Direct from Sonneberg to Pittsburgh." The address side of the 1910 postcard has the following message: "The Pittsburgh Dry Goods Co. wishes to announce that their Doll Samples are ready and invite your inspection of same, bought personally from the Manufacturer." The last sentence on the address side of the postcard reads: "Published by R.H. for the Pittsburgh Dry Goods Co., Pittsburgh, Pa.; Made in Germany." This postcard also shows the strong business partnerships that existed between Sonneberg doll factories and American wholesale and retail companies.

Ernst Dressel had eight children, one of whom was Cuno Dressel. He spent many years working abroad, contacting owners of large stores. In 1876 the Dressel doll factory participated in the Philadelphia World Exposition. My original 1876 *Philadelphia World Exposition* booklet lists the Cuno & Otto Dressel doll factory as participants in the trade fair. The Dressel products listed for the event included: "dolls and toys of wood, papier-mâché and porcelain, as well as glassware, wax-ware, porcelain-ware, baskets and musical instruments."

Throughout doll history, individual dolls with realistic portrait-like features have been produced. Sculptors trained at industrial schools like the Sonneberg and Lichte schools of modeling and painting were encouraged by their teachers to create dolls of all kinds. Often they were portraits of well-known personalities. In 1898 the Dressel doll factory was commissioned to create a group of portrait dolls of the Spanish-American War heroes. When first considered, this decision is puzzling since the Spanish-American war lasted for only a year, and the dolls had limited appeal from a long-term sales standpoint. But when we understand the history of the Dressel doll factory's solid base of American customers, it is understandable why this particular doll factory was chosen and why the Dressel doll factory decided to market a series of dolls that would appeal to the United States doll market alone.

Dressel ordered the heads from the Simon & Halbig porcelain factory and then relied upon his own doll factory and home trade workers to make the composition-jointed bodies, clothing and military-like accessories. The portrait dolls representing heroes of the Spanish-American War resemble William Thomas Sampson, commander of the Western Atlantic Squadron, who established the blockade of Cuba; Charles Dwight Sigsbee, commander of the battleship Maine at the time it was sunk; Richmond Pearson Hobson, who sank the Merrimac in Santiago harbor in a effort to contain the Spanish fleet; Winfield Scott Schley, who commanded the "Flying Squadron" from Norfolk; George Dewey, commander of the Asiatic Squadron who scored a victory at the Battle of Manila Bay and William McKinley, president during the Spanish-American War.

The majority of bisque-head dolls sold by the Dressel doll factory wore wigs, most of which were made by home workers who lived in the Sonneberg area. We are able to study a group of original wigs worn by Dressel composition and bisque-head dolls because of an exhibit in the basement of the Sonneberg Doll Museum. After being awarded the grand prize at the 1910 Brussels World Exposition, the entire exhibit was moved from Brussels to the building that now houses the Sonneberg doll museum, where it remains today. All of the original 1910 Dressel dolls are still sitting on the seats of the carousel, which remains in perfect working order.

This eye-catching exhibit represented the entire town of Sonneberg. Individual doll factories were not allowed to compete in the Brussels World Exposition, so thirty-seven Sonneberg doll factories worked together to create the component parts of the elaborate display. The exhibit was designed in 1910 by Professor Reinhard Möller, director of the Sonneberg Industrial School. Möller began his sculpting career at the A.W. Fr. Kister porcelain factory, and was then in charge

Cuno & Otto Dressel Doll Factory

4. This late-1880s photograph shows Otto Dressel mounted on his favorite horse. He traveled extensively throughout the United States, taking orders for dolls and toys produced by the Dressel doll factory. (Photo: Courtesy Deutsches Spielzeugmuseum, Sonneberg)

of the modeling department for the Hertwig porcelain factory before becoming the director of the Sonneberg School of Industry.

The scene is of a Thuringian village fair, including a large carousel, on which a number of large dolls are seated. There are also doll and toy booths in the exhibit, filled with a variety of toys, dolls and doll parts. A circus procession is a focal point of the scene, and a group of townspeople are gathered on each side of the procession. Some of the materials used in the display include papier-mâché, textiles, wood, metal, cardboard and animal skins. Special features of the realistic scene include typical Sonneberg slate-covered, half-timbered houses and a shooting gallery. Along with Professor Möller's students, Sonneberg carpenters, cabinetmakers, painters, mechanics, decorators, metal workers, fence makers and saddle makers contributed to the completion of the elaborate scene.

The exhibit allows visitors to see Sonneberg as it was in 1910. If one looks closely, the social structure of Sonneberg is evident. The woman delivering dolls with her tall basket is an onlooker, rather than a participant in the festivities. Other interesting sights include an elderly man offering a sausage to a child, an organ grinder, a musician, farmers, a doll clinic and a woman selling fruits.

The original doll wigs, worn by the composition and bisque-head dolls sitting on the carousel, demonstrate the importance of a wig to the appearance of a doll. The wigs were originally made by Sonneberg tress makers, braid makers and wig makers. There were very different occupations for home workers, and reflect the division of labor relating to hair. Women and children generally worked on tress making, braid making and wig making. Tresses were made by tress makers for the wig makers. This important step involved working with hair strands.

In the book *Sonneberg Stories of Dolls, Slate Pencils and Cuckoo Whistles*, we learn about tress making and braid making.

> We worked mainly on artificial hair that we got in various colors in large skeins from the Breitung doll factory in Sonneberg. We opened the skeins and divided them into pieces that would conform to the needed hair lengths. From these pieces we always took a small bundle and pulled it over a nail board called a *Hechel* (hackle). For that reason this part of the work was known as *Hecheln* (hackling). It served to remove matted hairs.
>
> On the edge of the kitchen table, the two tress pegs were fastened. Between these rods we stretched either three threads for the skeins or four threads for the part in the hair. It was most often children who knitted the hair strands together. With our small fingers we could knot them up quickly and needed only 5-7 minutes to make one hair strand. For adults it was more difficult. The length of the strand was determined by the hairstyle and the size of the doll head. Generally such a hair-strand was enough for a wig. We worked every spare minute in our living room/kitchen, before school, after school, and often deep into the night. My mother watched that we worked neatly.
>
> To make curls from these hair-strands, we wound the hair onto metal rods. We then laid the rods into a hot oven. Naturally we had to watch that the temperature did not get too hot and singe the hair. Through the heat the hair formed into curls. The size of the curls depended on the diameter of the rods. We used thin rods for small curls and thick rods for large curls. Curls were also made in another way. We pressed a hot curling iron made of metal into a piece of beeswax and 'burned' curls or waves into the straight hair. The beeswax held the curls or waves in place.
>
> The finished wigs were carefully removed from the wooden forms. We children stuffed them with tissue paper and packed them in single layers into large cartons. Sometimes we brought the already painted doll

Chapter 1

heads, in which the eyes were already set, from the doll factory. Before we could glue the wigs on, we had to glue the opening on the back of the head shut with a cardboard lid. Twice a week we children delivered the wigs or heads in a wagon to the dollmakers in Sonneberg, and brought back new materials.

On Saturdays Untere Market Square in Sonneberg was the scene of the exchanges of thousands of doll-related goods. It must have been a sight to behold. From every village that surrounded Sonneberg, women and children carried doll parts to the town's many doll factories. The *Schanzen* (delivery baskets), filled with every part of a doll, were covered in white cloths to protect the precious cargo underneath. One historian described "Delivery Day" in vivid detail: "The women carrying the baskets look like gray ghosts as they emerge from the early morning haze." Archival photographs show that the baskets filled with dolls and doll parts sometimes towered six to seven feet over the shoulders of a delivery woman.

One document in the Sonneberg town archives documents the life of Ernestine Brand, a home worker who delivered dolls and doll parts. She walked from the Zinner doll factory in Schalkau to Sonneberg and back three or four times a week. Ernestine was born in Schalkau in 1825. For more than fifty years, she carried dolls and doll parts in the tall wicker basket fastened to her back with leather straps. The trip from Schalkau to Sonneberg took many hours on foot each way. Ernestine died in a roadside ditch on July 10, 1901, at the age of seventy-six, with her wicker basket still on her back. She is reported to have said before she died: "Whenever I feel unable to deliver, I want my life to come to an end."

The variety and the number of dolls assembled and sold by the Cuno & Otto Dressel doll factory outnumber all other doll factories in Sonneberg. One type of doll, described in original catalogs as a "teenaged" doll, was made for the United States market alone. The Simon & Halbig porcelain factory supplied the majority of bisque socket heads for these unique dolls. The wigs were usually short and bobbed to reflect the style popular in the United States during the 1920s. The composition body is very different from a standard child's fully jointed composition body; the long thin arms are un-jointed and the knee joint is much higher in order to show off the shorter skirts typical of this era. The most unusual feature of these flapper dolls is the composition feet, which are molded to accommodate high-heeled shoes.

Cuno & Otto Dressel co-owned the Dressel doll factory from 1873 until 1882, when Otto's two sons also became owners. When Cuno Dressel died in 1893, Otto Dressel and his two sons, Otto Junior and Ernst Friedrich Dressel Jr., remained as co-owners. When Otto died in 1908, his two sons became sole owners. Otto Dressel, Jr. retired in 1914 and his son, Dr. Hans Dressel, and his son-in-law, Hermann Ortelli, became the owners of the Dressel doll factory. Ortelli died in 1939 and Hans Dressel owned the factory until his death in 1942. Shortly after his death, the Dressel doll factory closed, having been in business for more than two hundred years.

5. The large Otto Dressel villa is still standing on Eller Street in Sonneberg. (Photo: Mary Krombholz)

6. Cuno Dressel (3/3/1829-2/1/1893) also lived in a villa on Eller Street, a few yards from his brother Otto's home. (Photo: Mary Krombholz)

Cuno & Otto Dressel Doll Factory

7. After the 1910 Brussels World Exposition closed, the entire Sonneberg competitive exhibit was moved to the basement of the Sonneberg Doll Museum (see Part Two: Introduction, illustration 10). In 1910 the building was the site of the School of Industry, where students learned skills relating to dollmaking. The exhibit titled "Parish Fair of Thuringia" has been on public view in the Sonneberg Doll Museum since it opened in 1929. The realistic scene was designed by Professor Möller, director of the Sonneberg School of Industry in 1910. His students created hundreds of designs for the component parts of the realistic scene, which were then produced by thirty-seven Sonneberg doll factories. Like World Fairs held in cities all over the world since 1815, the Brussels exposition was an important public show that displayed the finest products of industry, science and art. The large exposition sample and display rooms were filled with spectators during the months the exhibit was open to the public. (Photo: Courtesy Deutsches Spielzeugmuseum, Sonneberg)

8. This photograph shows a dollmaker's booth filled with dolls and doll parts. A home worker, dressed in a blue work apron, is leaning over her delivery basket, which is partially covered with a patterned cloth. (Photo: Courtesy Deutsches Spielzeugmuseum, Sonneberg)

9. A circus procession on the streets of Sonneberg is a focal point of the exhibit. The realistic modeling of the townspeople is one of the reasons the display was awarded the Grand Prize in Brussels. (Photo: Courtesy Deutsches Spielzeugmuseum, Sonneberg)

10. A large carousel is the main feature of the display. For almost one hundred years, an important group of Cuno & Otto Dressel dolls, with composition as well as bisque heads, have been seated on the carousel. The dolls sit on green wooden benches on the top tier of the carousel, and ride on wooden and composition animals on the lower tier. Photo: Courtesy Deutsches Spielzeugmuseum, Sonneberg)

Chapter 1

ANFERTIGEN DER PERÜCKEN.

11. This 1911 photograph, which has been hand colored, shows a group of women making wigs in a doll factory. The original wigs on the carousel dolls were made by hand in the Dressel doll factory at similar worktables. Author's Archival Paper Collection.

12. This carousel doll is wearing a dress with a full skirt, which partially covers the realistic wooden reindeer. The four photographs on the facing page picture dolls with similarly sculpted heads. (Photo: Courtesy Deutsches Spielzeugmuseum, Sonneberg)

14. A closer view of the composition head of the doll in illustration 13 shows the multi-stroke eyebrows; upper molded eyelids and upper painted eyelashes; stationary glass eyes and closed mouth. The original clothing and wigs differ on each of the carousel dolls, although many of the heads were made from identical master molds. Courtesy Deutsches Spielzeugmuseum, Sonneberg. (Photo: Christiane Gräfnitz)

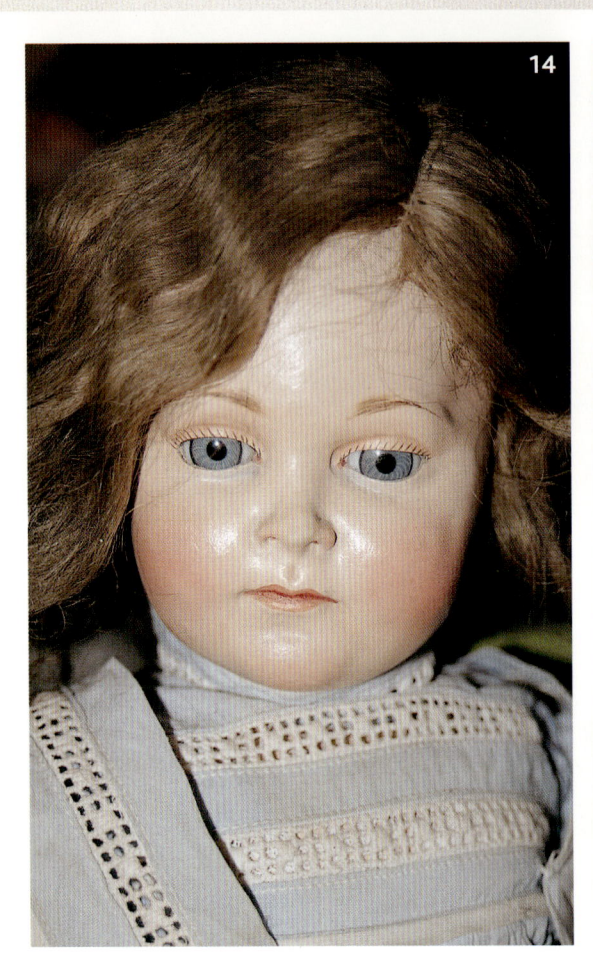

13. This 19½-inch Dressel doll has an original wig, clothing, composition head and body. The exposition date of 1910 is important because it provides irrefutable evidence that all of the dolls on the carousel were made before the completed exhibit was previewed by Sonneberg residents on March 13, 1910. All of the carousel dolls wear original clothing, which provides information on doll clothing and accessories popular at the beginning of the German character-doll movement. The doll's blue dress is an excellent example of the sewing details found on the clothing worn by each of the carousel dolls. (Courtesy Deutsches Spielzeugmuseum, Sonneberg.) (Photo: Christiane Gräfnitz)

200

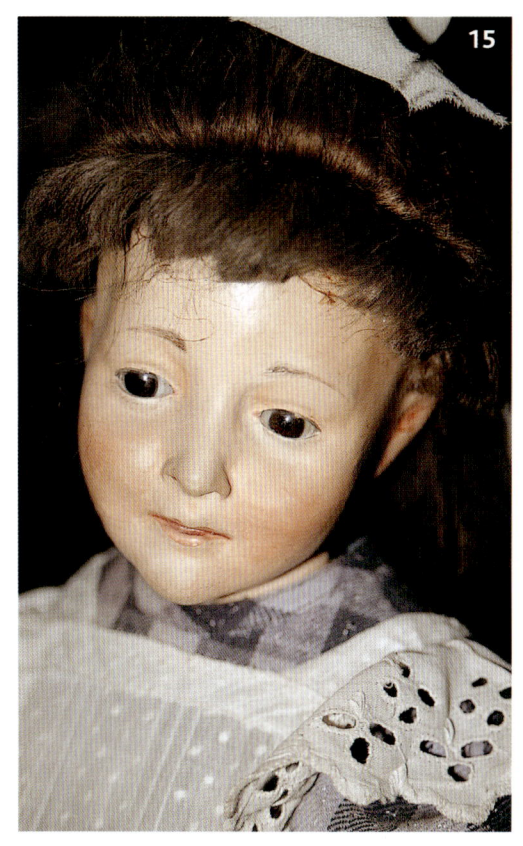

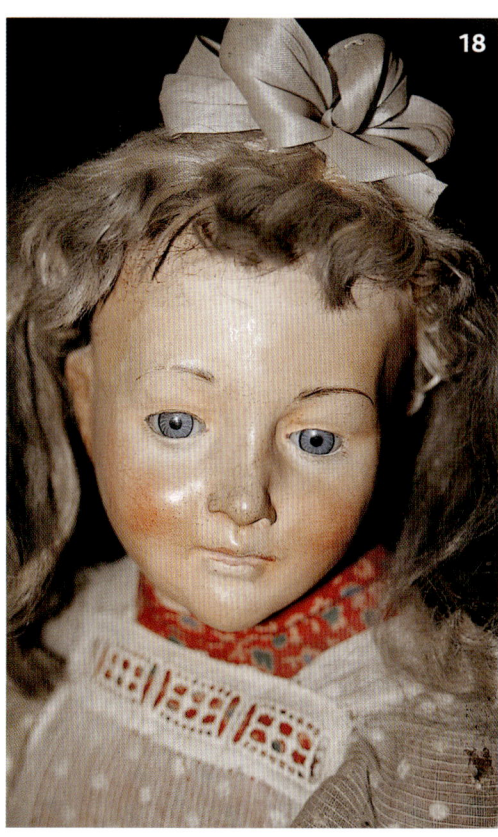

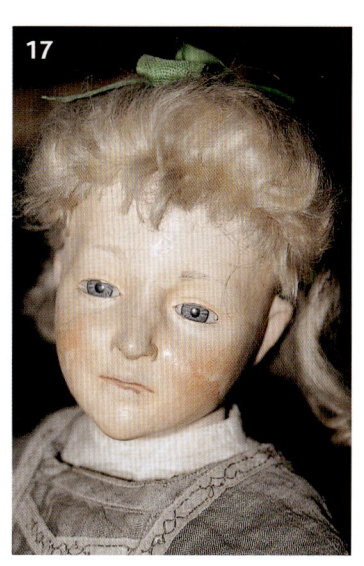

Cuno & Otto Dressel Doll Factory

15. This composition-head doll, with long brown hair pulled back and held in place with a large ribbon, is wearing a white pinafore over its blue-checked dress. Like the dolls in illustrations 16, 17, 18, 20 and 21, this doll has multi-stroke eyebrows, molded upper eyelids, stationary glass eyes and a closed mouth. The words papier-mâché and composition are used interchangeably to describe the carousel dolls' heads because the recipes for Thuringian papier-mâché and composition are similar; both have a base of material that includes wet wood pulp and/or paper pulp, dry plaster of Paris and hot glue. Some of the mixtures dried as hard as wood in about three hours, and were then sanded to create a smooth painting surface. Papier-mâché mixtures contained more paper pulp, while composition mixtures contained more wood pulp and plaster of Paris. Courtesy Deutsches Spielzeugmuseum, Sonneberg. (Photo: Christiane Gräfnitz)

16. This doll is wearing a straw hat and a wig with a center-parted hairstyle and bangs. The lace-trimmed neckline showcases the unusual patterned dress. As the carousel turns to make a complete circle, each doll stands out because the dresses, wigs and hats are so different. Courtesy Deutsches Spielzeugmuseum, Sonneberg. (Photo: Christiane Graefntiz)

17. This Dressel carousel doll has a long hairstyle that features hair pulled back from the forehead and held in place by a green bow. The blue dress is trimmed with an insert of white material decorated with a contrasting geometric pattern. Courtesy Deutsches Spielzeugmuseum, Sonneberg. (Photo: Christiane Gräfnitz)

18. A big satin bow and a white pinafore over a red-patterned dress change the appearance of this Dressel composition-head doll. The polka-dotted pinafore is trimmed with openwork created by home workers. Courtesy Deutsches Spielzeugmuseum, Sonneberg. (Photo: Christiane Gräfnitz)

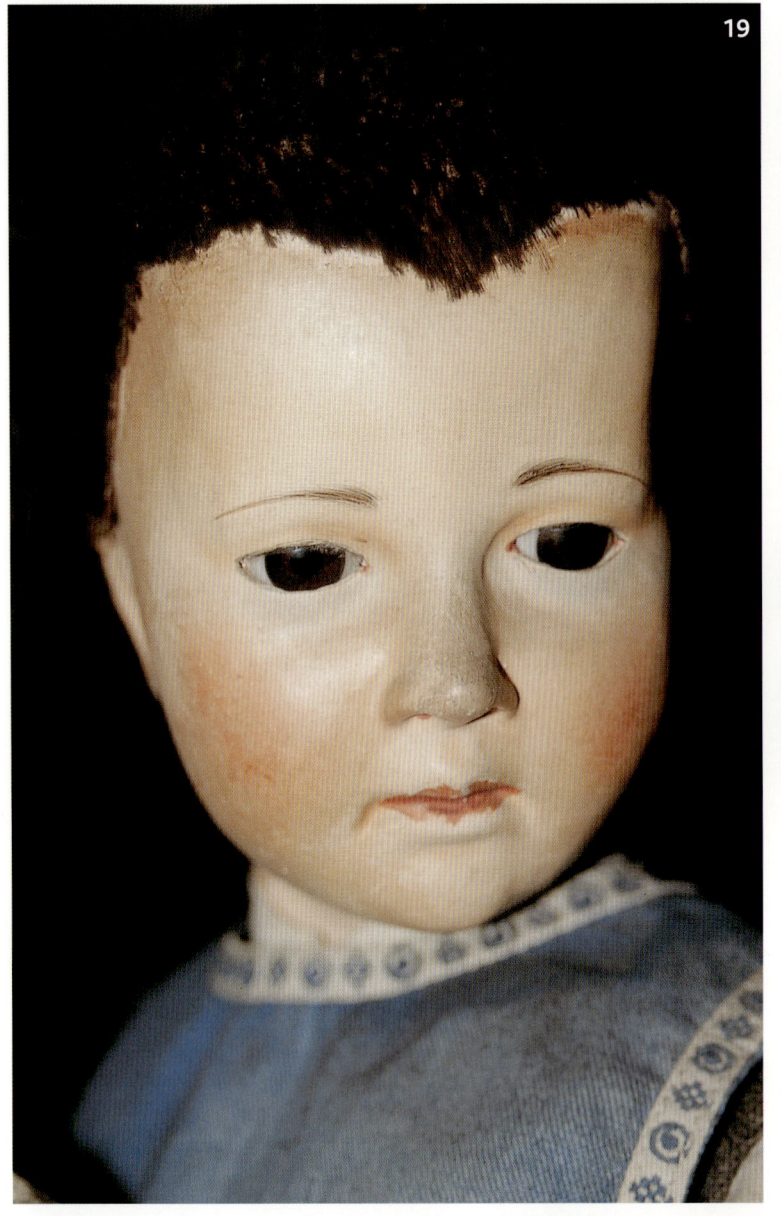

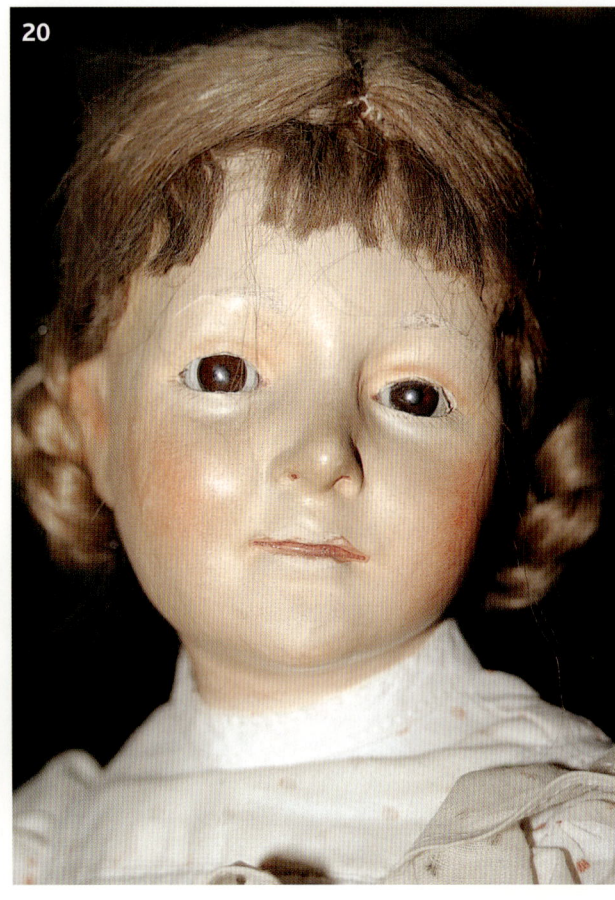

Chapter 1

19. The composition-head boy dolls on the carousel were also made from identical master molds, but their appearances vary because of the types of wigs they wear. This Dressel boy is wearing a brown skin wig that comes to a point in the center of the forehead. Courtesy Deutsches Spielzeugmuseum, Sonneberg. (Photo: Christiane Gräfnitz)

20. This Dressel doll has a center-parted hairstyle with coiled braids over the ears. The hairstyle, popular in Germany for decades, is the one Marion Kaulitz claimed she first used on the Munich Art Dolls. Her claim was challenged by the doll and toy director of the Tietz department stores, who said dolls with this hairstyle were sold at the Tietz stores before the Munich Art Dolls were introduced. Courtesy Deutsches Spielzeugmuseum, Sonneberg. (Photo: Christiane Gräfnitz)

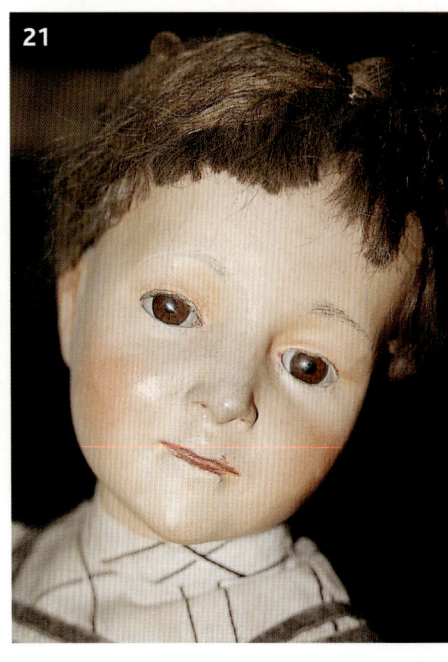

21. This doll is wearing a wig that is styled in a short hairstyle with bangs. The large blue-edged collar trims the striped-cotton dress Courtesy Deutsches Spielzeugmuseum, Sonneberg. (Photo: Christiane Gräfnitz)

22. This composition-head boy has red painted hair with brushmarks across the forehead. Dressel sculptors and modelers were responsible for creating new head models yearly. They used many inspiration sources, including family members and neighborhood children. Courtesy Deutsches Spielzeugmuseum, Sonneberg. (Photo: Christiane Gräfnitz)

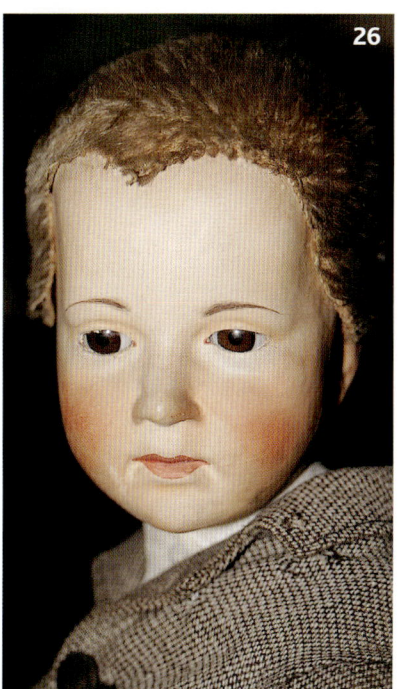

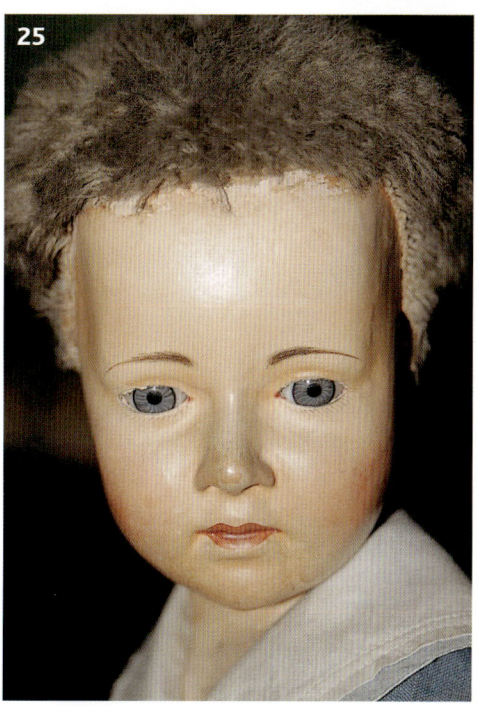

Cuno & Otto Dressel Doll Factory

23. This 19-inch composition-head boy, marked with the Dressel winged helmet trademark, was designed by Professor Reinhardt Möller, director of the Sonneberg School of Industry in 1910. Möller was the perfect choice to design and supervise the creation of the Brussels exhibit, having studied art and sculpture at the Nuremberg Academy of Fine Arts before working as a sculptor at the A.W. Fr. Kister and the Hertwig porcelain factories. Courtesy Deutsches Spielzeugmuseum, Sonneberg. (Photo: Christiane Gräfnitz)

24. This 20-inch girl also has a Dressel-marked composition body, according to the original inventory sheet in the Sonneberg doll museum archives. The carousel dolls pictured in illustrations 24, 27, 28, 29, 30 and 34 have composition heads made from the same master mold and multi-stroke eyebrows, molded eyelids with upper painted eyelashes, stationary glass eyes and closed mouths. This doll has a center-parted hairstyle with coiled braids arranged above the ears, on each side of the part. Its dress is trimmed with wide-patterned braid at the neckline, short sleeves and around the waist of the pleated skirt. A 1911 *Playthings* magazine pictured girl dolls wearing colorful plaid and patterned cotton dresses that resemble the clothing the carousel dolls wear. Courtesy Deutsches Spielzeugmuseum, Sonneberg. (Photo: Christiane Gräfnitz)

26. Doll wigs were made in a variety of colors, as this light-colored wig illustrates. The heads on the boy dolls pictured in illustrations 19, 22, 25 and 26 are dome-shaped, without a cut crown. Courtesy Deutsches Spielzeugmuseum, Sonneberg. (Photo: Christiane Gräfnitz)

25. The front section of the wig on this composition-head boy is trimmed to expose the high forehead, and thereby change the doll's appearance. The clothing on the carousel boy dolls pictured in illustrations 19, 22, 25 and 26 varies in color and styling, but the dolls all have multi-stroke eyebrows, stationary glass eyes and a closed mouth. Courtesy Deutsches Spielzeugmuseum, Sonneberg. (Photo: Christiane Gräfnitz)

Chapter 1

27. This 19-inch doll also has a marked Dressel composition body. The large lace-trimmed picture hat and eyelet-trimmed garments resemble the type of clothing worn by children pictured in fashion plates during the Gibson-Girl era. A 1910 sales catalog published by Macy's department store pictures children dressed in lawn dresses trimmed with lace. In 1911, *Playthings* magazine pictured girl dolls wearing lacy dresses with big ruffled hats. Courtesy Deutsches Spielzeugmuseum, Sonneberg. (Photo: Christiane Gräfnitz)

28. This Dressel doll is wearing a sailor-type hat and clothing. The jacket features include a large braid-trimmed collar, a cotton tie and eight brass buttons. The pleated skirt is full and covers several layers of petticoats slightly visible under the skirt. The 1910 Christmas Butler Brothers catalog pictured dolls wearing sailor clothing with matching hats. This clothing style was popular for decades, and was worn by both girl and boy dolls. Courtesy Deutsches Spielzeugmuseum, Sonneberg. (Photo: Christiane Gräfnitz)

30. A straw hat and a brown curly wig change the appearance of this 19-inch doll with a marked Dressel body. The red-patterned dress has puffed sleeves and a wide border around the gathered skirt. Macy's department store pictured children wearing straw hats trimmed with ribbon bows or braid in their 1910 sales catalog. Sears, Roebuck & Co. and Montgomery Ward mail-order catalogs were also important sources of inspiration for doll clothing designed in Thuringia. Courtesy Deutsches Spielzeugmuseum, Sonneberg. (Photo: Christiane Gräfnitz)

29. This 19-inch Dressel doll has a composition head and marked Dressel body. It wears a patterned cotton apron over a braid-trimmed dress. The dolls were designed and dressed to resemble children aged five to eight. The Sonneberg resident responsible for painting the carousel animals on which the dolls are sitting was a talented artist and decorator named Rempel. Courtesy Deutsches Spielzeugmuseum, Sonneberg. (Photo: Christiane Gräfnitz)

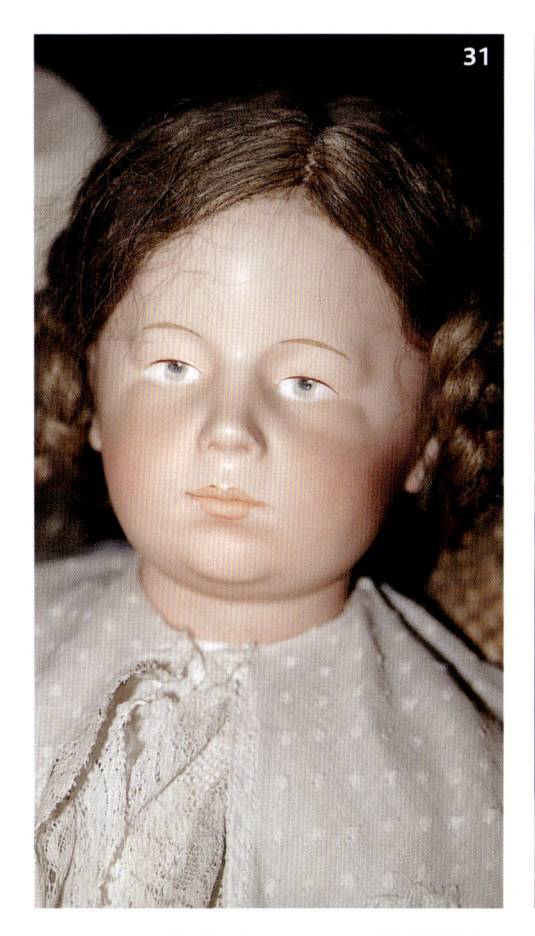

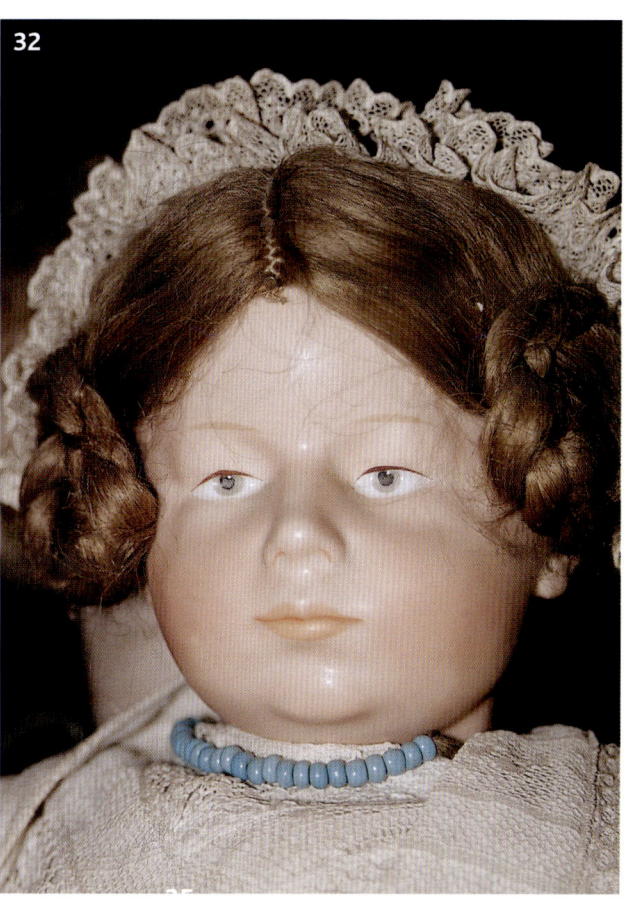

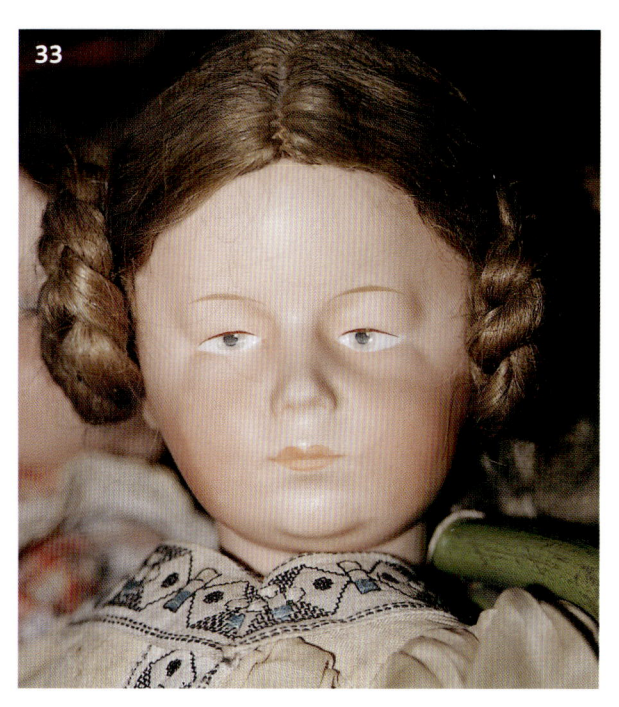

Cuno & Otto Dressel Doll Factory

31. Bisque socket head for the Cuno & Otto Dressel doll factory; original wig and clothing; single-stroke eyebrows; painted eyes with outlined upper eyelids and white highlights; closed mouth; 19½-inch doll; circa 1910; marked: **COD//A/6½**. Like the composition-head dolls on the carousel, each of the bisque-head dolls on the carousel varies in appearance due to its wig and clothing. This doll wears a lace dress with a large collar, and the hairstyle features large coiled braids covering the ears. Courtesy Deutsches Spielzeugmuseum, Sonneberg. (Photo: Christiane Gräfnitz)

32. Bisque socket head for the Cuno & Otto Dressel doll factory; wig; single-stroke eyebrows; painted eyes with outlined upper eyelids and white highlights; closed mouth; 20½-inch doll; marked: **COD//A/7**. This doll is wearing a beautiful lace dress and matching hat. Unlike the unmarked composition heads on the carousel dolls, the bisque heads are marked COD and a size number. The lack of mold marks or trademarks on the bisque heads however, make it difficult to identify the porcelain factory responsible for making the heads. Courtesy Deutsches Spielzeugmuseum, Sonneberg. (Photo: Christiane Gräfnitz)

34. A very large straw hat and wavy center-parted hair change the appearance of this composition-head carousel doll, which is wearing a simple white cotton dress with a full skirt gathered at the waist and trimmed with two separate rows of matching wide ruffles. The most popular fabrics used for doll clothing in the early 1900s were silk (for First Quality dolls), cotton, wool and linen. Courtesy Deutsches Spielzeugmuseum, Sonneberg. (Photo: Christiane Gräfnitz)

33. Bisque socket head for the Cuno & Otto Dressel doll factory; original wig and clothing; single-stroke eyebrows; painted eyes with outlined eyelids and white highlights; closed mouth; 17-inch doll; circa 1910; marked: **COD//A/6**. The doll has a brown center-parted wig with a large coiled braid over each ear. A wide strip of patterned braid is sewn around the neckline and puffed sleeves, down the front of the dress and around the pleated skirt. Courtesy Deutsches Spielzeugmuseum, Sonneberg. (Photo: Christiane Gräfnitz)

Chapter 1

35. Bisque socket head for the Cuno & Otto Dressel doll factory; original wig and clothing; single-stroke eyebrows; painted eyes with outlined upper eyelids and white highlights; closed mouth; 20-inch doll; circa 1910; marked: **COD//A/7**. This doll is wearing sailor-style clothing that features a long striped jacket with eight pearl buttons, a braid-trimmed collar and a simple cotton tie. The large hat, with a braid-trimmed brim, covers the top of the head and showcases the long braids tied with navy-blue ribbons. Courtesy Deutsches Spielzeugmuseum, Sonneberg. (Photo: Christiane Gräfnitz)

Cuno & Otto Dressel Doll Factory

36. Bisque socket head for the Cuno & Otto Dressel doll factory; original wig; single-stroke eyebrows; painted eyes with outlined upper eyelids and white highlights; closed mouth; 17-inch doll; marked: COD//A/6½. This doll is wearing a plaid cotton dress trimmed with eyelet ruffles, and has a center-parted wig with large coiled braids over the ears. Courtesy Deutsches Spielzeugmuseum, Sonneberg. (Photo: Christiane Gräfnitz)

38. The fully jointed composition body on the doll in illustration 37 is identical to the composition bodies on the carousel dolls. It is also identical to the composition bodies on the majority of the Munich Art Dolls in the Sonneberg Doll Museum shown in Part One: Chapter 1. My two Munich Art dolls, pictured in illustration 18 in Part One: Chapter 1, have identical fully jointed composition bodies marked with the Dressel winged-helmet trademark. Susan Moore Collection. (Photo: John Cummings)

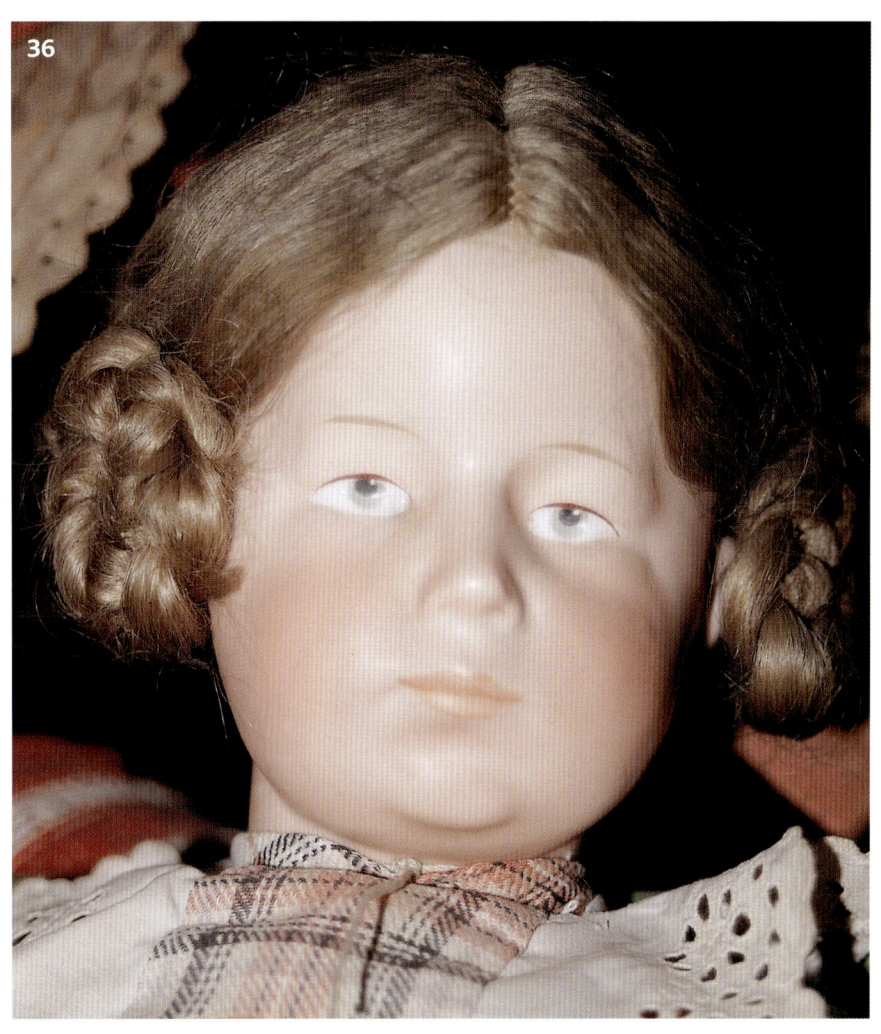

37. The bisque head on this 13-inch doll was made from a master mold identical to the one used for the Dressel bisque-head dolls on the carousel. The flesh-colored complexion coat is darker on this head than on the dolls pictured in illustrations 31, 32, 33, 35, 36 and 41, and the eyes are painted to suggest the doll is looking up rather than straight ahead, like the eyes on the carousel dolls. Bisque head for the Cuno & Otto Dressel doll factory; pierced ears; pale-blond single-stroke eyebrows; reddish-brown upper-eyelid outlines; painted eyes with tiny white highlights on upper right pupils; closed pouty mouth. Susan Moore Collection. (Photo: John Cummings)

CHAPTER 1

39. The incised markings on the back of the bisque head of the doll in illustrations 37 and 38, **COD//A/3**, are identical to those on the bisque-head dolls on the carousel. The composition body is marked with the Dressel winged-helmet trademark. Susan Moore Collection. (Photo: John Cummings)

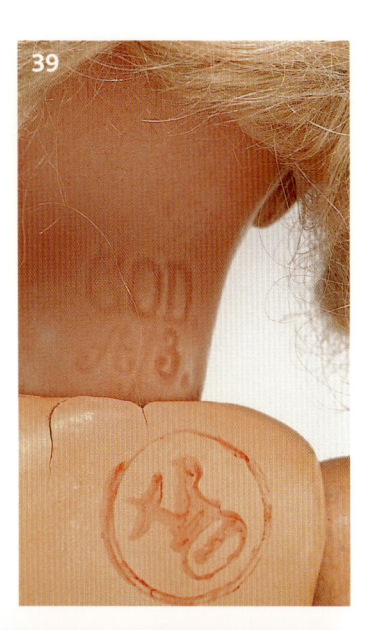

41. Bisque socket head for the Cuno & Otto Dressel doll factory; original wig and clothing; single-stroke eyebrows; painted eyes with outlined upper eyelids and white highlights; closed mouth; 21½-doll; circa 1910; marked: **COD//A/7**. This doll is wearing a straw hat trimmed with a band and bow over a coiled-braid hairstyle. The dress features a gathered ruffle with a machine-sewn leaf pattern around the neckline and covering the shoulders. The shoes and socks of each of the carousel dolls differ in color and style. Courtesy Deutsches Spielzeugmuseum, Sonneberg. (Photo: Christiane Gräfnitz)

40. Jutta bisque socket head by Simon & Halbig for the Cuno & Otto Dressel doll factory; wig; multi-stroke eyebrows; glass sleep eyes; open mouth with upper teeth; 22½-inch doll; circa 1914; marked: **Jutta//1914//S&H**. Courtesy Historisches Coburger Puppenmuseum/Lossnitzer Collection. (Photo: Christiane Gräfnitz)

208

Cuno & Otto Dressel Doll Factory

42. A closer view of the head of the doll in illustration 40 shows the beautiful facial modeling and painting details often found on Simon & Halbig Jutta heads. Historisches Coburger Puppenmuseum/Lossnitzer Collection. Photo: (Christiane Gräfnitz)

43. Jutta bisque socket head by Simon & Halbig for the Cuno & Otto Dressel doll factory; original wig and clothing: fully jointed composition Dressel body; 23-inch doll; circa 1914; marked: **52//Jutta//1914//12**. A Jutta circular paper tag is still attached to the doll's original chemise. Courtesy Deutsches Spielzeugmuseum, Sonneberg. (Photo: Christiane Gräfnitz)

44. Jutta bisque socket head by Simon & Halbig for the Cuno & Otto Dressel doll factory; multi-stroke eyebrows; painted upper and lower eyelashes; glass sleep eyes; open mouth with upper teeth and separate tongue; circa 1914; 23-inch doll; marked: **Jutta//9.1914R**. Courtesy Ladenburger Spielzeugauktion/Goetz Seidel. (Photo: Christiane Gräfnitz)

45. This Dressel bisque socket head, marked **A/3½,** was also made from a master mold identical to those used for the dolls on the carousel. The flesh-colored complexion coat is much lighter on this 3½-inch head than on the head pictured in illustration 37. Bisque head features include pale-gray single-stroke eyebrows; dark reddish-brown outline of upper eyelids, painted irises that match the gray eyebrows; white highlights on the top right side of left pupil only and a closed mouth. Beth Karp Collection. (Photo: Gregg Smith)

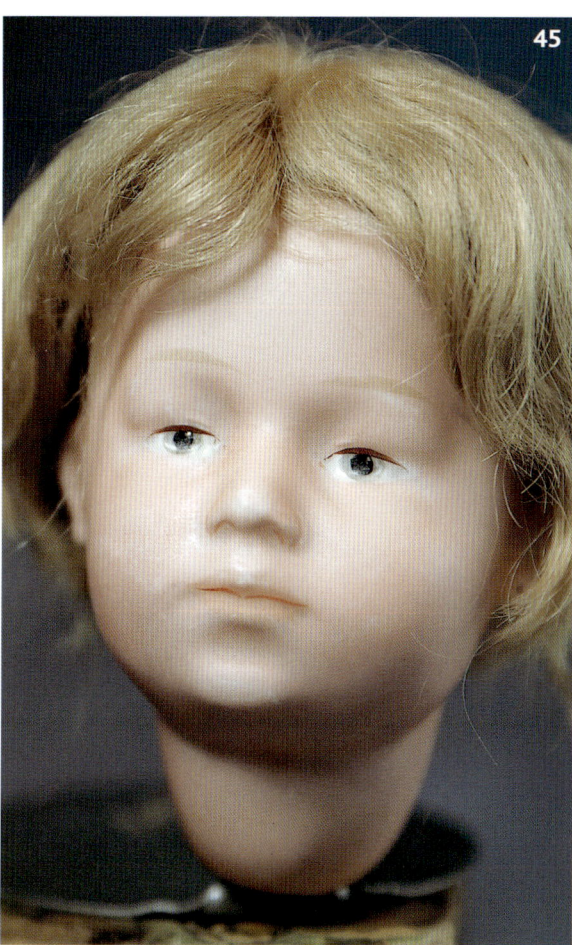

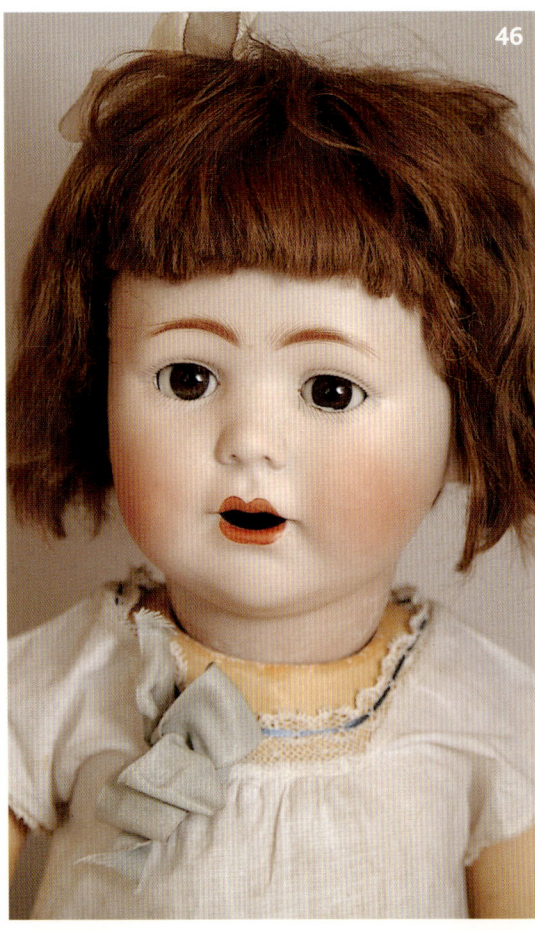

Chapter 1

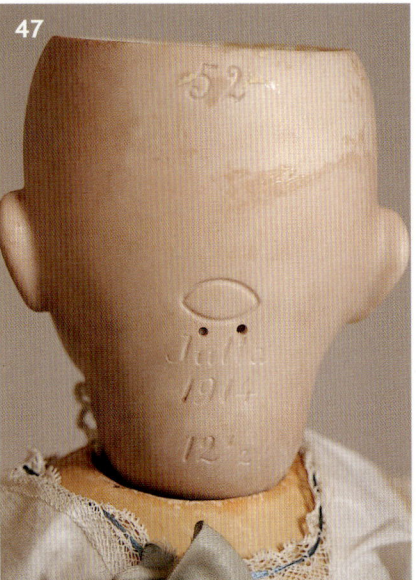

46. A closer view of the doll in illustration 43 shows the bisque head by Simon & Halbig for the Cuno & Otto Dressel doll factory with its multi-stroke eyebrows; painted upper and lower eyelashes; glass sleep eyes and open mouth with upper teeth. Courtesy Deutsches Spielzeugmuseum, Sonneberg. (Photo: Christiane Gräfnitz)

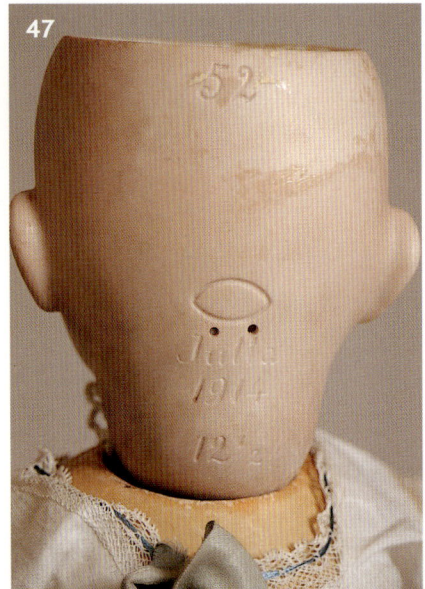

47. The back of the head of the doll in illustrations 43 and 46 shows the incised marks: **52//Jutta/1914//12**. Courtesy Deutsches Spielzeugmuseum, Sonneberg. (Photo: Christiane Gräfnitz)

48. An original 1920s Leipzig Fair photograph shows another important venue used by Thuringian doll and porcelain factories to increase doll-related sales. Thousands of buyers and sellers attended the semi-annual fairs, held in the spring and fall. The large number of people on the street, and the many signs hanging from the buildings, reflect the importance of Leipzig fairs to wholesale and retail doll sales. Author's Archival Paper Collection.

49. This original 1910 postcard was printed in Germany especially for the Pittsburgh Dry Goods Company, as advertising for a new sales line. Members of the Dressel family made numerous trips to the United States to locate buyers, and were successful in establishing strong business relationships with many wholesale and retail stores. The German words on the bottom of the postcard read: "*Aus der Spielwarenstadt*" (from the toy factory town). Author's Archival Paper Collection.

Cuno & Otto Dressel Doll Factory

50. Two circa-1898 bisque-head dolls with Simon & Halbig bisque heads, from the Cuno & Otto Dressel Portrait Series, represent American naval officers who fought in the 1898 Spanish-American War. The taller doll on the left resembles Charles Dwight Sigsbee (1845-1923), Commander of the battleship Maine when it was sunk. The doll on the right is a portrait of Richmond Pearson Hobson (1870-1937), responsible for sinking the Merrimac in Santiago harbor in an effort to contain the Spanish fleet. Beth Karp Collection. (Photo: Gregg Smith)

51. Richard Pearson Hobson bisque socket head by Simon & Halbig for the Cuno & Otto Dressel doll factory's Portrait Series; original hat and clothing; molded hair; molded multi-stroke eyebrows; gray intaglio-painted eyes with white highlights; closed mouth partially covered by large molded mustache; molded ribbed socks and buckled shoes painted black to resemble boots; 12½-inch doll; circa 1898, unmarked. Beth Karp Collection. (Photo: Gregg Smith)

52. Charles Dwight Sigsbee bisque socket head by Simon & Halbig for the Cuno & Otto Dressel doll factory's Portrait Series; original hat and clothing; molded hair; single-stroke wavy eyebrows; painted upper and lower eyelashes; large, stationary glass eyes; closed mouth partially covered by large mustache; painted lower lip without molding; white hands painted to look like gloves; 15-inch doll; circa 1898; marked: **24D**. Beth Karp Collection. (Photo: Gregg Smith)

53. Bisque socket head by Simon & Halbig for the Cuno & Otto Dressel doll factory's Portrait Series; original hat and military uniform; molded gray hair and large mustache; single-stroke eyebrows; painted upper and lower eyelashes; upper and lower stationary glass eyes; molded lower lip, upper lip hidden under mustache; 13½-inch doll; circa 1898; unmarked. The uniform, head modeling and painted facial features on this portrait doll vary slightly from the other portrait dolls in this series, making it difficult to identify the Naval officer the doll resembles. Kathy and Mike Embry Collection. (Photo: Ann Hanat)

Chapter 1

54. Rear Admiral William Sampson bisque socket head by Simon & Halbig for the Cuno & Otto Dressel doll factory; original hat and military uniform; molded gray hair; single-stroke wavy eyebrows; painted upper and lower eyelashes; stationary glass eyes; molded gray mustache and beard; 8½-inches; circa 1898; marked: **17-SP**. This is a portrait doll of William Sampson (1842-1902), credited with establishing the blockade of Cuba during the Spanish American War. This bisque head was also sold with a brown mustache and beard. Author's Collection. Photo: (Red Kite Studio)

55. Commodore George Dewey socket head by Simon & Halbig for the Cuno & Otto Dressel doll factory; original hat and military uniform; molded hair; molded multi-stroke eyebrows; large gray mustache, intaglio-painted eyes with white eyelashes; lower lip under mustache, chin dimple; 15-inch doll; circa 1898; marked: **1D**. This is a portrait doll of George Dewey (1837-1917), Commander of the Asiatic Squadron who scored a victory at the Battle of Manila Bay. Kathy and Mike Embry Collection. (Photo: Ann Hanat)

56. Bisque socket head by Simon & Halbig for the Cuno & Otto Dressel doll factory; flapper-type composition body with long, slender un-jointed arms and legs jointed above the knees; wig; single-stroke eyebrows; painted upper and lower eyelashes; small glass sleep eyes; closed mouth; 15-inch doll; circa 1920; marked: **1469//S&H//C&O Dressel//Germany//5**. Kathy and Mike Embry Collection. (Photo: Kathy Embry)

57. A side view of the doll in illustration 55 shows the decorated hat and profile of the bisque head with realistic nose and ears. Kathy and Mike Embry Collection. (Photo: Ann Hanat)

212

Cuno & Otto Dressel Doll Factory

58. Bisque socket-head doll sold by the Cuno & Otto Dressel doll factory; flocked hair; single-stroke eyebrows; intaglio-painted eyes, open/closed mouth with molded tongue; circa 1920; marked: **COD A//9/0//Germany**. The Dressel doll factory purchased bisque heads from so many Thuringian porcelain factories that it is difficult to tell which factory made this head, due to the absence of mold marks. Author's Collection. (Photo: Gregg Smith)

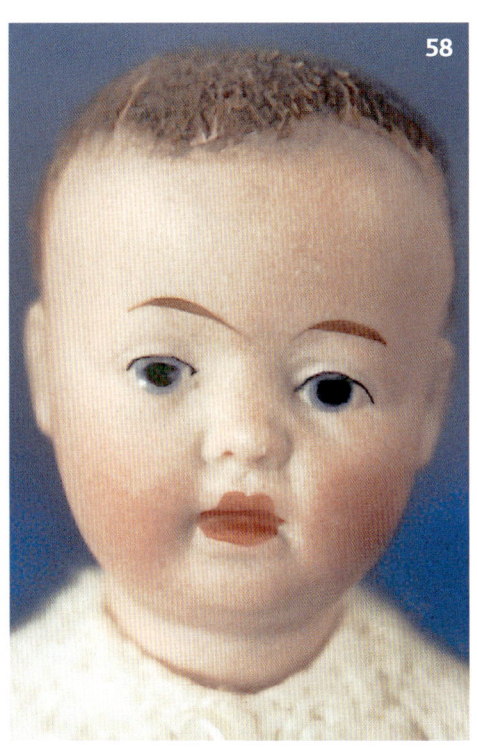

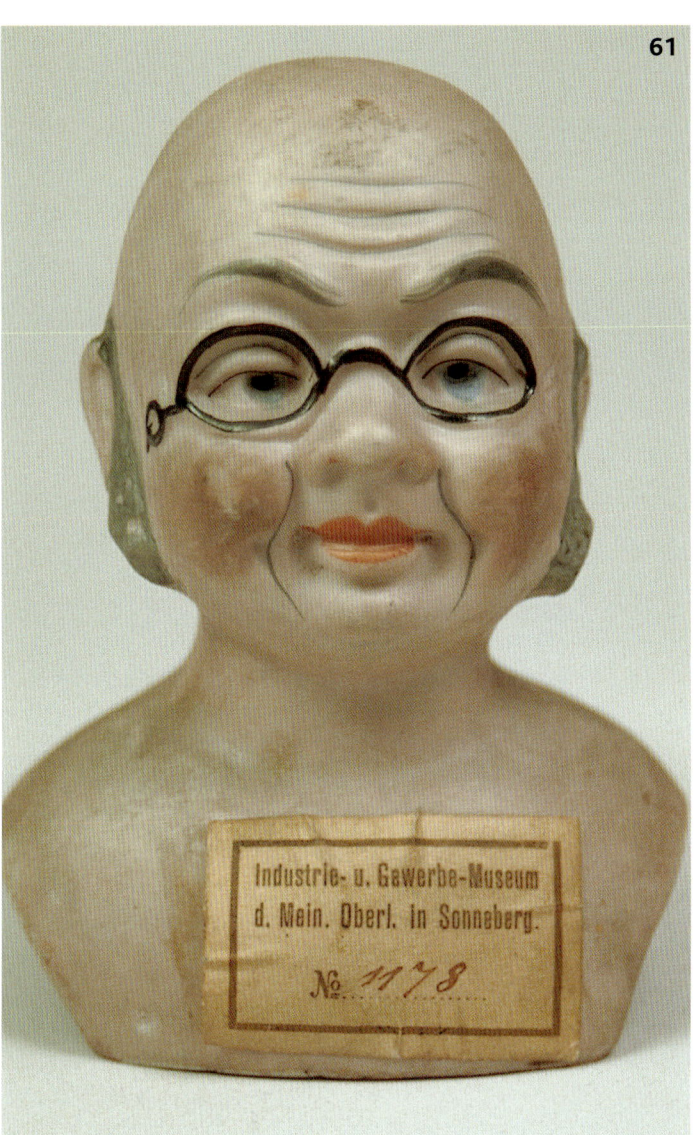

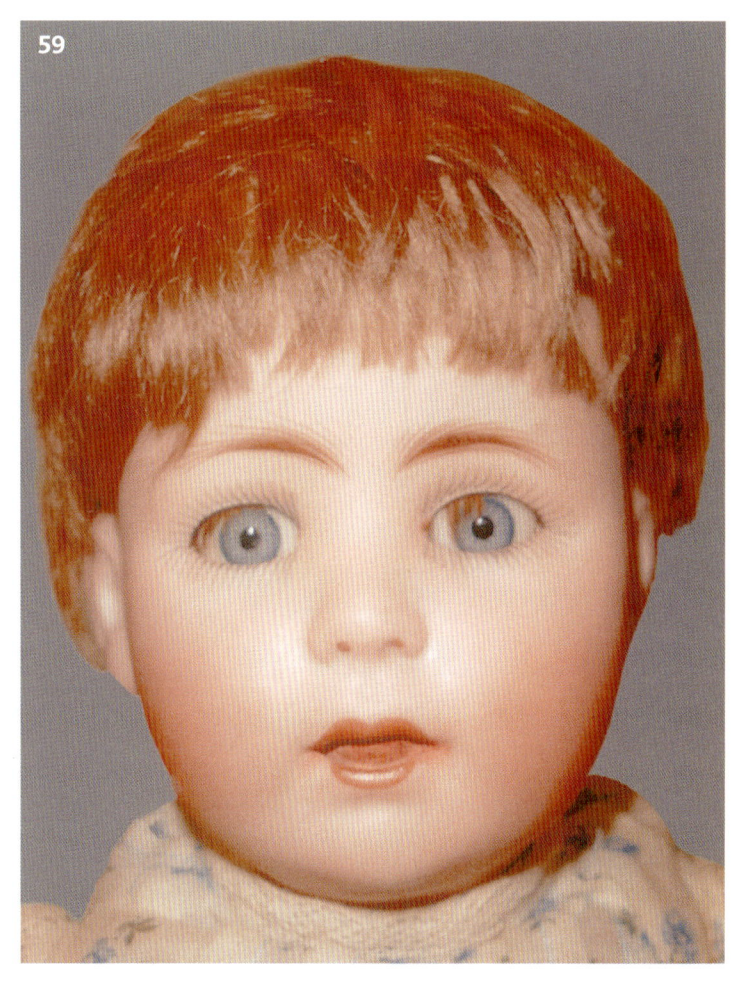

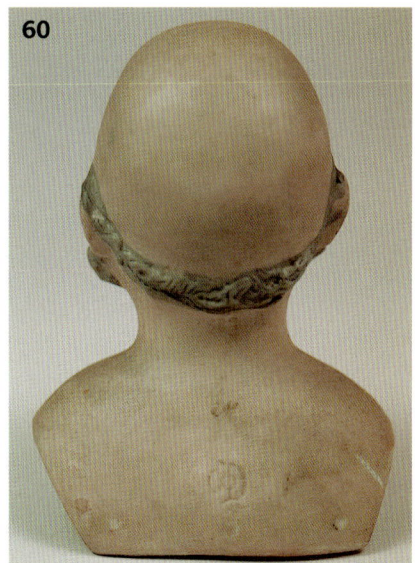

59. Bisque socket-head doll by Simon & Halbig for the Cuno & Otto Dressel doll factory; wig; multi-stroke eyebrows; painted upper and lower eyelashes; upper hair eyelashes; open/closed mouth; 11-inch doll; circa 1914; marked: **Jutta//1914**. Beth Riley Collection. (Photo: Andrea Jones)

60. The back of the 2½-inch shoulder head in illustration 61 shows the bald head and Dressel COD trademark. Courtesy Deutsches Spielzeugmuseum, Sonneberg. (Photo: Christiane Gräfnitz)

61. An original paper label glued inside this bisque shoulder head reads: "Cuno & Otto Dressel, 1908." The original handwriting inside the head spells out the name: "Karl Höhn." The Höhn doll factory was founded in Sonnberg in 1903 and the sole owner in 1925 was Ernst Höhn. The factory specialized in making a variety of leather bodies for bisque shoulder-head dolls. The molded glasses and age wrinkles are unusual features on this elderly man. Courtesy Deutsches Spielzeugmuseum, Sonneberg. (Photo: Christiane Gräfnitz)

Part Two
CHAPTER 2

Arthur Schoenau Doll Factory and Schoenau & Hoffmeister Porcelain Factory

1. The circa-1884 Arthur Schoenau doll factory still stands near the railroad station in Sonneberg. The building was enlarged several times as orders for doll-related products increased during the dollmaking years. (Photo: Mary Krombholz)

The histories of the Arthur Schoenau doll factory and the Schoenau & Hoffmeister porcelain factory are well-known in Sonneberg because of the role Hanns Schoenau played in preserving the town's doll history. Schoenau was the official "doll historian" of Sonneberg. He marked the location of the majority of doll factories in Sonneberg and Köppelsdorf on a series of maps in articles he wrote for the Ciesliks' *Puppenmagazins*. The articles were later bound into a soft-cover book, which is a treasure for doll collectors interested in locating the remaining Sonneberg-area doll factories. In addition, homes of the owners of the larger Sonneberg-area doll factories are pictured in the book. Hanns Schoenau also wrote articles for the Ciesliks' *Puppenmagazins* about specific dolls made by his family's doll and porcelain factories, such as the portrait doll of Princess Elizabeth.

In 1980 Hanns Schoenau wrote a detailed history of the Arthur Schoenau doll factory and the Schoenau & Hoffmeister porcelain factory for the Sonneberg Doll Museum archives. A few paragraphs read as follows:

The founding of the doll factory was 1884. That same year, Arthur Schoenau from Oberweissbach married Caroline Jacob, the daughter of the Commissioner Louis Jacob.

Arthur Schoenau was born the 15th child of the local pharmacist. His father-in-law advised him to build a slate-covered building that housed his residence and business on Robertstrasse 2, on the upper train station road. The business made jointed dolls and soon had a good reputation and some big customers. In the beginning they manufactured for only 4 or 5 customers. Soon they had to start working overtime in order to meet all their orders.

On January 1, 1885, the inventory was worth about 4,000 German Marks. In 1901, Arthur Schoenau and Carl Hoffmeister (he was the father of Professor Cuno Hoffmeister who was the astronomer who founded the Sonneberg observatory) started the porcelain factory Schoenau & Hoffmeister in Burggrub near Sonneberg. In 1907, Hoffmeister resigned due to financial reasons.

Following Hoffmeister's resignation, the Schoenau family retained the Schoenau & Hoffmeister porcelain factory name. The Schoenau family continued to make bisque doll heads and doll parts at the porcelain factory in Burggrub, a small village near Sonneberg, until 1926, when the porcelain factory was purchased by Leube and Eversburg. A few of the factory's American distributors for bisque-head dolls were Butler Brothers, S.S. Kresge & Co. and Geo. Borgfeldt & Co.

Between the 1884 founding of the Arthur Schoenau doll factory and the 1901 founding of the Schoenau & Hoffmeister porcelain factory, the Arthur Schoenau doll factory bought bisque heads from the following Thuringian porcelain factories: Simon & Halbig, Gebrüder Kuhnlenz, Recknagel, Baehr & Proeschild, Gebrüder Beck and Carl Müller (the only porcelain factory located in the town of Sonneberg).

Hanns Schoenau's memoirs continue as follows.

> Arthur Schoenau died in 1911. His son Curt Schoenau took over the doll factory and Arthur's son Hans Schoenau took over the porcelain factory. Hans Schoenau died in 1914 in World War I. From then on, Curt ran both businesses. He moved the residence out of the building on Robertstrasse and turned the building into doll manufacturing space. He also enlarged the customer base and went on sales trips, mostly to England.
>
> After World War I, Curt built a three-story addition to the doll factory. It had a complete cardboard-stamping business on the first floor. He also had elevators and central heating installed. At that time, they not only made jointed dolls but also babies. The business employed 70 people and had its own eye-inserting business. The customer base kept growing and the business was mainly for export. Our customers were in Holland, Belgium, Switzerland, Sweden, Hungary and Overseas.
>
> In 1923, the company had a walking doll patented. In 1921 and again in 1927, the doll factory building on Robertstrasse was enlarged. In 1926 the porcelain factory Burgrubb was sold to Mr. Leube from Lippelsdorf and Leube's son-in-law, Eversburg. Business declined about half during the World Depression and with it the devaluation of the British pound.
>
> However, the creation of two dolls helped the business. It was the doll 'Princess Elizabeth' (today's Queen of England) and the 'Bebe Carmencita' (a doll with a softly stuffed body and hard limbs). On his sales trips Curt also sold the products of smaller doll factories from Neustadt, Mengersgereuth and Schalkau. After Hitler took office, there was a further decline in business. World-known customers like Marks & Spencer in London and the Hudson Bay Company in Canada would no longer purchase from German companies.

2. The old Arthur Schoenau villa is still standing in Huttensteinach. The large curved stairway leads to a front doorway that features a fancy script "S." (Photo: Mary Krombholz)

> During World War II, the Arthur Shoenau doll factory kept assembling and exporting dolls, and denied to manufacture arms. On January 21, 1945, owner Curt Schoenau died. His son, Hanns Arthur Schoenau, who was a soldier, became the new owner of the business. After the war ended, Hanns Schoenau returned home from the war and with 5 other old factory workers they were able to resume production and export trade in June of 1945.
>
> In 1946, the Leipzig Fair started up again and our company was able to obtain their first export orders from Switzerland. In 1950, the trade volume achieved the numbers of the years shortly before the war. After 1953, business increased greatly. That year, the company manufactured 5,000 dolls. In 1954, business was about 400,000 Mark. In 1955, it was 680,000 Mark; in 1956 it was 750,000 Mark; in 1957 it was 950,000 Mark; in 1958 and 1959 it was 1,150,000 Mark and in 1961 it was 1,300,000 Mark.

I was privileged to know Hanns Schoenau personally for many years. My last letter from him is dated August 2002. He died in September 2002. It was a joy to visit Sonneberg year

Chapter 2

3. The Schoenau & Hoffmeister porcelain factory in Burggrub was founded in 1901. Dolly-faced bisque heads and character bisque heads were made in this building. The village of Burggrub is about four miles from Sonneberg. (Photo: Courtesy of Hanns Schoenau)

after year and see Hanns Schoenau walking the streets of his beloved hometown. He was always very gracious about answering my many doll-related questions. One of my most treasured memories is of sitting with him in the café across the street from the Sonneberg Museum. One summer I asked him why there were no examples of Schoenau & Hoffmeister Princess Elizabeth dolls in the museum.

His answer began with a description of finding a porcelain factory to make the bisque heads. He told me his family had sold the Schoenau & Hoffmeister porcelain factory to the company's managing directors Leube and Eversburg in 1926. Although the Schoenau doll factory did not own a porcelain factory after 1926, his family's former factory was the perfect choice to make the Princess Elizabeth bisque character heads because they could guarantee absolute secrecy from competitors, according to Schoenau.

His father hired Caesar Schneider to design the head from a Marcus Adams' photo of three-year-old Princess Elizabeth. The body had a composition torso and one-piece composition arms and legs. A prototype of the doll was ready for approval by the Duke and Duchess of York in 1929, and the first examples were finished in 1930. The doll was introduced in January 1930 in three sizes. According to Schoenau, however, the doll was not the big success they hoped it would be. Orders dropped after the first year because of the world's economic crisis. Production of the doll ended in 1933. Schoenau recalled that when he took over the family doll factory in 1945, there was not a single Princess Elizabeth doll in Sonneberg. He later found one, and kept it in his show room for many years; unfortunately, it was stolen from the show room in 1960.

During the years the porcelain factory in Burggrub was owned by the Schoenau family, they sold bisque doll heads to the following doll factories: Hermann von Berg, Köppelsdorf; Curt Bruckner, Sonneberg; Cuno & Otto Dressel, Sonneberg; Canzler & Hoffmann, Sonneberg; Gebrüder Eckhardt, Oberlind near Sonneberg; E. Edelmann, Sonneberg; Edmund Knoch, Monchroden near Coburg; R. Leschhorn, Sonneberg; Ernst Maar & Sohn, Rödental near Coburg; H. Sussenguth, Neustadt near Coburg; Friedrich Voight, Sonneberg and Carl Zinner & Söhne, Schalkau near Sonneberg.

Many Schoenau dolls are listed in a catalog I bought as part of the Arthur Krauss doll factory papers. Several doll factories in Sonneberg sold dolls called "Carla." The 1934 Carla catalog describes "Quality Dolls by the A. Schoenau Company: The finest Mama dolls, sleeping eyes with eyelashes, beautiful dresses, elegant underwear, in the finest presentation. The same doll is available with an elegant straw hat, also with a mama voice and rascal eyes."

The Schoenau "Doll for the Best Taste" is described as: "Doll with mama voice, dressed in a blue or pink silk dress, first class underwear, sleeping eyes and curly hair." Other A. Schoenau factory dolls are listed as: "Mama Dolls; Girls with Sweaters and Pleated Skirts; Red Riding Hood; Extra Beautiful Baby with Ruffled Dress and Sitting Baby with Hand-crocheted Blue or Pink Pants and Shirt."

According to Hanns Schoenau, bisque-head dolls continued to be assembled at the A. Schoenau doll factory into the 1950s. The majority of bisque-head dolls were marked with a large star that contained the initials "PB," which stood for the porcelain factory in Burggrub. The "S" and "H" found on each side of the star are the factory initials. Like Cuno & Otto Dressel, Schoenau & Hoffmeister used Butler Brothers as a distributor for the majority of dolls that were sold in America.

The Arthur Schoenau doll factory and the Schoenau & Hoffmeister porcelain factory were unique because they made and dressed dolls from start to finish. There were very few doll and porcelain factories in Thuringia that made complete dolls. Two other examples are the J. D. Kestner doll and porcelain factory in Waltershausen and the Hermann Steiner doll and porcelain factory in Neustadt. All three of these combined factories made, assembled and dressed bisque-head character dolls.

Although it is not possible to travel back in time to witness the assembly of dolls in the Arthur Schoenau doll factory, an oral history given by a daughter of a Sonneberg doll-parts

Arthur Schoenau Doll Factory and Schoenau & Hoffmeister Porcelain Factory

MODELLIERSTUBE.

4. Doll-related porcelain products made by the Schoenau & Hoffmeister porcelain factory were assembled into complete dolls in the Arthur Schoenau doll factory in Sonneberg. Two porcelain factory modelers are examining bisque doll heads in this 1911 photograph, which has been hand colored. The German text reads: "*Modellierstube*" (modeling room). A large plaster working mold is visible on the worktable. Author's Archival Paper Collection.

maker and assembler in the Sonneberg book titled *Sonneberg Stories of Dolls, Slate Pencils and Cuckoo Whistles* explains the process.

> The dollmaker completed the masterful preliminary work of the tress maker, the wig maker, the molder, the cardboard processor, the doll shoemaker, the seamstress, the porcelain head maker, the eye installer, the painter, the voice maker and the box maker who delivered their products to him twice a week.
>
> After the manufacturing stage on the parts, the next step in the work took shape. For example, we received arms, legs and bodies of papier-mâché as unfinished parts. They had only been cleaned, but not yet colored or lacquered. That was mostly our work. We had to dip them in color first, and let them dry, then dip them again and let them dry. The drying took place on boards with pegs.
>
> The voice boxes my father glued into the backs of the finished bodies. My mother was creative and clever. She designed the hairdos and dresses for our dolls, braided the tresses, sewed the wigs, and even set the hair according to her design. We obtained the porcelain or composition heads already painted and with eyes set in. With little cardboard covers and glue my mother closed the opening on the back of the head before she glued the wig on. With the help of rubber bands and a wire hook my father attached first the head, then the arms and legs to the body. By this fastening system, they remained movable.
>
> Next the doll received a beauty treatment, for my mother always designed and produced the newest styles in doll clothing. I helped her since age twelve, turned my energies to the little dresses, sewed on bows and buttons. The quality of the material used to make the dolls, and the expenditure of work time and ornamentation were in keeping with the economic status of the future doll-mommy. This also related to the shoes and stockings, too. We once more curled the hair and provided the appropriate decorations which were suitable for the outfit.
>
> My mother sewed the dressed-up dolls cleverly with a few stitches into boxes of the proper size, which had been brought to us by the boxmaker from Untere Marktstrasse. That way, nothing could happen to the dolls on their way to the doll-mommies. To our business came buyers and shopkeepers who valued individual style which our dolls had. Many thousands of our dolls went by train and ship on the big trip to distant lands and continents and surely we had a small share in making our Sonneberg famous as the Number One City of Dolls and Toys.

Although her oral history describes the assembly work done in a very small doll factory, the process was the same in the Arthur Schoenau doll factory on Robertstrasse. Some of the parts were made by home workers in the area; the rest of the work was done in the factory. Hand-colored illustrations from my archival paper collection show the various types of work necessary to assemble a complete doll.

Chapter 2

5. Although complete dolls were assembled in the Arthur Schoenau doll factory, home workers in the Sonneberg area furnished many composition body parts. The German text on this 1911 photograph, which has been hand colored, translates as "Home Industry" (on the left) and "Taking Parts out of Their Molds" (on the right) Many composition body parts are stacked on the worktable and window sill. Author's Archival Paper Collection.

HAUSINDUSTRIE.   AUSFORMEN DER PUPPENTEILE.

My original Shoenau & Hoffmeister bisque dolly-faced doll shows the quality of the dolls once made by this important Sonneberg doll and porcelain factory. The red-and-white label on the cardboard box is in excellent condition. The name "Rosebud" is printed on the label that is glued to the end of the box. A barefoot doll in a chemise, with arms outstretched, is pictured on the right side of the label. Under the name "Rosebud," are the two words "Registered Markenschutz" (Trademark Protected). The color of the doll's eyes, the hair color and the number and size of the doll are listed over the label phrase "Made in Germany."

The original box is made of heavy cardboard, well stapled at each corner. Inside the box, under the doll, is a paper mattress stuffed with excelsior. The back of the doll's bisque head has the incised Schoenau-Hoffmeister trademark star containing the initials SHB, indicating the factory name and the location of the porcelain factory (Burggrub). The #5200 mold number is incised under the star. The date 1906 is incised over the initials SH. When I asked Hanns Schoenau about the date (1906), he explained that it was the year of initial production.

My 102-year-old doll is dressed in a blue silk dress trimmed in wide lace at the neck, bodice, sleeves and hemline, and a matching blue cotton, lace-trimmed slip under her dress. A matching blue satin ribbon is tied in several loops over each ear. The doll wears blue cotton socks and white boots trimmed with blue buttons. It is surprising that she is wearing a standard chemise under her lace-trimmed underwear and slip. The majority of inexpensive German bisque-head dolly-faced dolls were sold wearing only a chemise of cheap gauze-like cotton, trimmed in colored edging or inexpensive lace. A chemise is seldom found on a doll wearing beautifully made lace-trimmed underwear.

The attention to detail in the dressing of Rosebud leads me to believe this doll was sold as a "First-Quality" doll. There are several examples of fine workmanship. Tiny hand stitches encircle each buttonhole. The wide blue-ribbon sash around the waistline of the dress has hand-tied knots on each end. The hair bows are attached with a carefully twisted and sewn matching ribbon. Rosebud's bisque face is beautifully blushed and hand-painted with care. The doll has hair eyelashes as well as painted upper and lower eyelashes. In the open mouth are four porcelain applied upper teeth. A deep dimple is modeled in the chin.

We will never know the exact details of Rosebud's assembly and delivery to her first owner. But by comparing dolls sold during the same time period, we can estimate an original sales price. A 1910 *Harpers Bazar* advertisement pictures a very similar bisque-head dolly-faced doll priced at $5.45 and described as: "Finest quality fully-jointed composition body, beautiful large bisque head, sleeping eyes with lashes, hand curled wig. Extra fine underwear. All clothes come off. One of the handsomest dresses possible to put on a doll. Elaborate China-silk dress edged with lace and beautiful ribbon trim. Fine leather shoes and stockings. Height, 21 inches."

An average weekly wage in Sonnberg for a male factory worker in 1900 was about four dollars a week. A woman worker received the equivalent of three U.S. dollars a week for working in a doll factory for a week. In 1900, a U.S. dollar equaled 4.20 Marks. One family of four home workers in 1900 received fifty cents for sixteen hours of work.

It is difficult to locate information on the Thuringian doll and porcelain factories during and after World War II. About a year before he died, Hanns Schoenau sent me a copy of speech he gave years ago on the history of Sonneberg. He also gave me permission to use his words in books and maga-

Arthur Schoenau Doll Factory and Schoenau & Hoffmeister Porcelain Factory

6. The large punch press machine pictured in this 1906 photograph, which has been hand colored, was used to "Stamp Out Small Body Parts," according to the German text on the bottom of the photograph. Completed composition arms and legs are visible on the tray next to the worker. The punch press is like a giant, but more elaborate, paper punch. The worker is applying pressure to the hand wheel, which in turn applies pressure to the metal-cutting device. The paper calendar hanging on the wall dates the photo as November 27, 1906. Author's Archival Paper Collection.

STANZEN KLEINER PUPPENTEILE.

zines to help others understand what life was like in Sonneberg during and after this war. A few paragraphs from his speech follow.

> In 1928, Sonneberg had about 20,000 residents; many new buildings were built, including a larger Town Hall.
>
> After the New York stock market crash in 1929, doll production in Sonneberg decreased in a dramatic way. Unemployment and poverty rose until Hitler began his preparations for World War II. Some Sonneberg companies made money by producing equipment for Hitler's army, like uniforms and parachutes for the Air Force. Only a few Sonneberg doll factories continued to produce dolls and toys. During the war, Sonneberg lost over 2,000 soldiers who fought in the Nazi army. The town only lost a few buildings.
>
> In April, 1945, the U.S. army conquered Sonneberg. In July, 1945, according to the Jalta agreement of the Allies, the Soviet army began the occupation of middle Germany. The town of Sonneberg became the border between Russia and the Free World, between East and West Germany. When East and West Germany were founded, the East German Government (GDR) fenced in the border around the town of Sonneberg with barbed wire. These conditions stood until the end of the East German State in 1989.
>
> While the GDR existed, nearly every company in Sonneberg was expropriated, unreliable personalities were evacuated, and everybody who wished to visit the town had to face a large number of soldiers and policemen. Despite these developments, the 'Volkseigene' (East German State Industries) in our area boomed. The main customer was the Soviet Union. Sonneberg products at this time were dolls and toys, of course; household and electrotechnical porcelain products; men's uniforms and clothing; vacuum cleaners; plastic products; glass products from Lauscha; radios and engines. None of these products were sold on the free market.
>
> So, after our peaceful revolution in 1989, industry, commerce, culture, social and political realities had a new life. Today you can see successful development again. We have less unemployed people than most of the other states in our country. Industries and the home-craft establishments are in a good position, and we all hope Sonneberg will be a well-known place for dolls and toys in the future.

Hanns Schoenau left quite a legacy in Sonneberg. Because of his love of doll history, the names and locations of the majority of old doll factories are recorded for posterity. In November 2002 the Sonneberg Town Council re-named the square near his house "Hanns Schoenau Square." The square is at the well-known Sonneberg land triangle in the center of the town, which is bordered by Bahnhofstrasse, Cuno-Hoffmeisterstrasse and Bismarckstrasse. (*Strasse* is the German word for "street.") In the square are children's play figures, benches and moving water. It has become a favorite meeting place for residents and visitors alike.

Chapter 2

7. After making the doll-body parts, workers applied paint to the parts. The translated German words on the bottom of this 1911 photograph, which has been hand colored, read: "Covering with Paint." Long wooden sticks with cross bars on top were used to hold the doll bodies while they were being painted and were left inside the bodies until the paint dried. Author's Archival Paper Collection.

8. Removing the sticks from the painted, dried composition body parts was the next step in doll-body production, according to the German wording on this 1911 photograph, which has been hand colored. Author's Archival Paper Collection.

9. Composition bodies were attached to bisque shoulder or socket heads made at the Schoenau & Hoffmeister porcelain factory in Burggrub. This 1930s photograph, which has been hand colored, shows a worker stirring porcelain slip before he fills the plaster working molds stacked behind him. The German text on the photograph (which is not visible in this image) translates as: "Filling of the Molds." Author's Archival Paper Collection.

10. After the bisque heads were taken out of the plaster molds and fired, they were taken to the painting department. This 1936 photograph, which has been hand colored, shows a female worker painting bisque doll heads with a small paintbrush. The painted heads are drying on the large tray next to the artist. Author's Archival Paper Collection.

11. By the 1930s the painting department in a Thuringian doll factory had changed in appearance from the way it looked in the 1911 photograph seen in illustration 7. One of the major changes in doll-body painting was the use of airbrushes instead of hand painting or hand dipping the body parts. Airbrushes were also used to paint hair and eyebrows on many 1920s bisque-head baby dolls. Author's Archival Paper Collection.

12. The assembly process also changed in the 1930s, as mass-production techniques were introduced. This 1936 photograph, which has been hand colored, is an example of a body-assembly department in a doll factory like the Arthur Shoenau doll factory in Sonneberg. Doll arms and legs are neatly stacked in separate wooden boxes. The woman in the foreground is using a variety of body-stringing devices, including pliers and gripping tools, which are laid out in front of her on the worktable. The completed dolls are stacked in front of the workers at the left end of the table. Author's Archival Paper Collection.

Arthur Schoenau Doll Factory and Schoenau & Hoffmeister Porcelain Factory

14. Doll socks were always an important part of a dressed doll. This original sock sample board shows the variety of sock colors and sizes offered to buyers. Doll factories, like the Wagner & Zetsche doll factory in Ilmenau, specialized in doll socks. According to Hanns Schoenau, the Schoenau doll factory bought doll socks from the Wagner & Zetsche doll factory and also from Sonneberg home workers. Courtesy Schloss Tenneberg Museum, Waltershausen. (Photo: Christiane Gräfnitz)

13. An original sample box of doll shoes is on permanent display at the doll museum in Waltershausen. Each pair of shoes is different, and reflects the variety of accessories made to coordinate with dresses or other clothing. Home workers living in the small villages that surrounded Sonneberg supplied shoes for the majority of Sonneberg doll factories, including the Arthur Schoenau doll factory. Courtesy Schloss Tenneberg Museum, Waltershausen. (Photo: Christiane Gräfnitz)

Chapter 2

15. An original 1890s stereoscopic card shows the type of doll-dressing scene that took place in the Arthur Schoenau doll factory, as well as in home-workers' houses and other Thuringian doll factories. The text on the back of the card explains the double photograph in the following way: "Doll Factory, Dressing Dolls, Sonneberg, Germany. Did you ever think how many hands it takes to make toys for the children of the world? Even the making and dressing of dolls keeps many people very busy. In the toy factory pictured, one person does the same thing over and over again. One person molds dolls' heads. Another puts in the eyes. One makes the hands, the body, the legs or the feet. One person must put the different parts of the doll together. When the doll is entirely made it must be dressed. Dolls' clothes are so small that many dresses are made by hand. That is what these women are doing. What beautiful dresses they are making. Many of your toys are made in Germany and that is where this factory is. Did you ever stop to think that your doll Bessie or Florence or Mary made a long journey across the big ocean before she became your baby or your little girl? Do you think she enjoyed the journey? Copyright by: The Keystone View Company." Author's Archival Paper Collection.

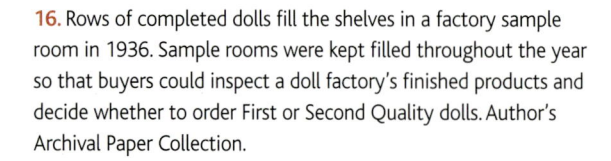

16. Rows of completed dolls fill the shelves in a factory sample room in 1936. Sample rooms were kept filled throughout the year so that buyers could inspect a doll factory's finished products and decide whether to order First or Second Quality dolls. Author's Archival Paper Collection.

17. Bisque socket head by Schoenau & Hoffmeister; wig; multi-stroke eyebrows; painted upper and lower eyelashes; glass sleep eyes; open mouth with upper teeth, 14-inch doll; circa 1905; marked: **S(PB** inside **star)H**. Author's Collection. (Photo: Gene Abbott)

18. Dark-brown bisque socket head by Schoenau & Hoffmeister; original wig and clothing; single-stroke eyebrows; stationary glass eyes; open mouth with upper teeth; 7½-inch doll; GM 1903; marked: **5000//S/(PB** inside **star)H//Dep//12/0**. Author's Collection. (Photo: Gregg Smith)

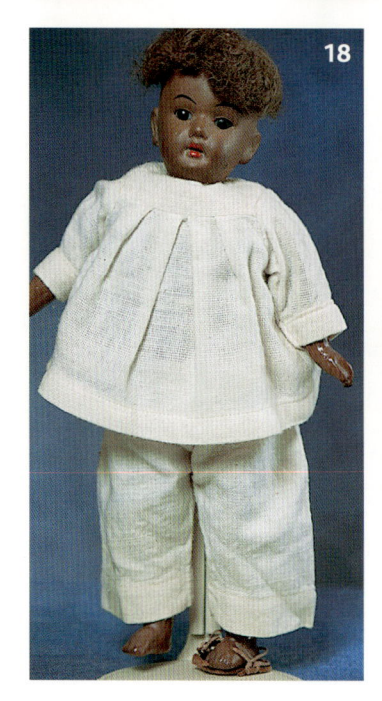

Arthur Schoenau Doll Factory and Schoenau & Hoffmeister Porcelain Factory

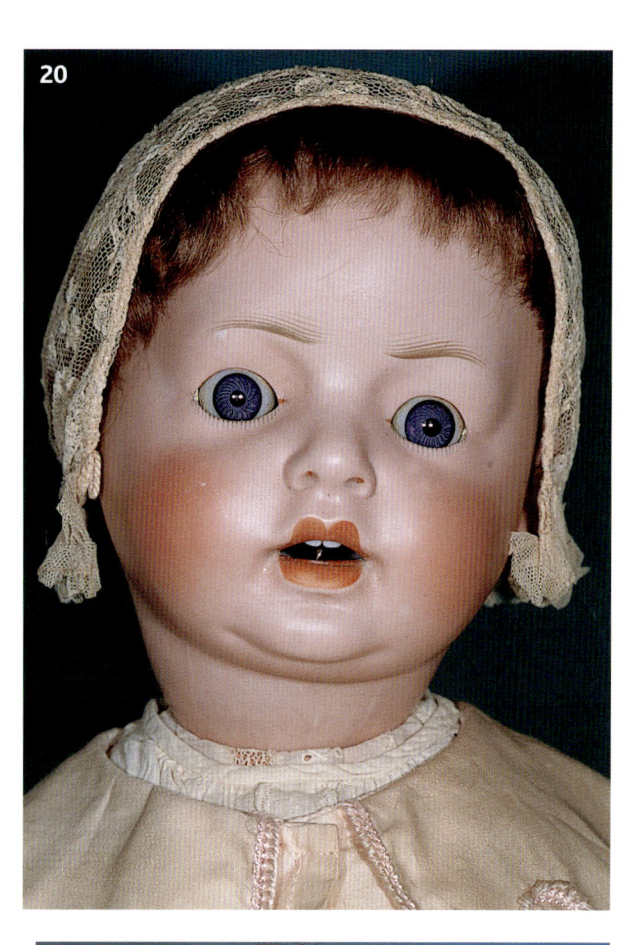

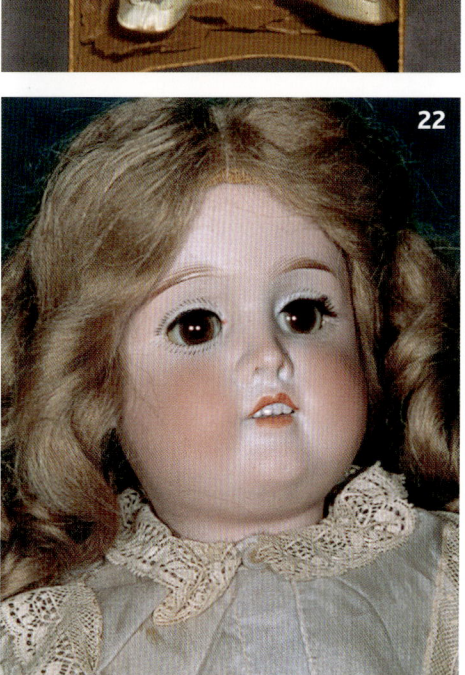

19. This 23-inch Schoenau & Hoffmeister bisque dolly-faced doll is still tied in her original cardboard box marked Rosebud. The doll lies on a paper mattress filled with excelsior. The cushion protected First Quality dolls from breakage during shipment to their final destinations. The clothing and accessories reflect the attention to detail lavished on the top-of-the-line dolls. Author's Collection. (Photo: Gregg Smith)

20. Hanna bisque socket head by Schoenau & Hoffmeister; wig; multi-stroke eyebrows; painted lower eyelashes; glass sleep eyes; open mouth with upper teeth; 23-inch doll; circa 1920; marked: Germany//S(PB inside star)H//Hanna//7. Author's Collection. (Photo: Gene Abbott)

21. Light-brown bisque head by Schoenau & Hoffmeister; original wig and clothing; single-stroke eyebrows; painted upper and lower eyelashes; glass sleep eyes; open mouth with upper teeth; 6¾-inch doll; circa 1920; marked: Germany//S(PB inside star)H//Hanna//12/0. Author's Collection. (Photo: Gregg Smith)

22. A closer view of 23-inch Rosebud, seen in illustration 19, shows the original wig and clothing; multi-stroke eyebrows; painted lower eyelashes and upper eyelashes of hair; glass sleep eyes and open mouth with upper teeth. The circa-1905 doll is marked: S(PB inside star)H. Author's Collection. (Photo: Gregg Smith)

Chapter 2

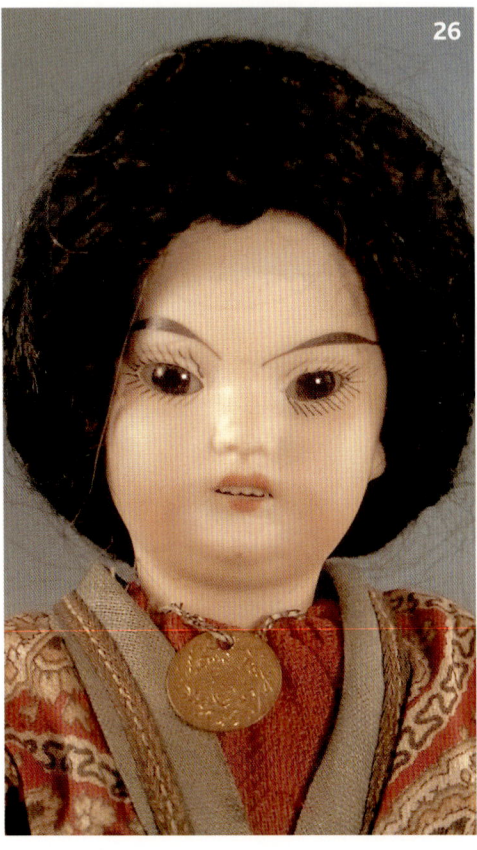

23. Bisque socket head by Schoenau & Hoffmeister; wig; multi-stroke eyebrows; painted lower eyelashes; glass sleep eyes; open mouth with upper teeth; 10-inch doll; circa 1920; marked **S(PB inside star)H//Hanna 3/0//Germany**. Susan Moore Collection. (Photo: John Cummings)

26. Light-brown bisque socket head by Schoenau & Hoffmeister; original wig and clothing; slanting, single-stroke eyebrows; painted upper and lower eyelashes; almond-shaped stationary glass eyes; open mouth with upper teeth; 9-inch doll; circa 1905; marked: **4900//S(PB inside star)H//11/0**. Beth Karp Collection. (Photo: Lee Krombholz)

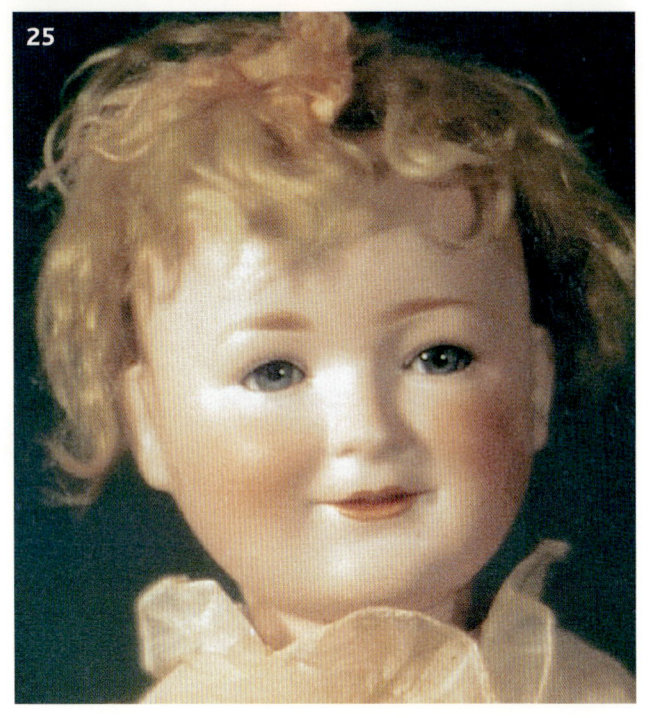

24. The creation of a new model head required patience and skill. Caesar Schneider designed the head of the well-known character doll Princess Elizabeth from a Marcus Adams photograph of three-year-old Elizabeth. This 1930s photograph, which has been hand colored, shows a model head on a pedestal and a modeler examining a bisque doll head. The modeling technique remained the same during the many years bisque doll heads were made in Thuringia. Author's Archival Paper Collection.

25. Princess Elizabeth bisque socket head by the Eversberg porcelain factory in Burggrub, formerly the Schoenau & Hoffmeister porcelain factory; wig; multi-stroke eyebrows; painted upper and lower eyelashes; glass sleep eyes; open mouth with upper teeth; 23-inch doll; made from January 1930 to 1933; marked: **Porzellanfabrik//Burggrub//Princess Elizabeth//Made in Germany**. Private Collection. (Photo: Christiane Gräfnitz)

Arthur Schoenau Doll Factory and Schoenau & Hoffmeister Porcelain Factory

27. Light-brown bisque socket head by Schoenau & Hoffmeister; original wig and clothing; single-stroke eyebrows; painted upper and lower eyelashes; glass sleep eyes; open mouth with upper teeth; 9-inch doll; circa 1920; marked: S(PB inside star)H//Hanna//7/0. Beth Karp Collection. (Photo: Lee Krombholz)

Chapter 2

Arthur Schoenau Doll Factory and Schoenau & Hoffmeister Porcelain Factory

28. Princess Elizabeth; bisque socket-head doll sold by the Arthur Schoenau doll factory; composition torso and one-piece composition arms and legs; 23 inches. See page 216 for more information on this doll's modeling and production. Private Collection. (Photo: Christiane Gräfnitz)

29. Bisque socket head by Shoenau & Hoffmeister; smooth head with painted hair; single-stroke eyebrows; painted upper and lower eyelashes; glass sleep eyes; closed mouth; 18-inch-doll; circa 1920; marked: S(PB inside star)H//NB. Christiane Gräfnitz Collection. (Photo: Christiane Gräfnitz)

30. Bisque socket head by Schoenau & Hoffmeister; wig; multi-stroke eyebrows; painted lower eyelashes; glass sleep eyes; open mouth with upper teeth; 24-inch doll; circa 1912; marked: S(PB inside star)H. Private Collection. (Photo: Christiane Gräfnitz)

31. Bisque socket head by Schoenau & Hoffmeister; wig; multi-stroke eyebrows; painted lower eyelashes and upper eyelashes of hair; glass sleep eyes; open mouth with upper teeth and separate tongue; 15-inch doll; marked: S(PB inside star)H. Courtesy Ladenburger Spielzeugauktion/Goetz Seidel. (Photo: Christiane Gräfnitz)

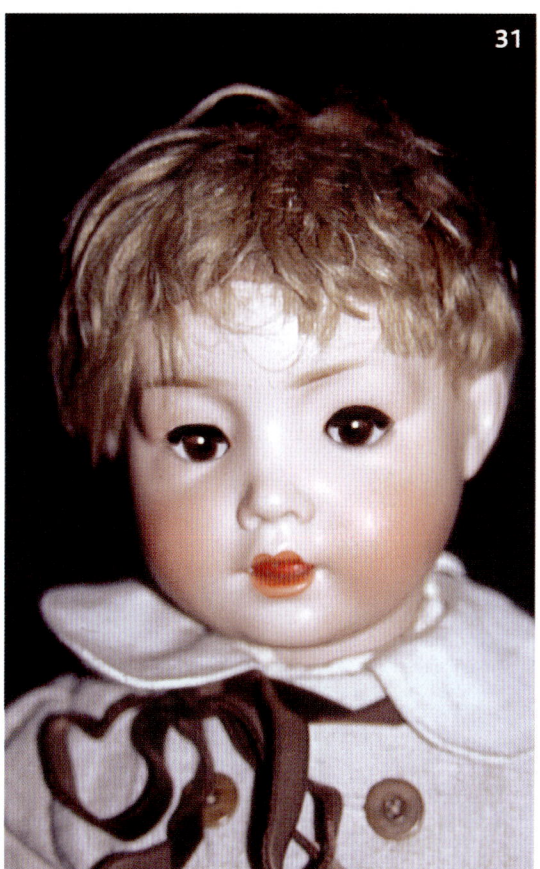

Chapter 2

32. My Cherub bisque socket head by Schoenau & Hoffmeister; smooth head with painted hair; single-stroke eyebrows; painted upper and lower eyelashes; glass sleep eyes; open mouth with upper teeth; 12½-inch doll; circa 1924; marked: **MB**. The incised MB initials found on bisque doll heads are credited to the Arthur Schoenau doll factory. Ferna Nolte Collection. (Photo: Christiane Gräfnitz)

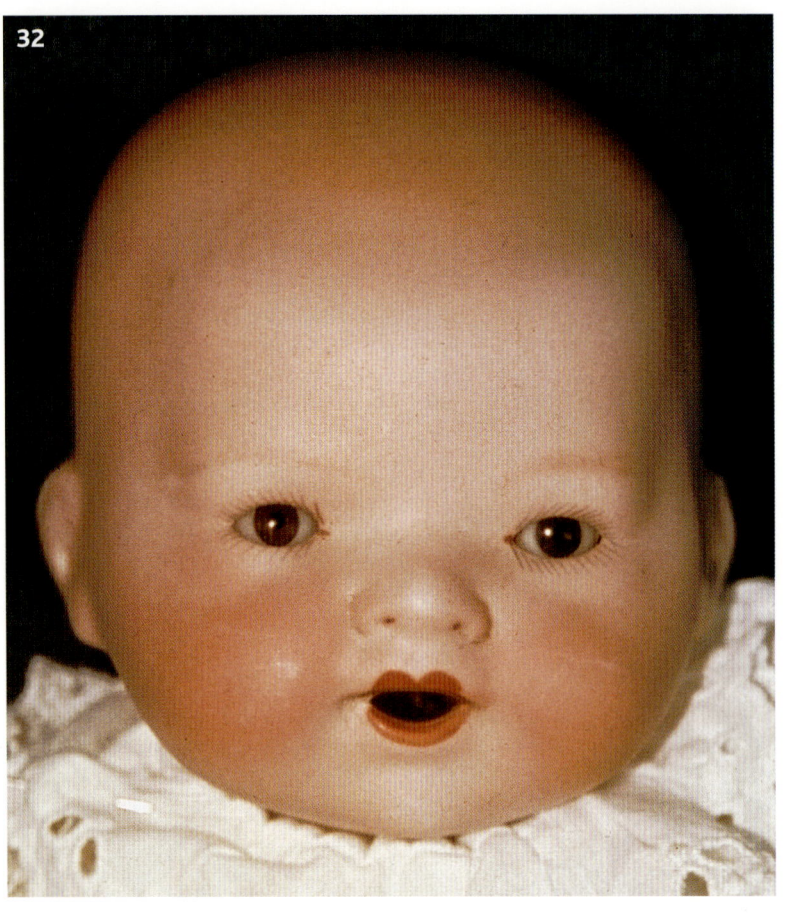

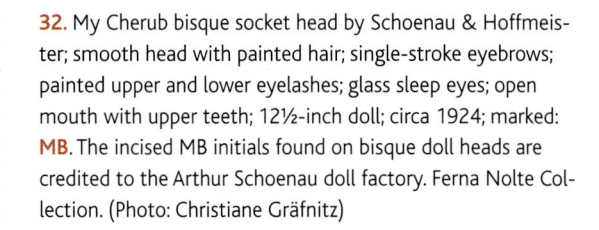

33. A closer view of the Schoenau & Hoffmeister bisque-head doll seen in illustration 34 shows the original wig and clothing; single-stroke eyebrows, painted eyes and open mouth with painted teeth. Courtesy Deutsches Spielzeugmuseum, Sonneberg. (Photo: Christiane Gräfnitz)

34. The Zinner & Söhne doll factory in Schalkau made this 11-by-13-inch pull toy for the Karl Seidler doll factory in Sonneberg, according to the original label on the base. The character doll in back has a Schoenau & Hoffmeister bisque head marked: **S(PB inside star)H//14/0//Germany**. The doll in front has a bisque head marked **13//225**, made by Armand Marseille in 1920. Courtesy Deutsches Spielzeugmuseum, Sonneberg. (Photo: Christiane Gräfnitz)

228

Arthur Schoenau Doll Factory and Schoenau & Hoffmeister Porcelain Factory

35. Smaller Schoenau & Hoffmeister bisque heads were used on a variety of novelty items, including this 6-inch doll riding a cloth stork. The doll's features include an original wig and clothing; multi-stroke eyebrows; painted upper and lower eyelashes, stationary glass eyes and an open mouth with upper teeth. The doll's body, lower arms and legs are made of wood, and connected to the body with wire. The circa-1905 bisque head is marked: **4600 20//S**(**PB** inside **star**) **H**. Beth Karp Collection. (Photo: Lee Krombholz)

37. Hanns Schoenau referred to his home in Sonneberg as his "domicile." (Photo: Mary Krombholz)

38. I enjoyed my May 2002 talk with Hanns Schoenau on top of the 1930s Town Hall in Sonneberg. He showed me the oldest doll factories in town and compared them to the doll factories built in the early 1900s. (Photo: Susan Moore)

36. In this 1950s photograph, Hanns Schoenau holds a doll made at the Arthur Schoenau doll factory. (Photo: Courtesy Deutsches Spielzeugmuseum Archives, Sonneberg)

Part Two

CHAPTER 3

Armand Marseille Porcelain Factory

1. The Armand Marseille villa is still standing in Köppelsdorf, but is completely hidden by overgrown trees and other vegetation. The porcelain factory once stood directly across the street from the Marseille villa. (Photo: Mary Krombholz)

The Sonneberg Doll Museum archives are an excellent source of information on the life of Armand Marseille, including the years he manufactured bisque-head character dolls. For many years, there has been speculation about his French-sounding name. A few early doll researchers believed he adopted the French-sounding name as a marketing ploy. Nothing could be further from the truth: Armand Marseille's ancestors were French Huguenots.

Armand Marseille was born on May 15, 1856, in St. Petersburg (now Leningrad), Russia. His father was employed as an architect for the Imperial Court of the Russian Czar. During his education at the Royal Court of St. Petersburg, Armand Marseille became proficient in several foreign languages.

Following the assassination of Czar Alexander II on March 13, 1881, Marseille, with his father, mother and siblings left Russia to travel in Europe in search of a new home. After riding in horse-drawn coaches throughout France, Germany and Switzerland, the family decided to settle in the Thuringian town of Coburg. Although small in size, Coburg is described in history books as having been a cultured town filled with accomplished artists and musicians.

During the years he lived in Coburg, Marseille loved to travel the countryside on horseback or in a horse-drawn coach. He visited nearby Sonneberg often. In 1884, at the age of twenty-eight, Marseille became so impressed with the rapidly growing doll production in the area that he decided to buy the Lambert doll and toy factory in Sonneberg.

The Lambert doll factory was originally named the Lambert & Samhammer doll factory. In 1881, Matthias Lambert and Philipp Samhammer ended their partnership and founded new doll factories. The year 1884 was important to Armand Marseille for another reason: that year he married Hilda Sieder, the daughter of a Sonneberg dollmaker whose small home still stands in Sonneberg today, near the old town hall. Their son Hermann was born in 1885.

A year after buying the Lambert doll factory, Marseille bought the Liebermann & Wegescher porcelain factory, which made pipe heads, beer steins and pitchers. Although he had no experience in producing porcelain, Marseille's natural talent for business became readily apparent. In 1889 he advertised for workers in the Sonneberg newspaper using the following words: "Looking for immediate hiring, 15 women that specialize in the molding of doll heads and one experienced molder. Employment is for an undetermined time."

In 1890 Marseille fired his first bisque doll heads. One of his first registered doll heads was made for the Cuno & Otto Dressel doll factory. The heads (made from sizes 0 to 10) were marked: "C.O.D. 93 Dep." The 93 mold number is an abbreviation for the 1893 registration date. By 1893 the Marseille porcelain factory employed two hundred and fifty workers devoted to making bisque doll heads and bathing dolls. His

2. The Armand Marseille porcelain factory in Köppelsdorf was torn down in 2004. (Photo: Carol Nagel)

dedication to hard work combined with his policy of treating all of his customers fairly resulted in ever-increasing doll orders. From 1890 to 1929, the Marseille employees worked two shifts a day. The shifts included work at the porcelain factory in Neuhaus (a suburb of Köppelsdorf), which Armand Marseille built in 1905. This factory only made electro-technical porcelain products.

In 1900 Marseille built a large villa on the ten-acre property across the street from his porcelain factory. He turned the villa grounds into a beautiful horticultural paradise, planted with examples of rare plants gathered from many areas of the world. His head gardener and three assistants kept the grounds in pristine condition year round. He entertained often, and enjoyed showing his guests the Russian icons marked with the initials of his father's family. On special occasions, he flew a Russian flag from his roof.

Unlike other Thuringian porcelain factory owners, Marseille refused to advertise or participate in town fairs. Instead, he used his knowledge of foreign languages to establish business contacts, which, in turn, increased sales. In 1904 the Marseille porcelain factory won the Grand Prize in the St. Louis World's Fair. By 1910, the factory employed eight hundred workers. The Armand Marseille twenty-fifth-commemorative-anniversary booklet states: "The Armand Marseille factory is the largest union in the milieu of the German doll and toy industry."

In 1918, at the age of sixty-two, Marseille had a heart attack. Poor health forced him to retire and turn the leadership of the porcelain factory over to his son Hermann in 1919. Marseille died of a heart attack on April 23, 1925, after a walk through the public gardens near Lichtenfels, Germany. He was sixty-nine years old. He is the only member of his family to be buried in the Köppelsdorf cemetery. The rest of his immediate family is buried in the Coburg cemetery.

The Armand Marseille and Ernst Heubach porcelain factories had much in common. They were located a short distance from one another in the small village of Köppelsdorf. In 1915 Armand Marseille's daughter Beatrix married Ernst Heubach's son, Ernst, Jr. The two porcelain factories merged in 1919. The name of the combined factories was: "The United Köppelsdorf Porcelain Factories." Hermann Marseille and Ernst Heubach, Jr. had many arguments in the years following the merger because their personalities were so different. Hermann Marseille was much like his father, agreeable and calm in temperament, and treated his workers much like his father had, with respect and admiration for their loyalty and hard work. After only thirteen years of joint ownership the Armand Marseille and Ernst Heubach porcelain factories separated in 1932.

Under Hermann's leadership, the Marseille porcelain factory was very successful. Hermann made many trips to the United States to locate new customers. In 1921 he married Marianne Heumann, whose father was the director of the Deutsche Bank of Coburg. They had a son named Hermann,

Chapter 3

who died in the battle of Stalingrad in World War II.

Armand Marseille bisque-head dolls are often a first purchase for antique-doll collectors, and so are found in most antique-doll collections. Prolific is the word we generally hear when this factory is mentioned. The Armand Marseille porcelain factory made millions of dolly-face dolls in the low-to-medium-price range for more than forty years. Because the majority of dolls were sold to American importers, a doll collector can usually find examples of Marseille dolly-faced dolls at doll shows or auctions across America. The most common shoulder-head doll made by this factory is mold number 370, and the same mold in a socket head is number 390. Dolls marked with these mold numbers can be appealing, but the quality can also vary considerably.

The majority of Armand Marseille bisque dolly-faced dolls were sold wearing simple gauze-like chemises, which kept production costs down. Thuringian home workers were able to enhance the plainest doll face with bonnets and beautifully trimmed dresses in every color and style. The cotton fabric used to make the chemises was inexpensive, but when it was stiffened, trimmed with braid or lace and pressed, the result was a very attractive dress. When boxed, these dolls, though cheap in price, were extremely appealing.

There were many reasons for the low cost of making dolls in Köppelsdorf. It is a very short walk from the center of Sonneberg to the Marseille porcelain factory. When the Marseille factory was founded, there were more home workers in this area of Germany that in any other area of the country. Considering the number of doll orders the factory filled every year, it was imperative to have large numbers of home and factory workers who could fill orders in a short amount of time. The Armand Marseille porcelain factory concentrated on the lower-priced doll market. Many women who lived on farms in the Midwest as little girls can still remember opening a box on Christmas that contained a beautiful Armand Marseille doll ordered from Sears, Roebuck & Co. Inexpensive dolls were just as appealing as the higher-priced dolls to the average child.

Most of Armand Marseille's dolly-faced dolls and character dolls had stationary or sleep eyes, rather than painted eyes. The old Köppelsdorf railroad station is directly across the street from the Ernst Heubach doll factory. The station sign illustrates the importance of Köppelsdorf as a recipient of millions of glass doll eyes. For many years, the sign on the station read "Laucha Branch Railroad Station." Glass-eye blowers in Lauscha made the majority of glass eyes for the Marseille factory. Lauscha and Köppelsdorf are only 9.2 miles apart. During the years of character dollmaking, Lauscha delivery women delivered eyes daily, or at least twice a week, to the doll factories in this Sonneberg suburb.

Lauscha has been the world's doll-eye center for more than four hundred years. The first glass factory opened there in 1597. The April 25, 1936, Lauscha newpaper described glass doll-eye delivery with the following words:

> Messenger woman Louise Petzold can look back on 25 years of daily activity. Mrs. Petzold is in the 68th year of her life and in spite of this advanced age continues in the fast pace of her work. In unbroken activity, she practices her business in wind and rain day in and day out. Already hours before the daily departure of the train for Sonneberg—this small, vigorous woman is seen at the station in Lauscha, ready to receive doll eyes to be delivered to the Sonneberg doll factories. In Sonneberg she is equally well-known. When she returns on the afternoon or the evening train because of more orders, she displays a very energetic zeal toward the various glassblowers waiting for monies brought back.

I have had the opportunity to visit the homes of several different Lauscha glassblowers during my many trips to Thuringia. I marvel at the skill it must have taken to create glass doll eyes from a simple glass tube. During the years glass doll eyes were made by the thousands, very little equipment was necessary, and many Lauscha glassblowers worked at home from a bench in a dining room or kitchen. The table used for blowing glass had a gas burner to provide the heat required to soften and blow the glass. A foot pedal controlled the air required to produce a hotter flame.

As I watched one glassblower heat the glass tube and blow a glass bubble, I wondered whether his father or grandfather had taught him this skill. Skills such as glassblowing were often passed down from generation to generation. It is amazing to watch as the iris and the pupil are attached to the blown eyeball. A clear crystal outer layer is often applied to the completed eyeball to create paperweight eyes.

Glassblowers did not make much money during the years character dolls were made. At the turn of the last century, a glassblower made only one dollar for blowing one hundred glass eyes. The Lauscha Industrial School taught glassblowing, and students worked for many years to become a "Glass Art Master" or "Doll Eye Master." During the years following World War II, a number of glassblowers combined their talents to form a company called Lauscha Glass Art. But after the reunification of East and West Germany, the company closed and many glass artists had a hard time finding work. Today, due to the popularity of glass Christmas ornaments, glassblowers have more work.

From the book *Sonneberg Stories of Dolls, Slate Pencils and Cuckoo Whistles*, we learn the process of blowing glass eyes. The oral history from a grandson of a Lauscha glassblower reads as follows.

> Earlier in my childhood, there was hardly a family in Lauscha who did not have something to do with the production and working of glass.
>
> There were many glass factories which produced

Armand Marseille Porcelain Factory

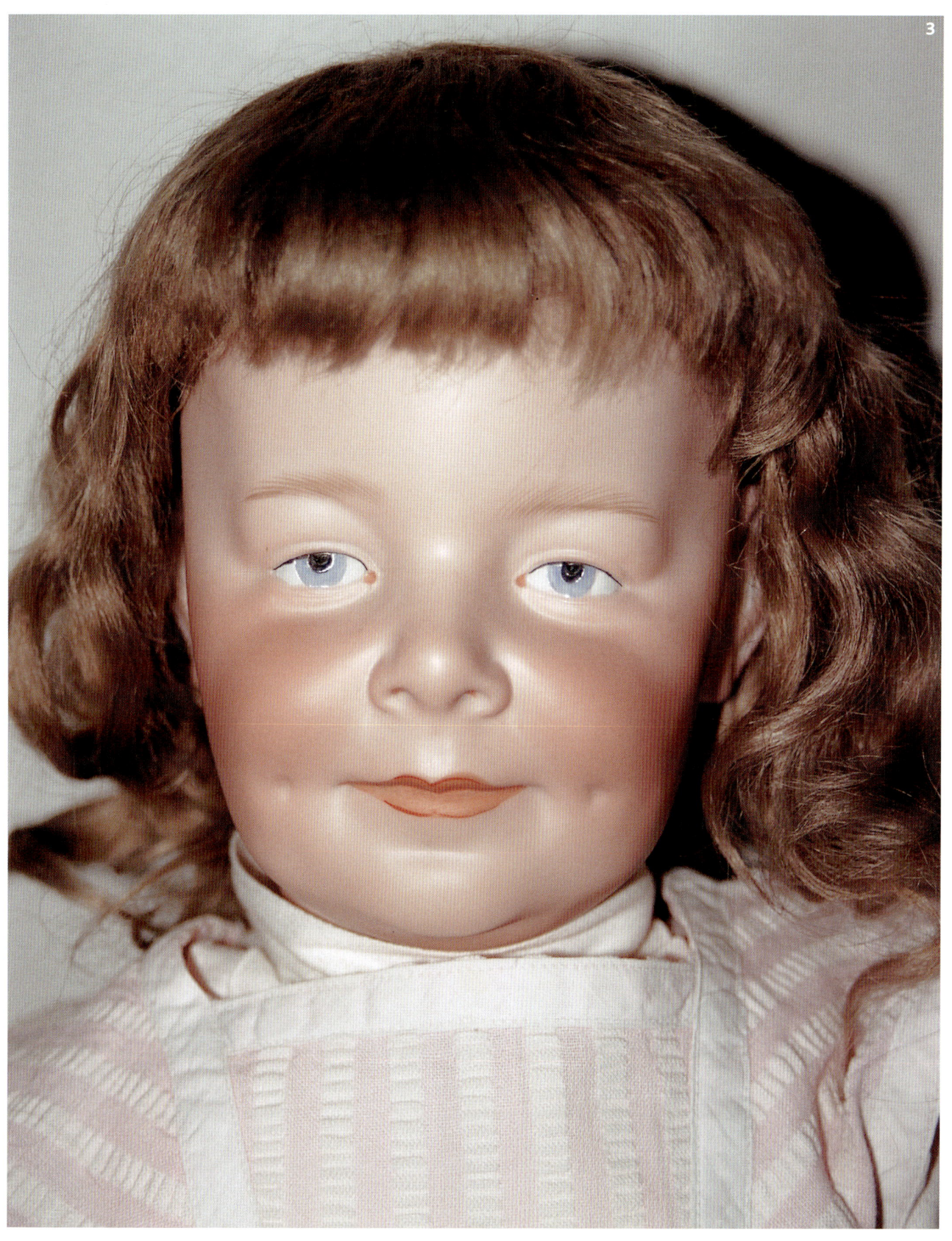

3. Bisque socket head by Armand Marseille; wig; well-defined eye sockets; multi-stroke eyebrows; painted eyes; closed mouth; cheek dimples; 24-inch doll; circa 1910; marked: **A7M**. Courtesy Rosalie Whyel Museum of Doll Art. (Photo: Christiane Gräfnitz)

Chapter 3

material for the glassblowers and glass shapers. Little by little the producers of glass objects became specialized. There were the doll eye makers, animal eye makers, figurine eye makers, and people eye makers, who specialized in eyes for show window figures and the people eye makers who specialized in prostheses. They all had different tools and resources, which they made, or had made to their specifications. In every family the talents and strategies were passed on from the elders to the young.

My parents were doll eye makers, my grandparents were figure eye makers and my uncle made people eyes. I already at age ten entered into glass eyemaking under my grandfather and father. At the same time I began to help with earning the family living.

The glassmakers' families could not live sumptuously. In 1900, for 100 eyes we received, according to size, about 3.60 Marks (86 cents in U.S. dollars during this time period). Together with our parents, we earned 45 Marks in a week. From that we subtracted the material costs, packaging and the gas to blow the glass object. So we were left with only 30 Marks to live on.

I learned from the glassblowers in the Lauscha Trade School and from my parents, how to be a doll eye maker. My parents made mostly simple, inexpensive doll eyes, oval eyes and reflex eyes, for which my father received a patent. The color palette was not large; we produced only eyes with a blue or a brown iris in various sizes.

My parents and I made glass doll eyes in the following way.

1. From a white tube, whose cross-cut pattern conformed to the desired doll eye size, the little tube was blown and shaped.

2. With a rod of colored glass the basic color of the iris was melted on.

3. The threads of the iris were then set on the doll eyes. I made these glass rods myself for figure eyes, on which I drew very thin colored threads on a colorless glass rod. Of course, through this, many nuances occurred, making the eye look even more natural.

4. Then the black pupil was set on.

5. For an especially flashing eye, a clear, colorless layer was set on. During the work procedure toward production, the iris was once again heated and re-blown, so that it became very flat and uniform.

6. Then the eyeball was blown to the needed size.

7. The finished eye was heated once more for the removal of the inner tension.

8. With a steel hammer I removed the remainder of the glass tube.

9. Because each eye had a very individual appearance, the pairing of the eyes was very important. An eye pairer with a practiced eye took on this chore.

Out of 100 finished eyes, only 60 to 70 were possible to be paired. The unmatched eyes were given back to the glassblower, so he could turn them in for pairing with the next order. The eye makers were paid by pairs of eyes.

Another group of home workers was responsible for the glass sleep eyes that allowed a dolly-faced doll or a character doll to open and close its eyes. The oral history of a Sonneberg eye installer provides insight as to the steps necessary to create these eyes. The daughter of this Sonneberg area doll-eye installer explains the process.

My family had a small family factory in which we worked independently as eye installers. We children got the finished painted porcelain or molded heads from the doll factory. They were packed individually in tissue paper and wood shavings. The unpacking was typically children's work, which we always did.

The doll eyes were of glass and were delivered to us by Lauscha glassmakers. Also in this we children were included in sorting the eyes according to the size of the doll head and the color of the iris (blue, gray or brown), and in placing the eyes into the eye holes. The qualified work, which required much skill and practice, was done by our parents. Usually one eye went through their hands 25 times before it was set into the head as prescribed, and functioned as a sleep eye.

The steps my parents took to make sleep eyes were:

1. With the help of a small board on which marks for the different sizes of doll heads had been placed, my father cut the wire. Then the wires were suitably bent to the eye interval and to the size of the eyes. On both ends he set a glass eye. In the middle between the eyes, he fastened a second wire, on whose end a lead ball was fastened and squeezed together with pliers. This lead ball served as the weight for the sleep function. When laid down, the doll closed her eyes; when lifted up they opened.

2. Then my father dipped the eyes in wax. After they were dry, he dipped them in an eyelid color and then again in wax. Again the wax had to dry. With a pointed knife my father marked the edge of the lid, cut it clean and very carefully lifted the lid off with the point of the knife.

3. The eyelashes were glued to a very thin piece of paper. Either he or my mother glued the eyelash strip with bone glue directly inside the top of the eye hole. When this glue dried, my mother then glued the waxed and painted eyelid onto the glass eye again. The eyelashes were then trimmed to the desired length with special eyelash scissors.

4. My father then fastened each holder with two

Armand Marseille Porcelain Factory

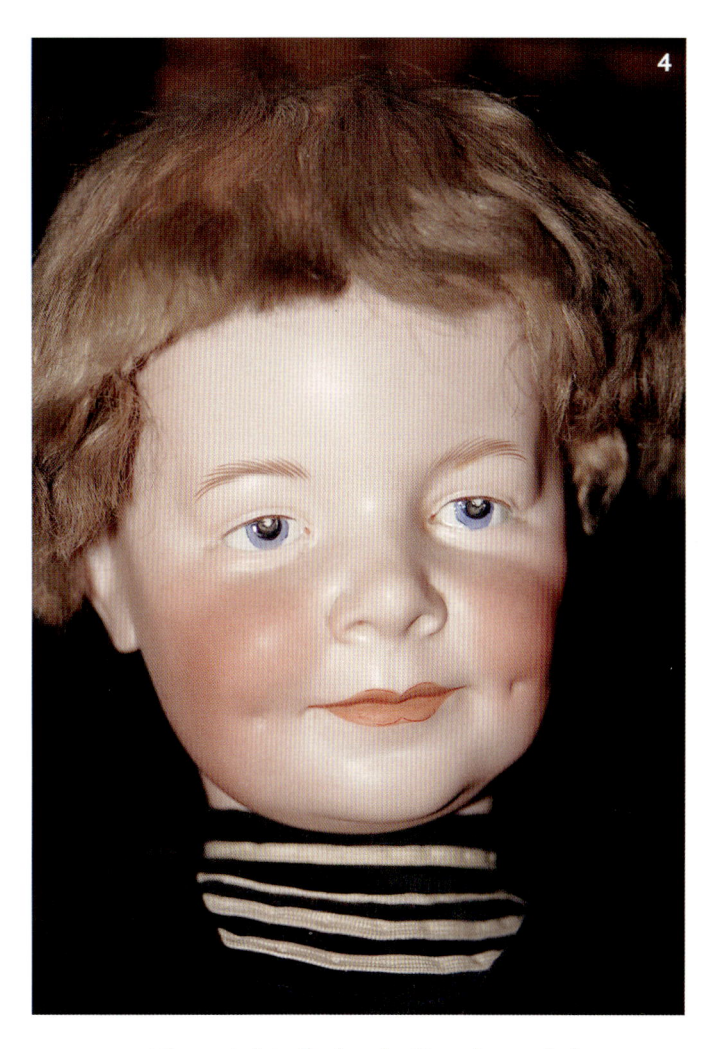

eyes at the ends into the head with a clump of plaster. Now he had the last chance to adjust the distance between the eyes so that they would fit exactly into the eyeholes.

5. The finished heads were now placed on a board with pegs. Our help was sought again now. As a child I had to vibrate the boards so the eyes remained movable as the plaster dried. When the plaster was dry, we children wrapped the finished heads in tissue paper and packed them with wood shavings in individual compartments in a large box. Two times a week we delivered the heads to the doll factory, and then picked up heads without eyes.

The Marseille porcelain factory sold a wide variety of bisque-head dolls with stationary and glass sleep eyes, including Native American dolls, googlies and character dolls. An Armand Marseille googly doll with very expressive features is marked "Nobbi Kid" on the back of the bisque head. The New York importers Geo. Borgfeldt & Co. introduced the Nobbi Kid in 1914. The Borgfeldt company was one of the largest importers of German dolls and toys (see Part One: Chapter 4). One of the main purposes of an import/export company was to locate the most reasonably priced doll-related products and reorder similar products year after year. The ability to buy

4. The Armand Marseille porcelain factory made a group of exceptional bisque socket heads marked with the initials "AM," separated by a size number. They are excellent examples of the factory's First Quality bisque character heads. This 22-inch doll, circa 1910, is sitting on a carousel in the basement of the Sonneberg Doll Museum. The carousel was part of an exhibit created by thirty-seven Sonneberg doll factories for the 1910 World Exposition in Brussels. The bisque head features a wig; multi-stroke eyebrows; painted eyes with white highlights; closed mouth and deep cheek dimples. The white-eye highlights are placed between the outlined upper lid and the top edge of the pupils. Marked: **A7M**. Courtesy Deutsches Spielzeugmuseum, Sonneberg. (Photo: Christiane Gräfnitz)

5. Bisque socket head by Armand Marseille; wig, well-defined eye sockets; multi-stroke eyebrows; painted eyes with white highlights; closed mouth; 19-inch doll; circa 1910; marked: **A6M**. The head sculpting and facial painting on the earliest group of Armand Marseille character dolls varies slightly, but the dolls are all marked in the same way, with the AM initials separated by a size number. The bisque head on this doll has a much thinner nose that the noses of the dolls pictured in illustrations 3 and 4. Courtesy Rosalie Whyel Museum of Doll Art. (Photo: Christiane Gräfnitz)

and sell under a competitor's price yearly resulted in repeat orders, but often, unfortunately, in dolls of lower quality.

Geo. Borgfeldt & Co. was able to sell dolls at very reasonable prices by buying large quantities of dolls and toys from so many Thuringian doll and porcelain factories. For decades, the Armand Marseille factory sold millions of inexpen-

Chapter 3

sive bisque shoulder and socket head dolls to the Borgfeldt company. The heads were attached to bodies and dressed by home workers in dozens of Sonneberg doll factories. Large orders from one company, like the Geo. Borgfeldt & Co. importing company, were profitable because payment was made immediately after the invoice and shipping papers were received. But the danger was that a buyer like Borgfeldt would find another source and a large percentage of sales would be lost. Large customers often applied pressure to lower prices, and yet the overall number made was usually worth the price consideration given to the best customers. An American doll and toy store like F.A.O. Schwarz consistently ordered more merchandise of top quality than of low quality. American mail-order companies such as Sears, Roebuck & Company and Montgomery Ward sold as many low-to-medium-priced dolls as high-priced dolls.

The 1920s can be called the decade of the infant doll. Bye-Lo Babies and My Dream Babies were the most popular baby dolls. My Dream Babies were introduced in 1924, and millions were sold, primarily to American buyers. The Armand Marseille porcelain factory made the bisque-head dolls marked with the mold numbers 341 and 351 for the New York-based distributor, the Arranbee Doll Company.

My Dream Babies were an immediate success. According to the Coleman research published in *The Collector's Encyclopedia of Dolls, Volume II*: "In 1925, the factory had to work overtime to fill the orders. Dream Babies sold for $2.25 to $5.00; and, a cheaper but similar line sold for a dollar less." Following the record sales of My Dream Babies, the Armand Marseille factory introduced a number of similarly sculpted doll heads. Each variation resembled the original #341 and #351 dolls, but differed in subtle modeling details. Marseille molds #345, #372 and #375 were bisque-head dolls (circa 1926) in the Kiddiejoy line sold by the New York importers Jacobs and Kassler.

The Marseille mold known as Baby Gloria is an older-looking variation of the original My Dream Baby mold. The bisque head resembles a year-old baby with dimples, a smiling face and molded hair, with a large curl in the center of the doll's forehead. The company Roth, Baitz & Lipsitz distributed the dolls. Another variation was Baby Phyllis. Marseille made the Baby Phyllis Dream Baby look-a-like for the Baby Phyllis Doll Company, a New York company in business from 1919 to 1929. Other names for My Dream Babies included Lullaby Baby, Rock-A-Bye-Baby and Tee Wee the pillow doll. One of the most unusual My Dream Baby variations was the crying A.M. bisque-head baby marked: "A.M. Germany//347/3."

One group of popular baby dolls was a doll designed in 1914 and copyrighted by the New York importers Louis Amberg and Son (1906-1930). It was designed by Juno Juszko and given the name: New Born Babe. Armand Marseille used the mold number 371 for their version of the Newborn Babe. The Recknagel porcelain factory also made the New Born Babe, using the mold number 886.

Dorothy S. Coleman wrote an excellent article in the April 1942 issue of *Antiques Journal*, which sheds light on the New-born Babe. Coleman includes several *Playthings* magazine ads in her article. The January 9, 1914, issue of *Playthings* advertised the New Born Babe (G45520) as a very young infant (two days old) sculpted from life, with half-closed eyes, flattened nose, sunken chin, full cheeks, faun-like ears and general new-born features. Also in January 1914, the New Born Babe was listed among the doll lines ready for delivery on February 1. According to the *Antiques Journal* article, the 1912, 1913 and 1915 Louvre department store catalogs contained advertisements for New Born Babies. In 1925, in response to the re-issue of the New Born Babe, *Playthings* quoted a doll wholesaler as follows: "We've secured a reserve stock of one-half a million in various sizes. The New Born Baby doll is the biggest success we have had for years."

Baby dolls were popular for many years following the introduction of the Bye-Lo-Baby in 1922. My Dream Baby dolls were sold in record numbers because of their appeal and low sales price. For years, the Thuringian doll factories competed for American mail-order business. Each doll factory tried to locate different markets. The price of a doll often dropped depending upon the size of the order and the chance that there might be repeat orders from the same buyer. And, of course, the main reason the Thuringian doll and porcelain factories were able to offer dolls at such low prices was due to the low wages paid to home and factory workers in towns like Sonneberg and Köppelsdorf.

The Armand Marseille porcelain factory made bisque doll heads for the following companies: Louis Amberg & Son; Arranbee Doll Company; C.M. Bergmann; Geo. Borgfeldt & Co.; Butler Brothers; W.A. Cissna & Co.; Cuno & Otto Dressel; Gebrüder Eckardt; Foulds & Freure; Otto Gans; Max Handwerck; Hitz, Jacobs & Co.; B. Illfelder; Koenig & Wernicke; E. Maar & Son; Montgomery Ward; F.A.O. Schwarz; Sears, Roebuck & Company; Peter Scherf; E.U. Steiner; Wagner & Zetsche; Adolf Wislizenus; Wanamakers Department Stores and Louis Wolf & Co.

American importers were Armand and Hermann Marseille's best customers. The four largest New York importers sold Marseille bisque-head dolly-face and character dolls. These were: Louis Wolf, founded in 1870; Butler Brothers, founded in 1877; Louis Amberg & Sons, founded in 1878 and Geo. Borgfeldt & Co., founded in 1882. American department and toy store representatives were well known in Sonneberg and Köpplesdorf. During the 1870s, American department stores began to add doll and toy departments. The well-known department store R.H. Macy added a doll and toy department in 1875. The Chicago-based department store Marshall Field and Company added a doll and toy department store in 1889. During this same period of time, the John Wanamaker and Woodward & Lothrop department stores also sold dolls and toys.

American doll importers like Geo. Borgfeldt & Co. placed annual orders for one thousand or more dolls. It seems likely that the Armand Marseille porcelain factory was always con-

Armand Marseille Porcelain Factory

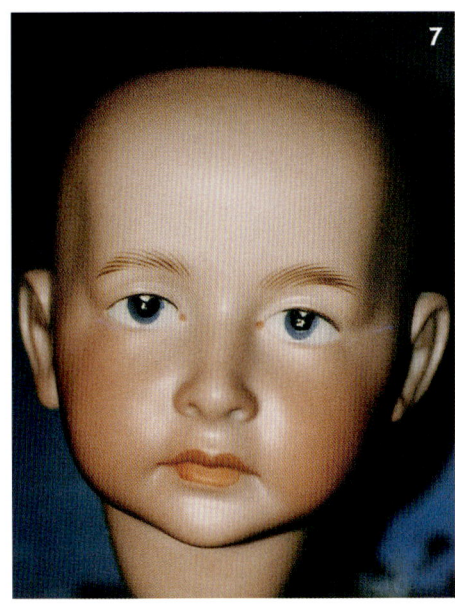

7. Bisque socket head by Armand Marseille; multi-stroke eyebrows; painted eyes with white highlights; closed mouth; 5-inch head; circa 1910; marked: **A6M**. The high crown is visible in this photograph. Courtesy Deutsches Spielzeugmuseum, Sonneberg. (Photo: Christiane Gräfnitz)

6. Bisque socket head by Armand Marseille; wig; multi-stroke eyebrows; painted eyes with white highlights; closed mouth; cheek dimples; 19½-inch doll; circa 1910; marked: **A6M**. Julie Blewis Collection. (Photo: Fanilya Gueno)

8. Bisque socket head by Armand Marseille; wig; multi-stroke eyebrows; painted eyes with white highlights; closed mouth; 15-inch doll; circa 1910; marked: **A3M**. Julie Blewis Collection. (Photo: Fanilya Gueno)

9. Bisque socket head by Armand Marseille; wig; multi-stroke eyebrows; painted eyes with white highlights; closed mouth; cheek dimples; 23-inch doll; circa 1910; marked: **A6M**. Julie Blewis Collection. (Photo: Fanilya Gueno)

sidered a source for large doll orders. Unlike smaller doll factories, Armand Marseille was able to provide large numbers of bisque heads, clothing and accessories in a short period of time thanks to the large number of home workers living in the immediate vicinity.

The Armand Marseille porcelain factory made bisque heads from 1890 until 1949, when Armand's son Hermann moved to West Germany for political reasons. The Armand Marseille porcelain factory was torn down in 1994. The March 1994 issue of the Ciesliks' *Puppenmagazin* provides the following details of the demolition of the factory. "Beginning in July of this year, the building in which millions of doll heads were made will be torn down. In its place, a new apartment and business building will be erected. After the re-unification, the building had again become the property of the Marseille family. The heirs, who live in Austria now, sold the property to an investor who wants to open his new building by Christmas, 1995."

The 1900 Marseille villa is still standing today in Köppelsdorf, but is badly in need of repair. It is completely hidden by overgrown trees and shrubs that were once part of the ten-acre horticultural haven. Year after year, Armand Marseille crossed the street that divided his home from his porcelain factory. Those years are long over, but his memory lives on in the thousands of dolls found in doll collections today.

An oral history from a former Armand Marseille porcelain factory worker can be found in *Spinning Wheel's Complete Book of Dolls*. Genevieve Angione's article titled "Armand Marseille Dolls" includes an interview with a man who worked in the Marseille porcelain factory during the last years of production. He states:

> Although they did not make kid bodies or bisque forearms, A.M. did make completely jointed papier-mâché bodies, including bodies with jointed ankles. The latter were not too popular, however, for a factory-strung body will stand alone, and jointed ankles made the dolls fall over too easily.
>
> Tiny heads were made four to a mold; medium sizes were three to a mold; the large ones were molded individually. The coloring of the lips, cheeks, etc. was done by whole families, including small children, yet these home workers barely made a living.

The worker's oral history is very important because it offers proof that the Armand Marseille porcelain factory made "completely jointed bodies" in the factory. We can therefore surmise that factory workers assembled bisque-head dolls in the factory with composition bodies created by home workers or employees of the porcelain factory. In the 1946 book *More About Dolls* by Janet Pagter Johl, Fred Kolb states that the Armand Marseille and the Ernst Heubach porcelain factories were two of the largest manufacturers of bisque doll heads in Thuringia.

Armand Marseille bisque-head character dolls are often characterized as being poorly modeled and painted. Marseille focused on ever-increasing sales, and therefore located buyers like Geo. Borgfeldt & Co., who ordered a variety of inexpensive dolls year after year. When bisque-head dolls from the Sonneberg-area porcelain factories are compared to those made by Waltershausen-area porcelain factories, the quality of the bisque, molding and painting is often described as excellent on those made in the Waltershausen area and poor on those made in the Sonneberg area. The quality of Armand Marseille bisque head dolls is apparent, however, when one studies the painted-eye 500 mold number series and the exquisite character dolls marked only with the A.M. initials and a size number.

Arthur Krauss Doll Factory

The Arthur Krauss doll factory is still standing next door to the old Armand Marseille villa today. The Marseille porcelain factory was formerly directly across the street from the Krauss factory, causing the factory to cast a shadow on the Krauss doll factory on sunny days. A special highlight on one of my trips to the Sonneberg area was meeting and interviewing Arthur Krauss's son, Helmut. Following in his father's footsteps, Helmut lived in and operated a doll factory in his father's home/factory, which was founded in 1919.

Shortly before he died, Helmut Krauss sold many of his business ledgers, company order records and sales catalogs to me. By studying the translated Krauss records, I am better able to understand the role a small doll factory in the Sonneberg area played in the production of bisque-head character dolls. The Krauss doll factory ledgers document the years 1925, 1928, 1930 and 1942, and list the dates bisque-doll heads were ordered from the Armand Marseille, Ernst Heubach and other porcelain factories in the area. The business ledgers also list the doll factories that bought complete dolls assembled by the Krauss doll factory, including the doll factories of Martin Eichhorn and Welsch & Co. in Sonneberg and Max Oscar Arnold in Neustadt.

When I toured the attic of the Krauss doll factory in 2001, I noticed a large box of doll heads next to some open shelves. Helmut Krauss kindly gave me one of the bisque character heads still in the box. The incised marks cover the entire back of the small head. The marks are the initials "M.O.A." inside an incised eight-pointed star (the Max Oscar Arnold trademark), the mold number "150" and "Made in Germany//Welsch//9/0" (size number). This doll head offers definitive proof of the alliance that existed between the Sonneberg-area Max Oscar Arnold and Welsch & Co. doll factories. When doll orders were too large for small doll factories to fill, larger doll and porcelain factories in the area made bisque heads and other parts to help the smaller factory fill its orders on time.

The Krauss sales catalogs are of special interest to antique-doll collectors. The doll-related items listed in the 1925 catalog include dressed character babies in undershirts, babies with clockwork eyes, dollhouse dolls and dressed dolly-faced

Armand Marseille Porcelain Factory

10. Bisque socket head by Armand Marseille; wig; multi-stroke eyebrows; painted eyes; uncommon open/closed mouth with painted teeth; 19½-inch doll; circa 1910; marked: **A6M**. Julie Blewis Collection. (Photo: Fanilya Gueno)

Chapter 3

dolls. The 1925 Krauss doll parts' list includes: porcelain, celluloid and papier-mâché heads; bodies made of fabric and papier-mâché; composition and bisque arms and legs; wigs; shoes; stockings; dresses; underwear; and hats. The sales catalogs also list many items for making and repairing dolls including: loose non-movable eyes; parts for sleep eyes and eyelashes; rubber cord in all sizes; head spirals for attaching bodies; wooden cranks; hooks and eyes; celluloid material; make-up, lacquer and eye paint.

During my visit to his home/factory, Krauss showed me a very unusual character head. The head is referred to as "Gladdie" by doll collectors. Although the Krauss doll factory bought bisque doll heads from many Sonneberg-area porcelain factories, the majority of entries in the Krauss original business records are for bisque heads made by the Armand Marseille porcelain factory. In my opinion, the Marseille porcelain factory quite possibly made the earthenware head that Krauss is holding in the photo in illustration 94 on page 261. When I asked him, through a translator, who made the head, he pointed towards the location of the former Armand Marseille porcelain factory.

The Arthur Krauss doll factory is empty now, and the home/factory is badly in need of repair. It is fortunate that the business records remained in the Krauss home because the 1920s ledgers and business records now in my collection provide valuable information on the entire production of character dolls in the Sonneberg area.

The Arthur Krauss factory continued to buy composition-head dolls from the Armand Marseille porcelain factory until 1948. According to a document in the Sonneberg Doll Museum archives, in the early 1940s the Armand Marseille porcelain factory made doll heads in bisque using the same molds, the same porcelain mixture and the same serial numbers as those used before 1939.

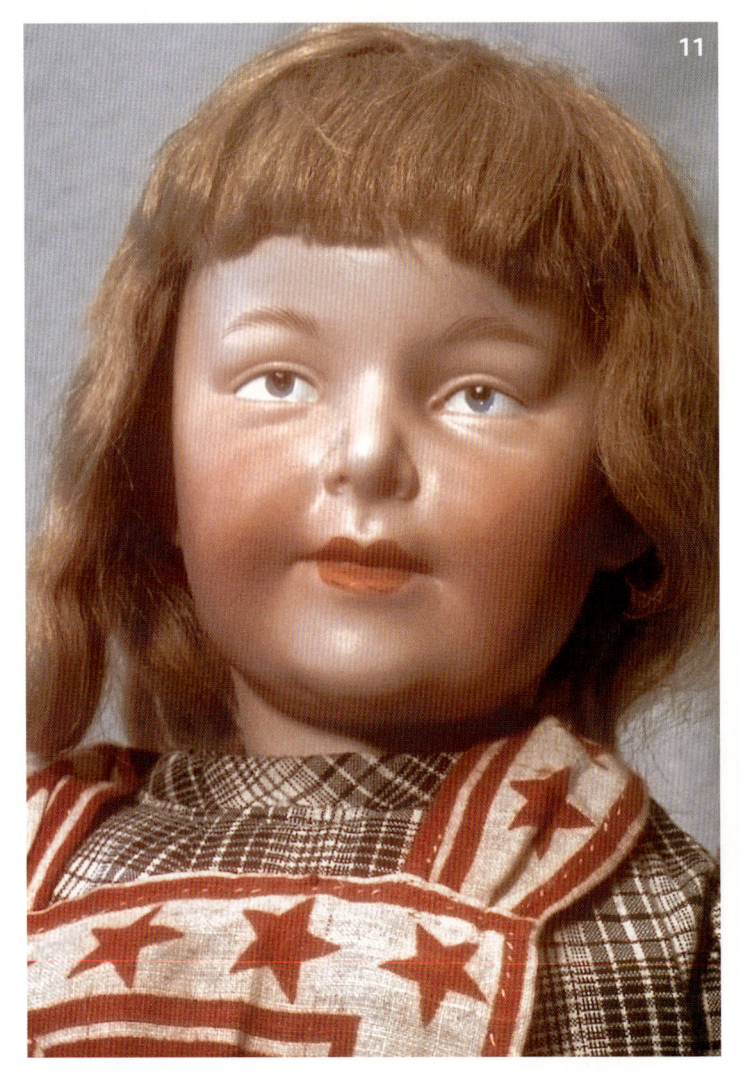

11. Bisque socket head by Armand Marseille; wig; multi-stroke eyebrows; painted eyes with white highlights; closed mouth; 21½-inch doll; circa 1910; marked: **A6M**. Julie Blewis Collection. (Photo: Fanilya Gueno)

12. Bisque socket head by Armand Marseille; wig; multi-stroke eyebrows; painted eyes with white highlights; closed mouth; chin dimple; 31-inch doll; circa 1910; marked: **A14M**. Julie Blewis Collection. (Photo: Fanilya Gueno)

Armand Marseille Porcelain Factory

13. Two bisque socket-head googlies by Armand Marseille; molded hair; single-stroke eyebrows; side-glancing intaglio-painted eyes with white highlights; open/closed smiling mouths with molded tongues; 6- and 6½-inch dolls; GM 1911; marked: **210//A. 10/0. M.// Germany// D.R.G.M**. Beth Karp Collection. (Photo: Lee Krombholz)

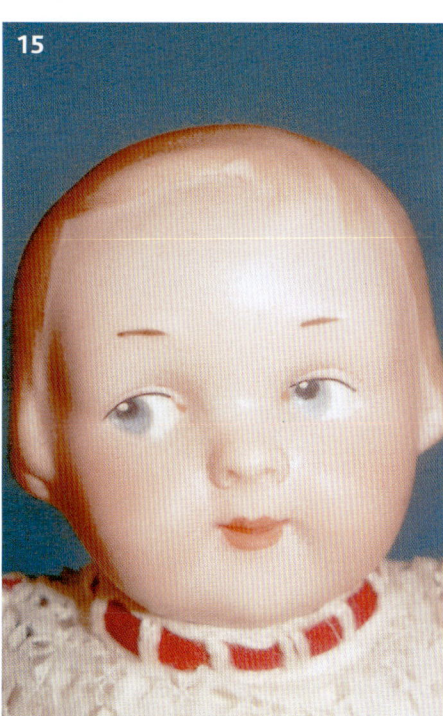

16. Bisque socket-head googly by Armand Marseille; single-stroke eyebrows; painted upper and lower eyelashes; side-glancing glass sleep eyes; open/closed mouth with molded tongue; 8-inch doll; GM 1911; marked: **200//A. 10/0 M.//Germany //D.R.G.M.//243/1**. The Marseille factory sold large numbers of googlies and baby dolls to a variety of wholesale and retail buyers in the United States, including the Sears, Roebuck and Montgomery Ward catalogs, which reached ten million households by 1910, according to the book *Remembering Woolworth's* by Karen Plunkett-Powell. Beth Karp Collection. (Photo: Lee Krombholz)

14. Bisque socket-head googly by Armand Marseille; molded hair; single-stroke eyebrows; side-glancing intaglio-painted eyes with white highlights; closed mouth; 13¾-inch doll; GM 1911; marked: **210//A.M.//Germany//D.R.G.M**. Courtesy Rothenburg Puppenmuseum/Katharina Engels Collection. (Photo: Christiane Gräfnitz)

15. Bisque socket-head googly by Armand Marseille; molded hair; single-stroke eyebrows; side-glancing intaglio-painted eyes with white highlights; open/closed mouth with molded tongue; 9¾-inch doll; GM 1911; marked: **210//A. 10/0. M. // Germany//D.R.G.M**. Andrea Jones Collection. (Photo: Andrea Jones)

Chapter 3

17. Two bisque socket-head googlies by Armand Marseille; molded hair; single-stroke eyebrows; side-glancing painted eyes; closed smiling mouths; 5- and 6-inch dolls; circa 1912; doll on left marked: **D.R.G.M.//248//A. 11/0. M//Germany**; doll on right marked: **254//A. 11/0. M. Germany**. Beth Karp Collection. (Photo: Lee Krombholz)

18. Fany bisque socket head by Armand Marseille; flocked hair; single-stroke eyebrows; painted upper and lower eyelashes; glass sleep eyes; closed pouty mouth; 15½-inch doll; circa 1912; marked: **Fany.230//A.4.M**. The wigged Fany is marked 231. The 230 and 231 mold numbers are based on a child's head sculpture by Italian sculptor Francois Duquesnoy, known as Il Fiammingo in Italy. Norah Stoner Collection. (Photo: Norah Stoner)

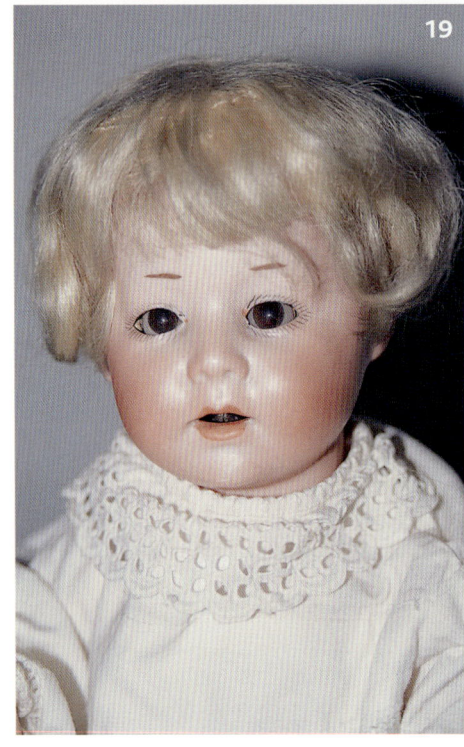

19. Bisque socket head by Armand Marseille; wig; single-stroke eyebrows; painted upper and lower eyebrows; glass sleep eyes; open mouth with upper teeth; 9-inch doll; circa 1920; marked: **233//A.M**. Courtesy Hessisches Puppenmuseum, Hanau, Wilhelmsbad. (Photo: Christiane Gräfnitz)

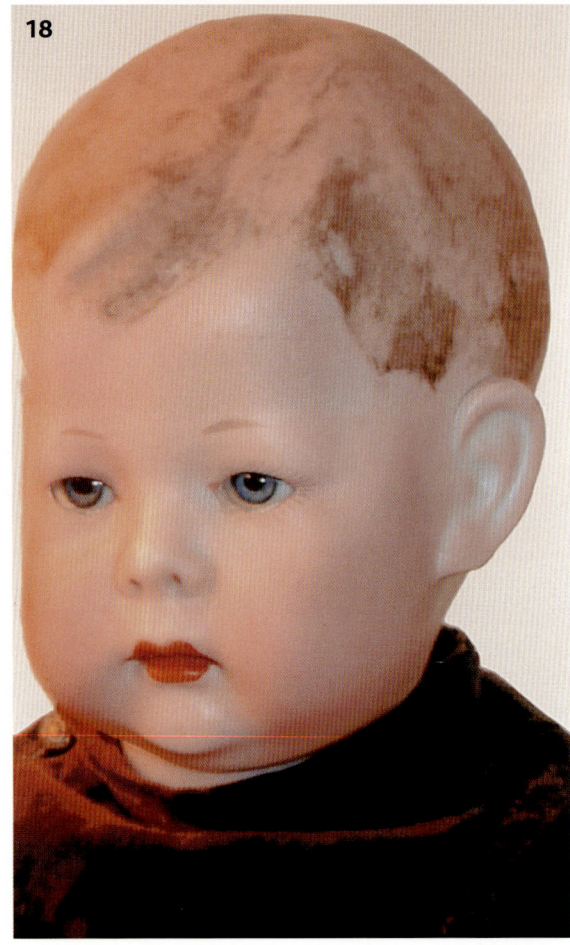

Armand Marseille Porcelain Factory

20. Bisque socket head by Armand Marseille for Geo. Borgfeldt & Co.; molded hair; single-stroke eyebrows; intaglio-painted eyes with white highlights; open/closed mouth with molded tongue; 10-inch doll; GM 1912; marked: **GB 250//A.1.M.// D.R.G.M. 248**. Georgia Alarcon Collection. (Photo: Estelle Johnston)

21. Bisque socket head by Armand Marseille for Geo. Borgfeldt & Co.; molded hair; single-stroke eyebrows; intaglio-painted eyes with tiny white highlights; open/closed mouth with molded tongue; 8-inch doll; GM 1912; marked: **GB 250//A. 5/0. M.// Germany//D.R.G.M. 248**. Beth Karp Collection. (Photo: Lee Krombholz)

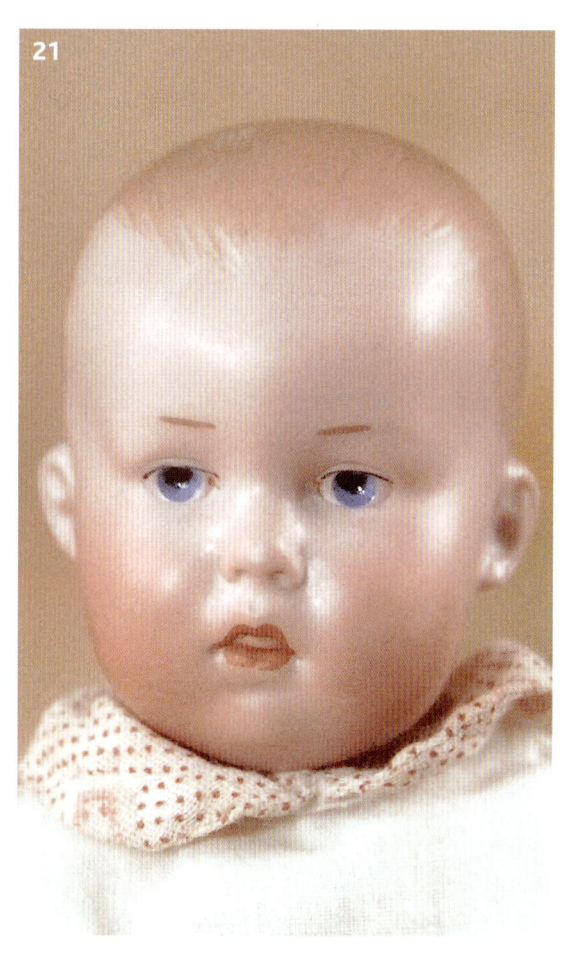

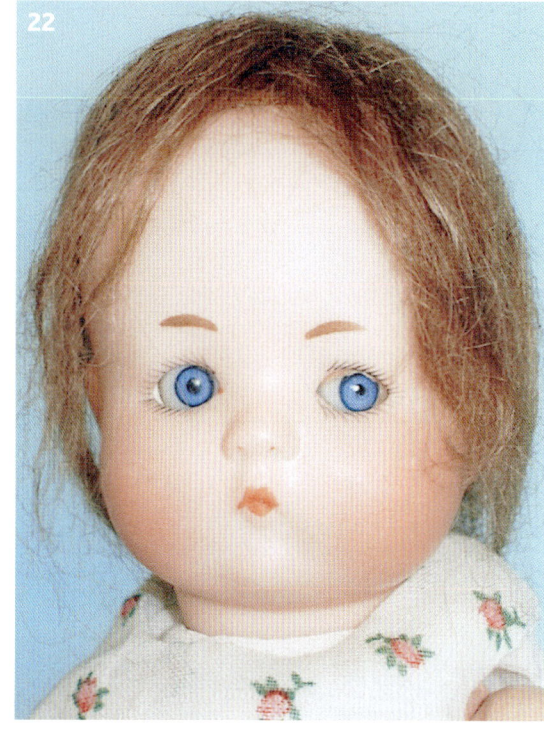

22. Just Me bisque socket-head googly by Armand Marseille for Geo. Borgfeldt & Co.; wig; single-stroke eyebrows; painted upper and lower eyelashes; side-glancing glass sleep eyes; tiny closed mouth; 9 inches; circa 1929; marked: **Just Me//Registered//Germany//A. 310. 7/0. M.** Andrea Jones Collection. (Photo: Andrea Jones)

23. Bisque socket head by Armand Marseille for Geo. Borgfeldt & Co.; original wig and clothing; single-stroke eyebrows; painted upper and lower eyelashes; glass sleep eyes; open/closed mouth with molded tongue; 11-inch doll; GM 1912; marked: **251// GB Germany//A. 3/0. M.//D.R.G.M. 248 11**. Ann Cummings Collection. (Photo: John Cummings)

Chapter 3

24. Just Me bisque socket-head googly by Armand Marseille for Geo. Borgfeldt & Co.; wig; single-stroke eyebrows; painted upper and lower eyelashes; side-glancing, glass sleep eyes; tiny closed mouth; 10-inch doll; circa 1929; marked: **Just Me// Registered//Germany//A. 310 5/0.Mx**. Beth Karp Collection. (Photo: Lee Krombholz)

25. Just Me bisque socket-head googly by Armand Marseille for Geo. Borgfeldt & Co.; wig; single-stroke eyebrows; painted upper and lower eyelashes; side-glancing, glass sleep eyes; tiny closed mouth; 9-inch doll; circa 1929; marked: **Just Me//Registered//Germany//A. 310 7/0. M**. Kathy and Mike Embry Collection. (Photo: Ann Hanat)

27. Just Me painted bisque socket head by Armand Marseille for Geo. Borgfeldt & Co.; original wig and clothing; single-stroke eyebrows; glass sleep eyes; tiny closed mouth; 10-inch doll; circa 1929; marked: **Just Me//Reg. Germany//A. 310-7/0. M**. The facial features on painted bisque heads were painted after the initial high-temperature kiln firing, but they were not fired a second time at a lower temperature to set the colors. Ann Cummings Collection. (Photo: John Cummings)

26. Bisque socket-head googly by Armand Marseille; smooth head with painted hair; single-stroke eyebrows; side-glancing intaglio-painted eyes with white highlights; closed smiling mouth; 6½-inch doll; GM 1913; marked: **320//A. 11/0. M.//Germany**. Author's Collection. (Photo: Gregg Smith)

Armand Marseille Porcelain Factory

28. Bisque socket-head googly by Armand Marseille; wig; single-stroke eyebrows; painted upper and lower eyelashes; large, side-glancing glass eyes; closed smiling mouth; 7-inch doll; circa 1914; marked: Germany//323//A. 11/0. M. Beth Karp Collection. (Photo: Lee Krombholz)

29. The town of Lauscha was the world's largest center of glass eye production from the 1850s on. The roofs and sides of most of the buildings in Lauscha are covered with dark-gray slate, trimmed in patterns of light-gray slate. (Photo: Mary Krombholz)

30. Bisque socket-head googly by Armand Marseille; wig, single-stroke eyebrows; side-glancing glass eyes; closed mouth; 9½-inch doll; circa 1914; marked: Germany//323//A.6/0.M. Susan Moore Collection. (Photo: John Cummings)

31. Bisque socket-head googly by Armand Marseille; wig; single-stroke eyebrows; painted upper and lower eyelashes; large, side-glancing glass eyes; closed mouth; 6½-inch doll; circa 1914; marked: 323//Germany//A. 11/0. M. A comparison of the size numbers on the dolls pictured in illustrations 30 and 31 shows that the size numbers increased, rather than decreased, as bisque heads were sized down. Ann Cummings Collection. (Photo: John Cummings)

Chapter 3

32. The words on this 1911 photograph, which has been hand colored, translate as: "Installing of Glass Eyes." Five male workers are matching pairs of doll eyes and inserting them in large bisque doll heads. Author's Archival Paper Collection.

35. These two sets of glass sleep eyes are weighted with lead balls to enable porcelain-head dolls to open and close their eyes. The eyes on the right have traces of original eyelash strips. The eyes on the left have original wax-coated eyelids that were initially painted with a flesh-toned color before they were dipped in wax. Author's Collection. (Photo: Gregg Smith)

33. The eye cuts on bisque doll heads, made when the heads were in the leather stage, vary in size and shape because they were cut by hand. The eye cuts made on this bisque head are larger than many of those on the 323 mold number googly dolls pictured in this chapter. Bisque socket head by Armand Marseille; wig; single-stroke eyebrows; large side-glancing glass eyes; closed mouth; 6½-inch doll; circa 1914; marked: **323//Germany//A. 11/0. M.** Kathy and Mike Embry Collection. (Photo: Ann Hanat)

34. A 1911 photograph, which has been hand colored, bears German text that translates as follows: "Home Industry" and "Blowing of Doll Eyes." Glass rods are stacked on the table in front of the two home workers. The male worker is heating a glass eyeball with a gas flame to make it malleable. Completed glass eyes are piled on the worktable, ready to be matched into pairs. Matching glass eyes to make pairs required fine eyesight and concentration. Delivery women from Lauscha traveled back and forth from Köppelsdorf daily, or at least bi-weekly, to bring glass doll eyes to the Armand Marseille and Ernst Heubach doll and porcelain factories. For many years, the Köppelsdorf railroad station bore a sign identifying it as the Lauscha Branch Railroad Station. Author's Archival Paper Collection.

Armand Marseille Porcelain Factory

36. Bisque socket-head googly by Armand Marseille; wig; single-stroke eyebrows; painted upper and lower eyelashes; large, side-glancing glass eyes; closed mouth; 9-inch-doll; circa 1914; marked: A.323.M. Beth Karp Collection. (Photo: Lee Krombholz)

37. Bisque socket-head googly by Armand Marseille for the Dennis Malley Company of London; wig; single-stroke eyebrows; painted upper and lower eyelashes; large, side-glancing glass eyes; closed mouth; 11-inch doll; circa 1914; marked: Demalcol//5/0//Germany. The word "Demalcol" was formed from some of the letters in the name Dennis Malley & Co. This bisque head looks like a 323 mold number head. Beth Karp Collection. (Photo: Lee Krombholz)

38. Bisque socket-head googly by Armand Marseille; wig; single-stroke eyebrows; painted upper and lower eyelashes; large, side-glancing glass eyes; closed mouth; 11½-inch doll; circa 1914; marked: A.323.M. Ursula Gauder Collection. (Photo: Christiane Gräfnitz)

39. Bisque socket-head googly by Armand Marseille; wig; single-stroke eyebrows; painted upper and lower eyelashes; side-glancing glass eyes; closed mouth; 9½-inch doll; circa 1914; marked: Germany//323. Kenneth Drew Collection. (Photo: Ann Hanat)

Chapter 3

40. Bisque socket head by Armand Marseille for Geo. Borgfeldt & Co.; wig; multi-stroke eyebrows; painted upper and lower eyelashes; glass sleep eyes; open mouth with upper teeth and separate tongue; 21-inch doll; GM 1913; marked: **G 327 B//Germany//A.11.M.** Ann Cummings Collection. (Photo: John Cummings)

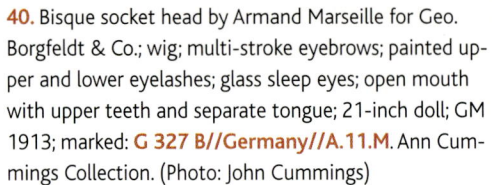

41. This is an old photograph of the Geo. Borgfeldt & Co. building in Sonneberg. Borgfeldt opened the Sonneberg branch of its New York-based exporting company in 1887. The Borgfeldt name is over the arched doorway. Courtesy Deutsches Spielzeugmuseum, Sonneberg Archives.

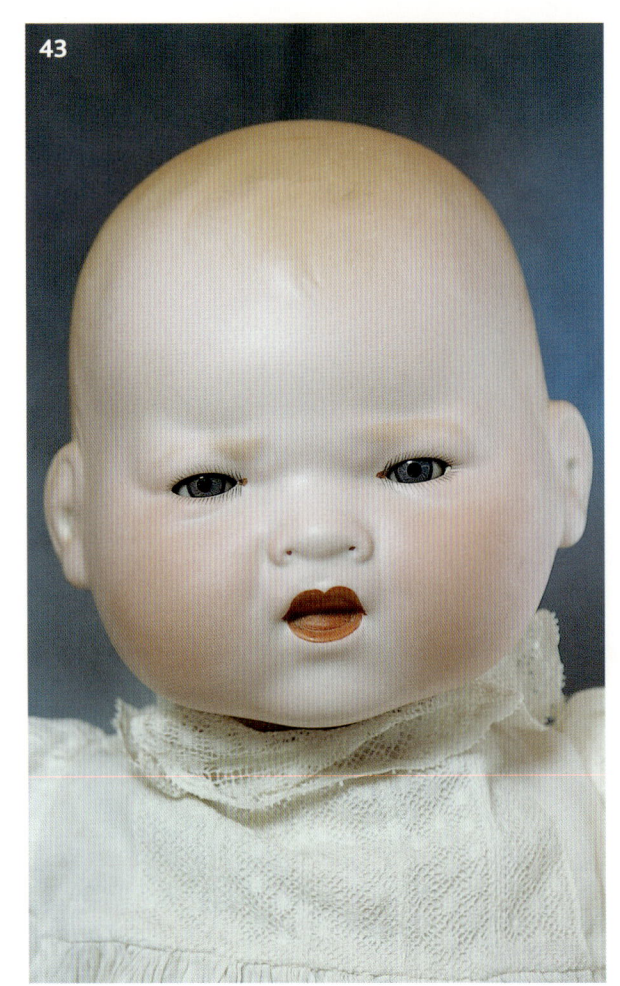

43. Bisque socket head by Armand Marseille; flange neck; molded hair; single-stroke eyebrows; painted upper and lower eyelashes; glass sleep eyes; open/closed crying mouth with molded tongue; 20-inch doll; circa 1926; marked: **A.M.//Germany//347/8.** Author's Collection. (Photo: Gregg Smith)

42. Bisque socket head by Armand Marseille for Geo. Borgfeldt & Co.; original wig and clothing; multi-stroke eyebrows; painted upper and lower eyelashes; glass sleep eyes; open mouth with upper teeth; 12-inch doll; GM 1913; marked: **Germany.//G. 329. B.//A. 1. M.//D.R.G.M. 267/1.** Author's Collection. (Photo: Gregg Smith)

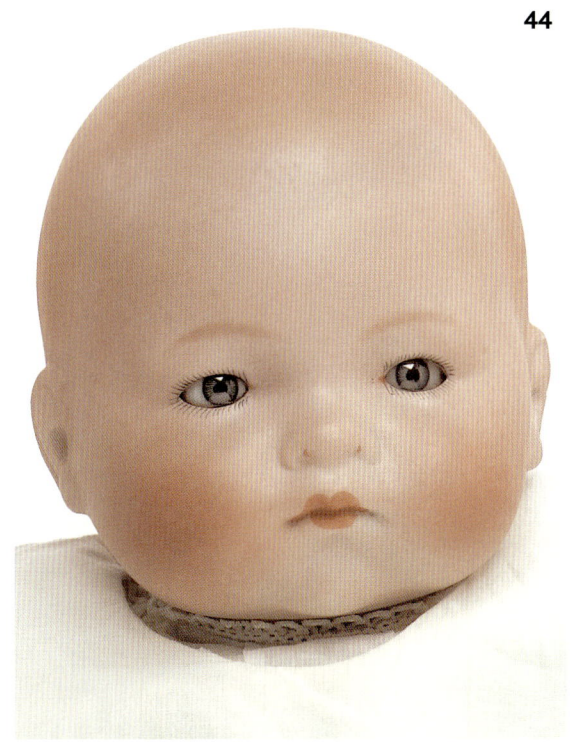

Armand Marseille Porcelain Factory

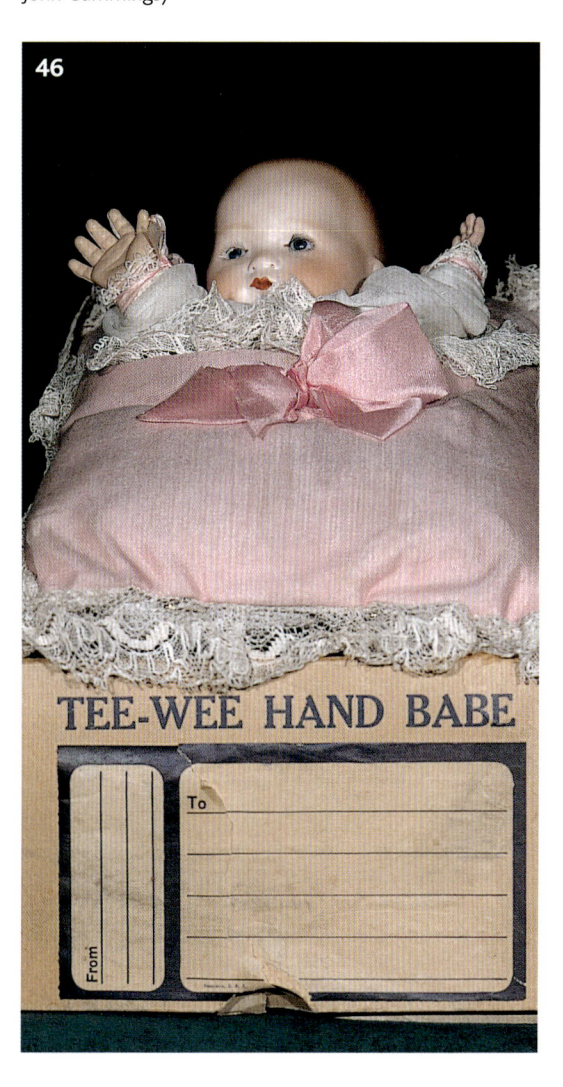

44. My Dream Baby bisque socket head by Armand Marseille for the Arranbee Doll Company; smooth head with painted hair; single-stroke eyebrows; painted upper and lower eyelashes; glass sleep eyes; closed mouth; 13-inch doll; GM 1926; marked: A.M.//Germany//341/4. Ann Cummings Collection. (Photo: John Cummings)

45. My Dream Baby bisque socket head by Armand Marseille for the Arranbee Doll Company; smooth head with painted hair; single-stroke eyebrows; painted upper and lower eyelashes; glass sleep eyes; closed mouth; 19-inch doll; GM 1926; marked: 341//AM. Susan Moore Collection. (Photo: John Cummings)

46. An Armand Marseille bisque-head doll, marked 341, in original clothing, is pictured with its original box marked: TEE-WEE HAND BABE. The hand-puppet head has glass sleep eyes that open and close by means of a lever on the back of the head, which is connected to the eyes. The description on the box reads: "Operate fingers freely to get any effect you desire. Looks so real you can love it. Tee Wee Hand Babe – The Living Doll." Private Collection. (Photo: Gene Abbott)

47. This 6-inch closed-mouth Armand Marseille My Dream Baby is marked with a Louis Amberg & Son original cloth tag that reads: "The Original//Newborn Babe// Jan. 9th 1914// Amberg Dolls//The World Standard." Bisque head; flange neck; smooth head with painted hair; single-stroke eyebrows; painted eyes; closed mouth; 6 inches; marked: A.M.//Germany. Author's Collection. (Photo: Gregg Smith)

Chapter 3

48. Baby Phyllis bisque head by Armand Marseille for the Baby Phyllis Doll Company of New York; flange neck; smooth head with painted hair; single-stroke eyebrows; painted upper and lower eyelashes; glass sleep eyes; closed mouth; 3-inch head; circa 1925; marked: **AM//Germany//Baby Phyllis**. Courtesy Deutsches Spielzeugmuseum, Sonneberg. (Photo: Christiane Gräfnitz)

49. The Recknagel porcelain factory also made bisque-head Newborn Babes for Louis Amberg & Son. This 8-inch, circa-1925 Dream Baby look-alike has a flange neck; smooth head with painted hair; glass sleep eyes; single-stroke eyebrows; painted upper and lower eyelashes; and a closed mouth. It is marked: **L.A.& Son//Germany//O//127A**. Author's Collection. (Photo: Gene Abbott)

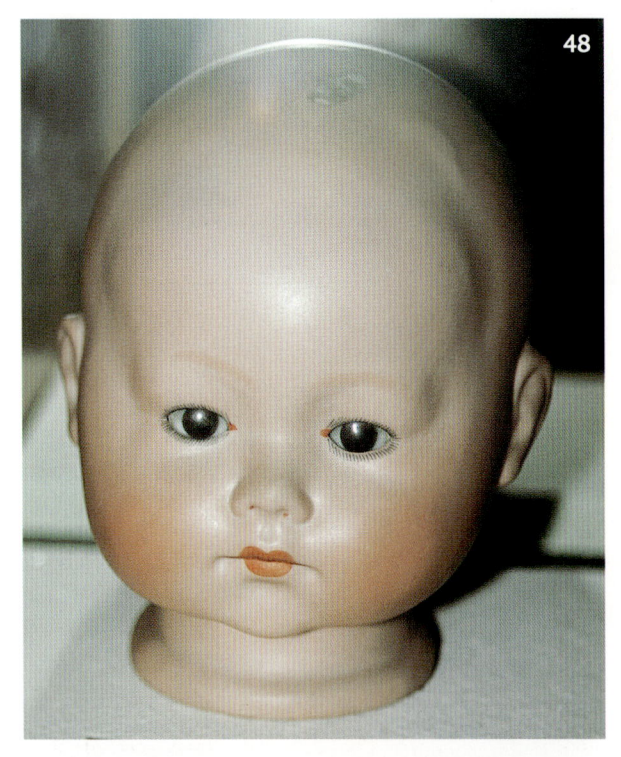

50. Dark-brown bisque socket head by Armand Marseille for the Baby Phyllis Doll Company of Brooklyn, New York; smooth head with painted hair; single-stroke eyebrows; painted upper and lower eyelashes; glass sleep eyes; closed mouth; 18-inch doll; circa 1925; marked: **A.M.//Germany//Baby Phyllis**. Ann Cummings Collection. (Photo: John Cummings)

51. Two My Dream Babies with dark-brown bisque socket heads by Armand Marseille; smooth heads with painted hair; single-stroke eyebrows; painted upper and lower eyelashes; glass sleep eyes; standing doll (8 inches) has closed mouth and is marked: **A.M.//Germany//341.14/0**; seated doll (6½ inches) has open mouth with lower teeth and is marked: **Germany//351.6/0. xk.**; circa 1925. Beth Karp Collection. (Photo: Lee Krombholz)

Armand Marseille Porcelain Factory

52. My Dream Baby bisque socket head by Armand Marseille; smooth head with painted hair; single-stroke eyebrows; painted upper and lower eyelashes; glass sleep eyes; open mouth with lower teeth; 13-inch doll; circa 1925; marked: **A.M.//Germany//351.3.k**. Ann Cummings Collection. (Photo: John Cummings)

53. Sleeping side of the two-faced bisque head seen in illustrations 54 and 55 by Armand Marseille; smooth head with painted hair; single-stroke eyebrows; closed eyes with molded eyelids and painted lower eyelashes; closed mouth; 11-inch doll. Beth Karp Collection. (Photo: Lee Krombholz)

54. The two-faced Armand Marseille bisque-head doll seen in illustrations 53 and 55 has a cloth body with celluloid hands, and is jointed at the shoulders and hips. Two touching ears are molded on each side of the head. Beth Karp Collection. (Photo: Lee Krombholz)

55. Smiling side of a two-faced bisque head by Armand Marseille, also seen in illustrations 53 and 54; flange neck; smooth head with painted hair; single-stroke eyebrows; painted upper and lower eyelashes; glass sleep eyes; open mouth with upper teeth; 11-inch doll; circa 1920s; unmarked. Beth Karp Collection. (Photo: Lee Krombholz)

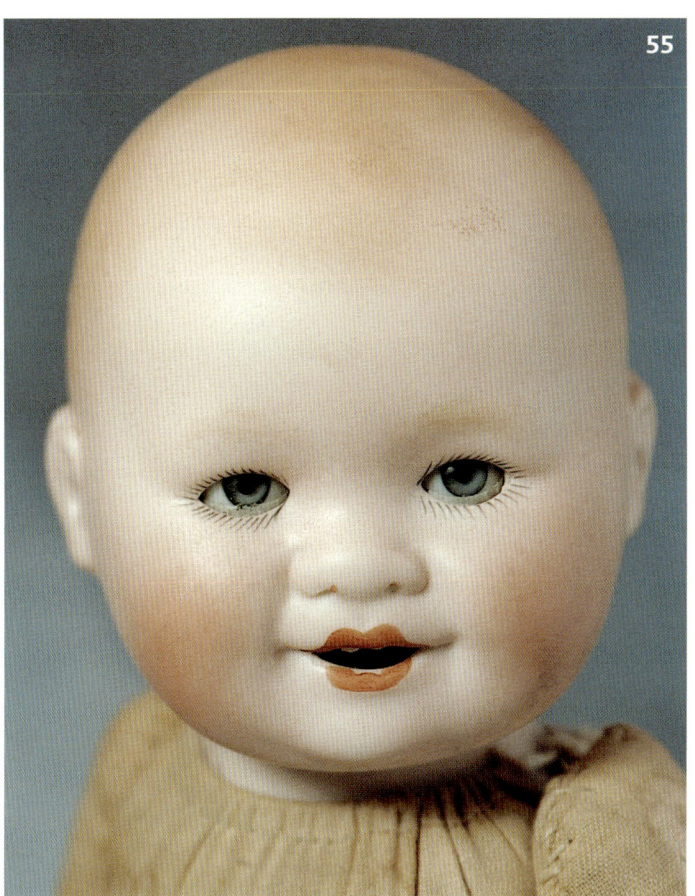

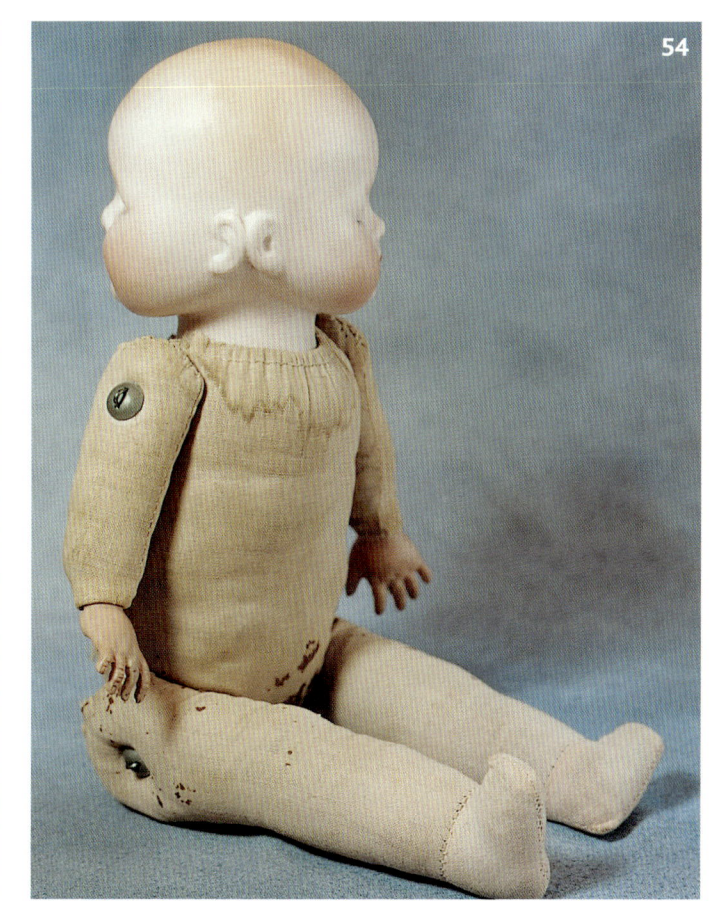

Chapter 3

56. Bisque socket head by Armand Marseille; molded hair; single-stroke eyebrows; painted upper and lower eyelashes; glass sleep eyes; open mouth with upper teeth; 19¾-inch doll; GM 1930; marked: **AM//352 8**. Historisches Coburger Puppenmuseum/Lossnitzer Collection. (Photo: Christiane Gräfnitz)

58. Kiddiejoy bisque shoulder head by Armand Marseille for the New York importing company, Hitz, Jacobs and Kassler; molded hair; multi-stroke eyebrows; glass sleep eyes; open/closed laughing mouth with upper teeth; 19-inch doll; circa 1925; marked: **Germany//Kiddiejoy//372//A.1.M**. Beth Karp Collection. (Photo: Lee Krombholz)

59. Bisque socket head by Armand Marseille; wig; multi-stroke eyebrows; painted upper and lower painted eyelashes; glass sleep eyes; closed mouth; 18½-inch doll; GM 1926; marked: **A.M.//400**. Norah Stoner Collection. (Photo: Norah Stoner)

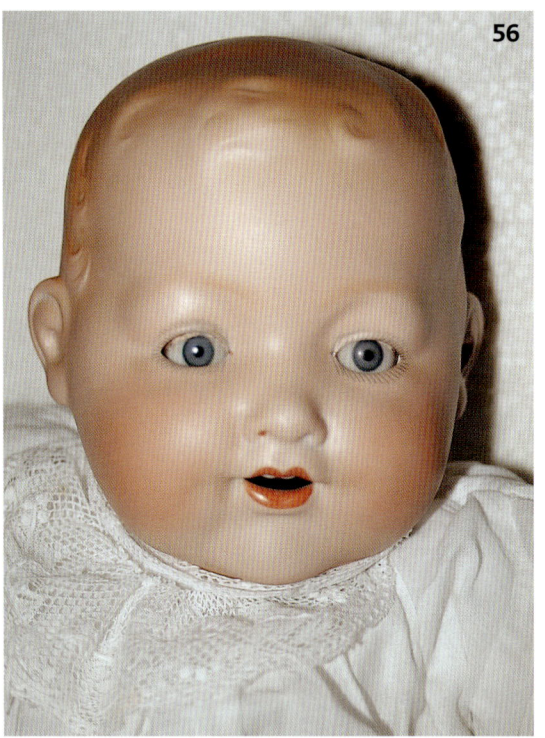

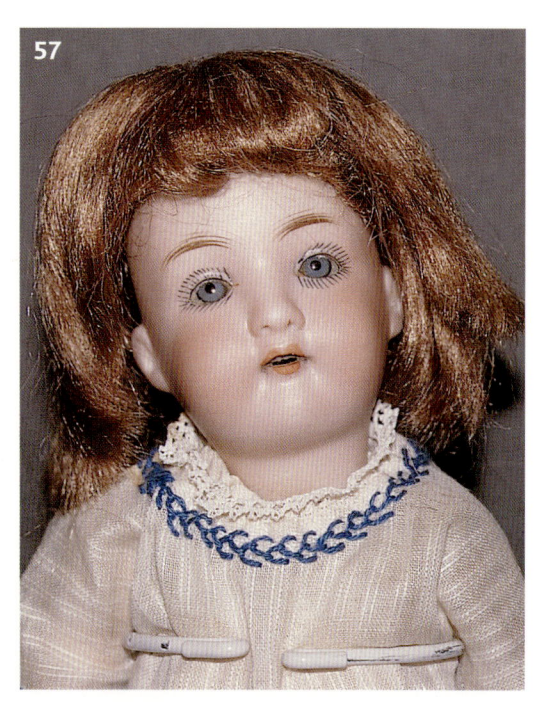

57. Bisque socket head by Armand Marseille; wig; multi-stroke eyebrows; painted upper and lower eyelashes; glass sleep eyes; open mouth with upper teeth; 8-inch doll; circa 1925; marked: **Germany//395//A. 12/0x. M**. Kathy and Mike Embry Collection. (Photo: Kathy Embry)

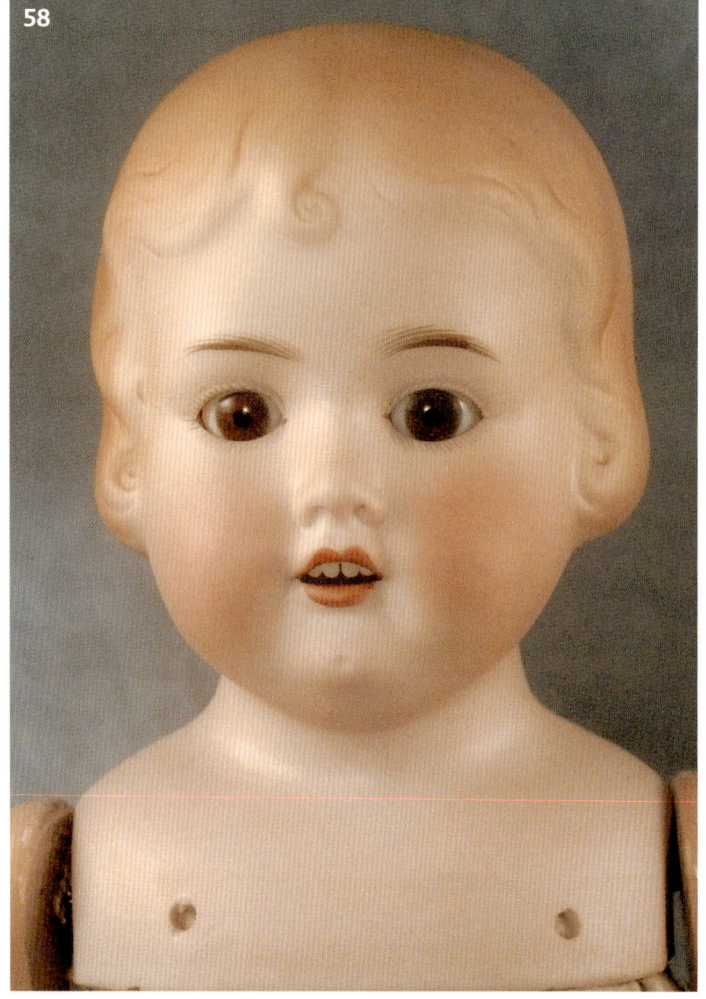

252

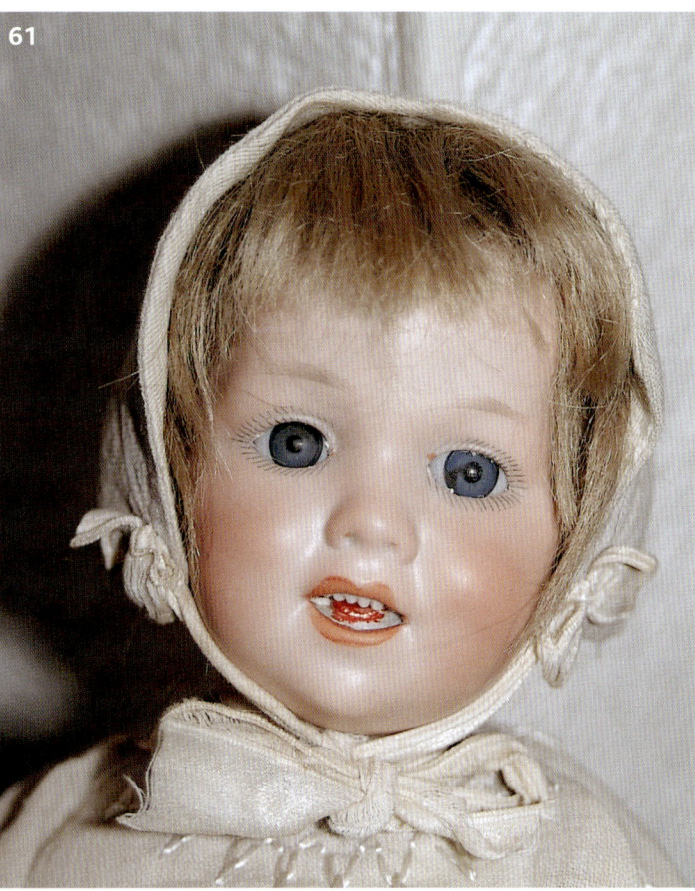

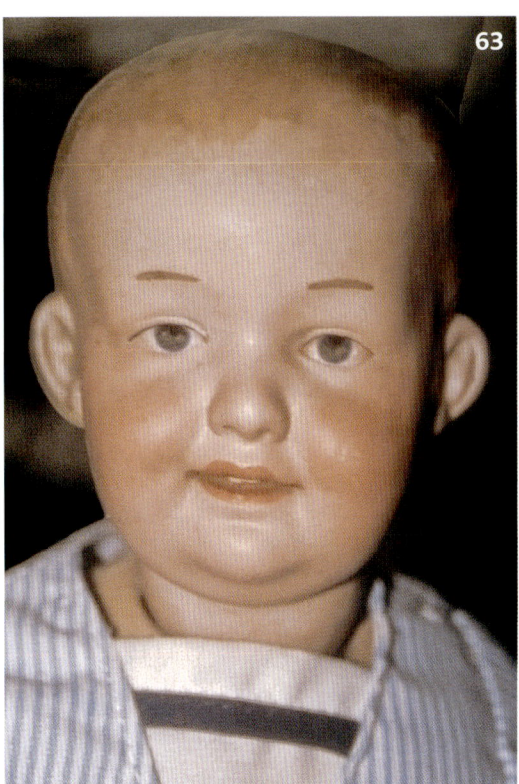

Armand Marseille Porcelain Factory

60. Bisque socket head by Armand Marseille; wig; multi-stroke eyebrows; painted upper and lower eyelashes; glass sleep eyes; closed mouth; 13-inch doll; GM 1926; marked: **Armand Marseille//Germany//400//A. 4/0. M**. Kathy and Mike Embry Collection. (Photo: Ann Hanat)

61. Bisque socket head by Armand Marseille for the Robert Maaser doll factory in Sonneberg; wig; multi-stroke eyebrows; painted upper and lower eyelashes; glass sleep eyes; open mouth with upper teeth and tongue; 10½-inch doll; GM 1913; marked: **410//4/0**. The American mail-order house Montgomery Ward advertised mold number 410 dolls on flapper-type bodies as late as 1930. Courtesy Rothenburg Puppenmuseum/Katharina Engels Collection. (Photo: Christiane Gräfnitz)

62. Bisque socket head by Armand Marseille; molded hair; single-stroke straight eyebrows; intaglio-painted eyes; closed mouth; dimples; 10-inch doll; GM 1910; marked: **500//Germany//A.4/0.M//D.R.G.M**. The head, of fine quality, is mounted on an original Neustadt five-piece, high-heeled body of poor quality, made of ground sawdust and glue. Author's Collection. (Photo: Gregg Smith)

63. Bisque socket head by Armand Marseille; molded hair; single-stroke eyebrows; intaglio-painted eyes; open/closed mouth with upper teeth; 11½-inch doll; GM 1910; marked: **AM//560**. Courtesy Ladenburger Spielzeugauction/Goetz Seidel. (Photo: Christiane Gräfnitz)

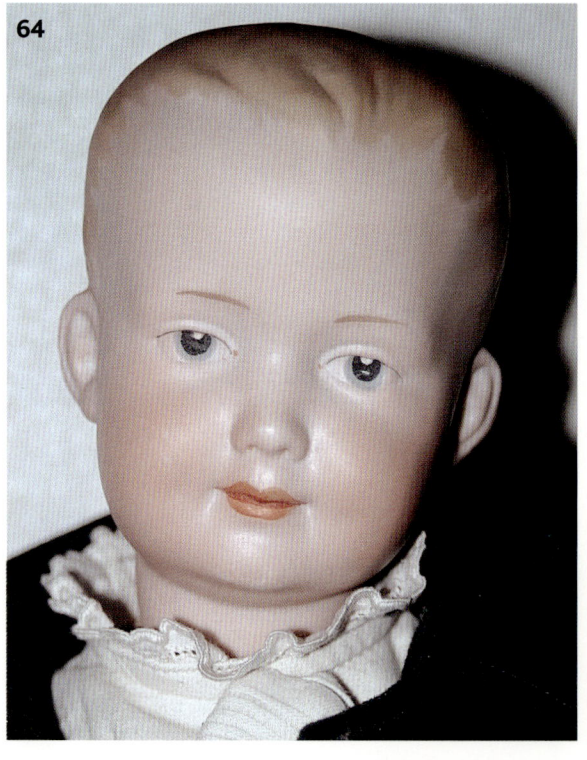

Chapter 3

64. Bisque socket head by Armand Marseille; molded hair; single-stroke eyebrows; painted eyes with white highlights; closed mouth; 17-inch doll; GM 1910; marked: **A.4.M.//D.R.G.M.** Although this head is not marked with a mold number, it resembles the mold number 500 bisque head. Historisches Coburger Puppenmuseum/Lossnitzer Collection. (Photo: Christiane Gräfnitz)

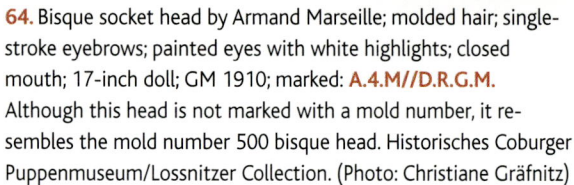

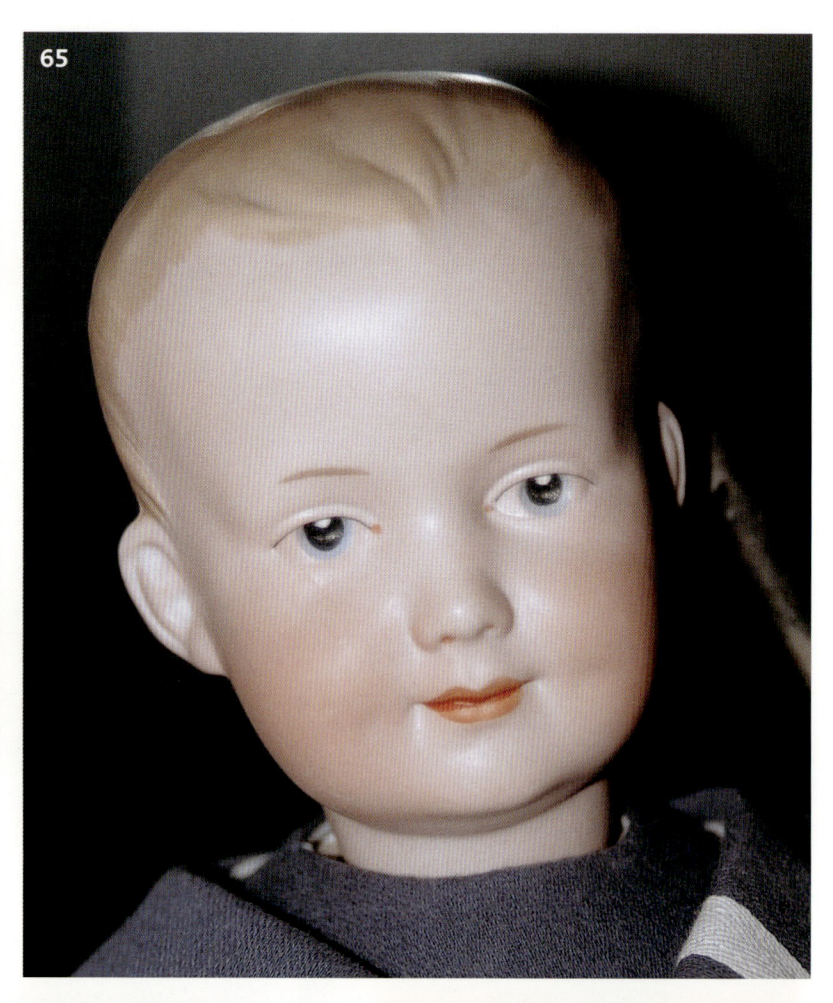

65. Bisque socket head by Armand Marseille; molded hair; single-stroke eyebrows; intaglio-painted eyes with white highlights; closed mouth; 16½-inch doll; GM 1910; marked: **500//A.M.//D.R.G.M.//Germany**. Rothenburg Puppenmuseum/Katharina Engels Collection. (Photo: Christiane Gräfnitz)

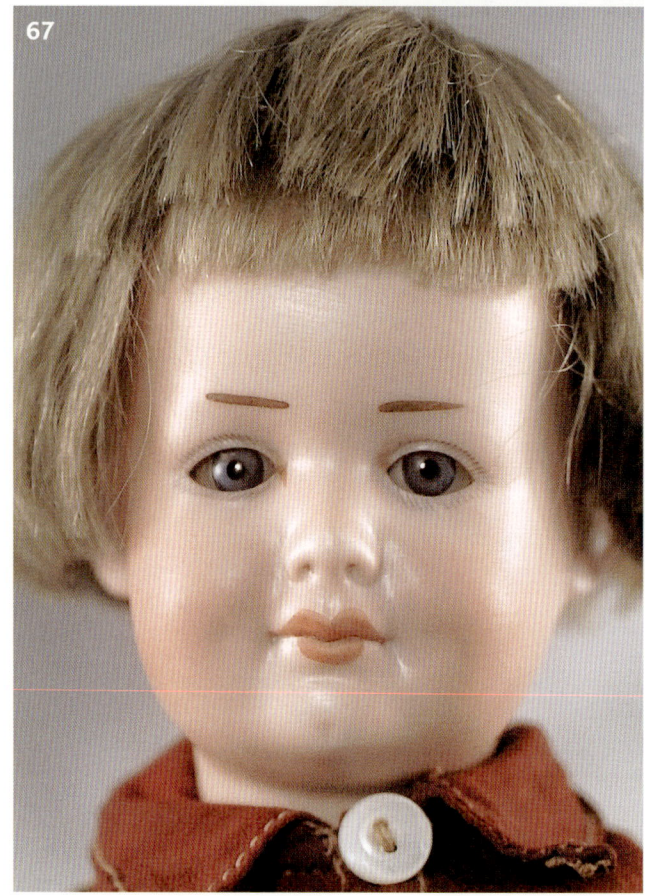

67. Bisque socket head by Armand Marseille; wig; single-stroke straight eyebrows; painted upper and lower eyelashes; glass sleep eyes; closed mouth; chin dimple; 12-inch doll; circa 1910; marked: **Germany//550//A.1.M.//D.R.G.M.** Beth Karp Collection. (Photo: Lee Krombholz)

66. Bisque socket head by Armand Marseille; wig; multi-stroke eyebrows; painted upper and lower eyelashes; glass sleep eyes; open mouth with upper teeth; 22-inch doll; circa 1926; marked: **Made in Germany//Armand Marseille//560a//A.7.M.//D.R.G.M.** Carol Wood Collection. (Photo: Lee Krombholz)

Armand Marseille Porcelain Factory

68. Bisque socket head by Armand Marseille; wig; single-stroke eyebrows; painted upper and lower eyelashes; glass sleep eyes; open mouth with upper teeth and tongue; 14-inch doll; circa 1926; marked: **590//A.4.M.//Germany//D.R.G.M**. Ann Cummings Collection. (Photo: John Cummings)

70. Bisque socket head by Armand Marseille; wig; single-stroke eyebrows; intaglio-painted eyes; closed mouth; chin dimple; 12-inch doll; circa 1920; marked: **700//4/0**. Norah Stoner Collection. (Photo: Norah Stoner)

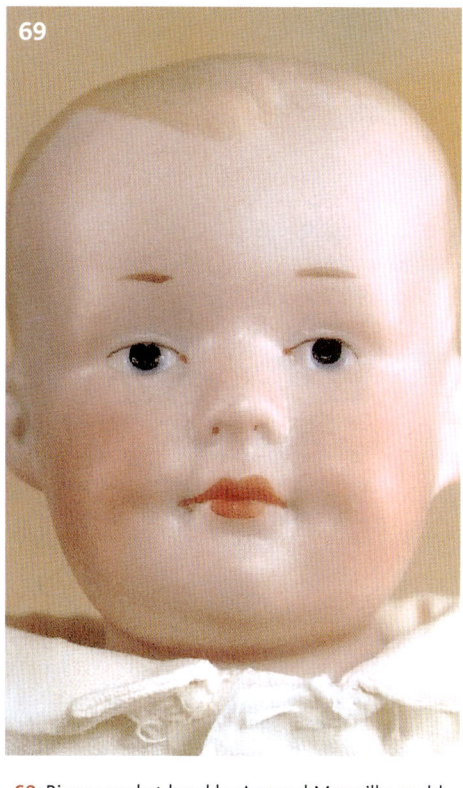

69. Bisque socket head by Armand Marseille; molded hair; single-stroke eyebrows; intaglio-painted eyes; closed mouth; 11-inch doll; GM 1910; marked: **600//A. 5/0/ M.//Germany//D.R.G.M**. Beth Karp Collection. (Photo: Lee Krombholz)

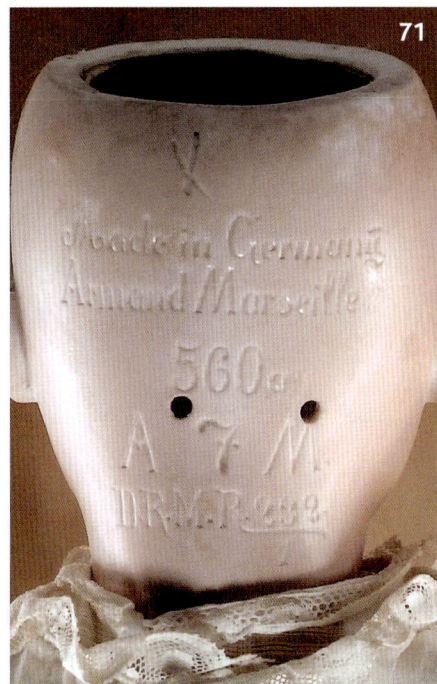

71. The detailed incised marks on the back of the head seen in illustration 66 are easily read. Carol Wood Collection. (Photo: Lee Krombholz)

255

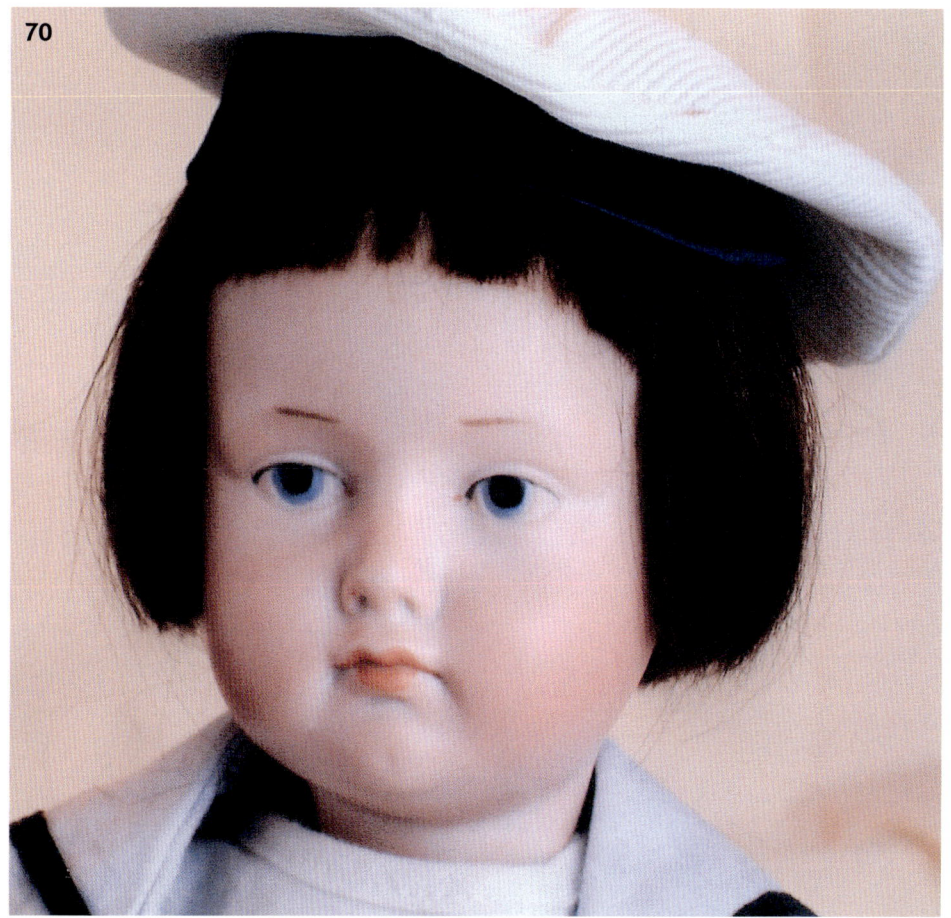

Chapter 3

72. Bisque socket head by Armand Marseille; wig; single-stroke eyebrows; intaglio-painted eyes; closed mouth; 12-inch doll; circa 1920; marked: **700//4/0**. Kathy and Mike Embry Collection. (Photo: Kathy Embry)

73. Bisque socket head by Armand Marseille; wig; multi-stroke eyebrows; painted upper and lower eyelashes; glass sleep eyes; open mouth with upper teeth; 9½-inch doll; GM 1913; marked: **Armand Marseille//750//D.R.G.M. 258//A.4/0.M**. Christiane Gräfnitz Collection. (Photo: Christiane Gräfnitz)

75. Painted bisque head by Armand Marseille; wig, multi-stroke eyebrows; upper eyelashes of hair; glass sleep eyes; open mouth with upper teeth and tongue; 21-inch doll; GM 1938; marked: **A.M.//966//8**. Andrea Jones Collection. (Photo: Andrea Jones)

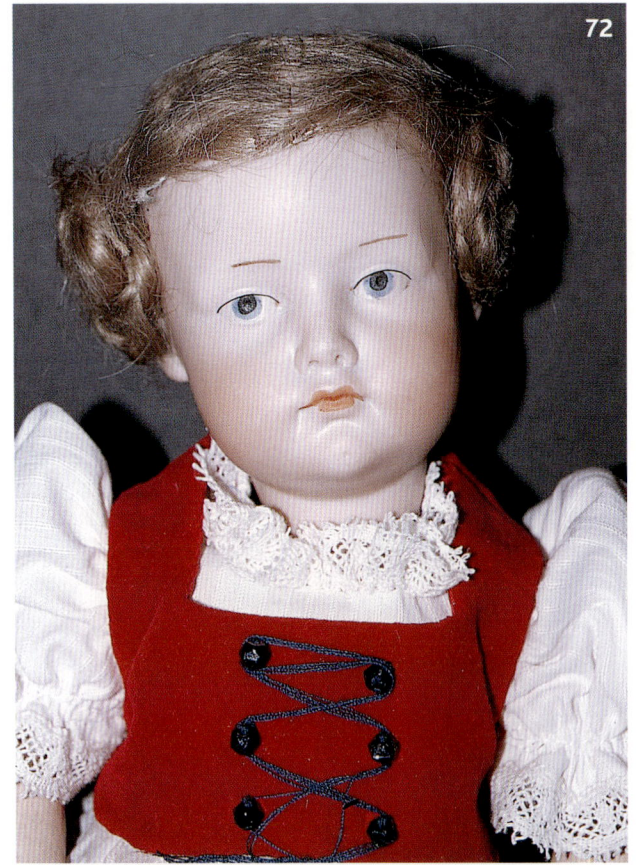

74. Bisque head by Armand Marseille; wig; multi-stroke eyebrows; painted upper and lower eyelashes; glass sleep eyes; open mouth with upper teeth; 12-inch doll; GM 1913; marked: **971//Germany//A. 4/0. M**. Kenneth Drew Collection. (Photo: Ann Hanat)

Armand Marseille Porcelain Factory

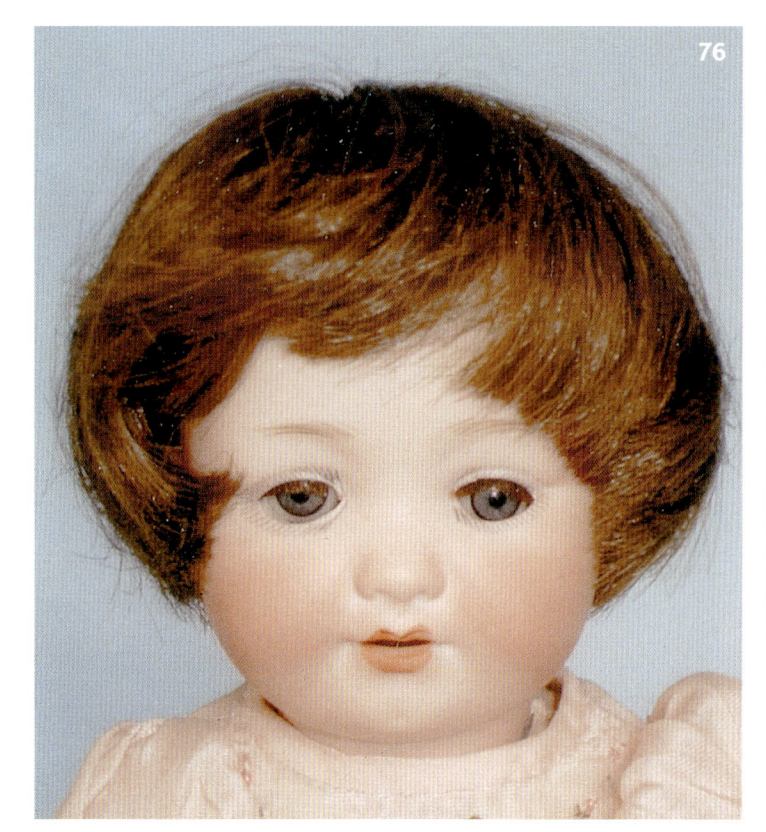

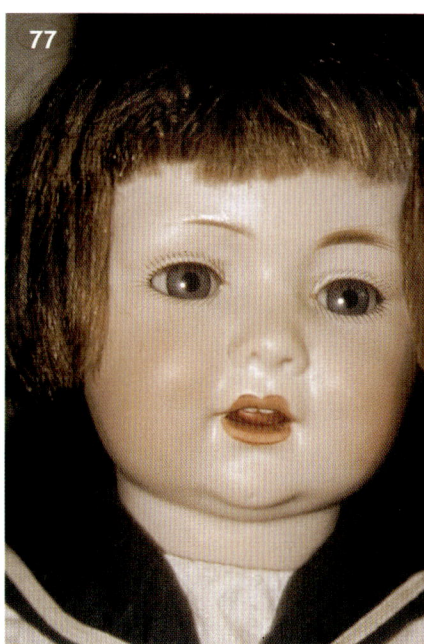

77. Bisque head by Armand Marseille; wig; multi-stroke eyebrows; painted upper and lower eyelashes; glass sleep eyes; open mouth with upper teeth and tongue; 13½-inch doll; GM 1913; marked: **971//Germany//A. 4/0. M**. Courtesy Museum Schloss Tenneberg, Waltershausen. (Photo: Christiane Gräfnitz)

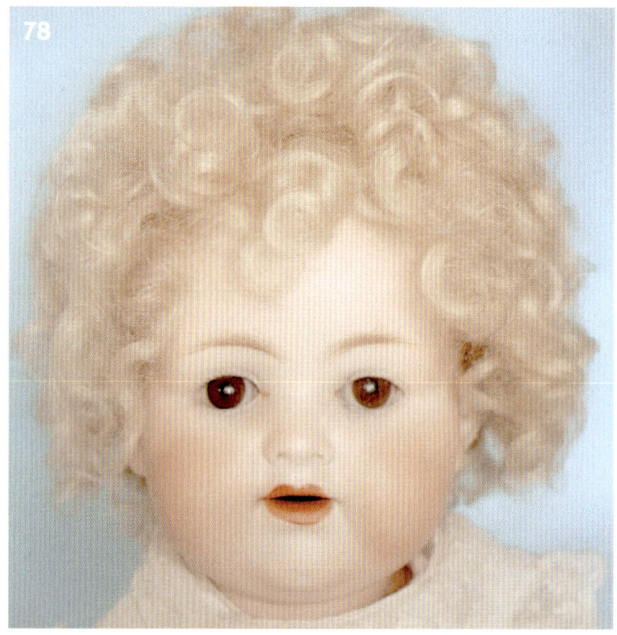

76. Bisque socket head by Armand Marseille for the Otto Gans doll factory in Waltershausen; wig; multi-stroke eyebrows; painted upper and lower eyelashes; glass sleep eyes; open mouth with upper teeth; 10-inch doll; circa 1922; marked: **Armand Marseille//A.975.M.//Germany//5/0**. Andrea Jones Collection. (Photo: Andrea Jones)

78. Bisque socket head by Armand Marseille; wig; multi-stroke eyebrows; painted upper and lower eyelashes; glass sleep eyes; open mouth with upper teeth; 15-inch doll; circa 1925; marked: **Armand Marseille//Germany//990//2½**. Andrea Jones Collection. (Photo: Andrea Jones)

79. Bisque socket head by Armand Marseille; wig; multi-stroke eyebrows; painted upper and lower eyelashes; glass sleep eyes; open mouth with upper teeth; 16-inch doll; circa 1925; marked: **Armand Marseille//Germany//990//A.1.M**. Ann Cummings Collection. (Photo: John Cummings)

Chapter 3

80. Melitta bisque socket head by Armand Marseille for the Edmund Edelmann doll factory in Sonneberg; wig; multi-stroke eyebrows; painted upper and lower eyelashes; glass sleep eyes; open mouth with upper teeth and tongue; 15½ inch doll; circa 1922; marked: **Melitta//A. Germany.M.** Rothenburg Puppenmuseum/Katharina Engels Collection. (Photo: Christiane Gräfnitz)

81. Baby Peggy bisque socket head by Armand Marseille for Louis Amberg & Son; wig; multi-stroke eyebrows; painted upper and lower eyelashes; glass sleep eyes; closed, smiling mouth; 18-inch doll; GM 1926; marked: **Germany//19©24//LA&S-N-Y//30//973/3.** Private Collection, formerly Jane Walker Collection. (Photo: C.W. Walker)

82. This red brick multi-storied apartment building with balconies, remodeled a few years ago, was once used as a Sonneberg branch office for the New York importers Louis Amberg & Son. (Photo: Mary Krombholz)

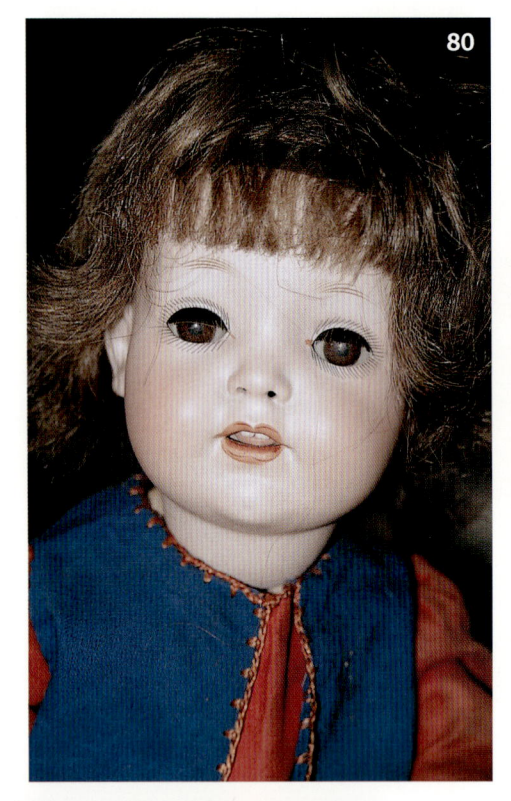

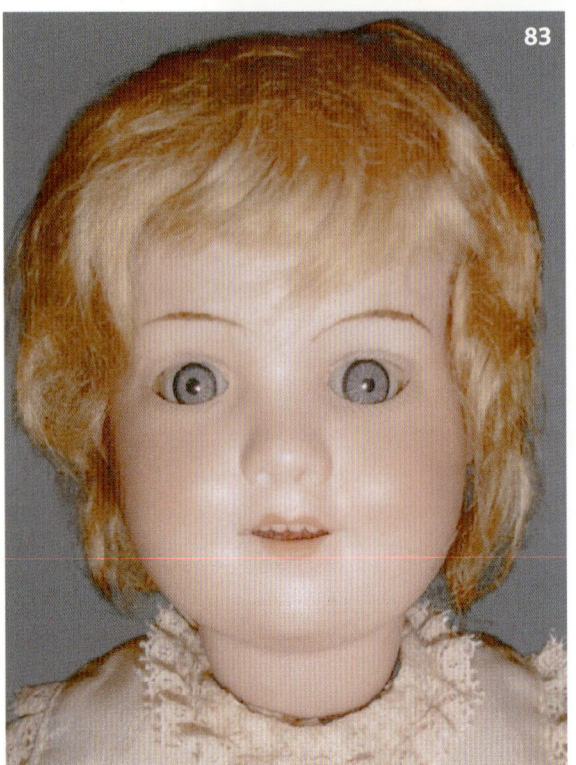

83. Baby Betty bisque socket head by Armand Marseille; wig; single-stroke eyebrows; painted upper and lower eyelashes; glass sleep eyes; open mouth with upper teeth and separate tongue; 14-inch doll; circa 1912-1914; marked: **A.M.//Baby//3/0x//Betty//D.R.G.M.** The New York importers Butler Brothers listed dolls with Baby Betty heads for sale in 1912. Andrea Jones Collection. (Photo: Andrea Jones)

Armand Marseille Porcelain Factory

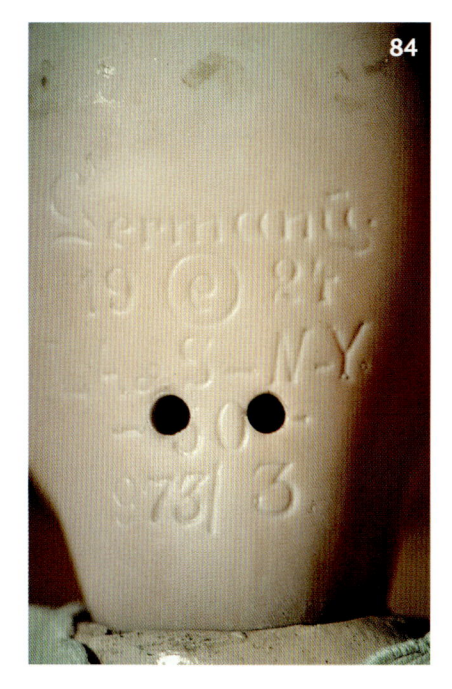

84. The incised marks on the back of the bisque head of the doll seen in illustration 81 include the Louis Amberg & Son initials. The distinctive incised "G" and "y" in "Germany" aid in the identification of Armand Marseille dolls. Baby Peggy Montgomery was a well-known Hollywood child actress in the 1920s. Private Collection, formerly Jane Walker Collection. (Photo: C.W. Walker)

85. Bisque socket head by Armand Marseille for Louis Amberg & Son; smooth head with painted hair; single-stroke eyebrows; painted upper and lower eyelashes; glass sleep eyes; closed mouth; 13-inch doll; circa 1914; marked: **(c)LA&S 1914//G '45520**. The Armand Marseille and Recknagel porcelain factories used identical master molds to make Newborn Babes for Louis Amberg & Son. Ann Cummings Collection. (Photo: John Cummings)

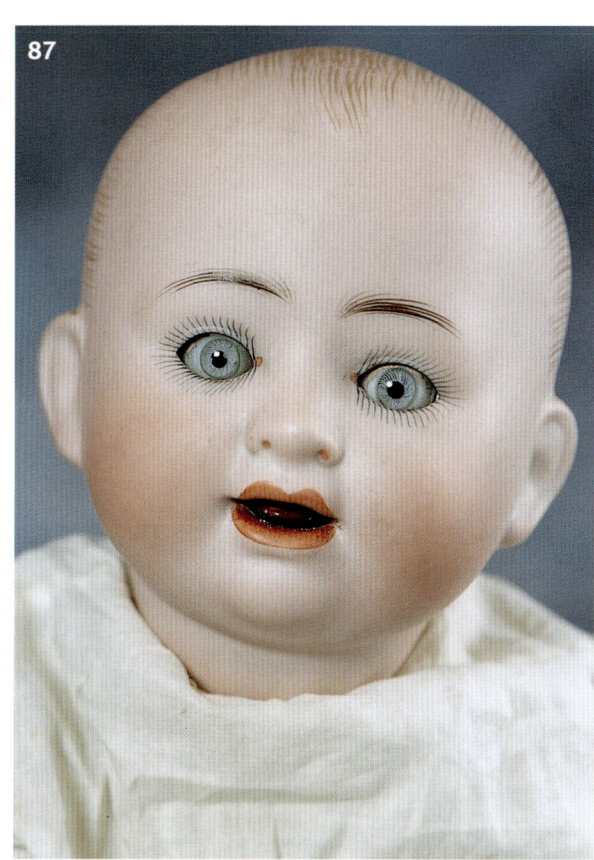

86. The old Louis Wolf & Co. building is still standing in Sonneberg at #5 Cuno Hoffmeister Street, close to the railroad station. The Louis Wolf & Co. doll importers (1870-1930s) had branch offices and sample rooms in many cities, including New York, Boston, Nuremberg and Sonneberg. (Photo: Mary Krombholz)

87. Bisque socket head by Armand Marseille; molded hair; multi-stroke eyebrows; painted upper and lower eyelashes; glass sleep eyes; open mouth with separate tongue; 11-inch doll; circa 1920s; marked: **30//L.W. & Co.//A.M.//3**. Author's Collection. (Photo: Gregg Smith)

259

Chapter 3

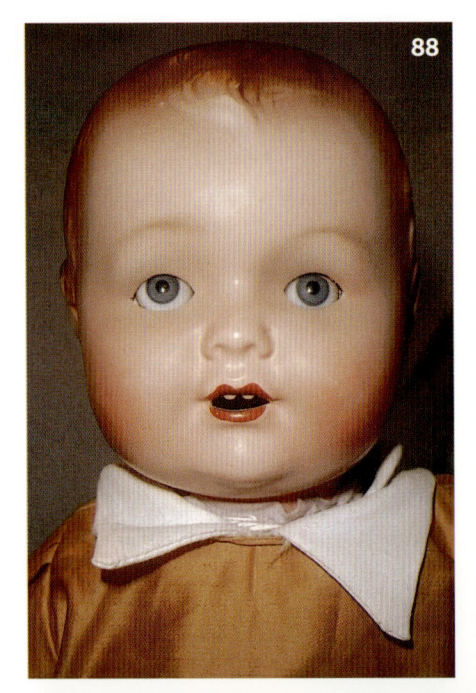

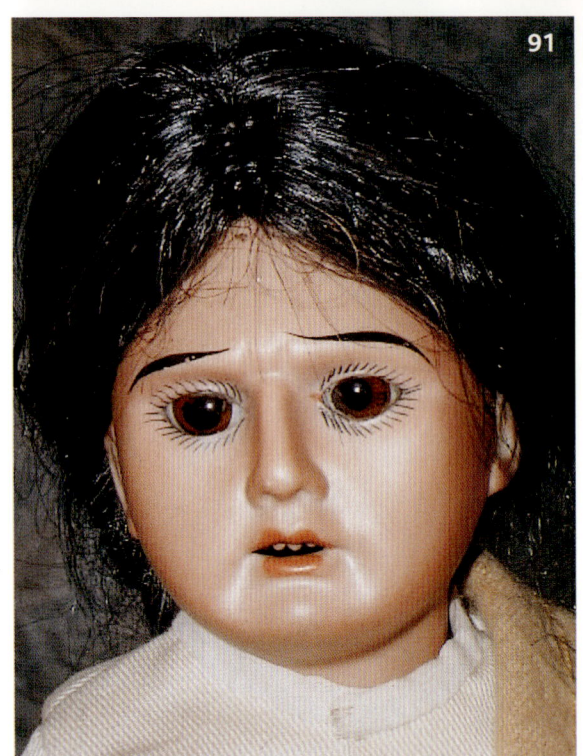

89. Two brown bisque Native-American-type socket heads by Armand Marseille; original wigs and clothing; scowling, single-stroke wavy eyebrows with frown lines between eyebrows; painted upper and lower eyelashes; stationary glass eyes; open mouth with upper teeth; 10-inch dolls; circa 1890s on; marked: **AM//6/0**. Beth Karp Collection. (Photo: Lee Krombholz)

88. Painted bisque socket head by Armand Marseille; flange neck; molded hair; single-stroke eyebrows; glass sleep eyes; open mouth with upper teeth; 14-inch-doll; circa 1930; marked: **A.M.//2542. 0½. 2¼**. Beth Riley Collection. (Photo: Andrea Jones)

91. Brown bisque Native-American-type socket head by Armand Marseille; wig; scowling single-stroke eyebrows with frown lines between eyebrows; painted upper and lower eyelashes; stationary glass eyes; open mouth with upper teeth; 13½-inch doll; circa 1890s on; marked: **Made in Germany**. The similarity of this doll to those in illustrations 89 and 90 identifies it as a product of the Armand Marseille porcelain factory. Kenneth Drew Collection. (Photo: Ann Hanat)

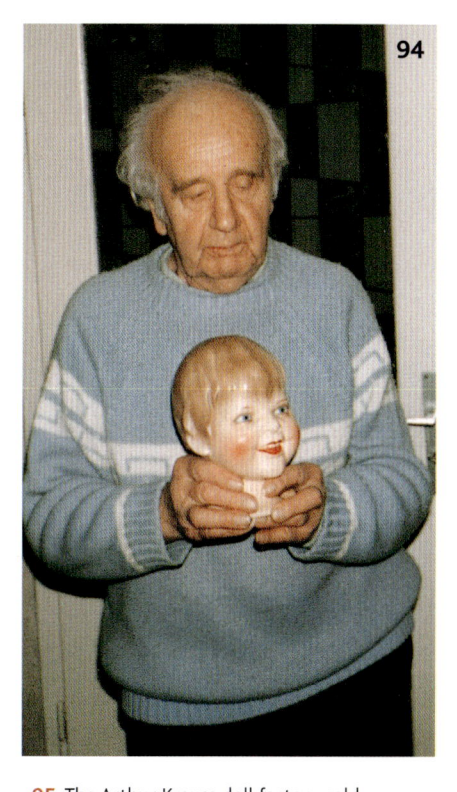

Armand Marseille Porcelain Factory

92. The Krauss doll factory sold many twirling musical Marottes on sticks with Armand Marseille bisque heads, according to my original Krauss sales receipts. Bisque shoulder head by Armand Marseille; round cylinder music box; original wig and clothing; one-stroke eyebrows; painted upper and lower eyelashes; stationary glass eyes; open mouth with upper teeth; GM 1896; marked: **3200//110-6x DEP**. Beth Karp Collection. (Photo: Lee Krombholz)

93. The Arthur Krauss doll factory is still standing in Köppelsdorf. The Krauss property adjoins the Armand Marseille villa property. (Photo: Mary Krombholz)

94. In 2001, inside the Arthur Krauss doll factory in Köppelsdorf, his son Helmut holds a biscaloid (an imitation bisque-like composition) Gladdie head, which he said came from the Armand Marseille factory. (Photo: Mary Krombholz)

90. Two brown bisque Native-American-type socket heads by Armand Marseille; original wigs and clothing; scowling, single-stroke wavy eyebrows with frown lines between eyebrows painted upper and lower eyelashes; stationary glass eyes; open mouth with upper teeth; circa 1890s; 7½-inch doll marked with larger size number: **Germany//8/0**; 9-inch doll marked: **Germany//7/0**. Author's Collection. (Photo: Gregg Smith)

95. The Arthur Krauss doll factory sold thousands of dolly-faced dolls with 390 mold number bisque heads. The Krauss business records in my archival paper collection record the frequency with which this mold number was ordered during the years following World War I, and whether the dolls were First Quality or Second Quality. This 12-inch bisque-head doll, wearing original clothing and accessories, is marked: **Made in Germany//390//A.2/0.M**. The silk dress, lace-trimmed underwear and shoes trimmed with rosettes indicate it was sold as a First Quality doll. Private Collection. (Photo: Gene Abbott)

Chapter 3

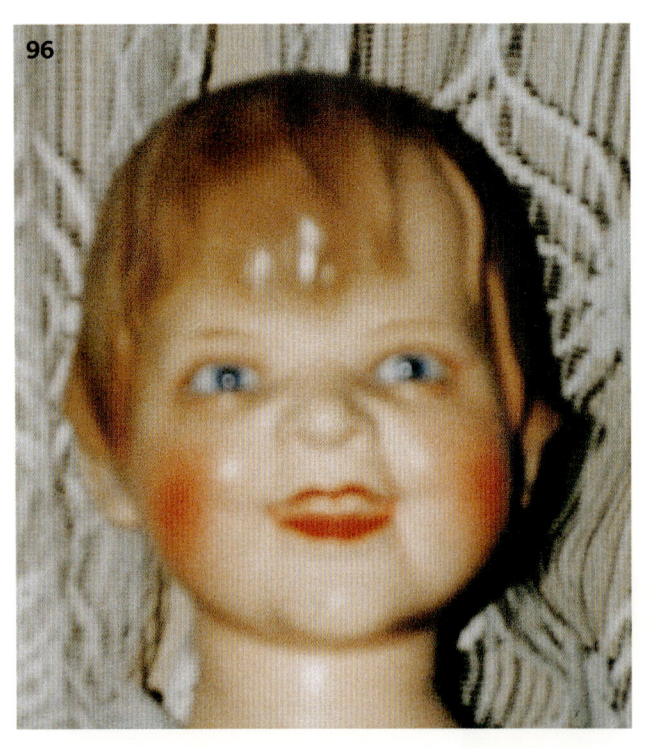

96. This photo of the biscaloid Gladdie owned by Helmut Krauss more clearly shows the difference between the biscaloid doll and the bisque Gladdies seen in illustrations 98 and 99. (Photo: Mary Krombholz)

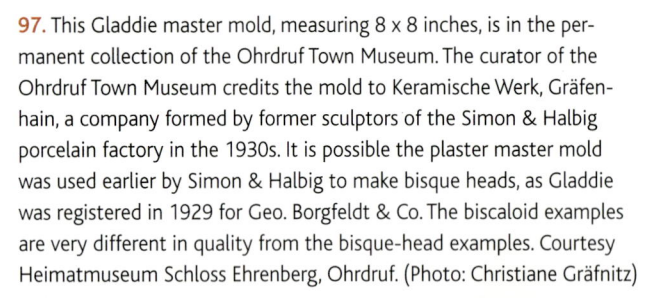

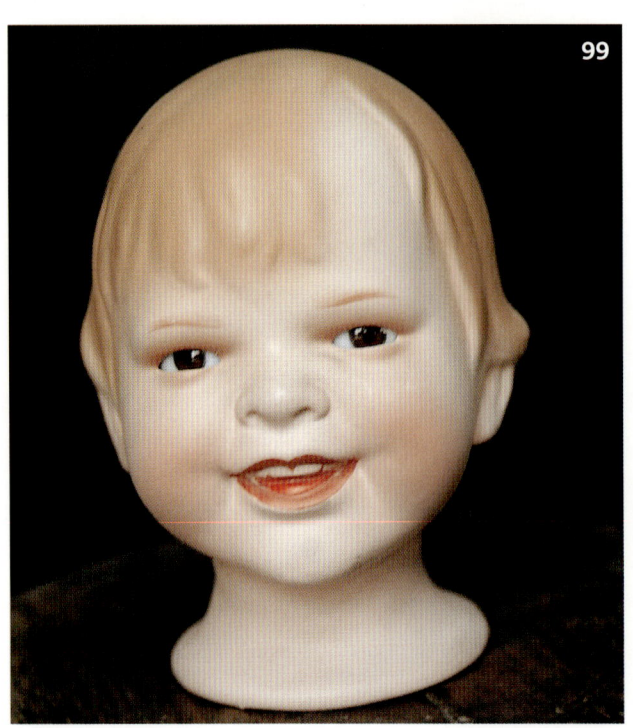

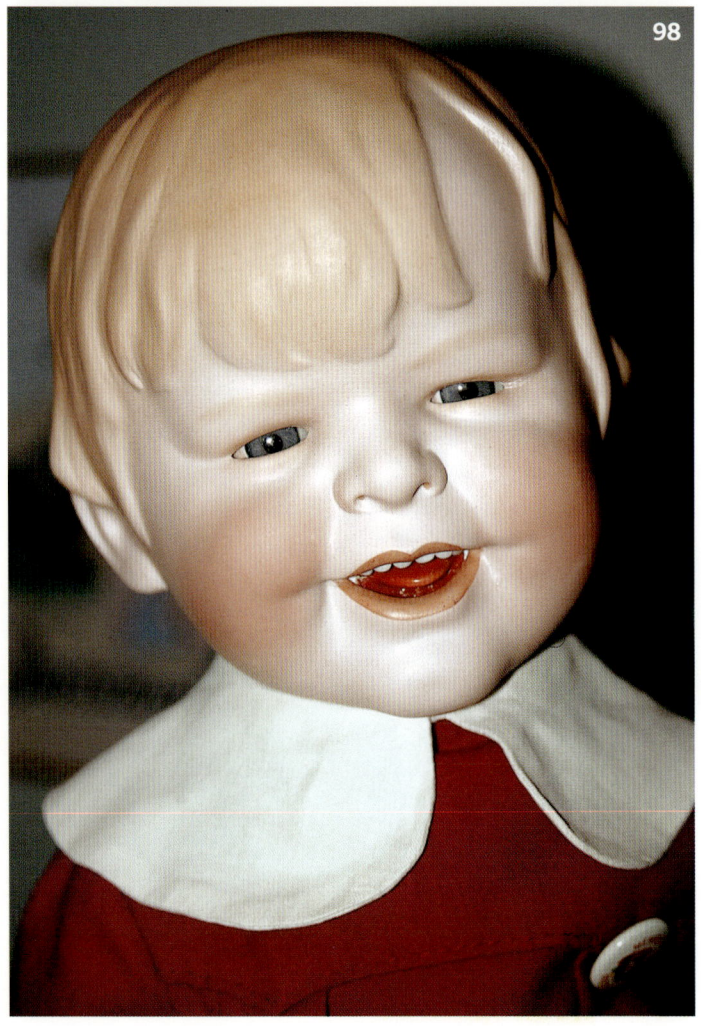

97. This Gladdie master mold, measuring 8 x 8 inches, is in the permanent collection of the Ohrdruf Town Museum. The curator of the Ohrdruf Town Museum credits the mold to Keramische Werk, Gräfenhain, a company formed by former sculptors of the Simon & Halbig porcelain factory in the 1930s. It is possible the plaster master mold was used earlier by Simon & Halbig to make bisque heads, as Gladdie was registered in 1929 for Geo. Borgfeldt & Co. The biscaloid examples are very different in quality from the bisque-head examples. Courtesy Heimatmuseum Schloss Ehrenberg, Ohrdruf. (Photo: Christiane Gräfnitz)

Armand Marseille Porcelain Factory

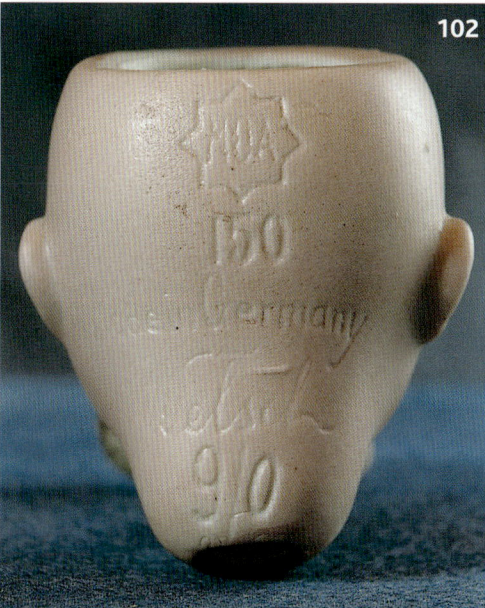

98. This 28-inch Gladdie bisque-head doll is the permanent collection of the Rosalie Whyel Museum of Doll Art in Bellevue, Washington. The fine modeling on the head is enhanced by the facial features that include molded hair, stationary glass eyes, dimples and an open/closed mouth with molded teeth and a realistic tongue. The doll is marked: **Gladdie//Copyriht By//Helen W. Jensen//Germany**. Courtesy Rosalie Whyel Museum of Doll Art. (Photo: Christiane Gräfnitz)

99. Gladdie bisque head, possibly by Simon & Halbig for Geo. Borgfeldt & Co.; flange neck; molded hair; single-stroke eyebrows; half-closed, stationary glass eyes; open/closed laughing mouth with upper teeth and realistic tongue; circa 1929; marked in handwritten script: **Gladdie//Copyriht By//Helen W. Jensen//Germany**. The word "copyright" is misspelled on all the bisque heads. Although American designer Helen Jensen used her own two-year-old daughter Ann as the model for the Gladdie heads, Gladdie dolls are usually dressed as boys. Courtesy Heimatmuseum Schloss Ehrenberg, Ohrdruf. (Photo: Christiane Gräfnitz)

100. A box of old bisque doll heads was still in the attic of the Arthur Krauss doll factory when I visited it with Roland Schlegel and Susan Bickert. The doll head in the left foreground is typical of the bisque character heads purchased by the Arthur Krauss factory from Sonneberg-area doll factories. (Photo: Susan Bickert)

101. Helmut Krauss gave me the bisque character head in the box pictured in illustration 100. The back of the bisque head is marked: **MOA (inside star)//150//Made in Germany//Welsch//9/0**. The 150 mold number, circa 1920, was made by Max Oscar Arnold for the Welsch & Co. doll factory in Sonneberg, following the Arnold purchase of the Knoch porcelain factory in 1919. Author's Collection. (Photo: Gregg Smith)

102. The back of the head seen in illustration 101 shows the incised marks that start at the crown and end at the neck socket. Author's Collection. (Photo: Gregg Smith)

Part Two

CHAPTER 4

Ernst Heubach Porcelain Factory

1. The old Ernst Heubach villa in Köppelsdorf was still standing in May 2007, when I last visited the site. New apartment buildings now stand on some of the original Heubach property. (Photo: Mary Krombholz)

The Ernst Heubach porcelain factory is one of four porcelain factories located in the Sonneberg suburb of Köppelsdorf. The others include the Hering & Sohn, the Swaine & Co. and the Armand Marseille porcelain factories.

Touring the old Heubach factory in 2003 taught me a great deal about the porcelain products made shortly before it closed a few years ago. The largest beehive kiln I have ever seen filled one downstairs room. Many molds were stacked around the kiln. I was surprised to see that so many of the molds were used to made porcelain insulation and plumbing products. The electro-technical branch of the factory continued to produce porcelain long after most of the porcelain factories in the area had closed due to lack of orders.

The porcelain factory was founded in 1887 by Ernst Heubach. Before the factory was built, the Sonneberg newspaper *Sonneberg Tageblatt* published the following description: "A porcelain factory for approximately 80 workers is going to be constructed by E. Heubach in nearby Köppelsdorf at the Lauscha branch railway station. The production of doll heads is assumed." The newspaper reference to the Lauscha branch railroad station is interesting because the old sign on the building now reads: "*Sonneberg Ost*" (East). The small railroad station was originally built to transport home workers who were delivering glass doll eyes from Lauscha to Köppelsdorf. The original name of the station substantiates the size of doll-eye orders placed year after year by the Ernst Heubach and Armand Marseille doll and porcelain factories.

In 1888 bathing dolls and doll heads were listed as products. In 1891 Ernst Heubach installed a workshop to make electro-technical porcelain products. The factory was enlarged several times during the next few years, and by 1913 it operated five kilns and employed two hundred and fifty workers. In 1915 Ernst's sons Ernst, Jr. and Hans began working at the factory. That same year Ernst, Jr. married Armand Marseille's daughter Beatrice. After World War I, Ernst, Jr. operated the factory alone, due to the death of his brother Hans during World War I.

Following Armand Marseille's heart attack in 1918, Ernst Heubach and Armand Marseille merged their two factories in 1919 under the name "United Porcelain Factory at Köppelsdorf, earlier Armand Marseille and Ernst Heubach." Although

2. I was standing in front of the old Lauscha/Sonneberg branch railroad station when I took this 2002 photograph of the Ernst Heubach porcelain factory in Köppelsdorf. (Photo: Mary Krombholz)

the combined factories continued to separately produce doll heads, the largest income resulted from the sale of electro-technical products. The Armand Marseille and Ernst Heubach porcelain factories separated permanently in 1932, after having been combined for only thirteen years. Following the separation, Ernst Heubach kept the name "United Köppelsdorf Porcelain Factories."

All of the bisque doll heads made by the Ernst Heubach porcelain factory during the first decade of production were dolly-faced dolls. In 1910 the factory began to produce character dolls. The majority of bisque character-doll heads were purchased by the doll factories in nearby Sonneberg. But, like the majority of other porcelain factories in the area, the Ernst Heubach porcelain factory also made bisque character-doll heads for doll factories in the Waltershausen area. Although the main customers of the Heubach porcelain factory were the Sonneberg doll factories of Cuno & Otto Dressel, Gebrüder Ohlhaver and August Luge & Co., the Adolf Wislizenus and Seyfarth & Reinhardt doll factories in Waltershausen also ordered doll heads from Heubach. The Albin Hess doll factory in Schalkau and the Priska Sander doll factory of Neustadt on the Orla River also used Ernst Heubach character heads on their dolls. Examples of the Sander and Hess character dolls are pictured in this chapter. Character dolls were successful products for the factory, and in 1914 the number of employees had grown to three hundred and twenty.

Today the old Heubach villa and the Armand Marseille villa still stand on the same side of the street, a short distance from each other. According to doll historian Hanns Schoenau, officials of the East German government arrested Ernst Heubach on August 4, 1945. The Heubach villa was then used as the headquarters for the East German border troops. Following the defeat of Germany in 1945, the country was divided into four military zones, controlled by American, British, French and Soviet troops. In the Soviet Zone of Germany, the Communists set up a Communist government and continued to control their zone until 1989.

The Ernst Heubach villa was restored after the reunification of East and West Germany. In May 2007, I walked down the hill from the Sonneberg Doll Museum to Köppelsdorf to see if the Heubach villa had been torn down since I last visited Sonneberg. Most of the land that once belonged to the Ernst

Chapter 4

Heubach family is now filled with large apartment buildings. While still standing, the villa is in very poor condition, and will probably be torn down in the near future, much like the majority of other buildings that were once part of the Thuringian dollmaking scene.

Ernst Heubach character dolls are favorites with antique-doll collectors because the faces are so expressive. They vary in many ways and often include special molded details, like the realistic bug applied to the nose of a Heubach character doll pictured in this chapter. Many of the character heads are mounted on "chunky" composition bodies and have molded white-painted socks and blue or brown-painted shoes.

It is unusual to find the names of character-doll sculptors listed in porcelain factory correspondence. One exception is an Ernst Heubach sculptor named Hans Homberger, whose brother was an Armand Marseille sculptor. Homberger must have had a wonderful sense of humor, considering the number of Heubach character dolls with unusual expressions credited to him.

One of the most unusual Ernst Heubach dolls is pictured in this chapter. It is a two-faced character doll with a laughing and a crying face. The head is incised with the marks "Priska Sander Neustadt/Orla/353 DRGM 2." Priska Sander was a doll artist who lived in the town of Neustadt on the Orla River, according to the Cieslik's research published in the August 1990 issue of *Puppenmagazin*. (The town of Neustadt on the Orla River is quite a distance from the town of Neustadt, which is located a little over a mile from Sonneberg.) Sander registered the design for her "Twin Doll" in 1925, and registered the two-faced character head in 1930. The 353 mold number indicates the head was made by the Ernst Heubach porcelain factory.

The bisque socket head has blue sleep eyes. The crying side of the face has a molded tear on each side of the nose. The laughing mouth has two upper porcelain teeth, while the crying mouth has two lower teeth. The doll was originally sold with a cloth baby body. Priska Sander advertised the doll in the 1930 *Guide for the Toy Industry*, where the two-faced doll is pictured as a swaddled baby that laughs and cries. In an advertisement pictured in the Cieslik's 1990 *Puppenmagazin*, both views of the babies show the dolls inside a ruffled blanket tied with two large bows. Sander also offered the doll as a standing baby.

It was important for Thuringian porcelain factories to offer new types of dolls every year. The Ernst Heubach porcelain factory often turned to exotic lands for modeling inspiration. Dolls that represented Asians, American Indians and South Sea Islanders appealed to buyers because they differed from the majority of dolls pictured in factory sample books and seen in displays at trade fairs like the semi-annual Leipzig fairs.

One group of 1920s dolls proved to be very profitable for the Ernst Heubach porcelain factory. Named "South Sea Babies," they were made exclusively for the August Luge doll factory in Sonneberg. A large variety of South Sea Babies were pictured in the 1930 August Luge doll factory catalog. Luge became well known for these dolls, and they were his best-selling products in the 1930s. The dark coloring was included in the porcelain slip used to make the bisque heads and the composition bodies were painted to match the heads. Dark glass eyes, black wigs and authentic clothing added to the appeal for customers in Europe and other countries.

It was important to carefully market novelty dolls, because they did not appeal to all buyers. This type of distribution often required the expertise of large American importing companies like Louis Amberg & Son, Butler Brothers or Geo. Borgfeldt & Co. These three American importers built large buildings in Sonneberg to stockpile doll-related products until they were needed to fill orders. These importers bought directly from the porcelain factories in the Sonneberg and the Waltershausen areas, and were very successful in locating buyers for dolls in every price range.

Prior to attending the semi-annual Leipzig fairs, buyers for the largest Amercian importing companies came to Sonneberg to contact suppliers and place orders before the doll-related products reached the general market. The following American importers and wholesalers had branches in Sonneberg: Louis Amberg & Co., American Wholesale Corporation, Arlington Toy Company, Inc., Geo. Borgfeldt & Co., Butler Brothers, S.S. Kresge & Co., F.W. Woolworth and Gebrüder Eckardt for Strauss-Eckardt of New York City.

The Ernst Heubach porcelain factory used a variety of doll bodies on their bisque-head dolls. Although character dolls were best sellers for many years, the factory continued to make and sell dolly-faced dolls. When I first toured the factory in 1999, I learned from a former employee that some dolls were assembled in the factory, particularly for Christmas orders. Sonneberg-area home workers furnished composition-body parts for Ernst Heubach and other porcelain factories in the Köppelsdorf vicinity.

The book *Sonneberg Stories of Dolls, Slate Pencils and Cuckoo Whistles* provides important information on the wooden parts used in the majority of Thuringian jointed-composition bodies. The workers who made wooden body parts were taught to become wood-lathe operators, also called "turners." One daughter of a lathe operator tells the following story about her father.

> One occupational group that arose out of the abundance of wood in our region and steadily developed itself further was the turners. Here in Forschengereuth, near Sonneberg, there were many turners who worked with their families in the home industry.
>
> My father specialized in wooden doll limbs in various sizes. Every year the forest management auctioned off wood that was ready to be cut. With this opportunity my father increased his yearly supply of spruce wood. The lumberman felled the tree, cut up

Ernst Heubach Porcelain Factory

3. A massive beehive kiln filled a room on the first floor of the factory. (Photo: Mary Krombholz)

4. Plaster working molds were stacked next to the kiln, just as bisque doll-head molds were once stacked in this room. The molds pictured were for electro-technical porcelain products. (Photo: Mary Krombholz)

6. Ernst Heubach porcelain factory workers once made bisque-character heads inside the old red brick factory building pictured in illustration 2. This 1936 photograph, which has been hand colored, shows the airbrushing department of a typical Thuringian porcelain factory. Ernst Heubach 1920s bisque-head babies often had airbrushed hair and eyebrows. Author's Archival Paper Collection.

5. During the years bisque-head character baby dolls were popular, storage rooms inside the Ernst Heubach porcelain factory were filled with finished heads ready to be shipped to buyers in many countries, including the United States. Author's Archival Paper Collection.

Chapter 4

the tree trunks, and delivered it to us at home.

My father sawed the largest pieces of trunk into the needed lengths. He braced them on the joiner's bench and split them with a cutting knife into numerous pieces. On the lathe, he shaped limbs for lower arms, upper arms, lower and upper legs, as well as small balls which served as joints. Then he drilled a hole through them.

When I arrived home after school my portion of the work already lay ready for me. Little time remained for doing school assignments. Quickly I changed clothes and began my work. My mother and I scoured the rough edges off of the wooden doll-body parts with a very sharp knife and reamed out the ends of the holes in the limbs, through which rubber bands would tie the limbs to the body. I would never have given my sons or grandsons such a sharp knife to use.

In those days no one gave it a thought. If the family wanted to survive, all family members had to help. We often worked deep into the night. Sometimes I fell asleep and cut my fingers. In addition, we had to work on our small farm, which principally fed us. Delivery was also a typical chore for women and children. We delivered the wooden limbs to doll factories in the Neustadt and Sonneberg areas. The delivery basket, which was towering high and had the goods bound together, was very heavy. I easily lost my balance when I carried it on my back. I was small and thin. After all, I had little counterweight to offer. Therefore, I was allowed to travel by train when I delivered to Neustadt. Homeward I went on foot with the empty, lighter basket.

After my father was killed in World War I, my mother and I continued the business alone. How else might we have supported ourselves? The workplace and the tools were already there. Now my childhood was definitely at an end. Day and night we worked for our meager sustenance, on the farm and in the workshop.

The number of wooden parts used to assemble a body varied by factory. Composition body parts were cheaper, but did not last as long as wooden ones. Therefore, dolls of first quality had more wooden parts than those of second quality.

Robert E. Roentgen's book titled *Marks on German, Bohemian and Austrian Porcelain, 1710 to the Present* is an excellent source of information on Thuringian porcelain factory products because it lists the variety of porcelain products made by each factory. From this well-researched book we learn that the Heubach porcelain factory operated as the United Köppelsdorf Porcelain Factories from 1919 until 1950. From 1950 until 1964, the Ernst Heubach porcelain factory made household porcelain, electro-technical and sanitary porcelain under the name VEB United Porcelainworks Köppelsdorf. In 1964 the factory became a branch of the VEB Electroceramic Works Sonneberg and operated under that name until 1990. After a short period of semi-privatization as Tridelta GmbH from 1990 to 1996, the VEB Electroceramic Works Sonneberg were fully privatized and named CERAM Elektrokeramik Sonneberg GmbH in 1996. The porcelain factory closed a few years ago.

7. The large rooms on the top floor of the factory once served as doll assembly rooms, according to a factory employee. This worker is assembling jointed composition bodies in 1936. Author's Archival Paper Collection.

Ernst Heubach Porcelain Factory

HAUSINDUSTRIE.   AUSFORMER-FAMILIE.

8. Once the doll parts had been assembled into complete dolls, the dolls were dressed and shipped from the Ernst Heubach porcelain factory. In this 1936 photograph, which has been hand colored, women factory workers are creating a variety of wigs. The wigs are on stands in front of several workers. Author's Archival Paper Collection.

9. Bisque socket-head googly by Ernst Heubach; molded hair; single-stroke eyebrows, large side-glancing painted eyes with white highlights, open/closed mouth with protruding upper lip and molded upper teeth; cheek dimples; 8½-inch-doll; GM 1914; marked Germany//EH 262. 14/0//D.R.G.M. Courtesy Deutsches Spielzeugmuseum, Sonneberg. (Photo: Christiane Gräfnitz)

10. Much like other Thuringian porcelain factories, the Ernst Heubach factory depended on home workers to furnish doll-body parts, which were assembled inside the factory. Doll-body parts were also made and assembled by home workers inside their own homes. The German text on this 1911 photograph, which has been hand colored, translates to read: "Family takes parts out of molds." Large composition doll bodies are stacked on the worktable and on the drying racks behind the group of workers. Author's Archival Paper Collection.

11. The railroad station across the street from the Ernst Heubach porcelain factory once had a large sign that read Lauscha Branch Railroad Station. Delivery women transported glass doll eyes in their *Schanzen* (delivery baskets) from Lauscha to the Köppelsdorf railroad station daily or several times a week, depending on the number of doll-eye orders. The original framed photograph of this group of women with their delivery baskets hangs on a wall in the Lauscha Glass Museum. (Photo: Courtesy Deutsches Spielzeugmuseum, Sonneberg Archives)

Chapter 4

12. Three bisque socket heads by Ernst Heubach; one with single-stroke eyebrows, two with multi-stroke eyebrows; all three heads have glass sleep eyes; painted upper and lower eyelashes; open mouths with upper teeth; 17-, 19-, and 22-inch dolls; circa 1915; marked: **E.H. 275** and a size number. Author's Collection. (Photo: Gene Abbott)

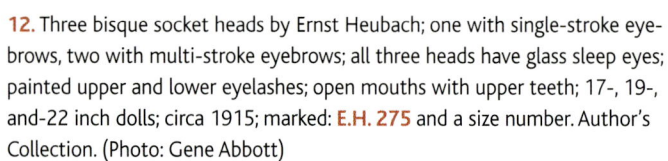

13. Bisque socket head by Ernst Heubach; wig; multi-stroke eyebrows; painted upper and lower eyelashes; glass sleep eyes; open mouth with upper teeth and separate tongue; cheek and chin dimples; 22¾-inch doll; circa 1920; marked: **Heubach.Koppelsdorf//300.8**. Courtesy Deutsches Spielzeugmuseum, Sonneberg. (Photo: Christiane Gräfnitz)

14. Bisque socket head by Ernst Heubach; molded hair with brushstrokes; single-stroke eyebrows; intaglio-painted eyes, glancing upwards; white highlights on pupils; closed mouth; 6½-inch doll; GM 1914; marked: **Germany//EH 269.15/0//DRGM**. Beth Karp Collection. (Photo: Lee Krombholz)

15. Three bisque socket heads by Ernst Heubach; wigs; multi-stroke eyebrows; painted upper and lower eyelashes; glass sleep eyes; open mouths with upper teeth; 11-, 13- and 16-inch dolls; circa 1920; marked: **Heubach.Koppelsdorf//300** and a size number. Author's Collection. (Photo: Gene Abbott)

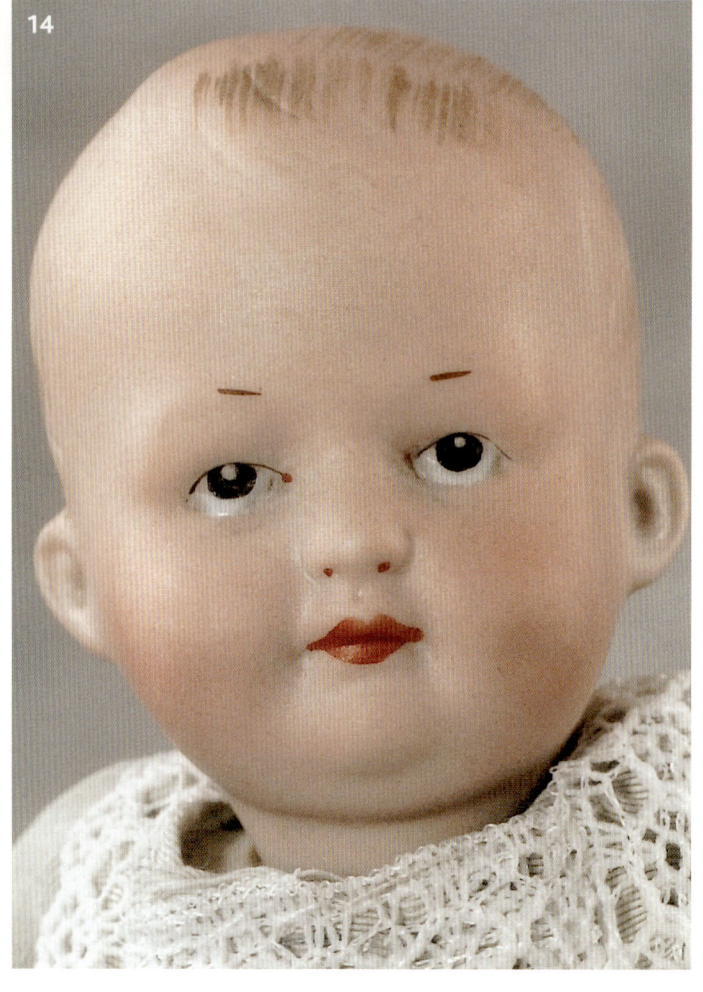

16. Bisque socket head by Ernst Heubach; molded hair with topknot; prominent ears; single-stroke eyebrows; painted eyes; closed smiling mouth; 7¼-inch doll; GM 1915; marked **EH//276//DRGM**. The "crossed" eyes are created by painting the irises and white highlights on the pupils close to the nose rather than centered in the eye socket. The realistic green and black beetle is molded in the center of the nose. Susan Moore Collection. (Photo: John Cummings)

270

Ernst Heubach Porcelain Factory

Chapter 4

17. Bisque socket head by Ernst Heubach; wig; multi-stroke eyebrows; painted upper and lower eyelashes; glass sleep eyes; open/closed mouth with upper teeth and separate tongue; 12-inch inch doll; circa 1920; marked: **300//11/0**. Roswitha Lucke Collection. (Photo: Christiane Gräfnitz)

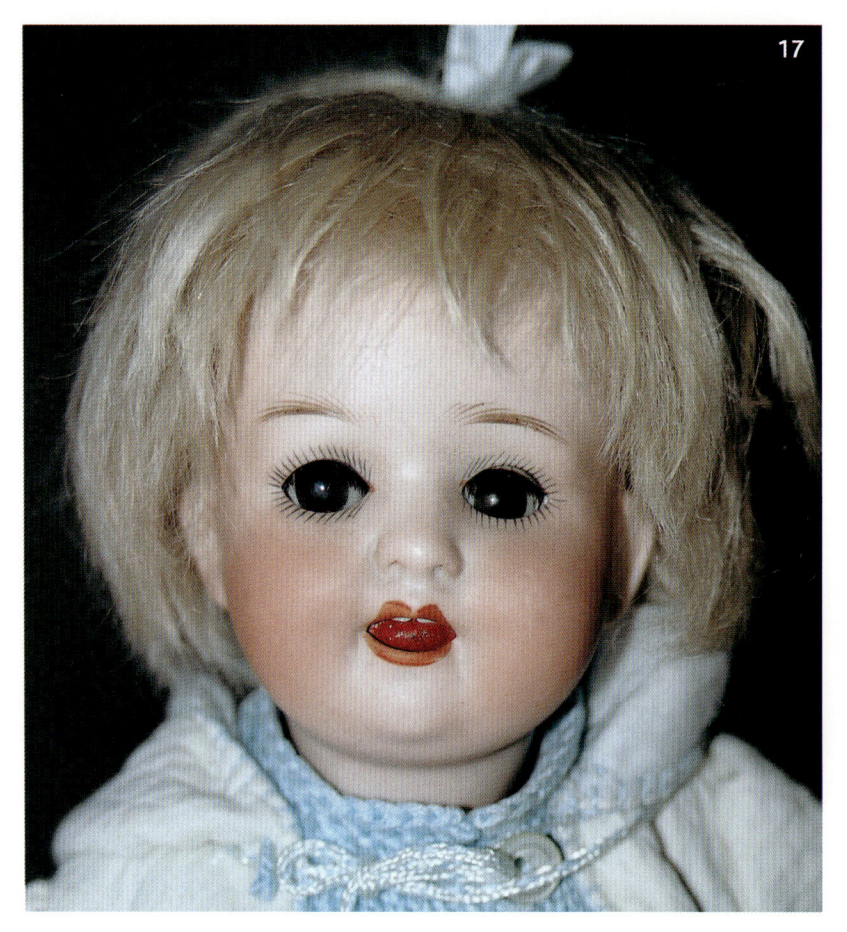

20. Bisque socket head by Ernst Heubach; wig; multi-stroke eyebrows; painted lower eyelashes and upper eyelashes of hair; glass sleep eyes; open mouth with upper teeth and separate tongue; 15-inch doll; circa 1920; marked: **Heubach. Koppelsdorf**. Courtesy Hessisches Puppen museum, Hanau-Wilhelmsbad. (Photo: Christiane Gräfnitz)

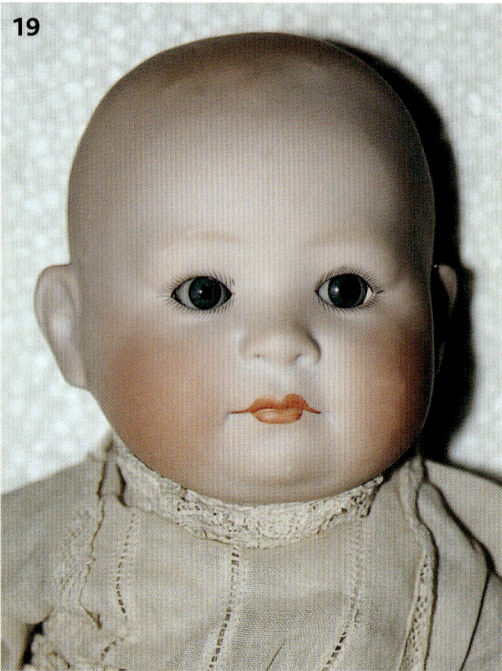

18. Bisque socket head by Ernst Heubach; original mohair wig and clothing; multi-stroke eyebrows; painted upper and lower eyelashes; glass sleep eyes; pierced nostrils; open mouth with upper teeth; 10-inch doll; circa 1920; marked **Heubach.Koppelsdorf//320-12/0//Germany**. Author's Collection. (Photo: Gregg Smith)

19. Bisque socket head by Ernst Heubach; flange neck; slightly molded hair; single-stroke eyebrows; painted upper and lower eyelashes; glass sleep eyes; closed mouth; 15-inch doll; circa 1925; marked: **339//3/0**. Historisches Coburger Puppenmuseum/Lossnitzer Collection. (Photo: Christiane Gräfnitz)

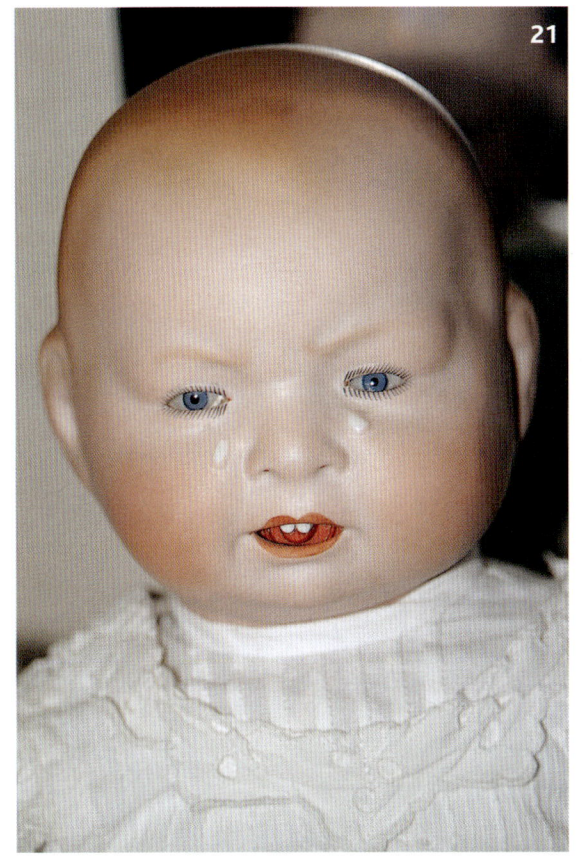

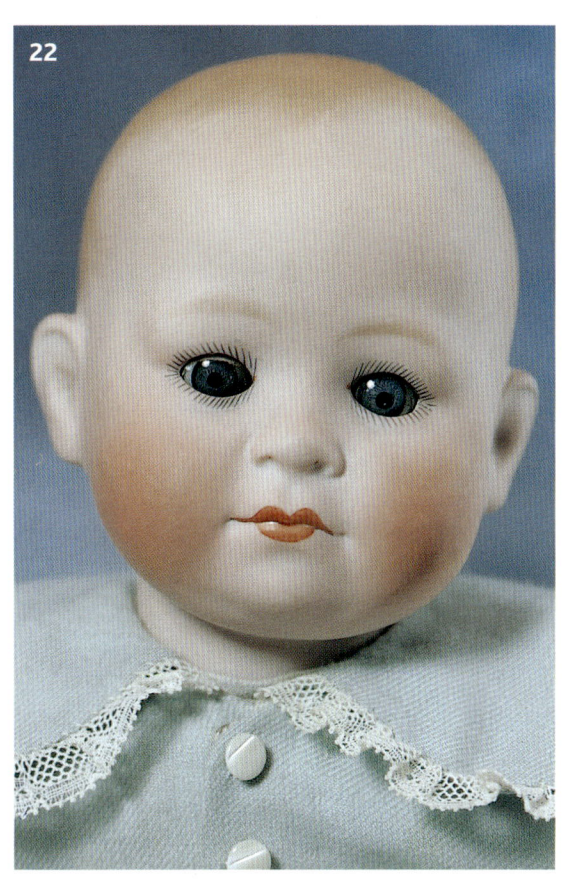

Ernst Heubach Porcelain Factory

21. Crying side of two-faced bisque socket head seen in illustration 24 by Ernst Heubach for the Priska Sander doll factory; flange neck; smooth head with painted hair; single-stroke eyebrows; painted upper and lower eyelashes; tiny, glass sleep eyes; molded tear below each eye; open mouth with upper teeth and tongue; 14-inch doll; GM 1930; marked: **Priska Sander//Neustadt/Orla//353//DRGM 2**. Courtesy Museum Schloss Tenneberg, Waltershausen. (Photo: Christiane Gräfnitz)

22. Bisque socket head by Ernst Heubach; flange neck; slightly molded hair; single-stroke eyebrows; painted upper and lower eyelashes; glass sleep eyes; closed mouth; 13-inch doll; circa 1925, marked: **Heubach. Koppelsdorf//339//5/0**. Beth Karp Collection. (Photo: Lee Krombholz)

23. Dark-brown South Sea Baby bisque socket head by Ernst Heubach for the August Luge doll factory in Sonneberg; original clothing; pierced ears with large hoop earrings; smooth head with painted hair; single-stroke eyebrows; painted upper and lower eyelashes; tiny, glass sleep eyes; closed mouth; 8-inch doll; GM 1930; marked: **Heubach. Koppelsdorf//399-15/0//DRGM//Germany**. In 1893, Theodor Recknagel applied for a design patent that included blending the coloring into the porcelain mixture. Sonneberg-area porcelain factories, like the Ernst Heubach porcelain factory, used this method to pre-color porcelain for ethnic bisque heads. Beth Karp Collection. (Photo: Lee Krombholz)

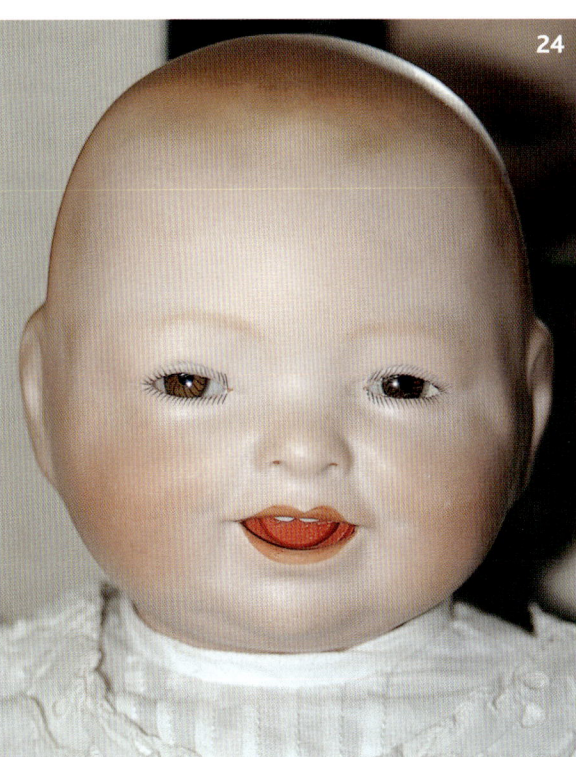

24. Laughing side of two-faced bisque socket head seen in illustration 21 by Ernst Heubach for the Priska Sander doll factory; smooth head with painted hair; single-stroke eyebrows; painted upper and lower eyelashes; glass sleep eyes; open, smiling mouth with upper teeth and tongue; 14-inch doll; GM 1930; marked: **Priska Sander//Neustadt/Orla//353/DRGM/2**. Courtesy Museum Schloss Tenneberg, Waltershausen. (Photo: Christiane Gräfnitz)

Chapter 4

25. Bisque socket-head googly by Ernst Heubach; original wig and clothing; multi-stroke eyebrows; upper eyelashes painted with straight brushstrokes; side-glancing glass sleep eyes; open mouth with upper teeth; chin dimple; 10½-inch doll; circa 1926; marked: **Heubach.Koppelsdorf//417-10/0//Germany**. Author's Collection. (Photo: Gregg Smith)

26. Bisque socket-head googly by Ernst Heubach; original wig and clothing; multi-stroke eyebrows; upper eyelashes painted with straight brushstrokes; side-glancing glass sleep eyes; open mouth with upper teeth; 12-inch doll; circa 1926; marked: **Heubach.Koppelsdorf//417-8/0//Germany**. Beth Karp Collection. (Photo: Lee Krombholz)

27. Light-brown bisque socket head by Ernst Heubach; original wig and clothing; gold ball metal earrings attached to non-pierced ears; single-stroke eyebrows; painted upper and lower eyelashes; glass sleep eyes; closed mouth; 8½-inch doll; circa 1926; marked: **Heubach.Koppelsdorf//444-15/0**. Beth Karp Collection. (Photo: Lee Krombholz)

28. Reddish-brown bisque socket head by Ernst Heubach; molded hair; original wig and Gypsy-styled clothing; gold molded earrings; multi-stroke eyebrows; painted upper and lower eyelashes; glass sleep eyes; open mouth with upper teeth; 9½-inch doll; circa 1928; marked: **Heubach.Koeppelsdorf//452.14/0//Germany**. Beth Karp Collection. (Photo: Lee Krombholz)

29. Two bisque socket-head googlies by Ernst Heubach porcelain factory for the Albin Hess doll factory in Schalkau, Thuringia; doll on right holds light-bulb fixture, wire goes through the body from a hole in the sole of one foot; wig; lamp shade is a large ball-like straw hat that covers the light bulb; single-stroke eyebrows; painted, straight upper eyelashes; large, side-glancing glass sleep eyes; closed smiling mouth; 11-inch doll; GM 1923; marked: **Heubach.Koppelsdorf//318 7/0//Germany A.H. Schalkau D.R.G.M.**. This rare doll is a documented lamp doll. The head was modeled by Albin Hess from his "1922 registered design for an Electric lamp-doll," according to the Cieliks' research in the January 25, 1991, issue of their *Puppenmagazin*. See illustration 30 for description of larger doll. Julie Blewis Collection. (Photo: Fanilya Gueno)

Ernst Heubach Porcelain Factory

30. Bisque socket-head googly by Ernst Heubach porcelain factory; original wig and jockey clothing; single-stroke eyebrows; painted, straight upper eyelashes; large, side-glancing glass sleep eyes; closed down-turned mouth; 15-inch doll; GM 1923; marked: Heubach.Koppelsdorf//319.3//A.H. Schalkau. Julie Blewis Collection. (Photo: Fanilya Gueno)

Part Two

CHAPTER 5

Gebrüder Heubach Porcelain Factory

1. This photograph of Richard Heubach is a black-and-white photocopy of a 1931 portrait on porcelain painted by Louis Scherf, a former student of the Gebrüder Heubach School of Art and Modeling. Richard Heubach was a co-owner of the Gebrüder Heubach porcelain factory from 1904 until the 1930s. (Photocopy: Courtesy Deutsches Spielzeugmuseum, Sonneberg, with permission from the Eisenach Museum in Eisenach, owner of the original porcelain portrait)

The Gebrüder Heubach porcelain factory is unique because, unlike the other Thuringian porcelain factories that made doll-related porcelain products in the nineteenth and twentieth centuries, it continues to make porcelain products in Thuringia today, under the name Lichte Porcelain, Ltd. The Heubach porcelain factory has produced fine-quality porcelain products for 165 years. The factory was founded in Lichte, Thuringia, by Johann Heinrich Leder in 1804. The first products were blue painted cups and pipe ends made of earthenware. In 1833 Wilhelm Liedermann bought the pottery factory. In 1840 the brothers Christoph and Philipp Heubach of Laucha purchased the factory. Hard-paste porcelain was not produced at the factory until September 16, 1843, when the Prince of Sachsen-Meiningen granted the Heubach brothers the "Privilege" needed to operate a porcelain factory in Lichte. An article in *Spinning Wheel's Complete Book of Dolls*, written by Genevieve Angione, notes that: "In *Dolls, Makers and Marks*, Dorothy S. Coleman states that "The trade address was Sonneberg, but the actual factory was in Lichte, near Wallendorf, north and west of Sonneberg."

An article titled *VEB Lichte, Combined Porcelain Works*, currently in the archives of the Sonneberg Doll Museum, provides important information on the town of Lichte and the Gebrüder Heubach porcelain factory. The mid-1800s are described as a "time of poverty and need" in the Thuringian forest. Lichte and many other towns in this Thuringian doll-making area were very isolated because they were not connected to railroad lines.

In order to generate more business, a few Thuringian porcelain factories decided to work together to create porcelain products of higher quality, which would, in turn, increase sales and thereby create more jobs for the factory workers living in each town, markedly improving the economy of the entire Thuringian area. To accomplish these far-reaching changes, the Art and Business Society of Sonneberg asked

276

2. This original 1900 postcard shows the small valley town of Lichte and the Thuringian mountains that surround it. Until railroad tracks connected Lichte to other doll factories in Thuringia and to the main German shipping ports in Bremen and Hamburg, transportation of doll-related porcelain products was difficult. Author's Archival Paper Collection.

the Rudolstadt and Meiningen government to financially support the area's porcelain factories. The Sonneberg group also asked for government permission to found a painting and modeling school in Lichte. The Prince of Sachsen-Meiningen approved the request, and the Lichte School of Modeling and Painting was founded on August 15, 1862.

The first director of the school was Munich sculptor Georg Mayer. The students came from five nearby villages. By 1883, 122 students attended the school. They were divided into eight groups to learn drawing and modeling. Fundamental skills were taught and practiced. Students analyzed animal and human anatomy to acquire detailed knowledge of the sculptures they would be required to create and to reproduce each form accurately on the drawing board. These skills were indispensable for a sculptor or painter. Students spent many months learning basic skills before they were allowed to paint on porcelain for the first time.

The students of the Lichte School of Modeling and Painting had excellent role models. Professor Louis Hutschenreuther was the second director of the school. Under his leadership, the artistic level of the student's education improved considerably. He taught new techniques for porcelain decoration, which created specialties among the students. His students were soon able to paint beautiful scenes and portraits on porcelain plaques. During the years character dolls were made, sculptor Otto Thiem also worked at the school. He was well known throughout Europe for his exceptional oil paintings. Two other graduates of the Lichte School of Modeling and Painting were the Scherf Brothers, Louis and Albert. They lived in Lichte for many years and consulted often with the current instructors of the school. Louis Scherf's paintings were awarded gold medals at five World Expositions. The Pitti Palace in Florence owns more than eighty of his oil paintings on porcelain.

The Gebrüder Heubach porcelain factory made tableware and simple figurines until 1876, when they began making decorative porcelain. Their porcelain plaques, tiles and figurines won awards at the Paris, St. Louis and Brussels World Expositions. Other products made by the factory included vases, chandeliers, children's china sets, writing utensils, bowls, containers for holy water, tableware, plaques with paintings and portraits on porcelain that were based on photographs.

It was a natural progression for the Heubach porcelain factory to modify figurine heads to create doll heads. A master mold was created from a figurine head, which was then attached to a shoulder plate or adapted to serve as a socket head. The first doll heads made by the factory in 1910 were bisque character heads. Dolls with Gebrüder Heubach bisque heads sold well because the character faces were so expressive. The modeling of the facial features was unique in comparison to other character dolls on the market. The Gebrüder

Chapter 5

Heubach porcelain factory made more bisque character heads with expressions that portrayed human emotion than any other Thuringian porcelain factory. Due to the skilled modeling of their facial features, Heubach character dolls laughed, cried, smiled and pouted. Facial painting similarities are apparent between the heads on figurines, piano babies and dolls, indicating the work of a particular factory artist.

One of the most unusual features of a Gebrüder Heubach character doll is the sculpting of the eyes. Heubach intaglio eyes have semi-spherical impressed or incised pupils. They are surprisingly realistic. The majority of Heubach character dolls have intaglio-painted eyes rather than glass eyes.

The incised marks on the back of the heads vary, and may include the Heubach name in a square with "HEU" on the top line and "BACH" underneath. Another identification mark is the Heubach "sunburst," a rising sun on a half-circle containing the initials "G" over "H". Mold numbers are often incised on each side of the Heubach trademark square or the sunburst. Small green stamped numbers are also a characteristic mark of this porcelain factory.

The Gebrüder Heubach porcelain factory in Lichte sold bisque-head character dolls to a variety of doll factories in the Waltershausen and Sonneberg areas, including the Sonneberg-area doll factories of Cuno & Otto Dressel and Gottlieb Zinner & Söhne. The Heubach factory also provided bisque heads for the Waltershausen-area doll factories of Wagner & Zetsche and Adolf Wislizenus. As a way to lower prices on some of their bisque character heads, the Gebrüder Heubach porcelain factory used pink pre-tinted bisque. In other words, the porcelain slip was colored pink before it was poured into the plaster molds. The majority of doll heads were not pre-tinted, and to my knowledge, all other Heubach porcelain products were made of pure white bisque.

The character dolls made by this prolific Thuringian porcelain factory remain popular with antique-doll collectors. One googly bisque head was made by the Gebrüder Heubach porcelain factory for the Eisenmann & Co. doll factory of Fürth. It is marked with the name "Einco" and the mold number "8723." Other popular Heubach dolls include the Winker and Coquette. Many character dolls were made primarily for the American market, including Coquette. Originally Heubach bisque-character heads were made to appeal to customers in the lower-priced doll market. The majority of Heubach bisque-head characters are mounted on jointed composition bodies, assembled at the many Thuringian doll factories that purchased the heads. The bodies on Gebrüder Heubach character dolls vary considerably. Some of the socket heads are on crude five-piece stick bodies made of varnished papier-mâché. Others are on realistic composition toddler bodies with slant hips. Many Heubach heads are mounted on five-piece composition baby bodies. The factory also sold heads that required special bodies; for example, the Whistler required a body with a voice box. When pressing the bellows mechanism that was originally inserted into the body, a whistling sound seems to come out of the doll's pursed lips. Dolls like the Whistler represent the skilled work of voice makers who lived and worked in the Sonneberg area.

An automaton pictured in this chapter features three Gebrüder Heubach bisque-head dolls having a tea party. The music box was made by the Gottlieb Zinner & Söhne doll factory in nearby Schalkau. The Zinner doll factory made mechanical toys that included dolls with voices and various other mechanisms designed to simulate lifelike movements.

Zinner specialized in this type of "mechanical toys with voices," as the Ciesliks describe them in their *German Doll Encyclopedia*, from 1879 until the late 1930s. The factory's products were sold in England, France, Russia, South America and the United States. Many of their doll-related products were attributed to French dollmakers. The Zinner doll factory was an early participant in the semi-annual Leipzig Fairs. Advertising cards given to potential customers made the following claim: "This enterprise is number one in mechanical toys, doll automata, etc in the world."

As early as 1820, Gottlieb Zinner's father Karl carved wooden animals, houses and figures during the long Thuringian winters. In 1845 Gottlieb founded his own business with dolls and toys that closely resembled his father's wooden products. Until about 1876, Gottlieb Zinner sold his products exclusively to Sonneberg wholesalers and import houses. An 1879 Sonneberg Doll Museum document records the participation of the Zinner doll factory in an exhibition of "Arts and Trade in Sonneberg" with "mechanical toys with music."

The factory added movable, dressed dolls to its line in 1860. These dolls were named "Automatons" and proved to be very popular with both French and American toy stores. Zinner's doll-and-toy related products were especially popular during the Christmas season. Automatons with bisque heads continued to be made by the Zinner doll factory through the 1930s.

The factory depended on voice makers in the Sonneberg area to furnish the sound mechanisms for their dolls and toys. Thanks to an oral history in the book *Sonneberg Stories of Dolls, Slate Pencils and Cuckoo Whistles,* we can learn how these sound mechanisms were made. The main village responsible for making voice boxes was located in the Sonneberg suburb of Neufang.

The daughter of a Neufang voice-box maker describes voice-box making as follows.

> Since the beginning of the 19th century clever toy manufacturers tried to give voices to their dolls. My father had learned violin making from my grandfather. Work got so bad that he decided to work as a doll-body stuffer. Then he decided to retrain himself and learned voice-box making at the Steiner Company in Sonneberg. Later he made doll and bear voices in a small workshop in our house.

Gebrüder Heubach Porcelain Factory

3. The Gebrüder Heubach porcelain factory is quite large, as evidenced by this recent photograph of the back of the factory. The factory was founded as an earthenware factory in 1804. Porcelain production began in 1843 and continues to this day. (Photo: Mary Krombholz)

4. This 9-inch Gebrüder Heubach figurine of a young girl admiring her doll is marked with the factory's red-stamped sunburst trademark. The sun-rays cover the top half of the circle, and the initials "HG" and "SCHÜTZ-MARKE" fill the bottom half of the circle. The letters DEP are inside an attached oval below the circle trademark. Author's Collection. (Photo: Gregg Smith)

5. This view of the porcelain factory from the Heubach home shows the white street-side section of the factory that bears the current signage: "Lichte Porzellan." (Photo: Mary Krombholz)

6. A former Heubach home is still standing in Lichte, across the street from the Gebrüder Heubach porcelain factory. (Photo: Mary Krombholz)

Chapter 5

The whole family helped. For the first voice boxes we made, my father procured iron underparts. These iron pieces we children had to rub smooth with a file, as part of the finishing process, so that the brass plates lay flat on them. We cut these plates out of brass sheet metal and bound them to the iron pieces with twine. Then my father tuned each of them individually. He blew into it and bent the sheet metal until the sound matched his idea. These bound and tuned voice boxes we glued onto small rectangular pieces of wood or goat leather that was drilled at this spot. With a second little board of paper or goat leather, bone glue and a fine, thin spring a small bellows was made. When pressing the bellows, air went through the boring on the upper board in the voice box and sounded the tone. The spring brought both boards back to the original position.

In a week we finished 500 to 600 such voice boxes. For every dozen we received 70 Pfennig, allowing for expenses. Every Saturday we made delivery in a large back basket to the doll factories in the area. On the way home my mother always bought a quarter-pound of candy for my brother and me as a reward for our after school help.

In addition to the work, we maintained a small farm that supported us half way. We did not need to go hungry, especially when the potato harvest was good. Potatoes in their jackets we had every day. We ate either herring in thick milk occasionally, or on Saturdays a piece of sausage. Before Christmas when the orders were completed we celebrated with a butchering festival, and butchered a pig. Sausage, ham, bacon, lard, salted and smoked meat my mother divided so that it lasted over the whole year. Later my brother learned the voice-making craft and became a master voice maker. He continued our family business. Today after the reunification there are no longer any voice-box makers in Neufang.

According to Robert E. Roentgen, author of *Marks on German, Bohemian and Austrian Porcelain, 1710 to the Present*, until 1945 the Lichte porcelain factory operated under the name Gebr. Heubach AG. After World War II, the factory was expropriated. Three years later it was nationalized and became a branch of VEB Ceramics with the name Porcelain Factory Lichte, under which it operated from 1948 until 1954. From 1954 until 1972, the factory name was VEB Porcelainworks Lichte. From 1972 until 1990, the porcelain factory operated as United Decorative Porcelainworks Lichte. After the dissolution of the VEB Decorative Porcelainworks in 1990, the porcelain factory became a holding company. In 1994 the factory name became Lichte Porcelain, Ltd., and it continues to make porcelain products under that name today.

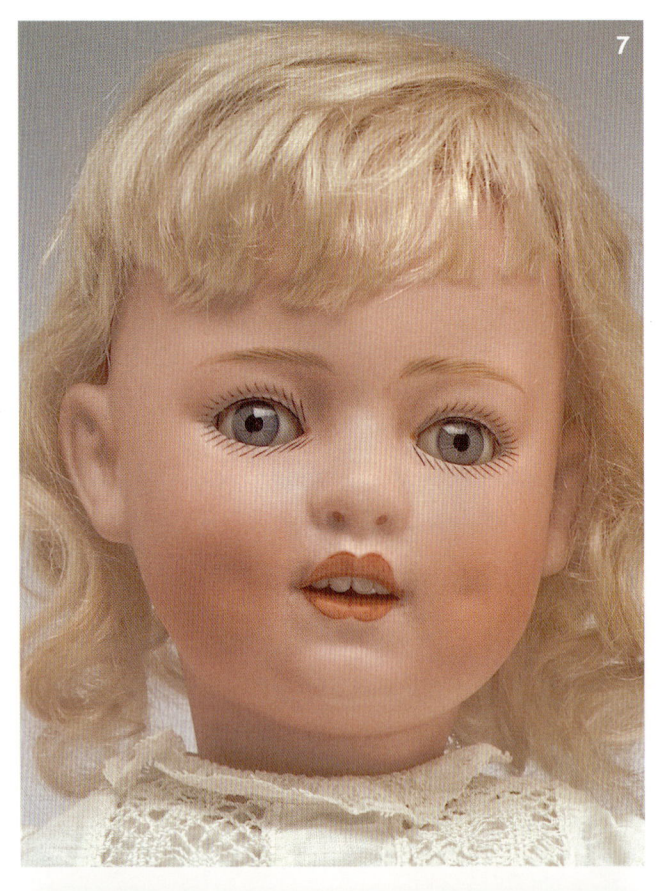

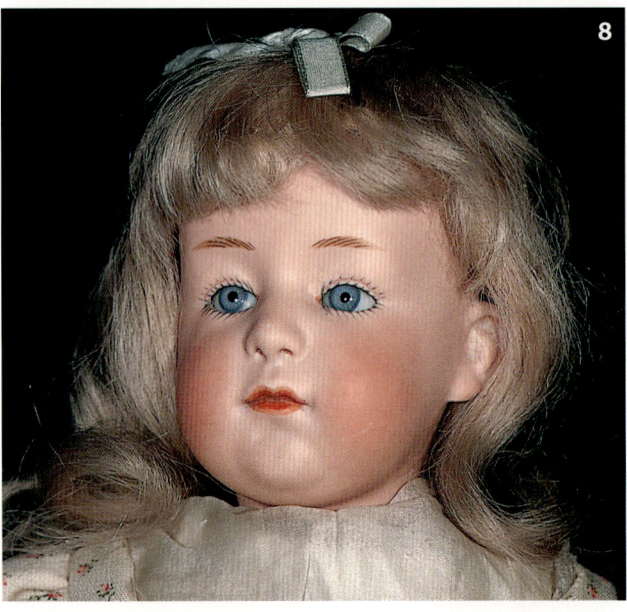

7. Dolly Dimple bisque socket head by Gebrüder Heubach for the Hamburger & Co. doll factory in Berlin and the American importing company Butler Brothers; wig; multi-stroke eyebrows; painted upper and lower eyelashes; glass sleep eyes; open mouth with upper teeth; cheek and chin dimples; 14½-inch doll; circa 1913; marked: **DEP//Dolly Dimple H//Germany//6½//sunburst** (mark). Susan Moore Collection. (Photo: John Cummings)

8. Bisque socket head by Gebrüder Heubach; wig; multi-stroke eyebrows; painted upper and lower eyelashes; glass sleep eyes; closed mouth; 14-inch doll; circa 1912; marked: **6970//Germany//4**. Private Collection, formerly Jane Walker Collection. (Photo: Gene Abbott)

Gebrüder Heubach Porcelain Factory

9. Bisque socket head by Gebrüder Heubach; wig; multi-stroke eyebrows; painted upper and lower eyelashes; glass sleep eyes; closed pouty mouth; 18-inch doll; circa 1912; marked: **6969**. Many bisque-character heads marked with the Gebrüder Heubach mold number 6969 were mounted on composition-bodied dolls marked with the Dressel winged-helmet trademark. Norah Stoner Collection. (Photo: Norah Stoner)

10. Bisque socket head by Gebrüder Heubach; wig; multi-stroke eyebrows; painted upper and lower eyelashes; glass sleep eyes; open mouth with upper teeth; 13-inch doll; circa 1920; marked: **10532//Heubach(square)//4**. Ann Cummings Collection. (Photo: John Cummings)

- **11.** Bisque socket head by Gebrüder Heubach; wig, multi-stroke eyebrows; painted upper and lower eyelashes; glass sleep eyes; closed pouty mouth; 20-inch doll; circa 1912; marked: **7247//8//Germany//sunburst**(mark). Ursula Gauder Collection. (Photo: Christiane Gräfnitz)

- **12.** Bisque socket head by Gebrüder Heubach; wig; multi-stroke eyebrows; painted upper and lower eyelashes; glass sleep eyes; closed pouty mouth; 16-inch doll; circa 1912; marked: **7247//5//Germany**. Norah Stoner Collection. (Photo: Norah Stoner)

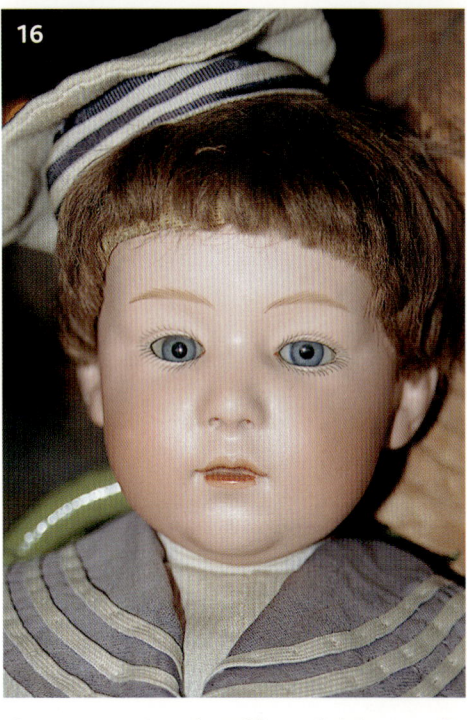

Chapter 5

13. Bisque socket head by Gebrüder Heubach; wig; multi-stroke eyebrows; painted upper and lower eyelashes; glass sleep eyes; open/closed mouth; 17-inch doll; circa 1910; marked: **7//sunburst**(mark)**//Germany**. This is one of four Gebrüder Heubach dolls sitting on the carousel in the basement of the Sonneberg Doll Museum. Note the resemblance to the Heubach 6970 mold number doll pictured in illustration 8. Courtesy Deutsches Spielzeugmuseum, Sonneberg. (Photo: Christiane Gräfnitz)

14. Bisque socket head by Gebrüder Heubach; wig; multi-stroke eyebrows; painted upper and lower eyelashes; glass sleep eyes; open/closed mouth; 17¼-inch doll; circa 1910; marked: **Germany//7**. This doll is also sitting on the carousel in the basement of the Sonneberg Doll Museum. The carousel dolls may have been some of the earliest dolls made by the factory because the entire Brussels exhibit was previewed by Sonneberg residents on March 13, 1910, and the production of Gebrüder Heubach bisque heads was first mentioned in commercial registers in 1910. Courtesy Deutsches Spielzeugmuseum, Sonneberg. (Photo: Christiane Gräfnitz)

15. Bisque socket head by Gebrüder Heubach; wig; multi-stroke eyebrows; painted upper and lower eyelashes; glass sleep eyes; closed mouth; 17½-inch doll; circa 1910; marked: **Germany//7**. This doll is also sitting on the carousel in the Sonneberg Doll Museum. Courtesy Deutsches Spielzeugmuseum, Sonneberg. (Photo: Christiane Gräfnitz)

16. Bisque socket head by Gebrüder Heubach; wig; multi-stroke eyebrows; painted upper and lower eyelashes; glass sleep eyes; open/closed mouth; 17½-inch doll; circa 1910; marked: **sunburst**(mark)**//7//Germany**. This doll is also sitting on the carousel in the Sonneberg Doll Museum. Courtesy Deutsches Spielzeugmuseum, Sonneberg. (Photo: Christiane Gräfnitz)

Gebrüder Heubach Porcelain Factory

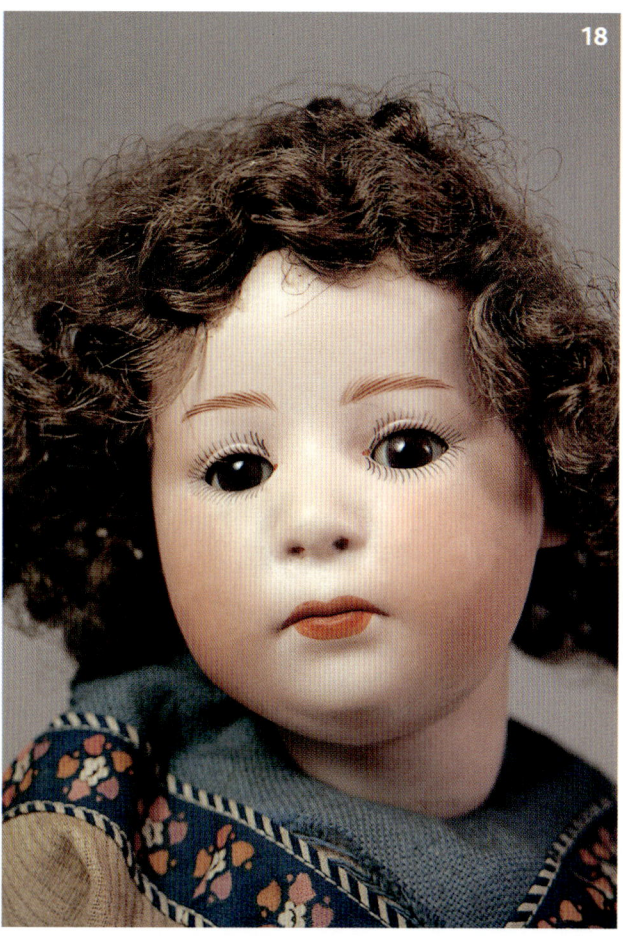

17. Bisque socket head by Gebrüder Heubach; molded hair; single-stroke eyebrows; intaglio-painted eyes with typical factory white highlights, centered close to upper eyelids; closed mouth; 13-inch doll; circa 1910; marked: **6//Germany**. The Gebrüder Heubach 5-inch glazed-porcelain dog is marked with a blue-stamped factory sunburst mark. Author's Collection. (Photo: Gene Abbott)

18. Bisque socket head by Gebrüder Heubach; wig; multi-stroke eyebrows; painted upper and lower eyelashes; glass sleep eyes; closed pouty mouth; circa 1910; 12½-inch doll; marked: **sunburst(mark)//Germany**. Courtesy Deutsches Spielzeugmuseum, Sonneberg. (Photo: Christiane Gräfnitz)

19. Bisque socket head by Gebrüder Heubach; wig; multi-stroke eyebrows; painted upper and lower eyelashes; glass sleep eyes, open mouth with upper teeth; chin dimple; 17¾-inch doll; circa 1910; marked: **sunburst(mark)//G.3.H**. Christa Dorner Collection. (Photo: Christiane Gräfnitz)

20. Bisque socket head by Gebrüder Heubach; molded hair; single-stroke eyebrows; intaglio-painted eyes with white highlights; closed pouty mouth; 9-inch doll; circa 1912; marked: **sunburst(mark)//7603//3**. Ann Cummings Collection. (Photo: John Cummings)

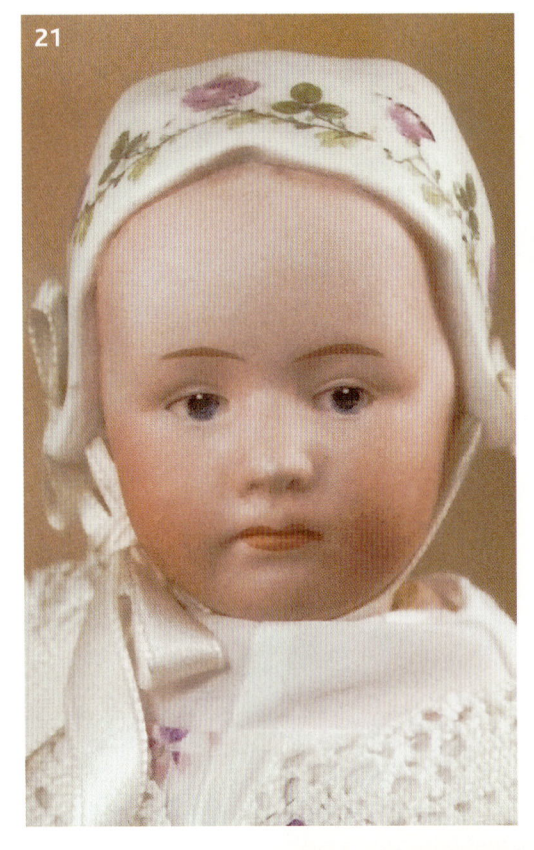

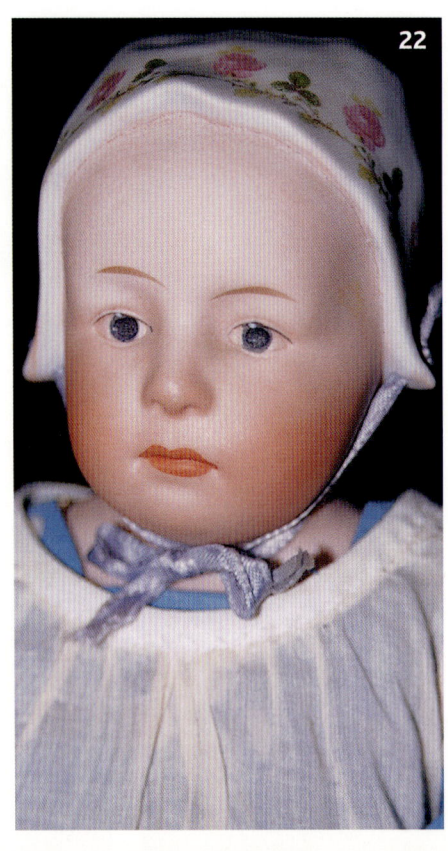

Chapter 5

21. Bisque socket head by Gebrüder Heubach; molded bonnet painted with leaves and flowers; single-stroke eyebrows; intaglio-painted eyes with white highlights; closed mouth; 8-inch doll; circa 1912; marked: **79sunburst(mark)//77DEP//Germany**. Beth Karp Collection. (Photo: Lee Krombholz)

22. Bisque shoulder head by Gebrüder Heubach; molded bisque bonnet, painted with leaves and flowers; single-stroke eyebrows; intaglio-painted eyes with white highlights; closed mouth; 12-inch doll; circa 1912; marked: **Germany//79sunburst(mark)77//DEP**. Courtesy Ladenburger Spielzeugauktion/Goetz Seidel. (Photo: Christiane Gräfnitz)

23. Bisque socket head by Gebruder Heubach; so-called Baby Stuart; molded bisque bonnet, painted with leaves and flowers; single-stroke eyebrows; intaglio-painted eyes with white highlights; closed mouth; 16-inch doll; circa 1912; marked: **5//Germany//79sunburst(mark)77//DEP**. Courtesy Deutsches Spielzeugmuseum, Sonneberg. (Photo: Christiane Gräfnitz)

24. Two bisque-head dolls with shoulder and socket heads by Gebrüder Heubach, circa 1912. Socket-head doll on right: flocked hair; single-stroke eyebrows; intaglio-painted eyes with white highlights; closed mouth; 12½-inch doll; marked: **7602sunburst(mark)//DEP//3//Germany**. Shoulder-head doll on left: molded hair; single-stroke eyebrows; intaglio-painted eyes with white highlights; smiling open/closed mouth with two molded upper teeth and tongue; cheek and chin dimples; 16-inch doll; marked: **sunburst(mark)//Germany//7064**. Beth Karp Collection. (Photo: Lee Krombholz)

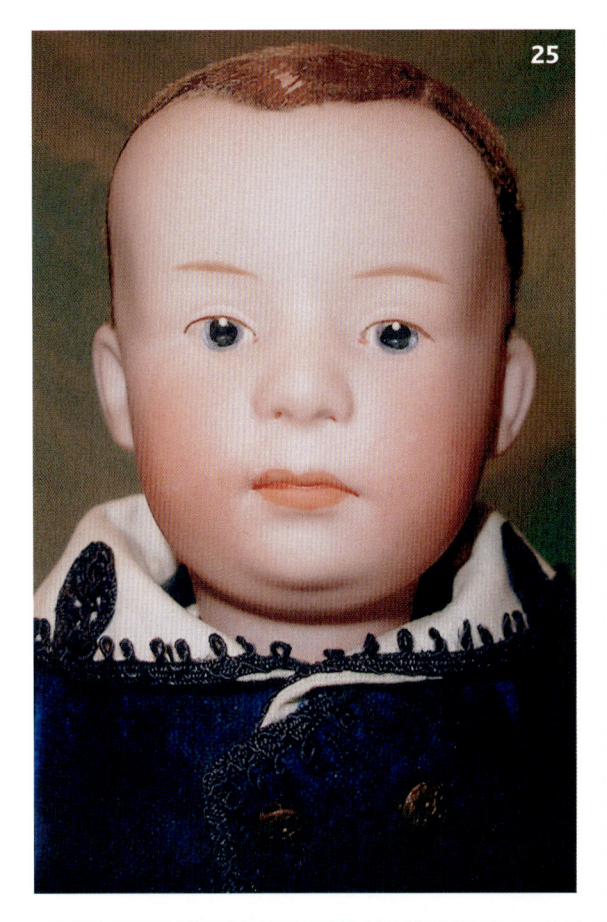

Gebrüder Heubach Porcelain Factory

25. Bisque socket head by Gebrüder Heubach; flocked hair; single-stroke eyebrows; intaglio-painted eyes with white highlights; closed mouth; 12½-inch doll; circa 1912; marked: **76 sunburst**(mark)**02//DEP**(inside oval)**3//Germany**. Note the typical factory white highlight, centered between the iris and pupil, close to the upper-lid outline. Andrea Jones Collection. (Photo: Andrea Jones)

26. Bisque socket head by Gebrüder Heubach; original boxed doll; molded hair; single-stroke eyebrows; intaglio-painted eyes with white highlights; closed pouty mouth; 10-inch doll; circa 1912; marked: **7603**. The German words printed on the box lid translate as follows: "Think of Our War Orphans! We Only Have One Will: To Win or Die." Author's Collection. (Photo: Gregg Smith)

27. Two bisque socket-head boys by Gebrüder Heubach; five-piece baby bodies; original chemises; flocked hair; intaglio-painted eyes with white highlights; closed pouty mouths; 6½-inch dolls; circa 1912; marked: **square**(mark)**//Germany**. Author's Collection. (Photo: Gregg Smith)

Chapter 5

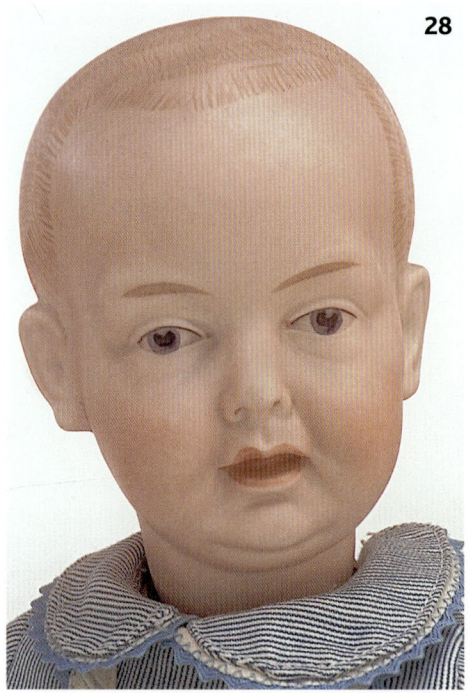

28. Bisque socket head by Gebrüder Heubach for the Eisenmann & Co. doll factory in Fürth; molded hair; single-stroke eyebrows; intaglio-painted eyes with white highlights; open/closed mouth; 13-inch doll; circa 1913; marked: Einco 1//Germany. Two other Einco-marked Gebrüder Heubach heads are the #8723 socket head googly with lever on back to move the eyes and the #8764 shoulder-head googly. Ann Cummings Collection. (Photo: John Cummings)

29. Three unmarked Gebrüder Heubach dolls are having a tea party on this 1912 Zinner & Söhne music box/automaton. The dolls raise their tea cups as the hand crank on the box is turned. The Zinner & Söhne doll factory in Schalkau made more mechanical dolls and toys than any other Thuringian doll factory. The factory used many Gebrüder Heubach and Simon & Halbig bisque heads on their moving toys. Beth Karp Collection. (Photo: Gregg Smith)

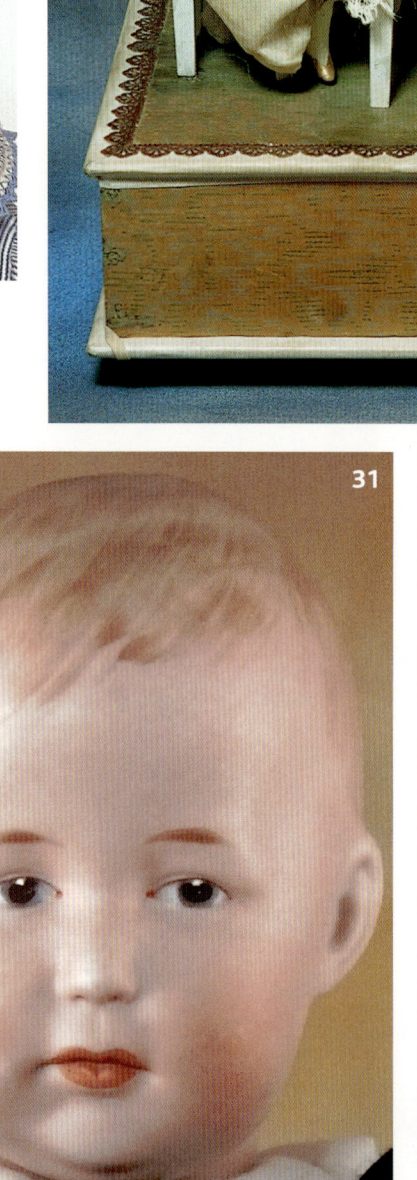

31. Bisque socket head by Gebrüder Heubach; molded hair; single-stroke eyebrows; intaglio-painted eyes with white highlights; closed pouty mouth; 12-inch doll; circa 1912; marked: 7759//square(mark)//Germany. Beth Karp Collection. (Photo: Lee Krombholz)

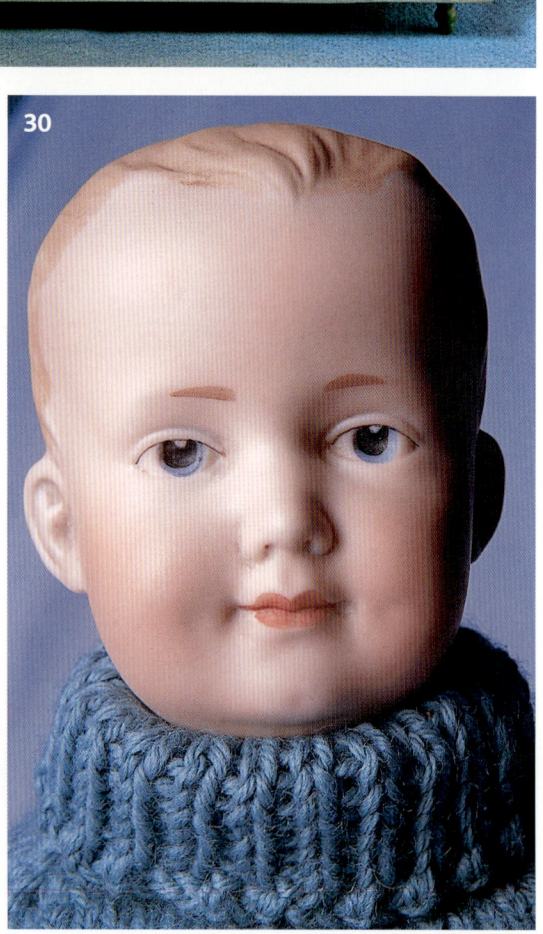

30. Bisque socket head by Gebrüder Heubach; molded hair; single-stroke eyebrows; molded upper eyelids; intaglio-painted eyes with white highlights; closed mouth; chin dimple; 4½-inch head; circa 1912; marked: square(mark)//Germany. Kenneth Drew Collection. (Photo: Ann Hanat)

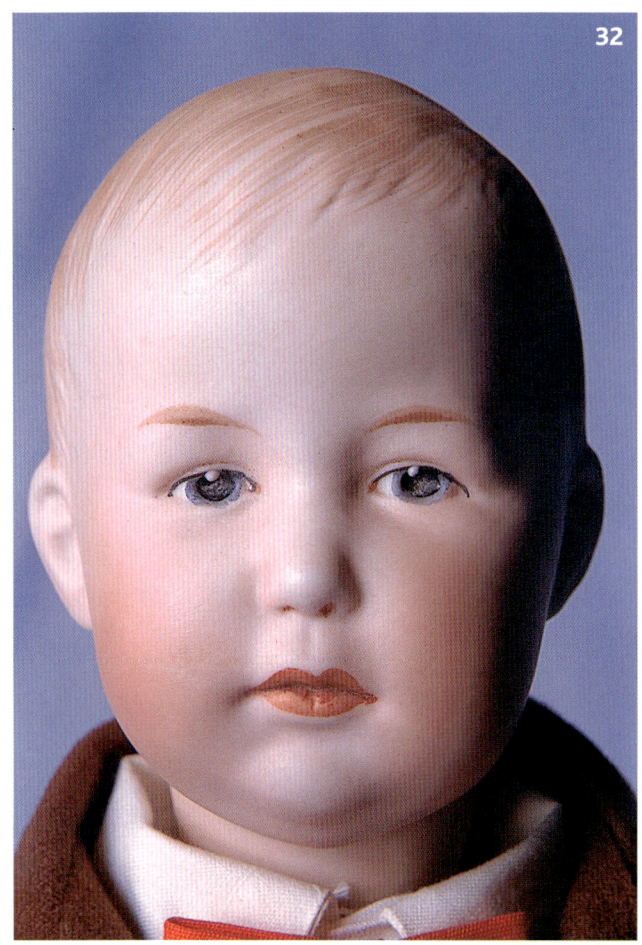

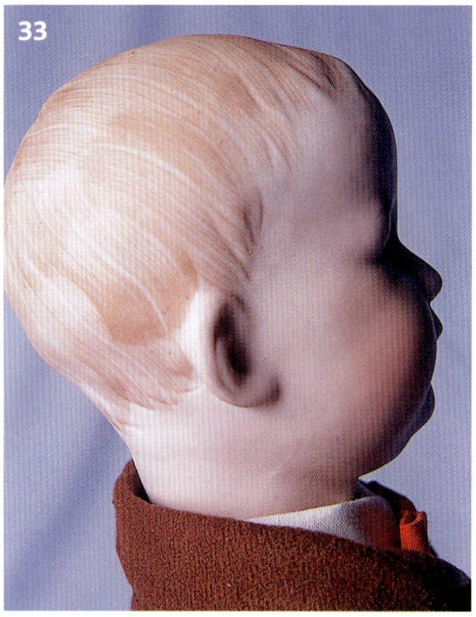

Gebrüder Heubach Porcelain Factory

32. Bisque shoulder head by Gebrüder Heubach; molded hair; single-stroke shaded eyebrows; intaglio-painted eyes with white highlights; closed mouth; 4-inch shoulder head; circa 1912; marked: **square**(mark)**//Germany)**. This is the shoulder-head version of socket head 7759, seen in illustration 31. Kenneth Drew Collection. (Photo: Ann Hanat)

33. A side view of the doll in illustration 32 shows the large molded ears and painted hair. Kenneth Drew Collection. (Photo: Ann Hanat)

34. Bisque shoulder head by Gebrüder Heubach; molded hair; single-stroke eyebrows; side-glancing intaglio-painted eyes with white highlights; open/closed mouth; 14½-inch doll; circa 1912; unmarked. Mold number 8035, seen in illustration 39, is the socket-head version of this shoulder head. Private Collection. (Photo: Christiane Gräfnitz)

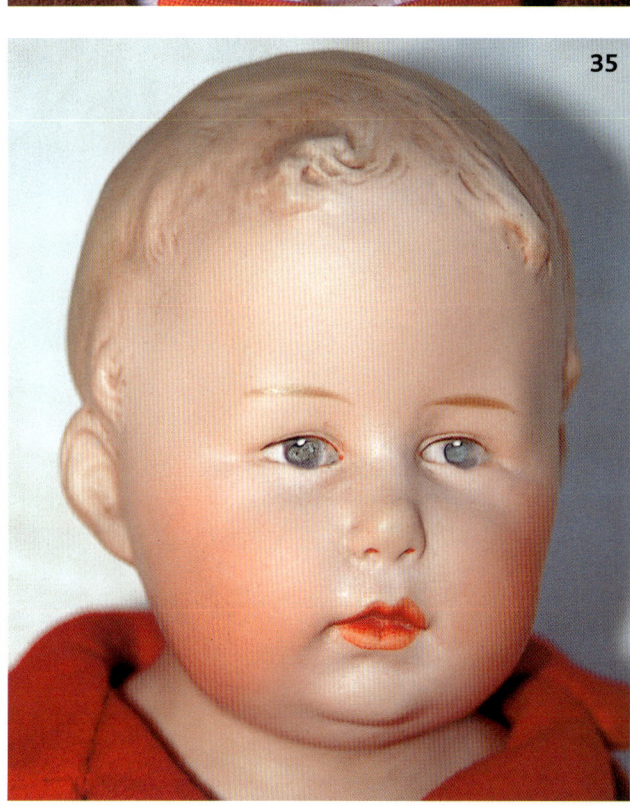

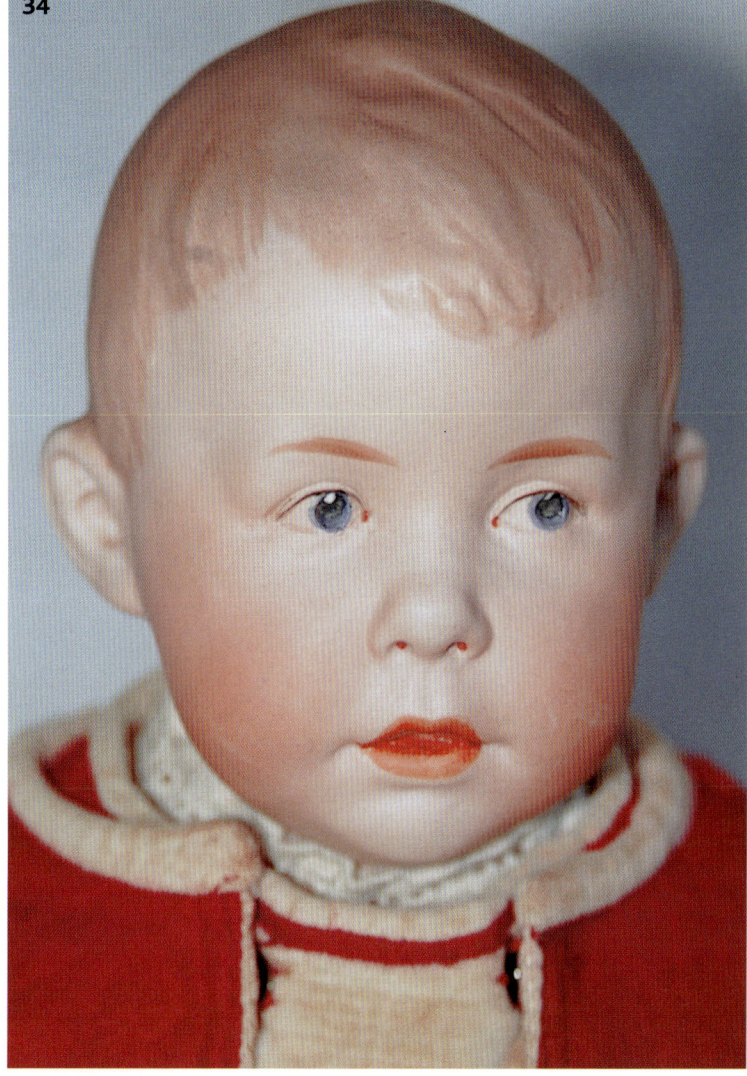

35. Bisque shoulder head by Gebrüder Heubach; molded hair; single-stroke eyebrows; intaglio-painted eyes with white highlights; open/closed mouth with molded tongue; 15½-inch doll; circa 1912; marked: **sunburst**(mark). Private Collection. (Photo: Christiane Gräfnitz)

287

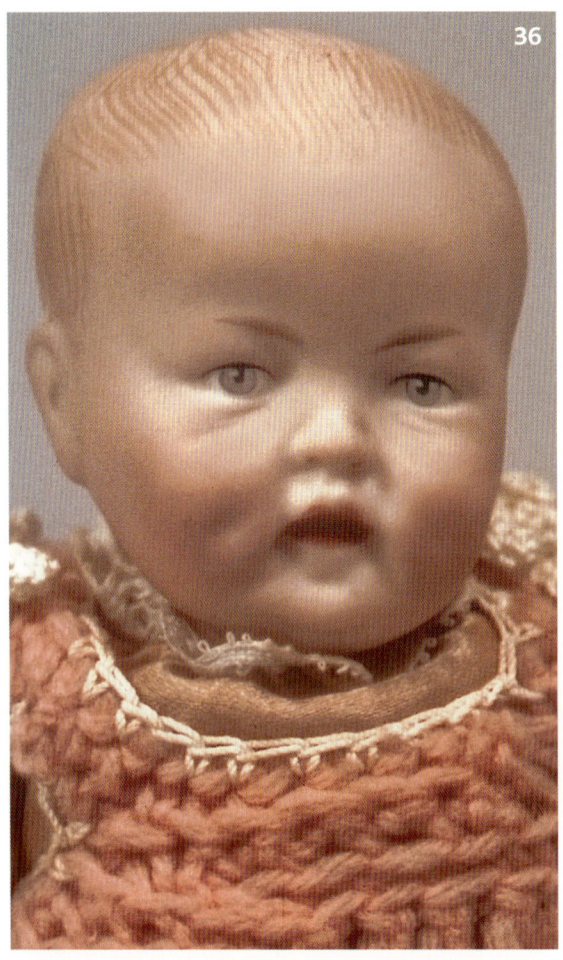

Chapter 5

36. Bisque socket head by Gebrüder Heubach; molded hair; outlined single-stroke eyebrows; intaglio-painted eyes with white highlights; open/closed mouth; cheek dimples; double chin; 8½-inch doll; circa 1912; marked: **GH**. Courtesy Deutsches Spielzeugmuseum, Sonneberg. (Photo: Christiane Gräfnitz)

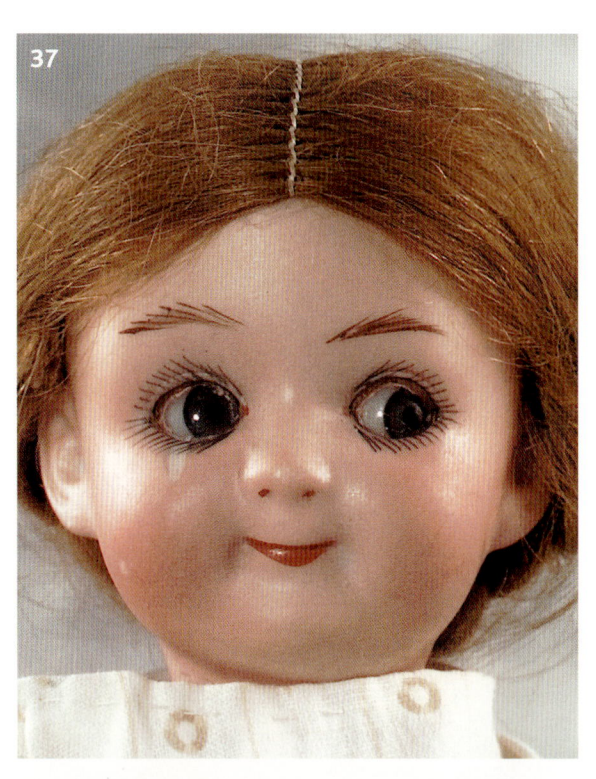

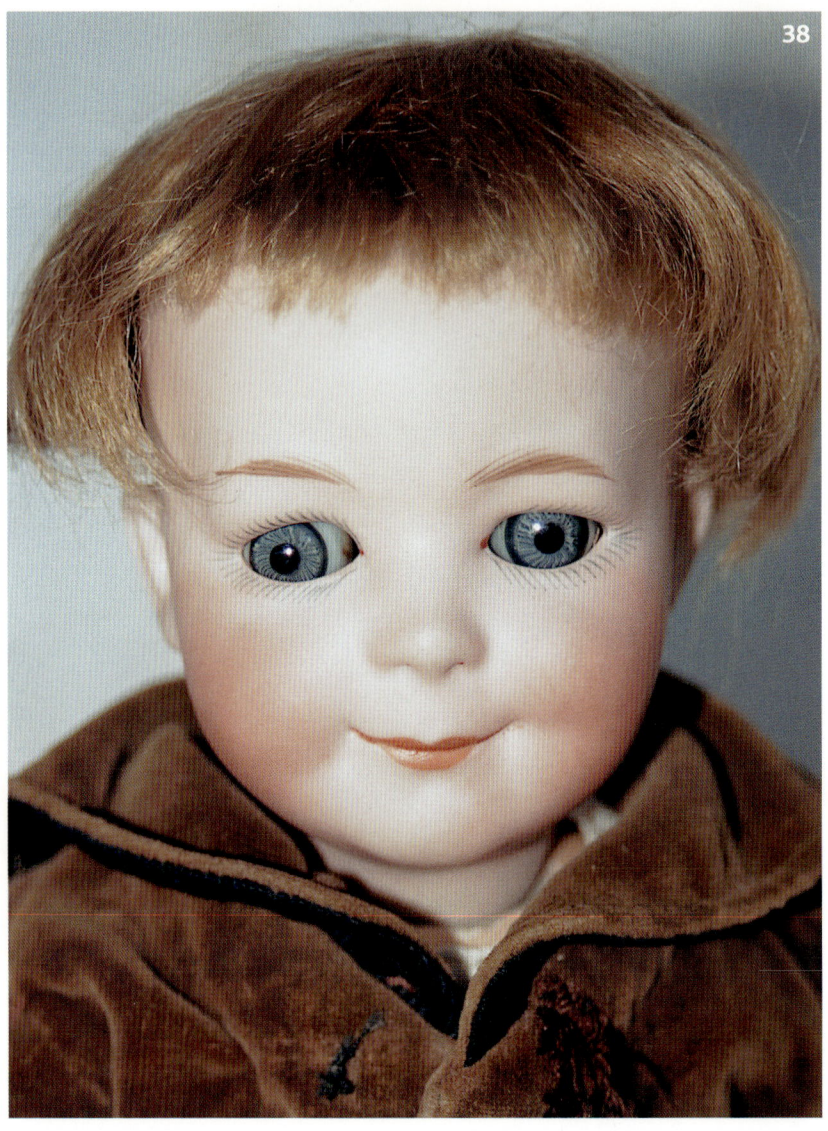

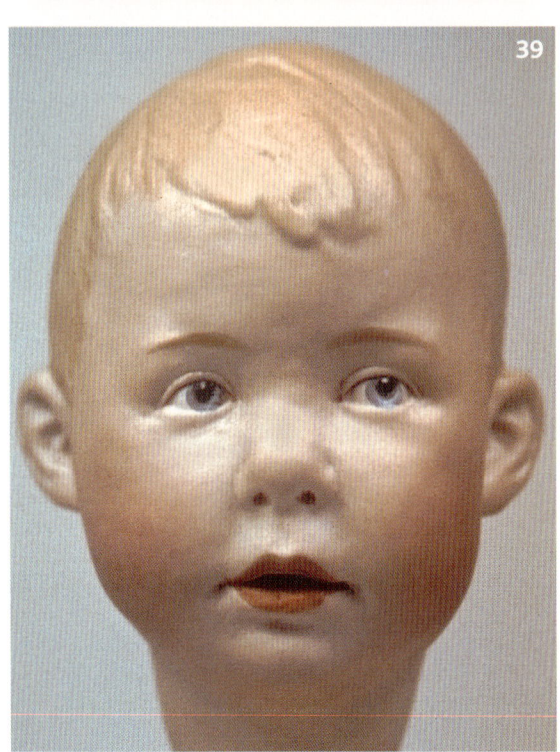

39. Bisque socket head by Gebrüder Heubach; molded hair; single-stroke eyebrows; side-glancing intaglio-painted eyes with white highlights; open/closed mouth; 4-inch head; circa 1912; marked: **8035**. Courtesy Deutsches Spielzeugmuseum, Sonneberg. (Photo: Christiane Gräfnitz)

Gebrüder Heubach Porcelain Factory

40. Bisque socket head by Gebrüder Heubach; molded hair; single-stroke eyebrows; molded upper eyelids; intaglio-painted eyes with white highlights; open/closed pouty mouth; 14-inch doll; circa 1912; marked: **7622**. Norah Stoner Collection. (Photo: Norah Stoner)

37. Bisque socket-head googly by Gebrüder Heubach; wig; multi-stroke eyebrows; painted upper and lower eyelashes; side-glancing glass sleep eyes; closed smiling mouth; 7½-inch doll; circa 1914; marked: **9573//3/0// square**(mark)**// Germany**. Beth Karp Collection. (Photo: Lee Krombholz)

38. Bisque socket head by Gebrüder Heubach; wig; multi-stroke eyebrows; painted upper and lower eyelashes; glass sleep eyes; closed smiling mouth; 13-inch doll; circa 1922; marked: **10671// square**(mark)**// Germany**. Private Collection. (Photo: Christiane Gräfnitz)

40

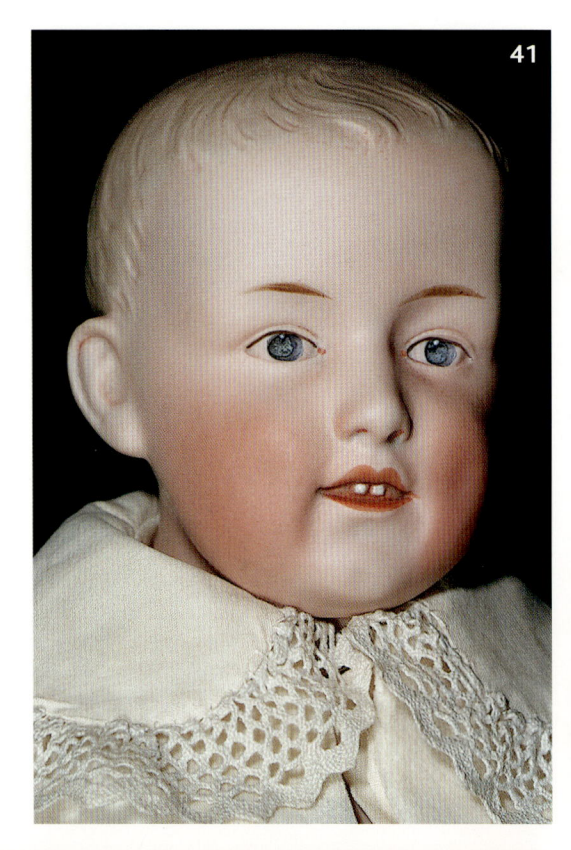

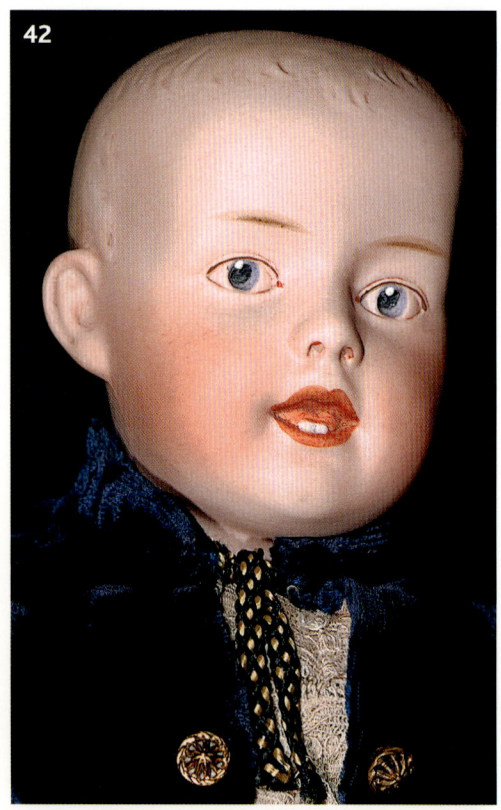

Chapter 5

41. Bisque shoulder head by Gebrüder Heubach; molded hair; two-tone single-stroke eyebrows; intaglio-painted eyes with white highlights; smiling open/closed mouth with two upper teeth and molded tongue; cheek and chin dimples; 15½-inch doll; circa 1912; marked: **3//sunburst**(mark)**//Germany//7054**. Author's Collection. (Photo: Gene Abbott)

42. Bisque shoulder head by Gebrüder Heubach; molded hair; two-tone single-stroke eyebrows; intaglio-painted eyes with white highlights; open/closed mouth with lower teeth and molded tongue; 17-inch doll; circa 1912; marked: **3//Germany**. Author's Collection. (Photo: Gene Abbott)

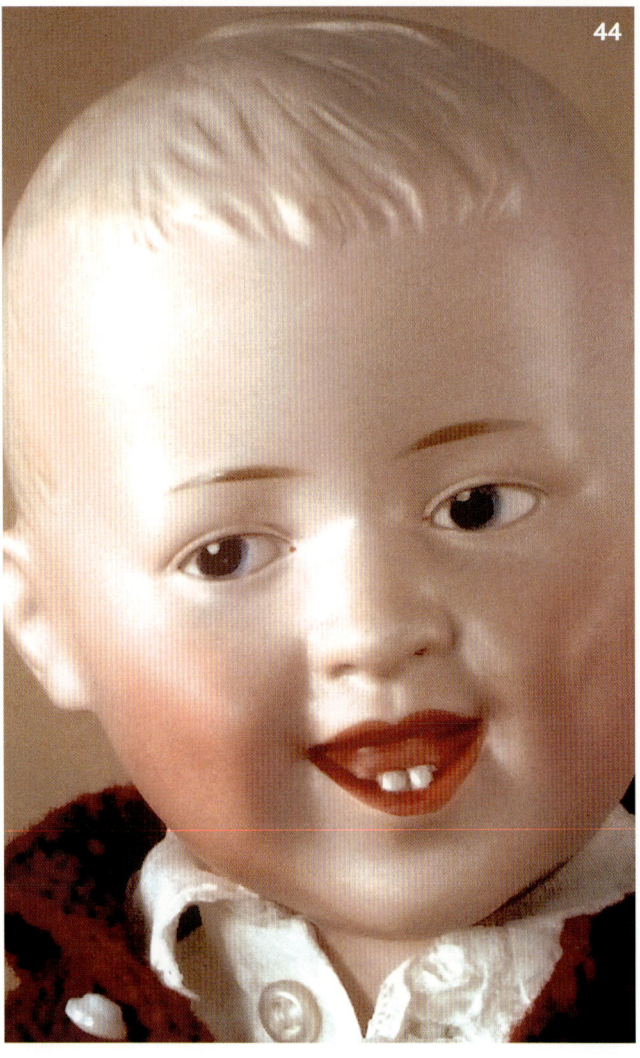

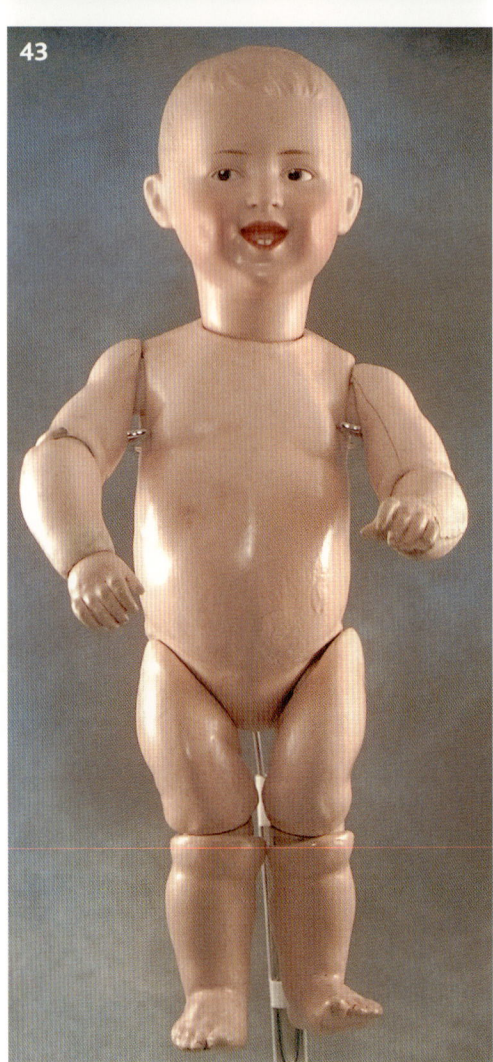

43. Bisque socket head by Gebrüder Heubach for the Adolf Wislizenus doll factory in Waltershausen; molded hair; single-stroke eyebrows; intaglio-painted eyes with white highlights; open/closed mouth with lower teeth; 16-inch doll; circa 1912; marked: **76sunburst**(mark)**04//DEP//7**. Note the unusual upper and lower limbs with molded fat wrinkles, typical of Wislizenus bodies. Beth Karp Collection. (Photo: Lee Krombholz)

44. A closer view of the bisque head in illustration 43 shows the well-modeled laughing mouth, molded tongue and typical Gebrüder Heubach white highlight in the top center of each painted eye. Beth Karp Collection. (Photo: Lee Krombholz)

290

Gebrüder Heubach Porcelain Factory

45. Bisque socket head by Gebrüder Heubach; wig; multi-stroke eyebrows; painted upper and lower eyelashes; glass sleep eyes; open/closed laughing mouth with lower molded teeth and tongue; 12-inch doll; circa 1912; marked: **5636//3sunburst**(mark)**DEP//Germany**. Beth Karp Collection. (Photo: Lee Krombholz)

46. Three bisque socket heads by Gebrüder Heubach show the range of facial expressions created by the talented factory artists and modelers. The tallest standing 14-inch boy has single-stroke wavy eyebrows; intaglio eyes with white highlights; open/closed mouth; and is marked: **square**(mark)**//Germany**. The standing 10-inch doll in red sweater has single-stroke eyebrows; squinting-intaglio eyes with white highlights; closed mouth; and is marked: **sunburst**(mark)**//Germany**. The seated circa-1912 12-inch boy has single-stroke eyebrows; intaglio side-glancing eyes; open/closed laughing mouth; upper and lower teeth and molded tongue. Beth Karp Collection. (Photo: Lee Krombholz)

47. Bisque socket head by Gebrüder Heubach; molded hair; single-stroke eyebrows; side-glancing intaglio-painted eyes with white highlights; open/closed laughing mouth with upper and lower teeth and molded tongue; 12-inch doll; circa 1912; marked: **DEP**(inside oval)**//square**(mark)**//6//8191//Germany**. This is the same doll that is shown seated in illustration 46. Beth Karp Collection. (Photo: Lee Krombholz)

291

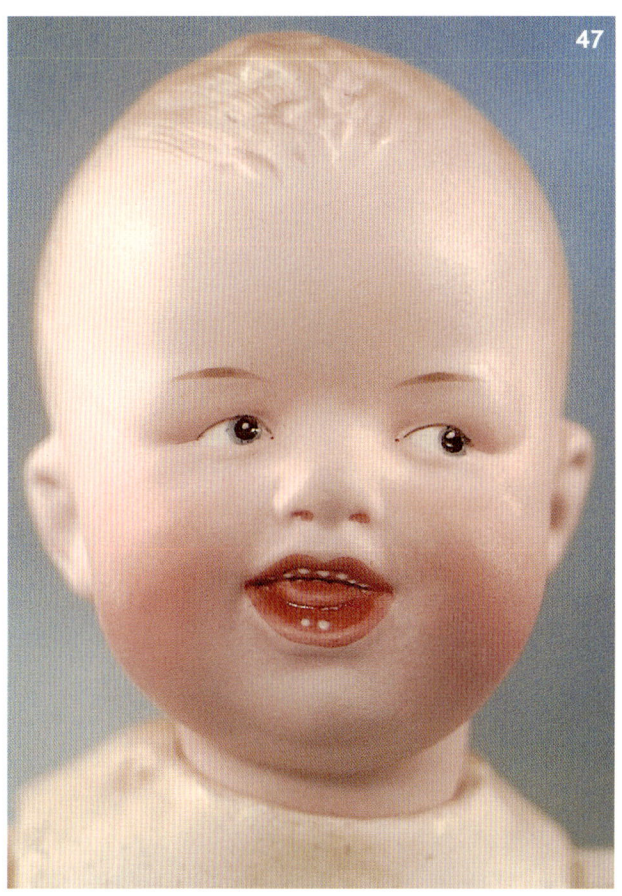

Chapter 5

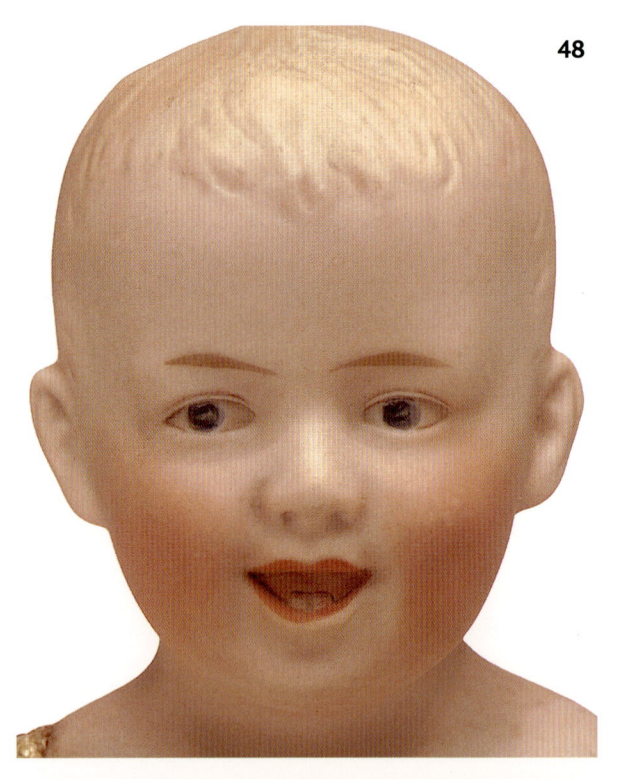

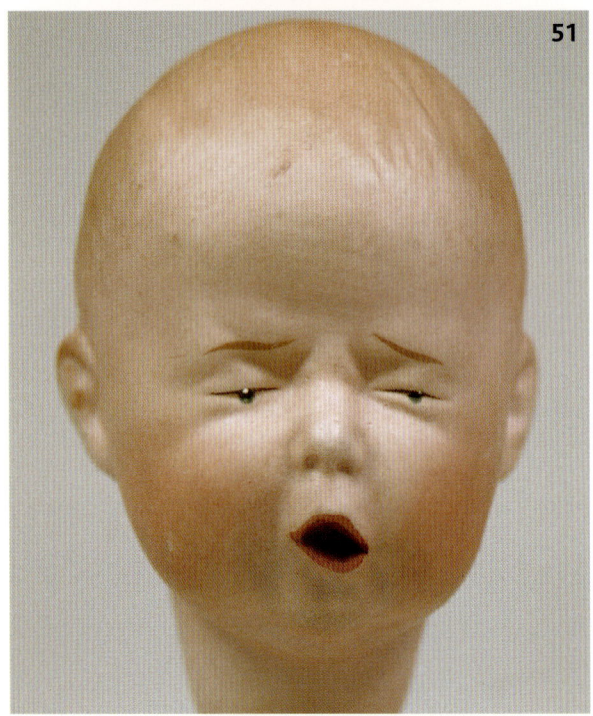

48. Bisque shoulder head by Gebrüder Heubach; molded hair; single-stroke eyebrows; intaglio-painted eyes; open/closed mouth with lower teeth and molded tongue; 11-inch doll; circa 1912; marked: **6897//Germany//sunburst**(mark). Susan Moore Collection. (Photo: John Cummings)

51. Bisque socket head by Gebrüder Heubach; molded hair; single-stroke eyebrows; molded upper and lower eyelids; squinting intaglio-painted eyes with white highlights; open/closed crying mouth; 3-inch head; circa 1912; marked: **77square**(mark)**61//Germany**. Courtesy Deutsches Spielzeugmuseum, Sonneberg. (Photo: Christiane Gräfnitz)

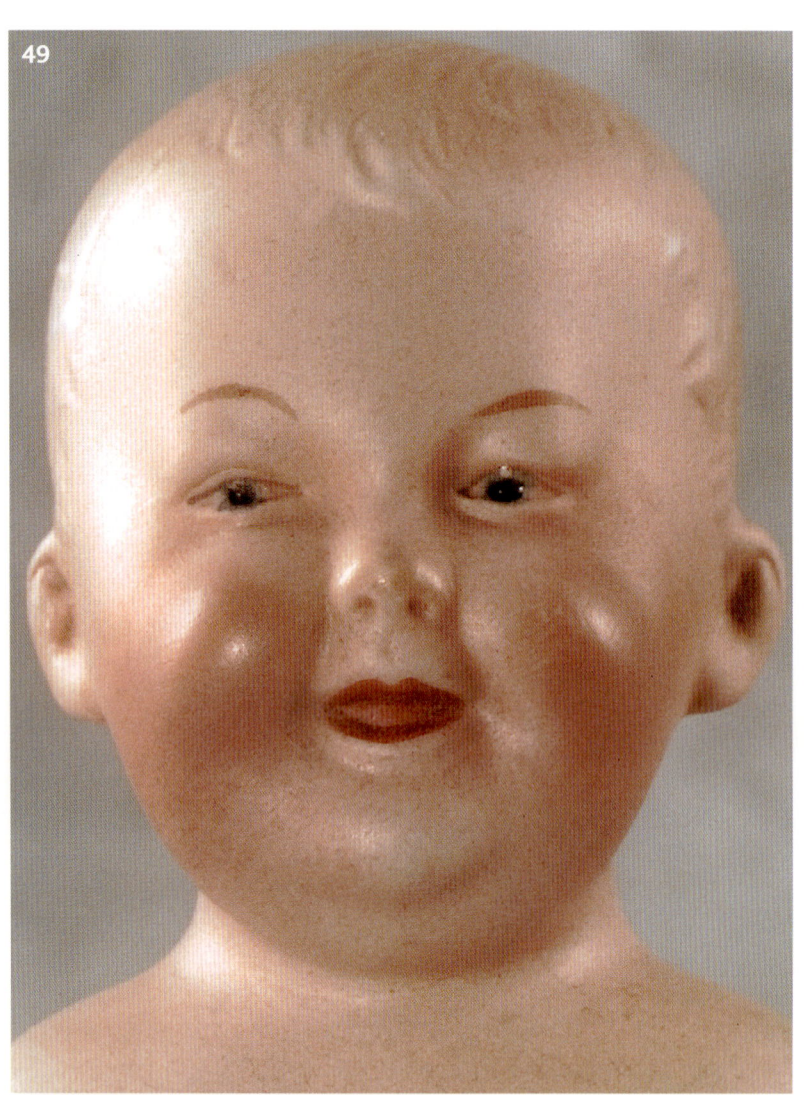

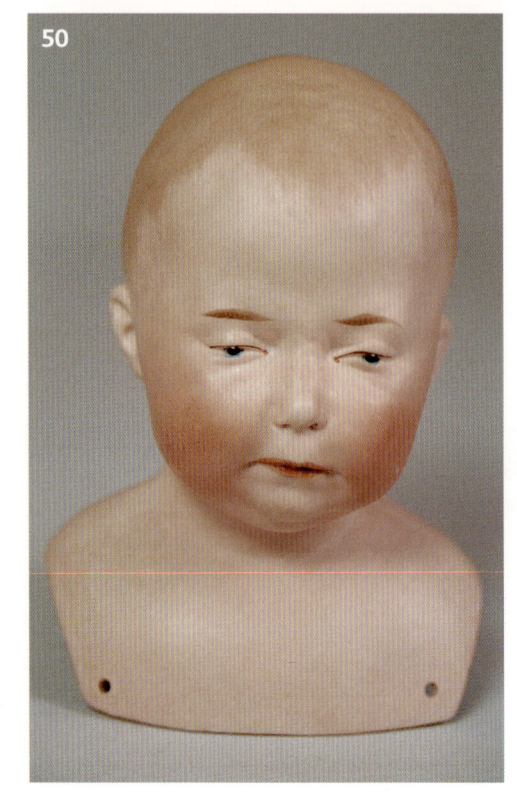

49. Bisque shoulder head by Gebrüder Heubach; molded hair; single-stroke eyebrows; intaglio-painted eyes with white highlights; open/closed laughing mouth with molded tongue; GM 1910; 12½-inch doll; marked: **2/0 D//sunburst**(mark)**//7644//Germany**. Beth Karp Collection. (Photo: Lee Krombholz)

50. Bisque shoulder head by Gebrüder Heubach with typical squared-off shoulder plate; molded hair; single-stroke eyebrows; molded upper and lower eyelids; intaglio-painted eyes; unusual open/closed mouth; 5½-inch shoulder head; circa 1912; marked: **6//sunburst**(mark)**//Germany**. Courtesy Deutsches Spielzeugmuseum, Sonneberg. (Photo: Christiane Gräfnitz)

Gebrüder Heubach Porcelain Factory

52. Bisque socket head by Gebrüder Heubach, so-called Winker; molded hair; single-stroke eyebrows; one large, open eye with painted upper eyelashes; one closed eye with painted upper eyelashes; closed mouth with lopsided smile; 2½-inch head; circa 1912; marked: **6/0//square**(mark)**//Germany**. Beth Karp Collection. (Photo: Lee Krombholz)

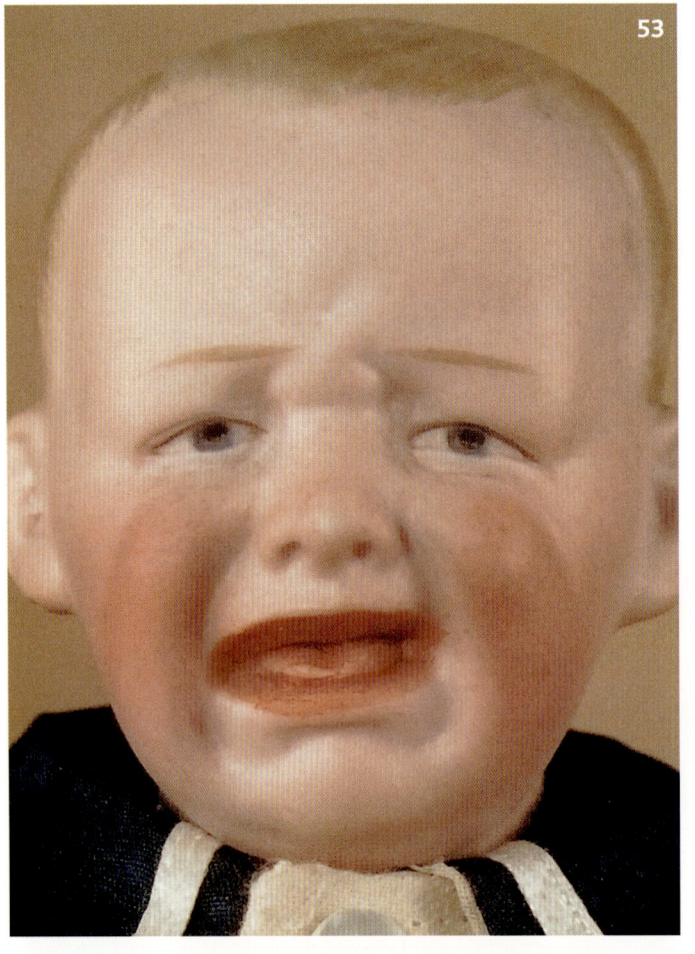

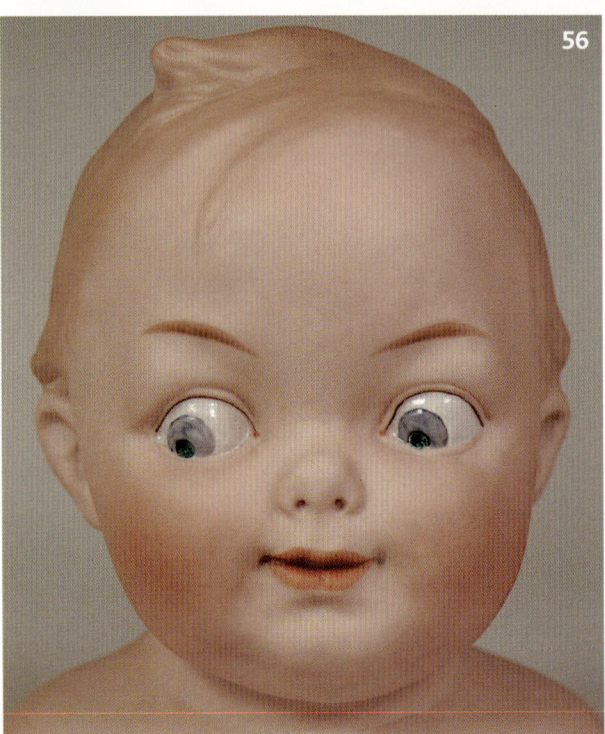

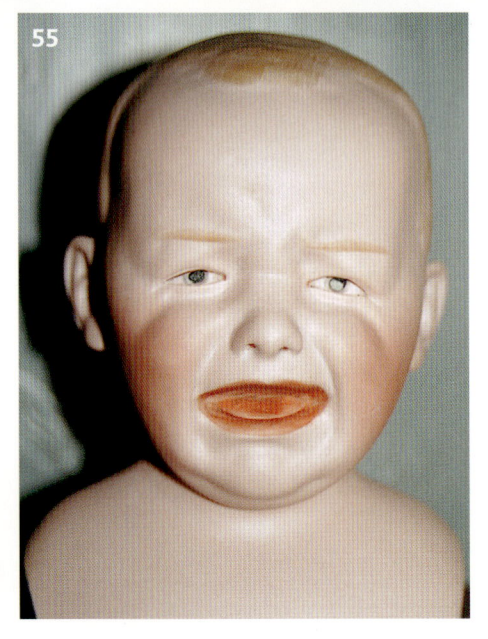

Chapter 5

53. This Gebrüder Heubach shoulder head was made from a master mold similar to the one used to make the shoulder head in illustration 55. A closer view of this head shows the expressive face, achieved through skilled factory facial modeling. This head must have been one of the first heads molded in the plaster working mold. Beth Karp Collection. (Photo: Lee Krombholz)

54. Two bisque socket heads by Gebrüder Heubach, on two different bodies, so-called Whistlers; molded hair; single-stroke eyebrows; side-glancing intaglio-painted eyes with white highlights; open/closed pursed mouths; sound achieved by pressing bellows voice box in center of body; 12- and 13-inch dolls; circa 1914; each marked: **8774//square**(mark)**//Germany**. Beth Karp Collection. (Photo: Gregg Smith)

55. Bisque shoulder head by Gebrüder Heubach, so-called Screamer; molded hair; single-stroke eyebrows; squinting intaglio-painted eyes; crying open/closed mouth with realistic molded tongue; 6-inch shoulder head; circa 1912; marked: **8//Germany//7634**. Courtesy Museum Schloss Tenneberg, Waltershausen. (Photo: Christiane Gräfnitz)

56. Bisque shoulder-head googly by Gebrüder Heubach; molded hair; two-tone single-stroke eyebrows; large, downward-glancing, bulging painted eyes; open/closed smiling mouth; 6½-inch shoulder head; circa 1914; marked: **8590//square**(mark)**//Germany**. Courtesy Deutsches Spielzeugmuseum, Sonneberg. (Photo: Christiane Gräfnitz)

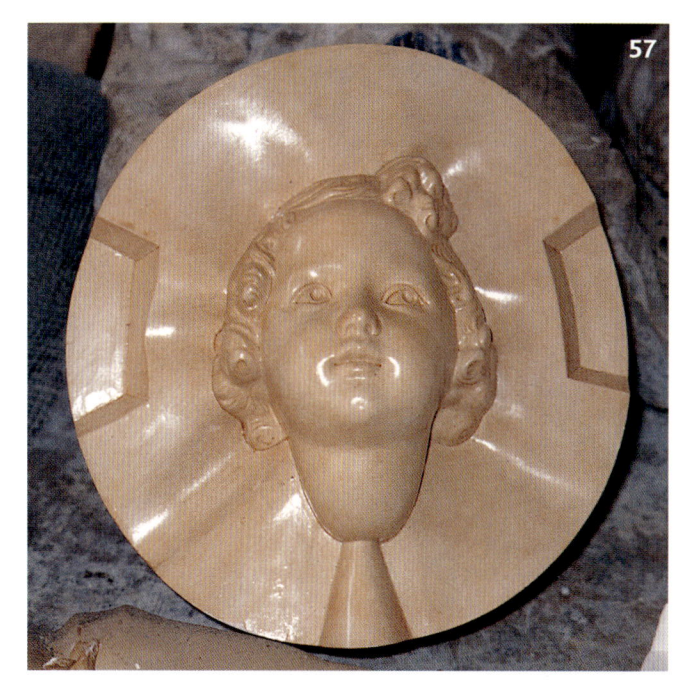

Gebrüder Heubach Porcelain Factory

57. This Gebrüder Heubach master mold features a girl with molded hair and a large hair ribbon. Master molds were heavily shellacked so that multiple working molds could be made from each master mold. Roland Schlegel Collection. (Photo: Mary Krombholz)

58. This bisque socket head by Gebrüder Heubach was made from a master mold identical to the one used to make the head pictured in illustration 59. This view of the head shows the typical factory white highlights on the top center of each eye. Susan Moore Collection. (Photo: John Cummings)

59. Bisque socket head by Gebrüder Heubach; molded hair and bonnet; single-stroke eyebrows; intaglio-painted eyes with white highlights; open/closed mouth with upper teeth and molded tongue; 10-inch doll; circa 1914; marked: **8649// square**(mark). Courtesy Museum Schloss Tenneberg, Waltershausen. (Photo: Christiane Gräfnitz)

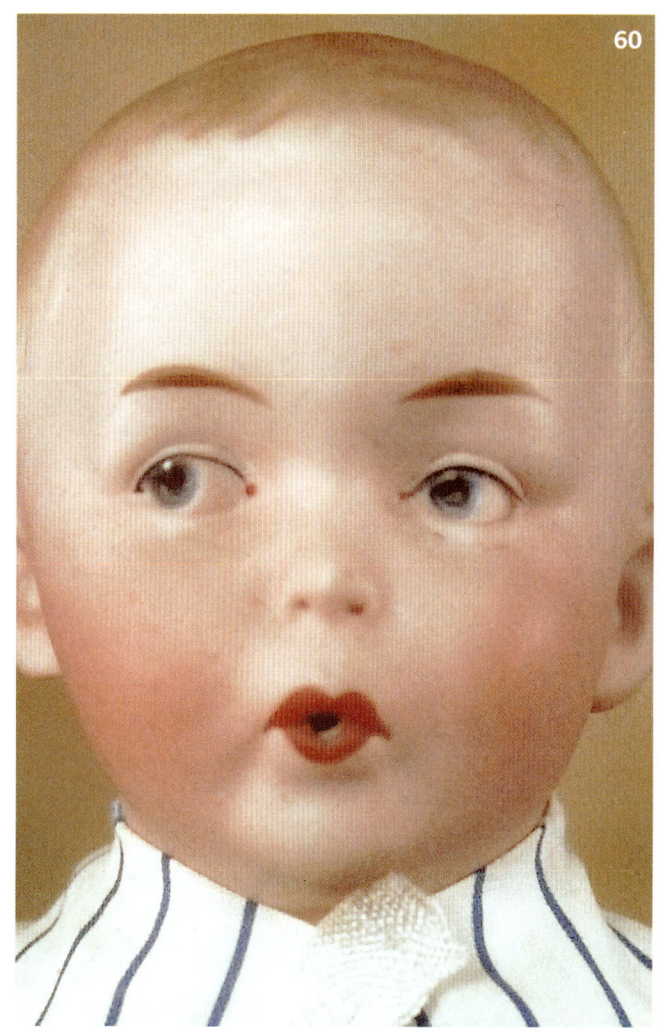

60. A closer view of the doll on the left in illustration 54 shows the pursed lips and hole in the center of the mouth, which gives the illusion that sound comes out of the mouth. This mold number was also used for the so-called Smoker, which had a porcelain cigarette in the mouth. Beth Karp Collection. (Photo: Lee Krombholz)

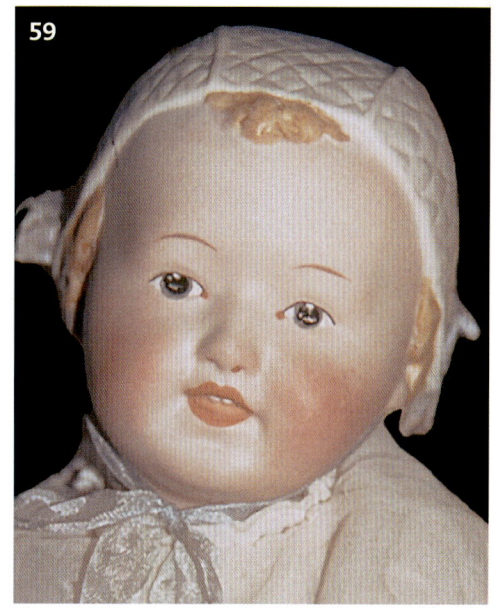

Chapter 5

61. Bisque socket head by Gebrüder Heubach; molded hair with molded ribbon; single-stroke eyebrows; molded upper eyelids; side-glancing intaglio-painted eyes with white highlights; open/closed mouth with molded tongue; 17-inch doll; circa 1912; marked: **4//77square**(mark) **64//Germany**. Susan Moore Collection. (Photo: John Cummings)

Gebrüder Heubach Porcelain Factory

62. Coquette bisque socket head by Gebrüder Heubach; molded hair with molded turquoise ribbon and bow; two-toned single-stroke eyebrows; side-glancing intaglio-painted eyes with white highlights; open/closed smiling mouth with upper teeth; 14-inch doll; circa 1912; marked: **77square**(mark)**88//Germany**. Beth Karp Collection. (Photo: Gregg Smith)

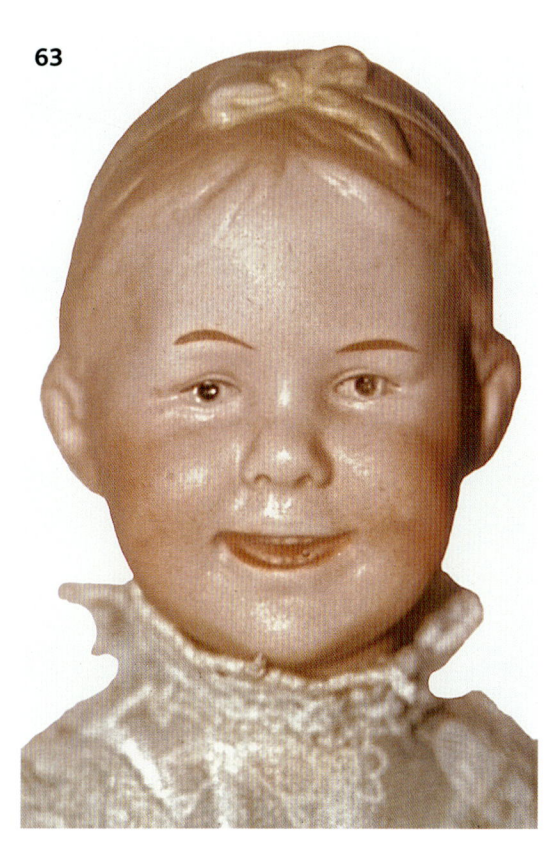

63. Bisque socket head by Gebrüder Heubach; molded hair and ribbon; single-stroke eyebrows; intaglio-painted eyes with while highlights; open/closed laughing mouth with upper and lower molded teeth and tongue; 10¼-inch doll; circa 1912; marked: **8050//square**(mark)**//Germany**. Historisches Coburger Puppenmuseum/Lossnitzer Collection. (Photo: Christiane Gräfnitz)

64. Bisque socket head Jubilee Doll by Gebrüder Heubach for the Emil Bauersachs doll factory in Sonneberg; original clothing; molded hair with large molded ribbon; single-stroke eyebrows; upper molded eyelids that cover half of the eye socket; half-closed intaglio-painted eyes; closed mouth; 14-inch doll; circa 1913; marked: **7865//square**(mark). This bisque head was one of a group of 7865 mold number heads commissioned by the Bauersachs doll factory to commemorate the one-hundredth anniversary of German liberation from French subjugation. Courtesy Deutsches Spielzeugmuseum, Sonneberg. (Photo: Christiane Gräfnitz)

65. Bisque shoulder head by Gebrüder Heubach; molded hair with hole between curls to hold a ribbon; single-stroke eyebrows; intaglio-painted eyes with white highlights; open/closed mouth; 7-inch shoulder head; unmarked. Courtesy Deutsches Spielzeugmuseum, Sonneberg. (Photo: Christiane Gräfnitz)

Chapter 5

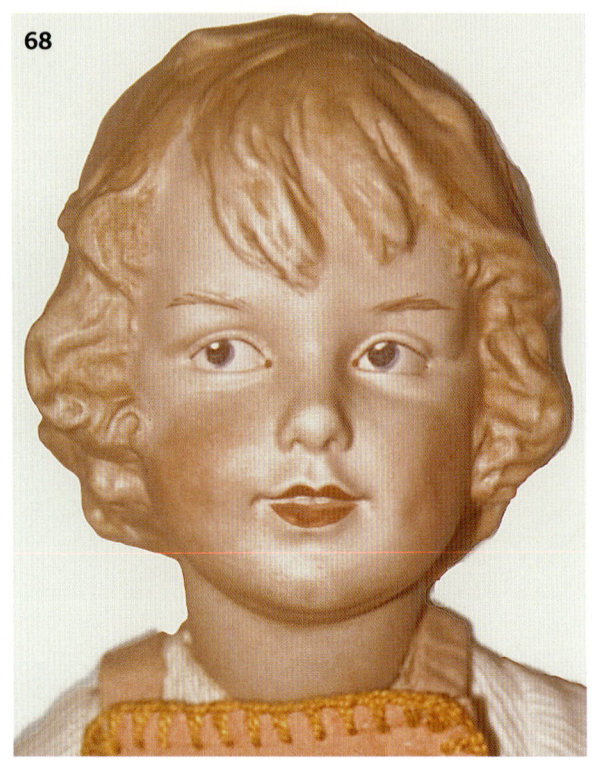

66. Coquette bisque shoulder head by Gebrüder Heubach; molded hair with molded turquoise ribbon and bow; single-stroke eyebrows; side-glancing intaglio-painted eyes with white highlights; open/closed smiling mouth with upper teeth; 11-inch doll; circa 1912; marked: **78square**(mark)**50//Germany**. This is the shoulder-head version of socket head mold number 7788. Beth Karp Collection. (Photo: Lee Krombholz)

67. Two 8-inch all-bisque unmarked Coquettes by Gebrüder Heubach; molded hair with turquoise headbands; intaglio-painted eyes with tiny white highlights; open/closed smiling mouths. The undressed example has the typical Coquette hands, with second and third fingers molded together. The dressed example, with the dark-tan molded shoes, was part of a group of three dolls marketed by Gebrüder Heubach in 1913 as *Unsere Goldigen Drei* (Our Golden Three). The Heubach advertisement read: "New artistically created bisque dolls designed by B. Zitzman, dressed in tasteful clothing from the best modern fabrics. Size: 8 inches tall. Available in every specialty store. If not available we will ship the three dolls directly to your house for 6 Marks against cash on delivery." A doll with short boyish hair and a doll with a pageboy hairstyle were included in the original boxed group of three dolls. Author's Collection. (Photo: Red Kite Studio)

68. Bisque socket head by Gebrüder Heubach; molded hair; multi-stroke eyebrows; intaglio-painted eyes with white highlights; open/closed mouth with upper teeth and tongue; cheek and chin dimples; 19¼-inch doll; circa 1912: marked: **7956//square**(mark). Coburg Historisches Coburger Puppenmuseum/Lossnitzer Collection. (Photo: Christiane Gräfnitz)

298

Gebrüder Heubach Porcelain Factory

69. These three unmarked Gebrüder Heubach all-bisque dolls were made in the 1920s as part of the extended marketing of the *Unsere Goldigen Drei* (Our Golden Three) dolls. A 1920 Gebruder Heubach catalog lists Size 1 as 6 inches and Size 2 as 8-8½-inch dolls. Unlike the 1913 Our Golden Three, the 1920s dolls were also sold singly. The 8-inch Coquette on the left has a turquoise headband without bow; one-stroke eyebrows; side-glancing eyes with white highlights; and a closed mouth. The 6-inch doll in the center has single-stroke eyebrows; intaglio-painted eyes; and a closed mouth. The 8-inch doll on the right has single-stroke eyebrows; intaglio-painted eyes; and a closed mouth. All three dolls have molded one-strap shoes with molded bows painted dark tan, typical of Our Golden Three dolls. Beth Karp Collection. (Photo: Lee Krombholz)

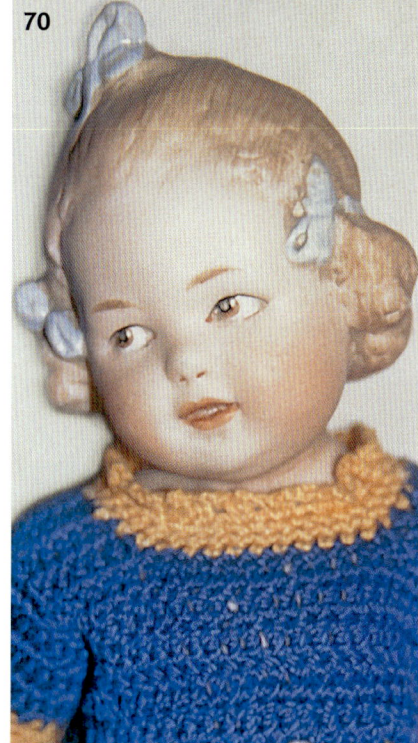

70. *Unsere Goldigen Drei* (Our Golden Three) all-bisque doll by Gebrüder Heubach; molded hair with three molded ribbons; jointed shoulders and slant hips; single-stroke eyebrows; side-glancing intaglio-painted eyes with white highlights; open/closed mouth with painted upper teeth; 9-inch doll; circa 1925; unmarked. This doll is also wearing dark-tan one-strap shoes with molded bows. Courtesy Historisches Coburger Puppenmuseum/Lossnitzer Collection. (Photo: Christiane Gräfnitz)

71. *Unsere Goldigen Drei* (Our Golden Three) Coquette all-bisque doll by Gebrüder Heubach; jointed shoulders and slant-hips; molded dark-tan one-strap shoes with molded bows; turquoise headband without bow; one-stroke eyebrows; side-glancing painted eyes with white highlights; closed mouth; circa 1920s; 8½-inch doll; unmarked. Courtesy Deutsches Spielzeugmuseum, Sonneberg. (Photo: Christiane Gräfnitz)

Chapter 5

72. *Unsere Goldigen Drei* (Our Golden Three) all-bisque doll by Gebrüder Heubach; molded hair with molded loop to hold ribbon; single-stroke eyebrows; side-glancing intaglio-painted eyes with white highlights; closed mouth; 8½-inch doll; unmarked. The museum's original inventory sheet dates the doll as 1924, and pictures the typical dark-tan one-strap shoes with molded bows. Deutsches Spielzeugmuseum, Sonneberg. (Photo: Christiane Gräfnitz)

73. All-bisque googly baby by Gebrüder Heubach; molded hair; single-stroke eyebrows; large, side-glancing painted eyes with white highlights; painted straight upper eyelashes; closed smiling mouth; 5-inch doll; circa 1912; unmarked. Hannelore Henze Collection. (Photo: Christiane Gräfnitz)

75. *Unsere Goldigen Drei* (Our Golden Three) all-bisque doll by Gebrüder Heubach; molded page-boy hairstyle with bangs; single-stroke eyebrows; side-glancing intaglio-painted eyes with white highlights; closed mouth; 8½-inch doll; unmarked. The original inventory sheet dates the doll as 1924, and pictures the typical dark-tan one-strap shoes with molded bows. Courtesy Deutsches Spielzeugmuseum, Sonneberg. (Photo: Christiane Gräfnitz)

74. This all-bisque Gebrüder Heubach doll has an especially expressive face. The head modeling and facial painting is often used on Heubach socket and shoulder head dolls, but is seldom seen on all-bisque dolls. Wig; multi-stroke eyebrows; painted upper and lower eyelashes; glass sleep eyes; open/closed mouth with lower teeth; 9-inch doll; unmarked. Beth Karp Collection. (Photo: Lee Krombholz)

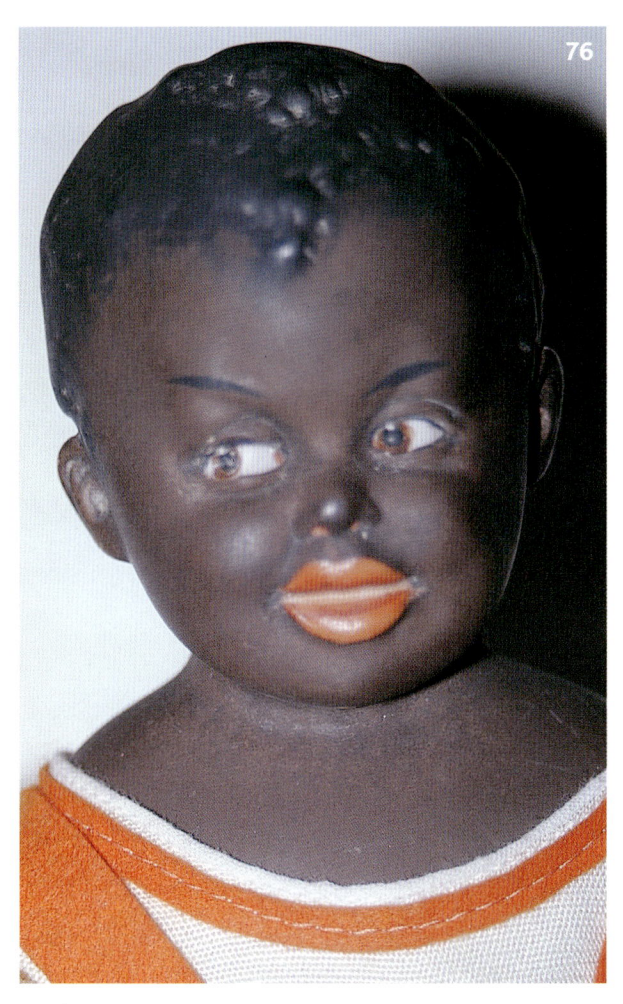

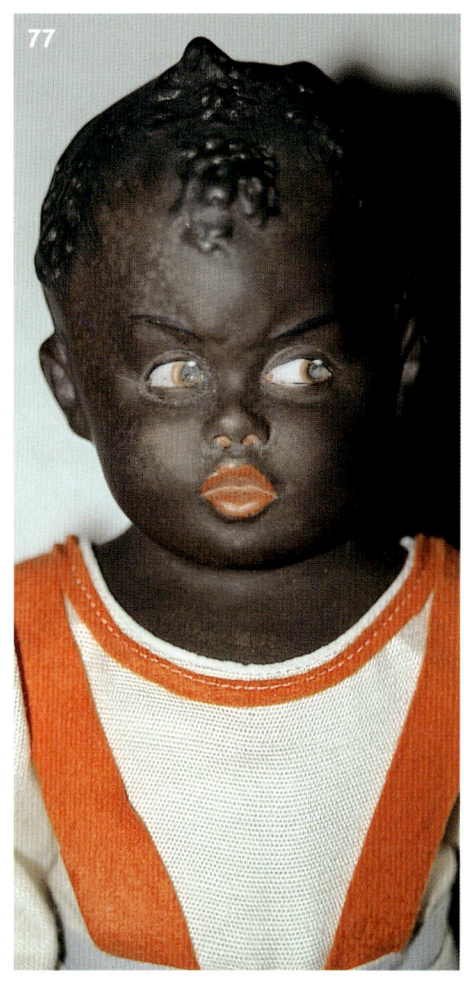

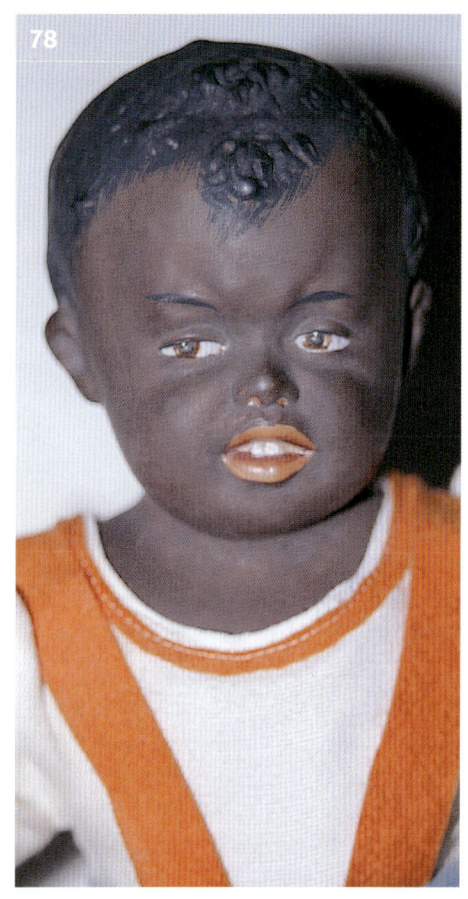

Gebrüder Heubach Porcelain Factory

76. Black bisque shoulder head by Gebrüder Heubach; molded hair; single-stroke eyebrows; side-glancing painted eyes; red painted nostril dots; open/closed mouth; 13½ inch doll; GM 1910; marked: **sunburst**(mark) **//7657//4**. (Photo: Courtesy Historisches Coburger Puppenmuseum/Lossnitzer Collection)

77. Black bisque shoulder head by Gebrüder Heubach; molded hair; single-stroke eyebrows; side-glancing painted eyes with white highlights; red painted nostril dots; open/closed mouth; 13¼-inch doll; GM 1910; marked: **sunburst**(mark) **//7659**. (Photo: Courtesy Historisches Coburger Puppenmuseum/Lossnitzer Collection)

78. Black bisque shoulder head by Gebrüder Heubach; molded hair; single-stroke eyebrows; molded upper eyelids; side-glancing painted eyes; open/closed mouth with lower teeth; 13¾-inch doll; GM 1910; marked: **sunburst**(mark)**//7658**. (Photo: Courtesy Historisches Coburger Puppenmuseum/Lossnitzer Collection)

79. Solid bisque shoulder head by Gebrüder Heubach, without a shoulder-plate indentation; open crown with original hat; light-orange, single-stroke molded eyebrows; barely visible squinting eyes with white highlights; open/closed screaming mouth with tongue and painted upper and lower teeth; 13½-inch doll; marked: **square**(mark)**//Germany**. This doll head may have been made with the solid shoulder plate for use as a paperweight. Beth Karp Collection. (Photo: Lee Krombholz)

Part Two
CHAPTER 6

Hertwig & Co. Porcelain Factory

1. This old beehive kiln smokestack was torn down in 2004, along with all but one of the Hertwig factory buildings. The remaining yellow-brick building was once used by the artists and modelers who designed and sculpted doll-related porcelain products for the factory. (Photo: Mary Krombholz)

The buildings that once made up the large Hertwig & Co. porcelain factory in Katzhütte have been torn down, with one exception: a two-story building that was once used as a studio for the factory's artists and modelers. The original factory was founded in 1566 and became the property of the ruling Duke in 1821. The earliest buildings in the large factory complex were once used as a smelting factory to separate the metal contained in iron ore. The economy of the area was extremely poor at this time. Christoph Hertwig, his brother-in-law Benjamin Beyermann and Carl Birkner bought the property and existing buildings from the ruling Duke on January 18, 1864. Under their leadership, within twenty-five years the Hertwig & Co. porcelain factory became the largest employer in the Schwarza valley.

The town of Katzhütte is only a few miles from Sonneberg. An article in the Cieshiks' March 1998 *Puppenmagazin* offers the following description of the town in 1862: "Katzhütte was comprised up of 129 homes, 6 barns, one church, a community center, nine smelting houses, one grinding mill and four cutting mills. The homes are mainly shingled huts, with little windows. Some even look like they are falling down and poor. A lot of men that work in the forest during the summer make little porcelain figures for the 'Scheiber' factory in the winter." (The neighboring villages of Scheibe and Alsbach are located a short distance from Katzhütte. The words "Scheiber factory" in the sentence above refers to the A.W. Fr. Kister porcelain factory, founded in 1835 in Sheibe-Alsbach).

The Cieshiks' description of the early changes to the porcelain factory continues: "Carl Birkner was the technical person and he started remodeling and adding to the old factory buildings. The old hammering works building was turned into a masse and gypsum mill. Next to it was the firing house with two kilns and right next to that was the painting building. In addition to those, there were several offices, a gypsum boiling area, a modeling shack and lots of room for stables and wagons."

A very important advertisement for the Leipzig Fair appeared in the Leipzig daily newspaper on April 25, 1865, which documents the manufacture of doll heads. "Hertwig

2. This photograph shows the factory grounds as they appeared following the demolition of the buildings. The graded earth hides tons of bisque-head shards that are buried below the surface. (Photo: Roland Schlegel)

& Co., porcelain factory from Katzhütte in Thuringia, display rooms with luxury and fantasy items, bathing children, doll heads, etc." This substantiates the production of doll heads the year after the Hertwig porcelain factory was founded.

In 1865 Christoph's son Ernst Hertwig became the manager of the factory at the age of eighteen. Ernst's leadership at such a young age caused problems with some of the employees and also caused co-owner Carl Birkner to sell his share of the company to Christoph Hertwig and Christoph's brother-in-law Benjamin Beyermann. Further difficulties arose when a large fire destroyed Beyermann's property in 1868. Despondent because his insurance did not cover his loss from the fire, Beyermann killed himself.

The following years were profitable years for the porcelain factory because a railroad line connected Katzhütte with many areas of Germany. From the 1870s until the 1940s, glazed-porcelain shoulder heads mounted on cloth bodies (Nanking dolls) led the list of dolls produced. In 1890 the factory employed three hundred factory workers and six hundred home workers. Several factors influenced the number of dolls made in the Hertwig porcelain factory, including the availability of workers. The thousands of people living in and around Katzhütte were unable to find work except as home or factory workers for the Hertwig porcelain factory once mining was no longer a viable industry. They played a major part in the production of Hertwig porcelain dolls from the beginning of doll-related production in 1865. Home workers in the nearby villages of Fehrenbach, Goldisthal, Grossbreitenbach, Heubach, Masserberg, Mellenbach, Meuselbach, Oelze, Schnett and Waffenrod did everything from sewing and stuffing bodies to dressing the finished dolls.

Ernst Hertwig led the company throughout the 1870s, until he developed rheumatism and moved to Egypt. This forced his father Christoph, who had assumed the daily operation of the factory, to hire an assistant named August Fischbach. On March 23, 1879, Ernst Hertwig died. Christoph Hertwig led the company until his death in 1886, when his sons Carl and Friedrich became owners of the porcelain factory. In the commercial register listings, Fritz Hertwig is listed as the owner in 1913. Fritz, Ernst F. and Hans Hertwig were listed as owners in 1920, at which time the factory employed five hundred people. Fritz Hertwig died in 1930, and as a result, Ernst F. and Hans became co-owners. The factory continued to produce doll-related porcelain products into the 1940s.

The success or failure of a porcelain factory often depended on whether it could fill large orders on time. To do this, porcelain factories like the Hertwig porcelain factory, operated day and night during the months before Christmas in order to produce an abundance of dolls to have on hand when orders increased. Inexpensive all-bisque Hertwig character dolls were sold at a variety of American stores like F.&W. Woolworth, the S.S. Kresge Company and Sears, Roebuck & Co. Hertwig all-bisque dolls were also sold at candy and hardware stores throughout the United States.

The majority of Thuringian doll-related porcelain products came from large, well-run factories that turned out a wide spectrum of products in huge kilns. The kilns were expensive to fire and operate in a cost-effective way, so every shelf in the kiln had to be carefully filled. It is evident that small all-bisque dolls offered a way to keep the kilns full at all times, regardless of the number of current orders. They filled the spaces between larger pieces, and if there were not enough orders of large pieces to fill the kilns, the smaller all-bisque products made up the difference. Also, the porcelain slip from which

Chapter 6

3. Hundreds of 1914 Hertwig & Co. porcelain factory employees stand in front of one of the many buildings that once made up the original porcelain factory site in Katzhütte, Thuringia. (Photo: Courtesy Katzhütte Town Museum)

the larger bisque heads were poured was mixed in large quantities, often resulting in an oversupply, which was then used to fill smaller plaster molds. The Hertwig factory workers filled the kilns daily with a variety of doll-related articles.

Methods of marketing also determined the success of a doll or porcelain factory. Even during the years Thuringian doll and toy making was carried out by the trade unions alone, a middleman or selling agent controlled the marketing of goods. The Butler Brothers importing company was by far the largest distributor of Hertwig doll-related porcelain products. To supplement the orders taken by middlemen, doll and porcelain factories displayed their current products at trade fairs like those held twice a year in Leipzig, Germany. The Leipzig Spring Fair opened the Sunday before Easter each year and lasted for three weeks. The Leipzig Fall Fair opened the last Sunday in August and also lasted three weeks.

The large number of orders destined for the United States and other foreign countries required the production of cardboard boxes and wooden crates. The Hertwig porcelain factory made all of their cardboard boxes and wooden crates on the factory site from the 1870s on. As orders increased, so did the need for more factory space to make the boxes and crates. A new factory building was constructed in 1873 for the sole purpose of producing cardboard boxes and wooden shipping crates.

The book *Sonneberg Stories of Dolls, Slate Pencils and Cuckoo Whistles* includes the oral history of a box maker. Sonneberg doll factories often hired young workers who served as apprentices to learn a particular dollmaking trade. When these workers became proficient in a specific type of work like box making, they looked for jobs in doll and/or porcelain factories located in the area, like the Hertwig porcelain factory. The son of a Sonneberg boxmaker explains the process of making boxes in a doll or porcelain factory.

> Boxmaking was a trained occupation. Mostly boys were trained for it in the doll factories, for the work required strength and space. Very few boxmakers work in the home workshops. After finishing school I began my apprenticeship in the Martin Eichhorn doll factory in Sonneberg. Here dolls were made and packed into cartons for shipping. We glued large carton panels with glue and colored paper. This work was called Kaschieren (to coat with paper).
>
> With special stamping machines we cut the outline of the carton from the panel. By notching and folding we joined the corners. With a large stapling machine and metal clips the suitable carton pieces were fastened together. For different sized dolls there were boxes of various sizes and types of cardboard. Cartons made for transport were of strong cardboard and not coated with paper. To attract the attention of little doll-mommies, thinner cardboard boxes were often brightly colored on the outside. For valuable, expensive dolls there was suitable and valuable packaging, lined with lace or even silk.
>
> When we had the cartons for an order appropriately finished, we took them to the finishing department of our company. With a needle and thread, the women sewed the dolls firmly to the carton back. The stitching,

Hertwig & Co. Porcelain Factory

4. A group of original Hertwig & Co. porcelain factory sample boards are on display in the Sonneberg Doll Museum. This board, circa 1925, holds twenty-one dolls, including a row of dollhouse dolls with cloth bodies and bisque limbs. The realistic portrait-like heads and original clothing identify the family members and servants. Courtesy Dr. Christoph Hertwig and the Deutsches Spielzeugmuseum, Sonneberg. (Photo: Christiane Gräfnitz)

however, did not injure the doll's appearance. The doll had to be fastened securely enough that its sleep mechanism as well as its clothing and hairdo would remain intact during transport. For such a doll, on its way for weeks along to doll-mommies in England and America, was often reloaded and transported along bumpy streets.

The Hertwig porcelain factory continued to expand as sales increased. The Ciesliks published a very interesting article about the Hertwig factory in the March 1998 issue of their *Puppenmagazin*. The article was written in 1888 by the Berlin Export Bank. One important paragraph reads:

In addition to the work in the main building the company is manufacturing a great number of Nanking dolls in another building. The doll bodies are made from stuffed Nanking cotton fabric and have heads and limbs made from porcelain. They have three machines that punch out the fabric parts which are then sewn together and stuffed with saw meal. They punch out the torso, the upper arms and thighs and each machine punches out ten-dozen pieces of fabric at one time. The sewing and stuffing, etc. is done mostly at people's homes and done by about 600 people with about 45 sewing machines. In the summer time, these people make about 1000 to 1200 dozen and in winter

Chapter 6

about 2,000 dozen dolls each day. Most people in Katzhütte make their money working for the doll industry. The Hertwig business also founded a health insurance for their workers. In addition, the company opened a public pool for summer tourists and the residents of the area.

There is also a very distressing report about the factory in the Ciesliks' March 1998 article, in which they note that: "In the 1970s and 1980s, the GDR regime was trying hard to get their hands on western currency."

In the 1980s, the "art robbers" came dressed in black leather jackets without warning. They locked down the area and first viewed the inventory. The porcelain archives were immense. You could compare it to the Steiff archives in Giengen. Every product that had ever been made was neatly organized and kept. It was the perfect loot for the art robbers who were backed by the regime's secret police. There were workers who spoke up and demanded that the most important items were to be given to the Sonneberg Museum. Their influence was so massive that even the Ministry for State Security gave in. Over 50% of the archives had already been looted when Hans Grauss, Director of the Deutches Spielzeugmuseum, Sonneberg picked out and took the "museum worthy" pieces. Those were not that many because Mr. Gauss did not have much time for his work – only a few hours. Mr. Gauss said the following about saving the sample boards for the Sonneberg Museum: "The material could be taken over just like it had been in the sample room at the factory – on sample cards or mounted on samples boxes or in its original box." The plundering of the archives took place for almost ten years.

Many of the original Hertwig sample boards in the Sonneberg Doll Museum hold all-bisque dolls. Attributing a maker to Thuringian all-bisque dolls is difficult because so few dolls are marked. Fortunately we can positively identify a large number of Hertwig all-bisque character dolls because they are still tied to their original sample boards and are on permanent display in the Sonneberg Doll and Toy Museum. They are on loan to the museum from Dr. Christoph Hertwig and Frau Sophie Berlinger. Christoph Hertwig inherited his sample boards from his father, Ernst Friedrich Hertwig. Sophie Berlinger inherited her sample boards from her father, Hans Hertwig.

The dolls, dressed and undressed, are still securely tied to each board. Some of the dolls are individually boxed, and the boxes are tied to the boards. Several all-bisque babies are in original baskets, and they are also tied to the boards. There are sturdy little boy dolls wearing shirts and dolls with molded

5. The Sonneberg branch of the American importing company Butler Brothers, founded in 1877, was still acting as a middleman between porcelain factories and retail stores in the 1930s. Butler Brothers was the main distributor of the doll-related products of the Hertwig & Co. porcelain factory. (Photo: Mary Krombholz)

clothing. Headbands are featured on a number of molded-hair dolls. Nine all-bisque dollhouse dolls fill one row of a sample board.

One of the most appealing groups of all-bisque character dolls, still tied to an original sample boards, are the "flower" girls. Ten of these dolls, wearing identical outfits, are tied to one board. They range in size from approximately eight inches down to two inches. The modeling is different depending on the size of the doll. Each doll has a molded-flower wreath around her hair, painted in a variety of bright colors. The painted flowers are shaded and quite detailed on the larger dolls. The flowers on the wreaths of the smaller dolls are solid colors with a contrasting center color.

Molded hats change the appearance of many of the all-bisque sample board dolls. There are pointed hats with pom-poms, triangular hats and big hats with hatbands that almost cover the faces. The triangular hat on one doll is a separate accessory, while a molded shoulder strap and dagger are part of the original mold on another all-bisque doll.

The Hertwig & Co. porcelain factory made a large variety of all-bisque character dolls in molded clothing, often dressed in sailor suits. The legs are fixed, while the arms are wire-jointed. The molded hair is generally blonde, and the sailor suits are painted in various shades of blue trimmed in white. Genevieve Angione describes the Hertwig sailors with molded clothing in her book titled *All-Bisque & Half-Bisque Dolls*. Identical dolls are described and pictured in the Fall 1908 *Butler Brothers Wholesale Catalog*. The price for a dozen in the 4½-inch size was forty-one cents.

Another group of all-bisque dolls pictured in the Butler Brothers Catalog can be described as the "pigeon-toed" dolls. The toes turn slightly inward, allowing the dolls to stand eas-

Hertwig & Co. Porcelain Factory

6. Three boxed all-bisque character dolls are still tied to the top row of the sample board in illustration 4. They wear original crocheted sweaters and socks made by home workers. Courtesy Dr. Christoph Hertwig and the Deutsches Spielzeugmuseum, Sonneberg. (Photo: Christiane Gräfnitz)

7. Three all-bisque dolls, tied to the bottom row of the sample board pictured in illustration 4, wear molded clothing. The two dolls dressed in sailor suits were advertised in a 1908 Butler Brothers Fall Wholesale Catalog. The dolls were described as follows: "Sailor Boy Bisque Dolls. Big Value – 5 and 10 cents. F 4072 – 4 inches. Flesh-tinted faces, hands and legs, painted features and hair, white costume and hat, blue painted trimmings, shoes and socks. 1 dozen in box. Per dozen, 41 cents." Courtesy Dr. Christoph Hertwig and the Deutsches Spielzeugmuseum, Sonneberg. (Photo: Christiane Gräfnitz)

8. A group of Hertwig all-bisque dolls with molded clothing, 3½ to 6 inches tall, illustrate the variety of dolls sold by the Butler Brothers Company. The same shades of blue paint were used for many years to trim the molded clothing and hats worn by Hertwig all-bisque dolls. Author's Collection. (Photo: Gregg Smith)

Chapter 6

ily without support. A group of these dolls is also pictured on the sample boards in the Sonneberg Doll Museum. Ten examples are pictured on page 302 in *All-Bisque & Half-Bisque Dolls*. Angione describes the pre-colored all-bisque dolls as follows: "These dolls are listed in the December 1925 *Butler Brothers Wholesale Catalog*. They cost 84 cents a dozen in the 4½-inch size." Angione also describes the pigeon-toed dolls with clothes in the 3¾-inch size: "Boys and girls, 3¾-inches tall are also listed at $1.80 a dozen at the wholesale price, with two-color fancy costumes and hats. The costumes are made of cloth and braid or ribbon rather than being molded on the dolls."

Hertwig all-bisque character dolls were made in a variety of sizes and featured many different molded details. The girls often had molded hair ribbons or a hole in the molded hairstyle capable of holding a silk ribbon. Many of these pink pre-tinted all-bisque dolls have a very distinctive identification feature: The eyebrows are painted with an upward stroke, creating a surprised look on each tiny face. The dolls were also offered in mesh bathing suits as well as other clothing styles.

Two other interesting character dolls on the sample boards are a Hertwig Kewpie dressed in a simple dress and a Snow Baby. A Hertwig Snow Baby is pictured on page 228 of *All-Bisque & Half-Bisque Dolls* and described as follows.

> Unmarked, 5 inches tall, hip and shoulder-jointed with hard wire, this is an excellent Snow Baby. It has a fine, white grog finish which is not sharp or unpleasant to the touch. The suit is molded to the figure like a fuzzy snowsuit, the peaked cap is quite thick, and the peak, the edge of the hood and the tops of the shoes are lightly glazed. The complexion tinting is bright and glossy like a child's while playing outside in winter, the deeply molded mouth is painted in two sections, and there are dimples in the cheeks." Hertwig sales catalogs listed Snow Babies as "winter sports figures."

In his book *Marks on German, Bohemian & Austrian Porcelain, 1710 to the Present*, Robert E. Roentgen provides the following information about the Hertwig & Co. porcelain factory: "Hertwig & Co. Porcelain Factory, Ernst F. and Hans Hertwig, 1864 – 1958, gift articles, figurines, dolls and household earthenware. In 1958 nationalized as VEB Decorative Ceramics. After some attempts at privatization, the factory closed in 1990."

9. This original Hertwig & Co. sample board, circa 1925, holds twenty-three all-bisque dolls, including a boy with a removable three-corner hat, a Kewpie and a pair of hip-and shoulder-jointed character dolls. Many dolls on the board, wearing original hats and matching shirts, are jointed at the shoulders only. Courtesy Sophie Berlinger and the Deutsches Spielzeugmuseum, Sonneberg. (Photo: Christiane Gräfnitz)

10. The all-bisque boy wearing a molded dagger and removable tri-corner hat is tied to the upper left corner of the sample board in illustration 9. The shirt on the smaller doll is not hemmed because this type of sewing detail added to the cost of the dressed doll. Courtesy Sophie Berlinger and the Deutsches Spielzeugmuseum, Sonneberg. (Photo: Christiane Gräfnitz)

Hertwig & Co. Porcelain Factory

11. A Hertwig & Co. Kewpie is still tied to the bottom row of the sample board in illustration 9. Note the original Kewpie trademark heart marked: "KEWPIE//Germany" beneath the original gathered dress. Many Thuringian porcelain factories made Kewpies for American importer Geo. Borgfeldt & Co. because the initial producer, the Kestner & Co. porcelain factory, was unable to fill the large orders. Courtesy Sophie Berlinger and the Deutsches Spielzeugmuseum, Sonneberg. (Photo: Christiane Gräfnitz)

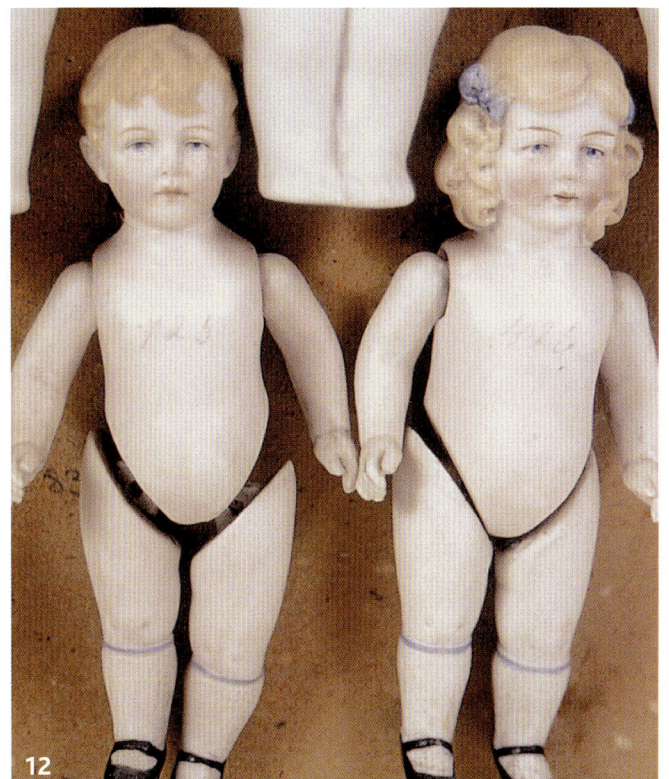

12. These two all-bisque character dolls are tied on the bottom row of the sample board pictured in illustration 9. Courtesy Sophie Berlinger and the Deutsches Spielzeugmuseum, Sonneberg. (Photo: Christiane Gräfnitz)

13. This is a 2-inch example of the all-bisque dolls wearing flower wreaths on the sample board pictured in illustration 14. The pigeon-toed Hertwig all-bisque dolls were made in a variety of sizes and feature different molded accessories, such as molded hair ribbons. The pre-tinted dolls often have a very distinctive facial feature; the eyebrows are painted with one small upward line, which creates a surprised facial expression. (See illustration 9 for many examples.) The molded and painted flower details are simplified on the wreaths of the smaller dolls. The pigeon-toed stance enables the doll to stand alone without support. Author's Collection. (Photo: Red Kite Studio)

Chapter 6

14. Twenty-seven all-bisque dressed dolls are tied to this Hertwig & Co. sample board. The ten dolls on the board wearing molded flower wreaths are dressed in identical dresses. This sample board is valuable because it provides information on the original clothing worn by a variety of all-bisque dolls. Two small all-bisque dolls (tied to the top left corner) are dressed in original crocheted clothing. This type of dressed miniature doll was previously attributed to the Carl Horn doll factory in Dresden but, in fact, the dolls were made at the Hertwig porcelain factory. They were dressed in a variety of crocheted outfits by the factory's home workers. Courtesy Dr. Christoph Hertwig and the Deutsches Spielzeugmuseum, Sonneberg. (Photo: Christiane Gräfnitz)

16. Twenty-four all-bisque dolls and babies, wearing original clothing, are still tied to this sample board in the Sonneberg museum. Two pairs of twins are in the top row. Many Hertwig doll-related porcelain products, like the doll on the far right of the bottom row, were placed in individual cardboard boxes made at the factory. Courtesy Dr. Christoph Hertwig and the Deutches Spielzeugmuseum, Sonneberg. (Photo: Christiane Gräfnitz)

17. This original sample board, circa 1925, holds sixteen wigged all-bisque dolls, wire-jointed at the shoulders only. The dolls on the top row are wearing molded shoes and socks. The chubby dolls on the lower two rows have typical factory pigeon-toed bare feet. Courtesy Dr. Christoph Hertwig and the Deutches Spielzeugmuseum, Sonneberg. (Photo: Christiane Gräfnitz)

18. This Hertwig & Co. family of dolls, from 4 to 7 inches tall, is made up of grandparents, parents and children. An unusual aspect of these dolls is the realistic upper torsos, which feature an array of colorful molded clothing, including ties and scarves. The dolls all have cloth lower torsos, arms and legs. The bisque hands have realistic finger delineation. Susan Moore Collection. (Photo: Frank McAloon)

15. A closer view of the doll's head in illustration 19 on page 312 shows the details of the molded hair and bonnet, the single-stroke wrap-around eyebrows, the blue side-glancing painted eyes, the heavily blushed cheeks and the slightly open/closed mouth. Susan Moore Collection. (Photo: John Cummings)

Hertwig & Co. Porcelain Factory

Chapter 6

19

19. This 12½-inch Hertwig & Co. parian-like shoulder-head doll has typical factory garter bows and molded high-heeled shoes that help identify cloth-bodied Nanking dolls made by this factory. The back shoulder plate is marked with the size number **2/0**. Susan Moore Collection. (Photo: John Cummings)

22. Two dolls representing young boys with decorated shoulder plates, 4 and 6 inches tall, wear white molded vests trimmed with large blue bows. The boy on the left is pictured on page 20 in the book *Hertwig & Co. Archives, 1890-1937*. The picture caption describes the doll as an "older boy," and notes that it was pictured in the 1914 Hertwig fiftieth anniversary catalog as model number 217, from the "better series." This boy was available in twenty sizes and cost twice as much as the parian-like bonnet heads advertised in the same catalog. The original Hertwig sample board that holds identical examples of these boys is dated 1928/30. Susan Moore Collection. (Photo: John Cummings)

23. Three Hertwig dolls, measuring from 4½ to 6½ inches in height, wear molded braids across the top of their heads. This type of hairstyle was popular in Germany for many years, and the molded vests and blouses are typical of the clothing young girls wore during this period of time. Susan Moore Collection. (Photo: John Cummings)

Hertwig & Co. Porcelain Factory

20. The 6- and 6½-inch grandparents pictured in illustration 18 wear molded head coverings and molded vests that end at the waist. Susan Moore Collection. (Photo: John Cummings)

21. The 6½-inch parents pictured in illustration 18 wear colorful molded clothing: suspenders and a tie on the mustached father and a white-knotted scarf over a green-molded vest on the mother. Susan Moore Collection. (Photo: John Cummings)

313

Chapter 6

24. These three Snow Babies are typical of the many thousands of Snow Babies made by the factory from the 1880s through the 1940s. The Snow Babies playing with the round porcelain-encrusted ball are 2½ inches tall. The 5-inch Snow Baby has wire-jointed arms and legs. The dolls were featured in many American doll and toy catalogs, including the 1914 Marshall Field catalog, in which they were described as "Alaska Tots." Author's Collection. (Photo: Gregg Smith)

25. A closer view of two of the Hertwig Snow Babies in illustration 24 shows the snowsuits, hats and typical factory facial painting. Author's Collection. (Photo: Gregg Smith)

Hertwig & Co. Porcelain Factory

26. Five Hertwig bonneted and hatted shoulder-head dolls, measuring approximately seven inches in height, are still tied inside an original cardboard box made at the porcelain factory. The layers of handmade detailed underwear, slips, and dresses made by Katzhütte area home workers differ slightly on each doll. The molded boots and bonnets vary in color, and coordinate with the clothing. Author's Collection. (Photo: Gregg Smith)

27. The German text on this 1911 photograph, which has been hand colored, translates as: "Making Boxes." The photograph shows the type of box-making equipment used at the Hertwig porcelain factory before and after World War I. The young boy in the foreground is operating a cardboard-box stapling machine, which inserts wire staples into the corners of the boxes. A spool of wire is attached to the left side of the machine. The boy on his right is operating a folding machine that folds the cardboard sheets into the sizes needed for finished boxes. The man standing at the table is cutting cardboard sheets into various sizes. A large pile of completed cardboard boxes can be seen in the right foreground. Author's Archival Paper Collection.

28. The Hertwig porcelain factory made a large variety of all-bisque dolls wearing flocked clothing. This 7-inch boy wears Native-American-styled clothing, including a large simulated feather headdress. Author's Collection. (Photo: Gregg Smith)

Chapter 6

30. The shipping department of the Hertwig porcelain factory was similar to the shipping department pictured in this 1936 photograph, which has been hand colored. The factory workers are placing cardboard boxes into large wooden shipping crates. Author's Archival Paper Collection.

31. These twelve 4-inch all-bisque Hertwig dolls are still tied in an original factory box. The brightly colored tissue paper lining the box is meant to attract the attention of buyers visiting the Hertwig sample rooms. The original label on top of the box indicates that the Hertwig porcelain factory sold this box of dolls to the Carl Horn doll factory in Dresden. The Hertwig factory also made miniature all-bisque dolls dressed in crocheted clothing for the Carl Horn doll factory. Author's Collection. (Photo: Gregg Smith)

Hertwig & Co. Porcelain Factory

29. By the late 1930s the packing and shipping departments in Thuringian porcelain factories had been modernized with improved types of equipment. This 1936 photograph, which has been hand colored, illustrates the finishing and packaging department typical of the Hertwig and other Thuringian porcelain factories in the 1930s. The large room is subdivided; the women on the left are assembling dolls and the women on the right are sewing the finished dolls into cardboard boxes. Stacks of long doll boxes are visible in each room. Author's Archival Paper Collection.

32. This 1911 photograph, which has been hand colored, bears the German words that translate as: "Finishing and Packing." The Hertwig porcelain factory made cardboard boxes and wooden shipping crates on the factory site from the 1870s on. In 1873 a new factory building was constructed to provide more space for the construction of boxes and crates. In this photograph, the seated woman on the left is attaching a wig to a doll's head. The large wooden box on her left holds wigged dolls, while the box behind her holds dolls waiting for wigs. A large pile of trademarked cardboard boxes are stacked next to the man checking orders at the tall desk in the right foreground. Author's Archival Paper Collection.

33. This 2¼-inch Hertwig all-bisque "knotter" depicts an American comic character. The only moving part of the doll is the neck, which enables the doll to nod its head; the rest of the doll is un-jointed. All-bisque dolls with nodding heads were originally called "knotters" because of the large stringing knot found on the top of each head or back torso. The Hertwig porcelain factory made thousands of knotter dolls yearly for decades. Author's Collection. (Photo: Gene Abbott)

Part Two

CHAPTER 7

Other Sonneberg-Area Porcelain Factories

1. Bisque shoulder head by Goebel; wig; multi-stroke eyebrows; hair upper eyelashes; glass sleep eyes; open mouth with upper teeth; 22-inch doll; circa 1913; marked: **Bee**(mark)**// B1-3Germany**. Courtesy Historisches Coburger Puppenmuseum//Lossnitzer Collection. (Photo: Christiane Gräfnitz)

There were once sixty-one porcelain factories producing doll-related porcelain products within twenty-five miles of Sonneberg. I have chosen to profile four of them in order to show additional character dolls made in this area from 1910 until the 1940s. Character dolls were made by the majority of the porcelain factories in this area, and the quality and the price per doll varied. Inexpensive dolls were sold by retailers like the F.W. Woolworth "Five and Dime" stores, while more expensive dolls of higher quality were sold at stores like Gimbel Bros., located in New York and Philadelphia.

WM. UND F. & W. GOEBEL PORCELAIN FACTORY

The Goebel toy factory was founded in 1867 by William Goebel and initially produced children's marbles and slate pencils. It was incorporated in the commercial register in 1871. In 1876 William's father, Franz Detleff Goebel, who had been an employee of the Hermann Hutschenreuther porcelain factory, located in the Thuringian town of Gräfenthal, joined his son at the toy factory and together they decided to found a porcelain factory. The Goebels chose a beautiful location in Oeslau for their porcelain factory, which provided access to rich clay deposits as well as water from the River Röden, and called their factory Wilhelmsfeld.

The ruling Duke of Coburg initially refused to allow the Goebels to build a porcelain factory in Oeslau because he feared that fires from the kilns would destroy the nearby forests. After a few years of making earthenware products only, the Goebels tried again to persuade the ruling Duke to grant them permission to make hard-paste porcelain products. He finally agreed, and in 1879 the father and son began firing tableware in a newly constructed porcelain kiln. The factory now used the name F&W Goebel, reflecting the father's and son's names: Franz and William.

The first bisque-head dolls were produced in 1887, and the Goebel porcelain factory continued to make bisque-head dolls through the 1930s. In 1893 the factory produced 129 models with shoulder heads, socket heads and straight (flange) necks.

318

2. Today, a large M.I. Hummel figurine welcomes visitors to the Goebel porcelain factory in Rödenthal. The porcelain factory was founded in Oeslau, Thuringia in 1879. Oeslau became part of the "newly formed" town of Rödenthal in 1971. (Photo: Mary Krombholz)

One Goebel bisque-head character doll popular with doll collectors is the American Schoolboy. The back of the shoulder head is incised with the letter "B" and the mold number "30." Goebel also made the bisque heads bearing the mold number "31" in 1890. In 1893 Franz Detleff sold his interest in the factory to his son and the name of the firm became William Goebel. Over the following years, the Goebel porcelain factory made a variety of glazed and unglazed doll-related porcelain products, including shoulder and socket heads, bathing dolls, half-dolls and Kewpie-like dolls.

As he grew older, William Goebel felt that the prime market for increased sales of his products was America. In order to develop this market, he sent his sixteen-year-old son, Max Louis, to the United States to work with possible clients. Max Louis did well and was soon taking orders from the Marshall Field department store in Chicago. When William Goebel died in 1911, his son became the new owner of the W. Goebel porcelain factory. At that time the factory had four hundred workers and four kilns.

Max Louis Goebel hired some of Europe's finest sculptors to work at the porcelain factory. Rampant inflation after World War I forced many Thuringian porcelain factories to close but Goebel continued to produce porcelain, year after year. In 1926 the factory added fine-grained earthenware to their product line. The year 1929 was a difficult one for the company; Max Louis died after leading the Goebel porcelain factory for only eighteen years. The American stock market crash also severely impacted sales. The factory survived due to the leadership of Max Louis's son, Franz Goebel, and his son-in-law, Dr. Eugen Stocke.

In 1934 Franz Goebel discovered the artwork of a gifted academy-trained artist and nun, Sister Maria Innocentia Hummel, whose depictions of country children on note cards and postcards were very popular. According to a current Goebel sales catalog, he decided that it would be a good time to introduce a new line of products depicting "the gentle innocence of children." Late that year he contacted Sister Hummel, asking permission to create three-dimensional figurines based upon her artwork, and she agreed. Goebel sculptors Arthur Möller and Reinhold Unger began to create the figurines, all of which were approved by Sister Hummel herself. The first Hummel line was introduced at the Leipzig Fair in March 1935 and was an immediate success. Made of earthenware, the figurines are still produced today, painted in the same soft colors by means of a special factory process.

A large replica of a Hummel figurine in front of the main porcelain factory building helps visitors locate the W. Goebel porcelain factory in Rödenthal, Bavaria. (On July 1, 1920, the residents of Oeslau voted to join the West German state of Bavaria rather than remain residents of Thuringia and in 1971, the town name (Oeslau) was changed to Rödenthal to reflect the name of the nearby River Röden, again by a vote of the town's residents.) My visit to the factory's outlet shop in May 2007 was a pleasant surprise. The quality of the porcelain products is unchanged from the years doll-related products were made. The large variety of items includes tableware,

Chapter 7

figurines and household accessories like mirrors and lamps. The Goebel factory celebrated its 135th anniversary in 2006. According to a factory booklet, the company employs eighteen hundred people worldwide.

The W. Goebel porcelain factories made dolly-faced dolls from the late 1880s into the 1930s. The bisque-head character dolls made by the factory, ranging in height from about five inches to over twenty, are quite appealing, and the googlies are especially collectible. The first Goebel bisque-head character doll is marked with the 50 mold number. Introduced in 1910, it is also marked with the wide-spread "WG" initials and the Goebel trademark crown. The Goebel molded-hair girl marked with the 73 mold number was made beginning in 1914. The Goebel porcelain factory made a number of character dolls marked with the 100 mold number series, including 102, 103, 106, 107, 110, 111, 114, 120, 121, 122, 123, 124, 125 and 126. The 102 and 103 mold numbers are circa 1912, while the rest of the 100 number series are circa 1921.

In later years, the Goebel porcelain factory specialized in half-dolls. The modeling reflects the talents of the artists and sculptors who have made Goebel products factory through the years. The factory continues to produce porcelain products of fine quality today.

Gebrüder Knoch Porcelain Factory

The Gebrüder Knoch porcelain factory was founded in Neustadt by the Knoch brothers, Ernst and Christian, in 1887. The talents of the two founders complemented one another. Ernst was the dollmaker, while Christian was the merchant in charge of sales. In 1895 Königsee resident Carl Hofmann became a co-owner of the porcelain factory. The factory listed doll heads as a product in 1900. In 1910 character-doll heads were advertised, along with "doll arms in finest and simplest quality." The words "finest quality" and "simplest quality" indicate the range of quality offered by this porcelain factory, and the resulting difference in price.

Under the Gebrüder Knoch heading for the year 1913 in the *German Doll Encyclopedia*, the Ciesliks list the following porcelain products made by this factory: "Bisque doll heads with socket and breast plate, with or without hairstyle, with stationary and sleeping eyes, character doll heads, china doll heads with painted hair for Nanking dolls, all doll joints, half arms and full arms, swivel arms, heads in natural size for shop windows."

The town of Neustadt, former home of the Gebrüder Knoch porcelain factory, is only 1.7 miles from Sonneberg. Porcelain factories like the Knoch factory supplied bisque-doll heads to area doll factories, which were then sold and shipped from Sonneberg to countries all over the world. The Gebrüder Knoch porcelain factory made a large number of dolly-face bisque heads before starting to make bisque character heads in 1910.

During its thirty-two-year history, the factory made a number of character heads as part of their doll line. Founders Ernst and Christian Knoch had an unusual trademark, which is often found incised on the back of the dolls' heads: a pair of crossed bones with the initials "GK" over the bones. The letter "N" for Neustadt is often found underneath the bones. The character doll pictured as illustration number 18 in this chapter, marked with the #216 mold number, has the complete Knoch trademark. Character heads may only be marked "Ges. Nr. Gesch" and a mold number.

The Gebrüder Knoch mold numbers 181, 185, 189, 190, 193, 201, are dolly-faced bisque socket heads made from 1900 until 1910. The first Gebrüder Knoch bisque-head character doll produced circa 1910 is marked with the 203 mold number. Other bisque-head character dolls are marked with the following mold numbers: 204, 205, 206, 208, 211, 216, 217, 221, 223, 229, 230, 232, 233, 237, 238, 241 and 246.

The Max Oscar Arnold doll factory in Neustadt bought the Gebrüder Knoch porcelain factory in 1919. The Arnold doll factory made and dressed bisque-head dolly-faced dolls from 1907 on. The Arnold doll factory patented a number of talking mechanisms for their dolls. In 1901 they advertised "Arnola, the Talking and Singing Doll" and in 1910 gramophone rollers were made in the factory. One version of the phonograph doll has a megaphone that releases the sound via the doll's mouth. The other version has sound holes in the back of the doll's head.

The Arnola doll was able to sing, pray and speak in three languages, according to the original advertising. The description of the voice is as follows: "The clockwork is situated in the doll's body, the rolls of which can be exchanged, and this is the best that has been made in this field. By pressing a small pin on the doll, one initiates the clockwork without any trouble. The rolls offer text in German, English and French."

The bell-mouth of the gramophone ended directly in the mouth of the doll, giving the impression that the words or songs were actually spoken by the doll. Armand Marseille and Gebrüder Kuhnlenz bisque dolly-face heads were used on the Arnold gramophone doll. Large orders of this doll were listed in 1914, but the factory stopped making dolls due to the onset of World War I. Doll production resumed after 1918.

A bisque socket head marked with the Max Oscar Arnold trademark star and the name of the Welsch doll factory is pictured as illustration number 101 in Part Two: Chapter 3. This bisque character head was still in a large cardboard box in the attic of the Arthur Krauss doll factory in Köppelsdorf when I visited the doll factory in 2001. The head is important because it proves that the Max Oscar Arnold doll and porcelain factory made bisque-head character dolls after buying the Gebrüder Knoch porcelain factory in 1919. The Ciesliks note in the "Remarks" section of the Max Oscar Arnold doll factory entry in the *German Doll Encyclopedia*: "Bisque doll heads were found with neck marks 'MOA' and 'Welsch' which obviously

Other Sonneberg-Area Porcelain Factories

3. Three American Schoolboy bisque heads by Goebel; molded hair; multi-stroke eyebrows; painted upper and lower eyelashes; stationary glass eyes; closed mouths; 9-, 16½- and 20-inch dolls; circa 1890; each doll marked: **30B**. Two dolls have shoulder heads, while the smallest doll has a socket head. Beth Karp Collection. (Photo: Lee Krombholz)

4. **American Schoolboy** bisque shoulder head by Goebel; molded hair; multi-stroke eyebrows; painted upper and lower eyelashes; stationary glass eyes; closed mouth; 20 inches; circa 1890; marked: **Germany//30B//8½**. Beth Karp Collection. (Photo: Lee Krombholz)

had been produced after 1920 in the porcelain factory of Max Oscar Arnold for Welsch & Co., Sonneberg."

The Max Oscar Arnold doll and porcelain factory became the Max Oscar Arnold Electrotechnical Works in 1919. The factory became affiliated with Bing Werke in 1924. Bisque character doll heads were made until 1931, when the porcelain factory was purchased by Philip Rosenthal of Selb.

RECKNAGEL PORCELAIN FACTORY

The Recknagel porcelain factory was founded in Alexandrienthal in 1886 by Theodor Recknagel. The factory closed in 1934, and the building was torn down about twenty years ago. A sports center now stands on the old factory site. During the years that dolly-faced dolls and character dolls were made in the porcelain factory, most of the village's residents were employed there. The name Alexandrienthal is no longer listed on regional maps because the village became part of the newly formed town of Rödenthal in 1971. (The cities of Coburg and Alexandrienthal are located in the German state of Bavaria rather than Thuringia, due to a vote of the residents on July 1, 1920.)

The majority of character dolls made by the Recknagel porcelain factory were inexpensive, but unusual. The factory artists created expressive faces that are unlike the character dolls made by any other Thuringian porcelain factory. Many of the character babies wear molded bonnets or hair ribbons. Molded details used often by a particular porcelain factory can serve as clues to identification of a particular group of dolls. The Recknagel porcelain factory made a number of character dolls with two tiny, separate lower teeth in an open/closed mouth. Three of the Recknagels pictured in this chapter have these similarly molded and painted teeth. (See illustrations 30, 31 and 32.)

The Sonneberg-area porcelain factories that primarily made doll heads of lower quality, like the Recknagel porcelain factory, are often judged unfairly. The 16-inch character boy (illustration 28) in this chapter is an excellent example of the porcelain products this factory was capable of making. The bisque is smooth and fine in quality, and the painted facial features, particularly the open/closed mouth with painted teeth, are representative of a "First Quality" product. Recknagel character dolls like this example are seldom seen, but they are a very nice addition to any character-doll collection. The factory's dolls are easily identified by their distinctive trademark, consisting of crossed nails, inside of which are the letters "RA."

The large numbers of dolly-faced dolls made by the fac-

Chapter 7

5. Bisque shoulder head by Goebel for Geo. Borgfeldt & Co.; original wig and clothing; Mama-type body by K&K Toy Co.; cloth label reads: "K and K, The Doll of Quality, and a patent number." Donilee Popham Collection. (Photo: Scott Popham)

6. A closer view shows the bisque head by Geobel; original wig; multi-stroke eyebrows; upper and lower painted eyelashes; glass sleep eyes; open mouth with upper teeth and separate tongue; 14-inch doll; circa 1920s; marked: **Made in Germany// K&K//38//Thuringia.** Donilee Popham Collection. (Photo: Scott Popham)

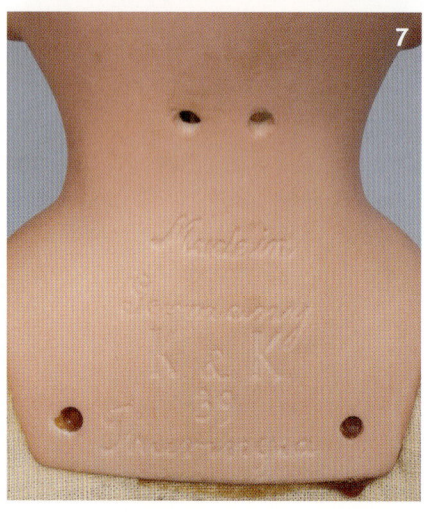

7. Back shoulder plate of the Goebel doll pictured in illustrations 5 and 6 shows the incised marking, including the rarely seen factory location "Thuringia." Donilee Popham Collection. (Photo: Scott Popham)

tory were easily sold because they were attractively dressed and inexpensive. The Recknagel factory made dolly-faced and character dolls with painted or glass eyes, open or closed mouths, wigs or molded hair and socket heads in a large variety of sizes. The original clothing has lasted well because cotton clothing was used to keep the costs down. The factory also made black dolls. Two dated entries in the Ciesliks' *German Doll Encyclopedia* note: "1897: GM '2 doll heads, Black and Mulatto. 1912: Character doll head of porcelain with bonnet and cloth ribbon drawn through." According to Robert E. Roentgen in his book *Marks on German, Bohemian & Austrian Porcelain, 1710 to the Present*, "the Recknagel porcelain factory made decorative porcelain, figurines and dolls' heads from 1886 until 1934."

Swaine & Co. Porcelain Factory

The Swaine & Co. porcelain factory was located in Hüttensteinach, just outside the town of Köppelsdorf. The portion of the factory that is still standing is located a few feet from the railroad tracks that connect the village to Sonneberg and to the shipping ports of Hamberg and Bremen. Accessible rail transportation was very important to the Swaine porcelain factory, as the Sonneberg-area porcelain factories were difficult to reach by any other means of transportation. The Thuringian mountains often prevented the successful construction of roads, and the roads that did exist were snow-covered for much of the winter.

The Swaine porcelain factory was founded in 1810 on the grounds of a former iron-ore smelting factory by William Swaine and the Shoenau brothers (Gebrüder). In 1853 the Shoenau brothers decided to leave Swaine to operate their own factory across the street. The Gebrüder Schoenau porcelain factory is still standing today across the street from the Swaine factory.

In 1856 William Swaine is listed as the sole owner. He died in 1914, and Albert Schoenau was listed as the new owner of the porcelain factory. In 1923 the name of the porcelain factory was changed from Swaine & Co. to Gebr. Schoenau, Swaine &

Other Sonneberg-Area Porcelain Factories

Co. During the years of production, in addition to doll heads, the Swaine/Gebrüder Schoenau porcelain factory made household, table, decorative and technical porcelain products.

The character heads made by the Swaine porcelain factory from 1910 on are beautifully modeled, and the bisque is as smooth and finely textured as that of any other Thuringian porcelain factory. Many of the bisque character heads must have been sold to customers in the United States, considering the number of Swaine dolls in American collections, compared to the examples on display in German museums. According to the Ciesliks' research published in their *German Doll Encyclopedia*, the Swaine & Co. porcelain factory made bisque doll heads for a very short time.

The incised marks include: "D//Lori//I, D.I.P., D.V., DI/4, B.P/4, and F.P/O." Another Swaine trademark is stamped rather than incised. It is a green circle within which are the words "GESCHÜTZT GERMANY" and the initials S&CO, which are printed in the center of the green circle.

One very uncommon character doll made by the Swaine porcelain factory is marked with the letters "F.P." The expressive laughing face has an open/closed mouth. Most of the character babies feature a sweet, placid expression. My Swaine character baby, illustration number 39, has deeply carved black pupils as part of her intaglio eyes. The irises are also incised, and have a white-iris highlight under the molded eyelid. A very fine black line outlines each upper eyelid. The multi-stroke eyebrows are light brown. The mouth is closed, with a hint of a tongue painted between the upper and lower lips. The cheek blushing is pale, as is the molded, painted hair. The five-piece composition baby body is well made, with bent arms molded in different positions.

According to Robert E. Roentgen in *Marks on German, Bohemian & Austrian Porcelain, 1710 to the Present*, the Gebrüder Schoenau, Swaine & Co. porcelain factory was nationalized in 1954, and named VEB Ceramic Works Sonneberg. The factory closed in 1990. Thuringian porcelain factories like the Swaine factory are part of a dollmaking scene that has completely faded from view. It is fortunate that these appealing character dolls are still in antique-doll collections today to remind us of the products made by the hundreds of porcelain factories that were once located, as a current Waltershausen Tourist Office booklet describes, in the "green heart of Germany."

8. Bisque socket head by Goebel; molded hair with Dutch-style molded bonnet; single-stroke eyebrows; painted eyes; closed mouth; 6-inch doll; marked: Bee (mark)//WG//G2//Germany. Beth Karp Collection. (Photo: Lee Krombholz)

9. Two bisque socket heads by Goebel; original clothing; molded hair and flowers; single-stroke eyebrows; painted eyes; open/closed smiling mouths with upper teeth; 6½-inch dolls; GM 1912; each marked: Bee(mark)//R/23x. Beth Karp Collection. (Photo: Lee Krombholz)

Chapter 7

10. Bisque shoulder-head googly by Goebel; molded hair; single-stroke eyebrows; painted, long, straight upper eyelashes; large "crossed" painted eyes with white painted highlights; open/closed mouth; 4-inch shoulder head; circa 1913; marked: **54B**. Courtesy Heitmatmuseum Ehrenberg, Ohrdruf. (Photo: Christiane Gräfnitz)

13. This is a closer view of part of the large Max Oscar Arnold/Gebrüder Knoch doll and porcelain factory. This factory is directly across the street from the Neustadt railroad station, which facilitated the transporting of dolls and doll parts. Neustadt is only 1.7 miles from Sonneberg. (Photo: Mary Krombholz)

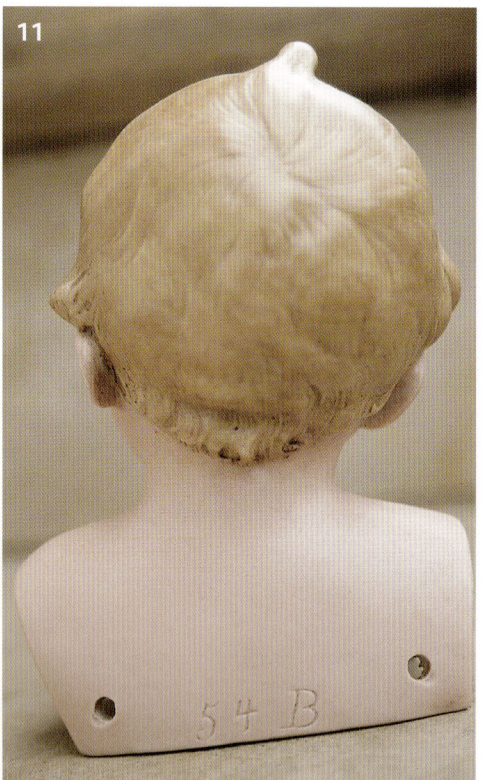

11. The back shoulder plate of the Goebel googly seen in illustration 10 shows the mark: **54B**. Courtesy Heitmatmuseum Ehrenberg, Ohrdruf. (Photo: Christiane Gräfnitz)

12. The back of head of the uncommon googly seen in illustration 14 shows the incised Goebel porcelain factory marks and molded hair. Kenneth Drew Collection. (Photo: Ann Hanat)

324

Other Sonneberg-Area Porcelain Factories

14. Bisque socket-head googly by Goebel; molded hair; single-stroke molded eyebrows; painted, closely spaced upper eyelashes; large painted side-glancing eyes with white highlights; open circular mouth with molded tongue; 3-inch head; circa 1912; marked: **Bee**(mark)**/N/WG//3/0//Germany**. Kenneth Drew Collection. (Photo: Ann Hanat)

Chapter 7

15. The Max Oscar Arnold/Gebrüder Knoch doll and porcelain factory still stands in Neustadt, Thuringia. The Gebrüder Knoch porcelain factory made bisque heads in Neustadt from 1887 until 1919, when the Max Oscar Arnold doll factory bought the Knoch porcelain factory. The bisque doll heads pictured in this chapter were made by the Gebrüder Knoch porcelain factory before the 1919 purchase. (Photo: Mary Krombholz)

17. White-bisque socket head by Gebrüder Knoch; skin wig; single-stroke eyebrows; clown-like facial painting on forehead, cheeks and chin; open mouth with upper teeth; 7-inch doll; circa 1900; marked: **Made in Germany//193 22/0//DEP**. The application of clown-like facial painting changed dolly-faced bisque heads into character-like heads. Author's Collection. (Photo: Gregg Smith)

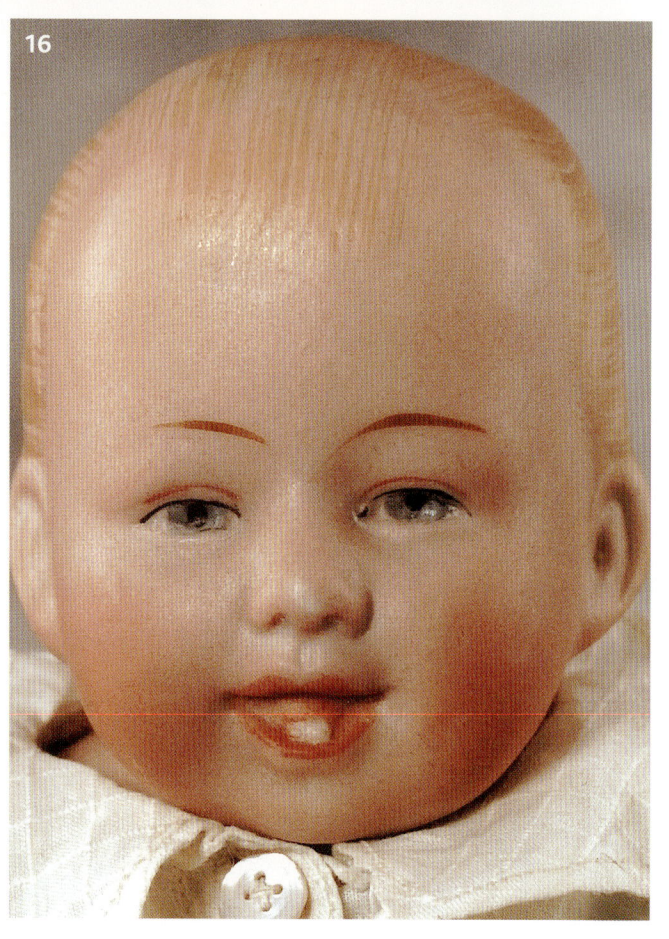

16. Bisque shoulder head by Gebrüder Knoch; molded hair; single-stroke eyebrows; intaglio-painted eyes with white highlights; open/closed laughing mouth with lower teeth and molded tongue; 10-inch doll; circa 1912; marked: **G(crossed bones)K//Made in Germany//ges. No.216**. Beth Karp Collection. (Photo: Lee Krombholz)

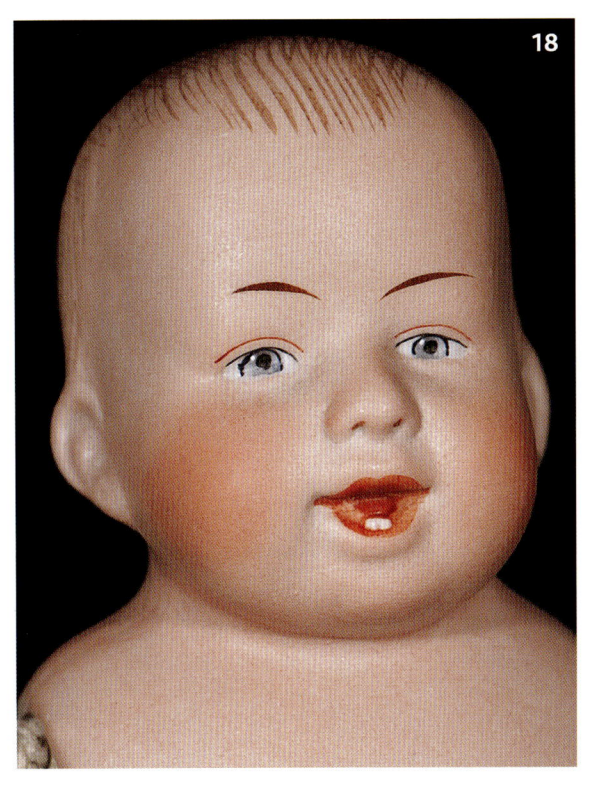

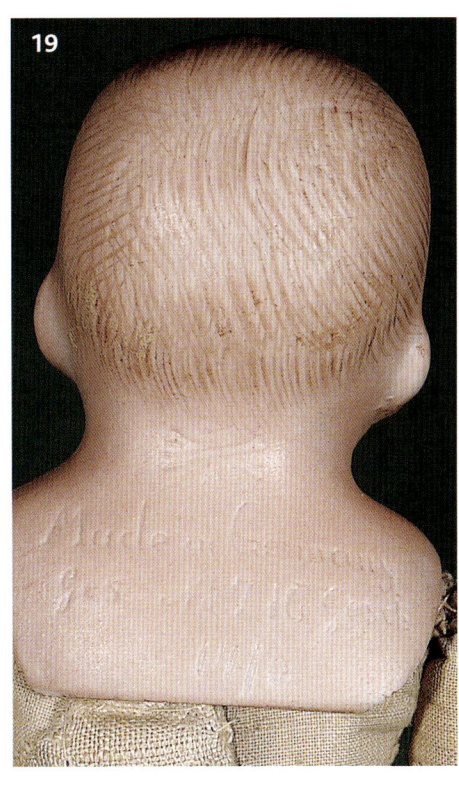

Other Sonneberg-Area Porcelain Factories

18. Bisque shoulder head by Gebrüder Knoch; molded hair; single-stroke eyebrows; intaglio-painted eyes with white highlights; open/closed mouth laughing mouth with lower teeth and molded tongue; 11-inch doll; circa 1912; marked: **GK(crossed bones)N// Made in Germany//ges. No.216 gesch.//14/0**. Author's Collection. (Photo: Gene Abbott)

19. The back shoulder plate of the doll seen in illustration 18 shows the incised markings. Author's Collection. (Photo: Gene Abbott)

20. A side view of the doll seen in illustration 21 shows the incised molding, scalloped edge and colorful designs on the bonnet. Historisches Coburger Puppenmuseum/Lossnitzer Collection. (Photo: Christiane Gräfnitz)

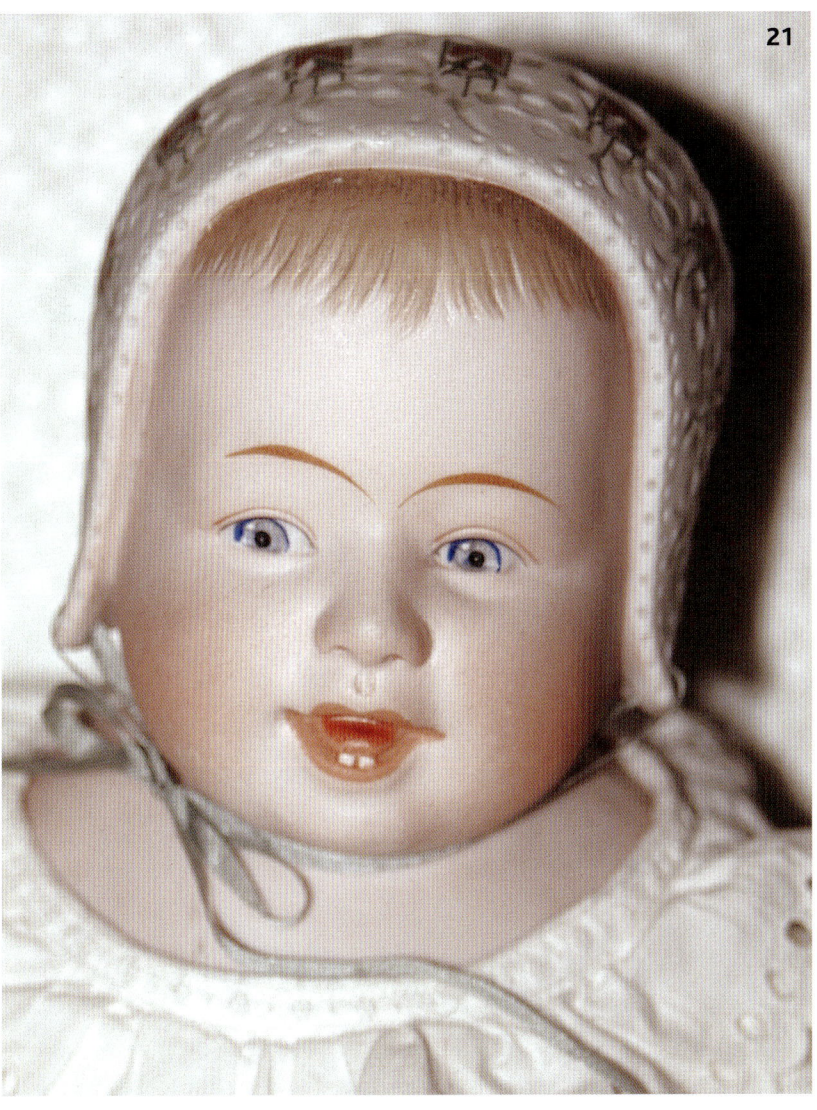

21. Bisque shoulder plate by Gebrüder Knoch; molded hair partially covered with bisque molded bonnet tied with a silk ribbon; single-stroke eyebrows; intaglio-painted eyes with white highlights; open/closed laughing mouth with lower teeth and molded tongue; 12-inch doll; circa 1912; marked: **Made in Germany// ges. No. 233 gesch**. Historisches Coburger Puppenmuseum/Lossnitzer Collection. (Photo: Christiane Gräfnitz)

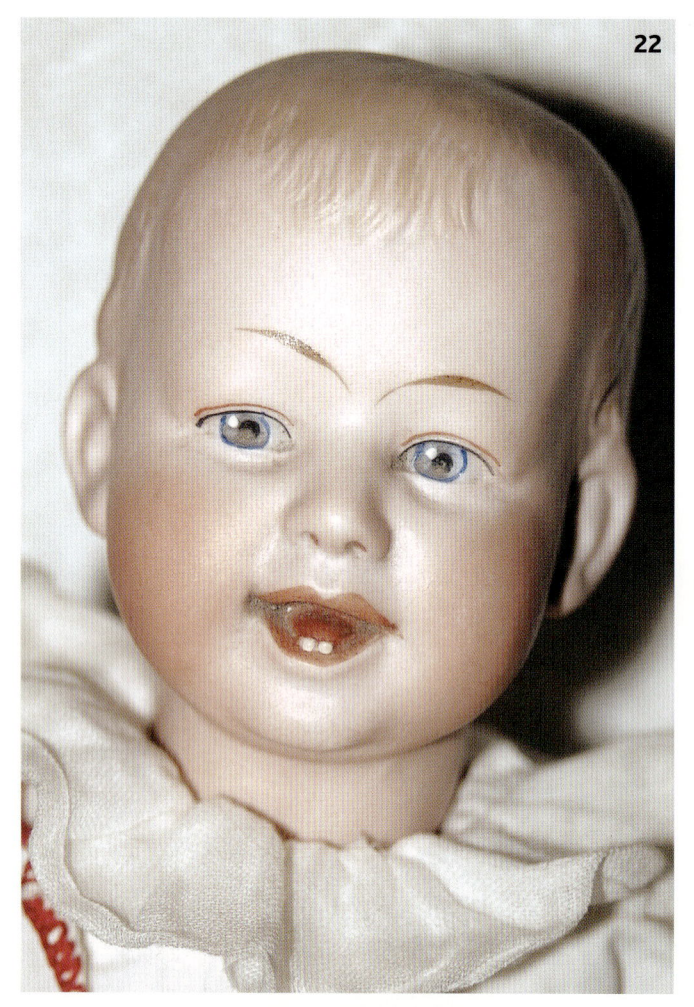

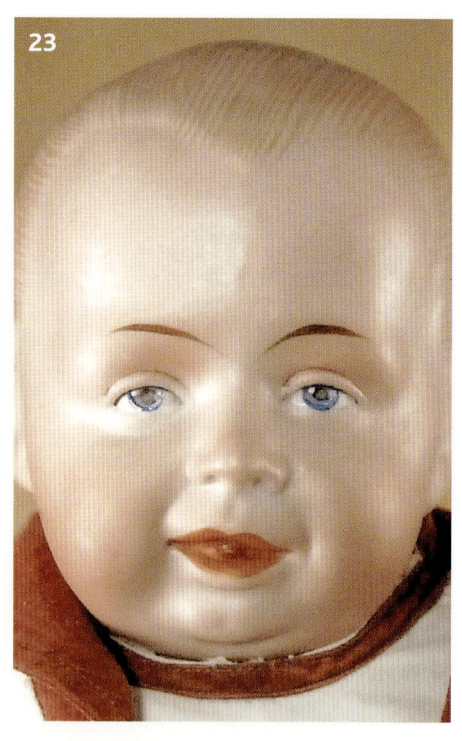

Chapter 7

22. Bisque socket head by Gebrüder Knoch; molded hair; single-stroke eyebrows; intaglio-painted eyes with white highlights; open/closed laughing mouth with lower teeth and molded tongue; 13½ inches; circa 1912; marked **GKN 217**. Courtesy Historisches Coburger Puppenmuseum/Lossnitzer Collection. (Photo: Christiane Gräfnitz)

23. Bisque shoulder head by Gebrüder Knoch; molded hair; single-stroke eyebrows; molded upper eyelids; intaglio-painted eyes with white highlights; open/closed smiling mouth with molded tongue; 18-inch doll; circa 1910; marked: **GKN(crossed bones)//Made in Germany//205**. Beth Karp Collection. (Photo: Lee Krombholz)

24. Bisque socket head by Gebrüder Knoch; molded hair; single-stroke eyebrows; intaglio-painted eyes with white highlights; open/closed smiling mouth with lower teeth; 3½-head; circa 1910; marked: **Made in Germany//206 13/0//DRGM**. Courtesy Deutsches Spielzeugmuseum, Sonneberg. (Photo: Christiane Gräfnitz)

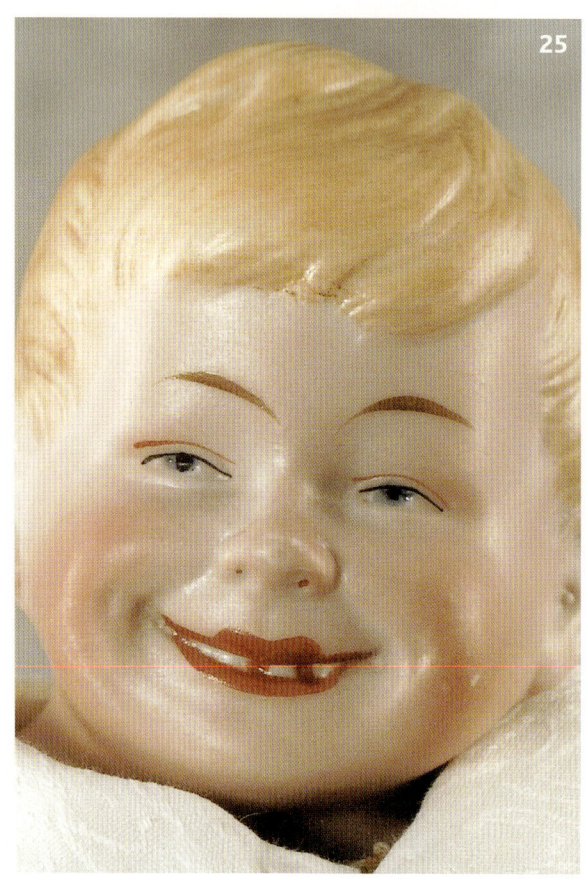

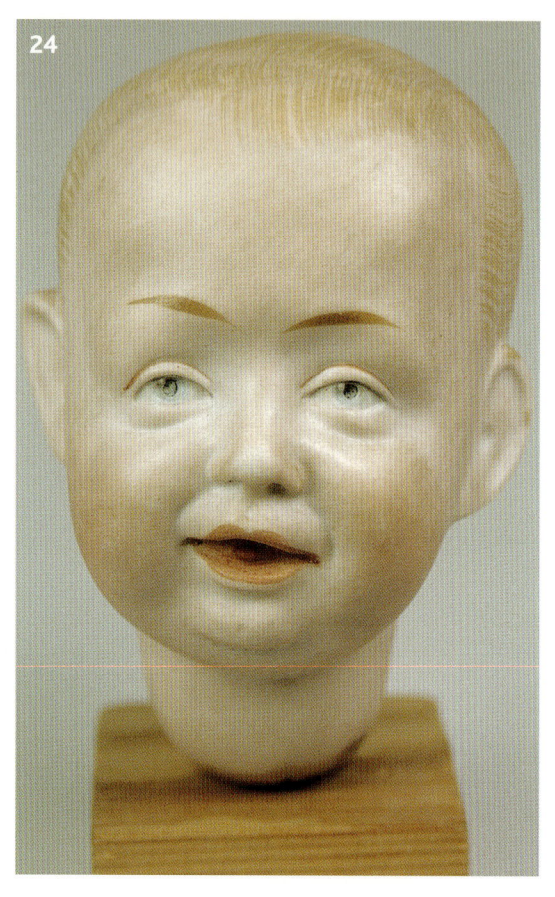

25. Bisque shoulder head by Gebrüder Knoch; molded hair; single-stroke eyebrows; painted eyes; open/closed smiling mouth with large lower teeth; cheek dimples; 11½-inch doll; circa 1912; marked: **Made in Germany//ges. 241/gesch//16/0**. Beth Karp Collection. (Photo: Lee Krombholz)

Other Sonneberg-Area Porcelain Factories

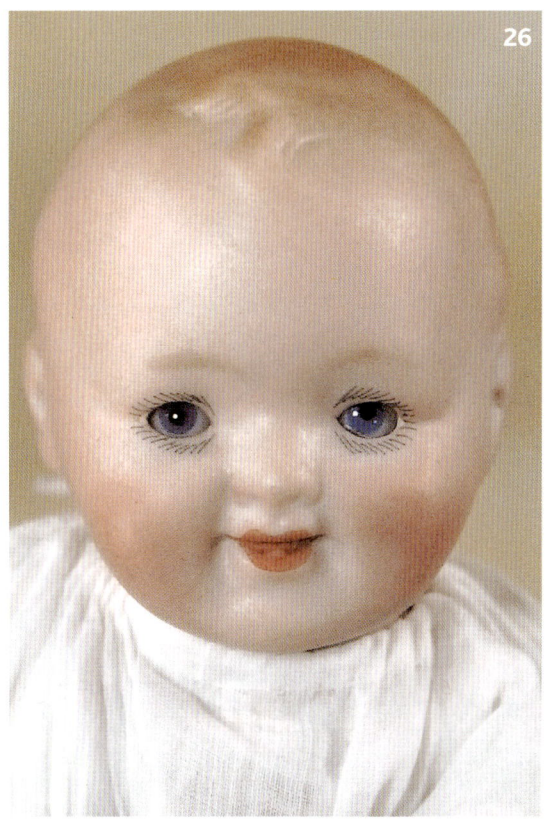

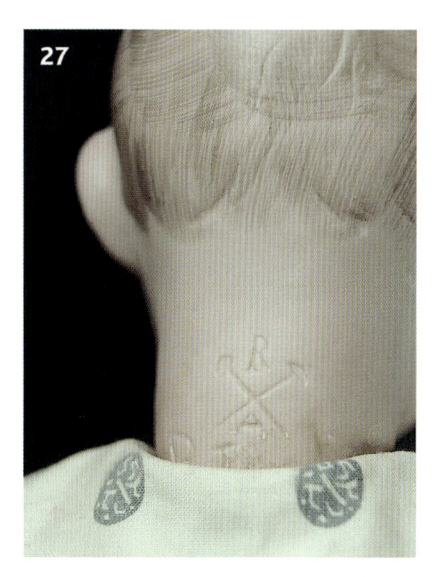

26. Bisque socket head by Recknagel; molded hair; single-stroke eyebrows; painted upper and lower eyelashes; glass sleep eyes; open/closed smiling mouth; 7½-inch doll; marked **A 2/0 R**. The Recknagel porcelain factory used the initials AR as well as RA on their bisque-head dolly-faced dolls and character dolls. Beth Karp Collection. (Photo: Gregg Smith)

27. The back of the head seen in illustration 28 shows the incised marks, including the Recknagel crossed-nails trademark. Beth Karp Collection. (Photo: Lee Krombholz)

28. The Recknagel porcelain factory, founded in 1886 by Theodor Recknagel, was torn down many years ago. Bisque socket head by Recknagel; molded hair; single-stroke eyebrows; intaglio-painted eyes with white highlights; open/closed smiling mouth with upper teeth and tongue; cheek dimples; 16-inch doll; marked: **R(crossed nails)A//RA-0**. Beth Karp Collection. (Photo: Gregg Smith)

29. Bisque socket head by Recknagel, smooth head with painted hair; painted upper and lower eyelashes; single-stroke eyebrows; glass sleep eyes; closed mouth; 20½-inch doll; circa 1925; marked **R141A**. Courtesy Historisches Coburger Puppenmuseum/Lossnitzer Collection. (Photo: Christiane Gräfnitz)

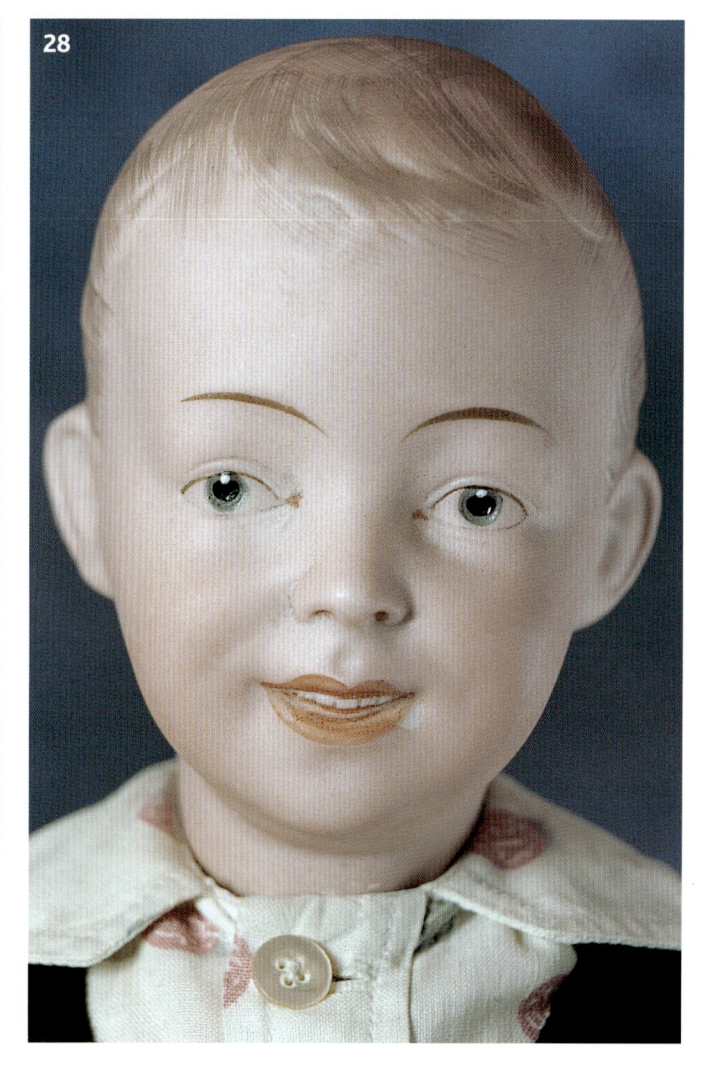

Chapter 7

30. Bisque socket head attributed to Recknagel; single-stroke eyebrows; intaglio-painted eyes; open/closed laughing mouth with molded tongue and lower teeth; 8½ inches; circa 1912; unmarked. If we compare the molding and painting of the mouth of the marked Recknagel doll pictured in illustration 31 to this doll, it is apparent the Recknagel factory also made this doll. Private Collection, formerly Jane Walker Collection. (Photo: Gene Abbott)

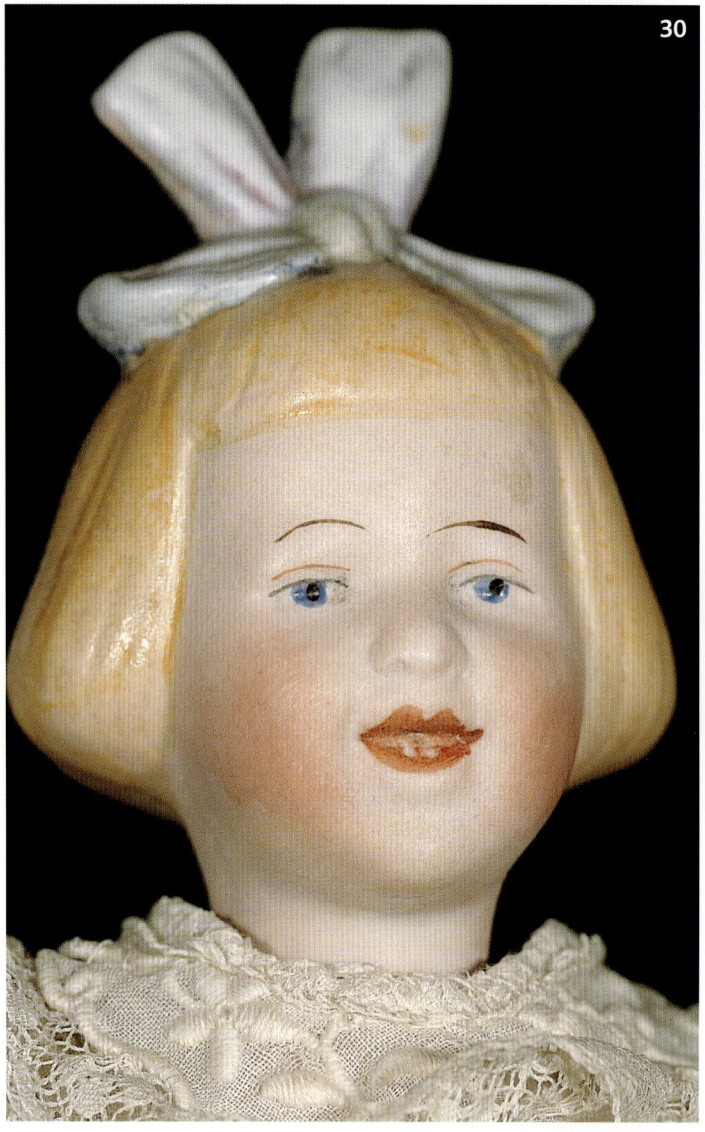

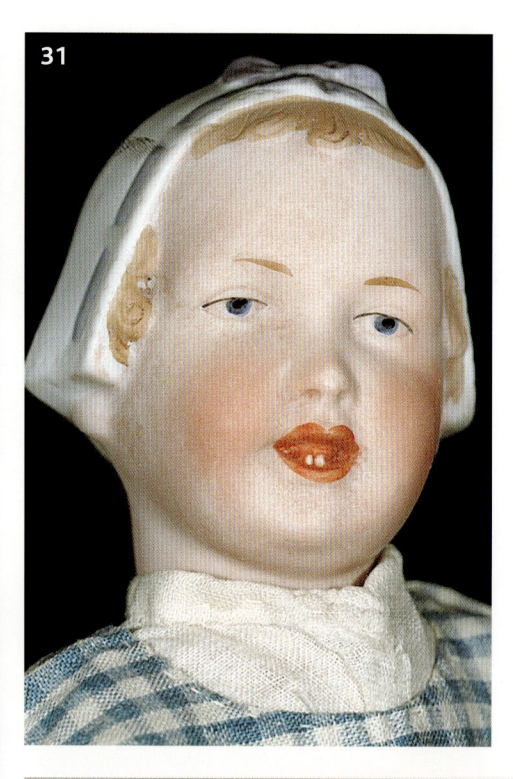

31. Bisque socket head by Recknagel; molded hair and bonnet; single-stroke eyebrows; intaglio-painted eyes; open/closed mouth with molded lower teeth and tongue; 9-inch doll; GM 1912; marked: **26-12/0**. Private Collection, formerly Jane Walker Collection. (Photo: Gene Abbott)

33. Dark-brown bisque socket head by Recknagel; molded hair; single-stroke eyebrows; white painted eyes; open/closed laughing mouth with upper teeth and molded tongue; 2½-inch head; GM 1914; marked: **55//9/0**. Courtesy Deutsches Spielzeugmuseum, Sonneberg. (Photo: Christiane Gräfnitz)

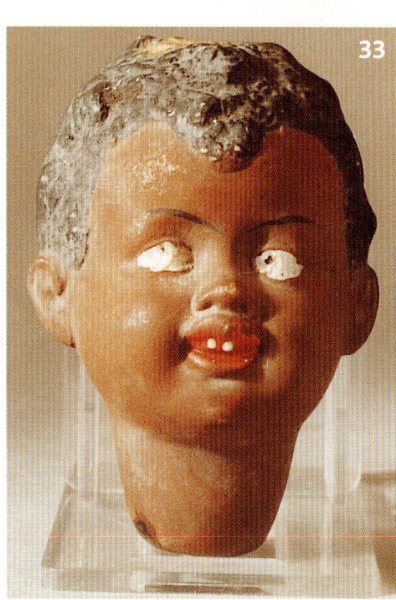

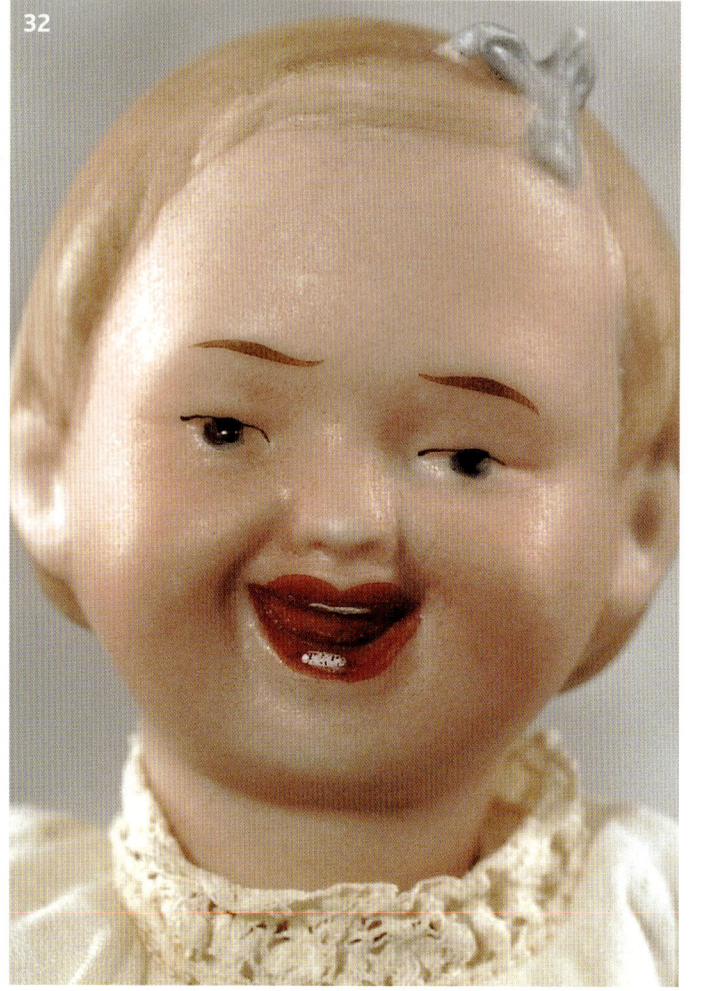

32. Bisque socket head by Recknagel; molded hair and ribbon; single-stroke eyebrows; intaglio-painted eyes; open/closed laughing mouth with upper and lower teeth and molded tongue; 7½-inch doll; circa 1912; marked: **R 57 A//12/0**. Beth Karp Collection. (Photo: Lee Krombholz)

330

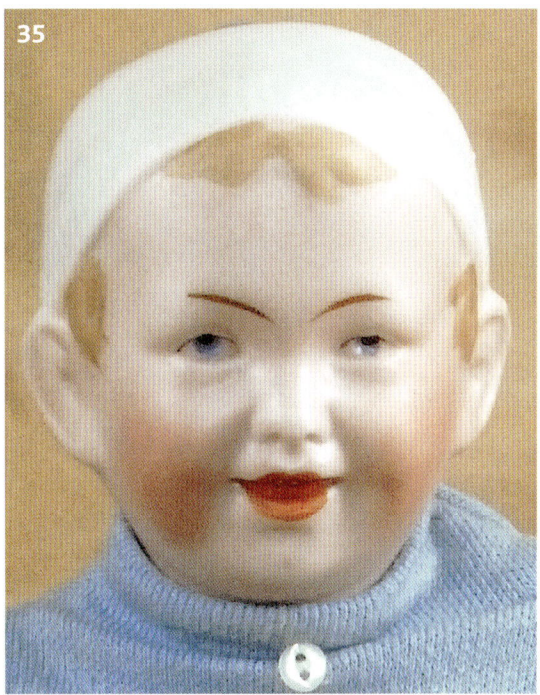

Other Sonneberg-Area Porcelain Factories

35. Bisque socket head by Recknagel; molded hair and cap; single-stroke eyebrows; intaglio-painted eyes; open/closed laughing mouth with tiny upper teeth and molded tongue; cheek and chin dimples; 8½-inch doll; GM 1912 marked: **28-7/0**. A comparison of the Second Quality doll pictured in illustration 34 with this First Quality doll illustrates the difference in First and Second Quality bisque character heads. The bisque heads were made from identical master molds, but the one in illustration 34 does not have the detail of this one. Beth Karp Collection. (Photo: Lee Krombholz)

34. Bisque socket head by Recknagel; molded hair and cap; single-stroke eyebrows; intaglio-painted eyes; open/closed laughing mouth with upper teeth and molded tongue; cheek dimples; 8-inch doll; GM 1912 marked: **RA//28-12.0**. Author's Collection. (Photo: Gregg Smith)

36. Two bisque socket-head googlies by Recknagel; molded hair; single-stroke eyebrows; side-glancing intaglio-painted eyes; closed mouth; 8-and-10-inch dolls; GM 1914; larger doll marked: **33-7/0**; smaller doll marked: **33-12/0**. Note that the size numbers increase as the head size decreases. Author's Collection. (Photo: Gregg Smith)

331

Chapter 7

37. Bisque socket head googly by Recknagel; wig; single-stroke eyebrows; painted upper and lower eyelashes; glass side-glancing eyes; open/closed smiling mouth; 7-inch doll; GM 1914; marked: **R37A//13/0**. Author's Collection. (Photo: Gregg Smith)

38. Bisque socket-head googly by Recknagel; molded hair; single-stroke eyebrows; large, round, convex painted eyes with intaglio black pupils; long, narrow, open/closed smiling mouth; 8-inch doll; circa 1915; marked: **R73A//13/0**. Beth Karp Collection. (Photo: Lee Krombholz)

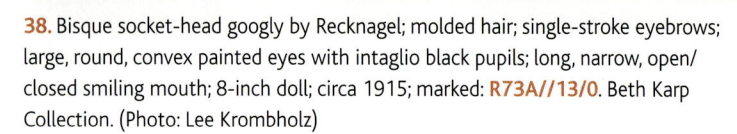

40. The old Swaine & Co. porcelain factory is still standing in Hüttensteinach, a suburb of Köppelsdorf. The Armand Marseille, Ernst Heubach, J. Hering & Sohn, Gebrüder Schoenau and Swaine & Co. porcelain factories were once located in the neighboring villages of Köppelsdorf and Hüttensteinach, which adjoin Sonneberg. The Swaine & Co. porcelain factory displayed character dolls at a Leipzig fair booth during the years 1910-1913. (Photo: Mary Krombholz)

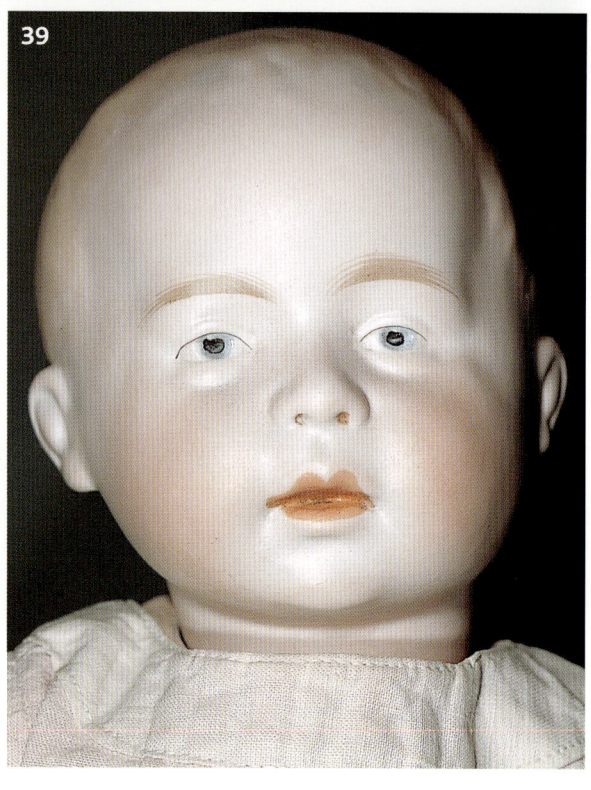

39. Bisque socket head by Swaine; molded hair; multi-stroke eyebrows; defined eye sockets; intaglio-painted eyes with white highlights; open/closed mouth; 14-inch doll; circa 1910; marked: **D.I.//4** and stamped green circle trademark. Author's Collection. (Photo: Gene Abbott)

332

Other Sonneberg-Area Porcelain Factories

41. Bisque socket-head googly by Recknagel; molded hair with pink bow over each ear; single-stroke eyebrows; intaglio-painted side-glancing eyes; round open/closed mouth with molded tongue; 8½-inch doll; GM 1914; marked: **R50A//14/0**. Beth Karp Collection. (Photo: Lee Krombholz)

Chapter 7

42. Bisque socket head by Swaine; wig; multi-stroke eyebrows; intaglio-painted eyes with white highlights; open/closed laughing mouth with upper teeth; 17 inches; circa 1910; marked: **B.P.//6**. Courtesy Rosalie Whyel Museum of Doll Art. (Photo: Courtesy Rosalie Whyel Museum of Doll Art)

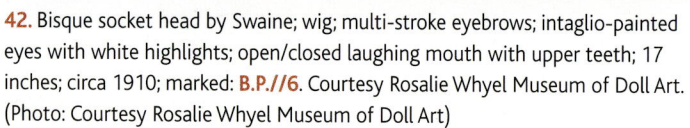

43. Bisque socket head by Swaine; wig; multi-stroke eyebrows; painted upper and lower eyelashes; glass sleep eyes; closed mouth; 15½-inch doll; circa 1910; marked **DEP 5//S&Co.** and stamped green circle trademark. Courtesy Ladenburger Spielzeugauktion/Goetz Seidel. (Photo: Christiane Gräfnitz)

44. Bisque socket head by Swaine; molded hair; multi-stroke eyebrows; intaglio-painted eyes with white highlights; open/closed mouth; 16-inch doll; circa 1910; marked: **D.I.** and stamped green circle trademark. Beth Karp Collection. (Photo: Lee Krombholz)

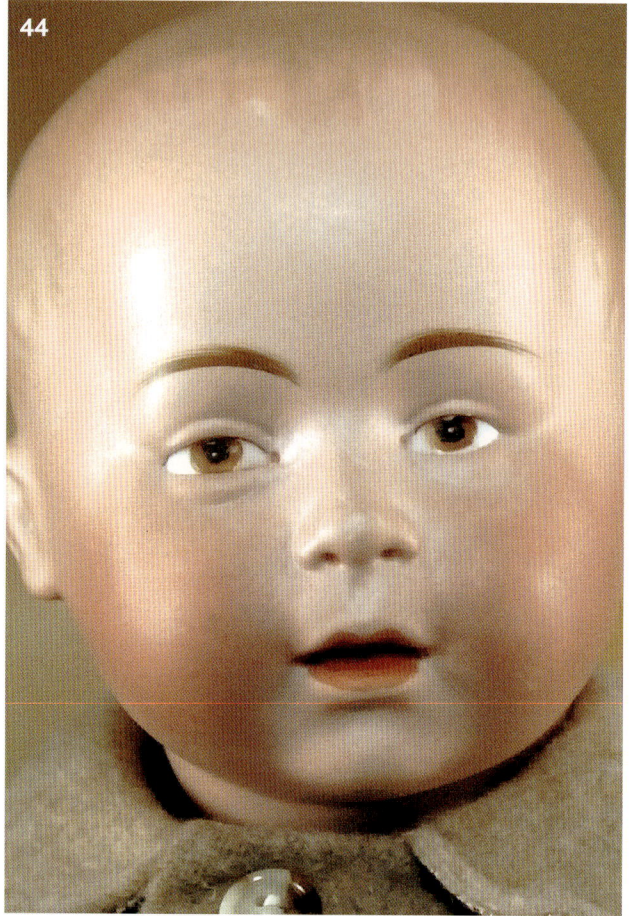

Other Sonneberg-Area Porcelain Factories

45. Bisque socket head by Swaine; original wig and maid's uniform; single-stroke eyebrows; intaglio-painted eyes; open/closed laughing mouth with upper teeth; 14-inch doll; circa 1910; marked **BP//4** and stamped green circle trademark. Kathy and Mike Embry Collection. (Photo: Kathy Embry)

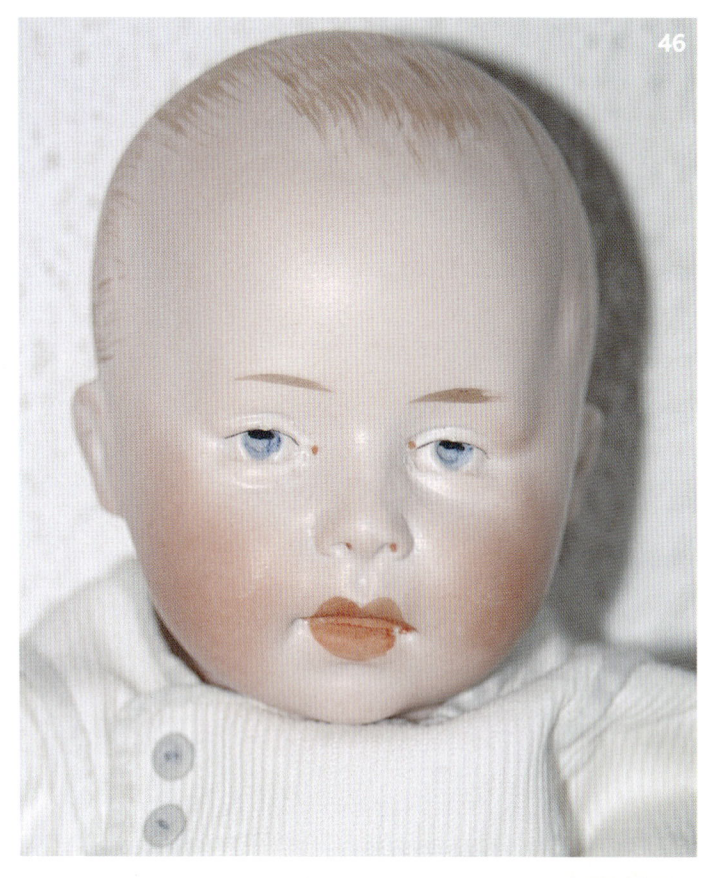

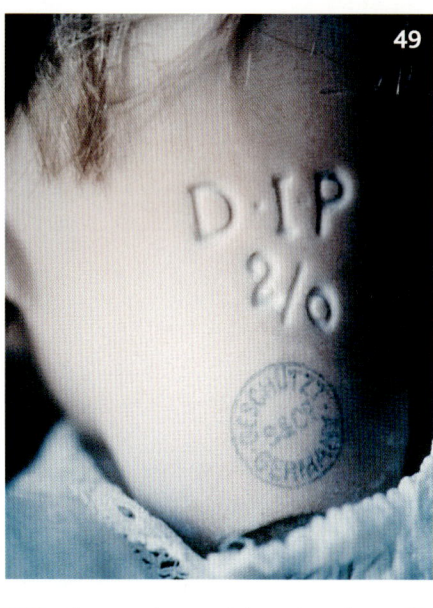

Chapter 7

46. Bisque socket head by Swaine; molded hair; single-stroke eyebrows; intaglio-painted eyes; open/closed mouth; 13½-inch doll; circa 1910; marked: **D.II.**. Courtesy Rothenburg Puppenmuseum/Katharina Engels Collection. (Photo: Christiane Gräfnitz)

47. Bisque socket head by Swaine; wig; single-stroke eyebrows; painted upper eyelashes; glass sleep eyes; open/closed mouth; 12-inch doll; circa 1910; marked: **D.I.P.//3** and stamped green circle trademark. Kathy and Mike Embry Collection. (Photo: Ann Hanat)

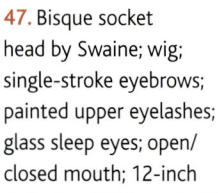

48. Bisque socket head by Swaine; wig; single-stroke eyebrows; painted upper eyelashes; glass sleep eyes; open/closed mouth; 12-inch doll; circa 1910; marked: **D.I.P.//2/0** and stamped green circle trademark. Private Collection; formerly Jane Walker Collection. (Photo: C.W. Walker)

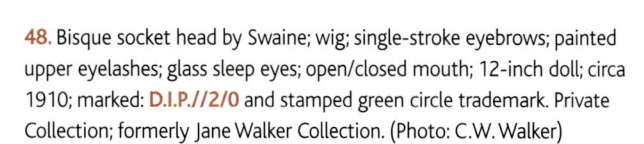

49. The back of the head seen in illustration 48 shows the incised marks and Swaine stamped green trademark circle. The initials "S&C" are in the center of the circle and the words inside the circle read: "GESCHÜTZT GERMANY." Private Collection, formerly Jane Walker Collection. (Photo: C.W. Walker)

Other Sonneberg-Area Porcelain Factories

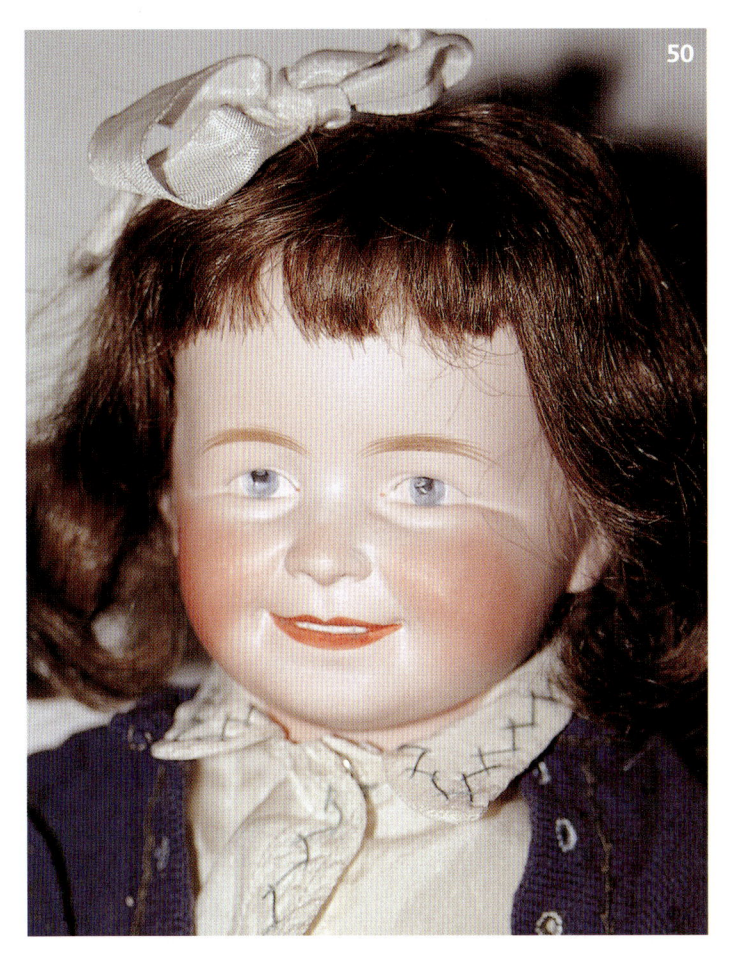

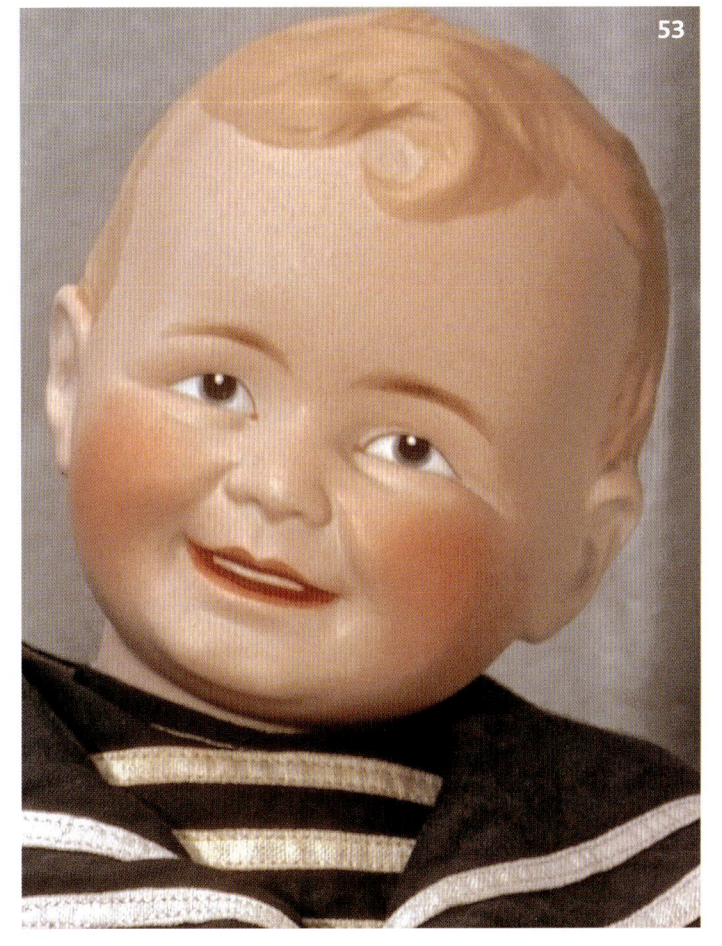

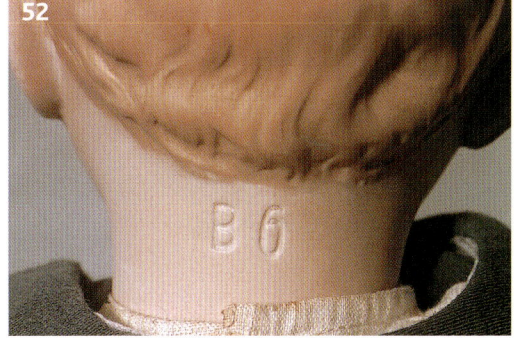

50. Bisque socket head by Swaine; wig; multi-stroke eyebrows; intaglio-painted eyes; open/closed laughing mouth with upper teeth; 16½-inch doll; circa 1910; marked: **BP//6** and stamped green circle trademark. Courtesy Historisches Coburger Museum/Lossnitzer Collection. (Photo: Christiane Gräfnitz)

51. Bisque socket head by Swaine; wig; single-stroke eyebrows; intaglio-painted eyes; open/closed laughing mouth with upper teeth; 14½-inch doll; circa 1910; marked: **BP//4** and stamped green circle trademark. Julie Blewis Collection. (Photo: Fanilya Gueno)

52. The back of the head seen in illustration 53 shows the molded hair and deeply incised **B6** mark. Julie Blewis Collection. (Photo: Fanilya Gueno)

53. Bisque socket head by Swaine; rare molded-hair boy; multi-stroke eyebrows; intaglio-painted eyes with white highlights; open/closed laughing mouth with upper teeth; 16-inch doll; circa 1910; marked: **B6**. Julie Blewis Collection. (Photo: Fanilya Gueno)

Bibliography

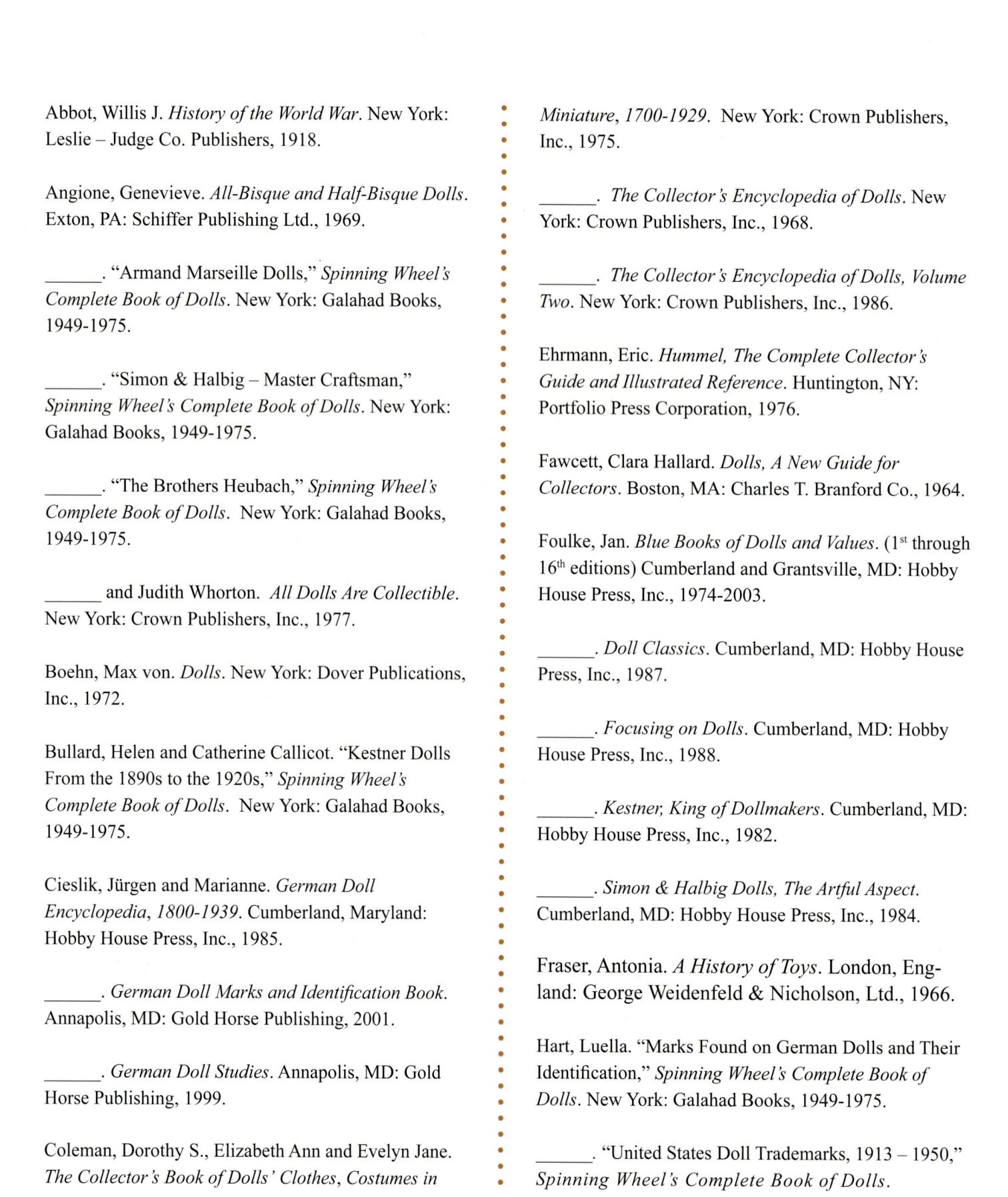

Abbot, Willis J. *History of the World War*. New York: Leslie – Judge Co. Publishers, 1918.

Angione, Genevieve. *All-Bisque and Half-Bisque Dolls*. Exton, PA: Schiffer Publishing Ltd., 1969.

_____. "Armand Marseille Dolls," *Spinning Wheel's Complete Book of Dolls*. New York: Galahad Books, 1949-1975.

_____. "Simon & Halbig – Master Craftsman," *Spinning Wheel's Complete Book of Dolls*. New York: Galahad Books, 1949-1975.

_____. "The Brothers Heubach," *Spinning Wheel's Complete Book of Dolls*. New York: Galahad Books, 1949-1975.

_____ and Judith Whorton. *All Dolls Are Collectible*. New York: Crown Publishers, Inc., 1977.

Boehn, Max von. *Dolls*. New York: Dover Publications, Inc., 1972.

Bullard, Helen and Catherine Callicot. "Kestner Dolls From the 1890s to the 1920s," *Spinning Wheel's Complete Book of Dolls*. New York: Galahad Books, 1949-1975.

Cieslik, Jürgen and Marianne. *German Doll Encyclopedia, 1800-1939*. Cumberland, Maryland: Hobby House Press, Inc., 1985.

_____. *German Doll Marks and Identification Book*. Annapolis, MD: Gold Horse Publishing, 2001.

_____. *German Doll Studies*. Annapolis, MD: Gold Horse Publishing, 1999.

Coleman, Dorothy S., Elizabeth Ann and Evelyn Jane. *The Collector's Book of Dolls' Clothes, Costumes in Miniature, 1700-1929*. New York: Crown Publishers, Inc., 1975.

_____. *The Collector's Encyclopedia of Dolls*. New York: Crown Publishers, Inc., 1968.

_____. *The Collector's Encyclopedia of Dolls, Volume Two*. New York: Crown Publishers, Inc., 1986.

Ehrmann, Eric. *Hummel, The Complete Collector's Guide and Illustrated Reference*. Huntington, NY: Portfolio Press Corporation, 1976.

Fawcett, Clara Hallard. *Dolls, A New Guide for Collectors*. Boston, MA: Charles T. Branford Co., 1964.

Foulke, Jan. *Blue Books of Dolls and Values*. (1st through 16th editions) Cumberland and Grantsville, MD: Hobby House Press, Inc., 1974-2003.

_____. *Doll Classics*. Cumberland, MD: Hobby House Press, Inc., 1987.

_____. *Focusing on Dolls*. Cumberland, MD: Hobby House Press, Inc., 1988.

_____. *Kestner, King of Dollmakers*. Cumberland, MD: Hobby House Press, Inc., 1982.

_____. *Simon & Halbig Dolls, The Artful Aspect*. Cumberland, MD: Hobby House Press, Inc., 1984.

Fraser, Antonia. *A History of Toys*. London, England: George Weidenfeld & Nicholson, Ltd., 1966.

Hart, Luella. "Marks Found on German Dolls and Their Identification," *Spinning Wheel's Complete Book of Dolls*. New York: Galahad Books, 1949-1975.

_____. "United States Doll Trademarks, 1913 – 1950," *Spinning Wheel's Complete Book of Dolls*.

New York: Galahad Books, 1949 - 1975.

Hillier, Mary. *Dolls and Dollmakers*. New York: G.M. Putnam's Sons, 1968.

Johl, Janet Pagter. *The Fascinating Story of Dolls*. New York: H.L. Lindquist Publications, 1941.

_____. *More About Dolls*. New York: H.L. Lindquist Publications, 1941.

_____. *Still More About Dolls*. New York: H.L. Lindquist Publications, 1946.

_____. *Your Dolls and Mine, A Collectors' Handbook*. New York: H.L. Lindquist Publications, 1952.

King, Constance Eileen. *The Collector's History of Dolls*. New York: St. Martin's Press, 1978.

Langer, Christa. *Charakterpuppen*. Duisburg, Germany: Verlag Puppen & Spielzeug, 1993.

MacDowell, Robert and Karin. *The Collector's Digest of German Character Dolls*. Cumberland, MD: Hobby House Press, Inc., 1981.

Mateaux, Clara. "The Wonderland of Work," *Doll Collectors Manual*. Doll Collectors of America, Inc., 1964. Originally published by Cassell, Petter, Galvin & Co. in 1898.

Mathes, Ruth E. and Robert C. *Toys and Childhood, The Mathes Collection and Philosophy*. Cumberland, MD: Hobby House Press, Inc., 1987.

Merrill, Madeline O. *The Art of Dolls, 1700 – 1940*. Cumberland, MD: Hobby House Press, Inc., 1985.

Müller, Marion Christiana. *Reise ins Spielzeugland*. Erfurt, Germany: VHT Verlaghaus, Thueringen, 1997.

Noble, John. *A Treasury of Beautiful Dolls*. New York: Hawthorne Books, Inc., 1971.

Richter, Lydia. *Heubach Character Dolls and Figurines*. Cumberland, MD: Hobby House Press, Inc., 1992.

Roentgen, Robert E. *Marks on German, Bohemian and Austrian Porcelain, 1710 to the Present*. Atglen, PA: Schiffer Publishing Ltd., 1997.

Scherf, Helmut. *Thueringer Porcelain*. Wiesbaden, West Germany: Ebeling, 1980.

_____ et al. *On the Porcelain Road*. Rudolstadt, Germany: Rudolstadter Heimathefte, 1995.

Smith, Patricia. *German Dolls, Featuring Character Children and Babies*. Paducah, KY: Collector Books, 1979.

_____. *Kestner and Simon & Halbig Dolls, 1804 – 1930*. Paducah, KY: Collector Books, 1979.

Stanton, Carol Ann. *Heubach's Little Characters, Doll and Figurines, 1850 – 1930*. Enfield, Middlesex, England: Living Dolls Publications, 1978.

Tarnowska, Maree. *Rare Character Dolls*. Cumberland, MD: Hobby House Press, Inc., 1987.

Tessmer, Angelika. *Sonneberger Geschichten*. Hildburghausen, Germany: Verlag Frankenschwelle, 1995.

_____. *Sonneberger Geschichten, Von Puppen, Griffeln und Kuckspfeifen*. Hildburghausen, Germany: Verlag Frankenschwelle, 1996.

Theriault, Florence. *Hertwig & Co. Archives, 1890 – 1937*. Annapolis, MD: Gold Horse Publishing, 2000.

Wendl, Martin and Ernst Schafer. *Spass am Sammeln, Altes Thueringer Porzellan*. Rudolstadt, Germany: Griefenverlag, 1984 and 1990.

Winkler, John K. *Five and Ten, The Fabulous Life of F.W. Woolworth*. New York: Robert M. McBride & Co., 1940.

Index of Mold Markings

23: 323	150: 149, 238, 263	251: 243
26: 330	151: 91, 150	254: 242
28: 331	152: 150	255: 180
33: 331	154: 151	257: 178
37: 332	158: 153	260: 179
50: 333	159: 152	262: 183, 269
55: 330	160: 153	266: 179
57: 330	165: 153, 154	269: 270
73: 332	166: 154	275: 270
100: 14, 53, 55	167: 154	276: 271
101: 57, 59, 60	168: 156	290: 91
101x: 61	169: 155	300: 270, 272
102: 61, 62	172: 81, 155, 157, 167	310: 243, 244
105: 63	174: 168	314: 69
106: 63	173: 168	318: 274
107: 64, 65	177: 169	319: 274, 275
109: 64, 65	178: 169	320: 244, 272
111: 84, 85	179: 169	323: 245-247
112: 65, 66, 67	181: 170	327: 248
112x: 66	182: 171	329: 248
114: 68, 69	184: 168	339: 272, 273
115: 70	185: 168, 172	399: 273
115A: 70	186: 170	341: 249, 250
116: 71	193: 326	347: 248
116A: 71, 72	200: 241	351: 250, 251
117: 72, 73	201: 60	352: 252
117A: 73, 74	205: 328	353: 273
117n: 73-75	206: 328	372: 252
117x: 75	208: 170, 183	390: 261
118: 75	210: 18, 241	394: 141
119: 76	211: 173	395: 252
120: 84, 85	216: 326, 327	399: 273
121: 76, 77	217: 328	400: 252, 253
122: 77	219: 173	410: 253
123: 77	221: 174, 175	417: 274
124: 77	222: 158	444: 274
126: 78, 79	225: 129, 228	452: 274
127: 79, 81	230: 242	500: 253, 254
127n: 79	233: 242, 327	520: 130, 132
128: 80	237: 174	525: 130
129: 85	241: 328	526: 130
131: 80	243: 176	531: 133
138: 147	244: 131	536: 133
140: 147	245: 176	537: 134
141: 148, 329	247: 176, 177	546: 134, 135
142: 148	248: 242	548: 134
143: 165, 166	249: 178	550: 254
149: 148	250: 243	560: 253

340

560a: 254, 255	1361: 112	8050: 297
567: 136	1391: 114	8191: 291
570: 193	1394: 120	8590: 294
582: 136	1418: 119	8649: 295
584: 137	1428: 99	8774: 294, 295
585: 137	1430: 117	9573: 288
590: 255	1448: 99, 100, 113	10532: 281
600: 91, 255	1450: 112	10671: 289
604: 137	1468: 100	
616: 193	1469: 100	13/AW: 102
686: 138	1488: 100	17SP: 212
680: 183	1489: 101	24D: 211
692: 141	1914: 208-210, 213	30/B: 321
700: 255, 256	2046: 139	54/B: 324
701: 60	2048: 139	AOM//570
717: 74	2072: 140	A3M: 237
728: 81	2094: 140	A6M: 235, 237, 239, 240
750: 256	2542: 260	A7M: 233, 235
759: 91	3200: 261	A14M: 240
919: 91	3900: 261	13AW: 102
966: 256	4600: 229	B1: 318
970: 257	4900: 224	B6: 337
971: 256	5000: 222	BP//4: 335, 337
973: 258, 259	5636: 291	BP//6: 334, 337
975: 257	6897: 292	COD: 213
990: 257	6969: 281	COD//A/3: 208
1005: 120	6970: 280	COD//A3½: 209
1070: 177	7054: 290	COD//A/6½: 205, 207
1159: 92	7064: 284	CP 210: 18
1199: 93	7247: 281	FB//616: 193
1249: 93	7602: 284, 285	H1: 102
1257: 104	7603: 283	K&H: 159
1259: 93	7604: 290	M1: 103
1262: 104	7622: 289	N1: 103
1267: 105	7634: 294	S1: 101
1271: 104	7644: 292	S&H 5: 19
1279: 93	7657: 301	TH 7: 193
1295: 105	7658: 301	WG//G2: 323
1299: 93, 105	7659: 301	
1301: 94	7759: 286, 287	D: 101
1303: 95-97	7761: 292	D.I.: 334
1304: 95	7764: 296	D.II.: 336
1307: 98	7788: 297	D.I.P.: 336
1321: 111	7850: 298	JIO: 115, 116, 117, 118, 121
1329: 98	7865: 297	PR: 13
1353: 111	7956: 298	RA: 329-332
1357: 111	7977: 284	S&C: 334
1358: 98	8035: 287, 288	TH: 193

General Index

Alt, Beck & Gottschalck porcelain factory: 86, 106-123
Alt, Johann Georg Wilhelm and family: 86, 107
Amberg, Louis, & Son: 236, 258, 259
American Schoolboy: 321
Arranbee Doll Company: 236, 249, 251
Arnold, Max Oscar, doll factory: 238, 263, 320, 321, 324, 326
AT-type Kestner: 166
Automaton: 278, 286
Averill, Georgene Hendren: 110, 120

Baby: 53, 55, 59
Baby Betty: 258
Baby Bo Kaye: 109, 120
Baby Peggy: 258, 259
Baby Phyllis: 250
Baby Phyllis Doll Company: 236, 250, 259
Baby Stuart: 284
Baehr, George and family: 124
Baehr & Proeschild porcelain factory: 54, 124-141
Bartenstein, Fritz: 90
Bauersachs, Emil, doll factory: 297
Beck, Gottlieb: 106
Beehive Kiln: 267
Bergmann, C.M., doll factory: 19, 90, 92, 236
Bergmann, Joseph, doll factory: 126
Bergner, Carl: 90
Bergner, Carl, doll factory: 90, 104
Bierschenk, Fritz: 193
Bing Werke (Works):   54, 58, 88, 92, 321
Biscaloid: 261, 262
Bonnie Babe: 110, 120, 121
Borgfeldt, Geo. & Co.:   92, 108, 118, 144, 145, 164, 235, 236, 238, 248
Brussels World Exposition of 1910/Carousel Dolls: 59, 196, 197, 199-208, 282
Bru-type Kestner: 166
Burkowitz, Heinz: 63
Butler Brothers: 90, 236, 258, 306, 307
Bye-Lo Baby: 108-110, 115, 118-120, 142, 145

Campbell Kid: 143, 144, 155, 156
Carl: 58, 61, 64, 65
Catterfelder Puppenfabrik: 18, 164, 165, 173, 183
Century Baby Doll: 180

Century Doll Company: 180
Chamotte: 127
Children's Work Act: 161
Coquette: 297-299
Cranach, Wanda V.:   37, 39, 47
Cymbalier: 129

Das Wunderkind (The Wonder Child):   168
Demalcol: 247
Dewey, George: 196, 212
DiDi: 110, 115, 118, 121
Doll, celluloid head: 50, 52, 54, 74, 81
Doll, cloth: 81
Doll, clown: 95, 326
Doll, flapper: 100, 198, 212, 253
Doll, Jubilee: 142, 145, 155, 157, 297
Doll, knotter: 317
Doll, lamp: 274
Doll, molded clothing: 305, 307, 311, 313-315, 317
Doll, multi-faced: 90, 104, 136, 152, 251, 273
Doll, Native American: 96, 131, 260
Doll, wax head: 47
Dolly Dimple: 280
Drayton, Grace Gebbie: 143, 144, 155, 156
Dream Baby, see also **My Dream Baby**:   236, 249-251
Dressel, Cuno & Otto doll factory: 32, 59, 90, 92, 100-103, 193-213, 216, 265
Dressel, Johann Friedrich, and family: 35, 194-198
Duquesnoy, Francois: 13, 70, 139, 151, 242

Edelmann, Edmund, doll factory: 258
Ehrenberger, Carl: 106
Einco: 278, 286
Eisenmann & Co.:   286
Elise: 64, 65
Erika: 101

Fany: 242
Fiammingo: 13, 70, 139, 151, 242
Fly-Lo Baby: 109, 119
Frobenius, Lillian: 20, 22, 25

Gans, Otto, doll factory: 19, 56, 80, 236, 257
Georgene, Madame: 110
George Washington: 90, 92, 102

342

Index

Gibson, Charles Dana: 167
Gibson Girl: 167
Gladdie: 240, 261, 262
Goebel, William and family: 318, 319
Goebel, Wm. und F&W, porcelain factory: 318-325
Goldschiner, Alfred: 24
Gottschalck, Johann Theodor and family: 86, 106, 107
Gretchen: 52, 66, 68, 69

Hahn, Paul: 144, 159
Halbig, Carl and family: 52, 86, 88-90, 92
Hamburger & Co.: 92, 280
Handwerck, Heinrich and family: 50, 53, 55-85, 92
Handwerck, Heinrich, doll factory: 50, 56, 82-85, 90, 92
Hanna: 223-225
Hans: 52, 66, 69
Hartmann, Carl, doll factory: 101
Hegemann, Alice: 20, 22, 25
Hertel, August: 142, 146
Hertel, Schwab & Co. porcelain factory: 119, 142-159
Hertwig, Christoph, and family: 302, 303
Hertwig & Co. porcelain factory: 164, 302-317
Hertwig sample boards: 305-311
Hess, Albin, doll factory: 274
Heubach, Ernst and family: 264-266
Heubach, Ernst, porcelain factory: 127, 264-275
Heubach, Richard, and family: 276
Heubach, Gebrüder, porcelain factory: 127, 276-301
Hexe: 90, 102
Hilda: 174, 176-178
Hitz, Jacobs & Kassler: 252
Hobson, Richard Pearson: 196, 211
Höhn, Karl: 213
Hoffmeister, Carl and family: 214
Hornlein, Theodor: 192, 193
Hülss, Adolf: 17, 90, 92

Just Me: 243, 244
Jutta: 194, 208-210, 213

K&K Toy Co.: 109, 120
Kämmer & Reinhardt doll factory: 26, 51, 48-83, 87, 90, 92
Kämmer, Ernst: 48, 50
Kallus, Joseph L.: 109, 120
Kaulitz, Marion Magdalena: 10, 20-31, 33, 37
Keramisches Werk GmbH: 92, 103, 108, 262
Kestner, Johann Daniel, Jr. and family: 16, 17, 160-162, 184
Kestner doll and porcelain factory: 54, 118, 160-187
Kestner Sample Book: 162, 163, 184-187
Kewpie: 108, 123, 164, 182, 308, 309
Kiddiejoy: 252
Kley & Hahn doll factory: 92, 125, 130, 131, 133-136, 144, 147, 151-155, 158, 159, 179, 183
Kley, Albert: 144, 159
Kling, C.F. & Co., porcelain factory: 119
Knoch, Christian and Ernst: 108
Knoch, Gebrueder, porcelain factory: 320, 321, 324, 326-328
Koenig & Wernicke doll factory: 54, 126, 142, 236
Kolb, Fred: 108
Krauss, Arthur, doll factory: 238, 240, 320
Krauss, Helmut: 238, 261-263
Krausser, Karl: 50, 54, 87
Kruse, Käthe: 13, 26, 52, 154

Leipzig Fairs: 56, 58, 66, 144, 210, 266
Lichte School of Modeling and Painting: 277, 278
Lewin-Funcke, Professor Arthur: 52, 53, 56, 57, 61-63
Luge, August, doll factory: 265, 266, 273

Maaser, Robert, doll factory: 253
Marc-Schnür, Marie: 20-22, 25, 26, 47
Marie: 56, 59, 60
Marotte: 261
Marseille, Armand, porcelain factory: 230-261
Marseille, Armand, and family: 19, 230-232
Max: 77, 181, 182
Mein Goldherz (My Goldheart): 125, 139
Mein Liebling (My Darling): 50, 72-74
Mein Lieblingsbaby (My Darling Baby): 72, 78, 79
Mein Fett Klein Liebling (My Fat Little Darling): 78
Mein Klein Liebling (My Little Darling): 76, 77
Mein Neuer Liebling (My New Darling): 72-75
Melitta: 258
MiMi: 110, 115, 116, 121
Möller, Professor Reinhard: 196, 197, 199, 203
Molds, master: 262, 295
Molds, plaster working: 217, 220
Moritz: 77, 181, 182
Müller, Friedrich: 142
Munich Art Dolls: 10, 13, 20-47
My Cherub: 228
My Dream Baby: 236, 249-251

Nanking doll: 305, 312

Index

Neumann, Kurt: 24
Newborn Babe: 236, 249, 250, 259
Nuessle, Gottlieb: 56

O'Neill, Rose: 108, 123, 164
Orsini, Jeanne I.: 110, 115-118, 121
Our Fairy: 142, 158
Our Golden Three (Unsere Goldigen Drei): 298-300

Peter: 58-61
Plaster Working Mold: 217, 220
Plaster Master Mold: 295
Pretty Peggy: 109, 110, 114
Princess Elizabeth: 216, 224, 226
Proeschild, August: 124
Putnam, Grace Storey: 108, 109, 118, 119

Rauschert, Paul porcelain factory: 13
Recknagel porcelain factory: 321, 322, 329-333
Recknagel, Theodor: 321
Reinhardt, Franz: 14, 26, 48, 51
Rheinische Gummi und Celluloid-Fabrik: 50, 54, 74, 81
Riemerschmid, Professor Richard: 21, 22
Rockwell, Grace Corry: 109, 114
Rosebud: 218, 223
Rosenbusch, Hugo: 142, 145

Sampson, William Thomas: 196, 212
Sander, Priska, doll factory: 266, 273
Schanzen: 191, 199, 269
Schmey, Gustav: 58
Schmidt, Bruno, doll factory: 54, 125, 129, 132-135, 138-141
Schmidt, Franz & Co., doll factory: 54, 90, 92, 104, 105
Schoenau & Hoffmeister porcelain factory: 214-220, 222
Schoenau, Arthur, and family: 214-216, 218, 219, 229
Schoenau, Arthur, doll factory: 214-219, 221, 222
Schoenau & Hoffmeister porcelain factory: 214-229
Schoenau, Gebrüder, porcelain factory: 322, 323
Schreiber, Max: 10, 20, 21, 28
Schwab, Heinrich: 142
Screamer: 294
Sigsbee, Charles Dwight: 196, 211
Siewert, Klara: 40, 41
Simon & Halbig porcelain factory: 52-105
Simon, Wilhelm and family: 86, 89, 90, 107
Snow Baby: 314

Sonneberg Dollmaking Area: 11, 12, 14, 15, 188-193
Sonneberg Privilege of Trade: 188, 189, 190, 195
South Sea Baby: 266, 273
Spanish American War Heroes: 90, 196, 211, 212
Steudinger, Mueller & Co. porcelain factory: 162
Stickel, Aline: 24, 27, 29
Stier, Heinrich, department stores: 20-47, 124
Strobel & Wilken: 64, 92, 142, 144, 145, 155
Swaine & Co. porcelain factory: 322, 323, 332, 334-337
Swaine, William: 322
Sweetums: 180

Tee Wee Hand Babe: 249
Tietz, Hermann, department stores: 10, 11, 13, 14, 20

Uncle Sam: 90, 101
United Köppelsdorf Porcelain Factories: 231, 264, 265, 268
Unsere Goldigen Drei (Our Golden Three): 298-300

Verleger: 188, 189, 194
ViVi: 110, 117, 118, 121
Vogelsanger, Paul: 20-22, 25-27, 29-33, 36, 37, 39-41, 44, 45
Völker, Heinrich: 106

Wackerle, Joseph: 20-22, 25, 26, 29, 34, 35, 38, 39, 42-47
Wagner & Zetsche doll factory: 92, 221, 236, 278
Walter: 61, 62
Waltershausen Dollmaking Area: 11, 12, 14-19, 160, 161
Washington, George: 90, 102
Weingart, Ernst and Reinhold: 107, 121
Welsch & Co. doll factory: 90, 238
Wendy: 134
Whistler: 294, 295
Wiesenthal, Schindel & Kallenberg doll factory: 90, 92, 125, 142, 149
Winker: 293
Wislizenus, Adolf, doll factory: 90, 92, 102, 126, 140, 141, 236, 290
Wolf, Louis & Co.: 145, 158, 236, 259

Zinner, Gottlieb, and family: 278
Zinner, Gottlieb & Söhne (Sons), doll factory: 216, 228, 278, 286